McDougal Littell

Math Intervention

Book 1:
Whole Numbers

McDougal Littell
A DIVISION OF HOUGHTON MIFFLIN COMPANY
Evanston, Illinois • Boston • Dallas

Cover photo © Royalty-Free/Corbis

Illustrations George Barile/McDougal Littell/Houghton Mifflin Company and John Evans/McDougal Littell/Houghton Mifflin Company

Copyright © 2008 by McDougal Littell, a division of Houghton Mifflin Company.
All rights reserved.

Permission is hereby granted to teachers to reprint or photocopy in classroom quantities the pages or sheets in this work that carry a McDougal Littell copyright notice. These pages are designed to be reproduced by teachers for use in their classes with accompanying McDougal Littell material, provided each copy made shows the copyright notice. Such copies may not be sold and further distribution is expressly prohibited. Except as authorized above, prior written permission must be obtained from McDougal Littell, a division of Houghton Mifflin Company, to reproduce or transmit this work or portions thereof in any other form or by any other electronic or mechanical means, including any information storage or retrieval system, unless expressly permitted by federal copyright laws. Address inquiries to, Supervisor, Rights and Permissions, McDougal Littell, P.O. Box 1667, Evanston, IL 60204.

ISBN-13: 978-0-618-90046-6
ISBN-10: 0-618-90046-2

123456789—PBO—11 10 09 08 07

Book 1: Whole Numbers

Whole Number Concepts

Activity 1-1	Counting by Ones and Tens	**2**
Lesson 1-2	Read and Write Whole Numbers	**4**
Lesson 1-3	Skip Counting	**8**
Lesson 1-4	Place Value and Expanded Notation	**12**
Lesson 1-5	Compare and Order Whole Numbers	**16**
Lesson 1-6	Round Whole Numbers	**20**
	Mixed Practice for Lessons 1-2 to 1-6	**24**

Addition and Subtraction of Whole Numbers

Activity 1-7	Adding and Subtracting Numbers	**26**
Lesson 1-8	Combinations that Make the Same Number	**28**
Lesson 1-9	Addition and Subtraction Facts	**32**
Lesson 1-10	Addition and Subtraction Properties	**36**
Lesson 1-11	Add 2-digit Numbers Without Regrouping	**40**
Lesson 1-12	Add 2-digit Numbers With Regrouping	**44**
Lesson 1-13	Add 3-digit, 4-digit, and 5-digit Numbers	**48**
Lesson 1-14	The Meaning of Subtraction	**52**
Lesson 1-15	Subtract 1-digit and 2-digit Numbers Without Regrouping	**56**
Lesson 1-16	Multiples of 10 or 100 Minus a 1- or 2-digit Number	**60**
Lesson 1-17	Subtract 1-digit and 2-digit Numbers With Regrouping	**64**
Lesson 1-18	Subtract 3-digit, 4-digit, and 5-digit Numbers With Regrouping	**68**
Lesson 1-19	Mental Math Strategies for Addition and Subtraction	**72**
Lesson 1-20	Add 3 or More Numbers	**76**
	Mixed Practice for Lessons 1-8 to 1-20	**80**

CONTENTS cont.

Multiplication and Division of Whole Numbers

Activity 1-21	Multiplying and Dividing Numbers	82
Lesson 1-22	Understand Multiplication and Division	84
Lesson 1-23	Multiplication and Division Facts	88
Lesson 1-24	Multiply 2-digit Numbers by 1-digit Numbers	92
Lesson 1-25	Multiply and Divide by 10 and Multiples of 10, 100, and 1000	96
Lesson 1-26	Multiply 2-digit and 3-digit Numbers by a 2-digit Number	100
Lesson 1-27	Multiply 3-digit and 4-digit Numbers by a 3-digit Number	104
Lesson 1-28	Divide by 1-digit Numbers Without Remainders	108
Lesson 1-29	Divide by 1-digit Numbers With Remainders	112
Lesson 1-30	Divide by 2-digit Numbers	116
Lesson 1-31	Multiplication and Division Properties	120
Lesson 1-32	Exponents	124
Lesson 1-33	Order of Operations	128
Lesson 1-34	Solve Problems with Whole Numbers	132
	Mixed Practice for Lessons 1-22 to 1-34	136

Math Intervention
Book 1 Whole Numbers

McDougal Littell

Math Intervention

MATH INTERVENTION

- The Math Intervention program includes skill lessons, problem solving lessons, activities, and mixed practice materials covering a wide range of mathematical topics that are needed for success in middle school and high school mathematics.

- There are seven books in the Math Intervention program. Book 1 contains materials on Whole Number concepts and operations.

- In the Math Intervention books, lessons include worked-out Examples and Try this exercises to help you build understanding of a topic. The Practice section includes a variety of problems to give you the practice you need to develop your math skills. The Did You Get It? section checks your understanding of the lesson.

- Problem solving lessons suggest strategies for approaching real-world problem solving situations and promote the use of estimation to check reasonableness of solutions.

- Activities build your understanding of a topic through the use of models and games.

- Mixed Practice sections include practice of vocabulary, skills, and problem solving methods covering the material in a group of lessons.

- You may complete the work in selected lessons, or cover the book as a whole, as directed by your teacher.

Name _____   Date _____

Counting by Ones and Tens

> **Goal:** Count and group objects in ones and tens.
>
> Materials: elbow macaroni, counters, index cards

Getting Started You can use groups of objects to help you count. The groups make a model of a number. Let one counter be equal to **10** elbow macaroni.

Count to 23.

Step 1 **Count** to **23** by ones using the elbow macaroni.

Step 2 **Regroup** the macaroni into piles of **10**. Separate the **23** macaroni into two groups of **10** and one group of **3**.

Step 3 **Replace** each pile of **10** macaroni with one counter. Draw the new model.

Step 4 **Replace** the new model with a number. Remember that each counter equals **10**. Two counters and three macaroni equal **20 + 3**, or **23**.

MAKE IT A GAME!

- Form groups of **4** students. Each student should have piles of macaroni, counters, and **4** index cards.
- Each student writes a whole number under **25** on each of the **4** cards.
- Students switch cards, model the numbers with macaroni, and then with counters, and check each other's work.

Name _____ Date _____

EXAMPLE 2

Write 45 in words.

Step 1 Ask yourself questions about the number.

How many groups of tens are in 45? _____

How many ones are in 45? _____

Step 2 Write the number as groups of tens and ones.

45 equals **4** groups of ten and **5** ones.

ANSWER 45 = **4** tens + **5**

EXAMPLE 3

Write 3 hundreds + 9 tens + 2 as a number.

3 hundreds equals 3 groups of ____?

9 tens equals 9 groups of ____?

2 is how many ones? ____

ANSWER 3 hundreds + 9 tens + 2 = **392**

Practice

Tell what number the model represents.

1.
2.
3.

Draw a model for the number.

4. 54
5. 18
6. 61

7. **Make a Conjecture** Suppose a star ☆ represents 10 counters (the number 100). Based on your answers to Exercises 1–6, make a conjecture about how to show the number 245 with a model.

DID YOU GET IT? Write the expanded form as a number.

8. 6 tens + 7
9. 8 tens + 9
10. 9 tens

11. 7 hundreds + 9
12. 5 hundreds + 9 tens + 2

Name _____ Date _____

LESSON 1-2

Read and Write Whole Numbers

Words to Remember

Whole numbers: The numbers 0, 1, 2, 3, 4, 5, 6, 7, ...

Even: ⭐⭐   **Even numbers make pairs.**

Odd: ⭐⭐ ⭐   **Odd numbers have one left over.**

Getting Started   In Activity 1-1, you learned how to count, read, and write whole numbers in ones and tens. You can use the same methods to read and write greater whole numbers.

EXAMPLE 1   Writing Numbers Using Models

Write how many.

Hundreds	Tens	Ones

Solution

Step 1   Think **2** hundreds, **4** tens, **5** ones.

Step 2   Write the number as **245**.

TRY THIS   Write how many.

1.

Hundreds	Tens	Ones

2.

Hundreds	Tens	Ones

_____   _____

Math Intervention
Book 1 Whole Numbers

Name _____ Date _____

Counting Up Start at any whole number and add **1**. You will get the next whole number. Repeat adding **1** each time to count a sequence of numbers. You can represent the group of numbers on a number line.

EXAMPLE 2 Writing Numbers Using Number Lines

Fill in the missing numbers on the number line.

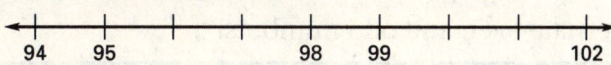

Solution

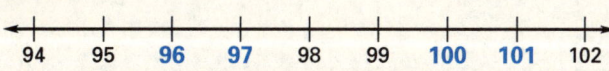

> **Remember**
> When you count to 99, the next number is 100.

TRY THIS Fill in the missing numbers on the number line.

3.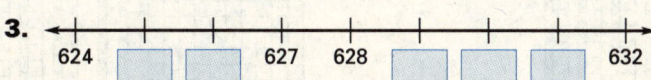

4.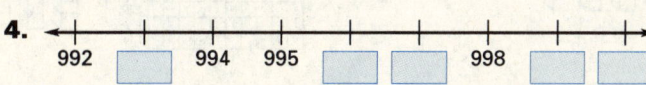

Even and Odd Numbers When you count, you alternate *even* and *odd* numbers. Even numbers make pairs. The numbers **2**, **4**, **8**, and **10** are all even. Odd numbers have one left over. The numbers **3**, **7**, **11**, and **21** are all odd.

EXAMPLE 3 Identifying Odd and Even Numbers

Tell whether the number 1047 is odd or even.

Solution

Look at the end of the whole number, at the ones' place. The number **7** in the ones' place is odd, so **1047** is odd.

> **Look Ahead**
> For help with finding **place value**, see Lesson 1-4 on page 12.

TRY THIS Tell whether the number is *odd* or *even*.

5. 8223 _____   6. 11,352 _____

7. 764,220 _____   8. 3,405,011 _____

Math Intervention
Book 1 Whole Numbers   5

Name _____ Date _____

> **Summarize**
>
> **Showing Numbers**
>
> You can show any number from **100** to **999** using hundreds, tens, and ones.
>
> **Even and Odd Numbers**
>
> Even numbers make pairs. The numbers **2**, **4**, **8**, and **10** are all even.
>
> Odd numbers have one left over. The numbers **3**, **7**, **11**, and **21** are all odd.
>
> When you count, you alternate even and odd numbers.

Practice

Write how many.

1.

2.

3.

4.

Fill in the missing numbers on the number line.

5. 99, ☐, 101, 102, ☐, 104, ☐, ☐, 107

6. 395, 396, ☐, ☐, 399, ☐, ☐, ☐, 403

7. 751, 752, ☐, ☐, 755, ☐, 757, ☐, ☐

Tell whether the number is *odd* or *even*.

8. 79
9. 102
10. 184
11. 301
12. 385
13. 400
14. 1875
15. 18,442

Name _____   Date _____

Solve each problem. Explain your answer.

16. The houses on one side of Eric's street all have even house numbers. The first three houses on that side are numbered **1024**, **1026**, and **1028**. If the same pattern continues, what are the next two houses on that side numbered?

    _____
    _____

17. Kristen is painting a wall mural to commemorate one million residents living in her city. How many zeroes will Kristen paint for the number one million?

    _____
    _____

18. If you begin counting from **100**, what will be the next number? Is it odd or even? Suppose you count down from **100**. What will be the next number? Is it odd or even?

    _____
    _____

DID YOU GET IT?

19. **Fill in the missing words.** The number **704** is modeled by seven _____ , zero _____ , and four _____ .

20. **Count up.** When you count up from **900** to **1000**, what are the last five numbers you count?

    _____

21. **Explain your reasoning.** Your friend says that when deciding if a number is even or odd, numbers greater than **1000** are more difficult than numbers less than **1000**. Is your friend correct? Explain why or why not.

    _____
    _____
    _____

LESSON 1-3: Skip Counting

Getting Started In Activity 1-1, you counted whole numbers by ones: for example 35, 36, 37, 38. When you count by ones, you are adding **1** to each number to get the next number. You can also count whole numbers by other units, such as twos, fives, and tens.

EXAMPLE 1 Skip Counting by 2s

Fill in the missing numbers on the number line.

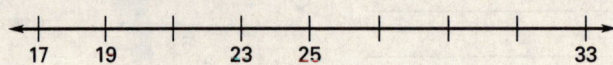

Solution

Step 1 Observe that **17** and **19** are **2** units apart. Count by **2s** to find the missing numbers.

Step 2 Complete the number line.

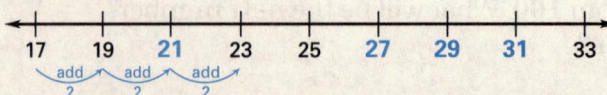

ANSWER The missing numbers are **21, 27, 29,** and **31**.

> **Remember**
> When you count by 2s from an even number, all the numbers you count will be even. When you count by 2s from an odd number, all the numbers will be odd.

TRY THIS Fill in the missing numbers on the number line.

1.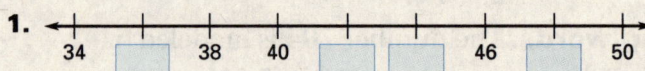

2.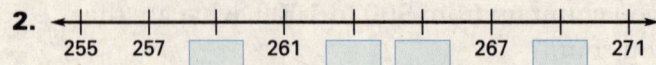

3.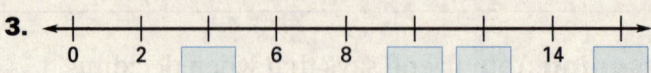

4.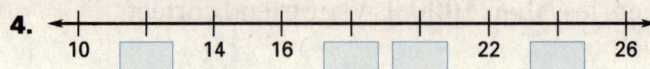

Name _____ Date _____

Skip Counting by 10s and 5s You can skip count to find the value of a group of coins.

 **Skip Counting by 10s**

How much are 4 dimes worth?

Solution

One dime is worth 10 cents (10¢) so you can skip count by 10s.

10¢   20¢   30¢   40¢

ANSWER Four dimes are worth 40¢.

TRY THIS Skip count to find the value of the group of coins.

5. 6 dimes _____

6. 8 dimes _____

 **Skip Counting by 5s**

How much are 6 nickels worth?

Solution

One nickel is worth 5 cents (5¢) so you can skip count by 5s.

5¢   10¢   15¢   20¢   25¢   30¢

ANSWER Six nickels are worth 30¢.

TRY THIS Skip count to find the value of the group of coins.

7. 7 nickels _____

8. 9 nickels _____

Math Intervention
Book 1 Whole Numbers

Name _____ Date _____

> **Summarize**
> **Skip Counting**
> You can count whole numbers by **2**s, **5**s, **10**s, or other whole numbers.
> An example of counting by **2**s is **31, 33, 35, 37, 39**.
> An example of counting by **5**s is **31, 36, 41, 46, 51**.
> An example of counting by **10**s is **31, 41, 51, 61, 71**.

Practice

Fill in the missing numbers on the number line.

1.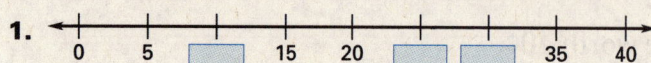

2.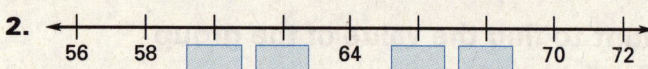

3.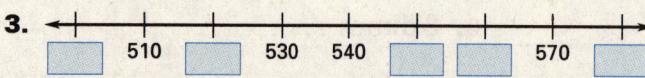

4.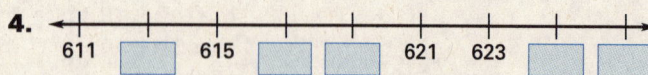

5.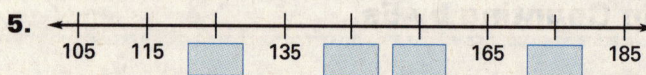

6.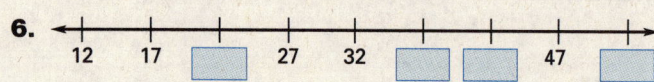

Find the value of the group of coins.

7.  _____

8.  _____

9.  _____

Math Intervention
Book 1 Whole Numbers

Name _____   Date _____

Solve the problem. Explain your answer.

10. At a museum's grand opening, every 10th ticket holder wins a free poster. The last three winners had ticket numbers **677**, **687**, and **697**. Will you win a poster if you have ticket number **700**? Why or why not?

    _____
    _____

11. Delaney has **25¢** in nickels. Draw and label by skip counting the number of nickels she has.

12. Nico runs **3** miles every morning. By Monday evening, he has run **3** miles. By Tuesday evening, he has run **6** miles for the week, and by Wednesday evening, he has run **9** miles for the week. How many miles will he have run by Sunday evening?

    _____
    _____

DID YOU GET IT?

13. **Fill in the missing words.** When you count by **10s** from **110**, the first three numbers are **110**, _____ , and _____ .

14. **Explain your reasoning.** When you count by **2s** from an even number, do you count all *even* or all *odd* numbers? Explain why.

    _____
    _____
    _____

15. **Use a number line.** Write a skip counting problem using the number line. Then solve the problem.

    ←——+——+——+——+——+——+——+——→

    _____
    _____
    _____

Math Intervention
Book 1 Whole Numbers   **11**

LESSON 1-4

Place Value and Expanded Notation

> **Words to Remember**
> Digit: Any of the numbers **0, 1, 2, 3, 4, 5, 6, 7, 8**, or **9**
> Place value: The value of a digit depends on its position in a number.

Getting Started You can write any number using the digits **0** to **9**. The place that a digit is in tells you how much the digit represents.

EXAMPLE 1 Using Place-Value Charts

Write how many in the place-value chart.

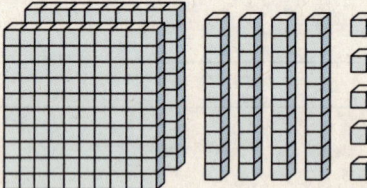

Solution
Think **2** hundreds, **4** tens, **5** ones.

Hundreds	Tens	Ones
2	4	5

TRY THIS Write how many in the place-value chart.

1.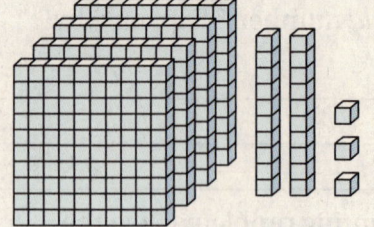

Hundreds	Tens	Ones

2.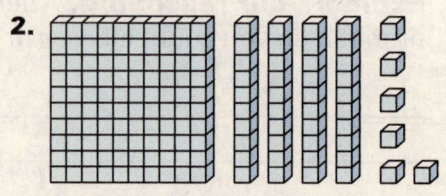

Hundreds	Tens	Ones

> **Place Value**
> The value of a digit depends on its place. The 4 in 423 has a value of 400. The 4 in 146 has a value of 40.

Math Intervention
Book 1 Whole Numbers

Name _____ Date _____

Zeros The zero in **10** means that there are no ones. Similarly, the zero in **508** means there are no tens.

EXAMPLE 2 Using Place Value to 10,000

Write how many in the place-value chart.

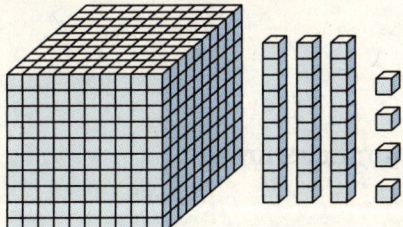

Solution

Think **1** thousand,
0 hundreds, **3** tens, **4** ones.

Thousands	Hundreds	Tens	Ones
1	0	3	4

TRY THIS Write how many in the place-value chart.

3.

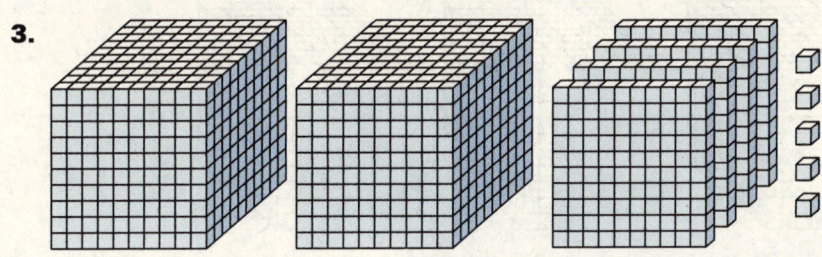

Thousands	Hundreds	Tens	Ones

EXAMPLE 3 Writing a Number in Expanded Form

Write 1034 in expanded form.

Solution

Show the values as addition.

   $1034 = 1000 + 30 + 4$

TRY THIS Write the value in expanded form.

4. 3708 = ▬▬ + ▬▬ + ▬

5. 9145 = ▬▬ + ▬ + ▬ + ▬

Math Intervention
Book 1 Whole Numbers

Name _____ Date _____

> **Summarize**
> **Place Value**
> The place that a digit is in tells you how much the digit represents.
> A number in expanded form is written as an addition of all the place values in the number.

Practice

Make a place-value chart and write the number shown.

1.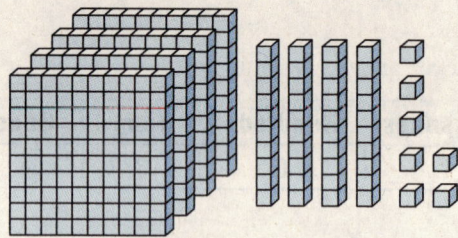

2.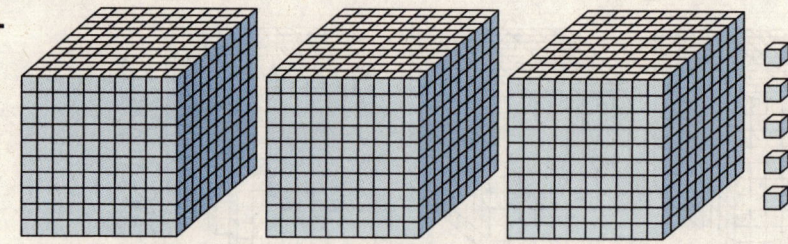

3.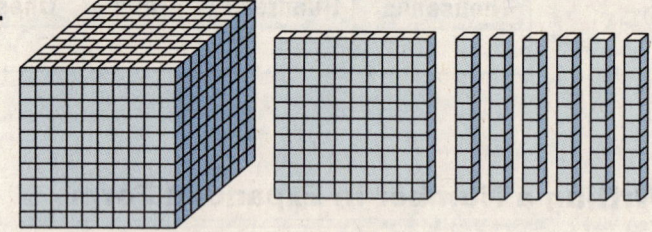

Write the value in expanded form.

4. 159   5. 264   6. 387

7. 107   8. 330   9. 690

10. 1001   11. 4890   12. 4906

13. 7020   14. 8044   15. 9719

Math Intervention
Book 1 Whole Numbers

Name _____ Date _____

Solve the problem. Explain your answer.

16. A tour guide accompanies each group of ten visitors to a historical site. Eighty students from your school visit the site on a field trip. How many tour guides meet the students?

_____
_____

17. There are **1466** contestants in a talent show. Write the number of contestants in the place-value chart. Then write the number in expanded form.

Thousands	Hundreds	Tens	Ones

_____

18. Tim's car repairs cost **$472**. Tim has **$100** bills, **$10** bills, and **$1** bills in his wallet. How many of each bill does he need to pay for the repairs?

_____
_____

DID YOU GET IT?

19. **Fill in the missing words.** The zero in **9093** means that there are zero _____ . The three means that there are three _____ .

20. **Explain your reasoning.** How is the value of the 5 in the number **1520** different from the value of the 5 in the number **1250**?

_____
_____
_____

21. **Write a number.** Write three numbers each having 3 hundreds and 4 tens.

_____
_____
_____

LESSON 1-5

Compare and Order Whole Numbers

Getting Started You can compare numbers to see if they are the same or if one number is greater. You can compare numbers by using models or a number line.

EXAMPLE 1 Comparing with Models

Are there more stars or hearts?

Solution

Method 1

Group the stars together and the hearts together. Compare the numbers of each.

4 hearts

6 stars

ANSWER There are more stars than hearts.

Method 2

Use a number line. There are 4 hearts and 6 stars.

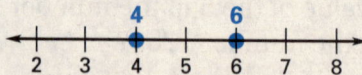

ANSWER The number 6 is to the right of 4, so 6 is greater than 4. There are more stars than hearts.

TRY THIS Circle the greater number.

1. 4 or 5
2. 9 or 8
3. 7 or 6
4. 10 or 11

Name _____   Date _____

Comparing Larger Numbers   You can compare numbers by looking at the digits. To compare three-digit numbers, compare hundreds first. Then compare tens. Then compare ones.

Symbols
To compare two numbers, use the symbol < for less than, the symbol > for greater than, and the symbol = for equal to.

EXAMPLE 2   Comparing Larger Numbers

Compare 376 and 320.

Solution

300 is equal to 300.   Compare the hundreds.

70 is greater than 20.   Compare the tens.

ANSWER   376 > 320

TRY THIS   Compare the pair of numbers.

5. 541 ● 218

6. 743 ● 748

Ordering Numbers   It is often easier to work with a group of numbers if they are in order. You can order numbers by comparing them to each other.

EXAMPLE 3   Ordering Numbers

Use a number line to show the numbers 25, 18, 27, and 17 in order.

Solution

Draw a number line and plot each number.

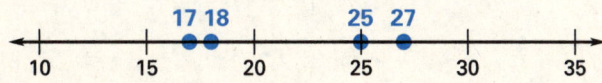

ANSWER   From least to greatest, the numbers are 17, 18, 25, and 27.

TRY THIS   Use a number line to show the numbers in order.

7. 220, 205, 180, 215

8. 380, 360, 410, 370

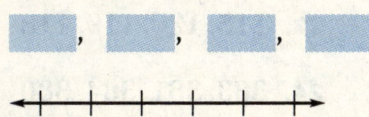

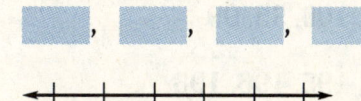

Math Intervention
Book 1 Whole Numbers   **17**

Name _____ Date _____

> **Summarize**
> **Comparing and Ordering Whole Numbers**
> On a number line, the greater number is on the right.
> You can compare numbers by looking at the digits. To compare three-digit numbers, compare hundreds first. Then compare tens. Then compare ones.
> You can order a group of numbers by plotting them on a number line.

Practice

Compare the numbers. Write <, >, or = in the ◯.

1. 8 ◯ 11
2. 15 ◯ 9
3. 18 ◯ 18
4. 21 ◯ 19
5. 20 ◯ 30
6. 29 ◯ 31
7. 92 ◯ 214
8. 99 ◯ 99
9. 87 ◯ 101
10. 271 ◯ 264
11. 181 ◯ 81
12. 158 ◯ 158
13. 887 ◯ 778
14. 178 ◯ 177
15. 365 ◯ 385

Use a number line to show the numbers in order.

16. 90, 110, 98, 101

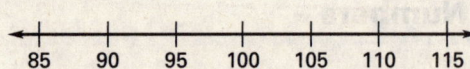

17. 533, 525, 531, 530

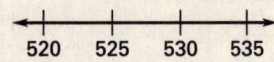

18. 600, 850, 725, 900

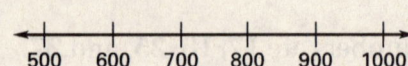

Write the numbers in order from least to greatest.

19. 23, 18, 33, 19
20. 48, 55, 41, 50
21. 101, 100, 95, 99
22. 115, 120, 119, 118
23. 201, 195, 196, 198
24. 383, 381, 384, 380
25. 530, 135, 242, 280
26. 681, 861, 168, 618

Name _____ Date _____

27. Four friends are planting flowers. Andre planted **83** flowers, Beth **65**, Camille **77**, and Donna planted **82** flowers. Write the friends in order from least number of flowers planted to greatest number planted.

_____
_____

28. Compare the lengths of Louise and Topaz.

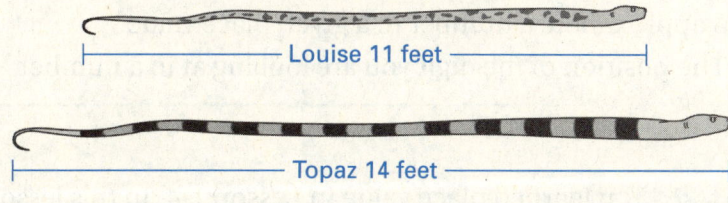

_____

29. A new movie plays every **3** hours at a theater. At the **10** A.M. show, **335** people attend. At **1** P.M., **320** people attend. At **4** P.M., **342** people attend. At **7** P.M., **299** people attend. Write the movie showtimes in order from least number attending to greatest number attending.

_____
_____

DID YOU GET IT?

30. Fill in the missing words. To compare two-digit numbers, compare the values in the _____ place. Then compare the values in the _____ place.

31. Explain your reasoning. When you compare numbers on a number line, is the greater number on the left or the right? Explain how you know.

_____
_____
_____

32. Use symbols. Write using symbols the comparison **13** is less than **18**. Explain how you know which symbol to use for *is less than*.

_____
_____
_____

Name _____ Date _____

LESSON 1-6

Round Whole Numbers

Words to Remember

Whole numbers: The numbers **0**, **1**, **2**, **3**, **4**, . . .
Digit: Any of the numbers **0**, **1**, **2**, **3**, **4**, **5**, **6**, **7**, **8**, or **9**
Rounding: To approximate a number to a given place value
Place value: The position of the digit you are looking at in a number

Getting Started You learned place value in Lesson 1-4. In this lesson you will round a whole number to a given place value.

EXAMPLE 1   Rounding a Number to the Nearest Thousand

Round 68,432 to the nearest thousand.

Solution

Step 1 Think of the number on a place-value chart.

Ten Thousands	Thousands	Hundreds	Tens	Ones
6	8	4	3	2

To round to thousands, you look here.

Remember
The value of a digit depends on its place in the chart. The 4 in 68,432 has a value of 400.

Step 2 Look at the column that you are rounding. You are rounding to thousands. Look to the *right* of the thousands' column, or at the hundreds' column.

Step 3 Ask yourself: Is the number in the hundreds' column a **5** or greater? No, the number is **4** and **4 < 5**. Since it isn't **5** or greater, you round *down* by leaving the thousands' column the same and replacing the hundreds' digit **4** with a **0**. Then also replace every other digit to the right of the **4** with a **0**.

ANSWER 68,432 to the nearest thousand is **68,000**.

TRY THIS Round the number to the nearest thousand.

1. 728,900 _____   2. 43,433 _____

Math Intervention
Book 1 Whole Numbers

Name _____ Date _____

Numbers in the Real World   Sometimes, numbers are easier to visualize or understand if they are rounded. For example, when you are talking about the population of a large city, you may not need to think about every digit in the number.

 **Rounding a Number to the Nearest Hundred Thousand**

In 2000, the U.S. Census stated that the population of Chicago, Illinois, was 2,896,016. Round to the nearest hundred thousand.

Solution

Step 1 Make a place-value chart.

Millions	Hundred Thousands	Ten Thousands	Thousands	Hundreds	Tens	Ones
2	8	9	6	0	1	6

To round to hundred thousands, you look here.

Step 2 Read the chart. The **8** is in the hundred thousands' place. The digit to the right of the **8** is **9**. The **9** is in the ten thousands' place.

Step 3 Ask yourself: Is the number in this column a **5** or greater? Yes, **9 ≥ 5**. Since the number is **5** or greater, you round *up* by increasing the digit to the left, the hundred thousands' digit, by **1**. You also replace the ten thousands' digit and every digit to its right with a **0**.

ANSWER 2,896,016 to the nearest hundred thousand is **2,900,000**.

Try This

Round the number to the nearest hundred thousand.

3. 818,700   4. 4,045,313

Round the number to the nearest hundred.

5. 18,702   6. 38,790

Round the number to the nearest ten thousand.

7. 748,702   8. 94,502

Name _____ Date _____

> **Summarize**
>
> Digit: Any of the numbers 0, 1, 2, 3, 4, 5, 6, 7, 8, or 9
> Rounding: To approximate a number to a given place value
> Place value: The position of the digit you are looking at in a number

Practice

Tell the place value for the digit 9 in the number.

1. 394 _____
2. 4915 _____
3. 29,803 _____
4. 1,290,600 _____

5. Fill in the missing information to round **42,631** to the thousands' place.

   Step 1 To round a number to the thousands' place, you look at the number in the _____ place.

   Step 2 If that number is **5** or more, then you round the thousands' place _____.

   Step 3 If the number in Step 1 is ____ ____ **5**, then you leave the thousands' place the same.

   Step 4 For **42,631**, the hundreds' place is ▪, so the thousands' place becomes ▪.

   Step 5 You change any digits to the right of the thousands' place to ▪.

   Step 6 Rounded to the thousands' place, **42,631** = ▪.

Round the number to the place value of the digit that is underlined.

6. 1<u>0</u>59
7. 2<u>6</u>,423
8. 3,8<u>8</u>7,332
9. 10<u>7</u>,090

10. 32,<u>3</u>00
11. <u>6</u>90,072
12. <u>1</u>00,998
13. <u>1</u>99,998

14. 4<u>0</u>,490
15. 7<u>0</u>20
16. <u>8</u>0,144
17. 2,32<u>9</u>,719

18. <u>1</u>594
19. 20,0<u>6</u>4
20. 2<u>3</u>,387
21. <u>1</u>0,700

22. 23,5<u>3</u>0
23. 6,9<u>7</u>8,880
24. <u>1</u>091
25. 4<u>8</u>3,290

Math Intervention
Book 1 Whole Numbers

Name _____ Date _____

Solve the problem. Explain your answer.

26. In 2000, the U.S. Census stated that the population of San Francisco, California, was **776,733**. Round to the nearest hundred thousand.

   _____
   _____
   _____

27. The area of Massachusetts is **27,336** square kilometers. Round to the nearest thousand.

   _____
   _____

28. According to the U.S. 2000 Census, the number of 10- to 14-year olds in Miami, Florida, was **22,182**. Round to the nearest thousand.

   _____
   _____

29. In 2003, the median household income in California was **$48,440**. Round to the nearest hundred.

   _____
   _____

DID YOU GET IT?

30. **Fill in the missing words.** To round **9780** to the nearest hundred, look at the _____ digit. Since the number is _____ than 5, round _____.

31. **Explain your reasoning.** Why does **6972** rounded to the nearest hundred round to **7000**?

   _____
   _____
   _____

32. **Write a number.** Write three numbers in the thousands that when rounded to the nearest hundred will give a result of **6800**.

   _____
   _____

Math Intervention
Book 1 Whole Numbers

Mixed Practice for Lessons 1-2 to 1-6

Vocabulary Review

Match the word with its mathematical meaning and everyday meaning.

Word	Mathematical meaning	Everyday meaning
1. even numbers ___, ___	A. position of a digit	X. numbers that make pairs
2. place value ___, ___	B. numbers whose ones' digits are 0, 2, 4, 6, or 8	Y. tens, hundreds, and so on

Fill in the missing words.

3. To write a number in expanded form, you should show the values as _____ of all the place values in the number.

4. The digit in the thousands' place for the number **456,782** is _____.

Write how many in the model.

5.

Hundreds	Tens	Ones
(1 flat)		5

6.

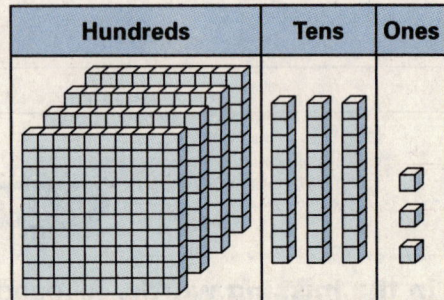

Hundreds	Tens	Ones
(4 flats)	3	3

Tell whether the number is *odd* or *even*.

7. 4338 _____   8. 734,120 _____   9. 12,555 _____   10. 1049 _____

Fill in the missing numbers on the number line.

11.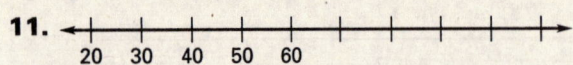
   20 30 40 50 60

12.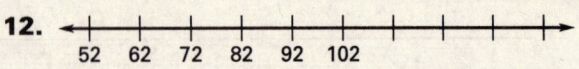
   52 62 72 82 92 102

13.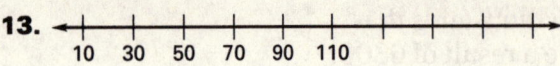
   10 30 50 70 90 110

14.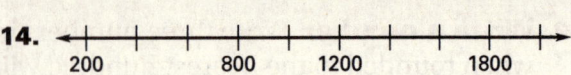
   200   800 1200   1800

Math Intervention
Book 1 Whole Numbers

Name _____ Date _____

Skip count to find the value of the group of coins.

15. 12 nickels = _____ ¢

16. 14 quarters = _____ ¢

Write the value in expanded form.

17. 7403   **18.** 688   **19.** 2001   **20.** 109

Show the numbers in order from least to greatest.

21. 240, 202, 190, 212

22. 340, 380, 270, 310

Compare the numbers. Write <, >, or = in the ●.

23. 82 ● 91   **24.** 30 ● 20   **25.** 182 ● 82

26. 9 ● 12   **27.** 178 ● 177   **28.** 998 ● 889

Round the number to the place of the underlined digit.

29. <u>4</u>7   **30.** 2<u>0</u>15   **31.** <u>7</u>6,348   **32.** 3,457,9<u>6</u>1

Solve each problem. Explain your answer.

33. The houses on one side of Splitrail Lane are all numbered with odd numbers. The first three numbers are **1033, 1035,** and **1037.** If the same pattern continues, what are the next two houses on that side numbered?

_____
_____
_____

34. Every Sunday a drawing is held at the ball park. Every **100**th ticket receives a team T-shirt. The last three winners held tickets **28,752, 28,852,** and **28,952.** Will you win if you have ticket number **29,002**? Why or why not?

_____
_____
_____

35. Jeffrey said that the value of the **4** in the number **1042** is different from the value of the **4** in the number **1402.** Is he right? Explain.

_____
_____
_____

Math Intervention
Book 1 Whole Numbers

Name _____ Date _____

 ## Adding and Subtracting Numbers

> **Goal:** Use concrete objects to understand that addition and subtraction are inverse operations.
> **Materials:** counters, Number Squares cards

Getting Started If you know an addition fact involving a group of numbers, you can write a subtraction fact about the numbers.

Consider addition as *counting on* and subtraction as *taking away*. Choose numbers and write addition and subtraction facts.

Step 1 **Choose** two numbers. For example, choose **8** and **6**.

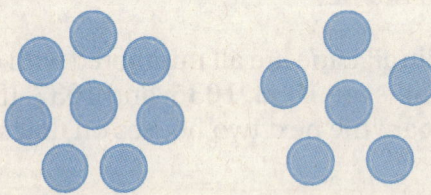

Count out **8** counters and **6** counters. Then put them together and count the total. What is the new total? _____

Step 2 **Rewrite** the addition fact you learned from the counters by filling in the boxes with numbers.

$\boxed{8} + \boxed{6} = \boxed{}$

Step 3 **Count** out a group of **14** counters. Then take away, or subtract, **6** counters from the group. What is the new total? _____

Step 4 **Rewrite** the subtraction fact you learned from the counters by filling in the boxes with numbers.

$\boxed{14} - \boxed{6} = \boxed{}$

Step 5 **Fill** in the boxes for a similar addition fact and subtraction fact.

If $\boxed{12} + \boxed{9} = \boxed{}$,

then $\boxed{21} - \boxed{} = \boxed{12}$.

Math Intervention
Book 1 Whole Numbers

Name _____ Date _____

MAKE IT A GAME!

- Form groups of two students.
- Cut out the number squares, mix them, and display them face up.
- Each student chooses three numbers that make an addition fact and then makes one subtraction fact with the numbers. Write the answers as shown below.
- The second student checks the facts. If both facts are correct, the first person gets **2** points. If either fact is wrong, the second student gets **1** point.
- Put the numbers back and choose three more. Repeat the steps.
- The first student who gets **10** points wins.

$$9 + 11 = 20$$

$$20 - 9 = 11 \longrightarrow 2 \text{ points}$$

Practice

1. Use counters to help you write three true statements using addition or subtraction with the numbers **7**, **12**, and **19**.

2. You know that $39 + 18 = 57$. Write two true subtraction facts.

3. Skip count to find the value of **8** dimes. Then subtract **2** dimes. What is the new value?

4. Skip count to find the value of **12** nickels. Then subtract **8** nickels. What is the new value?

5. **Make a Conjecture** Suppose you know that $18 + 48 = 66$. Make a conjecture about the result of $66 - 48 - 18 = ?$. Test your conjecture.

DID YOU GET IT? Fill in the missing information.

6. ☐ + 15 = 75, so 75 − 15 = ☐.

7. 42 − ☐ = 20, so 20 + ☐ = 42.

LESSON 1-8

Combinations that Make the Same Number

Words to Remember

Addends: Numbers you add	2 + 3
Sum: The total after you add	2 + 3 = 5
Plus sign: The sign + that tells you to add	
Equal sign: The sign = that means *is equal to*	
Subtract: To take away one quantity from another	5 − 2
Difference: The result after a subtraction	5 − 2 = 3
Minus sign: The sign − that tells you to subtract	

Getting Started There are many ways to relate numbers with addition and subtraction.

You can write **6 + 4 = 10** or say *six plus four equals ten* or draw a diagram.

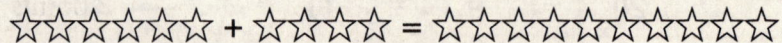

EXAMPLE 1 Relating Addition and Subtraction Facts

Use the numbers 3, 7, and 10 to write two addition facts and two subtraction facts.

Solution

Addition facts

7 + 3 = 10

3 + 7 = 10

Subtraction facts

10 − 7 = 3

10 − 3 = 7

TRY THIS Use the numbers to write an addition fact and a subtraction fact.

1. 4, 6, and 10

   ___ + ___ = ___

   ___ − ___ = ___

2. 1, 9, and 10

   ___ + ___ = ___

   ___ − ___ = ___

Math Intervention
Book 1 Whole Numbers

Name _____ Date _____

Drawing to Add You can draw a picture to help you add. To add using pictures, use any symbol or picture that makes sense to you. Be sure to write a note on your drawing to tell what the symbol represents.

EXAMPLE 2 Drawing to Add Larger Numbers

Draw a picture to add 30 + 70.

Solution

★ ★ ★   Draw 30 using ★ for 10.

★ ★ ★ ★ ★ ★ ★   Draw 70.

100 total   Count how many by 10s.

ANSWER 30 + 70 = 100

Pictures
In Example 2, the symbol ★ represents the value 10.

TRY THIS Draw a picture for each addition.

3. 80 + 20

4. 50 + 50

Equivalent Forms There are multiple ways to show the same number. For example, **5** is the same as **4 + 1** and **5** is also the same as **2 + 3** or **2 + 1 + 2**.

EXAMPLE 3 Using Equivalent Forms

Show the number 20 in eight different ways that include the number 14.

Sample solution

14 + 5 + 1	14 + 1 + 5	14 + 2 + 4
14 + 4 + 2	14 + 3 + 3	14 + 2 + 2 + 2
14 + 2 + 1 + 3	14 + 4 + 1 + 1	

TRY THIS

5. Show the number **20** in eight different ways that include the number **11**.

Math Intervention
Book 1 Whole Numbers **29**

Name _____   Date _____

> **Summarize**
>
> **Relating Addition and Subtraction Facts**
> These four facts are all related:
>   7 + 3 = 10   10 − 7 = 3   3 + 7 = 10   10 − 3 = 7
>
> **Using Equivalent Forms**
> There are multiple ways to show the same number. Here are a few ways to show 7.
>   4 + 3   6 + 1   2 + 5   2 + 2 + 3   1 + 1 + 1 + 4

Practice

Use the numbers to write two addition facts and two subtraction facts.

1. 2, 8, and 10   ___ + ___ = ___   ___ − ___ = ___

                       ___ + ___ = ___   ___ − ___ = ___

2. 5, 15, and 20   ___ + ___ = ___   ___ − ___ = ___

                       ___ + ___ = ___   ___ − ___ = ___

3. 40, 60, and 100   ___ + ___ = ___   ___ − ___ = ___

                       ___ + ___ = ___   ___ − ___ = ___

Draw a picture for each addition.

4. 30 + 20   5. 10 + 50

6. Show the number **20** in eight different ways that include the number 13.

_____
_____
_____

Math Intervention
Book 1 Whole Numbers

Name _____ Date _____

First decide whether you need to *add* or *subtract* to find the answer. Then solve the problem.

7. Riley wants to buy a DVD set costing **$28**. He has many **$1**, **$5**, and **$10** bills. Draw pictures to show three different ways that Riley could make **$28** with his bills.

8. Chelsea needs an extra **22** cents' worth of stamps to mail a package. She has sheets of **1** cent stamps, **2** cent stamps, and **5** cent stamps. Draw pictures to show four different ways that Chelsea could make **22** cents with her stamps.

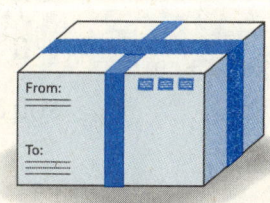

DID YOU GET IT?

9. **Fill in the missing words.** The plus sign tells you to _____ . The _____ sign tells you to subtract.

10. **Write equivalent forms.** Write the number 8 in three different ways.

    _____
    _____
    _____

11. **Use symbols.** Write a problem you could solve with $10 + 90 = 100$. Explain what each of the numbers **10**, **90**, and **100** represents.

    _____
    _____
    _____
    _____

Math Intervention
Book 1 Whole Numbers

Name _____ Date _____

LESSON 1-9
Addition and Subtraction Facts

Words to Remember
Fact family: Three numbers related by inverse operations

Getting Started One fact family shares the numbers **3**, **7**, and **10**. All the facts in this family are:

$7 + 3 = 10$ $\qquad\qquad$ $10 - 7 = 3$
$3 + 7 = 10$ $\qquad\qquad$ $10 - 3 = 7$

You can illustrate fact families using symbols or pictures.

EXAMPLE 1 Illustrating Facts

Illustrate the fact family.

$8 + 12 = 20$ $\qquad\qquad$ $20 - 12 = 8$
$12 + 8 = 20$ $\qquad\qquad$ $20 - 8 = 12$

Solution

Answers may vary. A sample answer is shown.

Illustrations

In Example 1, blue and white circles represent 12 and 8. Use any symbols or pictures you wish. They do not have to be fancy.

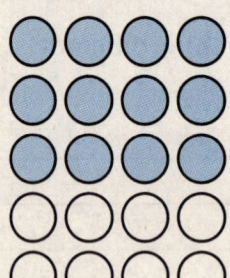

12 are blue.

8 are white.

There are 20 altogether.

TRY THIS Illustrate the fact family.

1. $4 + 6 = 10$
    $6 + 4 = 10$
    $10 - 6 = 4$
    $10 - 4 = 6$

2. $6 + 9 = 15$
    $9 + 6 = 15$
    $15 - 9 = 6$
    $15 - 6 = 9$

Math Intervention
Book 1 Whole Numbers

Name _____   Date _____

Pairs of Facts Each addition fact has a related subtraction fact. In the Try this exercises below, you will find pairs of addition and subtraction facts.

TRY THIS Match the related addition facts and subtraction facts.

Write the letter of the subtraction fact beside its related addition fact. The first one has been done for you. Each fact belongs in only one pair.

3. $14 + 6 = 20$ __F__   A. $8 - 4 = 4$

4. $8 + 7 = 15$ ____   B. $19 - 17 = 2$

5. $16 + 3 = 19$ ____   C. $19 - 16 = 3$

6. $2 + 12 = 14$ ____   D. $12 - 9 = 3$

7. $4 + 4 = 8$ ____   E. $14 - 2 = 12$

8. $0 + 8 = 8$ ____   F. $20 - 6 = 14$

9. $3 + 9 = 12$ ____   G. $15 - 7 = 8$

10. $12 + 7 = 19$ ____   H. $8 - 8 = 0$

11. $17 + 2 = 19$ ____   I. $19 - 12 = 7$

Write the letter of the addition fact beside its related subtraction fact. Each fact belongs in only one pair.

12. $12 - 1 = 11$ ____   J. $5 + 10 = 15$

13. $19 - 10 = 9$ ____   K. $15 + 1 = 16$

14. $18 - 0 = 18$ ____   L. $10 + 3 = 13$

15. $13 - 3 = 10$ ____   M. $13 + 3 = 16$

16. $15 - 10 = 5$ ____   N. $18 + 0 = 18$

17. $11 - 5 = 6$ ____   O. $7 + 11 = 18$

18. $18 - 7 = 11$ ____   P. $6 + 5 = 11$

19. $16 - 3 = 13$ ____   Q. $9 + 10 = 19$

20. $16 - 1 = 15$ ____   R. $11 + 1 = 12$

Math Intervention
Book 1 Whole Numbers

Name _____   Date _____

> **Summarize**
>
> **Fact Families**
> Fact families share the same three numbers.
>
> **Pairs of Facts**
> Each addition fact has a related subtraction fact.

Practice

Illustrate the fact family.

1. $8 + 5 = 13$
   $5 + 8 = 13$
   $13 - 8 = 5$
   $13 - 5 = 8$

2. $6 + 11 = 17$
   $11 + 6 = 17$
   $17 - 11 = 6$
   $17 - 6 = 11$

Write a related subtraction fact for the addition fact.

3. $0 + 20 = 20$ _____
4. $7 + 5 = 12$ _____
5. $14 + 2 = 16$ _____
6. $6 + 8 = 14$ _____
7. $16 + 1 = 17$ _____
8. $11 + 9 = 20$ _____

Write a related addition fact for the subtraction fact.

9. $12 - 0 = 12$ _____
10. $7 - 3 = 4$ _____
11. $20 - 18 = 2$ _____
12. $16 - 8 = 8$ _____
13. $9 - 1 = 8$ _____
14. $19 - 14 = 5$ _____

Math Intervention
Book 1 Whole Numbers

Name _____   Date _____

First decide whether you need to *add* or *subtract* to find the answer. Then draw a picture of the problem. Use your picture to solve the problem.

15. Carlos buys **15** books with his birthday money. Nine of the books are science fiction. The rest are puzzle books. How many puzzle books does he buy?

    _____
    _____

16. Shanequa had old dog toys for her puppy. Eric gave her **8** more. Now Shanequa has **19** dog toys. How many did she have to start with?

    _____
    _____

DID YOU GET IT?

17. **Fill in the missing words.** Each _____ fact has a corresponding subtraction fact. A group of facts sharing the same three numbers make up a _____ _____.

18. **Explain your reasoning.** A fact family uses the numbers 3, 13, and 16. In the addition facts, which number is the sum? How do you know?

    _____
    _____
    _____

Math Intervention
Book 1 Whole Numbers   35

LESSON 1-10
Addition and Subtraction Properties

Words to Remember

Commutative property of addition: The sum does not change when you change the order of addends.

$7 + 3 = 3 + 7$

Associative property of addition: The sum does not change when you change how addends are grouped.

$4 + (3 + 5) = (4 + 3) + 5$

Identity property of addition: When you add zero to a number, the sum is that same number.

$7 + 0 = 7$

Getting Started You have learned some addition and subtraction facts involving zero. When you add zero to a number, the sum is the same as the number. When you subtract zero from a number, the difference is the same as the number.

EXAMPLE 1 Adding Zero

Use a model to find the sum $3 + 0$.

Solution

$3 + 0 = 3$

EXAMPLE 2 Subtracting Zero

Use a model to find the difference $4 - 0$.

Solution

$4 - 0 = 4$

TRY THIS Find the sum or difference.

1. $0 + 37$  2. $42 - 0$

Math Intervention
Book 1 Whole Numbers

Rearranging Addends You can use the commutative property and associative property to rearrange addends. This may make it easier to find a sum.

EXAMPLE 3 Changing Addend Order

Use the commutative property and the associative property of addition to rearrange the addends and find the sum $9 + 9 + 1 + 1$.

Solution

$9 + 9 + 1 + 1 = 9 + 1 + 9 + 1$ Swap 9 and 1.
$ = (9 + 1) + (9 + 1)$ Group addends.
$ = 10 + 10$ Find the sum of each group.
$ = 20$ Add $10 + 10$.

Mental Math When you are adding many addends, look for ways to group the addends to form sums of **10**. Then combine the tens.

EXAMPLE 4 Forming Sums of 10

Rearrange the addends to find the sum $7 + 6 + 3 + 4$.

Solution

$7 + 6 + 3 + 4 = (7 + 3) + (6 + 4)$ Rearrange to form 10s.
$ = 10 + 10$ Find the sum of each group.
$ = 20$ Add $10 + 10$.

> **Ways to Make 10**
> Some ways to make 10 are: $9 + 1, 8 + 2, 7 + 3, 6 + 4,$ and $5 + 5$.

TRY THIS Find the sum.

3. $8 + 8 + 2 + 2$

4. $7 + 9 + 3 + 1$

5. $5 + 1 + 5 + 9 + 2$

6. $8 + 7 + 1 + 2 + 3$

7. $9 + 9 + 4 + 1$

8. $15 + 6 + 4 + 5$

Name _____ Date _____

> **Summarize**
>
> **Commutative property of addition**
> The sum does not change when you change the order of addends.
>
> **Associative property of addition**
> The sum does not change when you change how addends are grouped.
>
> **Identity property of addition**
> When you add zero to a number, the sum is that same number.

Practice

What property of addition does the model show?

1. [★★★★★] + [ ] = [★★★★★]   _____ property of addition

2. [▲▲] + [▲] = [▲] + [▲▲]   _____ property of addition

3. ([●●●●] + [●●●]) + [●●] = [●●●●] + ([●●●] + [●●])

   _____ property of addition

Find the sum or difference.

4. $0 + 27$ 5. $15 - 0$ 6. $33 + 0$ 7. $0 - 0$

8. Fill in the missing information to rearrange the addends in $4 + (2 + 6) + 8$ to find the sum.

   $4 + (2 + 6) + 8$ = $4 + (6 + \_\_) + 8$ Commutative property of addition
   = $(\_\_ + 6) + (\_\_ + 8)$ Associative property of addition
   = $\_\_ + \_\_$ Add.
   = $\_\_$ Add.

Use the properties of addition to find the sum.

9. $5 + 2 + 8 + 5$ 10. $3 + 0 + 7$ 11. $4 + 9 + 6 + 1$

12. $0 + 8 + 0 + 2$ 13. $5 + 10 + 0 + 5$ 14. $0 + 9 + 7 + 3$

15. Imelda and Zach empty their pockets to see if they have enough money to see a movie together. How much money do they each have? Can they each pay for a movie ticket costing **$8**?

_____
_____

16. By helping his neighbor, Jacob earns **$5** on Saturday, **$10** on Sunday, and **$3** on Monday. Emory earns **$3** on Saturday, **$7** on Sunday, and **$8** on Monday. How much money do they each have?

_____
_____

17. Tyler is recording the number of purple martins he sees in his yard for a birdwatching study. In the first hour, he records **9** purple martins. In the second hour, he sees none. How many purple martins does Tyler record altogether?

_____
_____

DID YOU GET IT?

18. Fill in the missing words. The sum of a number and zero is always _____ _____ . The difference of a number minus zero is always _____ _____ .

19. Explain with a drawing. Draw a sketch in the space below to show that $3 + 5 + 2 = 5 + 2 + 3$.

LESSON 1-11
Add 2-digit Numbers Without Regrouping

> **Words to Remember**
>
> Tens   Ones   ← Place value
> 3   8

Getting Started You have learned some simple addition facts. Using these facts, you can add numbers that have two digits.

EXAMPLE 1 Adding Two-Digit Numbers

Find the sum 24 + 12.

Solution

Step 1 **Add** the numbers one place at a time. Begin with the ones' place. **4 + 2 = 6**, so the sum has a **6** in the ones' place.

Tens	Ones
2	4
+ 1	2
	6

Step 2 **Add** the tens. **2** tens plus **1** ten equals **3** tens. So the sum has a **3** in the tens' place.

ANSWER 24 + 12 = 36

Tens	Ones
2	4
+ 1	2
3	6

CHECK your answer You can check the sum using a model.

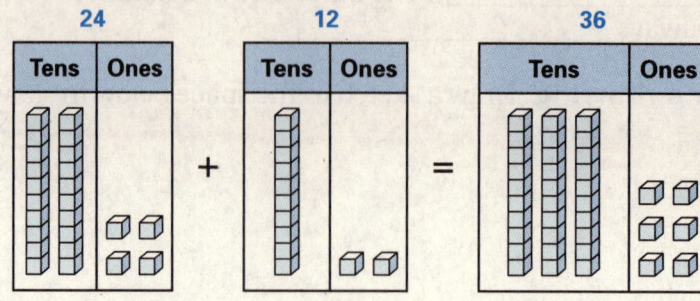

Name _____   Date _____

EXAMPLE 2 Adding Tens Without Ones

Find the sum 70 + 20.

Solution

Step 1 **Add** the numbers one place at a time. Begin with the ones' place. **0 + 0 = 0**, so the sum has a zero in the ones' place.

Tens	Ones
7	0
+ 2	0
	0

Step 2 **Add** the tens. **7** tens plus **2** tens equals **9** tens. So the sum has a **9** in the tens' place.

Tens	Ones
7	0
+ 2	0
9	0

ANSWER 70 + 20 = 90

EXAMPLE 3 Adding 1- and 2-Digit Numbers

Find the sum 64 + 5.

Solution

Step 1 **Write** 5 in the ones' column because five represents **5** ones. **4 + 5 = 9**, so the sum has a **9** in the ones' place.

Tens	Ones
6	4
+	5
	9

Lining Up the Ones
If you write the 5 in the tens' column, you will be adding 50, not 5.

Step 2 **Leave** the tens' column blank because there are no tens to add to **6**. The sum has a **6** in the tens' place.

Tens	Ones
6	4
+	5
6	9

ANSWER 64 + 5 = 69

TRY THIS   Find the sum.

1. 41 + 22
2. 16 + 11
3. 20 + 50
4. 10 + 60
5. 30 + 35
6. 22 + 6
7. 71 + 8
8. 9 + 50

Name _____ Date _____

> **Summarize**
>
> **Adding 2-digit Numbers**
>
> Add the numbers one place at a time. Add ones to ones and tens to tens. When adding vertically, be sure to line up the digits under the correct place value.

Practice

Match the addition problem with the model that represents it.

1. 40 + 26 ____
2. 4 + 25 ____
3. 12 + 13 ____
4. 21 + 6 ____

A.

B.

C.

D.

Write the sum.

5.
Tens	Ones
2	0
+ 1	8

6.
Tens	Ones
	6
+ 8	3

7.
Tens	Ones
6	1
+ 1	6

Find the sum.

8. 5 + 31
9. 20 + 78
10. 14 + 71
11. 30 + 67

12. 16 + 52
13. 17 + 52
14. 40 + 42
15. 5 + 62

Math Intervention
Book 1 Whole Numbers

Name _____ Date _____

Write the addition problem as a sum. Then add.

16. Before Malauna left for school, she noticed that **11** people had looked at her new web page. When she got home, **86** more people had looked at it. How many people altogether looked at her web page?

    _____
    _____

17. Sergio sent **51** text messages on his cellphone. He received **35** text messages. Altogether, how many text messages did he send or receive?

    _____
    _____

18. Yesterday, Anita read **38** pages of her library book. Today she read **61** pages. How many pages has she read so far?

    _____
    _____

DID YOU GET IT?

19. **Fill in the missing words.** When finding the sum $54 + 3$, you should write the 5 in the column for the _____ place and the 3 in the column for the _____ place.

20. **Explain your reasoning.** Doug adds $22 + 5$ and gets the sum 72. Explain what error Doug made.

    _____
    _____
    _____

21. **Use a model.** Draw a model in the space below to show the sum $27 + 21$. Then find the sum by adding vertically.

Math Intervention
Book 1 Whole Numbers

Name _____ Date _____

LESSON 1-12 Add 2-digit Numbers With Regrouping

> **Words to Remember**
> Regrouping: Writing a group of numbers as another number

Getting Started Sometimes when you add ones you get **10** or more. You can regroup **10** ones as **1** ten.

EXAMPLE 1 Regrouping Ones

Use the diagram shown. Regroup **15** ones so you have fewer than **10** ones.

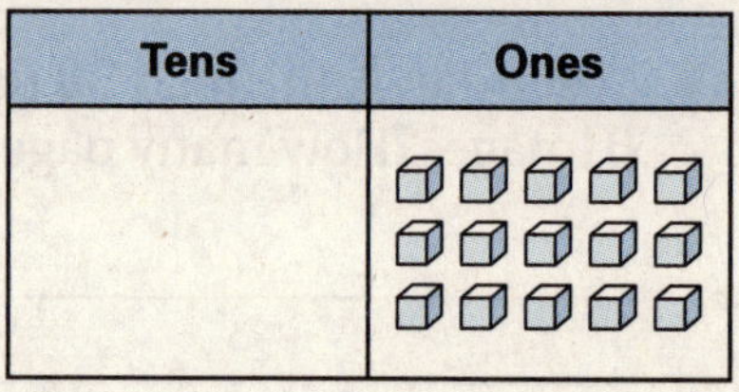

Solution

Regroup **10** of the ones as **1** ten.

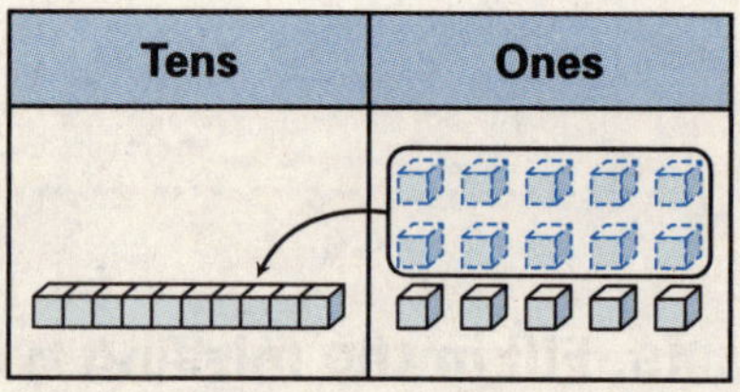

> **Regrouping**
> Regrouping is sometimes called **trading or renaming**.

ANSWER **1** ten **5** ones

EXAMPLE 2 Regrouping Ones as Multiple Tens

Regroup **23** ones so you have fewer than **10** ones.

Solution

Step 1 Show **23** ones.

Step 2 Regroup **10** of the ones as **1** ten. Regroup the next **10** of the ones as a second ten.

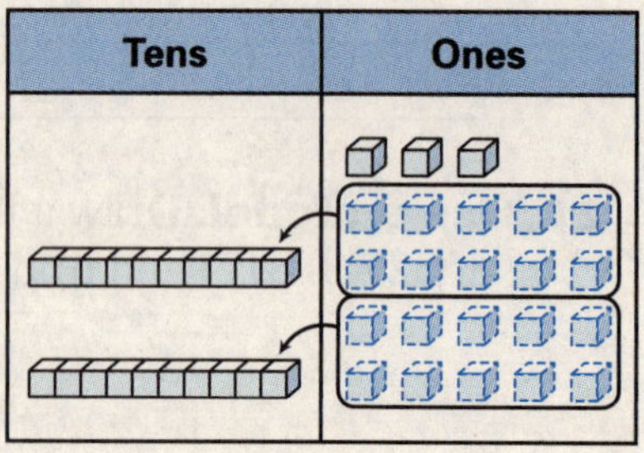

ANSWER **2** tens **3** ones

TRY THIS Regroup so you have fewer than 10 ones.

1. **1** ten **12** ones
2. **2** tens **11** ones
3. **2** tens **25** ones
4. **4** tens **38** ones

Name _____ Date _____

Regrouping After Adding Sometimes after you add, the sum has **10** or more ones.

EXAMPLE 3 Regrouping a Sum

Find the sum 27 + 18.

Solution

Step 1 **Show** each addend. Join the ones.

Tens	Ones

Step 2 **Regroup 15** ones as **1** ten **5** ones.

Tens	Ones

Step 3 **Add** the new **10** to the **3** tens.

Tens	Ones

ANSWER 27 + 18 = 45

TRY THIS Find the sum. Regroup so you have fewer than 10 ones.

5.
Tens	Ones
3	6
+ 3	5

6.
Tens	Ones
2	2
+	9

7.
Tens	Ones
3	9
+	6

Math Intervention
Book 1 Whole Numbers 45

Name _____   Date _____

> ### Summarize
> **Regrouping**
> Sometimes when you add ones you get **10** or more ones. You can regroup each group of **10** ones as **1** ten.

Practice

If you need to regroup the sum, write *yes*. If not, write *no*. Then find the sum.

1. | Tens | Ones |
    |------|------|
    | 4 | 3 |
    | + | 8 |

    _____

2. | Tens | Ones |
    |------|------|
    | 2 | 9 |
    | + | 3 |

    _____

3. | Tens | Ones |
    |------|------|
    | 5 | 4 |
    | + 2 | 5 |

    _____

Line up addends by tens and ones. Then add.

4. 64 + 16

Tens	Ones
+	

5. 4 + 88

Tens	Ones
+	

6. 1 + 79

Tens	Ones
+	

Add. Regroup if necessary.

7. | 5 | 6 |
    |----|---|
    | +1 | 5 |

8. | 7 | 7 |
    |----|---|
    | +1 | 0 |

9. | 6 | 8 |
    |----|---|
    | +1 | 2 |

10. | 3 | 0 |
    |----|---|
    | +1 | 4 |

11. | 2 | 9 |
    |----|---|
    | +3 | 8 |

12. | 4 | 1 |
    |----|---|
    | +4 | 8 |

13. | 6 | 0 |
    |----|---|
    | +1 | 0 |

14. | 2 | 3 |
    |----|---|
    | + | 8 |

15. | 5 | 4 |
    |----|---|
    | +4 | 3 |

Math Intervention
Book 1 Whole Numbers

Name _____   Date _____

16. Two groups of girl scouts are camping. There are **43** campers at one site and **19** at a second site. How many girl scouts are camping altogether?

_____
_____

17. On Saturday, Scott rode **17** miles of trails on his mountain bike. On Sunday, he rode **14** miles. How many miles did he bike that weekend in total?

_____
_____

18. Valerie's puppy weighed **16** pounds when she adopted it from the animal shelter. The puppy has since gained **38** pounds. What does the puppy weigh now?

_____
_____

19. Robin buys a webcam costing **$63** and a headset costing **$28**. How much does Robin spend altogether?

_____
_____
_____

DID YOU GET IT?

20. Write another way. After regrouping, a sum is **35**. Write three combinations of tens and ones that the sum could be before regrouping.

_____
_____
_____

21. Explain your reasoning. When you add two **2**-digit numbers, do you always need to regroup the sum? Explain why or why not with an example.

_____
_____
_____

Math Intervention
Book 1 Whole Numbers

Name _____ Date _____

LESSON 1-13 Add 3-digit, 4-digit, and 5-digit Numbers

Getting Started In Lesson 1-12 you learned how to add 2-digit numbers. Using the same methods, you can add numbers with more digits. For example, when you have **10** or more ones, you can regroup **10** ones as **1** ten. In the same way, when you have **10** or more tens, you can regroup **10** tens as **1** hundred.

EXAMPLE 1   Regrouping Tens as Hundreds

Find the sum 275 + 164.

Solution

Step 1 Add the numbers one place at a time. Begin with the ones' place. **5 + 4 = 9**, so the sum has a **9** in the ones' place. No regrouping is needed.

Hundreds	Tens	Ones
2	7	5
+ 1	6	4
		9

When to Regroup

Regroup only when necessary. Note that the sum of the digits in the ones' column is less than 10, so regrouping is not necessary.

Step 2 Add the tens. **7** tens plus **6** tens is **13** tens. Regroup **13** tens as **1** hundred and **3** tens. Write a **3** in the tens' place and a **1** in the hundreds' place.

Hundreds	Tens	Ones
	1	
2	7	5
+ 1	6	4
	3	9

Step 3 Add the hundreds. **1** hundred plus **2** hundreds plus **1** hundred is **4** hundreds. Write a **4** in the hundreds' place.

Hundreds	Tens	Ones
	1	
2	7	5
+ 1	6	4
4	3	9

ANSWER 275 + 164 = 439

TRY THIS   Find the sum.

1. 481 + 471 = ▮

2. 1233 + 3472 = ▮

Math Intervention
Book 1 Whole Numbers

Name _____ Date _____

Multiple Regrouping While adding, you may need to regroup more than once.

EXAMPLE 2 Regrouping Twice

Find the sum 86 + 88.

Solution

Step 1 Add the ones: $6 + 8 = 14$. Regroup 14 as 1 ten and 4 ones.

Hundreds	Tens	Ones
	1	
	8	6
+	8	8
		4

Step 2 Add the tens: $1 + 8 + 8 = 17$. Regroup 17 tens as 1 hundred and 7 tens.

Hundreds	Tens	Ones
	1	
	8	6
+	8	8
1	7	4

ANSWER $86 + 88 = 174$

TRY THIS Find the sum.

3. $269 + 274 =$ ☐

4. $1607 + 3519 =$ ☐

EXAMPLE 3 Regrouping Three Times

Find the sum 19,064 + 5257.

Solution

```
    1     1 1
    1 9 0 6 4
  +   5 2 5 7
    2 4 3 2 1
```

ANSWER $19{,}064 + 5257 = 24{,}321$

TRY THIS Find the sum.

5. $4708 + 2494 =$ ☐

6. $8774 + 26{,}098 =$ ☐

Math Intervention
Book 1 Whole Numbers **49**

Name _____ Date _____

> **Summarize**
>
> **Regrouping**
>
> You can regroup each group of **10** ones as **1** ten. Similarly, you can regroup each group of **10** tens as **1** hundred, and each group of **10** hundreds as **1** thousand.

Practice

Line up addends by hundreds, tens, and ones. Then add.

1. 305 + 94

Hundreds	Tens	Ones
+		

2. 407 + 209

Hundreds	Tens	Ones
+		

3. 515 + 97

Hundreds	Tens	Ones
+		

4. 824 + 76

Hundreds	Tens	Ones
+		

5. 742 + 108

Hundreds	Tens	Ones
+		

6. 283 + 177

Hundreds	Tens	Ones
+		

Add. Regroup if necessary.

7.
```
    1 0 9 7
+   4 6 0 3
```

8.
```
    3 4 6 4
+     7 8 2
```

9.
```
  1 1 9 9 9
+     1 9 9
```

10.
```
  8 0 3 5 6
+   8 7 5 6
```

11.
```
    2 4 0 8
+ 3 7 5 0 9
```

12.
```
  9 0 2 1 5
+   2 7 6 1
```

Math Intervention
50 Book 1 Whole Numbers

Name _____ Date _____

Find the sum.

13. 147 + 258

14. 325 + 989

15. 6105 + 944

16. 5217 + 2915

17. 6638 + 12,477

18. 65,498 + 1778

Write the addition problem as a sum. Then add.

19. When Gunnar bought a used car last year, the odometer read **37,757** miles. Since his purchase, he has driven the car **9450** miles. What does the odometer read now?

_____

_____

20. Next year, Autumn wants to spend **$2500** on a vacation in Europe and **$1550** on new computer equipment. How much money does Autumn need to save for both purchases?

_____

_____

DID YOU GET IT?

21. Give an example. Show how two 3-digit addends can have a 4-digit sum.

_____
_____
_____

22. Explain your reasoning. Could two 3-digit addends have a 5-digit sum? Explain why or why not.

_____
_____
_____

Name _____ Date _____

LESSON 1-14
The Meaning of Subtraction

Words to Remember

Subtract: To take away one quantity from another   5 − 2
Difference: The result after a subtraction   5 − 2 = 3
Minus sign: The sign − that tells you to subtract

Getting Started You know some subtraction facts. In this lesson you will explore when to use subtraction.

EXAMPLE 1 Finding How Many Are Left

Hannah picks **12** flowers in her garden to put in vases. She puts **5** flowers in one vase. How many flowers are left for a second vase?

Solution

Step 1 Draw how many you start with. Cross out the ones you subtract.

Start with **12** flowers.

Subtract **5**.

Step 2 Count how many are left.

  12 − 5 = 7

ANSWER There are **7** flowers left for the second vase.

TRY THIS Fill in the missing information to solve the problem.

1. Kyle orders **10** shirts from a clothing catalog. After trying them on, he returns **6** of them. How many shirts does Kyle keep?

   ▭ ● ▭ = ▭ shirts

Math Intervention
Book 1 Whole Numbers

Comparing   You can subtract to find how many more or fewer there are of something.

EXAMPLE 2 Comparing with Subtraction

Dee has 8 friends listed in her instant messaging software. Five friends are currently online. How many more friends are online than offline?

Solution

Step 1 Draw how many you start with. Cross out the ones you subtract.

Step 2 Count how many are offline.

8 − 5 = 3

Step 3 Count how many more are online than offline.

5 − 3 = 2

ANSWER There are 2 more friends online than offline.

> **Reading**
> **Read the question carefully.** Note that finding how many friends are offline is only part of the answer.

Undoing   You can think of a subtraction as undoing a related addition.

EXAMPLE 3 Undoing an Addition

If 18 + 7 = 25, what is 25 − 7?

Solution

Ask yourself, what number added to 7 has a sum of 25?

18 + 7 = 25, so the opposite must be true: 25 − 7 = 18.

TRY THIS   Fill in the missing information to solve the problem.

2. Judy's family have eaten 10 of the 19 bananas she bought at the grocery store. How many are left?

☐ ● ☐ = ☐ bananas

Name _____ Date _____

> **Summarize**
>
> **Subtracting**
>
> The number you get when you subtract one number from another is the difference. You subtract to find how many are left, to compare numbers, and to "undo" an addition.

Practice

Write how many there are in all. Write how many go away. Write how many are left.

1.

    _____
    _____
    _____

2.

    _____
    _____
    _____

3.

    _____
    _____
    _____

4.

    _____
    _____
    _____

Draw how many you start with. Cross out the ones you subtract. Write how many are left.

5. 6 − 3 = _____   6. 5 − 4 = _____

Math Intervention
Book 1 Whole Numbers

Name _____ Date _____

Subtract to find how many more or how many fewer shirts there are than pants.

7.

   ■ ● ■ = ■

8.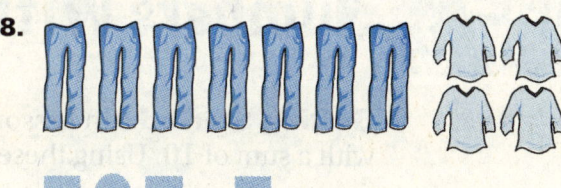

   ■ ● ■ = ■

Write a subtraction problem. Then find the difference.

9. Tristan gives **9** balls to his puppy. The puppy ruins **7** of them. How many balls are left?

   _____
   _____

10. Melissa has walked **4** kilometers of a **10** kilometer trail. How much farther does she have to walk?

    _____
    _____

DID YOU GET IT?

11. **Give an example.** Write a real-world problem that could be modeled by the subtraction $8 - 0 = 8$.

    _____
    _____

12. **Explain your reasoning.** Sketch **7** flowers. Use your sketch to explain how $7 + 1$ is unlike $7 - 1$.

    _____
    _____
    _____

Math Intervention
Book 1 Whole Numbers   **55**

LESSON 1-15
Subtract 1-digit and 2-digit Numbers Without Regrouping

Getting Started In Lesson 1-10, you learned about pairs of numbers with a sum of **10**. Using these pairs, you can subtract numbers from **10**.

EXAMPLE 1 Subtracting One-Digit Numbers

Find $10 - 7$.

Solution

$7 + 3 = 10$, so $10 - 7 = 3$.

Two-Digit Numbers You can subtract numbers that have two or more digits by subtracting one place at a time.

EXAMPLE 2 Subtracting Two-Digit Numbers

Find $47 - 12$.

Solution

Step 1 **Subtract** one place at a time. Begin with the ones' place. $7 - 2 = 5$, so the difference has a **5** in the ones' place.

Tens	Ones
4	7
− 1	2
	5

Step 2 **Subtract** the tens. **4** tens minus **1** ten equals **3** tens. So the sum has a **3** in the tens' place.

Tens	Ones
4	7
− 1	2
3	5

ANSWER $47 - 12 = 35$

TRY THIS Find the difference.

1. $10 - 4 = $ ▮
2. $10 - 8 = $ ▮
3. $63 - 11 = $ ▮
4. $89 - 51 = $ ▮

Math Intervention
Book 1 Whole Numbers

Ways to Make 100 You already know some ways to make 10, such as 9 + 1 and 8 + 2. You can apply these addition facts to write pairs of tens that add to make 100. Two examples are 90 + 10 and 80 + 20. You can use these facts to subtract tens.

EXAMPLE 3 Using a Model

Find 100 − 20.

Solution

Step 1 **Draw** how many you start with. Cross out the tens you subtract.

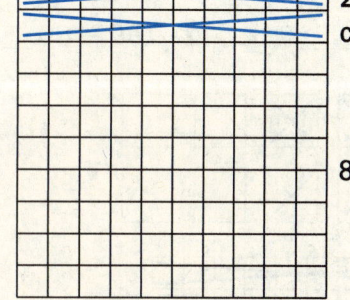

2 tens are crossed out.

8 tens are left.

Step 2 **Count** how many are left.

ANSWER 100 − 20 = 80

TRY THIS Use the model to find the difference.

5. 100 − 70

   _____

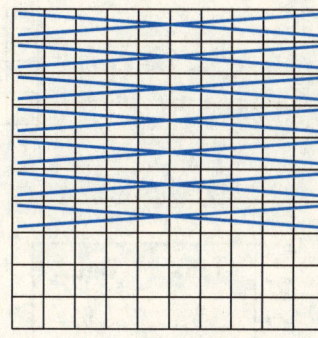

6. 100 − 40

   _____

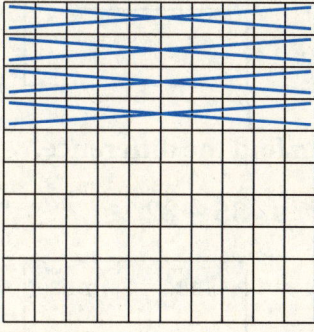

Math Intervention
Book 1 Whole Numbers **57**

Name _____ Date _____

> **Summarize**
>
> **Subtracting 2-digit Numbers**
>
> Subtract the numbers one place at a time. Subtract ones from ones and tens from tens.

Practice

Match the subtraction problem with the model that represents it.

1. 10 – 5 _____   2. 100 – 60 _____   3. 10 – 6 _____   4. 100 – 80 _____

A. 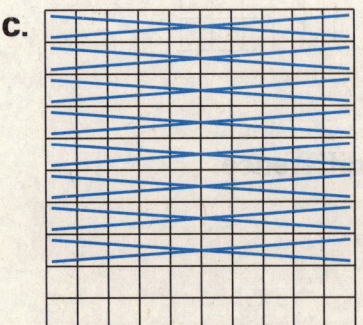   B.

C. 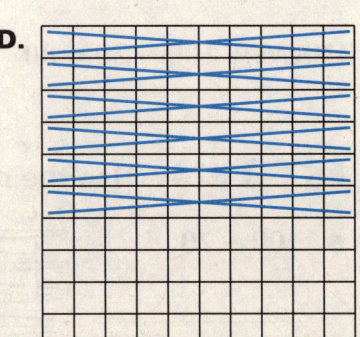   D.

Find the difference.

5.
Tens	Ones
4	9
– 1	8

6.
Tens	Ones
5	6
– 4	3

7.
Tens	Ones
6	1
– 1	0

Write the subtraction and then find the difference.

8. 25 – 13

Tens	Ones
–	

9. 95 – 82

Tens	Ones
–	

10. 70 – 10

Tens	Ones
–	

Name _____ Date _____

Find the difference.

11. 66 − 52   12. 57 − 23   13. 46 − 42   14. 95 − 64

15. 27 − 15   16. 47 − 36   17. 99 − 77   18. 100 − 90

Write the problem as a difference. Then subtract.

19. Alesha bought **12** posters to decorate her apartment. Today, she hung **9** of the posters. How many posters are left to hang?

_____

_____

20. On Saturday morning, the animal shelter had **27** kittens. By the end of the day, **14** had been adopted. How many kittens remained at the shelter?

_____

_____

21. Hayden has a DVD box set containing **59** episodes of his favorite television show. Last month, Hayden watched **13** episodes. How many episodes are left to watch?

_____

_____

DID YOU GET IT?

22. **Explain your reasoning.** To subtract **6** from **79**, do you subtract **6** from **7** or from **9**? Explain.

_____

_____

_____

23. **Use a model.** Draw a model in the space below to show **100 − 10**. Then find the difference.

Math Intervention
Book 1 Whole Numbers   **59**

LESSON 1-16
Multiples of 10 or 100 Minus a 1- or 2-digit Number

> **Words to Remember**
>
> Multiple: The product of a whole number and any nonzero whole number
>
> Multiples of 10: 10, 20, 30, 40, 50, ...

Getting Started In Lessons 1-8 and 1-10, you used pairs of numbers with a sum of **10** or **100**. Knowing these pairs will help you subtract numbers from multiples of **10** or **100**.

Regrouping Tens Sometimes you need to subtract more ones than you have so you need to regroup **1** ten as **10** ones.

EXAMPLE 1  Regrouping Tens as Ones

Find 30 − 7.

Solution

Step 1 **Regroup 3** tens as **2** tens and **10** ones.

Step 2 **Subtract 7** ones.

ANSWER 30 − 7 = 23

Another Way You can represent the regrouping modeled in Example 1 like this.

Tens	Ones
2	10
3̸	0̸
−	7
2	3

Math Intervention
Book 1 Whole Numbers

Name _____   Date _____

Two-Digit Numbers   You can subtract numbers that have two digits by subtracting one place at a time.

EXAMPLE 2   Subtracting Two-Digit Numbers

Find 70 − 12.

Solution

Step 1 **Subtract** one place at a time. Begin with the ones' place. Regroup **7** tens as **6** tens and **10** ones. **10** ones minus **2** ones equals **8** ones, so the difference has an **8** in the ones' place.

Tens	Ones
6	10
7̸	0̸
− 1	2
	8

Step 2 **Subtract** the tens. **6** tens minus **1** ten equals **5** tens. So the difference has a **5** in the tens' place.

Tens	Ones
6	10
7̸	0̸
− 1	2
5	8

ANSWER 70 − 12 = 58

EXAMPLE 3   Subtracting from 100

Find 100 − 60.

Solution

Step 1 **Subtract** the ones. 0 − 0 = 0

Step 2 **Regroup** 1 hundred as 10 tens.

Hundreds	Tens	Ones
0	10	
1̸	0̸	0
−	6	0
		0

> **Subtracting Zero**
>
> When you subtract zero, you are left with the original number. So 0 − 0 = 0.

Step 3 **Subtract** the tens. 10 − 6 = 4, so the difference has a **4** in the tens' place.

Hundreds	Tens	Ones
0	10	
1̸	0̸	0
−	6	0
	4	0

ANSWER 100 − 60 = 40

TRY THIS   Find the difference.

1. 40 − 4 = ▭
2. 60 − 8 = ▭
3. 50 − 18 = ▭
4. 100 − 10 = ▭

Math Intervention
Book 1 Whole Numbers

Name _____ Date _____

> **Summarize**
>
> **Regrouping**
> Sometimes you need to subtract more ones than you have so you need to regroup **1** ten as **10** ones. Similarly, you can regroup **1** hundred as **10** tens.

Practice

Which of A, B, or C shows the correct subtraction?

1. _____

A.
Hundreds	Tens	Ones
1	5̶ 6̶	10 0̶
	5	5
1	0	5

B.
Hundreds	Tens	Ones
1 1̶	10 6̶	0
	5	5
1	1	5

C.
Hundreds	Tens	Ones
0 1̶	10 6̶	0
	5	5
	5	5

2. _____

A.
Hundreds	Tens	Ones
0 2̶	10 0̶	0
	3	0
	7	0

B.
Hundreds	Tens	Ones
1 2̶	10 0̶	0
	3	0
2	7	0

C.
Hundreds	Tens	Ones
1 2̶	10 0̶	0
	3	0
1	7	0

Subtract. Regroup if necessary.

3.
Hundreds	Tens	Ones
1	0	0
	2	0

4.
Hundreds	Tens	Ones
1	5	0
	3	5

5.
Hundreds	Tens	Ones
2	8	0
	7	2

6.
Hundreds	Tens	Ones
4	0	0
	1	0

7.
Hundreds	Tens	Ones
3	7	0
	3	4

8.
Hundreds	Tens	Ones
5	8	0
	3	7

Math Intervention
Book 1 Whole Numbers

Name _____   Date _____

Write a subtraction problem to answer the question.

9. Leticia celebrated her **12**th wedding anniversary when she was **40** years old. How old was she when she got married?

   _____
   _____

10. To weigh his dog, Darryl picks up the dog and then steps on the bathroom scale. The scale reads **210** pounds. Then Darryl steps on the scale without the dog. The scale now reads **170** pounds. How much does the dog weigh?

    _____
    _____

11. At noon, the temperature at the airport was **90** degrees Fahrenheit. After a thunderstorm, the temperature dropped **15** degrees. What was the temperature after the storm?

    _____
    _____

DID YOU GET IT?

12. **Draw a model.** Subtract **9** from **30**. Then draw a model to illustrate how to find **30 − 9** by regrouping.

    _____

13. **Explain your reasoning.** When you subtract a 2-digit number from **100**, do you always need to regroup? Explain why or why not with an example.

    _____
    _____
    _____
    _____

Math Intervention
Book 1 Whole Numbers

Name _____ Date _____

LESSON 1-17
Subtract 1-digit and 2-digit Numbers With Regrouping

Getting Started In Lesson 1-16, you learned how to subtract numbers from multiples of **10** and **100**. In this lesson, you will subtract from numbers that are not multiples of **10** or **100**.

EXAMPLE 1   Subtracting 1-digit Numbers

Find 26 − 8.

Solution

Step 1 **Regroup** 2 tens 6 ones as **1** ten **16** ones.

Step 2 **Subtract 8** ones.

Step 3 **Decide** what is left. **1** ten and **8** ones are left.

ANSWER 26 − 8 = 18

> **Regrouping**
>
> When you regroup, remember that two values are regrouped, not just one. For example, when you regroup 2 tens in Step 1, the 2 in the tens' place and the 6 in the ones' place both change.

Another Way You can represent the regrouping modeled in Example 1 like this.

Tens	Ones
1	16
2̸	6̸
−	8
1	8

TRY THIS   Find the difference.

1. 42 − 8 = ____
2. 31 − 9 = ____

Two-Digit Numbers You can subtract numbers that have two digits by subtracting one place at a time.

Math Intervention
Book 1 Whole Numbers
64

Name _____ Date _____

EXAMPLE 2 — Modeling 2-digit Subtraction

Find 35 – 17.

Solution

Step 1 **Regroup** 3 tens 5 ones as 2 tens 15 ones.

Step 2 **Subtract** 7 ones.

Step 3 **Subtract** 1 ten. Decide what is left.

ANSWER 35 – 17 = 18

EXAMPLE 3 — Subtracting without Models

Find 71 – 19.

Solution

Step 1 **Regroup** 7 tens as 6 tens and 10 ones. Add the 10 ones to the 1 one already in the ones' place. Then subtract the ones.

Step 2 **Subtract** the tens.

ANSWER 71 – 19 = 52

TRY THIS Find the difference.

3. 63 – 26 = ☐

4. 81 – 12 = ☐

Name _____   Date _____

> **Summarize**
> **Regrouping**
> Subtract 2-digit numbers by regrouping and subtracting one place at a time.

Practice

Which of A, B, or C shows the correct subtraction?

1. ____

   A.
Tens	Ones
3	13
4	3
−	5
3	8

   B.
Tens	Ones
3	3
4	3
−	5
3	2

   C.
Tens	Ones
5	13
4	3
−	5
5	8

2. ____

   A.
Tens	Ones
	11
8	1
− 2	6
6	5

   B.
Tens	Ones
7	11
8	1
− 2	6
5	5

   C.
Tens	Ones
7	10
8	1
− 2	6
5	4

3. ____

   A.
Tens	Ones
6	10
7	4
− 6	9
	1

   B.
Tens	Ones
6	14
7	4
− 6	9
1	5

   C.
Tens	Ones
6	14
7	4
− 6	9
	5

Subtract. Regroup if necessary.

4.
Tens	Ones
3	2
− 1	8

5.
Tens	Ones
4	4
−	5

6.
Tens	Ones
5	6
− 2	9

Math Intervention
Book 1 Whole Numbers

Name _____ Date _____

Which of A, B, or C shows the correct difference?

7. 92 − 46 _____

   A. 36   B. 46   C. 56

8. 54 − 49 _____

   A. 5   B. 15   C. 10

Write a subtraction problem to answer the question.

9. Stacy has a coupon for **$14** off any poster. She chooses a poster costing **$52**. What does the poster cost after using the coupon?

   _____
   _____

10. Jay has read **55** pages of a **91** page report. How many pages does he have left to read?

    _____
    _____

11. A strip of carpet is **62** inches long. A decorator cuts **8** inches off the strip so the carpet will fit in a hallway. How long is the carpet strip now?

    _____
    _____

DID YOU GET IT?

12. **Fill in the missing numbers.** To subtract **19** from **70**, regroup 7 tens 0 ones as _____ tens _____ ones.

13. **Explain your reasoning.** Kevin says that when you regroup a 2-digit number during a subtraction, you cross out the number in the ones' place and write **10** above it. Kevin demonstrates **50 − 19 = 31** as an example. Does Kevin's method always work? Explain Kevin's mistake.

    _____
    _____
    _____
    _____

LESSON 1-18

Subtract 3-digit, 4-digit, and 5-digit Numbers With Regrouping

Getting Started   In Lesson 1-17, you practiced regrouping once during a subtraction. In this lesson, you will learn how to regroup more than once during the same subtraction problem.

EXAMPLE 1   Regrouping Twice

Find 321 − 78.

Solution

Step 1   Subtract 8 ones from 1 one, if possible. Show any regrouping necessary.

Hundreds	Tens	Ones
	1	11
3	2̸	1̸
−	7	8
		3

Regroup 2 tens as 1 ten and 10 ones. Add the 10 ones to the 1 one. 1 + 10 = 11 ones

Then subtract 8 ones.

> **Regrouping**
>
> **When you subtract, you must look carefully at the two digits in each column.** If the digit on the bottom is greater than the digit on the top, you must regroup.

Step 2   Subtract 7 tens from 2 tens, if possible. Show any regrouping necessary.

Hundreds	Tens	Ones
2	11	
3̸	2̸	11
		1̸
−	7	8
	4	3

Regroup 3 hundreds as 2 hundreds and 10 tens. Add the 10 tens to the 1 ten. 10 + 1 = 11 tens

Then subtract 7 tens.

Step 3   Subtract 0 hundreds from 2 hundreds.

Hundreds	Tens	Ones
2	11	
3̸	2̸	11
		1̸
−	7	8
2	4	3

Subtract 0 hundreds.

ANSWER   321 − 78 = 243

Math Intervention
Book 1   Whole Numbers

Name _____   Date _____

Subtracting Across Zeros Sometimes you need to regroup tens but there are no tens. So you have to first regroup hundreds as tens so you can regroup a ten as ones.

EXAMPLE 2 Subtracting Across Zeros

Find 402 − 37.

Solution

Step 1 Subtract 7 ones from 2 ones, if possible. Show any regrouping necessary.

Hundreds	Tens	Ones
3	10	
4̸	0̸	2
−	3	7

Regroup tens, if possible, to help regroup ones. But there are 0 tens to regroup.

So regroup 4 hundreds as 3 hundreds and 10 tens.

Step 2 Try again to subtract 7 ones from 2 ones. Show any regrouping necessary.

Hundreds	Tens	Ones
	9	12
3	10̸	
4̸	0̸	2̸
−	3	7
		5

Regroup 10 tens as 9 tens and 10 ones. Add the 10 ones to the 2 ones. 2 + 10 = 12 ones

Then subtract 7 ones.

Step 3 Subtract the tens and hundreds.

Hundreds	Tens	Ones
	9	12
3	10̸	
4̸	0̸	2̸
−	3	7
3	6	5

Subtract 3 tens from 9 tens.

Subtract 0 hundreds.

ANSWER 402 − 37 = 365

TRY THIS Find the difference.

1. 420 − 56 = ____
2. 732 − 89 = ____
3. 1704 − 859 = ____
4. 3042 − 2271 = ____

Name _____ Date _____

Summarize

Regrouping Across Zeros

Sometimes you need to regroup tens but there are no tens. So you have to first regroup hundreds as tens so you can regroup a ten as ones.

Hundreds	Tens	Ones
	9	10
	1̶0̶	
7̶	0̶	0̶
−	1	7
	8	3

Practice

Subtract. Regroup if necessary.

1.
Hundreds	Tens	Ones
5	0	2
−		8

2.
Hundreds	Tens	Ones
4	4	8
− 2	3	6

3.
Hundreds	Tens	Ones
6	0	3
− 2	7	9

4.
```
    5 7 0 0
  − 2 8 8 0
```

5.
```
    1 0 2 0 0
  −   4 0 9 0
```

6.
```
    3 2 0 0 0
  −   8 5 0 0
```

7.
```
    4 1 1 2 2
  − 1 8 0 8 1
```

8.
```
    1 0 0 0 0
  −       6 3
```

9.
```
    5 2 5 1 4
  −   7 5 9 5
```

Name _____ Date _____

Which of A, B, or C shows the correct difference?

10. 1050 − 96 _____

    A. 944   B. 954   C. 1044

11. 52,632 − 3885 _____

    A. 48,747   B. 48,847   C. 49,747

Write a subtraction problem to answer the question.

12. Sylvia has saved up **$147** toward her summer vacation airfare costing **$510**. How much more does Sylvia have to save?

    _____
    _____

13. Clayton is driving **230** miles to visit his sister. So far, he has driven **65** miles. How much farther does he have to drive?

    _____
    _____

14. The first year that Shannon's company held a Silly Hat Day, only **99** of **1000** employees wore a hat. How many employees did not wear a hat?

    _____
    _____

DID YOU GET IT?

15. **Fill in the missing words or numbers.** To subtract 9 from 100, regroup 1 hundred as 10 _____ and then regroup the result as _____ tens _____ ones.

16. **Explain your reasoning.** Use an example to explain how to regroup across a zero. How do you tell when regrouping is necessary?

    _____
    _____
    _____
    _____

Name _____ Date _____

LESSON 1-19
Mental Math Strategies for Addition and Subtraction

Words to Remember
Count on: To add
Count back: To subtract

Getting Started In this lesson, you will learn some simple mental math strategies. You know how to add numbers like $3 + 2$ in your head. You can also learn to add larger numbers.

EXAMPLE 1   Adding Tens

Find $40 + 20$.

Solution

40,   50,   60   Starting at 40, count on by 10s.
  $+10$ $+10$ 20 is 2 tens, so count on by 10s two times.

ANSWER $40 + 20 = 60$

Add Tens
Another way to find the sum is to think of addition facts. You know that $4 + 2 = 6$, so you know that 4 tens + 2 tens = 6 tens, or 60.

TRY THIS   Find the sum.

1. $30 + 40 =$ ☐

2. $50 + 30 =$ ☐

Mental Subtraction You can subtract $6 - 3$ in your head. You can also subtract larger numbers mentally.

EXAMPLE 2   Subtracting Tens

Find $50 - 20$.

Solution

50,   40,   30   Starting at 50, count back by 10s.
  -10 -10 20 is 2 tens, so count back by 10s two times.

ANSWER $50 - 20 = 30$

Math Intervention
Book 1 Whole Numbers

Name _____ Date _____

TRY THIS Find the difference.

3. 70 − 60 = ☐   4. 90 − 50 = ☐

EXAMPLE 3 Adding Two 2-digit Numbers

Find 14 + 43.

Solution

Step 1 Start at 14. Count on by 1s three times.

14, 15, 16, 17
    +1

Step 2 Start at 17. Count on by 10s four times.

17, 27, 37, 47, 57
    +10

ANSWER 14 + 43 = 57

EXAMPLE 4 Subtracting 2-digit Numbers

Find 86 − 23.

Solution

Step 1 Start at 86. Count back by 1s three times.

86, 85, 84, 83
    −1

Step 2 Start at 83. Count back by 10s two times.

83, 73, 63
    −10

ANSWER 86 − 23 = 63

TRY THIS Find the sum or difference.

5. 45 + 34 = ☐   6. 97 − 55 = ☐

Math Intervention
Book 1 Whole Numbers   73

Name _____   Date _____

> **Summarize**
>
> **Mental Math Strategies**
>
> To *add* one 2-digit number to another, count on by ones first. Then count on by tens.
>
> For **53 + 12**, count on by ones: **53, 54, 55**. Then count on by tens: **55, 65**.
>
> To *subtract* one 2-digit number from another, count back by ones first. Then count back by tens.
>
> For **75 − 23**, count back by ones: **75, 74, 73, 72**. Then count back by tens: **72, 62, 52**.

Practice

Find the sum or difference.

1. 20 + 60
2. 30 + 43
3. 50 + 12
4. 70 + 16
5. 90 − 30
6. 80 − 60
7. 78 − 22
8. 66 − 15

Which of A, B, or C shows the correct sum?

9. 35 + 32 _____

   A. 67   B. 57   C. 37

10. 48 + 21 _____

    A. 59   B. 68   C. 69

11. 82 + 11 _____

    A. 83   B. 93   C. 99

12. 28 + 61 _____

    A. 89   B. 88   C. 69

Which of A, B, or C shows the correct difference?

13. 70 − 40 _____

    A. 3   B. 30   C. 66

14. 87 − 32 _____

    A. 47   B. 55   C. 65

15. 93 − 61 _____

    A. 62   B. 34   C. 32

Math Intervention
Book 1 Whole Numbers

Name _____ Date _____

First tell whether you need to *add* or *subtract* to find the answer. Then solve the problem.

16. Quandalyn has **$20** in her wallet. She withdraws **$60** from a cash machine. How much money does she now have?

_____
_____
_____

17. Dan is driving to a client's office **38** miles away. He has already driven **12** miles. How many more miles does he have to drive?

_____
_____
_____

18. Richmond finds an old birthday card. Inside is written "Happy Birthday Richmond on your **15**th birthday – Nancy, August **1998**." In what year was Richmond born?

_____
_____
_____

DID YOU GET IT?

19. Explain your reasoning. When you add **23** and **14** mentally, you count on by **4** ones and then by **1** ten. So you are finding **23 + 4 + 10**. Explain why this is the same as **23 + 10 + 4**.

_____
_____
_____

20. Find the error. Dianne adds 17 to 30 by counting 17, 18, 19, 20. She writes **17 + 30 = 20**. How do you know Dianne made a mistake? Explain Dianne's error and describe what she should have done differently.

_____
_____
_____
_____

LESSON 1-20: Add 3 or More Numbers

> **Words to Remember**
> Addends: Numbers being added

Getting Started Now that you can add two numbers, you can extend this skill to adding three or more numbers.

EXAMPLE 1 — Adding Three 1-digit Numbers

Find $3 + 4 + 8$.

Solution

Step 1 Add the addends two at a time. First add 3 and 4.

$3 + 4 = 7$ There is no obvious way to regroup the addends to make tens, so just add the first two addends.

Step 2 Add the third addend.

$7 + 8 = 15$ Add the third addend to the sum in Step 1.

TRY THIS Find the sum.

1. $2 + 3 + 4 = $ ▢
2. $5 + 2 + 4 + 3 = $ ▢

EXAMPLE 2 — Adding Three 2-digit Numbers

Find $22 + 13 + 64$.

Solution

Tens	Ones
2	2
1	3
+ 6	4
9	9

Write the numbers in columns.

Add the ones. $2 + 3 + 4 = 9$

Then add the tens. $2 + 1 + 6 = 9$

TRY THIS Find the sum.

3. $12 + 23 + 14 = $ ▢
4. $25 + 31 + 11 = $ ▢

Math Intervention
Book 1 Whole Numbers

Name _____ Date _____

EXAMPLE 3 — Adding Three Numbers with Regrouping

Find $45 + 31 + 62$.

Solution

Look for Tens
Look for pairs of digits with a sum of 10. To add $4 + 3 + 6$, swap 3 and 6 to get $4 + 6 + 3$. Combine 4 and 6 to make 10. Then add 3.

Hundreds	Tens	Ones
1		
	4	5
	3	1
+	6	2
1	3	8

Write the numbers in columns.

Add the ones. $5 + 1 + 2 = 8$
Then add the tens. $4 + 3 + 6 = 13$
Regroup the 13 tens as 1 hundred 3 tens.
Add the hundreds. $1 + 0 = 1$

TRY THIS Find the sum.

5. $32 + 16 + 18 =$ ⬚　　**6.** $52 + 31 + 46 =$ ⬚

EXAMPLE 4 — Adding Three 3-Digit Numbers

Find $312 + 235 + 380$.

Solution

Hundreds	Tens	Ones
1		
3	1	2
2	3	5
+ 3	8	0
9	2	7

Write the numbers in columns.

Add the ones. $2 + 5 + 0 = 7$
Then add the tens. $1 + 3 + 8 = 12$
Regroup the 12 tens as 1 hundred 2 tens.
Add the hundreds. $1 + 3 + 2 + 3 = 9$

TRY THIS Find the sum.

7. $325 + 121 + 258 =$ ⬚　　**8.** $158 + 241 + 355 =$ ⬚

Name _____ Date _____

Summarize

Add 3 or More Numbers

To add three numbers, write them in columns. Add the ones, then the tens, then the hundreds. Regroup as necessary. Look for ways to combine digits to make tens.

Hundreds	Tens	Ones
	2	1
	7	6
	9	2
+	3	3
2	0	1

Practice

Find the sum.

1.
Tens	Ones
2	6
3	1
+ 4	2

2.
Tens	Ones
5	2
1	2
+ 3	3

3.
Tens	Ones
2	2
4	4
+ 1	3

4.
Tens	Ones
1	3
2	1
+ 5	3

5.
Tens	Ones
4	0
1	4
+ 2	1

6.
Tens	Ones
1	4
3	0
+ 5	4

7.
Hundreds	Tens	Ones
	5	2
	4	3
+	6	1

8.
Hundreds	Tens	Ones
	8	5
	4	8
+	7	5

9.
Hundreds	Tens	Ones
1	5	8
	6	6
+ 1	0	0

10.
Hundreds	Tens	Ones
2	6	5
1	2	2
+ 3	2	3

11.
Hundreds	Tens	Ones
2	0	6
	8	8
+ 1	7	7

12.
Hundreds	Tens	Ones
4	8	5
4	6	5
+	4	5

Math Intervention
Book 1 Whole Numbers

Name _____ Date _____

In Exercises 13–15, which of A, B, or C shows the correct sum?

13. 15 + 23 + 9 _____

    A. 47   **B.** 42   **C.** 37

14. 16 + 44 + 20 _____

    A. 70   **B.** 80   **C.** 82

15. 150 + 65 + 45 _____

    A. 210   **B.** 250   **C.** 260

16. In April, it rained about **5** inches, in May about **7** inches, and in June about **6** inches. About how much rain fell in the three months combined?

_____
_____

17. Julie knitted **3** scarves and sold them for **$23**, **$27**, and **$19**. How much did she earn altogether?

_____
_____

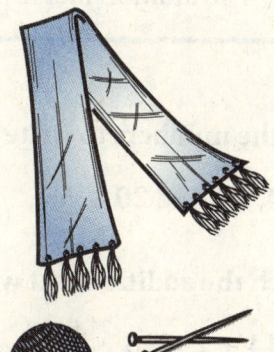

18. On a three-day roadtrip, Mason drove **125** miles the first day, **210** miles the second day, and **275** miles the third day. How far did Mason drive altogether?

_____
_____

DID YOU GET IT?

19. Explain your reasoning. When you are adding a string of digits, why do you look for pairs of numbers with a sum of **10**?

_____
_____
_____

20. Explain the error. Ezekiel adds 45 + 11 + 21 and gets 56. Explain Ezekiel's error.

_____
_____
_____

Name _____   Date _____

Mixed Practice for Lessons 1-8 to 1-20

Vocabulary Review

Match the word with its mathematical meaning and everyday meaning.

Word		Mathematical meaning	Everyday meaning

1. difference   ___, ___   A. the amount one thing is greater than or less than another   X. to arrange in a new grouping

2. regroup   ___, ___   B. to write a group of numbers as another number   Y. the condition of being unlike

Fill in the missing words.

3. Two subtraction facts from the sum $8 + 4 = 12$ are _____ and _____.

4. An addition fact from the subtraction fact $16 - 7 = 9$ is _____.

Use the numbers to write one addition fact and two subtraction facts.

5. 4, 16, and 20

6. 30, 70, and 100

Match the addition fact with its related subtraction fact.

7. $14 + 2 = 16$ _____   A. $18 - 8 = 10$

8. $11 + 9 = 20$ _____   B. $20 - 9 = 11$

9. $0 + 19 = 19$ _____   C. $16 - 14 = 2$

10. $8 + 10 = 18$ _____   D. $19 - 19 = 0$

Use the properties of addition to find the sum.

11. $4 + 10 + 6$ 12. $8 + 2 + 8$ 13. $6 + 0 + 10$

14. $5 + 5 + 7 + 3$ 15. $9 + 2 + 1 + 8$ 16. $(2 + 8) + (6 + 4)$

17. $(10 + 5) + 5$ 18. $2 + (7 + 8) + 3$ 19. $5 + (4 + 5) + 0$

20. Show the number 15 in six different ways that include the number 8.

_____   _____   _____

_____   _____   _____

Math Intervention
Book 1 Whole Numbers

Name _____ Date _____

Find the sum.

21. 20 + 30   **22.** 8 + 52   **23.** 34 + 14   **24.** 48 + 11

25. 18,650 + 3462   **26.** 701 + 213   **27.** 2090 + 3991   **28.** 118 + 211

Find the difference.

29. 532 − 24   **30.** 789 − 303   **31.** 420 − 312   **32.** 398 − 299

33. 1439 − 341   **34.** 3783 − 839   **35.** 8091 − 2391   **36.** 19,950 − 3072

Find the sum or difference.

37. 90,876 + 2872   **38.** 87,693 − 6593   **39.** 8960 + 900,569

40. 780,980 − 56,891   **41.** 254 + 34 + 651   **42.** 40 + 18 + 435

43. Fill in the missing information to solve the problem.

Arun has $82 in his wallet. He withdraws an additional $20 three times from a cash machine and puts the money in his wallet. How much money does he have now?

Step 1 Arun starts with $_____.

Step 2 He uses a cash machine ____ times and withdraws $_____ each time.

Step 3 The total he withdraws from the bank is $_____ + $_____ + $_____ = $_____.

Step 4 The total Arun has in his wallet now is $_____ + $_____ = $_____.

Solve the problem. Explain your answer.

44. A board is 14 feet long. A carpenter cuts off boards that are 1 foot, 3 feet, and 8 feet long. What is the length of board remaining?

_____
_____
_____

45. Kayla had 32,561 miles on her car's odometer when she went on a trip. After each stop, she recorded her new miles. After the first stop, her miles were 33,108, and after the second stop, her miles were 33,975. How many miles did she travel in all?

_____
_____
_____

Math Intervention
Book 1 Whole Numbers

Name _____ Date _____

Multiplying and Dividing Numbers

> **Goal:** Use concrete objects to understand how to multiply by repeated addition or divide by repeated subtraction.
>
> Materials: counters, index cards

Getting Started You learned how to add and subtract numbers using a model. You can also use models to multiply or divide numbers.

Use a model to show that $3 \times 5 = 15$.

Step 1 **Arrange** a column of 3 counters. Using 3 more counters, add another column next to the other column.

Step 2 **Repeat** adding columns of 3 until you have 5 columns of 3. Then count the counters. _____

Step 3 **Complete** the statement: 5 columns of _____ counters equals _____ counters.

This is the multiplication fact $3 \times 5 = 15$.

Step 4 **Repeat** Steps 1–3 with columns of 2 counters. Add columns of 2 counters until you reach 4 columns. Fill in the missing information to write a new multiplication fact.

☐ × 4 = ☐

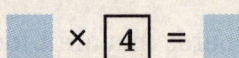

- Form groups of 4 students. Each student should have counters and 4 index cards.

- Each student writes a multiplication fact using numbers less than 20 on each of the 4 cards.

- The players switch cards, model the multiplication facts with counters, and check each other's work.

Math Intervention
Book 1 Whole Numbers

Name _____   Date _____

EXAMPLE 2

Use a model to show that 12 ÷ 4 = 3.

Step 1 **Start** with **12** counters. Subtract **4** counters. Now repeat subtracting **4** more counters at a time until there are none left. How many times were you able to subtract **4** counters? _____

Step 2 **Complete** the statement: You can subtract _____ groups of 4 counters from _____ counters.

This is the division fact **12 ÷ 4 = 3**.

Step 3 **Use 24** counters this time, subtracting **6** counters at a time. Fill in the missing information to write a new division fact.

☐ ÷ 6 = ☐

EXAMPLE 3

Show that 22 ÷ 4 = 5, with 2 left over.

Look Ahead
You will learn more about remainders in Lesson 1-29.

Using **22** counters, subtract **4** counters at a time. Fill in the missing information to write a new division fact with some counters left over, called the *remainder*.

                remainder
☐ ÷ 4 = ☐ + 2

Practice

1. Write the multiplication fact shown in the diagram.

2. Write the division fact shown in the diagram.

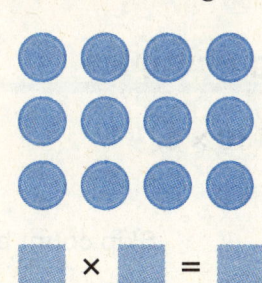

☐ × ☐ = ☐

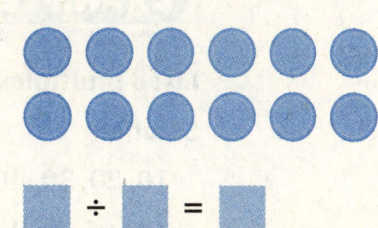

☐ ÷ ☐ = ☐

In Exercises 3–10, use counters to help you multiply or divide two numbers. Some division problems have a remainder.

3. 4 × 2   4. 6 × 4   5. 10 × 3   6. 5 × 5

7. 10 ÷ 2   8. 25 ÷ 5   9. 27 ÷ 4   10. 24 ÷ 10

11. **Make a Conjecture** Based on your answers to Exercises 1–10, make a conjecture about the results of **100 × 5** and **100 ÷ 5**.

Math Intervention
Book 1 Whole Numbers

LESSON 1-22
Understand Multiplication and Division

Words to Remember

Product: The result of multiplying two numbers $3 \times 6, x \cdot y$

Quotient: The result of dividing two numbers $10 \div 5, \frac{18}{3}$

Multiple: The product of a number and a nonzero whole number 48 is a multiple of 16 because $16 \times 3 = 48$.

Factor: The quotient of a number and a nonzero whole number with nothing left over (so, *a remainder* of **0**) $12 \div 4 = 3$, so 4 and 3 are factors of 12.

Getting Started There are several ways to multiply or divide numbers. For example, now that you can add numbers, you can use repeated addition to multiply two numbers.

EXAMPLE 1 Multiplying by Repeated Addition

Show that $12 \times 5 = 60$ by repeated addition.

Solution

Add **12** five times.

$0 + 12 = 12 \rightarrow 12 + 12 = 24 \rightarrow 24 + 12 = 36 \rightarrow$
$36 + 12 = 48 \rightarrow 48 + 12 = 60$

EXAMPLE 2 Counting Multiples

List 8 multiples of 10. Then find 10×5.

Solution

10, 20, 30, 40, 50, 60, 70, 80   Skip count by 10s.

$10 \times 5 = 50$ The product is the 5th multiple.

EXAMPLE 3 Multiplying Using a Model

Find 3×8.

Arrange **8** columns of **3**. Using stars to represent ones, you count **24** stars. **24** is a *multiple* of **3**.

Math Intervention
Book 1 Whole Numbers

Try This

1. Use repeated addition to find 5×20.

   $0 + 5 =$ ☐ → ☐ $+ 5 =$ ☐ → ☐ $+ 5 =$ ☐ → ......

2. 64 is what multiple of 2? Write a multiplication fact using 64 and 2.

EXAMPLE 4 Dividing Using Factors

Find the factors of 32. Then find $32 \div 4$.

Solution

$1 \times 32 = 32 \rightarrow 32 \div 1 = 32$
$2 \times 16 = 32 \rightarrow 32 \div 2 = 16$
$4 \times 8 = 32 \rightarrow 32 \div 4 = 8$
$16 \times 2 = 32 \rightarrow 32 \div 16 = 2$

The factors of 32 are 1, 2, 4, 8, 16, and 32.

Remember
A factor divides a number evenly without anything left over.

ANSWER $32 \div 4 = 8$

EXAMPLE 5 Dividing by Counting On

Find $57 \div 5$.

Solution

Count on by 5s until you reach a number equal to or over 57.

Count	1	2	3	4	5	6	7	8	9	10	11	12
	5,	10,	15,	20,	25,	30,	35,	40,	45,	50,	<u>55</u>,	60

ANSWER $57 - 55 = 2$, so $57 \div 5 = 11$ with 2 left over.

Look Ahead
You will see in Lesson 1-29 that remainders are often written using an "R." So, the answer to Example 5 is 11 R 2.

Try This Divide by using repeated subtraction.

3. Follow these steps to divide $80 \div 20$.

   Step 1 Subtract. $80 - 20 =$ ☐

   Step 2 Subtract 20 again from the result above. ☐ $- 20 =$ ☐

   Step 3 Repeat subtracting 20 until the result is less than 20. How many times did you subtract 20? _____

   Step 4 Did you have anything left over? If so, how much? _____

   Step 5 Use the results of Steps 3 and 4. $80 \div 20 =$ ☐ with remainder ☐

Name _____   Date _____

> **Summarize**
>
> **Understanding Multiplication and Division**
> - The result of multiplying two numbers is called the product.
> - You can find a product by counting multiples, adding repeatedly, or using a model.
> - The result of dividing two numbers is the quotient. If the remainder is **0**, then the second number is a factor of the first.
> - You can divide by finding the factors of a number or by repeated subtraction. Using factors gives you a remainder of **0**.

Practice

1. Give the first **10** multiples of **5**. Then find **5 × 8**.

Show how to find the products by repeated addition.

2. 6 × 7   3. 9 × 8   4. 11 × 5   5. 15 × 5

Match the product with the correct model.

6. 3 × 4 _____   7. 4 × 2 _____   8. 2 × 5 _____

A. 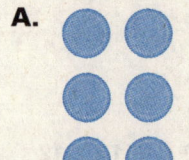   B.    C.

9. **75** is what multiple of **5**? Write a multiplication fact about **75** and **5**.

List all the factors of the given number.

10. 24   11. 10   12. 30   13. 49

14. List all the factors of **20**. Write three division facts using the factors.

In Exercises 15–18, show how to divide by repeated subtraction. Then give the answer.

15. 28 ÷ 7   16. 40 ÷ 10   17. 32 ÷ 5   18. 50 ÷ 8

Math Intervention
Book 1 Whole Numbers

Name _____   Date _____

In Exercises 19–26, find the quotient. State the remainder, if any.

19. 15 ÷ 3   **20.** 34 ÷ 17   **21.** 65 ÷ 5   **22.** 70 ÷ 10

23. 18 ÷ 3   **24.** 43 ÷ 3   **25.** 103 ÷ 5   **26.** 150 ÷ 25

27. You and a friend order a pizza. You pay **3** times as much as your friend. If your friend paid **$5**, how much did you pay? Justify your answer.

_____
_____

28. You want to buy a computer for **$800** and plan to save **$200** per month. How many months do you need to save? Justify your answer.

_____
_____

29. You want to start a training program for running a **26** kilometer race. The first week you run **4** kilometers and you plan to add **2** kilometers to your distance every week. In how many more weeks will you be running **26** kilometers? Justify your answer.

_____
_____

DID YOU GET IT?

30. Fill in the missing words. When finding the product 3 × 15 you should write _____ multiples of _____.

31. Write a word problem. Write a word problem using the numbers at the right. Then complete the calculation to solve the problem.

6 × 3 = ____

_____
_____

32. Explain your reasoning. Your friend says that if you split a **$32** fee for cutting grass **4** ways that each of you will get **$8**. Is your friend correct? Explain why or why not.

_____
_____

Lesson 1-23: Multiplication and Division Facts

> **Words to Remember**
>
> Product: The result of multiplying two numbers
>
> Multiple: The product of a number and a nonzero whole number
>
> Factor: The quotient of a number and a nonzero whole number with a remainder of **0**
>
> Multiplication table: The pattern you get when you multiply a number by **1, 2, 3, 4, 5, 6, 7, 8, 9,** and **10**

Getting Started In Lesson 1-22 you learned how to multiply and divide two numbers in several ways. If you memorize multiplication tables for numbers from **1** to **10**, multiplying and dividing can be quicker and easier.

EXAMPLE 1   Finding Multiplication Patterns

Use a pattern to find the next 2 products and sums.

Pattern of multiples	Repeated addition pattern
3 × 1 = 3	0 + 3 = 3
3 × 2 = 6	3 + 3 = 6
3 × 3 = 9	6 + 3 = 9
3 × 4 = 12	9 + 3 = 12
3 × ☐ = ☐	12 + ☐ = ☐
☐ × ☐ = ☐	☐ + ☐ = ☐

Solution

Pattern of multiples

The numbers in the second column go up by **1** and the products go up by **3**. The next **2** lines are 3 × 5 = 15 and 3 × 6 = 18.

Repeated addition pattern

3 is added repeatedly and the sum is then the first number in the next line. The next **2** lines are 12 + 3 = 15 and 15 + 3 = 18.

The results are the *same* using either the Pattern of multiples or the Repeated addition pattern.

Math Intervention
Book 1 Whole Numbers

Multiplication Tables If you continue the pattern in Example 1 until 3×10, you've done a multiplication table for 3. The products 3, 6, 9, 12, and so on, are multiples of 3. If you memorize the multiplication table for 3, finding the multiples of 3 is faster than using repeated addition.

TRY THIS Write a multiplication table to "times 10" for the number.

1. 2
2. 4

EXAMPLE 2 Listing Factors

What are the factors of 12?

Solution

Look at each pattern below.

$2 \times 4 = 8$	$3 \times 2 = 6$	$4 \times 1 = 4$
$2 \times 5 = 10$	$3 \times 3 = 9$	$4 \times 2 = 8$
$2 \times 6 = 12$	$3 \times 4 = 12$	$4 \times 3 = 12$

Since $2 \times 6 = 12$, 2 and 6 are factors of 12. Verify that the other factors of 12 are 1, 3, 4, and 12.

ANSWER A complete list of the factors of 12 are 1, 2, 3, 4, 6, and 12.

EXAMPLE 3 Finding a Factor

5 times what number is 20?

Solution

Multiplication and division undo each other. To find "5 times what number is 20", you can find "20 divided by 5 is what number."

$20 \div 5 = 4$ Use division.

ANSWER The remainder is 0, so 5 and 4 are each factors of 20 and $5 \times 4 = 20$.

TRY THIS Consider the numbers 7 and 21.

3. 7 times what number is 21?

   a. Use multiplication. 7 ◯ ▢ = 21

   b. Use division. 21 ◯ 7 = ▢

4. What are the factors of 21? _____

Math Intervention
Book 1 Whole Numbers **89**

Name _____ Date _____

> **Summarize**
>
> **Multiplication and Division Facts**
> - A multiplication table (to "times 10") is the pattern you get when you multiply a number by 1, 2, 3, 4, 5, 6, 7, 8, 9, and 10.
> - Memorizing a multiplication table may be faster than using repeated addition when you do a problem.
> - You can use division to find the factors of a number when one factor is known.

Practice

Write a multiplication table to "times 10" for each number. Memorize the table so that finding the product is automatic. Put a star in the box after you have memorized the table.

1. 1 ☐
2. 2 ☐
3. 3 ☐
4. 4 ☐
5. 5 ☐
6. 6 ☐
7. 7 ☐
8. 8 ☐
9. 9 ☐
10. 10 ☐

11. Test yourself: Recite the multiplication tables of 2s, 5s, and 10s from memory.

Write the factors of the number.

12. 6 _____
13. 8 _____
14. 15 _____
15. 16 _____
16. 26 _____
17. 36 _____
18. 52 _____
19. 80 _____
20. 7 _____
21. 23 _____
22. 31 _____
23. 53 _____

Math Intervention
Book 1 Whole Numbers

Name _____ Date _____

24. What do you notice about the factors for the numbers in Exercises 20–23? These numbers are called *prime numbers*. Explain what that might mean.

_____
_____
_____

Find a second factor of a number when one factor is known.

25. 4 times what number is 24?   **26.** 8 times what number is 72?

27. 41 times what number is 41?   **28.** 17 times what number is 51?

First tell if you are using a *multiple* or a *factor*. Then solve the problem. Explain your answer.

29. Your allowance is $8 per week for 5 weeks. What is the total you earn?

_____
_____
_____

30. You want to save $250 to buy an MP3 player and plan to save $25 per week. How many weeks do you need to save?

_____
_____
_____

Week 1 $25
Week 2 $50

Goal: $250
         Yeah!

DID YOU GET IT?

31. Give an example. Give an example of 3 numbers that have a factor of 4.

_____
_____

32. Explain your reasoning. There are 28 girls in a youth sports league. You want to make teams with 4 girls each. How many teams can you make?

_____
_____
_____

LESSON 1-24: Multiply 2-digit Numbers by 1-digit Numbers

Getting Started In Lesson 1-23 you learned your multiplication tables from **1** to **10**. You can use these multiplication facts to help you multiply larger numbers.

EXAMPLE 1 Multiplying without Regrouping

Find 24 × 2.

Solution

Tens	Ones
2	4
×	2
4	8

Write the numbers in columns.

Multiply the ones' digit by 2. Then multiply the tens' digit by 2.

Write the results below the line.

ANSWER 24 × 2 = 48

TRY THIS Find the product.

1. 13 × 3

2. 41 × 2

EXAMPLE 2 Multiplying with Regrouping

Find 28 × 3.

Solution Show regrouping.

Tens	Ones
2	
2	8
×	3
8	4

3 × 8 = 24, so regroup the 24 as 2 tens 4 ones.

3 × 2 = 6 and 6 + 2 = 8, so write 8 tens below the line.

ANSWER 28 × 3 = 84

CHECK 28 = 20 + 8, so you can use each partial product to check your result.

3 × 8 = 24

3 × 20 = 60

24 + 60 = 84, so 3 × 28 = 84.   Answer checks.

Math Intervention
Book 1 Whole Numbers

Name _____ Date _____

TRY THIS Find the product.

3. 15 × 4

Tens	Ones
×	

4. 29 × 3

Tens	Ones
×	

EXAMPLE 3 Multiplying with Regrouping

Find 37 × 6.

Solution

Step 1 Multiply 6 × 7 = 42.

Step 2 Regroup 42 as 4 tens 2 ones.

Step 3 Notice that 3 tens is 30. Multiply 6 × 30 = 180.

Step 4 Add 4 tens to 180.

40 + 180 = 220

ANSWER 220 + 2 = 222

Show regrouping.

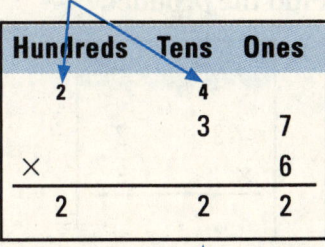

22 tens = 2 hundreds + 2 tens

Use Multiplication Tables

You always multiply numbers two at a time, and many of the individual products are ones you memorized when you learned your multiplication tables. **Keep practicing the tables!**

TRY THIS Fill in the missing information to find the product.

5. 53 × 5

Hundreds	Tens	Ones
×		

6. 72 × 4

Hundreds	Tens	Ones
×		

Math Intervention
Book 1 Whole Numbers

Name _____ Date _____

Summarize

Multiplying a 2-digit Number by a 1-digit Number

(1) Multiply the ones. Regroup tens if necessary.
(2) Multiply the tens. Regroup hundreds if necessary.
(3) Add down.

Tens	Ones
3	1
×	3
9	3

Hundreds	Tens	Ones
3	3	
	4	5
×		7
3	1	5

Practice

Find the product.

1.
Tens	Ones
3	2
×	3

2.
Tens	Ones
2	4
×	2

3.
Tens	Ones
1	2
×	4

4.
Tens	Ones
1	8
×	3

5.
Tens	Ones
2	7
×	2

6.
Tens	Ones
1	9
×	4

7.
Hundreds	Tens	Ones
	3	5
×		8

8.
Hundreds	Tens	Ones
	2	9
×		7

9.
Hundreds	Tens	Ones
	6	8
×		5

10.
Hundreds	Tens	Ones
	7	5
×		4

Name _____ Date _____

Which of A, B, or C shows the correct product?

11. 47 × 3 _____

    A. 121 B. 141 C. 1421

12. 99 × 9 _____

    A. 811 B. 891 C. 999

13. You and 5 friends each contribute $18 for a fund raiser at school. How much is contributed altogether?

    _____
    _____

14. Jacquin downloaded 47 songs from the Internet at a cost of $2 each. How much did he pay?

    _____
    _____

15. On a road trip, your family traveled 55 miles per hour for 6 hours, rested for 2 hours, then drove 52 miles per hour for 3 more hours. How many miles did you travel?

    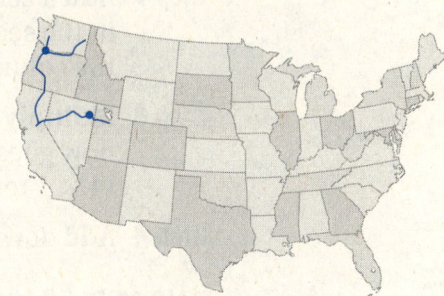

    _____
    _____

DID YOU GET IT?

16. **Draw a model.** Multiply 37 × 4. Draw a model to illustrate how you used regrouping.

    _____

17. **Find the error.** Joelene multiplies 84 × 3 and gets 242. Explain her error.

    _____
    _____

Math Intervention
Book 1 Whole Numbers

Name _____   Date _____

LESSON 1-25
Multiply and Divide by 10 and Multiples of 10, 100, and 1000

Getting Started   In Lesson 1-24 you learned how to multiply a 2-digit number by a 1-digit number. Now you can multiply or divide by 10 and multiples of 10.

EXAMPLE 1   Multiplying by 10

Multiply 524 × 10.

Solution

You need to have a thousands' column.

Step 1 **Multiply** each top number by **0**. Each product is **0**.

Step 2 **Add** a zero in the ones' column in the second row. This lines up the columns correctly.

Step 3 **Multiply** the top row by **1**. **1 × 4** now goes in the tens' column (**4 × 1** ten = **40**), and so on.

Step 4 **Add** down.

Thousands	Hundreds	Tens	Ones
	5	2	4
×		1	0
	0	0	0
+ 5	2	4	0
5	2	4	0

ANSWER 524 × 10 = 5240

TRY THIS   Find the product.

1. 230 × 10

2. 4281 × 10

Patterns of Zeros   When you multiply by **10**, **100**, or **1000**, there is a pattern you can use. Study Example 1. What do you notice? If you said that multiplying a whole number by **10** adds one zero to the end, you are right. You can multiply by **10** using this pattern.

   36 × 10 = 360   Add a zero on the end.

TRY THIS   Use a pattern.

3. Find 6537 × 10. _____

4. Find 100 × 10. _____

Math Intervention
Book 1 Whole Numbers

EXAMPLE 2 Multiplying by 100

Find 3724 × 100.

Solution

Step 1 **Count** the number of zeros in **100**. → 2 zeros

Step 2 **Add** two zeros to the end of **3724**. → 372400

Step 3 **Add** a comma to help you read the answer. Put a comma before the hundreds' place.

ANSWER 3724 × 100 = 372,400

EXAMPLE 3 Using a Place-Value Chart

Redo Example 2 with a place-value chart. What column in the chart contains the 3 before multiplying? after multiplying?

Hundred-Thousands	Ten-Thousands	Thousands	Hundreds	Tens	Ones
		3	7	2	4

Solution

Before multiplying, the **3** is in the thousands' place, as shown. After multiplying, the **3** is in the hundred-thousands' place. That is because adding **2** zeros "moves" the number over **2** places to the left.

EXAMPLE 4 Dividing a Multiple of 10 by 100

Look Ahead
You will learn more about dividing other types of numbers in later lessons.

Find 873,500 ÷ 100.

Solution

Step 1 **Count** the number of zeros in **100**.

2 zeros → 2 places

Step 2 **Remove** zeros. From the ones' place, count **2** places to the left. Cross out **2** zeros.   873500

ANSWER 873,500 ÷ 100 = 8735

TRY THIS Multiply or divide.

5. 5714 × 100

6. 7,321,000 ÷ 1000

Name _____ Date _____

Summarize
Multiplying and Dividing by 10, 100, and 1000

Multiplication by	Number of zeros to add	Words
10	1	Add 1 zero to the end of the number.
100	2	Add 2 zeros to the end of the number.
1000	3	Add 3 zeros to the end of the number.

Dividing a multiple of 10 by	Number of zeros to remove	Words
10	1	Remove 1 zero from the end of the number.
100	2	Remove 2 zeros from the end of the number.
1000	3	Remove 3 zeros from the end of the number.

Practice

Find the product.

1. | Hundreds | Tens | Ones |
    |---|---|---|
    | | 3 | 2 |
    | × | | 1 | 0 |

2. | Hundreds | Tens | Ones |
    |---|---|---|
    | | 2 | 8 |
    | × | | 1 | 0 |

3. | Hundreds | Tens | Ones |
    |---|---|---|
    | | 5 | 5 |
    | × | | 1 | 0 |

Multiply using a pattern.

4. 182 × 100
5. 1297 × 1000
6. 513 × 10
7. 787 × 100
8. 481 × 1000
9. 93 × 100

Divide using a pattern.

10. 8400 ÷ 10
11. 9,320,000 ÷ 100
12. 8200 ÷ 100
13. 7,605,000 ÷ 1000
14. 17,350,000 ÷ 1000
15. 93,400 ÷ 100

Math Intervention
Book 1 Whole Numbers

Name _____   Date _____

Which of A, B, or C is the correct place value for the first digit in the product?

16. 832 × 100 _____

   A. hundreds' place   B. thousands' place   C. ten-thousands' place

17. 9024 × 10 _____

   A. hundreds' place   B. thousands' place   C. ten-thousands' place

First tell if you need to *multiply* or *divide* to find the answer. Then solve the problem. Explain your answer.

18. You and 9 friends want to raise $220 for the entrance fee to a bike-a-thon fundraiser. How much should each of you raise?

   _____
   _____

19. Nassim saved $10 a week for each of 13 weeks. How much did he save altogether?

   _____
   _____

20. Evelyn has $100 per week deposited automatically into her checking account. How much does she save in a year?

   _____
   _____

DID YOU GET IT?

21. **Fill in the missing words.** To _____ a number by 100 using a pattern, add _____ zeros to the end of the number.

22. **Compare.** Which answer is larger, the product 4000 × 100 or the quotient 4000 ÷ 100? Explain how you know.

   _____
   _____

23. **Explain your reasoning.** Are multiplying by 10 and dividing by 10 inverse operations? Explain how you know.

   _____
   _____

LESSON 1-26
Multiply 2-digit and 3-digit Numbers by a 2-digit Number

Words to Remember

Estimate: To find an answer that is not exact

Estimates tell you *about how many* or *about how much*. You may find estimates helpful when you don't need to know the exact answer to solve a problem or when you want to make sure that the exact answer you find is reasonable.

Getting Started In Lesson 1-24 you learned how to multiply 2-digit numbers by 1-digit numbers. You will now multiply a 2- or 3-digit number by a 2-digit number.

Using Estimation You can estimate a product of numbers first to get a sense of its size. Then actually multiply the numbers and use the estimate to decide whether your exact calculation is reasonable.

EXAMPLE 1   Multiplying without Regrouping

Estimate 24 × 12. Then find the product.

Solution

Use rounding to estimate.

$24 \times 12 \rightarrow 25 \times 10$, or 250

Step 1 Multiply 24 × 2 = 48.

Step 2 Multiply 10 × 24 = 240.

Step 3 Add down.

Hundreds	Tens	Ones
	2	4
×	1	2
	4	8
+ 2	4	0
2	8	8

ANSWER 48 + 240 = 288

CHECK your answer Think of 12 as 2 + 10. Then you can check your answer if you think of the problem as 2 × 24 + 10 × 24, or 48 + 240.
48 + 240 = 288

CHECK using your estimate Compare your answer to your estimate. Since **288** is close to **250**, the answer is reasonable. If you put **250** on a place-value chart, it would be a number in the hundreds. If your answer to Example 1 came out with a different place value, you would need to retrace your steps to find your mistake.

TRY THIS   Find the product.

1. 32 × 13
2. 24 × 11
3. 103 × 23

Math Intervention
Book 1 Whole Numbers

EXAMPLE 2 Multiplying with Regrouping

Estimate 38 × 49. Then find the product.

Solution

Use rounding to estimate.

38 × 49 → 40 × 50, or 2000

> **Remember**
> When you multiply by a **tens' digit**, there will be a 0 in the ones' column.

Step 1 Multiply by the ones' digit. Regroup if necessary.

```
   7
  38
× 49
 342  ← 38 × 9
```

Step 2 Multiply by the tens' digit. Regroup if necessary.

```
   3
   7
  38
× 49
 342
+1520 ← 38 × 40
```

Step 3 Add the partial products to find 38 × 49.

```
   3
   7
  38
× 49
 342
+1520
 1862
```

ANSWER 38 × 49 = 1862

CHECK your estimate Compare your answer in Example 2 to the estimate. Since **1862** is close to **2000**, the answer is reasonable.

EXAMPLE 3 Multiplying by Multiples of 10

Find 75 × 50.

Solution

Step 1 Multiply by 0.

Step 2 Multiply 75 × 50 = 3750.

Step 3 Add down.

ANSWER 75 × 50 = 3750

```
          2
          7 5
×         5 0
          0 0
+     3 7 5 0
      3 7 5 0
```

TRY THIS Find the product.

4. 59 × 80

5. 95 × 43

6. 372 × 47

Name _____   Date _____

> **Summarize**
>
> **Multiplying Numbers by 2-digit Numbers**
> (1) Multiply by the ones' digit. Regroup tens if necessary.
> (2) Multiply by the tens' digit. Regroup hundreds if necessary.
> (3) Keep multiplying and regrouping.
> (4) Add down.
>
> | Hundreds | Tens | Ones |
> |---|---|---|
> | | 1 | |
> | | 3 | |
> | | 3 | 5 |
> | × | 2 | 7 |
> | 2 | 4 | 5 |
> | + 7 | 0 | 0 |
> | 9 | 4 | 5 |

Practice

Find the product.

1. 41 × 12
2. 91 × 11
3. 21 × 14

4. 11 × 28
5. 62 × 23
6. 154 × 27

7. 231 × 21
8. 25 × 25
9. 732 × 33

10. 986 × 78
11. 49 × 61
12. 143 × 84

Which of A, B, or C is a good estimate for the product shown?

13. 472 × 30 _____

   A. 1500
   B. 12,000
   C. 15,000

14. 49 × 98 _____

   A. 360
   B. 500
   C. 5000

Show how to multiply each of the following by using a multiple of 10 and repeated addition.

15. 98 × 40
16. 90 × 82
17. 124 × 40

Math Intervention
Book 1 Whole Numbers

Name _____ Date _____

18. A rock concert promoter still needs to sell **354** concert tickets at **$25** each for the concert to be a sell-out. What is the total price of the tickets?

_____
_____

19. Scott wanted to use his **$200** savings account to buy his **17** favorite DVDs at a cost of **$19** each. Was he able to buy all of them? Explain.

_____
_____

20. The monthly maintenance fee at a townhouse housing development is **$203**. How much does a homeowner pay over the course of **5** years?

_____
_____

DID YOU GET IT?

21. Use estimation. Estimate the product **148 × 98**. Then multiply and check your estimation.

_____
_____
_____

22. Explain the error. Juan multiplies **84 × 13** and gets **1082**. Explain his error.

_____
_____
_____

23. Solve a simpler problem. Pauline wants to know how to multiply **250** by **750**. How can she find the answer by solving a simpler problem?

_____
_____
_____

LESSON 1-27: Multiply 3-digit and 4-digit Numbers by a 3-digit Number

Getting Started In Lesson 1-26 you learned how to multiply 2- and 3-digit numbers by 2-digit numbers. You will now multiply a 3- or 4-digit number by a 3-digit number.

 **Multiplying a 3-digit Number by a 3-digit Number**

Find 314 × 204. Use a grid to make sure the numbers line up correctly.

Solution

Step 1 Multiply by the ones' digit. Regroup.

Step 2 Multiply by the tens' digit **0** and then by the hundreds' digit **2**.

Step 3 Add the partial products.

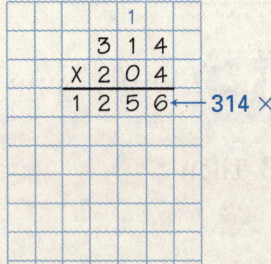

ANSWER 314 × 204 = 64,056

CHECK your answer Think of 204 as 200 + 4. Then you can check your answer if you think of the problem as 314 × 200 + 314 × 4, or 62,800 + 1256 = 64,056.

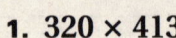 Find the product.

1. 320 × 413
2. 251 × 143
3. 372 × 257

 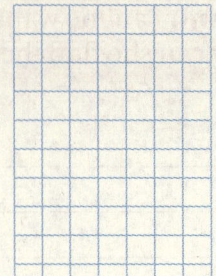 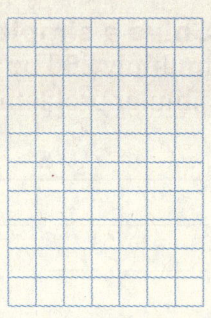

Math Intervention
Book 1 Whole Numbers
104

Name _____ Date _____

 **Multiplying a 4-digit Number by a 3-digit Number**

Estimate 7218 × 451. Then find the product.

Solution

Use rounding to estimate.

7218 × 451 → 7000 × 500, or 3,500,000

You can see that this is a large number, so multiply carefully!

Remember

When you multiply by the tens' digit, there will be a 0 in the ones' column.
When you multiply by the hundreds' digit, there will be a 0 in the tens' column and a 0 in the ones' column.

Step 1 **Multiply** by the ones' digit.

```
   7218
 ×  451
   7218  ← 7218 × 1
```

Step 2 **Multiply** by the tens' digit. Regroup if necessary.

```
    1 4
   7218
 ×  451
   7218
 360900  ← 7218 × 50
```

Step 3 **Multiply** by the hundreds' digit and add the partial products.

```
     3
   1 4
   7218
 ×  451
   7218
 360900
+2887200  ← 7218 × 400
 3255318   Add down.
```

Step 4 **Add** commas so the answer is easier to read.

ANSWER 7218 × 451 = 3,255,318

CHECK your estimate Compare your answer in Example 2 to the estimate. Since **3,255,318** is close to **3,500,000**, the answer is reasonable.

TRY THIS Find the product.

4. 1470 × 413   5. 2931 × 703   6. 3272 × 524

Math Intervention
Book 1 Whole Numbers **105**

Name _____ Date _____

> **Summarize**
>
> **Multiplying Numbers by 3-digit Numbers**
> (1) Multiply by the ones' digit. Regroup tens if necessary.
> (2) Multiply by the tens' digit. Regroup hundreds if necessary.
> (3) Multiply the hundreds. Regroup hundreds if necessary.
> (4) Continue multiplying if necessary.
> (5) Add down.

	Hundreds	Tens	Ones
	3	1 3	
	1	4	5
×		2 7	1
		1 4	5
	1 0	1 5	0
+	2 9	0 0	0
	3 9	2 9	5

Practice

Find the product.

1. 410 × 120
2. 901 × 111
3. 287 × 129

4. 191 × 281
5. 362 × 235
6. 154 × 127

7. 238 × 121
8. 3581 × 205
9. 2587 × 342

10. 9860 × 708
11. 490 × 611
12. 143 × 127

Which of A, B, or C is a good estimate for the product shown?

13. 512 × 300 _____

   A. 1500   B. 15,000   C. 150,000

14. 4967 × 96 _____

   A. 5000   B. 50,000   C. 500,000

Multiply each of the following by using a multiple of hundred and repeated addition.

15. 150 × 400
16. 900 × 700
17. 1240 × 300

Math Intervention
Book 1 Whole Numbers

Name _____ Date _____

18. Tuition at a local college is **$8700** a year. If there are **852** students in the freshman class, how much does the college receive in tuition from the those students?
_____
_____

19. Ross wants to save **$250** per month until he retires. What is his savings after **400** months if interest is not included?
_____
_____

20. Jermaine donates **$150** for each home run a baseball team makes during a season. At the end of a season, the team has a total of **272** home runs. How much does Jermaine donate?
_____
_____

DID YOU GET IT?

21. Use estimation. Estimate the product 2552 × 978. Then multiply and check your estimation.
_____
_____
_____

22. Eliminate choices. Marina wants to estimate how many digits are in the product 832 × 700. Her choices are 3, 4, 5, or 6 digits. Explain how she can eliminate choices.
_____
_____
_____

23. Solve a simpler problem. Akashi wants to know how to multiply 2500 by 200. How can he find the answer by solving a simpler problem?
_____
_____
_____

Math Intervention
Book 1 Whole Numbers   **107**

LESSON 1-28
Divide by 1-digit Numbers Without Remainders

Words to Remember

Divisor: The number you divide by — For $6\overline{)18}$, the divisor is 6.

Division symbol: $\overline{)}$ or ÷

Dividend: The number you divide — For $6\overline{)18}$, the dividend is 18.

Quotient: The result when you divide two numbers — For $6\overline{)18}$, the quotient is 3 since $3 \times 6 = 18$.

Multiple: The product of a number and a nonzero whole number

Getting Started In Lesson 1-24 you learned how to multiply a 2-digit number by a 1-digit number. In Lesson 1-23 you learned your multiplication tables. You can use these multiplication facts to help you divide two numbers.

EXAMPLE 1 — Dividing a 3-digit Number by a 1-digit Number

Find 208 ÷ 8.

Solution

Step 1 Place the first digit in the tens' place. Divide the tens.

$$\begin{array}{r} 2 \\ 8\overline{)208} \\ -16 \\ \hline 4 \end{array}$$

← $2 \times 8 = 16$
← $20 - 16 = 4$
Compare. $4 < 8$

Step 2 Bring down the ones.

$$\begin{array}{r} 2 \\ 8\overline{)208} \\ -16\downarrow \\ \hline 48 \end{array}$$

Bring down the 8.

Step 3 Divide the ones.

$$\begin{array}{r} 26 \\ 8\overline{)208} \\ -16 \\ \hline 48 \\ -48 \\ \hline 0 \end{array}$$

← $6 \times 8 = 48$
← $48 - 48 = 0$
Compare. $0 < 8$

Remember Pay careful attention to how the columns are lined up. In Step 1, you divide 20 by 8 so line up the result, 2, with the 0 in 208.

ANSWER The quotient is 26.

CHECK your answer $26 \times 8 = 208$, so 208 is a multiple of 8.

Repeated Subtraction You can also check your work in Example 1 by using repeated subtraction.

Verify that $208 - 26 - 26 - 26 - 26 - 26 - 26 - 26 - 26 = 0$.
How many times do you subtract 26? ▇ So, $208 ÷ 26 = $ ▇.

Math Intervention
Book 1 Whole Numbers

TRY THIS Find the quotient.

1. 729 ÷ 3
2. 504 ÷ 9

EXAMPLE 2 Dividing a 5-digit Number by a 1-digit Number

Find 43,278 ÷ 6.

Solution

> **Using a Grid**
> Using a grid can help you line up the numbers correctly.

Step 1 Place the first digit in the thousands' place. Divide the thousands, subtract, and bring down the hundreds.

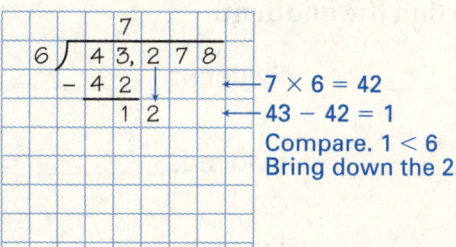

← 7 × 6 = 42
← 43 − 42 = 1
Compare. 1 < 6
Bring down the 2.

Step 2 Divide the hundreds, subtract, and bring down the tens.

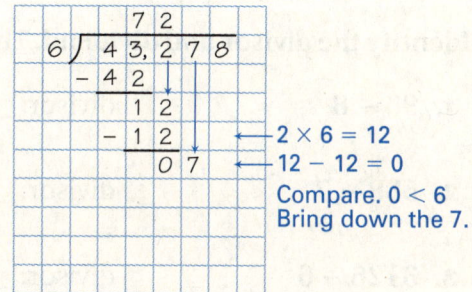

← 2 × 6 = 12
← 12 − 12 = 0
Compare. 0 < 6
Bring down the 7.

Step 3 Divide the tens, subtract, and bring down the ones.

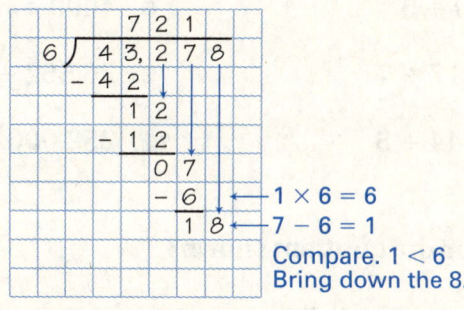

← 1 × 6 = 6
← 7 − 6 = 1
Compare. 1 < 6
Bring down the 8.

Step 4 Divide the ones. Subtract.

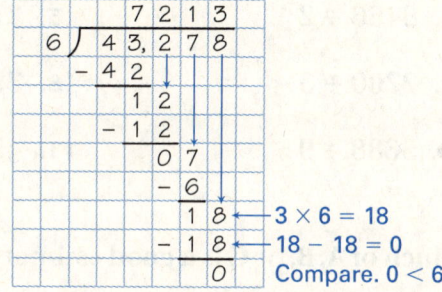

← 3 × 6 = 18
← 18 − 18 = 0
Compare. 0 < 6

ANSWER The quotient is 7213.

CHECK your answer 7213 × 6 = 43,278. 43,278 is a multiple of 6. Verify that 43,278 − 7213 − 7213 − 7213 − 7213 − 7213 − 7213 = 0.

Quotients with Zeros Sometimes, a quotient includes a zero. When do you think this may happen? Make sure you pay attention to using all digits when you divide, including zeros. In Try this exercise 4, you will have to bring down a zero.

TRY THIS Find the quotient.

3. 21,044 ÷ 4
4. 5760 ÷ 8

Math Intervention
Book 1 Whole Numbers

Name _____ Date _____

> **Summarize**
>
> **Dividing by a 1-digit Number**
>
> **Step 1** **Place** the first digit in the appropriate place.
> Here, place the digit in the hundreds' place.
> Divide the hundreds. Subtract.
>
> **Step 2** **Bring** down the tens. Divide the tens. Subtract.
>
> **Step 3** **Bring** down the ones. Divide. Subtract.
>
> ```
>       527
>     _____
>   6)3162
>    - 30
>     ____
>      16
>     - 12
>     ____
>       42
>     - 42
>     ____
>        0
> ```

Practice

Identify the divisor and dividend. Then find the quotient.

1. 96 ÷ 8   divisor: _____   dividend: _____   quotient: _____

2. 588 ÷ 7   divisor: _____   dividend: _____   quotient: _____

3. 3126 ÷ 6   divisor: _____   dividend: _____   quotient: _____

Find the quotient.

4. 8456 ÷ 2   5. 2750 ÷ 5   6. 4000 ÷ 5

7. 2700 ÷ 3   8. 39,417 ÷ 7   9. 26,562 ÷ 3

10. 5688 ÷ 9   11. 45,944 ÷ 8   12. 252,000 ÷ 4

Which of A, B, or C is a good estimate for the quotient shown?

13. 612 ÷ 3 _____

     A. 20   **B.** 200   **C.** 250

14. 4188 ÷ 8 _____

     A. 50   **B.** 500   **C.** 600

Show how to find each quotient by using repeated subtraction.

15. 32 ÷ 8   16. 25 ÷ 5   17. 45 ÷ 9

Name _____ Date _____

18. You and 5 friends buy a pizza for **$24**, drinks for $12, and salads for $18. You split the cost evenly. What is your share of the cost?

_____
_____

19. Tamika wants to use her **$200** savings account to buy CDs at a cost of **$8** each. How many can she buy? Explain.

_____
_____

20. Marilou wants a budget for her **$1200** per month salary. She divides the amount by **2** for her rent and the remainder equally by **3** for food, clothes, and other expenses. How much does she spend on clothes per month? Explain.

_____
_____

DID YOU GET IT?

21. Use estimation. Estimate the quotient $2670 \div 3$. Then divide and check your estimation.

_____
_____
_____

22. Explain the error. Jackie divides $3040 \div 4$ and gets **710**. Explain her error.

_____
_____
_____

23. Solve a simpler problem. Marcus wants to know how to divide **250,000** by **5**. How can he find the answer by solving a simpler problem?

_____
_____
_____

LESSON 1-29
Divide by 1-digit Numbers With Remainders

> **Words to Remember**
>
> Remainder: The number you have left over after dividing
>
> You can write a remainder of 3 as **R3**.
>
> Divisible: One number is divisible by another number if it is a multiple of the other number. For example, 27 is divisible by 3 because 27 is a multiple of 3. $9 \times 3 = 27$, so 27 is divisible by 3.

Getting Started   In Lesson 1-28 you learned how to divide numbers by a 1-digit number. There were no remainders (0 was the result of the last subtraction). In this lesson, you will have remainders when you divide.

EXAMPLE 1 Dividing a 4-digit Number by a 1-digit Number

Find 3162 ÷ 8.

Solution

Step 1 **Place** the first digit in the hundreds' place. Divide the hundreds. Subtract. Bring down the tens.

```
     3
  8)3162
   -24    ← 8 × 3 = 24
    76   ← 31 − 24 = 7
         Bring down
         the 6.
```

Step 2 **Divide** the tens. Subtract. Bring down the ones.

```
    39
  8)3162
   -24
    76
   -72    ← 8 × 9 = 72
    42   ← 76 − 72 = 4
         Bring down
         the 2.
```

Step 3 **Divide** the ones. Subtract. Rewrite the quotient with the remainder.

```
    395
  8)3162
   -24
    76
   -72
    42
   -40    ← 8 × 5 = 40
     2   ← 42 − 40 = 2
         The
         remainder
         is 2.
```

> **Remember**
> Pay careful attention to how the columns are lined up.

ANSWER The quotient is **395 R 2**.

CHECK your answer   Multiply the quotient by the divisor and add the remainder.

$(395 \times 8) + 2 = 3160 + 2 = 3162$

Math Intervention
Book 1 Whole Numbers

Name _____   Date _____

TRY THIS Find the quotient. Check your answer.

1. $751 \div 4$
2. $3525 \div 6$

EXAMPLE 2 Dividing a 5-digit Number by a 1-digit Number

One number is *divisible* by another if there is no remainder when you divide. Find $21{,}008 \div 5$ and tell if 21,008 is divisible by 5.

Solution

Step 1 Place the first digit in the thousands' place. Divide the thousands, subtract, and bring down the hundreds.

```
      4
  5)21008
   -20       ← 4 × 5 = 20
    10       ← 21 − 20 = 1
             Bring down the 0.
```

Step 2 Divide the hundreds, subtract, and bring down the tens.

```
      42
  5)21008
   -20
    10
   -10        ← 2 × 5 = 10
    00        ← 10 − 10 = 0
              Bring down the 0.
```

Step 3 Divide the tens, subtract, and bring down the ones.

```
     420
  5)21008
   -20
    10
   -10
    00
   -00        ← 0 × 5 = 0
    08        ← 0 − 0 = 0
              Bring down the 8.
```

Step 4 Divide the ones. Subtract. Rewrite the quotient with the remainder.

```
     4201
  5)21008
   -20
    10
   -10
    00
   -00
    08
     5        ← 1 × 5 = 5
     3        ← 8 − 5 = 3
              The remainder is 3.
```

ANSWER The quotient is **4201 R 3**. Since there is a remainder, **21,008** is *not* divisible by **5**.

CHECK your answer Multiply the quotient by the divisor and add the remainder.

$(4201 \times 5) + 3 = 21{,}005 + 3 = 21{,}008$

TRY THIS Find the quotient. Check your answer.

3. $62{,}000 \div 3$
4. $46{,}927 \div 9$

Math Intervention
Book 1 Whole Numbers   **113**

Name _____   Date _____

> **Summarize**
>
> Quotient: The number you get when you divide two numbers
> Remainder: The amount left over after division
>
> **Dividing With Remainders**
>
> Step 1 **Place** the first digit in the hundreds' place. Divide the hundreds. Subtract.
>
> Step 2 **Bring** down the tens. Divide the tens. Subtract.
>
> Step 3 **Bring** down the ones. Divide. Subtract. Write any remainder.
>
> ```
>      541
>   6)3248
>    -30
>     24
>    -24
>     08
>     -6
>      2    The remainder is 2.
> ```
> **ANSWER 541 R 2**

Practice

Find the quotient.

1. $86 \div 8$
2. $97 \div 7$
3. $8435 \div 2$
4. $3713 \div 6$
5. $6253 \div 8$
6. $8002 \div 5$
7. $2702 \div 3$
8. $30,417 \div 7$
9. $26,062 \div 3$
10. $598 \div 9$
11. $25,743 \div 6$
12. $962 \div 8$

Which division problem, A, B, or C, has a dividend that is an exact multiple of the divisor?

13. _____

    A. $8\overline{)98}$ B. $3\overline{)9700}$ C. $4\overline{)928}$

14. _____

    A. $6\overline{)90}$ B. $8\overline{)1298}$ C. $5\overline{)1208}$

Show how to find each quotient by using repeated subtraction.

15. $39 \div 8$
16. $86 \div 16$
17. $58 \div 6$

Math Intervention
Book 1 Whole Numbers

18. Nadine sells printed T-shirts in batches of **8** shirts. She has **692** shirts. How many batches can she make? How many shirts will she have left over?

_____
_____

19. Alex is in charge of games at a picnic. He divides up the students into groups of **5** students each. Each group plays a different game. If there are **78** students at the picnic, what is the most number of games that will be played? How many students will not get to play a game?

_____
_____

DID YOU GET IT?

20. Give an example. Using the numbers **2550** and **4**, write a word problem whose solution requires division.

_____
_____
_____

21. Explain your reasoning. Explain how to check if the following division is correct.

$3050 \div 4 = 762 \text{ R } 2$

_____
_____
_____

22. Write another way. Suppose you found that $887 \div 4 = 221 \text{ R } 3$. Show how you can check the quotient by writing a correct addition problem.

_____
_____
_____

LESSON 1-30

Divide by 2-digit Numbers

Words to Remember

Remainder: The number you have left over after dividing

Multiple: The product of a number and a nonzero whole number

Getting Started In Lessons 1-28 and 1-29 you learned how to divide number by a 1-digit number. In this lesson, you will divide by 2-digit numbers.

EXAMPLE 1   Dividing by a 2-digit Number

Find $1480 \div 26$.

Solution

Remember
When you compare two numbers, the difference must be less than the divisor.

Step 1 **Estimate** the quotient.

Think: **1480** is between **1400** and **1500**.

$$\begin{array}{r}70\\20\overline{)1400}\end{array} \quad \begin{array}{r}?\\26\overline{)1480}\end{array} \quad \begin{array}{r}50\\30\overline{)1500}\end{array}$$

So, the quotient is between **50** and **70**.

Step 2 **Place** the first digit of the quotient in the tens' place. Try 6.

$$\begin{array}{r}6\\26\overline{)1480}\\-156\end{array}$$ Place the 6.

← $6 \times 26 = 156$
Since $156 > 148$, try 5 instead.

Step 3 **Divide** the tens, subtract, and compare.

$$\begin{array}{r}5\\26\overline{)1480}\\-130\\\hline 18\end{array}$$ Place the 5.

← $5 \times 26 = 130$
← $148 - 130 = 18$
Compare. $18 < 26$

Step 4 **Bring** down the ones. Divide the ones and subtract. Write any remainder.

$$\begin{array}{r}56\\26\overline{)1480}\\-130\downarrow\\\hline 180\\-156\\\hline 24\end{array}$$

← $6 \times 26 = 156$
← $180 - 156 = 24$
Compare. $24 < 26$
The remainder is 24.

ANSWER $1480 \div 26 = 56 \text{ R } 24$

CHECK your work   Multiply, then add the remainder.

$56 \times 26 = 1456$

$1456 + 24 = 1480$

USE your estimate   56 is between 50 and 70. So, the answer is reasonable.

Math Intervention
Book 1 Whole Numbers

Name _____ Date _____

TRY THIS Find the quotient. Check your answer.

1. 1815 ÷ 36
2. 2480 ÷ 22

 **Dividing a Multiple of 10 by a 2-digit Number**

Find 117,600 ÷ 28. Use a grid.

Solution

Work Neatly
Pay careful attention to how the digits are lined up so you don't lose a place.

Step 1 **Place** the first digit in the thousands' place. Try **5**. Divide and compare to see if you need to try a higher or lower number.

```
      5
28)117,600   Since
   140       140 > 117,
             try 4
             instead.
```

Step 2 **Notice** that 5 is too high, so try **4**. Divide and compare. If the product is correct, subtract and bring down the next digit.

```
      4
28)117,600
  -112
     56
```

Step 3 **Divide** the tens, subtract, and compare. Bring down the **0**.

Step 4 **Continue** bringing down the zeros. Divide and subtract until no zeros remain.

```
       4200
28)117,600
  -112
     56
    -56
      00
     - 0
      00
     - 0
       0
```

Multiples
Notice that 117,600 is a multiple of 10 because it ends in a 0. It is also a multiple of 28 because there was no remainder after the division.

ANSWER 117,600 ÷ 28 = 4200

CHECK your answer Multiply the quotient by the divisor and add the remainder.

(4200 × 28) + 0 = 117,600

TRY THIS Find the quotient. Check your answer.

3. 60,800 ÷ 32
4. 86,400 ÷ 18

Math Intervention
Book 1 Whole Numbers **117**

Name _____ Date _____

> **Summarize**
> **Dividing by 2-digit Divisors**
> (1) Estimate the quotient and the starting value for the division. Divide and compare. If the product is less than the divisor, continue. If not, revise the starting value and repeat.
> (2) Continue to divide, subtract, and compare. Bring down the next number. Continue this until there are no digits remaining.
> (3) Write the quotient. Write any remainder. Check your work.

Practice

Find the quotient.

1. 860 ÷ 80
2. 2300 ÷ 20
3. 8480 ÷ 42
4. 3700 ÷ 16
5. 62,000 ÷ 15
6. 2688 ÷ 84
7. 24,000 ÷ 75
8. 20,232 ÷ 72
9. 9345 ÷ 15
10. 83,200 ÷ 16
11. 25,832 ÷ 24
12. 120,000 ÷ 84

Estimate the quotient. Then divide to check your answer.

13. 80)640   Estimate: _____
14. 30)8100   Estimate: _____

15. 40)48,000   Estimate: _____
16. 60)606,060 Estimate: _____

17. 50)250,000 Estimate: _____
18. 20)120,120 Estimate: _____

Math Intervention
Book 1 Whole Numbers

Name _____ Date _____

19. In one month, Richard sold **48** baseball T-shirts for a total income of **$960**. What was the price of each shirt? Explain your answer.

_____
_____
_____

20. A school is planning a field trip to a science museum. There are **175** students signed up for the field trip. Each bus can hold **45** students. How many buses will be needed?

_____
_____
_____

21. In one year, Tracey earned **$51,000**. If she earned the same amount each month, what was her monthly income?

_____
_____
_____

DID YOU GET IT?

22. Fill in the missing words. When you divide, the steps are to estimate, revise your _____ , divide, _____ , and compare. Continue this until there are no more digits. Then write the _____ and _____ .

23. Work backwards. Pamela knows that a certain number divided by **25** is **62 R 10**. What is the number? Explain your reasoning.

_____
_____
_____

24. Explain the error. Marjean said, "**88,080 ÷ 40 = 2210**." Is she correct? If not, explain her error.

_____
_____
_____

Math Intervention
Book 1 Whole Numbers

Name _____ Date _____

LESSON 1-31 — Multiplication and Division Properties

> **Words to Remember**
>
> **Multiplication property of 0:** The product of any number and 0 is 0.
> $0 \cdot a = a \cdot 0 = 0$, for any number a $4 \cdot 0 = 0 \cdot 4 = 0$
>
> **Multiplication property of 1:** The product of a number and 1 is the number.
> $1 \cdot a = a \cdot 1 = a$, for any number a $8 \cdot 1 = 1 \cdot 8 = 8$
>
> **Division property of 1:** The quotient of a number and 1 is the number.
> $a \div 1 = a$, for any number a $9 \div 1 = 9$

Identity Property

The Multiplication property of 1 is also called the Identity property of multiplication. A number does not change when it is multiplied by 1.

Getting Started In Lesson 1-24 you learned how to multiply a number by a 1-digit number, and in Lesson 1-28 you learned how to divide by a 1-digit number. If you know properties of multiplication and division, it can shorten some steps.

EXAMPLE 1   Using the Properties of 0 and 1

Study the following examples. Verify each step with mental math.

a. $(3 \cdot 5) \cdot (0 \cdot 2) = 0$

b. $(4 \cdot 2) \cdot (1 \cdot 3) = 24$

c. $(6 \cdot 5) \div (10 \div 1) = 3$

Solution

a. $(3 \cdot 5) \cdot (0 \cdot 2) = 15 \cdot (0 \cdot 2)$ Multiply $3 \cdot 5$.
$= 15 \cdot 0$ Multiplication property of 0
$= 0$ Multiplication property of 0

b. $(4 \cdot 2) \cdot (1 \cdot 3) = 8 \cdot (1 \cdot 3)$ Multiply $4 \cdot 2$.
$= 8 \cdot 3$ Multiplication property of 1
$= 24$ Multiply $8 \cdot 3$.

c. $(6 \cdot 5) \div (10 \div 1) = 30 \div (10 \div 1)$ Multiply $6 \cdot 5$.
$= 30 \div 10$ Division property of 1
$= 3$ Divide $30 \div 10$.

Math Intervention
Book 1 Whole Numbers

Name _____ Date _____

> **Checking Your Work**
>
> Check your answer to verify that you used the properties correctly.

TRY THIS   Simplify using properties and mental math.

1. $2(9 \cdot 0) + 3(8 \cdot 1)$
2. $12(1 \cdot 6) \div (8 \div 1)$

Other Properties of Multiplication   You used the commutative and associative properties of addition in Lesson 1-10. Similar properties are true for multiplication as well.

Commutative property of multiplication: You can multiply the factors of a product in any order.

$a \cdot b = b \cdot a$, for any numbers a and b $6 \cdot 3 = 3 \cdot 6 = 18$

Associative property of multiplication: Changing the grouping of numbers will not change their product.

$(a \cdot b) \cdot c = a \cdot (b \cdot c)$, for any numbers a, b, and c
$(4 \cdot 3) \cdot 8 = 4 \cdot (3 \cdot 8) = 96$

EXAMPLE 2   Using the Commutative and Associative Properties of Multiplication

Find the product $5 \cdot (41 \cdot 2)$ using mental math.

Solution

$5 \cdot (41 \cdot 2) = 5 \cdot (2 \cdot 41)$ Commutative property
$ = (5 \cdot 2) \cdot 41$ Associative property
$ = 10 \cdot 41$ Multiply within parentheses.
$ = 410$ Multiply.

Using Mental Math   In Example 2, using the properties made it easier to multiply using mental math. When you solve a problem, you need to make decisions about how to approach the problem if you want to simplify the work.

TRY THIS   Use properties of multiplication and division to simplify the expression.

3. $2 \cdot (9 \cdot 5)$
4. $(8 \cdot 3) \cdot 3$
5. $0 \cdot (6 \cdot 9) + 4 \cdot 1$
6. $(30 \div 1) + (10 \cdot 1)$

Math Intervention
Book 1 Whole Numbers

Name _____ Date _____

> **Summarize**
> **Properties of Multiplication and Division**
>
> | Multiplication Property of 0 | The product of a number and 0 is 0. |
> |---|---|
> | Multiplication Property of 1 | The product of a number and 1 is the number. |
> | Division Property of 1 | The quotient of a number and 1 is the number. |
>
> | Commutative Property of Multiplication | You can multiply factors of a product in any order. |
> |---|---|
> | Associative Property of Multiplication | Changing the grouping of factors will not change their product. |

Practice

Simplify the expression using properties and mental math.

1. $86 \div 1$
2. $2340 \div 1$
3. $80 \cdot 0$
4. $3(7 \cdot 0) \div 5$
5. $32(1) \div 8$
6. $2(6 \cdot 1) \cdot 2$
7. $(9 \cdot 2) \cdot 2$
8. $0(23) + (21 \div 1)$
9. $(8 \cdot 4) \cdot 5$
10. $(16 \div 1) \div 2$
11. $0(5 \cdot 1) + (24 \div 1)$
12. $(4 \div 1) + (6 \div 1)$

Use the properties of multiplication and division to find the missing number. Name the property or properties you used.

13. ___ $\div 1 = 18$ _____

14. ___ $(8 \cdot 1) + 12 = 12$ _____

15. $(14 \div 1) \cdot$ ___ $= 6 \cdot 14$ _____

16. $3($ ___ $\cdot 1) \cdot 2 = 18$ _____

17. $(8 \cdot$ ___ $) \cdot 3 = 8 \cdot (3 \cdot 3)$ _____

18. $(12 \div 1) \cdot 0 + ($ ___ $\div 1) = 32$ _____

Math Intervention
Book 1 Whole Numbers

Name _____   Date _____

Tell what property of multiplication is shown.

19. $(3 \cdot 8) \cdot 6 = 3 \cdot (8 \cdot 6)$ _____

20. $2 \cdot 0 = 0$ _____

21. $45 \cdot 1 = 45$ _____

22. $99 \cdot 12 = 12 \cdot 99$ _____

23. You are going on a bike trip. You plan on riding an average of **11** miles per hour for **6** hours a day. You want to know how far you can travel in **5** days. Show how to write the problem so that it can be solved with mental math. Then solve the problem.

Distance traveled = (Average speed) · (Number of hours per day) · (Number of days)

_____
_____
_____

24. Michael was doing his homework and wrote the following equation: $18 \div 0 = 18$. Explain what is wrong with his equation. How would you correct what he wrote?

_____
_____
_____

DID YOU GET IT?

25. Fill in the missing words. For any number, the product of _____ and the number is **0**. For any number, you can multiply the _____ of a product in any _____ .

26. Write an example. Write a division problem that uses the division property of **1** so that the quotient is **15**.

_____
_____

27. Explain your reasoning. Explain how the properties of multiplication can help you find the product of the factors **8, 3, 0,** and **2** using mental math.

_____
_____
_____

LESSON 1-32

Exponents

Words to Remember

Power of a number: How many times the number is multiplied by itself

A power can also refer to a number that has an exponent. Since 2^7 is written with an exponent, 2^7 is called a power.

Exponent: The power to which you raise a number, called the base

In the power 2^7, the number 2 is the base and the number 7 is the exponent.

In 2^7, 2 is multiplied by itself 7 times.

$2^7 = 2 \cdot 2 \cdot 2 \cdot 2 \cdot 2 \cdot 2 \cdot 2 = 128$

Getting Started Sometimes expressions contain products that can be written using exponents. In this lesson you will learn how to read, simplify, and evaluate powers.

EXAMPLE 1 Writing an Expression with an Exponent

Write $3 \cdot 3 \cdot 3 \cdot 3 \cdot 3 \cdot 3 \cdot 3$ using an exponent.

Solution

The number of repeated factors in the product is related to the exponent in the power.

$$3 \cdot 3 \cdot 3 \cdot 3 \cdot 3 \cdot 3 \cdot 3 = 3^7$$

number of factors = the exponent
7 factors, power
base = number being multiplied repeatedly

EXAMPLE 2 Reading a Power

Describe the power in words.

a. 8^2 b. 5^3 c. y^4

Solution

a. 8^2 is $8 \cdot 8$, or 8 *to the second power*. 8^2 is also read "8 squared."

b. 5^3 is $5 \cdot 5 \cdot 5$, or 5 *to the third power*. 5^3 is also read "5 cubed."

c. y^4 is $y \cdot y \cdot y \cdot y$, or *y to the fourth power*.

Math Intervention
Book 1 Whole Numbers

Name _____ Date _____

TRY THIS

Write the product as a power.

1. $1 \cdot 1 \cdot 1$
2. $12 \cdot 12 \cdot 12$
3. $m \cdot m \cdot m \cdot m \cdot m$

4. Describe each power in words. Explain how the two powers are different.
   a. 2^6
   b. 6^2

EXAMPLE 3 Evaluating Powers

Evaluate the power.

a. 5^2
b. 2^5
c. 7^3
d. 3^4

Solution

Write the powers as a product. Group factors to help you multiply easily.

a. $5^2 = 5 \cdot 5 = 25$
b. $2^5 = 2 \cdot 2 \cdot 2 \cdot 2 \cdot 2 = 8 \cdot 4 = 32$
c. $7^3 = 7 \cdot 7 \cdot 7 = 49 \cdot 7 = 343$
d. $3^4 = 3 \cdot 3 \cdot 3 \cdot 3 = 9 \cdot 9 = 81$

Remember
To evaluate a power, rewrite it as the product of factors and simplify.

EXAMPLE 4 Simplifying Expressions with Powers

Show that $2^4 \cdot 2^7 = 2^{11}$.

Solution

$2^4 \cdot 2^7 = (2 \cdot 2 \cdot 2 \cdot 2) \cdot (2 \cdot 2 \cdot 2 \cdot 2 \cdot 2 \cdot 2 \cdot 2)$ 4 factors × 7 factors

$= 2 \cdot 2 \cdot 2 \cdot 2 \cdot 2 \cdot 2 \cdot 2 \cdot 2 \cdot 2 \cdot 2 \cdot 2$ Write without parentheses.

$= 2^{11}$ Count the factors.

Look Ahead
You will learn more about the properties of exponents and powers in Book 7.

TRY THIS

Evaluate the power.

5. $3^3 = \boxed{} \cdot \boxed{} \cdot \boxed{} = \boxed{}$
6. $4^4 = \boxed{} \cdot \boxed{} \cdot \boxed{} \cdot \boxed{} = \boxed{}$

Write the product as a single power.

7. $3^2 \cdot 3^5$
8. $5^4 \cdot 5^3$
9. $2^3 \cdot (2^5 \cdot 2^2)$

Math Intervention
Book 1 Whole Numbers

Name _____ Date _____

> **Summarize**
> **Working with Powers**
> A power is a way to write a repeated multiplication.
>
> To evaluate a power, write the power as a product and multiply the factors.
>
> 6 to the third power, or 6 · 6 · 6, is 6^3.
>
> $6^3 = 6 · 6 · 6 = 36 · 6 = 216$

Practice

Match the expression with the correct product.

1. 3^2 _____
2. 4^2 _____
3. 2^3 _____

A. 16   B. 9   C. 8

Tell whether the equation is true or false.

4. $6^2 = 6 · 6$
5. $2^5 = 2(5)$
6. $4^3 = 4 \div 4 \div 4$

Write the product using an exponent.

7. $8 \times 8 \times 8$
8. $6 \times 6 \times 6 \times 6$
9. 20×20
10. $11 \times 11 \times 11 \times 11 \times 11$
11. $7 \times 7 \times 7 \times 7 \times 7$
12. $15 \times 15 \times 15$

Describe the power in words.

13. 10^3
14. x^{40}
15. 3^4
16. 7^{66}
17. z^2
18. 3^{10}

Evaluate the power.

19. 5^3
20. 6^4
21. 2^6

Write the product as a single power.

22. $3^2 · 3^3$
23. $4^3 · 4^2$
24. $2^3 · 2^{10}$
25. $10^2 · 10^4$
26. $8^3 · 8^3$
27. $5 · 5^7$

Math Intervention
Book 1 Whole Numbers

Name _____ Date _____

28. In a cube, all the sides have the same length. The volume of a cube is **length × width × height**. Express the volume of a cube with side length **8** centimeters as a power. Then find the volume.

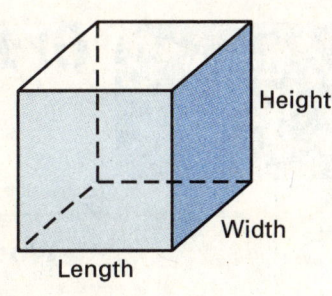

_____
_____
_____

29. Mrs. Tuttle is making a quilt. She is using **16** squares with side length **4** inches, **8** squares with side length **5** inches, and **24** squares with side length **3** inches. Write an expression for the total area of the squares. Then find the total area.

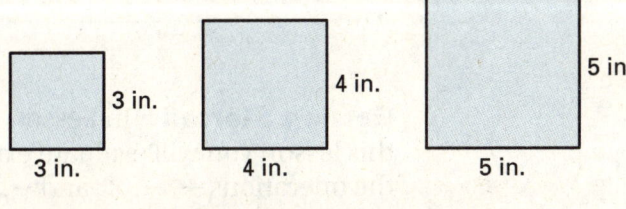

_____
_____
_____

DID YOU GET IT?

30. Fill in the missing words. 2 to the _____ power equals **16**. 7^8 is the _____ of **7**.

31. Describe a process. Explain why $(2^4)^2 = 2^8 = 256$ by using repeated multiplication. Show each step.

_____
_____
_____

32. Explain your reasoning. Your friend says $3^1 + 3^2 + 3^3 = 3^6$. Is your friend correct? Explain why or why not.

_____
_____
_____
_____

Name _____ Date _____

LESSON 1-33 Order of Operations

Words to Remember

Expression: Any combination of numbers, powers, and mathematical symbols

Evaluate: To find the value of an expression

Exponent: The number of times a number is multiplied by itself in a power

Order of operations: Rules you use to evaluate an expression

Getting Started In Lesson 1-32 you learned how to evaluate powers. In this lesson you will evaluate expressions containing powers, numbers, and the operations +, −, ×, and ÷.

Order of Operations

To evaluate an expression, use the following order.

1. Evaluate expressions inside grouping symbols. Parentheses and fraction bars are grouping symbols.
2. Evaluate powers.
3. Multiply and divide from left to right.
4. Add and subtract from left to right.

EXAMPLE 1 Using the Order of Operations

Evaluate the expression $8 + 12 \cdot 3 \div 6$.

Solution

$$
\begin{aligned}
8 + 12 \cdot 3 \div 6 &= 8 + 36 \div 6 && \text{Multiply } 12 \cdot 3 \text{ first.} \\
&= 8 + 6 && \text{Divide } 36 \div 6. \\
&= 14 && \text{Add } 8 + 6.
\end{aligned}
$$

Remember
Multiplying and dividing are done from left to right.

TRY THIS Evaluate the expression.

1. $18 + 24 \div 6 \div 4$
2. $30 - 8 \cdot 3 \div 6$

Math Intervention
Book 1 Whole Numbers

Name _____ Date _____

EXAMPLE 2 Using Grouping Symbols

> **Remember**
> Parentheses and fraction bars are grouping symbols.

a. Evaluate the expression $(12 + 8) \cdot 3$.

b. Evaluate the expression $\dfrac{9 \times 8}{3 + 3}$.

Solution

a. $(12 + 8) \cdot 3 = 20 \cdot 3$ Do parentheses first.

$= 60$ Multiply $20 \cdot 3$.

b. $\dfrac{9 \times 8}{3 + 3} = \dfrac{72}{6}$ Simplify the numerator and denominator first.

$= 12$ Divide $72 \div 6$.

TRY THIS Evaluate the expression.

3. $15 + 24 \div (12 \div 4)$

4. $\dfrac{24 + 12}{5 + 1}$

EXAMPLE 3 Using Exponents and the Order of Operations

Evaluate the expression $2(4 + 1) + 36 \div 3^2 - 4 \cdot 2$.

Solution

$2(4 + 1) + 36 \div 3^2 - 4 \cdot 2 = 2 \cdot 5 + 36 \div 3^2 - 4 \cdot 2$ Parentheses

$= 2 \cdot 5 + 36 \div 9 - 4 \cdot 2$ Power

$= 10 + 4 - 8$ Multiply and divide.

$= 6$ Add and subtract.

TRY THIS Evaluate the expression.

5. $20 - 2(3 - 1)$

6. $8 \cdot 6 + 2^4 \div 4$

7. $2(3 - 1) + 72 \div 2^2$

8. $2^4 \cdot 3 - 18 \div 3$

9. $3^4 - 2^5$

10. $2 \cdot 3^2 + 25 \div 5^2$

Name _____ Date _____

> **Summarize**
> **Using the Order of Operations**
> (1) Evaluate expressions inside grouping symbols.
> (2) Evaluate powers.
> (3) Multiply and divide from left to right.
> (4) Add and subtract from left to right.

Practice

Match the expression with the correct product.

1. $28 - 3^2$ _____
2. $20 - 6 \cdot 2$ _____
3. $2 \cdot 3 + 4 \cdot 5$ _____

A. 8
B. 26
C. 19

Tell whether the statement is true or false.

4. $12 - (10 + 1) = 12 - 11$ _____
5. $18 + 2^5 = 20^5$ _____
6. $24 + 2(18 \div 3) = 26 \cdot 6$ _____

Evaluate the expression.

7. $12 + 8 - 2$
8. $7 \cdot 4 + 2 \cdot 4$
9. $3 \cdot 2^3$

10. $\dfrac{18}{6-3}$
11. $2^3 \cdot 4^2$
12. $\dfrac{24-8}{4 \cdot 2}$

13. $\dfrac{5+2^2}{3}$
14. $\dfrac{24-12}{16-4}$
15. $\dfrac{6^2}{4 \cdot 3}$

16. $9 \cdot 3 + 2 - 6$
17. $18 - 12 + 2 \cdot 4$
18. $72 \div (8 \cdot 2 + 8)$

19. $120 \div (10 + 5 \cdot 10)$
20. $36 + 4 - (12 + 8)$
21. $(32 - 16) - (4 \cdot 2)$

Add parentheses to make the expression true.

22. $5 \cdot 2 + 4 - 6 = 24$
23. $30 \div 2 + 4 - 2 = 3$
24. $8 + 2 \cdot 3 + 4 = 70$

Math Intervention
Book 1 Whole Numbers

Name _____ Date _____

Solve the problem. Explain your answer.

25. You buy **3** notebooks at **$4** each and **5** pens at **$2** each. Find the total cost.
_____
_____
_____

26. A pack of paper costs **$4**. For every **10** packs of paper you buy, you receive a discount of **$11**. Find the cost of buying **36** packs of paper.
_____
_____
_____

27. Your band needs to buy **52** uniforms that cost **$75** each. Each student must do fundraising to earn **$40** towards the uniform, and the school contributes the rest. How much money will the school contribute?
_____
_____

DID YOU GET IT?

28. Fill in the missing words. When evaluating an expression, _____ go first, followed by _____ , then _____
and then_____.

29. Write an expression. Jorie and Kylie made **4** batches of **36** cookies and **3** batches of **24** cookies for a school bake sale. Write and evaluate an expression representing the number of cookies they made.
_____
_____
_____

30. Explain your reasoning. Your friend says $3 + 2(6 + 2) = 40$. Is your friend right? Explain why or why not.
_____
_____
_____

Name _____ Date _____

LESSON 1-34
Solve Problems with Whole Numbers

Strategies to Remember
To choose an operation when you solve a word problem:

Use **addition** when you need to:	Use **subtraction** when you need to:
• combine • join • add on • find a total	• compare • take away • find how many more are needed • find how many more are left
Use **multiplication** when you need to: • join together the total number of objects in groups of equal size	Use **division** when you need to: • find the number of equal groups • find the number in each equal group

EXAMPLE 1 Solving an Addition and Subtraction Problem

Martin needs to create a budget to help him manage his expenses. After keeping track of his expenses for six months, he found that monthly he spends the following amounts:

Rent	$980
Heat/electricity	$120
Clothing	$150
Movies	$40
Food	$285

Martin also wants to save $100 per month. If his salary is $2452 per month, can he live within his budget?

Solution

Step 1 **Identify** the operations needed. Since he needs to find a total, you need to add the expenses.

Step 2 **Add** the expenses.
$980 + 120 + 150 + 40 + 285 + 100 = 1675$
His expenses are $1675 per month.

Step 3 **Subtract** from the total since he needs to find out how much money is left.
$\$2452 - \$1675 = \$777$

ANSWER Since Martin still has $777 left over, he should be able to live within his budget.

> **Remember**
> There is often more than one way to solve a word problem. Martin could have done repeated subtraction until he had subtracted all expenses.

Math Intervention
Book 1 Whole Numbers

Name _____ Date _____

TRY THIS Fill in the missing information to solve the problem. Use Example 1.

1. Martin also wants to budget for items that are not monthly expenses. If he spends **$960** per year on gifts, how much should he add to the budget?

    Step 1 The phrase **$960** per year tells you that you need to _____ by **12** to find out how much he spends per month.

    Step 2 Calculate $960 ◯ 12 = $ _____.

    Step 3 He should add _____ to the budget. His total monthly budget is _____.

EXAMPLE 2 Solving Problems Using Multiple Operations

Mrs. Tuttle is making a quilt from **6** square yards of fabric (**7776** square inches). For the quilt, she needs to make **24** squares with side length **8** inches, **12** squares with side length **10** inches, and **24** squares with side length **12** inches. Does she have enough fabric?

Solution

> **Remember**
> Using an exponent is another way to show multiplication of a number by itself.

Step 1
Find the area of square **1**.
$8 \cdot 8 = 8^2 = 64$ in.²

Step 2
Find the area of square **2**.
$10^2 = 100$ in.²

Step 3
Find the area of square **3**.
$12^2 = 144$ in.²

Step 4 Find the total area.

$64 \cdot 24 = 1536$ in.²
$100 \cdot 12 = 1200$ in.²
$144 \cdot 24 = 3456$ in.²

```
   1 5 3 6
   1 2 0 0
 + 3 4 5 6
 ─────────
   6 1 9 2
```

ANSWER Yes. Since 7776 > 6192, she has enough fabric.

TRY THIS Use Example 2.

2. Suppose the quilt in Example 2 needs **15** more squares with side length **10** inches. Will Mrs. Tuttle still have enough fabric to complete her project? Explain.

Name _____ Date _____

> **Summarize**
> **Solving Word Problems**
> (1) Identify the operation or operations needed.
> (2) Perform the calculations and solve the problem.
> (3) Answer the question and check your answer for reasonableness.

Practice

Fill in the missing operation +, –, ·, or ÷ for the situation described.

1. Jake spent his **$20** allowance evenly over **5** days.   20 ◯ 5

2. Marylou's dog weighs **132** pounds and needs to lose **8** pounds.   132 ◯ 8

3. Nathan and **5** friends each put in **$5** to buy pizzas.   6 ◯ 5

4. Kim made a necklace from two other necklaces that were   8 ◯ 12
   8 inches and **12** inches long.

Identify the operation suggested by the phrase.

5. decreased by **$12**   6. split **4** ways   7. **8** feet and **10** feet

   _____   _____   _____

Fill in the missing information to solve the problem.

8. Gabe paid **$7200** for college tuition last year. This year the tuition was increased **$132**. What is his new tuition?

   Step 1 The word "increased" tells you that you need to _____.

   Step 2 Calculate 7200 ◯ 132 = _____.

   Step 3 The new tuition is $_____.

9. Gabe's parents will pay **$6000** of the tuition over a **12**-month period. How much do they pay each month?

   Step 1 The words "pay each month" tells you need to _____ by _____.

   Step 2 Calculate $6000 ◯ 12 = _____.

   Step 3 Their monthly payment is $_____.

Math Intervention
Book 1 Whole Numbers

Name _____ Date _____

First tell what operation(s) you need to use to find the answer. Then solve the problem. Explain your answer.

10. Johnathan sells baseball cards in groups of **12** cards. He has **1314** cards. How many groups can he make? How many will he have left over?

    _____
    _____
    _____

11. You buy **4** notebooks that cost **$3** each, **7** pens that cost a total of **$12**, and **3** markers for **$1** each. You give the cashier at the store **$30**. How much change do you receive?

    _____
    _____
    _____

12. Sheryl uses money from her **$750** savings account to buy **12** favorite DVDs at a cost of **$23** each and **9** CDs at a cost of **$14** each. She also wants to spend **$5** a week for **8** weeks at the school football games. Her parents give her **$10** a week allowance. How much money will she have left after **8** weeks?

    _____
    _____
    _____

DID YOU GET IT?

13. **Write a word problem.** Write a word problem using the numbers at the right. Then complete the calculation to solve the problem. Explain how you decided what operation to use.

    18 ● 4 = _____

    _____
    _____
    _____

14. **Explain your reasoning.** Jean and Joan baked **8** batches of **48** cookies and **6** batches of **32** cookies. They need to make **600** cookies for a bake sale. Joan says that they need to bake more cookies. Is Joan correct? Explain why or why not.

    _____
    _____
    _____

Math Intervention
Book 1 Whole Numbers 135

Name _____ Date _____

Mixed Practice for Lessons 1-22 to 1-34

Vocabulary Review

Match the word with its mathematical meaning and everyday meaning.

Word	Mathematical meaning	Everyday meaning
1. multiple ___, ___	A. the result of dividing two numbers	X. patterns like 3, 6, 9, 12, . . .
2. quotient ___, ___	B. product of a number and a nonzero whole number	Y. answer from division

Fill in the missing words.

3. The power of a number is how many times you multiply the number by _____.

4. An exponent is the _____ to which you raise a number called the _____.

Show how to find the products by repeated addition.

5. 3×7
6. 9×5
7. 12×4
8. 10×6

List all the factors of the given number.

9. 16
10. 32
11. 40
12. 81

Evaluate the power.

13. 5^3
14. 3^6
15. 8^3

Write as a single power.

16. $2^3 \cdot 2^2$
17. $9 \cdot 9^3$
18. $4^2 \cdot 4^5$

Multiply or divide using a pattern.

19. 192×100
20. 1387×1000
21. 5130×10
22. $900 \div 100$
23. $20,000 \div 1000$
24. $780 \div 10$

Math Intervention
Book 1 Whole Numbers

Name _____   Date _____

Use the properties of multiplication and division to find the missing number. Name the property used.

25. ☐ × 1 = 12 _____   26. (3 × 4) × 9 = 3(☐ × 9) _____
27. ☐ × 9 = 0 _____   28. 2(☐ × 18) = 2(18 × 7) _____

Find the product.

29. 32 · 3   30. 84 · 12   31. 34 · 16   32. 79 · 11
33. 65 · 34   34. 701 · 21   35. 2090 · 34 36. 1218 · 211

Find the quotient.

37. 144 ÷ 24 38. 96 ÷ 6   39. 420 ÷ 21   40. 3000 ÷ 25
41. 180 ÷ 12 42. 1050 ÷ 30 43. 7680 ÷ 48 44. 19,200 ÷ 12

Find the product or quotient.

45. 90,806 × 12   46. 17,984 ÷ 32
47. 8,561 × 38   48. 21,000 ÷ 50

Simplify.

49. 10 · 3 + 2 − 4   50. 28 − 12 + 2 · 8   51. 144 ÷ (4 · 2 + 8)
52. 120 ÷ (10 + 5 · 10)   53. 36 + 4 − (12 + 8)   54. (32 − 16) − (4 · 2)

Solve each problem.

55. Kalil earns $22 per week for 18 weeks selling newspapers. He saves all but $24. How much does he save?

56. You and 8 friends sell candy to raise money for band uniforms. The total you need to raise is $980 dollars. About how much money do each of you need to earn?

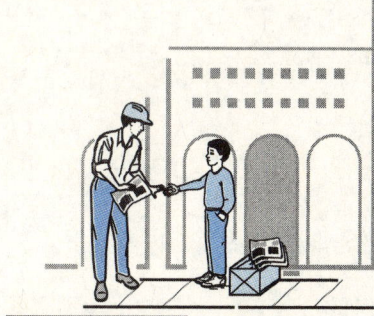

57. The Ryan family donates $80 every time their baseball team hits a home run. Their team hit 194 home runs last season. How much did they donate?

McDougal Littell

Math Intervention

Book 2:
Fractions and Decimals

McDougal Littell
A DIVISION OF HOUGHTON MIFFLIN COMPANY
Evanston, Illinois • Boston • Dallas

Cover photo © Photodisc Red/Getty Images

Illustrations George Barile/McDougal Littell/Houghton Mifflin Company and John Evans/McDougal Littell/Houghton Mifflin Company

Copyright © 2008 by McDougal Littell, a division of Houghton Mifflin Company.
All rights reserved.

Permission is hereby granted to teachers to reprint or photocopy in classroom quantities the pages or sheets in this work that carry a McDougal Littell copyright notice. These pages are designed to be reproduced by teachers for use in their classes with accompanying McDougal Littell material, provided each copy made shows the copyright notice. Such copies may not be sold and further distribution is expressly prohibited. Except as authorized above, prior written permission must be obtained from McDougal Littell, a division of Houghton Mifflin Company, to reproduce or transmit this work or portions thereof in any other form or by any other electronic or mechanical means, including any information storage or retrieval system, unless expressly permitted by federal copyright laws. Address inquiries to, Supervisor, Rights and Permissions, McDougal Littell, P.O. Box 1667, Evanston, IL 60204.

ISBN-13: 978-0-618-90047-3
ISBN-10: 0-618-90047-0

123456789—PBO—11 10 09 08 07

CONTENTS — Book 2: Fractions and Decimals

Number Concepts

Lesson 2-1	Prime Factorization	2
Lesson 2-2	Greatest Common Factor	6
Lesson 2-3	Least Common Multiple	10
	Mixed Practice for Lessons 2-1 to 2-3	14

Understanding Fractions

Lesson 2-4	Introduction to Fractions	16
Lesson 2-5	Equivalent Fractions	20
Lesson 2-6	Simplify Fractions	24
Lesson 2-7	Compare and Order Fractions	28
Lesson 2-8	Mixed Numbers and Improper Fractions	32
Lesson 2-9	Compare and Order Mixed Numbers and Improper Fractions	36
	Mixed Practice for Lessons 2-4 to 2-9	40

Operations with Fractions

Activity 2-10	Adding Fractions Using Models	42
Lesson 2-11	Add and Subtract Fractions with Like Denominators	44
Lesson 2-12	Add and Subtract Fractions with Unlike Denominators	48
Lesson 2-13	Add and Subtract Mixed Numbers	52
Lesson 2-14	Multiply Fractions	56
Lesson 2-15	Divide Fractions	60
Lesson 2-16	Multiply and Divide Mixed Numbers	64
Lesson 2-17	Solve Problems with Fractions	68
	Mixed Practice for Lessons 2-11 to 2-17	72

CONTENTS cont.

Understanding Decimals

Lesson 2-18	Decimals and Place Value	74
Lesson 2-19	Round Decimals	78
Lesson 2-20	Compare and Order Decimals	82
Lesson 2-21	Write Decimals as Fractions	86
Lesson 2-22	Write Fractions as Decimals	90
	Mixed Practice for Lessons 2-18 to 2-22	94

Operations with Decimals

Lesson 2-23	Add and Subtract Decimals	96
Lesson 2-24	Multiply Decimals by Whole Numbers	100
Activity 2-25	Multiplying Decimals Using Models	104
Lesson 2-26	Multiply Decimals	106
Lesson 2-27	Divide Decimals by Whole Numbers	110
Lesson 2-28	Divide by Decimals	114
Lesson 2-29	Estimate with Decimals	118
Lesson 2-30	Solve Problems with Decimals	122
	Mixed Practice for Lessons 2-23 to 2-30	126

Math Intervention
Book 2 Fractions and Decimals

McDougal Littell

Math Intervention

MATH INTERVENTION

- The Math Intervention program includes skill lessons, problem solving lessons, activities, and mixed practice materials covering a wide range of mathematical topics that are needed for success in middle school and high school mathematics.

- There are seven books in the Math Intervention program. Book 2 contains materials on Fraction and Decimal concepts and operations.

- In the Math Intervention books, lessons include worked-out Examples and Try this exercises to help you build understanding of a topic. The Practice section includes a variety of problems to give you the practice you need to develop your math skills. The Did You Get It? section checks your understanding of the lesson.

- Problem solving lessons suggest strategies for approaching real-world problem solving situations and promote the use of estimation to check reasonableness of solutions.

- Activities build your understanding of a topic through the use of models and games.

- Mixed Practice sections include practice of vocabulary, skills, and problem solving methods covering the material in a group of lessons.

- You may complete the work in selected lessons, or cover the book as a whole, as directed by your teacher.

LESSON 2-1 Prime Factorization

Words to Remember

Factor: When two or more numbers are multiplied together, they are called factors.

Prime number: A whole number greater than zero that has only itself and **1** as factors

Composite number: A whole number greater than **1** that has factors other than itself and **1**

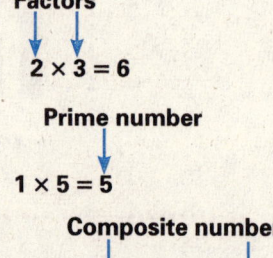

Factors
↓ ↓
2 × 3 = 6

Prime number
↓
1 × 5 = 5

Composite number
↓ ↓
1 × 6 = 6 *or* 2 × 3 = 6

Getting Started In Lesson 1-22 you learned how to find the product of two factors. You can also write numbers as the product of their factors.

EXAMPLE 1   Finding the Factors of a Number

Find all the factors of 24.

Solution

Step 1 Write 24 as a product of two factors in as many ways as possible.

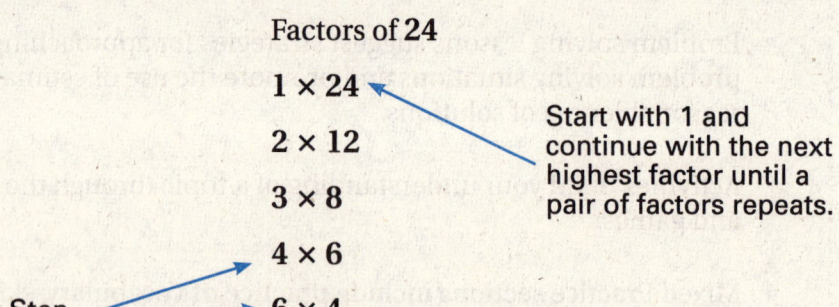

Factors of 24

1 × 24
2 × 12
3 × 8
4 × 6
Stop. → 6 × 4

Start with 1 and continue with the next highest factor until a pair of factors repeats.

Repeated Factors

When a factor repeats, you only list it once. For example, you can write 25 as 1 × 25 or as 5 × 5, but you say that the factors of 25 are 1, 5, and 25.

Step 2 List the factors in order from least to greatest.

ANSWER The factors of 24 are **1, 2, 3, 4, 6, 8, 12,** and **24**.

TRY THIS   Find all the factors of the number.

1. The factors of **18** are ▢, ▢, ▢, ▢, ▢, and ▢.

2. The factors of **35** are ▢, ▢, ▢, and ▢.

Math Intervention
Book 2 Fractions and Decimals

Name _____ Date _____

EXAMPLE 2 Identifying Prime and Composite Numbers

Tell whether the number is *prime* or *composite*.

a. 15   b. 11

Solution

a. The factors of 15 are 1, 3, 5, and 15, so 15 is composite.

b. The factors of 11 are 1 and 11, so 11 is prime.

TRY THIS Tell whether the number is *prime* or *composite*.

3. 43 _____   4. 27 _____

Prime Factorization Writing the prime factorization of a number means writing a number as the product of prime numbers. You can use a factor tree to write the prime factorization of a number.

EXAMPLE 3 Writing the Prime Factorization of a Number

Write the prime factorization of 168.

Solution

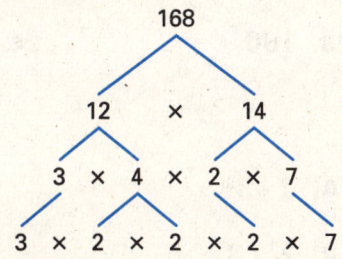

Write the given number as a product of any two factors.

Continue to write each factor as a product of two factors until all factors are prime numbers.

The prime number factors of 168 are 2^3, 3, and 7. The factor 2 has an exponent because it is used 3 times.

ANSWER The prime factorization of 168 is $2^3 \times 3 \times 7$.

TRY THIS Write the prime factorization of the number.

5. 200   ☐ × ☐ × ☐ × ☐ × ☐ = ☐^☐ × ☐^☐

6. 15   ☐ × ☐

Math Intervention
Book 2 Fractions and Decimals

Name _____ Date _____

> **Summarize**
>
> **Finding the Factors of a Number**
> Write the number as a product of two factors in as many ways as possible. List the factors from least to greatest.
>
> 40 → 1, 2, 4, 5, 8, 10, 20, 40
>
> **Writing the Prime Factorization of a Number**
> Write the number as a product of any two factors. Continue to write each factor as a product of two factors until all factors are prime.
>
>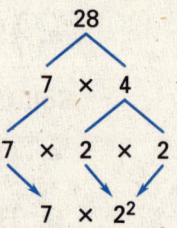

Practice

Find all the factors of the number.

1. 2
2. 8
3. 17
4. 25
5. 36
6. 49
7. 60
8. 73
9. 99
10. 108
11. 121
12. 200

Tell whether the number is *prime* or *composite*.

13. 9
14. 11
15. 21
16. 33
17. 47
18. 52
19. 65
20. 76
21. 91
22. 95
23. 100
24. 148

Match the number with its prime factorization.

25. 80 _____
26. 18 _____
27. 24 _____
28. 54 _____

A. $2 \cdot 3^3$
B. $2^3 \cdot 3$
C. $2^4 \cdot 5$
D. $2 \cdot 3^2$

Write the prime factorization of the number.

29. 7
30. 12
31. 20
32. 36
33. 43
34. 58
35. 64
36. 92
37. 125
38. 134
39. 157
40. 170
41. 220
42. 325
43. 344
44. 561

Math Intervention
Book 2 Fractions and Decimals

Name _____ Date _____

First tell whether you will *find factors, identify prime and composite numbers,* or *write a prime factorization* to find the answer. Then solve the problem. Explain your reasoning.

45. You are dividing **30** tomato plants into equal rows for planting. How many possibilities are there?

_____
_____
_____

46. Since you live at **240** Wilkens Lane, you decide to write **240** as a product of prime numbers and use each factor as a digit in a numerical password. How many digits will you have? Explain.

_____
_____
_____

47. You are using the number from a family member's birthday as the number on the back of your football jersey. You want the number to be divisible only by itself and **1**. Your family members were born on February **16**, June **13**, August **12**, and August **27**. Which birthday will you use?

_____
_____
_____

DID YOU GET IT?

48. Fill in the missing word. To write the prime factorization of a number, first write the number as a product of two _____.

49. Explain your reasoning. Your friend says the factors of **90** are all prime. Is your friend correct? Explain why or why not.

_____
_____
_____

LESSON 2-2 Greatest Common Factor

Words to Remember

Common factor: Any whole number that is a factor of two or more non-zero whole numbers

Greatest common factor (GCF): The largest whole number that is a factor of two or more non-zero whole numbers

Common factors of 8 and 12
Factors of 8: **1, 2, 4**, 8
Factors of 12: **1, 2**, 3, **4**, 6, 12

Greatest common factor of 8 and 12
Factors of 8: 1, 2, **4**, 8
Factors of 12: 1, 2, 3, **4**, 6, 12

Getting Started   In Lesson 2-1 you learned how to find the factors of a number. You can also use the factors of two or more numbers to find the greatest common factor (GCF).

EXAMPLE 1   Finding Common Factors

Find all the common factors of 20 and 30.

Solution

Step 1 List all the factors of 20 and 30.

Factors of 20: 1, 2, 4, 5, 10, 20
Factors of 30: 1, 2, 3, 5, 6, 10, 15, 30

Step 2 Circle the factors that appear in both lists.

Factors of 20: ①, ②, 4, ⑤, ⑩, 20
Factors of 30: ①, ②, 3, ⑤, 6, ⑩, 15, 30

ANSWER The common factors of 20 and 30 are 1, 2, 5, and 10.

TRY THIS   Find all the common factors of the numbers.

1. 14 and 34   Factors of 14: ▢, ▢, 7,

   _____   Factors of 34: ▢, ▢, ▢, 34

2. 28 and 72   Factors of 28: 1, 2, ▢, ▢, ▢,

   _____   Factors of 72: ▢, ▢, ▢, ▢, 6, ▢, ▢, 12, ▢, ▢, ▢, ▢

Name _____   Date _____

Repeated Factors

When a factor repeats, you only list it once. For example, for the factors of 36, only list the 6 once.

EXAMPLE 2   Finding the GCF Using a List

Find the greatest common factor of 36 and 48.

Solution

Step 1 List all the factors of 36 and 48.

Factors of 36: 1, 2, 3, 4, 6, 9, 12, 18, 36
Factors of 48: 1, 2, 3, 4, 6, 8, 12, 16, 24, 48

Step 2 Identify and circle the greatest factor that appears in both lists.

Factors of 36: 1, 2, 3, 4, 6, 9, ⓐ2, 18, 36
Factors of 48: 1, 2, 3, 4, 6, 8, ⓐ2, 16, 24, 48

ANSWER The GCF of 36 and 48 is 12.

TRY THIS   Make a list to find the GCF.

3. 16 and 24   4. 9 and 27

EXAMPLE 3   Finding the GCF Using Prime Factorization

Find the greatest common factor of 98 and 70.

Solution

Write the prime factorizations of 98 and 70.

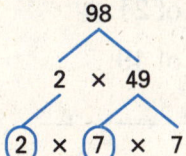 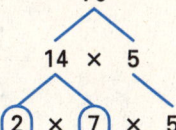   Circle all the common prime factors.

The common prime factors are 2 and 7. The GCF is the product of the common prime factors.

ANSWER The GCF of 98 and 70 is 2 × 7, or 14.

TRY THIS   Use prime factorization to find the GCF.

5. 52 and 96   6. 126 and 210

   52   96   126   210
   ∧   ∧   ∧   ∧

Math Intervention
Book 2 Fractions and Decimals   **7**

Name _____ Date _____

> **Summarize**
>
> **Finding the GCF Using a List**
>
> List all the factors of the numbers. Identify the greatest factor that appears in each list.
>
> 63: 1, 3, 7, 9, (21), 63   GCF is 21.
> 42: 1, 2, 3, 6, 7, 14, (21), 42
>
> **Finding the GCF Using Prime Factorization**
>
> Write the prime factorization of the numbers. Identify all the common prime factors. Multiply them together to find the GCF.
>
>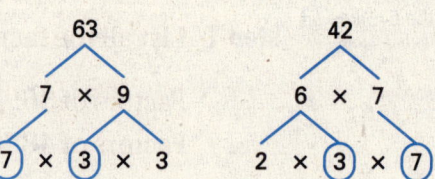
>
> GCF is 7 × 3 = 21.

Practice

Find all the common factors of the numbers.

1. 6 and 8
   Factors of 6: ▨, ▨, ▨, ▨
   Factors of 8: ▨, ▨, ▨, ▨
   _____

2. 9 and 18
   Factors of 9: ▨, ▨, ▨
   Factors of 18: ▨, ▨, ▨, ▨, ▨, ▨
   _____

3. 24 and 38
   _____

4. 30 and 75
   _____

Make a list to find the greatest common factor of the numbers.

5. 4 and 74
   Factors of 4: ▨, ▨, ▨
   Factors of 74: ▨, ▨, ▨, ▨
   GCF: _____

6. 21 and 49
   Factors of 21: ▨, ▨, ▨, ▨
   Factors of 49: ▨, ▨, ▨
   GCF: _____

7. 56 and 64
   GCF: _____

8. 15 and 105
   GCF: _____

Use prime factorization to find the greatest common factor of the numbers.

9. 16 and 72
   16   72
   GCF: _____

10. 60 and 90
    60   90
    GCF: _____

11. 45 and 120
    GCF: _____

12. 100 and 180
    GCF: _____

Name _____ Date _____

First tell whether you will find *common factors* or the *greatest common factor*. Then solve the problem. Explain your reasoning.

13. Ms. Randolf wants to divide Mr. Hunt's class of **14** students and Ms. Cary's class of **21** students into smaller groups of equal size. She does not want to mix the classes. What is the greatest number of students that she can put in one group?

   _____
   _____
   _____

14. You have **30** apples and **40** pears. You are dividing the fruit into equal groups without mixing types of fruit. Name all possible group sizes. The groups must have more than one piece of fruit.

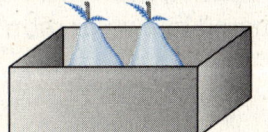 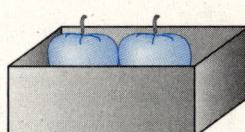

   _____
   _____
   _____
   _____

15. You have **220** black-and-white photos and **400** color photos to display on posters. You want to put the same number of photos on each poster without mixing black-and-white photos with color photos. What is the greatest number of photos you can put on each poster?

   _____
   _____
   _____

DID YOU GET IT?

16. **Fill in the missing word.** To find the GCF using prime factorization, determine the _____ of all the common prime factors.

17. **Work backwards.** The GCF of two numbers is **6**. What could the numbers be? Explain.

   _____
   _____

Math Intervention
Book 2 Fractions and Decimals

LESSON 2-3 Least Common Multiple

Words to Remember

Multiple: Any whole number that is a product of the number and another whole number

Multiples of 2
$2 \times 1 = 2$
$2 \times 2 = 4$
$2 \times 3 = 6$

Common multiple: A multiple shared by two or more numbers

Common multiples of 6 and 8

Multiples of 6: 6, 12, 18, **24**, 30, 36, 42, **48**, ...
Multiples of 8: 8, 16, **24**, 32, 40, **48**, 56, 64, ...

Least common multiple (LCM): The smallest multiple shared by two or more numbers

Least common multiple of 6 and 8

Multiples of 6: 6, 12, 18, **24**, 30, 36, 42, 48, ...
Multiples of 8: 8, 16, **24**, 32, 40, 48, 56, 64, ...

Getting Started In Lesson 1-22 you learned how to find the product of two whole numbers. You can use products to find the least common multiple (LCM).

EXAMPLE 1 Finding Multiples

List the multiples of 9 up through 80.

Solution

Multiply **9** by whole numbers starting with **1**. Each new product should be **9** greater than the previous product. List the products until you reach the product closest to, but not greater than, **80**.

$9 \times 1 = 9$ $9 \times 2 = 18$ $9 \times 3 = 27$ $9 \times 4 = 36$
$9 \times 5 = 45$ $9 \times 6 = 54$ $9 \times 7 = 63$ $9 \times 8 = 72$

ANSWER The multiples of **9** up through **80** are **9, 18, 27, 36, 45, 54, 63,** and **72**.

TRY THIS List the multiples of the number up through 100.

1. 20
   20 × ☐ = ☐
   20 × ☐ = ☐
   20 × ☐ = ☐
   20 × ☐ = ☐
   20 × ☐ = ☐

2. 16
   16 × ☐ = ☐
   16 × ☐ = ☐
   16 × ☐ = ☐
   16 × ☐ = ☐
   16 × ☐ = ☐
   16 × ☐ = ☐

Math Intervention
Book 2 Fractions and Decimals

Name _____   Date _____

EXAMPLE 2 **Finding the LCM Using a List**

Find the least common multiple of 6 and 14.

Solution

Step 1 **Start** listing the multiples of 6 and 14.

Multiples of 6: 6, 12, 18, 24, 30, 36, 42, 48, . . .
Multiples of 14: 14, 28, 42, 56, . . .

Step 2 **Identify** and circle the smallest multiple that appears in both lists.

Multiples of 6: 6, 12, 18, 24, 30, 36, ⓐ42, 48, . . .
Multiples of 14: 14, 28, ⓐ42, 56, . . .

ANSWER The LCM of 6 and 14 is 42.

TRY THIS Make a list to find the LCM.

3. 5 and 8   **4.** 2, 3, and 4

EXAMPLE 3 **Finding the LCM Using Prime Factorization**

Find the least common multiple of 42 and 56.

Solution

Step 1 **Write** the prime factorizations of 42 and 56. $42 = ②\times 3 \times ⑦$

Step 2 **Circle** all the common prime factors. $56 = ② \times 2 \times 2 \times ⑦$

Step 3 **Multiply** all the prime factors together, using each common factor only once.

Common factors   Remaining factors

$2 \times 7 \times 3 \times 2 \times 2 = 168$

ANSWER The LCM of 42 and 56 is 168.

TRY THIS Use prime factorization to find the LCM.

5. 32 and 48   **6.** 12, 120, and 180

Name _____ Date _____

> **Summarize**
>
> **Finding the LCM Using a List**
> Start listing multiples of the numbers. Identify the smallest multiple that appears in each list.
>
> 6: 6, 12, 18, 24, (30), 36, …
> 15: 15, (30), 45, …   LCM: 30
> 10: 10, 20, (30), 40, …
>
> **Finding the LCM Using Prime Factorization**
> Write the prime factorizations of the numbers. Find the product of all the prime factors. Use each common factor only once.
>
> $18 = 2 \times (3) \times (3)$
> $27 = (3) \times (3) \times 3$
> LCM: $3 \times 3 \times 2 \times 3 = 54$

Practice

1. Find the multiples of 7 through 75.

   7, ▢, ▢, ▢, ▢, ▢, ▢, ▢, ▢, ▢

2. Find the multiples of 6 through 80.

   ▢, ▢, 18, ▢, ▢, ▢, ▢, ▢, ▢, ▢, ▢, ▢, ▢

Make a list to find the least common multiple of the numbers.

3. 4 and 6
4. 3 and 15
5. 5 and 9
6. 8 and 10
7. 48 and 80
8. 3, 7, and 21

Use prime factorization to find the least common multiple of the numbers.

9. 27 and 36
10. 16 and 72
11. 4, 5, and 10
12. 12, 15, and 24
13. 39 and 52
14. 44 and 77

Name _____   Date _____

Solve the problem. Explain your reasoning.

15. Snack pouches come in packs of **8**, and drink boxes come in packs of **12**. For a class trip, there are just enough packs of each item so that each snack pouch is paired with one drink. How many pairs of snack pouches and drink boxes are there?

_____
_____
_____

16. Katy lifts weights every **4** days and swims laps every **6** days. Every **14** days she takes a yoga class. What day of her exercise routine is the first time she is supposed do all three activities?

_____
_____
_____

17. Carson inspects bike helmets at a factory. He notices that every **36**th helmet has a crack in the plastic. Every **48**th helmet is missing a buckle. Which is the first helmet that Carson will inspect that is both cracked and missing a buckle?

_____
_____
_____

DID YOU GET IT?

18. **Fill in the missing words.** When using a list to find the LCM, you identify the _____ of the common _____ that appears in each list.

19. **Work backwards.** The prime factorization of a number is $2^2 \times 3^2$. Find another number so that the LCM of both numbers is **180**.

_____
_____

Name _____   Date _____

Mixed Practice for Lessons 2-1 to 2-3

Vocabulary Review

Match the word with its definition.

Word	Definition
1. factor _____	A. a whole number greater than 1 that can only be evenly divided by itself and 1
2. prime _____	B. any whole number that is a product of two nonzero whole numbers
3. multiple _____	C. a number that is multiplied

Fill in the missing word(s).

4. The _____ _____ _____ is the smallest number that is a multiple of two numbers.

5. To find the greatest common factor of 2 numbers, you can list all factors of each number. Then find the _____ factor that appears in both lists.

6. Fill in the missing numbers to complete the prime factorization. Then identify the GCF and the LCM of **288** and **500**.

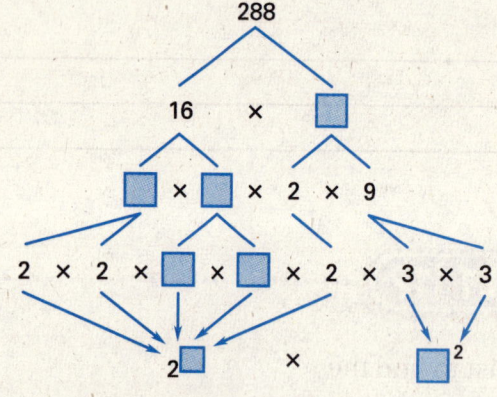
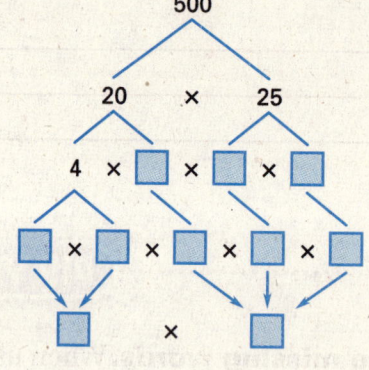

GCF of 288 and 500: _____

LCM of 288 and 500: _____

Find the greatest common factor of the numbers.

7. 27 and 9   8. 35 and 20   9. 18 and 42   10. 36 and 92

11. 40 and 28   12. 63 and 12   13. 43 and 86   14. 80 and 100

15. 30 and 225   16. 25 and 75   17. 99 and 54   18. 150 and 6

Name _____ Date _____

19. Fill in the missing information to solve the problem.

Your grocery store sells hamburger patties in packs of **6** and buns in packs of **8**. You buy just enough packs of each so you can match each patty with a bun. How many hamburger sandwiches can you make?

Step 1 The phrases "buy just enough packs" and "match each patty with a bun" tell you that you need to find the _____.

Step 2 Make two lists of multiples.

8: _____

6: _____

Step 3 You can make _____ hamburger sandwiches.

Find the LCM of the numbers.

20. 5 and 12   **21.** 2 and 6   **22.** 14 and 10   **23.** 16 and 20

24. 56 and 8   **25.** 9 and 15   **26.** 3 and 21   **27.** 35 and 25

28. 42 and 7   **29.** 11 and 2   **30.** 18 and 8   **31.** 40 and 85

First tell whether you need to find the *greatest common factor* or the *least common multiple* to find the answer. Then solve the problem. Explain your reasoning.

32. A T-shirt shop has **50** blue shirts and **20** gray shirts. An employee separates the shirts into equal-sized groups without mixing the colors. How many groups are there?

_____
_____

33. The accountant at a travel agency pays the water bill every **3** months and the insurance bill every **4** months. If both bills are paid together this month, in how many months will both bills be paid together again?

_____
_____

Name _____ Date _____

LESSON 2-4: Introduction to Fractions

Words to Remember

Fraction: A number written in the form $\frac{a}{b}$ that refers to parts of a set or parts of a whole

Fraction: $\frac{4}{5}$ ← fraction bar

Numerator: The number above the fraction bar that refers to the equal parts out of a set or whole

Denominator: The number below the fraction bar that refers to a whole or to the total number of equal parts in a set

$\frac{4}{5}$ ← Numerator
← Denominator

Getting Started In Lesson 1-2 you learned how to read, write, and represent whole numbers. You can also read, write, and represent fractions.

EXAMPLE 1 Reading and Writing Fractions

Reading Fractions

Denominators of fractions are named as follows:
- 2 → half
- 3 → third
- 4 → fourth
- 5 → fifth
- 6 → sixth
- 7 → seventh
- 8 → eighth
- 9 → ninth
- 10 → tenth
- 11 → eleventh
- 12 → twelfth
- 100 → hundredth

and so on ...

If the numerator is 1, use the form given above. If the numerator is greater than 1, add an *s* to make the denominator plural. The plural of *half* is *halves*.

a. Write the fraction $\frac{4}{9}$ in words.   b. Write six sevenths as a fraction.

Solution

a. Write the numerator followed by the appropriate name for the denominator.

$\frac{4}{9}$ → $\frac{\text{four}}{\text{ninths}}$

ANSWER four ninths

b. Write the first number, the numerator, over a fraction bar. Then write the second number, the denominator, under the fraction bar.

six sevenths $\frac{\text{six}}{\text{sevenths}}$

ANSWER $\frac{6}{7}$

TRY THIS Write the fraction in words or the words as a fraction.

1. $\frac{3}{5}$

_____ _____

2. one twelfth

Math Intervention
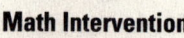

EXAMPLE 2 Representing a Fraction Using a Model

Draw a model that represents $\frac{5}{6}$.

Solution

Step 1 Draw a rectangle that is divided into six equal parts. The denominator tells the total number of equal parts. The denominator of $\frac{5}{6}$ is 6.

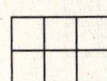

Parts of a Whole
The model drawn in Example 2 shows how fractions can represent parts of a whole.

Step 2 Shade five of the six parts. The numerator tells how many parts of the whole. The numerator of $\frac{5}{6}$ is 5.

ANSWER

TRY THIS Draw a model that represents the fraction.

3. $\frac{7}{10}$ 4. $\frac{2}{3}$

EXAMPLE 3 Writing a Fraction Represented by a Model

Write the fraction that is represented by the model.

Parts of a Set
The model in Example 3 illustrates how fractions can represent parts of a set.

Solution

Count the number of circled beads. That number is the numerator. Then count the total number of beads. That number is the denominator.

$$\frac{\text{number of circled beads}}{\text{total number of beads}} = \frac{3}{8}$$

ANSWER $\frac{3}{8}$

TRY THIS Write the fraction that is represented by the model.

5.    6.

Math Intervention
Book 2 Fractions and Decimals

Name _____ Date _____

> **Summarize**
>
> **Reading and Writing Fractions**
> Write the numerator over the denominator.
>
> The fraction "one half" is written as
> $\frac{1}{2}$ ← Numerator
>   ← Denominator
>
> **Using Models**
> The shaded parts in a model represent the numerator of a fraction. The total number of parts in a model represent the denominator of a fraction.
>
> = $\frac{8}{9}$

Practice

Write the fraction in words.

1. $\frac{5}{8}$ _____
2. $\frac{4}{5}$ _____
3. $\frac{9}{10}$ _____
4. $\frac{3}{7}$ _____
5. $\frac{8}{11}$ _____
6. $\frac{5}{6}$ _____
7. $\frac{16}{100}$ _____
8. $\frac{9}{12}$ _____
9. $\frac{7}{9}$ _____

Write the words as a fraction.

10. two thirds _____
11. three fourths _____
12. one sixth _____

13. four sevenths _____
14. two ninths _____
15. six elevenths _____

Draw a model that represents the fraction.

16. $\frac{1}{2}$
17. $\frac{3}{4}$
18. $\frac{4}{11}$
19. $\frac{7}{8}$
20. $\frac{1}{3}$
21. $\frac{2}{9}$
22. $\frac{5}{7}$
23. $\frac{2}{5}$

Write the fraction that is represented by the model.

24.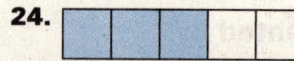

25.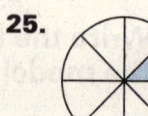

26.

27.

Math Intervention
Book 2 Fractions and Decimals

Name _____ Date _____

First identify the *numerator* and *denominator*. Then write a fraction to represent the situation. Explain your reasoning.

28. Three students in a class of eleven sign up for student council.

_____
_____
_____

29. The diagram shows the number of vacant apartments in one wing of an apartment complex.

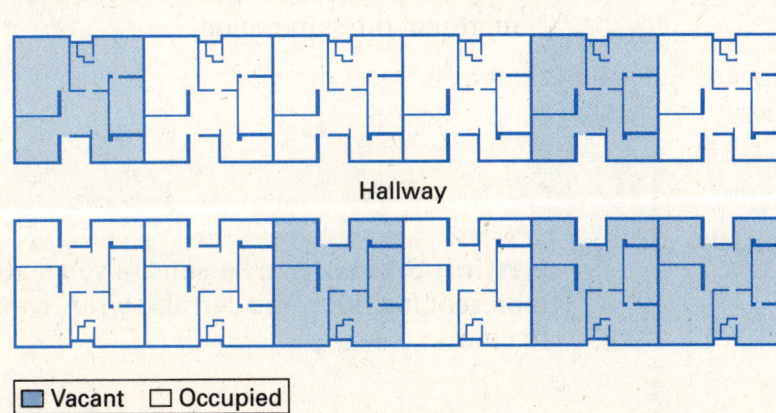

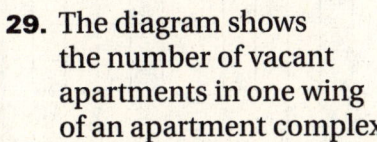

_____
_____
_____

30. Kim exercises four afternoons in seven days.

_____
_____
_____

DID YOU GET IT?

31. Fill in the missing words. The _____ of a fraction describes the equal parts of a whole. The _____ of a fraction describes the total number of parts.

32. Use a model. There is $\frac{2}{5}$ of a chicken pot pie left over from dinner last night. Fill in the blank model to represent this situation.

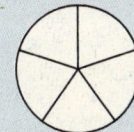

LESSON 2-5: Equivalent Fractions

Words to Remember
Equivalent fractions: Two fractions that represent the same value

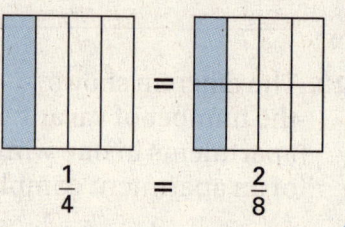

$$\frac{1}{4} = \frac{2}{8}$$

Getting Started In Lesson 2-4 you learned how to read, write, and represent fractions. You can also write, complete, and identify equivalent fractions.

EXAMPLE 1 Writing Equivalent Fractions

Write three fractions that are equivalent to $\frac{2}{5}$.

Solution

To write an equivalent fraction, multiply the numerator and denominator of a fraction by the same nonzero whole number.

$\frac{2}{5} = \frac{2 \times 2}{5 \times 2} = \frac{4}{10}$ Multiply the numerator and denominator by 2.

$\frac{2}{5} = \frac{2 \times 3}{5 \times 3} = \frac{6}{15}$ Multiply the numerator and denominator by 3.

$\frac{2}{5} = \frac{2 \times 4}{5 \times 4} = \frac{8}{20}$ Multiply the numerator and denominator by 4.

ANSWER The fractions $\frac{4}{10}$, $\frac{6}{15}$, and $\frac{8}{20}$ are equivalent to $\frac{2}{5}$.

TRY THIS Write three fractions that are equivalent to the given fraction.

1. $\frac{1}{12}$

2. $\frac{3}{7}$

Math Intervention
Book 2 Fractions and Decimals

EXAMPLE 2 Completing Equivalent Fractions

What number will complete the equivalent fraction in $\frac{4}{9} = \frac{12}{?}$?

Solution

Step 1 Think: 4 times what number is 12?

$\frac{4 \times ?}{9 \times ?} = \frac{12}{?}$ Write the problem.

$4 \times 3 = 12$ Find the unknown factor.

Step 2 Multiply the denominator 9 by the number you found in Step 1.

$\frac{4 \times 3}{9 \times 3} = \frac{12}{27}$

ANSWER 27

TRY THIS Complete the equivalent fraction.

3. $\frac{5}{6} = \frac{10}{\square}$

4. $\frac{1}{8} = \frac{\square}{56}$

EXAMPLE 3 Identifying Equivalent Fractions

Tell whether the models represent equivalent fractions.

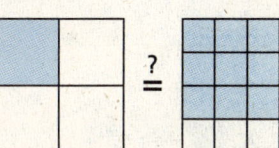

Using Models

Notice that even though the models are the same size, the total shaded area in the second model appears to be larger than the total shaded area in the first model.

Solution

$\frac{1}{4} \stackrel{?}{=} \frac{9}{16}$ Write the fractions represented by the models.

$\frac{1 \times ?}{4 \times ?} = \frac{9}{16} \rightarrow \frac{1 \times 9}{4 \times 4} = \frac{9}{16} \rightarrow 9 \neq 4$ Determine whether 1 and 4 are multiplied by the same number to get 9 and 16.

ANSWER Since 1 and 4 are multiplied by different numbers to get 9 and 16, the models do not represent equivalent fractions.

TRY THIS

5. Tell whether the models represent equivalent fractions.

Name _____ Date _____

Summarize

Writing Equivalent Fractions

Multiply the numerator and denominator by the same nonzero whole number to write an equivalent fraction.

$$\frac{3}{11} = \frac{3 \times 2}{11 \times 2} = \frac{6}{22}$$

Completing Equivalent Fractions

Find the number that when multiplied by the smaller numerator or denominator gives the larger numerator or denominator. The numerator and denominator are multiplied by the same nonzero whole number.

$$\frac{4}{5} = \frac{16}{?}$$

$$\frac{4 \times ?}{5 \times ?} = \frac{16}{?} \rightarrow \frac{4 \times 4}{5 \times ?} = \frac{16}{?} \rightarrow \frac{4 \times 4}{5 \times 4} = \frac{16}{20}$$

Identifying Equivalent Fractions

Determine whether the smaller numerator and denominator are multiplied by the same number to get the larger numerator and denominator.

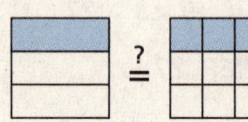

$$\frac{1}{3} \stackrel{?}{=} \frac{3}{9}$$

$$\frac{1 \times ?}{3 \times ?} = \frac{3}{9} \rightarrow \frac{1 \times 3}{3 \times 3} = \frac{3}{9} \rightarrow 3 = 3, \text{ so } \frac{1}{3} = \frac{3}{9}$$

Practice

Write three fractions that are equivalent to the fraction.

1. $\frac{3}{4}$ ___, ___, ___
2. $\frac{7}{10}$ ___, ___, ___
3. $\frac{1}{6}$ ___, ___, ___
4. $\frac{2}{9}$ ___, ___, ___
5. $\frac{4}{7}$ ___, ___, ___
6. $\frac{11}{12}$ ___, ___, ___

Complete the equivalent fraction.

7. $\frac{1}{10} = \frac{7}{\square}$
8. $\frac{2}{7} = \frac{18}{\square}$
9. $\frac{3}{5} = \frac{6}{\square}$
10. $\frac{8}{9} = \frac{\square}{45}$
11. $\frac{3}{8} = \frac{\square}{16}$
12. $\frac{7}{12} = \frac{\square}{36}$

Tell whether the models represent equivalent fractions.

13.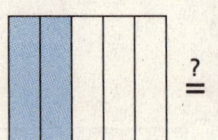
14.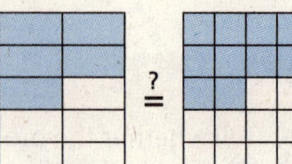
15.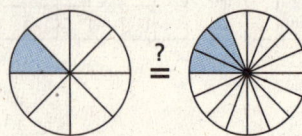
16.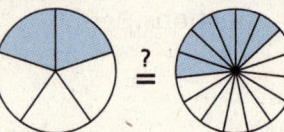

Math Intervention
Book 2 Fractions and Decimals

Name _____ Date _____

First tell whether you need to *write, complete,* or *identify* equivalent fractions. Then solve the problem. Explain your reasoning.

17. The diagram shows your marble collection and a friend's marble collection. Your friend says she has the same fraction of blue marbles in her collection as you have in yours. Is she correct?

 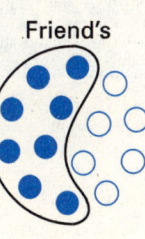

_____
_____
_____

18. Out of **12** students in the math club, **5** are baseball players. The drama club has **36** members. That club has the same fraction of baseball players as the math club. How many baseball players are in the drama club?

_____
_____
_____

19. A deli sells boxes with different kinds of sandwiches. In each box, $\frac{3}{8}$ of the sandwiches are ham and cheese. Suppose there were two boxes of sandwiches, or three boxes, or more. Name three other ways the fraction of ham and cheese sandwiches could be expressed.

_____
_____
_____

DID YOU GET IT?

20. Fill in the missing words. _____ _____ are two fractions that represent the same value.

21. Use a model. About $\frac{3}{4}$ of the blossoms on a tree are fully open. Represent an equivalent fraction by filling in the blank model.

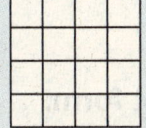 $\frac{3}{4} = \frac{}{}$

Name _____ Date _____

LESSON 2-6 Simplify Fractions

> **Words to Remember**
>
> **Simplest form:** The form of a fraction where the greatest common factor of the numerator and denominator is 1
>
> $\frac{5}{8}$ GCF of 5 and 8 is 1.
> So, $\frac{5}{8}$ is in simplest form.
>
> $\frac{9}{12}$ GCF of 9 and 12 is 3.
> So, $\frac{9}{12}$ is *not* in simplest form.

Getting Started In Lesson 2-2 you learned how to find the greatest common factor (GCF) of two numbers. In Lesson 2-5 you learned how write equivalent fractions. You can use the GCF of the numerator and the denominator to write an equivalent fraction that is in simplest form.

Identifying Fractions in Simplest Form To decide whether a fraction is in simplest form, find the greatest common factor of the numerator and the denominator. If the GCF is **1**, the fraction is in simplest form. If it is not **1**, then the fraction is not in simplest form.

EXAMPLE 1 Identifying Fractions in Simplest Form

Tell whether the fraction is in simplest form.

a. $\frac{3}{8}$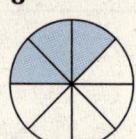

b. $\frac{4}{6}$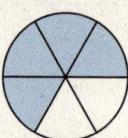

> **Reading**
> Simplest form is also called *the reduced form for a fraction*.

Solution

a. $\frac{3}{8}$ is in simplest form because the GCF of **3** and **8** is **1**.

   ANSWER The fraction $\frac{3}{8}$ is in simplest form.

b. $\frac{4}{6}$ is *not* in simplest form because the GCF of **4** and **6** is **2**.

   ANSWER The fraction $\frac{4}{6}$ is not in simplest form.

TRY THIS Tell whether the fraction is in simplest form. Write *yes* or *no*.

1. $\frac{4}{16}$ _____

2. $\frac{2}{11}$ _____

Math Intervention
Book 2 Fractions and Decimals

Simplifying A fraction that is not in simplest form can be written as an equivalent fraction that is in simplest form. To *simplify* a fraction, divide the numerator and the denominator by the GCF.

EXAMPLE 2 Writing Fractions in Simplest Form

Simplify the fraction.

a. $\frac{16}{20}$

b. $\frac{8}{8}$

Solution

> **Remember**
> When you simplify $\frac{16}{20}$, you are writing an equivalent fraction. The equivalent fraction has the smallest possible numbers in the numerator and denominator.

a. List the factors of 16 and 20.
16: 1, 2, 4, 8, 16
20: 1, 2, 4, 5, 10, 20

The GCF of 16 and 20 is 4.   Find the GCF of 16 and 20.

$\frac{16 \div 4}{20 \div 4} = \frac{4}{5}$ Divide 16 and 20 by 4.

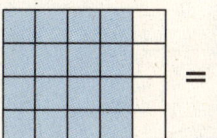 =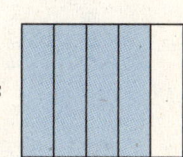

Look at models that represent $\frac{16}{20}$ and $\frac{4}{5}$. The shaded parts in each model are the same size. That is how you know the fractions are equivalent.

ANSWER $\frac{4}{5}$

b. List the factors of 8: 1, 2, 4, 8

The GCF of 8 and 8 is 8.   Find the GCF of 8 and 8.

$\frac{8 \div 8}{8 \div 8} = \frac{1}{1} = 1$ Divide 8 and 8 by the GCF.

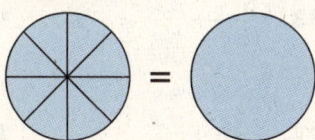

Look at the model that represents $\frac{8}{8}$. All the parts are shaded. So, 8 parts of 8 is equal to one whole, or 1.

ANSWER 1

TRY THIS Simplify the fraction.

3. $\frac{14}{26} \rightarrow$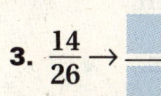

4. $\frac{11}{11} \rightarrow$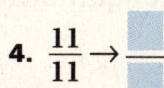

5. Which fraction represents the simplest form of the model? _____

A. $\frac{1}{4}$

B. $\frac{1}{2}$

Name _____ Date _____

Summarize

Identifying Fractions in Simplest Form
Find the GCF of the numerator and denominator.

$\frac{5}{9}$ GCF is 1.
So, $\frac{5}{9}$ is in simplest form.

$\frac{6}{8}$ GCF is 2.
So, $\frac{6}{8}$ is not in simplest form.

Simplifying Fractions
Divide the numerator and denominator by the GCF.

$\frac{7}{21}$ $\quad \frac{7 \div 7}{21 \div 7} = \frac{1}{3}$

$\frac{3}{3}$ $\quad \frac{3 \div 3}{3 \div 3} = \frac{1}{1} = 1$

Practice

Tell whether the fraction or model is in simplest form. Write *yes* or *no*.

1. $\frac{7}{12}$ _____
2. $\frac{6}{9}$ _____
3. $\frac{5}{5}$ _____
4. $\frac{8}{15}$ _____

5. $\frac{2}{5}$ _____
6. $\frac{3}{7}$ _____
7. $\frac{18}{24}$ _____
8. $\frac{25}{50}$ _____

9.  _____
10. 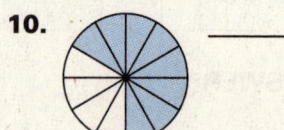 _____

Simplify the fraction.

11. $\frac{3}{9} \rightarrow \frac{\square}{\square}$
12. $\frac{8}{18} \rightarrow \frac{\square}{\square}$
13. $\frac{6}{15} \rightarrow \frac{\square}{\square}$
14. $\frac{12}{28} \rightarrow \frac{\square}{\square}$

15. $\frac{30}{40} \rightarrow \frac{\square}{\square}$
16. $\frac{24}{36} \rightarrow \frac{\square}{\square}$
17. $\frac{14}{49} \rightarrow \frac{\square}{\square}$
18. $\frac{10}{100} \rightarrow \frac{\square}{\square}$

19. $\frac{27}{60} \rightarrow \frac{\square}{\square}$
20. $\frac{25}{90} \rightarrow \frac{\square}{\square}$
21. $\frac{55}{65} \rightarrow \frac{\square}{\square}$
22. $\frac{48}{96} \rightarrow \frac{\square}{\square}$

Match each model with the equivalent fraction in simplest form.

23. 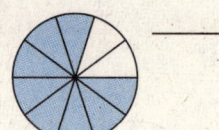 _____
24. 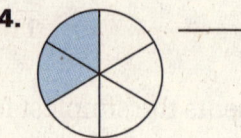 _____
25. 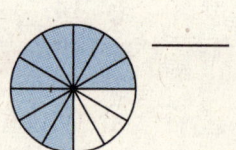 _____

A. $\frac{3}{4}$
B. $\frac{4}{5}$
C. $\frac{1}{3}$

Math Intervention
Book 2 Fractions and Decimals

Name _____ Date _____

Write a fraction to represent the situation. Then simplify the fraction to answer the question.

26. You are copying a picture for art class. The diagram shows how much you have finished so far. What fraction of the picture have you drawn?

_____

27. You have completed 18 of the 24 problems on a quiz. What fraction of the quiz have you completed?

_____

28. After school, you studied for a total of 25 minutes. You spent 10 minutes working on math homework. What fraction of your study time was spent on math homework?

_____

DID YOU GET IT?

29. Fill in the missing words. When a fraction is in _____ _____, the GCF of the numerator and denominator is 1.

30. Use a model. Use the blank models at the right to represent a fraction that is not in simplest form and an equivalent fraction that is in simplest form.

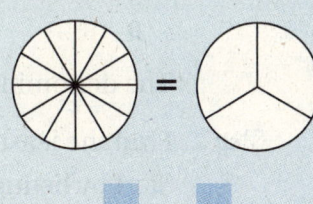

31. Explain your reasoning. You have read 15 pages of a 20-page short story. You tell your friend that you are $\frac{3}{4}$ of the way through the story. Is your statement correct? Explain.

_____
_____
_____

Name _____ Date _____

LESSON 2-7 Compare and Order Fractions

> **Words to Remember**
>
> Least common denominator (LCD): The least common multiple (LCM) of the denominators of two or more fractions
>
> For example: $\frac{3}{4}$ and $\frac{1}{6}$ ← denominators
>
> 4, 8, **12**, 16, 20, ...
> 6, **12**, 18, 24, ...   least common multiple (LCM) = 12
>
> The LCD of $\frac{3}{4}$ and $\frac{1}{6}$ is 12.   LCM = LCD

Getting Started In Lesson 2-3 you learned how to find the least common multiple. You can use the least common multiple of two or more denominators to compare and order fractions. The least common multiple of the denominators of two or more fractions is also known as the *least common denominator*, or LCD.

EXAMPLE 1 Finding the LCD

Find the least common denominator of $\frac{3}{8}$ and $\frac{5}{12}$.

Solution

Step 1 **Identify** the denominators of the fractions.

$\frac{3}{8}$ $\frac{5}{12}$

The denominators are **8** and **12**.

Step 2 **Find** the least common multiple of the denominators.
Start by listing the multiples for each number.
8, 16, **24**, 32, 40, ...
12, **24**, 36, 48, 60, ...

The LCM of 8 and 12 is 24.

Step 3 **Find** the least common multiple of the denominators. This number is the least common denominator (LCD).

ANSWER The LCD of $\frac{3}{8}$ and $\frac{5}{12}$ is 24.

TRY THIS Find the LCD.

1. $\frac{2}{9}$ and $\frac{3}{9}$ _____

2. $\frac{4}{5}$ and $\frac{7}{10}$ _____

Math Intervention
Book 2 Fractions and Decimals

EXAMPLE 2 — Comparing Fractions Using the LCD

Compare $\frac{1}{4}$ and $\frac{1}{6}$.

Solution

Step 1 Find the least common denominator of $\frac{1}{4}$ and $\frac{1}{6}$.

4, 8, **12**, 16, 20, . . .   6, **12**, 18, 24, 30, . . .   The LCD is **12**.

Step 2 Use the LCD to write equivalent fractions:

$$\frac{1 \times 3}{4 \times 3} = \frac{3}{12} \qquad \frac{1 \times 2}{6 \times 2} = \frac{2}{12}$$

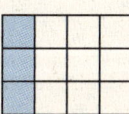   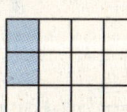

Using a Model
Notice that there is more shading in the model of $\frac{3}{12}$ than in the model of $\frac{2}{12}$.

Step 3 Notice that $3 > 2$, so $\frac{3}{12} > \frac{2}{12}$.

ANSWER You know that $\frac{3}{12} > \frac{2}{12}$, so $\frac{1}{4} > \frac{1}{6}$.

TRY THIS Compare the fractions. Complete the statement with <, >, or =.

3. $\frac{5}{8}$ ● $\frac{3}{4}$

4. $\frac{5}{6}$ ● $\frac{6}{7}$

EXAMPLE 3 — Ordering Fractions Using the LCD

Order the fractions $\frac{2}{3}, \frac{3}{5},$ and $\frac{7}{15}$ from least to greatest.

Solution

Step 1 Use the LCD to write equivalent fractions. The LCD of $\frac{2}{3}, \frac{3}{5},$ and $\frac{7}{15}$ is **15**.

$$\frac{2 \times 5}{3 \times 5} = \frac{10}{15} \qquad \frac{3 \times 3}{5 \times 3} = \frac{9}{15} \qquad \frac{7 \times 1}{15 \times 1} = \frac{7}{15}$$

Step 2 Notice that $7 < 9 < 10$, so $\frac{7}{15} < \frac{9}{15} < \frac{10}{15}$ or $\frac{7}{15} < \frac{3}{5} < \frac{2}{3}$.

ANSWER The fractions in order from least to greatest are $\frac{7}{15}, \frac{3}{5},$ and $\frac{2}{3}$.

TRY THIS Order the fractions from least to greatest.

5. $\frac{1}{9}, \frac{1}{4},$ and $\frac{1}{12}$

6. $\frac{1}{6}, \frac{7}{8},$ and $\frac{2}{3}$

Name _____ Date _____

> **Summarize**
> **Finding the Least Common Denominator**
> Find the LCM of the denominators. The LCM of the denominators is the least common denominator.
> **Comparing Fractions**
> Use the LCD to write equivalent fractions. Then compare the fractions.
> **Ordering Fractions**
> Use the LCD to write equivalent fractions. Then order the fractions.

Practice

Find the least common denominator of the fractions.

1. $\frac{1}{2}$ and $\frac{11}{14}$ ____
2. $\frac{5}{6}$ and $\frac{4}{9}$ ____
3. $\frac{3}{5}$ and $\frac{1}{7}$ ____

4. $\frac{2}{3}$ and $\frac{5}{8}$ ____
5. $\frac{7}{15}$ and $\frac{3}{4}$ ____
6. $\frac{9}{10}$ and $\frac{5}{6}$ ____

7. $\frac{1}{4}, \frac{5}{14}$, and $\frac{3}{28}$ ____
8. $\frac{1}{2}, \frac{3}{10}$, and $\frac{9}{16}$ ____
9. $\frac{1}{6}, \frac{7}{15}$, and $\frac{4}{5}$ ____

Complete the statement with <, >, or =.

10.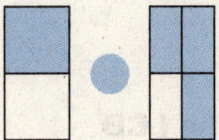
11.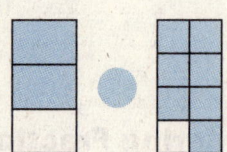
12.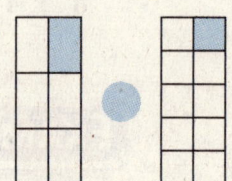

13. $\frac{8}{11}$ ◯ $\frac{10}{11}$
14. $\frac{1}{2}$ ◯ $\frac{3}{6}$
15. $\frac{2}{3}$ ◯ $\frac{4}{9}$

16. $\frac{3}{8}$ ◯ $\frac{2}{7}$
17. $\frac{7}{10}$ ◯ $\frac{4}{5}$
18. $\frac{9}{20}$ ◯ $\frac{5}{12}$

Order the fractions from least to greatest.

19. $\frac{1}{9}, \frac{1}{3}$, and $\frac{1}{12}$
20. $\frac{4}{7}, \frac{3}{4}$, and $\frac{5}{8}$
21. $\frac{5}{6}, \frac{9}{10}$, and $\frac{5}{12}$

22. $\frac{7}{9}, \frac{5}{6}$, and $\frac{5}{18}$
23. $\frac{7}{10}, \frac{4}{5}$, and $\frac{3}{20}$
24. $\frac{11}{16}, \frac{3}{8}$, and $\frac{13}{32}$

25. $\frac{1}{4}, \frac{5}{16}$, and $\frac{4}{15}$
26. $\frac{9}{20}, \frac{5}{12}$, and $\frac{3}{5}$
27. $\frac{6}{7}, \frac{7}{9}$, and $\frac{3}{4}$

Math Intervention
Book 2 Fractions and Decimals

Name _____ Date _____

Solve. Explain your answer.

28. The diagram shows the number of books you have read on your summer reading list. Your friend has read $\frac{2}{5}$ of the books on the list. Who has read more books on the list?

Read   Not read

_____
_____
_____

29. You are sewing lace onto some pillows. The lengths of lace that you need for three pillows are $\frac{7}{9}$ yard, $\frac{3}{4}$ yard, and $\frac{5}{6}$ yard. Order these measurements from least to greatest.

_____
_____
_____

30. You are building a shelf over a fireplace. You have just attached a $\frac{7}{12}$-inch piece of wood to the shelf. The next piece of wood you attach needs to be slightly shorter. Should you use a piece that measures $\frac{9}{16}$ inch or $\frac{5}{8}$ inch?

_____
_____
_____

DID YOU GET IT?

31. **Fill in the missing words.** The _____ _____ _____ of two fractions is the least common multiple of the denominators of the fractions.

32. **Use a model.** Use the blank models at the right to write a comparison statement with < or >. Then write the comparison using numbers.

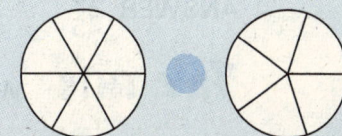

Math Intervention
Book 2 Fractions and Decimals   **31**

Lesson 2-8: Mixed Numbers and Improper Fractions

Words to Remember

Mixed number: A number that represents the sum of a whole number and a fraction

Mixed number: $5 + \frac{1}{4} = 5\frac{1}{4}$

Whole number part — Fraction part

Improper fraction: A fraction with a numerator that is greater than or equal to the denominator

Improper fraction: $\frac{10}{3}$

$10 > 3$

numerator > denominator

Getting Started In Lesson 2-4 you learned how to read, write, and represent fractions. You can also read, write, and represent mixed numbers and improper fractions.

EXAMPLE 1 — Writing Improper Fractions as Mixed Numbers

Write $\frac{13}{5}$ as a mixed number.

Solution

Step 1 Divide 13 by 5.

Denominator → $5\overline{)13}$ ← Whole number part (2)

$\frac{10}{3}$ ← Numerator in fraction part

$13 \div 5 = 2\ R\ 3$

Step 2 Write the mixed number. The quotient, or answer, is the whole number part of the mixed number. The remainder becomes the numerator of the fraction part of the mixed number. Keep the denominator from the improper fraction.

ANSWER $2\frac{3}{5}$

Using a Model

You can use a model to represent an improper fraction. Shade the model the same way you would shade a model for a proper fraction. Each whole has 5 equal parts. Shade 13 of the parts.

There are 2 wholes plus $\frac{3}{5}$. So, $\frac{13}{5} = 2\frac{3}{5}$.

TRY THIS
Write the improper fraction as a mixed number.

1. $\frac{7}{2} =$ ☐/☐

2. $\frac{16}{9} =$ ☐/☐

Math Intervention
Book 2 Fractions and Decimals

EXAMPLE 2 — Writing Mixed Numbers as Improper Fractions

Write $6\frac{3}{4}$ as an improper fraction.

Solution

Step 1 Multiply the whole number by the denominator. Then add the numerator. The sum becomes the numerator of the improper fraction.

$(6 \times 4) + 3 = 27$

Step 2 Write the improper fraction. Keep the denominator from the mixed number.

ANSWER $\frac{27}{4}$

TRY THIS Write the mixed number as an improper fraction.

3. $3\frac{1}{6} = \dfrac{(\square \times \square) + \square}{\square} = \dfrac{\square + \square}{\square} = \dfrac{\square}{\square}$

4. $1\frac{4}{7} = \dfrac{(\square \times \square) + \square}{\square} = \dfrac{\square + \square}{\square} = \dfrac{\square}{\square}$

EXAMPLE 3 — Using a Model

Use a model to write $1\frac{2}{3}$ as an improper fraction.

Solution

Step 1 Model $1\frac{2}{3}$ by shading 1 circle and $\frac{2}{3}$ of another circle.

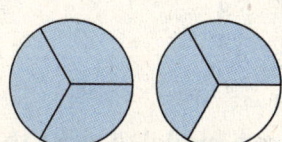

Step 2 Count the total number of shaded parts. This is the numerator of the improper fraction. The number of equal parts in each circle is the denominator. There are 5 shaded parts and 3 equal parts in each circle.

ANSWER $\frac{5}{3}$

TRY THIS

5. Use the model to write $2\frac{1}{4}$ as an improper fraction.

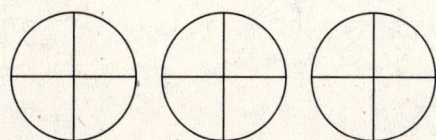

Name _____   Date _____

> ### Summarize
>
> **Writing Improper Fractions as Mixed Numbers**
>
> Divide the numerator by the denominator. The quotient is the whole number part of the mixed number. The remainder is the numerator of the fraction part of the mixed number. The denominator stays the same.
>
> $\dfrac{11}{2} \to 2\overline{)11} \to 5\dfrac{1}{2}$
>
> **Writing Mixed Numbers as Improper Fractions**
>
> Multiply the whole number by the denominator. Then add the numerator. This becomes the numerator of the improper fraction. Keep the denominator the same.
>
> $3\dfrac{2}{5} = \dfrac{(3 \times 5) + 2}{5} = \dfrac{17}{5}$
>
> **Using Models**
>
> The model represents a mixed number, $1\dfrac{3}{8}$, and an improper fraction, $\dfrac{11}{8}$.
>
>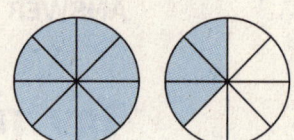

Practice

Write the improper fraction as a mixed number.

1. $\dfrac{12}{7}$ 2. $\dfrac{14}{5}$ 3. $\dfrac{15}{2}$ 4. $\dfrac{8}{3}$

5. $\dfrac{7}{4}$ 6. $\dfrac{17}{6}$ 7. $\dfrac{21}{10}$ 8. $\dfrac{25}{9}$

Write the mixed number as an improper fraction.

9. $2\dfrac{7}{8}$ 10. $5\dfrac{1}{4}$ 11. $3\dfrac{2}{3}$ 12. $1\dfrac{4}{9}$

13. $4\dfrac{3}{7}$ 14. $3\dfrac{2}{5}$ 15. $5\dfrac{1}{10}$ 16. $6\dfrac{5}{12}$

Use a model to write the mixed number as an improper fraction.

17. $2\dfrac{2}{5} = \dfrac{\square}{\square}$ 18. $1\dfrac{1}{9} = \dfrac{\square}{\square}$ 19. $2\dfrac{3}{10} = \dfrac{\square}{\square}$

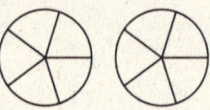   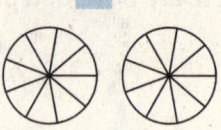   

20. $1\dfrac{5}{6} = \dfrac{\square}{\square}$ 21. $1\dfrac{7}{16} = \dfrac{\square}{\square}$ 22. $2\dfrac{5}{8} = \dfrac{\square}{\square}$

   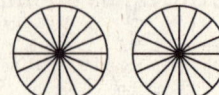   

Math Intervention
Book 2 Fractions and Decimals

Name _____ Date _____

Solve. Show all your work.

23. Thom served $2\frac{1}{2}$ pitchers of punch at a birthday party. Write this amount as an improper fraction.

_____

24. A recipe for pizza dough needs $\frac{11}{2}$ cups of flour. What is $\frac{11}{2}$ written as a mixed number?

_____

25. The diagram shows the number of seats that were filled at a dinner party. Write the amount as a mixed number.

_____

DID YOU GET IT?

26. Fill in the missing words. A(n) _____ _____ represents the sum of a whole number and a fraction. In a(n) _____ _____, the numerator is greater than or equal to the denominator.

27. Find the error. Stacy shows her steps as she writes $5\frac{4}{9}$ as an improper fraction. Describe and correct the error in Stacy's work.

$5\frac{4}{9} = \frac{5 \times 4}{9} = \frac{20}{9}$

_____
_____
_____

28. Use a model. There are $4\frac{1}{2}$ inches of snow on the ground. Fill in the blank model to represent this situation. Then write the amount as an improper fraction.

_____

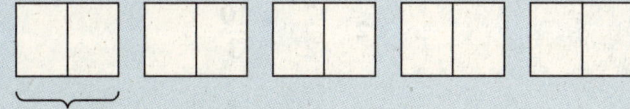

1 inch

Math Intervention
Book 2 Fractions and Decimals

Name _____   Date _____

LESSON 2-9: Compare and Order Mixed Numbers and Improper Fractions

Getting Started In Lesson 2-7 you learned how to compare and order fractions. You can also compare and order mixed numbers and improper fractions.

EXAMPLE 1   Comparing Mixed Numbers

Compare the mixed numbers.

a. $2\frac{8}{9}$ and $1\frac{11}{12}$

b. $4\frac{3}{5}$ and $4\frac{7}{15}$

Solution

a. Compare the whole numbers.

   ANSWER You know that $2 > 1$, so $2\frac{8}{9} > 1\frac{11}{12}$.

b. Compare the fraction parts. Use the LCD to write equivalent fractions.

   $\frac{3}{5} = \frac{3 \times 3}{5 \times 3} = \frac{9}{15}$ $\frac{7}{15}$

   ANSWER You know that $\frac{9}{15} > \frac{7}{15}$, so $\frac{3}{5} > \frac{7}{15}$. That means that $4\frac{3}{5} > 4\frac{7}{15}$.

Take Note!
In part (b), the whole number parts are equal, so compare the fraction parts.

EXAMPLE 2   Comparing Improper Fractions

Compare $\frac{9}{4}$ and $\frac{12}{5}$.

Solution

Use the LCD to write equivalent fractions.

$\frac{9}{4} = \frac{9 \times 5}{4 \times 5} = \frac{45}{20}$ $\frac{12}{5} = \frac{12 \times 4}{5 \times 4} = \frac{48}{20}$

ANSWER You know that $\frac{45}{20} < \frac{48}{20}$, so $\frac{9}{4} < \frac{12}{5}$.

TRY THIS   Complete the statement with < or >.

1. $1\frac{4}{9}$ ◯ $1\frac{13}{18}$

2. $\frac{7}{2}$ ◯ $\frac{10}{3}$

Math Intervention
Book 2 Fractions and Decimals

Name _____   Date _____

EXAMPLE 3 — Comparing Mixed Numbers and Improper Fractions

Compare $1\frac{3}{4}$ and $\frac{15}{8}$.

Solution

Step 1 Write the mixed number as an improper fraction.

$$1\frac{3}{4} = \frac{4 \times 1 + 3}{4} = \frac{7}{4}$$

Step 2 Use the LCD to write equivalent fractions.

$$\frac{7}{4} = \frac{7 \times 2}{4 \times 2} = \frac{14}{8} \qquad \frac{15}{8}$$

ANSWER You know that $\frac{14}{8} < \frac{15}{8}$, so $1\frac{3}{4} < \frac{15}{8}$.

TRY THIS Compare the numbers.

3. $3\frac{5}{8}$ ● $\frac{11}{3}$

4. $\frac{21}{5}$ ● $4\frac{2}{11}$

EXAMPLE 4 — Ordering Mixed Numbers and Improper Fractions

Order $\frac{17}{3}$, $3\frac{2}{3}$, and $3\frac{5}{9}$ from least to greatest.

Solution

Step 1 Write the mixed numbers as improper fractions.

$$3\frac{2}{3} = \frac{3 \times 3 + 2}{3} = \frac{11}{3} \qquad 3\frac{5}{9} = \frac{9 \times 3 + 5}{9} = \frac{32}{9}$$

Step 2 Use the LCD to write equivalent fractions.

$$\frac{17}{3} = \frac{17 \times 3}{3 \times 3} = \frac{51}{9} \qquad \frac{11}{3} = \frac{11 \times 3}{3 \times 3} = \frac{33}{9} \qquad \frac{32}{9}$$

You know that $\frac{32}{9} < \frac{33}{9}$ and $\frac{33}{9} < \frac{51}{9}$, so $3\frac{5}{9} < 3\frac{2}{3}$ and $3\frac{2}{3} < \frac{17}{3}$.

ANSWER The numbers in order from least to greatest are $3\frac{5}{9}$, $3\frac{2}{3}$, and $\frac{17}{3}$.

TRY THIS Order the numbers from least to greatest.

5. $2\frac{7}{12}$, $2\frac{1}{6}$, and $\frac{41}{24}$

6. $3\frac{4}{5}$, $\frac{67}{20}$, and $\frac{33}{10}$

_____   _____

Math Intervention
Book 2 Fractions and Decimals

Name _____ Date _____

> **Summarize**
>
> **Comparing Mixed Numbers**
> Compare whole numbers. If they are equal, compare fraction parts.
>
> **Comparing Improper Fractions**
> Use the LCD to write equivalent fractions. Then compare the fractions.
>
> **Comparing and Ordering Mixed Numbers and Improper Fractions**
> Write the mixed numbers as improper fractions. Use the LCD to write equivalent fractions. Then compare and order the fractions.

Practice

Complete the statement with <, >, or =.

1. $3\frac{1}{3}$ ◯ $2\frac{5}{6}$
2. $7\frac{9}{10}$ ◯ $7\frac{4}{5}$
3. $6\frac{3}{8}$ ◯ $6\frac{2}{3}$

4. $\frac{19}{8}$ ◯ $\frac{11}{4}$
5. $\frac{23}{6}$ ◯ $\frac{29}{4}$
6. $\frac{16}{9}$ ◯ $\frac{17}{11}$

7. $1\frac{5}{6}$ ◯ $\frac{23}{12}$
8. $\frac{11}{5}$ ◯ $2\frac{1}{10}$
9. $4\frac{2}{3}$ ◯ $\frac{51}{12}$

Circle the number with the greatest value.

10. $\frac{12}{7}$ $\frac{25}{14}$ $1\frac{9}{14}$
11. $\frac{9}{2}$ $4\frac{1}{3}$ $\frac{17}{4}$
12. $8\frac{4}{5}$ $\frac{91}{10}$ $9\frac{2}{5}$

13. $\frac{14}{9}$ $1\frac{5}{8}$ $1\frac{11}{20}$
14. $2\frac{1}{8}$ $\frac{31}{16}$ $\frac{41}{20}$
15. $5\frac{3}{10}$ $\frac{59}{12}$ $\frac{35}{6}$

Order the numbers from least to greatest.

16. $3\frac{1}{16}, \frac{9}{4}, \frac{41}{16}$
17. $\frac{13}{8}, 1\frac{7}{12}, \frac{17}{12}$
18. $\frac{26}{9}, \frac{8}{3}, 2\frac{5}{6}$

_____   _____   _____

19. $\frac{8}{3}, 2\frac{1}{2}, \frac{18}{7}$
20. $\frac{41}{10}, 4\frac{2}{15}, \frac{49}{12}$
21. $5\frac{7}{12}, \frac{43}{8}, \frac{16}{3}$

_____   _____   _____

Math Intervention
Book 2 Fractions and Decimals

Name _____   Date _____

Solve. Explain your answer.

22. You use $3\frac{3}{4}$ cups of flour to bake bread and $3\frac{7}{16}$ cups of flour to bake a cake. Do you use more flour for the bread or the cake?

   _____
   _____
   _____

23. Order the letters from narrowest to widest.

   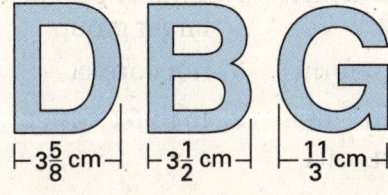

   _____
   _____
   _____

24. Sam walked $\frac{8}{3}$ miles. Jamila walked $\frac{11}{9}$ miles. Who walked farther?

   _____
   _____
   _____

DID YOU GET IT?

25. **Fill in the missing words.** To compare a mixed number and an improper fraction, first write the _____ _____ as a(n) _____ _____. Then use the _____ to write equivalent fractions.

26. **Explain your reasoning.** You are working on a painting for art class. To fit in a frame, the length of the canvas needs to be between $8\frac{5}{12}$ inches and $\frac{35}{4}$ inches. You cut your canvas so that it measures $8\frac{2}{3}$ inches. Will the canvas fit in the frame? Explain.

   _____
   _____
   _____

Name _____ Date _____

Mixed Practice for Lessons 2-4 to 2-9

Vocabulary Review

Match the word with its mathematical meaning and its everyday meaning.

Word	Mathematical meaning	Everyday meaning
1. simplify ___, ___	A. describes a fraction with a numerator greater than the denominator	X. smaller part of a larger group
2. improper ___, ___	B. to write a fraction in simplest form	Y. not correct
3. fraction ___, ___	C. a number written in the form $\frac{a}{b}$ that refers to parts of a set or parts of a whole	Z. to make easier

Fill in the missing word(s).

4. The fractions $\frac{3}{7}$ and $\frac{6}{21}$ are _____ because they represent the same value.

5. The _____ of a fraction refers to the whole, or number of equal parts in a set.

Identify the numerator and denominator of the fraction. Then shade in the model to represent the fraction.

6. $\frac{5}{8}$ 7. $\frac{2}{9}$ 8. $\frac{1}{5}$

Use the model to write the mixed number as an improper fraction.

9. $1\frac{1}{4}$ 10. $2\frac{5}{6}$ 11. $1\frac{2}{7}$

Complete the equivalent fraction.

12. $\frac{2}{3} = \frac{6}{\boxed{}}$ 13. $\frac{1}{10} = \frac{\boxed{}}{40}$ 14. $\frac{3}{5} = \frac{\boxed{}}{25}$ 15. $\frac{6}{7} = \frac{18}{\boxed{}}$

Order the numbers from least to greatest.

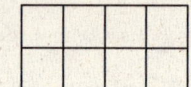

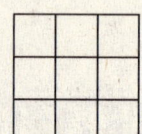

16. $\frac{3}{7}, \frac{3}{8}, \frac{4}{9}$ 17. $3\frac{5}{6}, \frac{25}{6}, 3\frac{2}{3}$ 18. $\frac{11}{4}, 2\frac{7}{8}, \frac{21}{8}$

Math Intervention
Book 2 Fractions and Decimals

Name _____   Date _____

19. Fill in the missing information to solve the problem.

Last year, sixth graders at a school spent an average of $\frac{3}{20}$ of each school day getting exercise. The principal wants to reorganize the school day next year to make more time for exercise. What fraction of the day should the school allow for exercise, $\frac{2}{9}$ or $\frac{1}{8}$?

Step 1 The phrase "more time" tells you that you need to compare the fractions $\frac{2}{9}$ and $\frac{1}{8}$ to the fraction $\frac{3}{20}$ to tell which one is _____.

Step 2 Compare: $\frac{2}{9}$ ◯ $\frac{3}{20}$ and $\frac{1}{8}$ ◯ $\frac{3}{20}$.

Step 3 The school should allow _____ of the day for exercise.

Simplify the fractions. Write any improper fractions as mixed numbers.

20. $\frac{6}{15}$ **21.** $\frac{9}{36}$ **22.** $\frac{8}{28}$ **23.** $\frac{16}{40}$

24. $\frac{26}{9}$ **25.** $\frac{33}{8}$ **26.** $\frac{14}{3}$ **27.** $\frac{65}{12}$

Complete the statement with <, >, or =.

28. $\frac{4}{5}$ ◯ $\frac{6}{7}$ **29.** $\frac{2}{9}$ ◯ $\frac{4}{11}$ **30.** $\frac{9}{4}$ ◯ $\frac{8}{5}$ **31.** $\frac{11}{3}$ ◯ $3\frac{1}{9}$

32. $4\frac{3}{4}$ ◯ $4\frac{3}{5}$ **33.** $1\frac{1}{6}$ ◯ $\frac{8}{3}$ **34.** $3\frac{1}{10}$ ◯ $2\frac{11}{12}$ **35.** $\frac{21}{8}$ ◯ $\frac{17}{4}$

Solve the problem. Explain your reasoning.

36. Three windows are on display at a store. The heights of the windows are $3\frac{7}{10}$ feet, $3\frac{4}{5}$ feet, and $\frac{41}{20}$ feet. Label each window in the diagram with its height.

 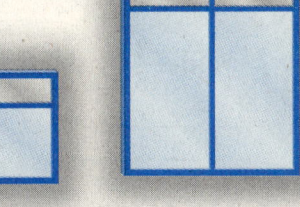 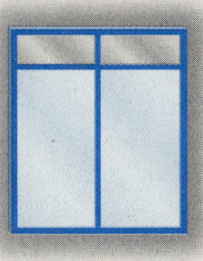

Height _____   Height _____   Height _____

_____
_____
_____

37. Jack is about $\frac{3}{8}$ of the way finished with his science project. Alexandra is about $\frac{5}{12}$ of the way finished with her science project. Who is farther along?

_____
_____
_____

Math Intervention
Book 2 Fractions and Decimals

Adding Fractions Using Models

Goal: Use models to understand how to add fractions.

Materials: Addition Expressions list, Game cards

Getting Started In Lesson 2-4 you learned how to represent a fraction using a model. You can also use models to add fractions.

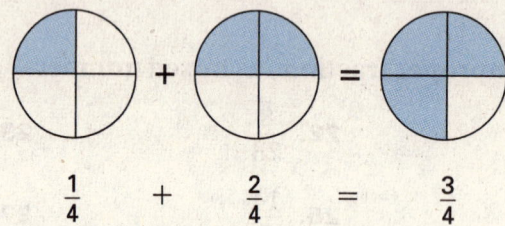

EXAMPLE

Use the following steps to model the sum: $\frac{1}{5} + \frac{3}{5}$

Step 1 Model $\frac{1}{5}$ by shading **1** out of **5** squares.

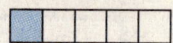

Step 2 Model $\frac{3}{5}$ by shading **3** out of **5** squares.

Step 3 Combine the models by shading **4** out of 5 squares.

Step 4 Write the result.

$$\frac{1}{5} + \frac{3}{5} = \frac{4}{5}$$

Math Intervention
Book 2 Fractions and Decimals

Name _____ Date _____

MAKE IT A GAME!

- Form groups of three or four students. Choose a caller.
- Give the caller the list of addition expressions. All other group members get a game card.
- The caller will call out the expressions at random. When an expression is called out, players look for a model on their card that represents the sum of the expression. If the model is there, the players mark it with an X.
- The first player in each group that marks three correct models in a row, column, or diagonal wins.

The caller called out:

$\frac{1}{3} + \frac{1}{3}$

$\frac{5}{12} + \frac{2}{12}$

$\frac{2}{4} + \frac{1}{4}$

So, this player wins.

Practice

In Exercises 1 and 2, use models to find the sum.

1. $\frac{6}{9} + \frac{1}{9} = \frac{\ }{\ }$

2. $\frac{1}{5} + \frac{1}{5} = \frac{\ }{\ }$

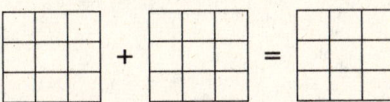

In Exercises 3–6, draw models to find the sum.

3. $\frac{1}{4} + \frac{2}{4}$ 4. $\frac{1}{3} + \frac{1}{3}$ 5. $\frac{2}{10} + \frac{5}{10}$ 6. $\frac{5}{12} + \frac{6}{12}$

7. **Make a Conjecture** Based on your answers to Exercises 1–6, make a conjecture about how to find the sum of two fractions without using models.

DID YOU GET IT? Use your conjecture to find the sum.

8. $\frac{2}{5} + \frac{2}{5} = \frac{\ }{\ }$

9. $\frac{1}{9} + \frac{4}{9} = \frac{\ }{\ }$

Name _____   Date _____

LESSON 2-11: Add and Subtract Fractions with Like Denominators

Words to Remember
Like denominators: Denominators that are equal

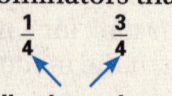

Like denominators

Getting Started In Activity 2-10 you learned how to add fractions using models. In this lesson you will learn to add and subtract fractions without using models.

EXAMPLE 1 — Adding Fractions Using Models

Use models to find the sum: $\frac{2}{9} + \frac{5}{9}$

Solution

Step 1 Model $\frac{2}{9}$ by shading 2 out of 9 squares.

Step 2 Model $\frac{5}{9}$ by shading 5 out of 9 squares.

Step 3 Model the sum by shading 7 out of 9 squares.

ANSWER $\frac{2}{9} + \frac{5}{9} = \frac{7}{9}$

TRY THIS Use models to find the sum.

1. $\frac{2}{7} + \frac{2}{7} = \frac{}{}$ 2. $\frac{1}{6} + \frac{4}{6} = \frac{}{}$

   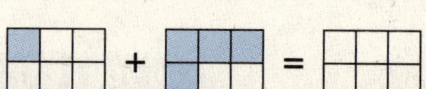

Adding Fractions To add fractions with like denominators, write the sum of the numerators over the denominator.

$$\frac{2}{9} + \frac{5}{9} = \frac{2+5}{9} = \frac{7}{9}$$

Name _____ Date _____

Simplifying the Sum If the answer is not in simplest form, simplify the fraction. If the answer is an improper fraction, write it as a mixed number.

EXAMPLE 2 — Adding Fractions with Like Denominators

Find the sum: $\frac{3}{5} + \frac{4}{5}$

Solution

$\frac{3}{5} + \frac{4}{5} = \frac{3+4}{5}$ Write the sum of the numerators over the denominator.

$= \frac{7}{5}$ Add.

$= 1\frac{2}{5}$ Write the improper fraction as a mixed number.

TRY THIS Find the sum.

3. $\frac{3}{8} + \frac{5}{8} = \frac{\square + \square}{\square} = \frac{\square}{\square} = \square$

4. $\frac{8}{16} + \frac{11}{16} = \frac{\square + \square}{\square} = \frac{\square}{\square} = \square\frac{\square}{\square}$

Subtracting Fractions To subtract two fractions with like denominators, write the difference of the numerators over the denominator.

$$\frac{7}{9} - \frac{2}{9} = \frac{7-2}{9} = \frac{5}{9}$$

EXAMPLE 3 — Subtracting Fractions with Like Denominators

Find the difference: $\frac{5}{6} - \frac{1}{6}$

Solution

$\frac{5}{6} - \frac{1}{6} = \frac{5-1}{6}$ Write the difference of the numerators over the denominator.

$= \frac{4}{6}$ Subtract.

$= \frac{2}{3}$ Simplify.

TRY THIS Find the difference.

5. $\frac{6}{7} - \frac{2}{7} = \frac{\square - \square}{\square} = \frac{\square}{\square}$

6. $\frac{7}{8} - \frac{3}{8} = \frac{\square - \square}{\square} = \frac{\square}{\square} = \frac{\square}{\square}$

Name _____   Date _____

> **Summarize**
>
> **Adding Fractions with Like Denominators**
> Write the sum of the numerators over the denominator. Simplify if possible.
> $$\frac{3}{7} + \frac{5}{7} = \frac{3+5}{7} = \frac{8}{7} = 1\frac{1}{7}$$
>
> **Subtracting Fractions with Like Denominators**
> Write the difference of the numerators over the denominator. Simplify if possible.
> $$\frac{7}{10} - \frac{3}{10} = \frac{7-3}{10} = \frac{4}{10} = \frac{2}{5}$$

Practice

Match the addition problem with the model that represents it.

1. $\frac{1}{2} + \frac{1}{2}$ _____
2. $\frac{1}{5} + \frac{2}{5}$ _____
3. $\frac{2}{9} + \frac{5}{9}$ _____

A.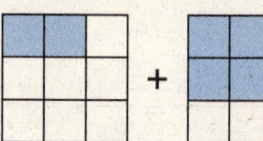
B.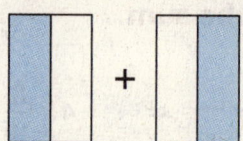
C.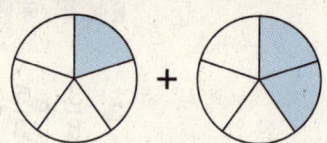

Shade in the models below to find the sum of the fractions.

4. $\frac{3}{5} + \frac{1}{5} = \frac{\square}{\square}$

5. $\frac{3}{4} + \frac{1}{4} = \frac{\square}{\square} = \square$

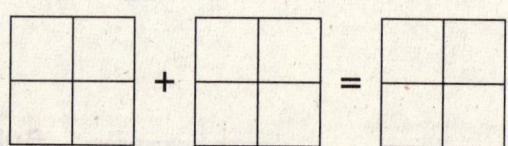

Find the sum.

6. $\frac{2}{11} + \frac{3}{11}$
7. $\frac{1}{7} + \frac{5}{7}$
8. $\frac{1}{3} + \frac{1}{3}$
9. $\frac{1}{2} + \frac{1}{2}$
10. $\frac{5}{9} + \frac{1}{9}$
11. $\frac{3}{10} + \frac{5}{10}$
12. $\frac{1}{6} + \frac{5}{6}$
13. $\frac{2}{5} + \frac{1}{5}$
14. $\frac{7}{10} + \frac{9}{10}$
15. $\frac{5}{8} + \frac{7}{8}$
16. $\frac{8}{11} + \frac{2}{11}$
17. $\frac{4}{9} + \frac{2}{9}$

Find the difference.

18. $\frac{8}{9} - \frac{1}{9}$
19. $\frac{4}{5} - \frac{1}{5}$
20. $\frac{14}{17} - \frac{3}{17}$
21. $\frac{4}{6} - \frac{2}{6}$
22. $\frac{5}{8} - \frac{1}{8}$
23. $\frac{5}{6} - \frac{5}{6}$
24. $\frac{7}{9} - \frac{4}{9}$
25. $\frac{9}{14} - \frac{7}{14}$
26. $\frac{9}{10} - \frac{7}{10}$
27. $\frac{15}{16} - \frac{5}{16}$
28. $\frac{11}{12} - \frac{7}{12}$
29. $\frac{14}{18} - \frac{5}{18}$

Math Intervention
Book 2 Fractions and Decimals

Name _____ Date _____

First tell whether you need to *add* or *subtract* to find the answer. Then solve the problem. Explain your reasoning.

30. You and a friend order a pizza. You eat $\frac{1}{8}$ of the pizza and your friend eats $\frac{3}{8}$ of the pizza. How much of the pizza did you and your friend eat?

_____
_____
_____

31. A tarnished plant bug is about $\frac{3}{16}$ inch long. A large milkweed bug is about $\frac{9}{16}$ inch long. How much longer is the milkweed bug than the tarnished plant bug?

_____
_____
_____

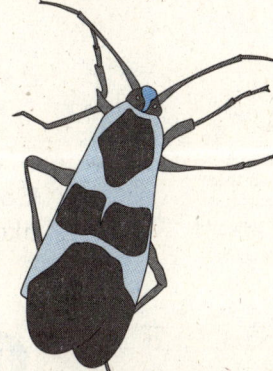

Tarnished plant bug   Large milkweed bug

DID YOU GET IT?

32. Fill in the missing words. To add two fractions with like denominators, write the _____ of the _____ over the _____.

33. Fill in the missing words. To subtract two fractions with like denominators, write the _____ of the _____ over the _____.

34. Use a model. Use blank models to write (a) an addition problem and (b) a subtraction problem involving fractions. Then solve the problems.

(a) 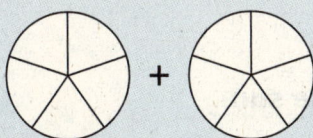   (b)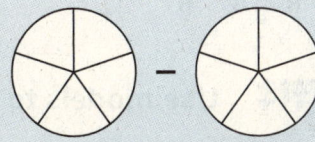

35. Explain your reasoning. Your friend says that the sum of $\frac{1}{6}$ and $\frac{1}{6}$ is $\frac{2}{12}$. Is your friend correct? Explain why or why not.

_____
_____
_____

Name _____ Date _____

LESSON 2-12
Add and Subtract Fractions with Unlike Denominators

Words to Remember

Unlike denominators: Denominators that are not equal

$$\frac{1}{6} \quad \frac{5}{12}$$

Unlike denominators

Getting Started In Lesson 2-11 you learned how to add fractions with like denominators. You can also add fractions with unlike denominators.

EXAMPLE 1   Adding Fractions Using Models

Use models to find the sum: $\frac{1}{4} + \frac{3}{8}$

Solution

Step 1 Model the fractions.

Step 2 Redraw the models so they are divided into the same number of equal parts. Redraw $\frac{1}{4}$ as $\frac{2}{8}$ instead.

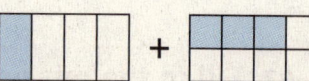

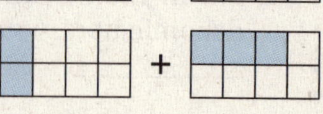

Step 3 Combine the models by shading 5 out of 8 squares.

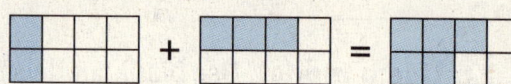

ANSWER $\frac{2}{8} + \frac{3}{8} = \frac{5}{8}$

TRY THIS Use models to find the sum.

1. $\frac{1}{2} + \frac{1}{4} = \frac{}{4} + \frac{1}{4} = \frac{}{}$

2. $\frac{2}{3} + \frac{1}{6} = \frac{}{6} + \frac{1}{6} = \frac{}{}$

Name _____ Date _____

EXAMPLE 2 — Adding Fractions with Unlike Denominators

Find the sum: $\frac{3}{5} + \frac{1}{2}$

Solution

$\frac{3 \times 2}{5 \times 2} = \frac{6}{10}$

Use the LCD to write equivalent fractions with like denominators.

$+\frac{1 \times 5}{2 \times 5} = +\frac{5}{10}$

$\frac{6+5}{10} = \frac{11}{10} = 1\frac{1}{10}$

Write the sum of the numerators over the denominator. Add and write as a mixed number.

Simplifying the Sum

If the sum is a fraction that is not in simplest form, write it as a fraction in simplest form. If the answer is an improper fraction, write it as a mixed number.

TRY THIS Find the sum.

3. $\frac{4}{9} + \frac{1}{3}$
4. $\frac{3}{4} + \frac{5}{6}$
5. $\frac{2}{7} + \frac{2}{5}$
6. $\frac{2}{3} + \frac{1}{2}$

EXAMPLE 3 — Subtracting Fractions with Unlike Denominators

Find the difference: $\frac{7}{12} - \frac{1}{4}$

Solution

$\frac{7}{12} = \frac{7}{12}$

Use the LCD to write equivalent fractions with like denominators.

$-\frac{1 \times 3}{4 \times 3} = -\frac{3}{12}$

$\frac{7-3}{12} = \frac{4}{12} = \frac{1}{3}$

Write the difference of the numerators over the denominator. Subtract and write the answer in simplest form.

TRY THIS Find the difference.

7. $\frac{5}{8} - \frac{1}{2}$
8. $\frac{4}{5} - \frac{1}{3}$
9. $\frac{8}{9} - \frac{5}{6}$
10. $\frac{11}{12} - \frac{1}{4}$

Math Intervention
Book 2 Fractions and Decimals

Name _____   Date _____

> ### Summarize
>
> **Adding Fractions with Unlike Denominators**
>
> Use the LCD to write equivalent fractions with like denominators. Write the sum of the numerators over the denominator. Simplify if possible.
>
> $\frac{1}{3} + \frac{3}{4} = \frac{4}{12} + \frac{9}{12}$
> $= \frac{4+9}{12} = \frac{13}{12} = 1\frac{1}{12}$
>
> **Subtracting Fractions with Unlike Denominators**
>
> Use the LCD to write equivalent fractions with like denominators. Write the difference of the numerators over the denominator. Simplify if possible.
>
> $\frac{4}{5} - \frac{3}{10} = \frac{8}{10} - \frac{3}{10}$
> $= \frac{8-3}{10} = \frac{5}{10} = \frac{1}{2}$

Practice

Find the sum using models.

1. $\frac{2}{9} + \frac{1}{3}$

2. $\frac{3}{5} + \frac{1}{10}$

3. $\frac{1}{3} + \frac{7}{12}$

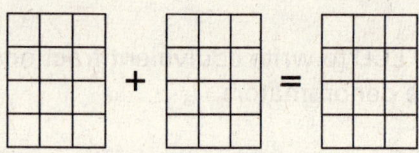

4. $\frac{3}{4} + \frac{1}{8}$

Find the sum.

5. $\frac{3}{4} + \frac{5}{8}$
6. $\frac{5}{6} + \frac{5}{12}$
7. $\frac{4}{7} + \frac{11}{14}$
8. $\frac{1}{4} + \frac{1}{6}$

9. $\frac{5}{18} + \frac{2}{9}$
10. $\frac{1}{2} + \frac{5}{8}$
11. $\frac{3}{4} + \frac{1}{5}$
12. $\frac{3}{8} + \frac{1}{2}$

Find the difference.

13. $\frac{11}{12} - \frac{1}{2}$
14. $\frac{8}{9} - \frac{2}{3}$
15. $\frac{3}{5} - \frac{1}{10}$
16. $\frac{5}{6} - \frac{3}{8}$

17. $\frac{3}{4} - \frac{3}{10}$
18. $\frac{1}{2} - \frac{1}{6}$
19. $\frac{4}{5} - \frac{7}{15}$
20. $\frac{7}{9} - \frac{1}{2}$

Math Intervention
Book 2 Fractions and Decimals

Name _____   Date _____

**First tell whether you need to *add* or *subtract* to find the answer.
Then solve the problem. Explain your reasoning.**

21. Kari and her grandmother are making a quilt. Over a holiday weekend, Kari sewed $\frac{1}{6}$ of the quilt. Her grandmother sewed $\frac{3}{8}$ of the quilt. How much of the quilt did they sew over the weekend?

_____
_____
_____

22. You put $\frac{1}{3}$ cup of flour in a 1-cup measuring cup. You then sprinkle $\frac{1}{4}$ cup of sugar on top of the flour. What fraction of the measuring cup is full?

_____
_____
_____

23. The distance from your house to the post office is $\frac{8}{9}$ mile. The distance from your house to the library is $\frac{2}{3}$ mile. How much farther from your house is the post office than the library?

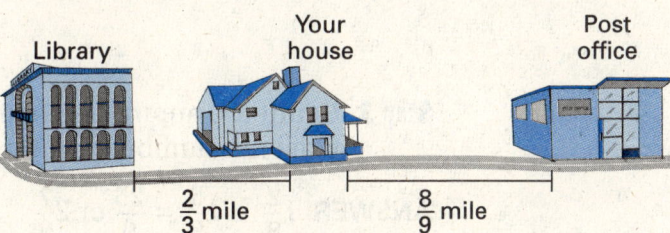

_____
_____
_____

DID YOU GET IT?

24. Fill in the missing words. To add two fractions with unlike denominators, first use the _____ to write _____ _____. Then write the _____ of the _____ over the _____.

25. Explain your reasoning. Your friend says that the difference of $\frac{7}{8}$ and $\frac{1}{4}$ is $\frac{6}{4}$, or $1\frac{1}{2}$. Is your friend correct? Explain why or why not.

_____
_____
_____

LESSON 2-13 Add and Subtract Mixed Numbers

Getting Started In Lessons 2-11 and 2-12 you learned to add and subtract fractions. In this lesson you will add and subtract mixed numbers.

EXAMPLE 1 Adding Mixed Numbers Using Models

Use models to find the sum: $1\frac{2}{9} + 1\frac{5}{9}$

Solution

Step 1 Model the mixed numbers. Since $1 = \frac{9}{9}$, model it by shading 9 out of 9 squares.

Step 2 Combine the models.

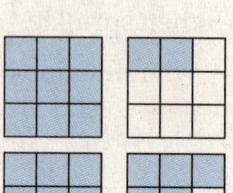

Step 3 Count the number of shaded parts, and write this number over the denominator, 9. $\frac{25}{9}$

ANSWER $1\frac{2}{9} + 1\frac{5}{9} = \frac{25}{9}$ or $2\frac{7}{9}$

TRY THIS   Use models to find the sum.

1. $1\frac{6}{8} + 1\frac{1}{8} = \frac{}{} = \blacksquare \frac{}{}$

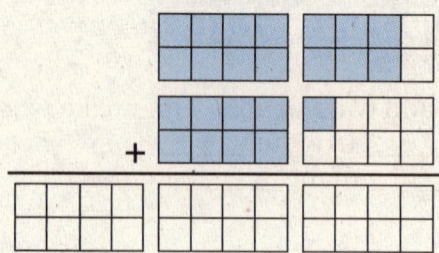

2. $2\frac{1}{6} + 1\frac{3}{6} = \frac{}{} = \blacksquare \frac{}{}$

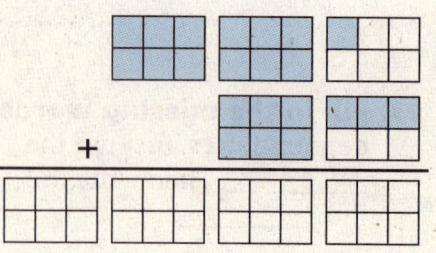

To Add Mixed Numbers without Using Models If the mixed numbers have the same denominator, you can add the whole numbers and fractions separately and combine the sums.

The problem in Example 1 is $1\frac{2}{9} + 1\frac{5}{9}$. When you add the whole numbers, you get $1 + 1 = 2$. When you add the fractions, you get $\frac{2}{9} + \frac{5}{9} = \frac{7}{9}$. Combining the sums gives an answer of $2 + \frac{7}{9}$ or $2\frac{7}{9}$.

Math Intervention
Book 2 Fractions and Decimals

EXAMPLE 2 Adding Mixed Numbers With Unlike Denominators

Find the sum: $1\frac{2}{3} + 2\frac{3}{4}$

Solution

$1\frac{2}{3} = \frac{5 \times 4}{3 \times 4} = \frac{20}{12}$ — Write each mixed number as an improper fraction.

$+ 2\frac{3}{4} = \frac{11 \times 3}{4 \times 3} = +\frac{33}{12}$ — Use the LCD to write equivalent fractions with like denominators.

$= \frac{20 + 33}{12} = \frac{53}{12} = 4\frac{5}{12}$ — Write the sum of the numerators over the denominator and simplify.

> **Remember**
> To write a mixed number as an improper fraction:
> - Multiply the whole number by the denominator.
> - Add the product to the numerator of the fraction.
> - Use the denominator from the mixed number.
>
> $3\frac{2}{3}$
> $3 \times 3 = 9$
> $9 + 2 = 11$
> $3\frac{2}{3} = \frac{11}{3}$

TRY THIS Find the sum.

3. $1\frac{3}{4} + 5\frac{3}{8}$

4. $2\frac{1}{2} + 1\frac{5}{6}$

5. $2\frac{1}{6} + 2\frac{4}{9}$

6. $1\frac{2}{5} + 1\frac{3}{10}$

EXAMPLE 3 Subtracting Mixed Numbers With Unlike Denominators

Find the difference: $1\frac{4}{5} - 1\frac{3}{10}$

Solution

$1\frac{4}{5} = \frac{9 \times 2}{5 \times 2} = \frac{18}{10}$ — Write each mixed number as an improper fraction.

$- 1\frac{3}{10} = \frac{13}{10} = -\frac{13}{10}$ — Use the LCD to write equivalent fractions with like denominators.

$= \frac{18 - 13}{10} = \frac{5}{10} = \frac{1}{2}$ — Write the difference of the numerators over the denominator and simplify.

TRY THIS Find the difference.

7. $7\frac{3}{7} - 4\frac{3}{14}$

8. $3\frac{3}{5} - 3\frac{1}{4}$

9. $3\frac{2}{3} - 2\frac{2}{5}$

10. $4\frac{1}{2} - 1\frac{1}{3}$

Name _____   Date _____

Summarize

Adding Mixed Numbers

Write the mixed numbers as improper fractions. Use the LCD to write equivalent fractions with like denominators. Write the sum of the numerators over the denominator and simplify.

$$1\tfrac{1}{4} = \tfrac{5}{4} = \tfrac{5}{4}$$
$$+\,1\tfrac{1}{2} = \tfrac{3 \times 2}{2 \times 2} = +\tfrac{6}{4}$$
$$= \tfrac{5+6}{4} = \tfrac{11}{4} = 2\tfrac{3}{4}$$

Subtracting Mixed Numbers

Write the mixed numbers as improper fractions. Use the LCD to write equivalent fractions with like denominators. Write the difference of the numerators over the denominator and simplify.

$$1\tfrac{5}{6} = \tfrac{11 \times 2}{6 \times 2} = \tfrac{22}{12}$$
$$-\,1\tfrac{1}{12} = \tfrac{13}{12} = -\tfrac{13}{12}$$
$$= \tfrac{22-13}{12} = \tfrac{9}{12} = \tfrac{3}{4}$$

Practice

Match the addition problem with the model that represents it. Then write the sum.

1. $1\tfrac{3}{8} + 1\tfrac{1}{8}$ _____
2. $1\tfrac{1}{5} + 1\tfrac{4}{5}$ _____
3. $1\tfrac{2}{7} + 1\tfrac{3}{7}$ _____

A.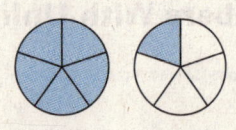
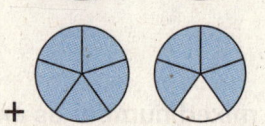
+ _____

B.
+ _____

C.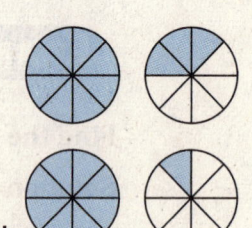
+ _____

Find the sum.

4. $2\tfrac{2}{5} + 1\tfrac{8}{15}$
5. $1\tfrac{2}{3} + 2\tfrac{1}{9}$
6. $1\tfrac{11}{20} + 3\tfrac{7}{10}$

7. $3\tfrac{1}{4} + 2\tfrac{1}{6}$
8. $5\tfrac{1}{2} + 1\tfrac{5}{8}$
9. $1\tfrac{5}{6} + 2\tfrac{2}{9}$

10. $4\tfrac{1}{2} + 1\tfrac{7}{9}$
11. $2\tfrac{3}{4} + 1\tfrac{3}{5}$
12. $2\tfrac{1}{6} + 1\tfrac{7}{18}$

Find the difference.

13. $2\tfrac{1}{2} - 1\tfrac{1}{6}$
14. $3\tfrac{4}{7} - 2\tfrac{1}{7}$
15. $5\tfrac{1}{4} - 2\tfrac{3}{10}$

16. $3\tfrac{1}{8} - 1\tfrac{11}{16}$
17. $4\tfrac{9}{10} - 3\tfrac{1}{2}$
18. $3\tfrac{3}{4} - 2\tfrac{1}{6}$

19. $1\tfrac{5}{7} - 1\tfrac{1}{2}$
20. $2\tfrac{2}{3} - 1\tfrac{11}{12}$
21. $3\tfrac{4}{5} - 1\tfrac{1}{4}$

Math Intervention
Book 2 Fractions and Decimals

Name _____ Date _____

First tell whether you need to *add* or *subtract* to find the answer. Then solve the problem. Explain your reasoning.

22. Your mom buys $2\frac{1}{2}$ yards of material. She returns to the store the next day and buys $1\frac{3}{4}$ yards of material. How much material does she buy in all?

_____
_____
_____

23. Last week your plant measured $2\frac{1}{3}$ inches tall. This week it measures $2\frac{11}{18}$ inches tall. How much has your plant grown?

_____
_____

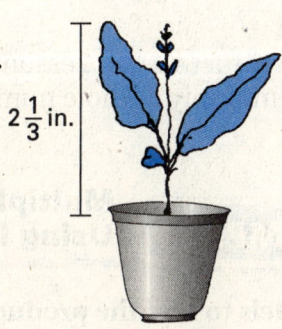
Last week

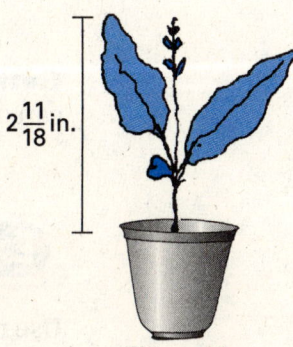
This week

24. A red carpet pad is $2\frac{5}{6}$ centimeters thick. A blue carpet pad is $1\frac{1}{4}$ centimeters thinner than the red pad. How thick is the blue pad?

_____
_____
_____

DID YOU GET IT?

25. Fill in the missing words. To subtract two _____ _____, first write the _____ _____ as _____ _____. Then write the _____ of the _____ over the _____.

26. Describe a process. How can you rewrite the mixed numbers $4\frac{1}{5}$ and $2\frac{7}{10}$ so that you can add them?

_____
_____
_____

Name _____   Date _____

LESSON 2-14
Multiply Fractions

Words to Remember

$\frac{2}{3}$ of 4 means $\frac{2}{3} \times 4$

$\frac{1}{4}$ of $\frac{1}{2}$ means $\frac{1}{4} \times \frac{1}{2}$

Getting Started In Lesson 1-22 you multiplied two whole numbers. You can also multiply a whole number and a fraction or two fractions.

EXAMPLE 1 **Multiplying a Fraction By a Whole Number Using Models**

Use models to find the product: $\frac{3}{4}$ of 8 or $\frac{3}{4} \times 8$

Solution

Step 1 Draw 8 squares. Arrange them in two rows of four. Notice that there are 4 columns and there are 2 squares in each column.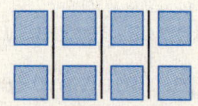

Step 2 Draw a circle around 3 of the 4 columns of squares. This represents $\frac{3}{4}$ of 8, or $\frac{3}{4} \times 8$. Notice that you have circled 6 squares.

ANSWER $\frac{3}{4} \times 8 = 6$

TRY THIS Use models to find the product.

1. $\frac{1}{3} \times 9$ 2. $\frac{2}{5}$ of 10

Multiplying a Fraction by a Whole Number To multiply a fraction by a whole number, write the product of the numerator and the whole number over the denominator. Then simplify if possible.

$\frac{3}{4}$ of 6 = $\frac{3}{4} \times 6 = \frac{3 \times 6}{4} = \frac{18}{4} = \frac{9}{2} = 4\frac{1}{2}$

Math Intervention
Book 2 Fractions and Decimals

Name _____ Date _____

EXAMPLE 2 Multiplying a Fraction by a Whole Number

Find the product: $14 \times \frac{1}{6}$

Solution

Write the product of the whole number and the numerator over the denominator and simplify.

$$14 \times \frac{1}{6} = \frac{14 \times 1}{6} = \frac{14}{6} = \frac{7}{3} = 2\frac{1}{3}$$

TRY THIS Find the product.

3. $15 \times \frac{3}{5} = \frac{\square \times \square}{\square} = \frac{\square}{\square} = \square$
4. $\frac{5}{6}$ of $12 = \frac{\square \times \square}{\square} = \frac{\square}{\square} = \square$

5. $\frac{2}{7} \times 21$
6. $\frac{2}{9}$ of 5

Another Way

You can also simplify a fraction before multiplying. In Try this 3,

$$\frac{15 \times 3}{5} = \frac{\overset{3}{\cancel{15}} \times 3}{\underset{1}{\cancel{5}}}$$
$$= \frac{9}{1}$$
$$= 9$$

Multiplying Two Fractions To multiply two fractions, write the product of the numerators over the product of the denominators. Then simplify if possible.

$$\frac{1}{9} \times \frac{3}{5} = \frac{1 \times 3}{9 \times 5} = \frac{3}{45} = \frac{1}{15}$$

EXAMPLE 3 Multiplying a Fraction by a Fraction

Find the product: $\frac{2}{3} \times \frac{3}{4}$

Solution

Write the product of the numerators over the product of the denominators and simplify.

$$\frac{2}{3} \times \frac{3}{4} = \frac{2 \times 3}{3 \times 4} = \frac{6}{12} = \frac{1}{2}$$

Watch Out!

Don't forget to multiply the denominators, too.

TRY THIS Find the product.

7. $\frac{3}{4}$ of $\frac{2}{5} = \frac{\square \times \square}{\square \times \square} = \frac{\square}{\square} = \frac{\square}{\square}$
8. $\frac{1}{6} \times \frac{3}{5} = \frac{\square \times \square}{\square \times \square} = \frac{\square}{\square} = \frac{\square}{\square}$

9. $\frac{5}{8} \times \frac{4}{9}$
10. $\frac{1}{4}$ of $\frac{2}{7}$

Name _____ Date _____

> **Summarize**
>
> **Multiplying a Fraction by a Whole Number**
> Write the product of the whole number and the numerator over the denominator. Simplify if possible.
>
> $2 \times \frac{4}{9} = \frac{2 \times 4}{9} = \frac{8}{9}$
>
> **Multiplying Two Fractions**
> Write the product of the numerators over the product of the denominators. Simplify if possible.
>
> $\frac{3}{8} \times \frac{2}{9} = \frac{3 \times 2}{8 \times 9} = \frac{6}{72} = \frac{1}{12}$

Practice

Match the multiplication problem with the model that represents it.

1. $\frac{4}{5}$ of 10 _____
2. $\frac{2}{3} \times 9$ _____
3. $\frac{5}{6} \times 12$ _____

A. B. C.

Write the multiplication problem that the model represents.

4. _____
5. _____
6. _____

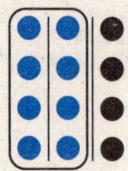  

Find the product of the fraction and whole number.

7. $\frac{4}{5} \times 20$
8. $\frac{5}{8}$ of 16
9. $\frac{3}{4} \times 16$
10. $\frac{1}{3} \times 14$
11. $\frac{2}{7}$ of 7
12. $\frac{5}{6}$ of 10
13. $\frac{1}{2}$ of 5
14. $\frac{4}{9} \times 21$
15. $\frac{3}{8} \times 4$

Find the product of the fractions.

16. $\frac{3}{4} \times \frac{4}{9}$
17. $\frac{1}{2}$ of $\frac{2}{5}$
18. $\frac{1}{6}$ of $\frac{9}{10}$
19. $\frac{5}{9}$ of $\frac{3}{7}$
20. $\frac{2}{3} \times \frac{6}{11}$
21. $\frac{3}{5}$ of $\frac{1}{3}$
22. $\frac{4}{11} \times \frac{1}{2}$
23. $\frac{5}{8} \times \frac{4}{7}$
24. $\frac{7}{10} \times \frac{5}{14}$

Math Intervention
Book 2 Fractions and Decimals

Name _____ Date _____

Solve the problem. Explain your reasoning.

25. Two-thirds of **21** students on a field trip brought a bag lunch. How many students brought a bag lunch?

_____
_____
_____

26. There is a $\frac{3}{4}$-mile walking trail around the lake at your park. You walk around this trail **5** times. What is the total distance that you walked?

_____
_____
_____

27. Your mom says she spent $\frac{1}{4}$ of $\frac{1}{2}$ hour reading through the mail. How much time did she spend reading through the mail?

_____
_____
_____

DID YOU GET IT?

28. Fill in the missing words. To multiply a fraction by a fraction write the _____ of the _____ over the _____ of the _____.

29. Use a model. Write and solve a multiplication problem using the blank model at the right.

_____
_____

30. Write a problem. Write a multiplication problem with two different fractions so that when they are multiplied together, you get the same answer as in the problem at the right.

_____
_____

LESSON 2-15

Divide Fractions

> **Words to Remember**
>
> **Reciprocals:** Two numbers whose product is **1**
>
> $\frac{2}{3}$ and $\frac{3}{2}$ are reciprocals because
> $\frac{2}{3} \times \frac{3}{2} = \frac{2 \times 3}{3 \times 2} = \frac{6}{6} = 1$
>
> 5 and $\frac{1}{5}$ are reciprocals because
> $5 \times \frac{1}{5} = \frac{5 \times 1}{5} = \frac{5}{5} = 1$
>
> **Inverse property of multiplication:** The product of a number and its reciprocal is **1**.
>
> $a \cdot \frac{1}{a} = 1$ and $\frac{1}{a} \cdot a = 1$

Getting Started In Lesson 2-14 you learned how to multiply fractions. You can also divide fractions by using a reciprocal.

EXAMPLE 1 Finding the Reciprocal of a Number

Find the reciprocal of the number.

a. $\frac{1}{8}$

b. 4

Solution

a. If the number is a fraction, write the denominator over the numerator.

   ANSWER $\frac{8}{1}$ or 8

b. If the number is a whole number, write it as a fraction. Then write the denominator over the numerator. $4 = \frac{4}{1}$

   ANSWER $\frac{1}{4}$

TRY THIS Find the reciprocal of the number.

1. $\frac{7}{11}$
2. $\frac{1}{15}$
3. 3

Dividing Fractions To divide two fractions, rewrite the problem as a multiplication problem. In the new problem, multiply the dividend by the reciprocal of the divisor. The dividend is the first number in a division problem. The divisor is the second number.

Math Intervention
Book 2 Fractions and Decimals

Name _____   Date _____

Dividing Fractions (*cont.*)   When dividing two fractions, the first fraction stays the same. The second fraction is rewritten as a reciprocal. The denominator becomes the numerator and the numerator becomes the denominator. The operation changes from division to multiplication.

$$\frac{1}{4} \div \frac{5}{6} = \frac{1}{4} \times \frac{6}{5}$$

Dividend   Divisor   Dividend   Reciprocal of the Divisor

EXAMPLE 2 — Dividing a Fraction by a Fraction

Divide: $\frac{2}{5} \div \frac{4}{9}$

Solution

$\frac{2}{5} \div \frac{4}{9} = \frac{2}{5} \times \frac{9}{4}$ Rewrite the problem so that the dividend is multiplied by the reciprocal of the divisor.

$= \frac{2 \times 9}{5 \times 4}$ Multiply the fractions.

$= \frac{18}{20} = \frac{9}{10}$ Simplify the answer, if possible.

TRY THIS   Divide.

4. $\frac{2}{3} \div \frac{1}{3}$ 5. $\frac{1}{4} \div \frac{4}{9}$ 6. $\frac{3}{5} \div \frac{7}{10}$

EXAMPLE 3 — Dividing Fractions and Whole Numbers

Divide.

a. $\frac{3}{8} \div 6$ b. $4 \div \frac{1}{6}$

Solution

a. $\frac{3}{8} \div \frac{6}{1}$ Write the whole number as a fraction.   b. $\frac{4}{1} \div \frac{1}{6}$

$= \frac{3}{8} \times \frac{1}{6}$ Rewrite the problem so that the dividend is multiplied by the reciprocal of the divisor. $= \frac{4}{1} \times \frac{6}{1}$

$= \frac{3 \times 1}{8 \times 6}$ Multiply the fractions. $= \frac{4 \times 6}{1 \times 1}$

$= \frac{3}{48} = \frac{1}{16}$ Simplify the answer, if possible. $= \frac{24}{1} = 24$

Check Your Answer

Multiply your answer by the divisor to see if you get the dividend.
In Example 3 part (a), $\frac{1}{16} \times 6 = \frac{6}{16} = \frac{3}{8}$. The dividend is $\frac{3}{8}$, so the answer checks.

TRY THIS   Divide.

7. $\frac{6}{11} \div 3$ 8. $\frac{5}{8} \div 5$ 9. $8 \div \frac{2}{3}$

Math Intervention
Book 2 Fractions and Decimals

Name _____   Date _____

Summarize

Finding the Reciprocal

Make sure the number is written as a fraction. Then write the denominator over the numerator and simplify.

Reciprocal of $\frac{2}{11}$: $\frac{11}{2} = 5\frac{1}{2}$

Reciprocal of 3 or $\frac{3}{1}$: $\frac{1}{3}$

Dividing Two Fractions

Rewrite the problem so that the dividend is multiplied by the reciprocal of the divisor. Multiply the fractions. Then, if possible, simplify your answer.

$\frac{4}{5} \div \frac{6}{5} = \frac{4}{5} \times \frac{5}{6} = \frac{2}{3}$

Dividing Whole Numbers and Fractions

Write the whole number as a fraction. Rewrite the problem so that the dividend is multiplied by the reciprocal of the divisor. Multiply and then simplify, if possible.

$3 \div \frac{4}{9} = \frac{3}{1} \times \frac{9}{4} = \frac{27}{4}$ or $6\frac{3}{4}$

$\frac{1}{2} \div 4 = \frac{1}{2} \div \frac{4}{1} = \frac{1}{2} \times \frac{1}{4} = \frac{1}{8}$

Practice

Find the reciprocal of the number.

1. $\frac{2}{7}$
2. $\frac{3}{4}$
3. $\frac{5}{12}$
4. $\frac{1}{11}$
5. $\frac{1}{2}$
6. 9
7. 15
8. 3

Match the division problem with the multiplication problem that represents it.

9. $\frac{3}{5} \div \frac{1}{4}$ _____

10. $\frac{3}{5} \div 4$ _____

11. $4 \div \frac{3}{5}$ _____

12. $\frac{1}{4} \div \frac{3}{5}$ _____

A. $\frac{3}{5} \times \frac{1}{4}$

B. $\frac{1}{4} \times \frac{5}{3}$

C. $\frac{3}{5} \times \frac{4}{1}$

D. $\frac{4}{1} \times \frac{5}{3}$

Divide.

13. $\frac{3}{7} \div \frac{4}{7}$
14. $\frac{5}{9} \div \frac{1}{3}$
15. $\frac{1}{10} \div \frac{2}{11}$
16. $\frac{4}{5} \div 3$
17. $\frac{7}{12} \div 2$
18. $\frac{2}{3} \div 8$
19. $5 \div \frac{3}{4}$
20. $6 \div \frac{1}{5}$
21. $9 \div \frac{6}{7}$
22. $\frac{7}{8} \div \frac{2}{3}$
23. $\frac{2}{5} \div 5$
24. $4 \div \frac{5}{8}$

Math Intervention
Book 2 Fractions and Decimals

Name _____ Date _____

Solve the problem. Explain your reasoning.

25. You use $\frac{2}{3}$ cup of sugar when you make a batch of brownies. How many batches could you make with **8** cups of sugar?

_____
_____
_____

26. How many $\frac{1}{8}$-gallon servings could you pour from $\frac{3}{4}$ gallon of milk?

_____
_____
_____

27. You have a poster board that is $\frac{5}{6}$ yard wide. You want to divide the poster into **10** equal sections. Find the width of one of these sections.

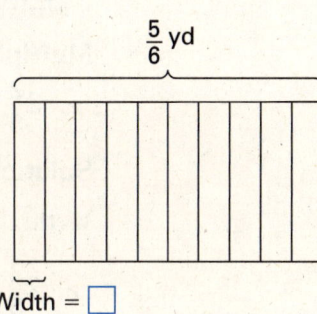

_____
_____

DID YOU GET IT?

28. Fill in the missing words. To find the reciprocal of a fraction write the _____ over the _____.

29. Explain your reasoning. Malik says that $\frac{8}{15} \div \frac{5}{6}$ is equal to $\frac{8}{15} \times \frac{5}{6}$, or $\frac{4}{9}$. Is he correct? Why or why not?

_____
_____
_____

30. Write a problem. Write a division problem that could be rewritten as the multiplication problem $\frac{4}{5} \times \frac{1}{4}$.

_____
_____
_____

LESSON 2-16: Multiply and Divide Mixed Numbers

Getting Started In Lessons 2-14 and 2-15 you learned how to multiply and divide fractions. You can also multiply and divide mixed numbers.

Multiplying and Dividing Mixed Numbers When you multiply or divide a mixed number, the first step is always to rewrite the mixed number as an improper fraction.

EXAMPLE 1 Multiplying Mixed Numbers and Fractions

Multiply.

a. $2\frac{2}{5} \times \frac{1}{4}$

b. $\frac{3}{10} \times 1\frac{2}{3}$

Solution

Write the mixed numbers as improper fractions and multiply.

a. $2\frac{2}{5} \times \frac{1}{4} = \frac{(2 \times 5) + 2}{5} \times \frac{1}{4}$

$= \frac{12}{5} \times \frac{1}{4}$

$= \frac{12 \times 1}{5 \times 4}$

$= \frac{12}{20} = \frac{3}{5}$

b. $\frac{3}{10} \times 1\frac{2}{3} = \frac{3}{10} \times \frac{(1 \times 3) + 2}{3}$

$= \frac{3}{10} \times \frac{5}{3}$

$= \frac{3 \times 5}{10 \times 3}$

$= \frac{15}{30} = \frac{1}{2}$

EXAMPLE 2 Multiplying Mixed Numbers and Whole Numbers

Multiply.

a. $1\frac{4}{9} \times 3$

b. $2 \times 1\frac{5}{6}$

Watch Out!
You also need to write the whole number as an improper fraction. Write the number over a denominator of 1.

Solution

Write the whole numbers as improper fractions and multiply as in Example 1.

a. $1\frac{4}{9} \times 3 = \frac{13}{9} \times \frac{3}{1}$

$= \frac{13 \times 3}{9 \times 1}$

$= \frac{39}{9} = 4\frac{1}{3}$

b. $2 \times 1\frac{5}{6} = \frac{2}{1} \times \frac{11}{6}$

$= \frac{2 \times 11}{1 \times 6}$

$= \frac{22}{6} = 3\frac{2}{3}$

Math Intervention
Book 2 Fractions and Decimals

EXAMPLE 3 — Dividing Mixed Numbers and Fractions

Divide.

a. $1\dfrac{3}{4} \div \dfrac{5}{12}$

b. $\dfrac{7}{8} \div 2\dfrac{5}{8}$

Solution

a.
$$1\dfrac{3}{4} \div \dfrac{5}{12} = \dfrac{7}{4} \div \dfrac{5}{12}$$ Write as an improper fraction.

$$= \dfrac{7}{4} \times \dfrac{12}{5}$$ Multiply by the reciprocal of the divisor.

$$= \dfrac{7 \times 12}{4 \times 5}$$ Multiply.

$$= \dfrac{84}{20} = 4\dfrac{1}{5}$$ Simplify.

b.
$$\dfrac{7}{8} \div 2\dfrac{5}{8} = \dfrac{7}{8} \div \dfrac{21}{8}$$ Write as an improper fraction.

$$= \dfrac{7}{8} \times \dfrac{8}{21}$$ Multiply by the reciprocal of the divisor.

$$= \dfrac{7 \times 8}{8 \times 21}$$ Multiply.

$$= \dfrac{56}{168} = \dfrac{1}{3}$$ Simplify.

Remember

When you divide by a fraction, you must multiply by the reciprocal of the divisor. To write a reciprocal, reverse the numerator and the denominator.

EXAMPLE 4 — Dividing Mixed Numbers and Whole Numbers

Divide.

a. $1\dfrac{4}{7} \div 4$

b. $6 \div 4\dfrac{1}{2}$

Solution

Write whole numbers as improper fractions. Then divide as in Example 3.

a.
$$1\dfrac{4}{7} \div 4 = \dfrac{11}{7} \div \dfrac{4}{1}$$

$$= \dfrac{11}{7} \times \dfrac{1}{4}$$

$$= \dfrac{11 \times 1}{7 \times 4}$$

$$= \dfrac{11}{28}$$

b.
$$6 \div 4\dfrac{1}{2} = \dfrac{6}{1} \div \dfrac{9}{2}$$

$$= \dfrac{6}{1} \times \dfrac{2}{9}$$

$$= \dfrac{6 \times 2}{1 \times 9}$$

$$= \dfrac{12}{9} = 1\dfrac{1}{3}$$

TRY THIS Multiply or divide.

1. $2\dfrac{1}{6} \times \dfrac{1}{3}$
2. $\dfrac{2}{5} \times 3\dfrac{1}{2}$
3. $2 \times 1\dfrac{7}{12}$
4. $2\dfrac{5}{8} \times 3$
5. $2\dfrac{2}{3} \div \dfrac{3}{4}$
6. $\dfrac{1}{2} \div 1\dfrac{5}{6}$
7. $4 \div 1\dfrac{1}{7}$
8. $3\dfrac{1}{8} \div 5$

Name _____ Date _____

> **Summarize**
>
> **Multiplying Mixed Numbers and Fractions**
> Write the mixed number as an improper fraction. Multiply and simplify.
>
> $1\frac{1}{2} \times \frac{4}{7} = \frac{3}{2} \times \frac{4}{7}$
> $= \frac{3 \times 4}{2 \times 7} = \frac{12}{14} = \frac{6}{7}$
>
> **Multiplying Mixed Numbers and Whole Numbers**
> Write the mixed number and whole number as improper fractions. Multiply and simplify.
>
> $8 \times 1\frac{3}{8} = \frac{8}{1} \times \frac{11}{8}$
> $= \frac{8 \times 11}{1 \times 8} = \frac{88}{8} = 11$
>
> **Dividing Mixed Numbers and Fractions**
> Write the mixed number as an improper fraction. Multiply the dividend by the reciprocal of the divisor and simplify.
>
> $\frac{5}{9} \div 1\frac{1}{3} = \frac{5}{9} \div \frac{4}{3}$
> $= \frac{5}{9} \times \frac{3}{4}$
> $= \frac{5 \times 3}{9 \times 4} = \frac{15}{36} = \frac{5}{12}$
>
> **Dividing Mixed Numbers and Whole Numbers**
> Write the mixed number and whole number as improper fractions. Multiply the dividend by the reciprocal of the divisor and simplify.
>
> $1\frac{2}{3} \div 3 = \frac{5}{3} \div \frac{3}{1}$
> $= \frac{5}{3} \times \frac{1}{3}$
> $= \frac{5 \times 1}{3 \times 3} = \frac{5}{9}$

Practice

Match the problem with a problem that is the same.

1. $4\frac{2}{5} \div 8$ _____
2. $8 \times 4\frac{2}{5}$ _____
3. $\frac{1}{8} \div 1\frac{3}{5}$ _____
4. $1\frac{3}{5} \times \frac{1}{8}$ _____

A. $\frac{22}{5} \times \frac{1}{8}$
B. $\frac{8}{5} \times \frac{1}{8}$
C. $8 \times \frac{22}{5}$
D. $\frac{1}{8} \times \frac{5}{8}$

Multiply.

5. $2\frac{3}{4} \times \frac{1}{7}$
6. $4\frac{1}{4} \times \frac{4}{5}$
7. $\frac{1}{6} \times 3\frac{3}{7}$
8. $\frac{9}{10} \times 1\frac{2}{3}$

9. $1\frac{5}{6} \times 4$
10. $3\frac{5}{8} \times 2$
11. $5 \times 1\frac{3}{4}$
12. $3 \times 2\frac{7}{12}$

13. $2\frac{1}{4} \times \frac{2}{3}$
14. $2 \times 4\frac{7}{10}$
15. $2\frac{2}{3} \times 5$
16. $\frac{3}{7} \times 2\frac{1}{3}$

Divide.

17. $1\frac{9}{10} \div \frac{2}{5}$
18. $1\frac{5}{12} \div \frac{1}{6}$
19. $\frac{7}{8} \div 2\frac{1}{2}$
20. $\frac{1}{6} \div 1\frac{1}{4}$

21. $3\frac{1}{5} \div 2$
22. $4\frac{4}{9} \div 4$
23. $5 \div 1\frac{1}{6}$
24. $9 \div 6\frac{2}{3}$

25. $2\frac{1}{3} \div \frac{2}{5}$
26. $8 \div 3\frac{1}{5}$
27. $\frac{4}{9} \div 1\frac{1}{9}$
28. $4\frac{2}{3} \div 3$

Name _____ Date _____

First tell whether you will *multiply* or *divide*. Then solve the problem. Explain your reasoning.

29. You are making 5 birdhouses. You need $1\frac{1}{4}$ quarts of paint to paint 1 birdhouse. How many quarts of paint will you need in all?

_____
_____
_____

30. Your bedroom window is $\frac{5}{9}$ yard tall. Your living room window is $2\frac{3}{5}$ times as tall as your bedroom window. How tall is your living room window?

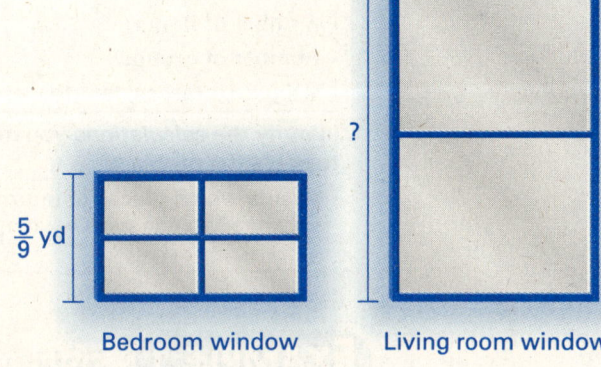

_____
_____
_____

31. You have 12 square feet of land that you are going to separate into sections of $2\frac{2}{5}$ square feet each. How many sections will you have?

_____
_____
_____

DID YOU GET IT?

32. Fill in the missing words. To multiply a mixed number by a fraction, first write the _____ _____ as a(n) _____ _____.

33. Explain your reasoning. Becca says that $7 \div 1\frac{2}{7}$ is the same as $\frac{7}{1} \times \frac{9}{7}$. Is she correct? Why or why not?

_____
_____
_____

Name _____   Date _____

LESSON 2-17
Solve Problems with Fractions

Strategies to Remember

To decide which information in a word problem is important and to order the steps you will follow:

Identify the *given information*:	Identify the *operation(s)* needed:
• dollar amounts • number of items • number of groups • weights, masses, lengths, etc.	• addition • subtraction • multiplication • division
Identify the *calculations* you must make to solve the problem:	*Order* the steps you will follow to solve the problem:
• decide which pieces of information you need to use with each operation	• decide on an order for the calculations

EXAMPLE 1 Solving an Addition Problem

A school's rain gauge catches $\frac{3}{8}$ inch of rain on Saturday and $\frac{1}{2}$ inch of rain on Sunday. What is the total rainfall for the weekend?

Solution

Step 1 **Identify** the operation needed. The word "total" tells you to *add*.

Step 2 **Add** the fractions: $\frac{3}{8} + \frac{1}{2} = \frac{3}{8} + \frac{4}{8} = \frac{7}{8}$

Step 3 **Check** for reasonableness. Because $\frac{3}{8}$ is almost $\frac{1}{2}$ and $\frac{1}{2} + \frac{1}{2} = 1$, the answer should be slightly less than 1. So, $\frac{7}{8}$ inch is reasonable.

ANSWER The total rainfall for the weekend is $\frac{7}{8}$ inch.

TRY THIS Fill in the missing information to solve the problem.

1. A package of 1 lb of hamburger meat loses $\frac{1}{4}$ lb when it is cooked. How much does the cooked hamburger meat weigh?

   Step 1 Identify the operation needed. The word "loses" tells you to ____.

   Step 2 Calculate: $1 \, \bigcirc \, \frac{1}{4} = \frac{\Box}{\Box}$

   Step 3 Check for reasonableness. Because $\frac{1}{4}$ is close to ____ and $1 - \Box = \Box$, the answer should be close to _____.

   Step 4 The cooked hamburger meat weighs _____ lb.

Math Intervention
Book 2 Fractions and Decimals

EXAMPLE 2 Solving a Division Problem

You are making dog leashes from a 50-foot length of rope. It takes $7\frac{1}{2}$ feet of rope to make each leash. How many leashes can you make?

Solution

Step 1 Identify the operation needed. To find how many $7\frac{1}{2}$-foot leashes can be made from 50 feet of rope, you need to *divide*.

Step 2 Calculate. Divide 50 by $7\frac{1}{2}$:
$$50 \div 7\frac{1}{2} = \frac{50}{1} \div \frac{15}{2}$$
$$= \frac{50}{1} \times \frac{2}{15}$$
$$= \frac{100}{15} = \frac{20}{3} = 6\frac{2}{3}$$

Step 3 Check that $6\frac{2}{3}$ leashes is reasonable. It does not make sense to make $\frac{2}{3}$ of a leash. So, 6 leashes is a more reasonable answer.

ANSWER You can make 6 leashes.

EXAMPLE 3 Solving Problems Using Multiple Operations

You fill $\frac{1}{2}$-liter bottles from a cooler containing $11\frac{1}{4}$ liters of water. How much water will be left in the cooler after filling 21 bottles?

Solution

Solve the problem. Identify the operations. Decide the order for the operations, then calculate. Check that your answer is reasonable.

Multiply, then subtract. $\quad \frac{1}{2} \times 21 = \frac{1}{2} \times \frac{21}{1} = \frac{21}{2}$ or $10\frac{1}{2}$

$$11\frac{1}{4} - \frac{21}{2} = \frac{45}{4} - \frac{21}{2}$$
$$= \frac{45}{4} - \frac{42}{4} = \frac{3}{4}$$

CHECK $11\frac{1}{4}$ is close to 11 and $11 - 10\frac{1}{2} = \frac{1}{2}$. So, $\frac{3}{4}$ liters is reasonable.

TRY THIS Solve the problem. Explain your reasoning.

2. You have a 30-foot roll of art paper. If an art project takes $1\frac{1}{3}$ feet of art paper, how much paper will be left over after you make 12 projects?

_____

_____

Math Intervention
Book 2 Fractions and Decimals

Name _____   Date _____

> **Summarize**
> **Solving Word Problems**
> (1) Identify the operation or operations needed.
> (2) Perform the calculations and solve the problem.
> (3) Check your answer for reasonableness.

Practice

Fill in the missing operation symbol +, −, ×, or ÷ for the situation described.

1. A student received $\frac{1}{5}$ of the class's 120 votes. $\frac{1}{5}\;\bigcirc\;120$

2. A cat weighs $1\frac{1}{2}$ pounds more than its usual weight of 9 pounds.
   $9\;\bigcirc\;1\frac{1}{2}$

3. Bracelets that are $6\frac{1}{4}$ inches long are being made from 72 inches of wire. $72\;\bigcirc\;6\frac{1}{4}$

4. You have $\frac{1}{3}$ cup less flour than the $2\frac{1}{2}$ cups the recipe suggests. $2\frac{1}{2}\;\bigcirc\;\frac{1}{3}$

Identify the operation suggested by the phrase.

5. took away $\frac{1}{4}$ pound

6. $\frac{2}{3}$ foot and $\frac{1}{2}$ foot

7. half of the 30 students

Read the problem. The first two steps of the solution are given. Number the steps of the solution to put them in order.

8. A kitten weighs $\frac{7}{8}$ pound. The kitten gains $\frac{1}{4}$ pound the first week and $\frac{1}{8}$ pound the second week. How much does the kitten weigh after 2 weeks?

   SOLUTION: ____ add: $1\frac{1}{8}+\frac{1}{8}$ ____ add: $\frac{7}{8}+\frac{1}{4}$

9. You need 4 pounds of pears for a dessert recipe. Each pear weighs about $\frac{2}{5}$ pound. After putting several pears on the scale in a grocery store, you still need $1\frac{3}{5}$ pounds of pears. How many pears are in the scale right now?

   SOLUTION: ____ subtract: $4-1\frac{3}{5}$ ____ divide: $2\frac{2}{5}\div\frac{2}{5}$

Math Intervention
Book 2 Fractions and Decimals

Name _____   Date _____

First identify the operation(s) needed to find the answer. Then solve the problem. Check your answer for reasonableness. Explain your reasoning.

10. Mario saves $\frac{1}{5}$ of his summer earnings for college. Last summer, Mario earned $2560. How much of this amount did he save for college?

   _____
   _____
   _____

11. The wait time at an amusement park ride is $1\frac{1}{2}$ hours. You have already been waiting in line for $\frac{3}{4}$ hour. How many minutes do you have left to wait?
   Hint: There are **60** minutes in **1** hour.

   _____
   _____
   _____

12. On Julio's computer, applications take up $\frac{9}{80}$ of the hard drive space and all other files take up $\frac{1}{20}$ of the hard drive space. What fraction of the hard drive space is left?

   _____
   _____
   _____

DID YOU GET IT?

13. **Write a word problem.** Write a word problem using the fractions at the right. Then solve the problem. Explain how you decided which operation to use.

   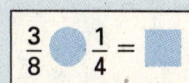

   _____
   _____

14. **Explain your reasoning.** Your friend says that the answer to the following problem is **4** shelves. Is your friend correct? Explain why or why not. A carpenter is cutting a **7**-foot-long board to make shelves for a bookcase. If the carpenter wants each shelf to be $\frac{15}{6}$ feet long, how many shelves can be made?

   _____
   _____
   _____

Name _____ Date _____

Mixed Practice for Lessons 2-11 to 2-17

Vocabulary Review

Match the word with its definition.

Word		Definition
1. operation	____	A. two fractions whose product is 1
2. difference	____	B. an action you perform on numbers, such as addition or multiplication
3. reciprocals	____	C. the answer when you subtract one number from another

Fill in the missing word(s).

4. After you solve a word problem, it is important to check for _____.

5. To subtract two fractions with unlike denominators, use the _____ _____ _____ to write the fractions with like denominators.

Shade the models below to find the sum or difference of the fractions.

6. $\frac{4}{7} - \frac{3}{7} = \frac{\Box}{\Box}$    7. $\frac{3}{6} + \frac{2}{6} = \frac{\Box}{\Box}$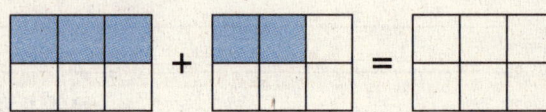

8. $1\frac{1}{4} - \frac{2}{4} = \frac{\Box}{\Box}$

9. $1\frac{2}{3} + \frac{2}{3} = \frac{\Box}{\Box}$

Add, subtract, multiply, or divide. Write your answer in simplest form.

10. $\frac{2}{7} + \frac{3}{7}$ 11. $\frac{2}{9} \times \frac{1}{3}$ 12. $\frac{3}{4} \div \frac{8}{3}$ 13. $\frac{7}{8} - \frac{2}{8}$

14. $\frac{5}{6} \div 7$ 15. $6\frac{5}{9} - 1\frac{4}{9}$ 16. $20 \times \frac{1}{4}$ 17. $\frac{3}{4} + \frac{3}{4}$

18. $\frac{3}{10} + 3\frac{1}{10}$ 19. $\frac{9}{10} \times \frac{2}{3}$ 20. $\frac{4}{5} \div \frac{2}{5}$ 21. $7\frac{5}{6} - 5\frac{1}{6}$

Math Intervention
72 Book 2 Fractions and Decimals

Name _____   Date _____

22. Fill in the missing information to solve the problem.

Students at a school are performing in a play. At the play, adults make up $\frac{2}{5}$ of the audience. One third of these adults are parents of the actors. What fraction of the audience are parents of the actors in the play?

Step 1 The phrase "$\frac{1}{3}$ of these adults" tells you that you need to _____.

Step 2 Calculate: $\frac{1}{3} \bigcirc \frac{2}{5} = \square$. So, parents of the actors make up $\square$ of the audience at the play.

Step 3 Check your answer for reasonableness. Since $\frac{1}{3}$ is close to $\square$ and $\frac{2}{5}$ is close to $\square$, their _____ should be about $\square$.

Add, subtract, multiply, or divide. Write your answer in simplest form.

23. $\frac{1}{2} + \frac{3}{8}$
24. $\frac{4}{5} - \frac{2}{3}$
25. $1\frac{3}{4} \times \frac{3}{7}$
26. $\frac{5}{8} \div \frac{5}{12}$

27. $2\frac{5}{8} \times 2\frac{1}{7}$
28. $3\frac{1}{4} + 6\frac{1}{3}$
29. $\frac{8}{9} \div 4\frac{2}{3}$
30. $3\frac{5}{6} - 1\frac{1}{2}$

31. $4\frac{1}{8} - 2\frac{3}{4}$
32. $3\frac{1}{5} \div 6\frac{2}{15}$
33. $5\frac{3}{4} + 2\frac{1}{5}$
34. $2\frac{1}{4} \times 1\frac{3}{5}$

35. $7\frac{5}{6} \div 2\frac{7}{12}$
36. $3\frac{1}{10} \times 2\frac{2}{3}$
37. $1\frac{2}{3} + 2\frac{5}{6}$
38. $7\frac{2}{7} - 1\frac{3}{5}$

Identify the calculations you must make to solve the problem. Order the steps you will follow. Then solve the problem.

39. A carpenter hammers a nail into a pair of boards. Each board is $1\frac{1}{8}$ inches thick. The nail stops $\frac{5}{8}$ inch from of the bottom of the second board. How long is the nail?

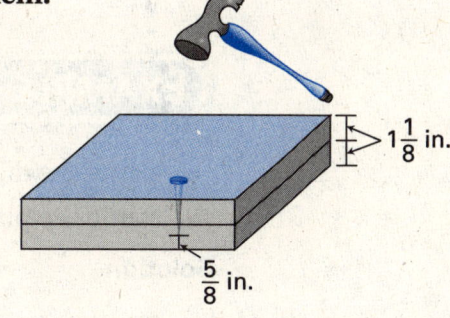

_____

_____

40. A chef makes 5 quarts of soup. Each soup bowl holds $\frac{2}{5}$ quart of soup. The chef has filled 7 bowls with soup. How much soup is left?

_____

_____

_____

Name _____ Date _____

LESSON 2-18

Decimals and Place Value

Words to Remember

Decimal: A number made up of digits and a decimal point

A decimal uses place values to refer to parts of a set or parts of a whole.

You read the decimal **1.7** as "one point seven" or "one and seven tenths."

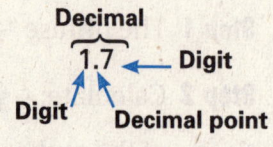

Getting Started In Lesson 2-4 you learned how to write and represent fractions. You can also write and represent decimals.

Place Value A decimal is written using place values. Each place value is ten times the place value to its right. Each digit in a decimal has a place value. In the decimal **18.416**, the digit **4** is in the tenths' place.

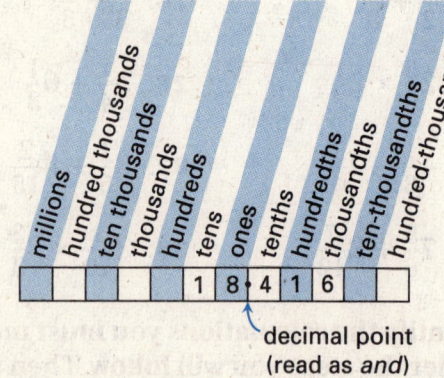

EXAMPLE 1 Identifying Place Value

a. Name the digit in the hundredths' place: **2.097**

b. Name the place value of the digit that is underlined: **41.03<u>5</u>**

Solution

a. The hundredths' place is located two places to the right of the decimal point.

2.097
 1 2

ANSWER 9

b. Three places to the right of the decimal point is the thousandths' place.

41.035
   1 2 3

ANSWER thousandths

TRY THIS Identify the digit or place value indicated.

1. Name the digit in the tenths' place: **43.215**

2. Name the place value of the digit that is underlined: **1.5<u>3</u>8**

Math Intervention
Book 2 Fractions and Decimals

Name _____   Date _____

EXAMPLE 2 Reading Decimals

Write the decimal in words.

a. 5.4   b. 0.007

Solution		Words	Numbers
a. **Step 1**	Write the whole number part. The word *and* represents the decimal point.	five and	5.4
Step 2	Write the number in the decimal part.	five and four	5.4
Step 3	Write the word for the place value of the rightmost digit.	five and four tenths	5.4 ↑ tenths
b. **Step 1**	Write the word for the decimal part. There is no whole number part.	seven	0.007
Step 2	Write the word for the place value of the rightmost digit.	seven thousandths	0.007 ↑ thousandths

Using Zeros

Use zeros to fill in where needed. Since the decimal part in part (a) is seventy-eight *thousandths*, you need to put a zero in the tenths' place so that the eight in seventy-eight is in the thousandths' place.

EXAMPLE 3 Writing Decimals

Write the words as a decimal.

a. twenty-four and seventy-eight thousandths   b. six tenths

Solution

a. twenty-four and seventy-eight thousandths   24.078 ← *Thousandths* is the place value of the rightmost digit.

The word *and* tells where to put the decimal point.

b. six tenths   0.6 ← *Tenths* is the place value of the rightmost digit.

TRY THIS Write the words as a decimal or the decimal in words.

3. 241.7   4. 0.549

5. three hundred four and twenty-seven thousandths   6. eighty-two hundredths

Math Intervention
Book 2 Fractions and Decimals

Name _____ Date _____

> **Summarize**
>
> **Identifying Place Value**
> Each place value is ten times the place value to its right.
>
> In 0.34, the 3 is in the tenths' place.
>
> **Reading and Writing Decimals**
> The word *and* represents the decimal point. Numbers before *and* are whole numbers. Numbers after *and* are less than 1. The rightmost digit in a decimal tells you which place value word belongs at the end of the spoken or written form of the decimal.
>
>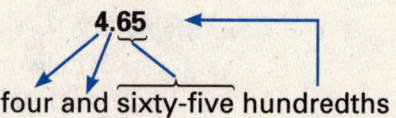
> four and sixty-five hundredths

Practice

Name the digit in the given place value.

1. 48.104; hundredths
2. 7.489; tenths
3. 0.012849; ten thousandths
4. 12.75684; thousandths

Name the place value of the digit that is underlined.

5. 9.4<u>7</u>58
6. 52.8349<u>7</u>
7. 234.0<u>7</u>
8. 200.7<u>8</u>6
9. 799.59<u>6</u>3
10. 24.<u>1</u>538
11. 86.5<u>7</u>9
12. 64.018<u>3</u>

Match the decimal with its description in words.

13. 271.6 _____   A. twenty-seven and sixteen hundredths
14. 27.16 _____   B. two hundred seventy-one and six tenths
15. 2.716 _____   C. two and seven hundred sixteen thousandths

Write the words as a decimal.

16. eight ten-thousandths
17. two hundred and three tenths
18. twenty-nine thousandths
19. forty-one and five hundredths
20. thirty-five hundredths
21. six and seven thousandths

Write the decimal in words.

22. 3.45
23. 71.404
24. 0.0009
25. 0.16
26. 214.01
27. 392.3
28. 19.002
29. 6.3477

Math Intervention
Book 2 Fractions and Decimals

Name _____ Date _____

Solve the problem. Explain your reasoning.

30. In the jumping event of a waterskiing tournament, Wesley's air time on his longest jump is **3.48** seconds. Write this decimal in words.

_____
_____
_____

31. Your coach tells you that you ran two and five hundred sixty-two thousandths miles. Write this distance as a decimal.

_____
_____
_____

32. A metric scale in your science class measures the mass of an object as **45.235** grams. Name the digit in the hundredths' place.

_____
_____
_____

DID YOU GET IT?

33. Fill in the missing words. The tenths' place is located _____ place(s) to the _____ of the _____ _____.

34. Use a model. The model represents two and five tenths. Write this as a decimal.

_____
_____
_____

35. Supply the number. Write a decimal that has the digit **5** in the thousandths' place. Then write the decimal in words.

_____
_____
_____

Math Intervention
Book 2 Fractions and Decimals

LESSON 2-19 Round Decimals

> **Words to Remember**
> Rounding: To approximate a number to a given place value
> 3.2 rounded to the nearest one is 3.

Getting Started In Lesson 1-6 you learned how to round whole numbers. You can also round decimals.

Using a Number Line You can see how to round decimals on a number line. Notice that there are **10** equal spaces between each whole number.

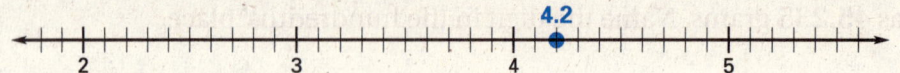

EXAMPLE 1 Rounding Decimals Using a Number Line

a. Use a number line to round **4.53** to the nearest *tenth*.

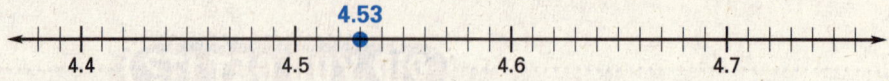

b. Use a number line to round **0.3497** to the nearest *thousandth*.

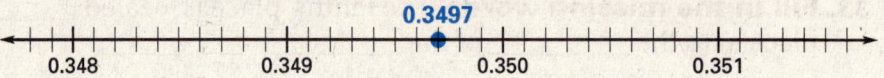

Solution

a. The decimal **4.53** is closer to **4.5** than **4.6**, so it rounds down.

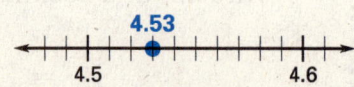

ANSWER 4.5

b. The decimal **0.3497** is closer to **0.350** than **0.349**, so it rounds up.

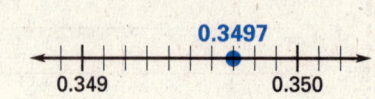

ANSWER 0.35

> **Using Zeros**
> If the rightmost digit to the right of the decimal point is a zero, you can drop it. So, in part (b), 0.350 is the same as 0.35.

TRY THIS Use a number line.

1. Round **0.2744** to the nearest *thousandth*.

Math Intervention
Book 2 Fractions and Decimals

Name _____ Date _____

Rounding a Decimal To round a decimal, look at the next digit to the right.
- If the digit is **4** or less, round down.
- If the digit is **5** or greater, round up.

SAMPLE: Round **0.48372** to the place value of the digit that is underlined.

0.4<u>8</u>372 The digit 3 is to the right of the 8.
Three is 4 or less, so round down.

0.48372 rounds down to **0.48**.

EXAMPLE 2 Rounding Decimals

Round the decimal to the place value of the digit that is underlined.

a. 57.<u>6</u>51   b. <u>0</u>.745

Solution

a. The digit to the right of **6** is **5**, so **57.651** rounds up to **57.7**.

b. The digit to the right of **0** is **7**, so **0.745** rounds up to **1**.

Rounding When 9 Is in the Given Place Value If the digit in the given place value is **9** and the number to its right is **5** or greater, first change the **9** to a **0**. Then increase the digit to the left of **9** by **1**.

SAMPLE: Round **2.796** to the nearest hundredth.

2.796   9 is in the hundredths' place, and
                              the digit to its right is a 6.
                              6 is greater than 5.

2.796 rounds up to **2.80**. Change 9 to 0 and increase 7 to 8.

EXAMPLE 3 Rounding to a Given Place Value

Round the decimal to the given place value.

a. 1.3023; hundredths   b. 4.964; tenths

Solution

a. The **0** is in the hundredths' place. The digit to its right is a **2**, so **1.3023** rounds down to **1.30**, or **1.3**.

b. The **9** is in the tenths' place. The digit to its right is a **6**, so **4.964** rounds up to **5.0**, or **5**.

TRY THIS Round the decimal to the place value of the digit that is underlined.

2. 22.<u>7</u>12   3. 16.4<u>8</u>5   4. <u>0</u>.315

Math Intervention
Book 2 Fractions and Decimals

Name _____ Date _____

Summarize
Rounding Decimals
To round to a given place value, look at the next digit to the right. If the digit is **4** or less, round down. If the digit is **5** or greater, round up.

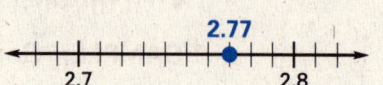

When rounding to the nearest *tenth*, 2.77 rounds up to 2.8.

Practice

Use a number line to round the decimal to the given place value.

1. 18.223; hundredths _____
2. 0.18; tenths _____
3. 2.0109; thousandths _____
4. 10.344; hundredths _____
5. 0.99; tenths _____

Match the rounded decimal with its original decimal.

6. 0.716 _____ 7. 0.72 _____ 8. 0.7 _____

A. 0.7162; tenths   B. 0.7162; hundredths   C. 0.7162; thousandths

Round the decimal to the place value of the digit that is underlined.

9. 3.4159
10. 1.9988
11. 0.71274
12. 45.39
13. 24.876
14. 0.4821
15. 30.62
16. 2.797
17. 5.6018
18. 9.551
19. 0.2449
20. 115.02

Round the decimal to the given place value.

21. 5.678; tenths
22. 0.497; hundredths
23. 7.32; ones
24. 0.625; hundredths
25. 1.784; tenths
26. 0.0078; thousandths

Math Intervention
Book 2 Fractions and Decimals

Name _____ Date _____

Solve the problem. Explain your reasoning.

27. You need to measure **8.62** milliliters of a substance for a science experiment. Your lab equipment measures only to the nearest *tenth* of a milliliter. Round **8.62** to the nearest *tenth*.

   _____
   _____
   _____

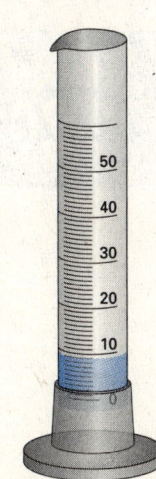

28. You divide **7** by **8** on a calculator and get **0.875**. Round **0.875** to the nearest *hundredth*.

   _____
   _____
   _____

29. A mail clerk tells you that the package you want to mail weighs **8.25** pounds. Round **8.25** pounds to the nearest *pound*.

   _____
   _____
   _____

DID YOU GET IT?

30. **Fill in the missing word.** To round a decimal to a given place value, look at the next digit to the _____.

31. **Use a number line.** Plot a decimal on the number line. Then give the rounded value when the decimal is rounded to the nearest *tenth*.

   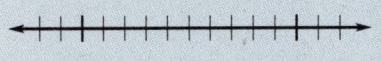   Decimal: _____

   Rounded to nearest tenth: _____

32. **Supply the numbers.** Write one decimal that rounds up to **3.18** and one decimal that rounds down to **3.18**.

   _____
   _____

Math Intervention
Book 2 Fractions and Decimals

Name _____ Date _____

LESSON 2-20
Compare and Order Decimals

Getting Started In Lesson 2-7 you learned how to compare and order fractions. You can also compare and order decimals.

Using a Number Line You can see how to order decimals on a number line. The numbers on a number line increase from left to right, so **2.44 > 2.32**.

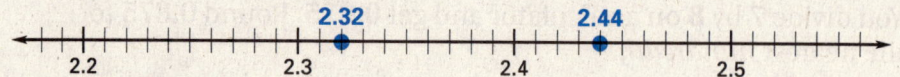

EXAMPLE 1 Ordering Decimals Using a Number Line

Use a number line to order the numbers from least to greatest.

0.81, 1, 0.9, 1.02, 0.74

Solution

Graph each number on a number line. Then list them in order from left to right.

ANSWER 0.74, 0.81, 0.9, 1, 1.02

TRY THIS Use a number line to order the numbers from least to greatest.

1. 3.3, 4.2, 2, 3, 4.9 _____

2. 1.79, 1.7, 1.66, 1.92, 1.8 _____

3. 13.03, 13.06, 12.93, 12.87, 13 _____

Name _____ Date _____

EXAMPLE 2 **Comparing Decimals with the Same Number of Decimal Places**

Compare the decimals.

  a. 4.61 and 4.62
  b. 7.91 and 7.83

Solution

Write the decimals in a column, lining up the decimal places. Compare the place values from left to right. When you come to a place value with different numbers, compare the numbers.

a. 4.61
    4.62
    same ↑↑ different
        same
    1 < 2

ANSWER 4.61 < 4.62

b. 7.91
    7.83
    same ↑↑ different
    9 > 8

ANSWER 7.91 > 7.83

TRY THIS Compare the decimals.

4. 14.42 and 14.47
5. 0.31 and 0.29

EXAMPLE 3 **Comparing Decimals with a Different Number of Decimal Places**

Compare the decimals: 5.02 and 5

Solution

Step 1 Write the decimals in a column, lining up the decimal places.

5.02
5.00 ← Add zeros after 5 to match 5.02.

Step 2 Add zeros so that each decimal has the same number of decimal places.

same ↑↑ different
    same

Step 3 Compare the place values from left to right.

ANSWER 2 > 0, so 5.02 > 5

TRY THIS Compare the decimals.

6. 0.16 and 0.092
7. 3 and 2.99

Math Intervention
Book 2 Fractions and Decimals **83**

Name _____   Date _____

> **Summarize**
>
> **Ordering Decimals**
>
> Graph the numbers on a number line. List the numbers in order from left to right (least to greatest).
>
>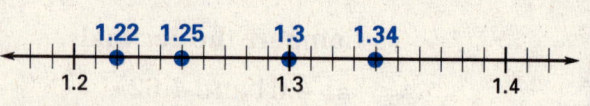
>
> The numbers in order from least to greatest are **1.22, 1.25, 1.3, 1.34**.
>
> **Comparing Decimals**
>
> Write the decimals in a column. If the decimals have a different number of decimal places, add zeros to make the number of decimal places the same. Compare the place values from left to right.
>
> 3.48 and 3.47   0.5 and 0.55
>   3.48   0.50
>   3.47   0.55
>   3.48 > 3.47   0.5 < 0.55

Practice

Use a number line to order the numbers from least to greatest.

1. 4.84, 4.94, 4.82, 5 _____

2. 1.08, 0.98, 1, 0.96 _____

3. 7, 5, 7.7, 6.3 _____

Match the statement with the number line that represents it.

4. 3.5 > 3.3 _____   A.

5. 3.19 < 3.2 _____ B.

6. 3.15 > 3.1 _____ C.

Complete the statement with <, >, or =.

7. 0.7 ◯ 0.6   8. 9.12 ◯ 9.14   9. 16.92 ◯ 16.91

10. 0.81 ◯ 0.9   11. 1.7 ◯ 1.74   12. 21 ◯ 21.4

13. 8.1 ◯ 8.01   14. 6.29 ◯ 6   15. 7 ◯ 6.54

16. 0.8 ◯ 0.80   17. 42.15 ◯ 42.18   18. 0.45 ◯ 0.06

19. 1.35 ◯ 1.31   20. 12.6 ◯ 12.07   21. 0.70 ◯ 0.74

Name _____ Date _____

Solve the problem. Explain your reasoning.

22. In a long jump competition, Mario jumped **4.45** feet and Cole jumped **4.49** feet. Who jumped farther?

_____
_____
_____

23. Order the dogs from lightest to heaviest.

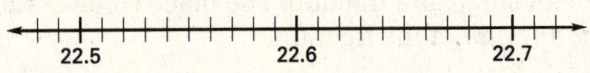

Dog	Weight (pounds)
Bonnie	22.6
Clyde	22.58
Mona	22.71
Lisa	22.68

_____
_____
_____

24. You type a paragraph in **3.68** minutes. Your friend types the same paragraph in **3.6** minutes. Who types faster, you or your friend?

_____
_____
_____

DID YOU GET IT?

25. Fill in the missing words. To compare two decimals, write the decimals in a(n) _____ . Then compare the _____ _____ from _____ to _____ .

26. Use a number line. Plot four numbers on the number line. Then list the numbers in order from least to greatest.

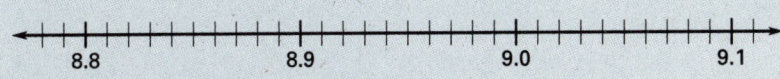

_____

27. Supply the number. Write a decimal with two decimal places that is less than **0.1**.

_____

Math Intervention
Book 2 Fractions and Decimals

LESSON 2-21

Write Decimals as Fractions

Getting Started In Lesson 2-8 you learned how to write mixed numbers as improper fractions. You can also write decimals as fractions and mixed numbers.

Using Place Value Use the place value of the rightmost digit in a decimal to help you write the decimal as a fraction. The place value of the rightmost digit tells the *denominator* of the fraction.

$0.\underline{1} \rightarrow$ one *tenth* $\rightarrow \frac{1}{10}$

$0.0\underline{1} \rightarrow$ one *hundredth* $\rightarrow \frac{1}{100}$

$0.00\underline{1} \rightarrow$ one *thousandth* $\rightarrow \frac{1}{1000}$

EXAMPLE 1 Writing Decimals as Fractions

Write the decimal as a fraction in simplest form.

a. 0.7   b. 0.42

Solution

a. Write 0.7 as a fraction.

$0.\underline{7} \rightarrow 7$ *tenths* $\rightarrow \frac{7}{10}$

$\frac{7}{10}$ is in simplest form.

ANSWER $\frac{7}{10}$

b. Write 0.42 as a fraction.

$0.4\underline{2} \rightarrow 42$ *hundredths* $\rightarrow \frac{42}{100}$

$\frac{42 \div 2}{100 \div 2} = \frac{21}{50}$ ←Use the GCF to simplify.

ANSWER $\frac{21}{50}$

> **Remember**
> To determine whether a fraction is in simplest form, look at the numerator and denominator. If they share a common factor, then the fraction is *not* in simplest form.

TRY THIS Write the decimal as a fraction in simplest form.

1. $0.3 = \frac{\square}{\square}$ 2. $0.27 = \frac{\square}{\square}$ 3. $0.115 = \frac{\square}{\square}$ 4. $0.75 = \frac{\square}{\square}$

Recognizing Common Decimals and Their Fraction Equivalents You can use what you know about money to help you recognize common decimals and their fraction equivalents.

$\$.25$ is $\frac{1}{4}$ of a dollar $\rightarrow 0.25 = \frac{1}{4}$

$\$.50$ is $\frac{1}{2}$ of a dollar $\rightarrow 0.5 = \frac{1}{2}$

$\$.75$ is $\frac{3}{4}$ of a dollar $\rightarrow 0.75 = \frac{3}{4}$

Math Intervention
Book 2 Fractions and Decimals

Name _____ Date _____

EXAMPLE 2 Writing Decimals as Mixed Numbers

Write the decimal as a mixed number in simplest form.

a. 1.6   b. 2.25

Solution

a. $1\frac{6}{10}$ Write 1.6, or one and six tenths, as a mixed number.

$1\frac{6 \div 2}{10 \div 2} = 1\frac{3}{5}$ Use the GCF to simplify the fraction part.

ANSWER $1\frac{3}{5}$

b. $2.25 = 2 + 0.25$ You can break 2.25 into 2 and the decimal 0.25.

$0.25 = \frac{1}{4}$ 0.25 is equal to one fourth $\left(0.25 = \frac{1}{4}\right)$.

$2 + 0.25 = 2 + \frac{1}{4}$ Two and twenty-five hundredths is the same as two and one fourth.

ANSWER $2\frac{1}{4}$ Write two and one fourth as a mixed number.

EXAMPLE 3 Writing Decimals with Zeros as Fractions or Mixed Numbers

Write the decimal as a fraction or mixed number in simplest form.

a. 0.006   b. 5.09

Solution

a. $\frac{6}{1000}$ Write 0.006, or six thousandths, as a fraction.

$\frac{6 \div 2}{1000 \div 2} = \frac{3}{500}$ Use the GCF to simplify.

ANSWER $\frac{3}{500}$

b. $5\frac{9}{100}$ Write 5.09, or five and nine hundredths, as a mixed number. The mixed number is in simplest form.

TRY THIS Write the decimal as a fraction or mixed number in simplest form.

5. 7.5 = ☐ $\frac{☐}{☐}$ 6. 4.45 = ☐ $\frac{☐}{☐}$ 7. 0.02 = $\frac{☐}{☐}$

Math Intervention
Book 2 Fractions and Decimals

Name _____   Date _____

Summarize

Writing Decimals as Fractions or Mixed Numbers

(1) Use place value to write the decimal as a fraction or mixed number.   0.59   fifty-nine *hundredths*
$= \frac{59}{100}$

(2) Learn to recognize common decimals and their fraction equivalents.   1.75 $0.75 = \frac{3}{4}$, so 1.75 is one and three fourths
$= 1\frac{3}{4}$

(3) Simplify if necessary.   2.05   two and five *hundredths*
$= 2\frac{5}{100} = 2\frac{1}{20}$

Practice

Match the decimal with the equivalent fraction in simplest form.

1. 0.5 ____   2. 0.25 ____   3. 0.75 ____   4. 0.125 ____

A. $\frac{3}{4}$ B. $\frac{1}{8}$ C. $\frac{1}{4}$ D. $\frac{1}{2}$

Match the decimal with the equivalent mixed number in simplest form.

5. 3.125 ____   6. 3.8 ____   7. 3.64 ____   8. 3.06 ____

A. $3\frac{4}{5}$ B. $3\frac{16}{25}$ C. $3\frac{1}{8}$ D. $3\frac{3}{50}$

Write the decimal as a fraction in simplest form.

9. 0.12   10. 0.4   11. 0.625   12. 0.35

13. 0.9   14. 0.46   15. 0.95   16. 0.28

17. 0.2   18. 0.255   19. 0.175   20. 0.6

Write the decimal as a fraction or mixed number in simplest form.

21. 9.15   22. 1.1   23. 3.315   24. 4.25

25. 2.76   26. 8.5   27. 2.02   28. 3.008

29. 0.09   30. 0.004   31. 7.65   32. 5.042

Math Intervention
Book 2 Fractions and Decimals

Name _____   Date _____

Solve the problem. Explain your reasoning.

33. You walk **0.25** mile and then jog **0.75** mile. Write these decimals as fractions.

_____
_____
_____

34. It takes you **3.04** minutes to download a song from an online music store. Write this decimal as a mixed number.

_____
_____
_____

35. A scrap piece of wood is one and seven tenths of a meter long. Write this number as a decimal and as a mixed number.

_____
_____
_____

DID YOU GET IT?

36. Fill in the missing words. When writing a decimal as a fraction, the _____ _____ tells the _____ of the fraction.

37. Find the error. Your friend says that to write **0.08** as a fraction, you should write eight tenths as $\frac{8}{10}$ and then simplify to $\frac{4}{5}$. Is your friend correct? Explain.

_____
_____
_____

38. Supply the number. Write a decimal so that its rightmost digit is in the hundredths' place. Then write your decimal as a fraction or mixed number.

_____
_____
_____

Name _____ Date _____

LESSON 2-22
Write Fractions as Decimals

> **Words to Remember**
>
> Terminating decimal: A decimal that has a final digit
>   0.2 and 0.47 are *terminating decimals*.
>
> Repeating decimal: A decimal that has one or more digits that repeat forever
>
> You can write a repeating decimal with a bar over the digits that repeat.
>   0.333... and 0.4545... are *repeating decimals* and can be written as $0.\overline{3}$ and $0.\overline{45}$.

Getting Started In Lesson 2-21 you learned how to write decimals as fractions. You can also write fractions as decimals.

EXAMPLE 1 Writing a Fraction as a Terminating Decimal

Write the fraction or mixed number as a decimal.

a. $\dfrac{13}{25}$ b. $1\dfrac{4}{5}$

Solution

a.
```
        0.52
    25)13.00
       12.5
          50
          50
           0
```
Divide the numerator by the denominator.
The remainder is 0 because the decimal is *terminating*.

ANSWER 0.52

b. $1\dfrac{4}{5} = \dfrac{(1 \times 5) + 4}{5} = \dfrac{9}{5}$ Write the mixed number as an improper fraction.

```
       1.8
     5)9.0
       5
       4 0
       4 0
         0
```
Divide the numerator by the denominator.
The remainder is 0 because the decimal is *terminating*.

ANSWER 1.8

Math Intervention
Book 2 Fractions and Decimals

Name _____ Date _____

TRY THIS Write the fraction or mixed number as a decimal.

1. $\frac{7}{20}$ 2. $\frac{9}{40}$ 3. $5\frac{3}{4}$ 4. $1\frac{3}{16}$

EXAMPLE 2 Writing a Fraction as a Repeating Decimal

Write $\frac{6}{11}$ as a decimal.

Solution

```
      0.5454...
  11)6.0000...
      5 5
        50
        44
         60
         55
          50
          44
           6
```

Divide the numerator by the denominator.

The digits 5 and 4 repeat. Write a bar over the 5 and 4.

Using a Decimal Bar
Remember, you can write repeating decimals with a bar over the digits that repeat.

ANSWER $0.\overline{54}$

Comparing Fractions and Decimals You can see how decimals and fractions relate on a number line. To compare a fraction and a decimal, write the fraction as a decimal.

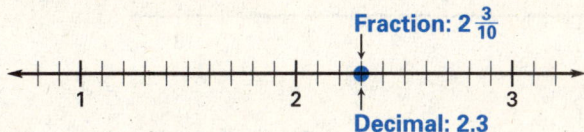

Fraction: $2\frac{3}{10}$
Decimal: 2.3

EXAMPLE 3 Comparing Fractions and Decimals

Compare: $\frac{3}{5}$ and 0.63

Solution

```
    0.6
  5)3.0
    3.0
      0
```
Write $\frac{3}{5}$ as a decimal.

$0.6 < 0.63$ Compare the decimals.

Using a Number Line
You can check your comparison by graphing the fraction and decimal on a number line. Multiply the numerator and denominator of $\frac{3}{5}$ by 2 to get $\frac{6}{10}$.

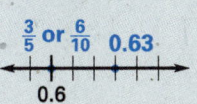

ANSWER $\frac{3}{5} < 0.63$

TRY THIS

5. Write $\frac{2}{3}$ as a repeating decimal.   6. Compare: $1\frac{3}{8}$ and 1.36

Math Intervention
Book 2 Fractions and Decimals

Name _____ Date _____

> **Summarize**
>
> **Writing Fractions or Mixed Numbers as Decimals**
>
> For a decimal, divide the numerator by the denominator. For a mixed number, write the mixed number as an improper fraction. Then divide the numerator by the denominator. Write repeating decimals with a bar over the digits that repeat.
>
> $\frac{4}{25}$
>
> $$25\overline{)4.00} = 0.16$$
> $$\underline{25}$$
> $$150$$
> $$\underline{150}$$
> $$0$$
>
> $\frac{1}{3}$
>
> $$3\overline{)1.000...} = 0.\overline{3}$$
> $$\underline{9}$$
> $$10$$
> $$\underline{9}$$
> $$10$$
> $$\underline{9}$$
> $$1$$
>
> **Comparing Fractions and Decimals**
>
> Write the fraction as a decimal. Then compare the decimals.
>
> Compare $\frac{9}{10}$ and 0.94. → $\frac{9}{10} = 0.9$
> $0.9 < 0.94$
> $\frac{9}{10} < 0.94$

Practice

Graph each fraction or mixed number on the number line below. Then give the decimal equivalent.

1. $\frac{9}{10}$ _____
2. $\frac{1}{2}$ _____
3. $1\frac{7}{10}$ _____
4. $2\frac{3}{5}$ _____

Match the fraction or mixed number with an equivalent decimal.

5. $\frac{4}{15}$ ___
6. $\frac{17}{20}$ ___
7. $1\frac{5}{18}$ ___
8. $1\frac{4}{5}$ ___

A. 1.8   B. 0.85   C. $0.2\overline{6}$ D. $1.2\overline{7}$

Write the fraction or mixed number as a decimal.

9. $\frac{2}{5}$
10. $\frac{3}{32}$
11. $1\frac{11}{40}$
12. $2\frac{13}{50}$
13. $\frac{1}{12}$
14. $\frac{7}{24}$
15. $4\frac{2}{3}$
16. $1\frac{4}{11}$

Complete the statement with <, >, or =.

17. $\frac{6}{25}$ ◯ 0.24
18. $\frac{19}{20}$ ◯ 0.97
19. $2\frac{3}{8}$ ◯ 2.37
20. $3\frac{1}{4}$ ◯ 3.28
21. $1\frac{1}{16}$ ◯ 1.05
22. $\frac{5}{80}$ ◯ 0.07

Math Intervention
Book 2 Fractions and Decimals

Name _____ Date _____

Solve the problem. Explain your reasoning.

23. You are mailing a letter that weighs $\frac{7}{8}$ of a pound. Write $\frac{7}{8}$ as a decimal.

_____
_____
_____

24. You measure the height of a young magnolia tree. Write the height as a decimal.

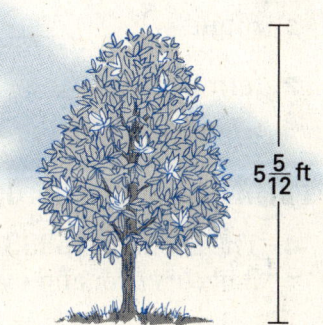

_____
_____

25. You are picking a colored paper to print a dozen flyers. The blue paper is $4\frac{7}{16}$ inches wide, and the yellow paper is **4.35** inches wide. Which paper is wider?

_____
_____
_____

DID YOU GET IT?

26. Fill in the missing word. A decimal that has a final digit is called a _____ decimal.

27. Use a number line. Graph a fraction on the number line. Then write a decimal that is equivalent to the fraction.

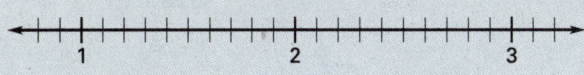

Fraction: _____

Decimal: _____

28. Solve the riddle. Three fractions with **12** in the denominator can be written as terminating decimals. Which fractions are they? (Hint: The fraction does not need to be in simplest form.)

_____
_____
_____

Name _____ Date _____

Mixed Practice for Lessons 2-18 to 2-22

Vocabulary Review

Match the word with its definition.

Word		Definition
1. round	_____	**A.** describes a decimal that has a final digit
2. terminating	_____	**B.** to write a decimal to a given place value
3. whole	_____	**C.** one unit

Fill in the missing word(s).

4. The decimal **0.5333…** is a _____ _____ because the 3 occurs over and over forever.

5. The _____ _____ of a decimal tells the denominator of its fraction equivalent.

Write the words as a decimal or the decimal in words.

6. fourteen and sixty-five thousandths

7. 105.61

Name the digit in the given place value. Then use the number line to round the decimal to the given place value.

8. 2.8375; hundredths

9. 1.96; tenths

Use the number line to order the numbers from least to greatest.

10. 5.268, 5.26, 5.271, 5.27

_____

11. 0.6, 0.45, 0.52, 0.5

_____

Complete the statement with <, >, or =.

12. 25.4 ⬤ 26.96

13. 30.1 ⬤ 30.01

14. 7.2 ⬤ $7\frac{1}{3}$

15. $4\frac{1}{4}$ ⬤ 4.15

16. $\frac{9}{10}$ ⬤ 0.9

17. 1.31 ⬤ $1\frac{2}{7}$

Math Intervention
Book 2 Fractions and Decimals

Name _____ Date _____

18. Fill in the missing information to solve the problem.

In gym class today, Meredith jumped a distance of **5.24** feet. Lydian jumped a distance of $5\frac{1}{4}$ feet. Who jumped the shorter distance?

Step 1 The word "shorter" tells you that you need to compare **5.24** and $5\frac{1}{4}$ to see which one is _____.

Step 2 Compare: 5.24 ◯ $5\frac{1}{4}$

Step 3 _____ jumped the shorter distance.

Write the decimal as a fraction or mixed number in simplest form.

19. 0.75   **20.** 0.02   **21.** 0.58   **22.** 3.6
23. 4.15   **24.** 2.84   **25.** 9.9   **26.** 0.005

Write the fraction or mixed number as a decimal.

27. $\frac{73}{100}$ **28.** $\frac{3}{8}$ **29.** $\frac{2}{25}$ **30.** $\frac{17}{20}$

31. $3\frac{1}{8}$ **32.** $1\frac{2}{5}$ **33.** $5\frac{61}{100}$ **34.** $1\frac{3}{4}$

Solve the problem. Explain your reasoning.

35. Jaime is mailing a rolled poster with a height of $8\frac{2}{5}$ inches. Will it fit into this mailing tube?

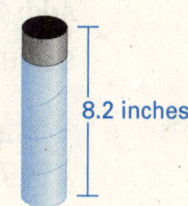
8.2 inches

_____
_____

36. At a grocery store, you order **4.25** pounds of ground turkey. The butcher rounds **4.25** to the nearest tenth and gives you that amount of ground turkey. Do you get more or less ground turkey than you ordered? Explain.

_____
_____

Math Intervention
Book 2 Fractions and Decimals   **95**

Lesson 2-23: Add and Subtract Decimals

> **Words to Remember**
> Regroup: To write a group of numbers as another number
>
> 214 can be regrouped as
> $2\overset{1}{\cancel{1}}\overset{11}{\cancel{1}}4$, or 1 hundred, 11 tens, and 4 ones.

Getting Started In Lessons 2-11 and 2-12, you learned how to add and subtract fractions. You can also add and subtract decimals.

Adding Decimals To add decimals, line up the decimal points. Then add the same way you would with whole numbers. Bring the decimal point down in your answer. You can add two or more numbers following the same steps.

```
   5.2
 + 5.3
 ─────
  10.5
```

 **Adding Decimals with the Same Number of Decimal Places**

Add: 4.29 + 7.18

Solution

```
    1
   4.79
 + 7.18
 ──────
  11.97
```

Write the decimals in a column, lining up the decimal points.

Add, regrouping as necessary. Bring the decimal point down.

ANSWER 11.97

 **Adding Decimals with a Different Number of Decimal Places**

Add: 5.061 + 2.3

Solution

```
   5.061
 + 2.3
```
Write the decimals in a column, lining up the decimal points or the digits in the ones' place.

```
   5.061
 + 2.300   ← Add zeros.
 ───────
   7.361
```
Add zeros so that both numbers have the same number of digits after the decimal.

Add, bringing the decimal point down.

ANSWER 7.361

Math Intervention
Book 2 Fractions and Decimals

Name _____ Date _____

TRY THIS Add.

1. 5.956 + 1.714
2. 3.292 + 14.5

Subtracting Decimals To subtract decimals, line up the decimal points. Then subtract the same way you would with whole numbers. Bring the decimal point down in your answer.

   3.8
 − 1.5
   ↓
   2.3

EXAMPLE 3 Subtracting Decimals with the Same Number of Decimal Places

Subtract: 3.16 − 1.76

Solution

Write the decimals in a column, lining up the decimal points.

Subtract, regrouping if necessary. Bring the decimal point down. The final digit is a zero, so you can drop it.

ANSWER 1.4

> **Don't Forget**
> **Drop the final digit if it is a zero.** So, 1.40 becomes 1.4.

EXAMPLE 4 Subtracting Decimals with a Different Number of Decimal Places

Subtract: 9 − 5.375

Solution

   9
− 5.375

Write the numbers in a column. If one of the numbers is a whole number, line up the digits in the ones' place.

  9.000
− 5.375
   ↓
  3.625

Add a decimal point to the whole number and zeros to the right of the decimal point. Both numbers should have the same number of digits after the decimal point. Subtract, regrouping if necessary. Bring the decimal point down.

ANSWER 3.625

TRY THIS Subtract.

3. 4.116 − 2.004
4. 27.1 − 18.2
5. 16 − 0.578
6. 6.44 − 3.9

Math Intervention
Book 2 Fractions and Decimals

Name _____ Date _____

> **Summarize**
>
> **Adding Decimals**
> Write the decimals in a column, lining up the decimal points.
> Add zeros to the right of the decimal point if necessary. Add, bringing the decimal point down.
>
> 2.25 + 4.2
> 2.25
> + 4.20
> 6.45
>
> **Subtracting Decimals**
> Write the decimals in a column, lining up the decimal points.
> Add zeros to the right of the decimal point if necessary.
> Subtract, bringing the decimal point down.
>
> 7.8 − 1.82
> 7.80
> − 1.82
> 5.98

Practice

Match the addition statement with the sum.

1. 7.007 + 0.7 + 1.07 _____   A. 7.067
2. 7.107 + 0.07 + 0.6 _____   B. 7.777
3. 7.07 + 0.6 + 0.1 _____   C. 8.777
4. 7 + 0.06 + 0.007 _____   D. 7.77

Add.

5. 9.171 + 4.784   6. 4.78 + 0.25   7. 1.24 + 8.87
8. 14.7 + 22.4   9. 10.04 + 5.8   10. 0.009 + 2.48
11. 6.781 + 8   12. 1.785 + 4.2   13. 5.2 + 0.08

Match the subtraction statement with the difference.

14. 9.99 − 4.78 _____   E. 5.19
15. 9.909 − 4.181 _____   F. 5.21
16. 9.9 − 4.71 _____   G. 5.728

Subtract.

17. 8.359 − 3.128   18. 5.67 − 3.22   19. 2.5 − 0.2
20. 24.3 − 10.3   21. 58.4 − 2   22. 3.02 − 0.78
23. 11 − 4.77   24. 6.235 − 4.04   25. 4.5 − 2.12

Math Intervention
Book 2 Fractions and Decimals

Name _____ Date _____

Solve the problem. Explain your reasoning.

26. What is the difference in the lengths of the two desks?

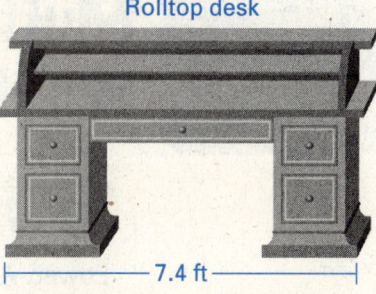

_____
_____
_____

27. You have $10.74. Your friend gives you $4.75. How much do you have now?

_____
_____
_____

28. Your driveway is **25.375** feet long. Your neighbor's driveway is **78.25** feet long. How much longer is your neighbor's driveway?

_____
_____
_____

DID YOU GET IT?

29. **Fill in the missing words.** To add or subtract decimals, you must write them in a column, lining up the _____ _____.

30. **Find the error.** Halley uses the method shown to add $12.14 + 1.03$. Is she correct? Why or why not?

$$\begin{array}{r} 12.14 \\ +\ 1.030 \\ \hline 2.244 \end{array}$$

_____
_____
_____

31. **Write a problem.** Write and solve a subtraction problem with decimals that have a different number of decimal places.

_____
_____
_____

Math Intervention
Book 2 Fractions and Decimals

LESSON 2-24: Multiply Decimals by Whole Numbers

> **Words to Remember**
>
> **Power:** An expression, such as 3^2, that represents a product with a repeated factor
>
> **Power of 10:** In a power of ten, the repeated factor is **10**. For example, $10^1 = 10 \times 1 = 10$ and $10^3 = 10 \times 10 \times 10 = 1000$. A number with **1** in the first place value followed by any number of zeros is a power of **10**.

Getting Started In Lessons 1-24 through 1-26 you learned how to multiply whole numbers. You can also multiply decimals by whole numbers.

Multiplying by Powers of Ten To multiply a decimal by a power of ten, first count the zeros in the power of ten. Then move the decimal point one place to the right for each zero.

$4.756 \times 100 = 475.6$

There are 2 zeros.   1 2

EXAMPLE 1 Multiplying Decimals by Powers of Ten

Multiply.

a. 0.1467×10 b. 4.3×1000

Solution

a. 0.1467×10 — Count the number of zeros in the power of ten.

There is 1 zero.

01.467 — Move the decimal point one place to the right for each zero in the power of ten.
1

1.467 — Drop the leftmost zero because the number is greater than 1.

ANSWER 1.467

b. 4.3×1000 — Count the number of zeros in the power of ten.

There are 3 zeros.

4.300 — Add zeros to the right of the decimal.

4300 — Move the decimal point one place to the right for each zero in the power of ten.
1 2 3

ANSWER 4300

Name _____   Date _____

TRY THIS Multiply.

1. 1.2 × 100

2. 0.007 × 10

Finding the Product of a Decimal and a Whole Number A *product* is the result of multiplying two numbers. A *factor* is one of the numbers being multiplied. The *product* of a decimal and a whole number has the same number of decimal places as the *decimal factor*.

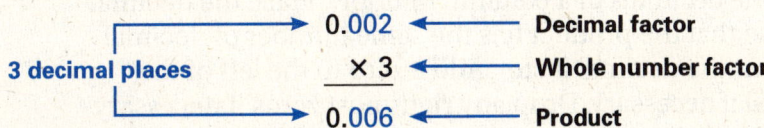

EXAMPLE 2 Multiplying a Decimal by a Whole Number

Multiply: 0.09 × 3

Solution

Step 1 Write the decimals in a column. You do not need to line up the decimal points or the ones' digits.

```
  0.09
×    3
    27
```

Step 2 Multiply as you would whole numbers.

Step 3 Decide how many decimal places are in the product. There are two decimal places in **0.09**. So, the product also needs two decimal places.

```
0.09
  12
```

Step 4 Count to the left from the rightmost digit of the product. Because **0.09** has two decimal places, count **2** digits to the left. Place the decimal point.

```
.27
 ʌʌ
 21
```

Step 5 Add a zero to the left of the decimal if necessary.   0.27

ANSWER 0.27

Remember
Drop any final zeros after you place the decimal point.
Example: 0.004 × 5 is 0.020, or 0.02.

TRY THIS Multiply.

3. 1.25 × 3

```
   1.25
×     3
```

____ decimal places

_____

4. 0.008 × 5

```
   0.008
×      5
```

____ decimal places

_____

Math Intervention
Book 2 Fractions and Decimals **101**

Name _____ Date _____

> **Summarize**
>
> **Multiplying a Decimal by a Power of Ten**
>
> Count the number of zeros in the power of ten. Add zeros to the right of the decimal if necessary. Move the decimal point one place to the right for each zero in the power of ten. Drop the leftmost zero if the product is greater than or equal to 1.
>
> $0.75 \times 1000 = 750$
>   1 2 3
>
> **Multiplying a Decimal by a Whole Number**
>
> Write the decimals in a column. Multiply. Place the decimal point so that the product has the same number of decimal places as the decimal factor. Add a zero to the left of the decimal if necessary. Drop any rightmost zeros if necessary.
>
> 1.5×2
>   1.5
> $\times\ 2$
>   30
>   3

Practice

Match the multiplication statement with the product.

1. 1000×14.487 _____   A. 0.06
2. 14.487×100 _____   B. 5.1
3. 8.01×4 _____   C. 32.04
4. 5×0.012 _____   D. 1448.7
5. 3×1.7 _____   E. 14,487

Multiply by a power of 10.

6. 4.729×10 7. 7.79×100 8. 12.5×10

9. 29.93×1000 10. 95.2×100 11. 144.03×10

12. 56.1×1000 13. 9.7913×1000 14. 8.4×100

Multiply.

15. 0.004×3 16. 0.08×14 17. 9×0.9

18. 0.016×5 19. 7×0.28 20. 4.5×8

21. 2×1.014 22. 1.343×6 23. 2.002×25

24. 5×2.24 25. 2.603×4 26. 32×0.005

27. 4.001×3 28. 12×2.306 29. 9×4.52

Math Intervention
Book 2 Fractions and Decimals

Name _____ Date _____

Solve the problem. Explain your reasoning.

30. One eraser costs **$.03**. How much does a pack of **100** erasers cost?

_____
_____
_____

31. The length across the spine of a reference book is **2.45** inches. If you place **8** of these books on a shelf side by side, what will the total length be?

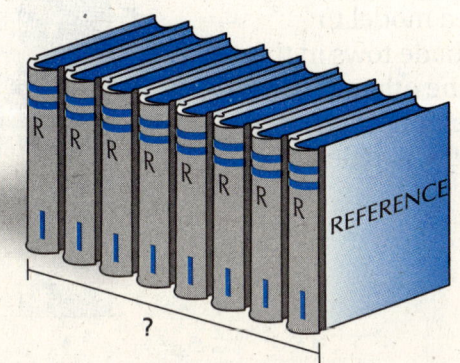

Spine = 2.45 in.

_____
_____
_____

32. One box of cereal weighs **0.8125** pound. If you put **30** boxes of this cereal in a crate, how much weight will the crate contain?

_____
_____
_____

DID YOU GET IT?

33. Fill in the missing words. When multiplying a decimal by a whole number power of ten, move the decimal point one place to the _____ for each _____ in the power of ten.

34. Find the error. Vladimir uses the method shown at the right to multiply **15.4 × 9**. Is he correct? Why or why not?

```
  15.4
×    9
─────
 1.386
```

_____
_____
_____

Math Intervention
Book 2 Fractions and Decimals **103**

Name _____ Date _____

Multiplying Decimals Using Models

Goal: Use area models to understand how to multiply decimals.

Getting Started You can use an area model to model multiplying decimals. Shade columns in the area model to represent one decimal. Shade rows in the area model to represent the other decimal. The squares that have the double shading represent the product of the two decimals.

$0.5 \times 0.3 = 0.15$

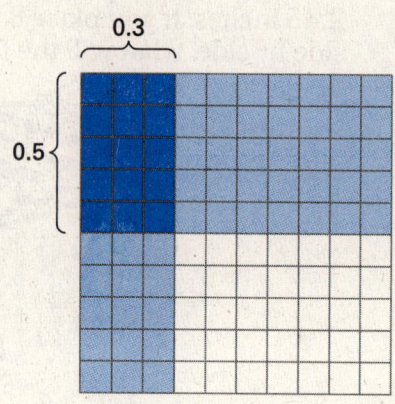

EXAMPLE

Use the following steps to model the product: 0.7×0.3

Step 1 Make a grid of 100 squares. The whole square represents 1. Each row and column of squares represents 0.1. Each small square represents 0.01.

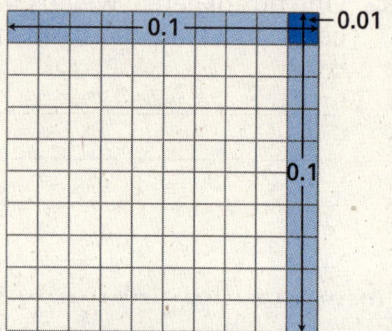

Step 2 Shade 7 rows of squares to represent 0.7. Then shade 3 columns to represent 0.3. There are 21 squares that have double shading.

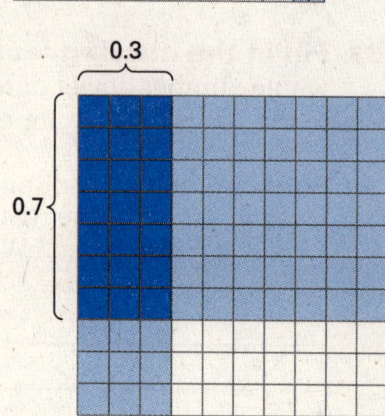

Step 3 Write the result.
$0.7 \times 0.3 = 0.21$

Math Intervention
Book 2 Fractions and Decimals

MAKE IT A GAME!

- Form groups of three students. Give each student two blank grids.
- In each group, have two students think of two different decimals between **0** and **0.9**.
- Have the third student model the product of the two decimals.
- Change roles within the group. Each student should get two chances to model a product.
- Tell the groups that each of their six collective products must be unique. The first group to accomplish this correctly wins.

First student says "**0.9**."

Second student says "**0.7**."

Third student models the product.

0.9 × 0.7 = 0.63

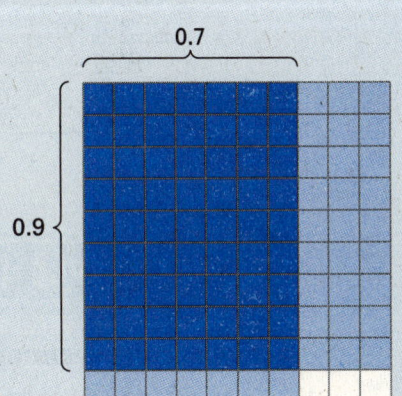

Practice

In Exercises 1 and 2, use models to multiply the decimals.

1. 0.4 × 0.4

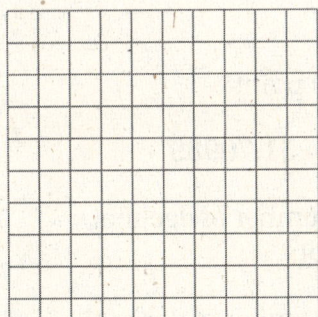

2. 0.9 × 0.5

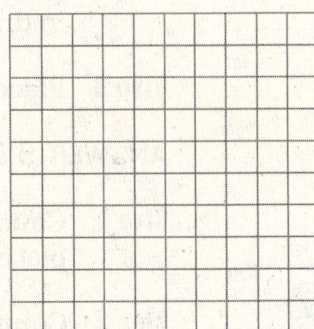

In Exercises 3–5, draw models to multiply the decimals. Then write the product.

3. 0.2 × 0.6
4. 0.4 × 0.3
5. 0.5 × 0.7

6. **Make a Conjecture** Based on your answers to Exercises 1–5, make a conjecture about how to multiply two decimals without using models.

LESSON 2-26 Multiply Decimals

Getting Started In Lesson 2-24 you learned how to multiply decimals by whole numbers. You can also multiply two decimals.

Multiplying Decimals To multiply decimals, write them in a column. Then multiply the same way you would whole numbers. Place the decimal point so that the product has the same number of decimal places as the total number of decimal places in the factors.

$$\begin{array}{r} 2.06 \\ \times\ 3.4 \\ \hline 824 \\ +\ 6180 \\ \hline 7.004 \end{array}$$

There are a total of 2 + 1 = 3 decimal places in the factors.

← There are 3 decimal places in the product.

EXAMPLE 1   Placing a Decimal Point in a Product

Place the decimal point in the product.

a. 9.523 × 5.43 = 5170989   b. 0.35 × 0.2 = 70

Solution

a. **Step 1** Count the total number of decimal places in the factors.

9.523 × 5.43 = 5170989
5 decimal places

Step 2 Count the same number of decimal places in the product that there are in the factors.

= 5170989

Step 3 Place the decimal point.

= 51.70989

ANSWER 9.523 × 5.43 = 51.70989

b. **Step 1** Count the total number of decimal places in the factors.

0.35 × 0.2 = 70
3 decimal places

Step 2 Count the same number of decimal places in the product that there are in the factors. Add zeros, if necessary.

= 0070

Step 3 Place the decimal point. Drop any rightmost zeros.

= 0.07

ANSWER 0.35 × 0.2 = 0.07

Using Zeros

Use rightmost zeros to help you place the decimal point correctly. Then drop any rightmost zeros in your final answer. So, 0.070 becomes 0.07.

Math Intervention
Book 2 Fractions and Decimals

Name _____ Date _____

EXAMPLE 2 Multiplying Decimals

Multiply.

a. 0.3×0.6 　　　　　　　　　　b. 0.04×0.15

Solution

a. **Step 1** Write the decimals in a column.

$$\begin{array}{r} 0.3 \\ \times\ 0.6 \\ \hline 18 \end{array}$$

Step 2 Multiply as you would whole numbers.

Step 3 Count the correct number of decimal places in the product. Place the decimal point. Add zeros to the left of the answer as needed.

0.18

Together, 0.3 and 0.6 have 2 decimal places.

ANSWER 0.18

CHECK your answer by thinking about fractions:
$0.3 \times 0.6 = 0.18$, because $\frac{3}{10} \times \frac{6}{10} = \frac{18}{100}$.

b.
$$\begin{array}{r} 0.15 \\ \times\ 0.04 \\ \hline 00060 \end{array}$$

The factors have a total of 4 decimal places. Add zeros to the left of the answer so that the decimal point can be placed correctly.

ANSWER 0.006

CHECK your answer by thinking about fractions:
$0.15 \times 0.04 = 0.0060$ or 0.006, because $\frac{15}{100} \times \frac{4}{100} = \frac{60}{10,000}$ or $\frac{6}{1000}$.

TRY THIS

Place the decimal point in the product.

1. $0.48 \times 0.5 = 240$ 　　　　　　　　2. $200.4 \times 10.26 = 2056104$

Multiply.

3. 0.7×0.08 　　　　　　　　4. 1.06×0.05

Name _____ Date _____

Summarize
Multiplying Decimals

(1) Multiply the same way you would whole numbers.

(2) Count the total number of decimal places in the factors.

(3) Moving from the right to the left, count the same number of zeros in the product that there are in the factors. Add zeros on the left of the product if necessary.

(4) Place the decimal point. Drop rightmost zeros in the final answer.

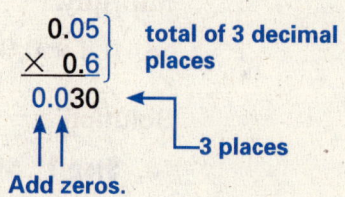

ANSWER 0.03

Practice

Place the decimal point in the product.

1. 1.24 × 0.08 = 992
2. 7.18 × 0.9 = 6462
3. 5.26 × 8.6 = 45236
4. 0.003 × 1.114 = 3342
5. 1.4 × 2.9 = 406
6. 3.75 × 0.6 = 2250
7. 4.28 × 0.05 = 2140
8. 123.1 × 2.45 = 301595

Match the multiplication sentence with the product that has the decimal point in the correct place.

9. 85.4 × 10.92 = 932568 _____
10. 8.54 × 1.092 = 932568 _____
11. 85.4 × 109.2 = 932568 _____
12. 8.54 × 10.92 = 932568 _____

A. 9.32568
B. 93.2568
C. 932.568
D. 9325.68

Multiply.

13. 0.14 × 0.2
14. 0.05 × 0.07
15. 0.4 × 0.009
16. 2.6 × 0.07
17. 18.5 × 0.2
18. 0.04 × 1.5
19. 0.24 × 2.4
20. 16.8 × 0.42
21. 36.03 × 1.3
22. 4.63 × 2.1
23. 5.08 × 0.36
24. 80.2 × 0.72
25. 412.9 × 0.011
26. 50.06 × 1.05
27. 9.344 × 7.8

Math Intervention
Book 2 Fractions and Decimals

Name _____ Date _____

Solve the problem. Explain your reasoning.

28. A machine that bottles lotion can pour **15.6** ounces of lotion in one minute. How many ounces can the machine pour in **8.5** minutes?

_____
_____
_____

29. Your kitten gains **0.6** pound in **1** month. At this rate, how much weight could the kitten gain in **4.25** months?

_____
_____
_____

30. You buy **0.75** pound of ground turkey priced at **$7.76** a pound. How much do you pay for the package of turkey?

_____
_____
_____

DID YOU GET IT?

31. Fill in the missing words. The product of two decimals has the same number of _____ _____ as the total number of _____ _____ in the factors.

32. Use a model. Use the model to multiply **0.6** by a decimal between **0** and **1** that has only one decimal place. Then write the product of the two decimals.

_____
_____

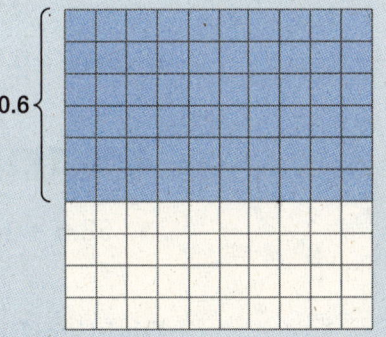

33. Explain your reasoning. When you multiply the digits of **3.45** and **7.2** you get **24840**. How do you write your final answer? Explain.

_____
_____
_____

LESSON 2-27 Divide Decimals by Whole Numbers

Getting Started In Lessons 1-28 through 1-30, you learned how to divide whole numbers by whole numbers. You can also divide decimals by whole numbers.

Dividing by Powers of Ten To divide a decimal by a power of ten, count the zeros in the power of ten. Then move the decimal point one place to the *left* for each zero. You may need to add zeros on the left of the answer to place the decimal correctly.

$$829.1 \div 100 = 8.291$$

There are 2 zeros.

EXAMPLE 1 Dividing Decimals by Powers of Ten

Divide: $9.457 \div 1000$

Solution

$9.457 \div 1000 = 0009457$ Count the zeros in the power of ten. There are 3. Count 3 place values to the left in the decimal. Add zeros as needed.

There are 3 zeros.

$= 0.009457$ Place the decimal point three places to the left.

ANSWER 0.009457

TRY THIS Divide.

1. $58.5 \div 100$
2. $467.72 \div 10$

Dividing Decimals by Whole Numbers To divide a decimal by a whole number, use long division. Bring the decimal point up from the dividend to the quotient, or answer.

```
              1.8   ← quotient
divisor → 2) 3.6   ← dividend
             -2
              16
             -16
               0
```

Math Intervention
Book 2 Fractions and Decimals

Name _____   Date _____

> ### EXAMPLE 2 Dividing Decimals by Whole Numbers
>
> **Divide:** $4.8 \div 8$
>
> **Solution**
>
> 0.6
> $8 \overline{)4.8}$
>
> Divide using long division. Bring the decimal point up from the dividend to the quotient.
>
> **ANSWER** 0.6
>
> ### TRY THIS Divide.
>
> **3.** $3.48 \div 3$ **4.** $3.927 \div 7$

Rounding a Decimal Quotient You may be asked to round your answer, or quotient, to the nearest tenth, hundredth, or thousandth. You learned how to round decimals in Lesson 2-19.

EXAMPLE 3 Rounding a Decimal Quotient

Divide $2.45 \div 5$. Round to the nearest tenth.

Solution

$$\begin{array}{r} 0.49 \\ 5\overline{)2.45} \\ -20 \\ \hline 45 \\ -45 \\ \hline 0 \end{array}$$

Divide using long division. Bring the decimal point up from the dividend to the quotient.

Round 0.49 to the nearest tenth. Since $9 > 5$, round 0.49 up to 0.5.

ANSWER 0.5

Using Zeros

If you are asked to round to the nearest hundredth but your answer only goes to the tenths' place, you do not need to add a 0 to the hundredths' place.

For example:

$1.6 \div 8 = 0.2$

Do not write 0.20 as the answer even if you were asked to round to the nearest hundredth.

TRY THIS

Divide. Round to the nearest hundredth.

5. $0.86 \div 4$ **6.** $12.5 \div 6$

Divide. Round to the nearest thousandth.

7. $6.15 \div 8$ **8.** $2.75 \div 5$

Name _____   Date _____

> **Summarize**
>
> **Dividing a Decimal by a Power of Ten**
>
> Count the number of zeros in the power of ten. Move the decimal point one place to the left for each zero in the power of ten. Add zeros before the number if they are needed to place the decimal correctly.
>
> $658.7 \div 100 = 6.587$
> $0.825 \div 100 = 0.00825$
> ↑ zeros added
>
> **Dividing a Decimal by a Whole Number**
>
> Use long division. Bring the decimal point up in the answer.
>
> $1.4 \div 2$
>
> ```
>   0.7
> 2)1.4
>  -1 4
>     0
> ```

Practice

Divide.

1. $114.5 \div 100$
2. $9.7 \div 10$
3. $2478.5 \div 100$
4. $0.6 \div 100$
5. $526.4 \div 1000$
6. $449.76 \div 10$
7. $91.8 \div 10$
8. $0.987 \div 1000$
9. $24.2 \div 1000$

Match the division statement with the correct quotient.

10. $68.2 \div 2$ _____   A. 2.4
11. $654.1 \div 10$ _____   B. 0.7
12. $3.5 \div 5$ _____   C. 0.6541
13. $65.41 \div 100$ _____   D. 65.41
14. $43.2 \div 18$ _____   E. 34.1

Divide. Round to the nearest hundredth.

15. $0.64 \div 8$
16. $4.5 \div 15$
17. $0.4 \div 4$
18. $1.23 \div 3$
19. $0.072 \div 9$
20. $19.4 \div 1000$
21. $0.406 \div 100$
22. $2.78 \div 10$
23. $17.52 \div 12$

Divide. Round to the nearest thousandth.

24. $68.509 \div 7$
25. $57.56 \div 100$
26. $0.825 \div 10$
27. $1.4375 \div 3$
28. $504.57 \div 11$
29. $23.364 \div 6$

Math Intervention
Book 2 Fractions and Decimals

Name _____ Date _____

Solve the problem. Explain your reasoning.

30. A sheet of paper is **8.5** inches wide. You fold the paper to divide it into **5** equal sections. What is the width of each section?

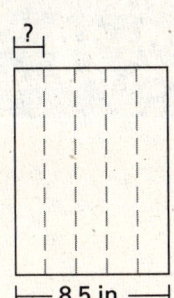

_____
_____
_____

31. A pack of **12** pencils costs **$.96**. How much does **1** pencil cost?

_____
_____
_____

32. You place **10** equal-sized sugar cubes on a metric scale and record a measurement of **16.7** grams. What is the mass of one of these sugar cubes?

_____
_____
_____

DID YOU GET IT?

33. **Fill in the missing words.** When dividing a decimal by a whole number power of ten, move the decimal point one place to the _____ for each _____ in the power of ten.

34. **Explain your reasoning.** Kayleigh uses the method shown at the right to divide $3.44 \div 2$. Is she correct? Why or why not?

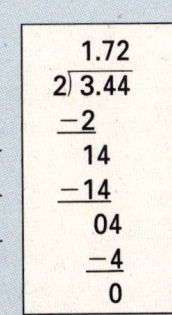

_____
_____
_____

Math Intervention
Book 2 Fractions and Decimals

Name _____ Date _____

LESSON 2-28 Divide by Decimals

Getting Started In Lesson 2-27, you learned how to divide decimals by whole numbers. You can also divide whole numbers by decimals and decimals by decimals.

Dividing by Decimals To divide by a decimal, change the decimal to a whole number. Do this by multiplying both the divisor and the dividend by a power of ten. This works because a division statement is also a fraction. Multiplying by the same number creates an equivalent fraction.

$$7.02 \div 5.4 = \frac{7.02}{5.4} \times \frac{10}{10} = \frac{70.2}{54} \text{ so } 5.4\overline{)7.02} \text{ is the same as } 54\overline{)70.2}.$$

EXAMPLE 1 Dividing by a Decimal

Divide.

a. $14.95 \div 6.5$ b. $1.68 \div 0.42$

Solution

a. **Step 1** Count the decimal places in the divisor. There is 1 decimal place, so you will multiply by 10.

$14.95 \div 6.5$
1 decimal place

Step 2 Multiply the divisor and dividend by 10.

$14.95 \div 6.5 = 149.5 \div 65$
Multiply by 10.

Step 3 Divide. Bring the decimal point up in the answer.

```
      2.3
65)149.5
    130
     195
     195
       0
```

b. **Step 1** Count the decimal places in the divisor. There are 2 decimal places, so you will multiply by 100.

$1.68 \div 0.42$
2 decimal places

Step 2 Multiply the divisor and dividend by 100. Drop the leftmost zero in the divisor.

$1.68 \div 0.42 = 168 \div 42$
Multiply by 100.

Step 3 Divide. Bring the decimal point up in the answer.

```
     4
42)168
   168
     0
```

TRY THIS Divide.

1. $2.52 \div 1.8$ 2. $0.72 \div 0.08$

Math Intervention
Book 2 Fractions and Decimals

Name _____   Date _____

Adding Zeros You will sometimes need to add zeros to the dividend when you multiply by a power of ten to make the divisor a whole number.

$$8.1 \div 0.09 = 8.10 \div 0.09 = 810 \div 9 \qquad \begin{array}{r} 90 \\ 9\overline{)810} \\ -81 \\ \hline 0 \end{array}$$

Multiply by 100.

EXAMPLE 2 Adding Zeros to Divide by a Decimal

Divide. Round to the nearest tenth.

a. $0.7 \div 0.005$
b. $95 \div 1.6$

Solution

a. $0.7 \div 0.005$
   3 decimal places

Count the decimal places in the divisor. There are 3 decimal places, so you will multiply by 1000.

$0.700 \div 0.005 = 700 \div 5$
Multiply by 1000.

Add 2 zeros to the right of the dividend. Multiply the divisor and dividend by 1000. Drop the leftmost zeros in the dividend and the divisor.

$$\begin{array}{r} 140 \\ 5\overline{)700} \\ 5 \\ \hline 20 \\ 20 \\ \hline 0 \end{array}$$

Divide. You do not need to round this answer.

ANSWER $0.7 \div 0.005 = 140$

b. $95 \div 1.6$
   1 decimal place

Count the decimal places in the divisor. There is 1 decimal place, so you will multiply by 10.

$950 \div 1.6 = 950 \div 16$
Multiply by 10.

Add 1 zero to the right of the dividend. Multiply the divisor and dividend by 10.

$$\begin{array}{r} 59.37 \\ 16\overline{)950.00} = 59.4 \\ 80 \\ \hline 150 \\ 144 \\ \hline 60 \\ 48 \\ \hline 120 \\ 112 \\ \hline 8 \end{array}$$

Divide. Because you should round to the nearest tenth, you can stop dividing when you reach the hundredths' place.

ANSWER To the nearest tenth, $95 \div 1.6 \approx 59.4$.

> **Whole Number Dividends**
>
> Notice that in part (b) you are dividing a whole number by a decimal. Even though the dividend is a whole number, you still need to multiply by a power of ten so that the divisor is a whole number.

TRY THIS Divide. Round to the nearest hundredth.

3. $4.6 \div 0.23$
4. $5.6 \div 0.007$
5. $3 \div 0.008$
6. $85 \div 6.4$

Name _____ Date _____

> **Summarize**
>
> **Dividing by a Decimal**
> Multiply both the divisor and the dividend by a power of ten so that the divisor is a whole number. Divide. Bring the decimal point up from the dividend to the quotient, or answer.
>
> $8.05 \div 1.4 \to 1.4\overline{)8.05} \to 14\overline{)80.5}$
> Multiply by 10.
>
> **Adding Zeros to Divide by a Decimal**
> When necessary, add zeros to the dividend when you are multiplying by a power of ten.
>
> $6 \div 0.15 \to 0.15\overline{)6} \to 15\overline{)600}$
> Add 2 zeros to 6 because it was multiplied by 100.

Practice

Match the equivalent division statements.

1. $6.96 \div 2.9$ _____   A. $29\overline{)6960}$
2. $0.696 \div 0.029$ _____   B. $29\overline{)69{,}600}$
3. $69.6 \div 0.29$ _____   C. $29\overline{)69.6}$
4. $6.96 \div 0.0029$ _____   D. $29\overline{)696}$

Divide. Round to the nearest tenth.

5. $1.05 \div 0.7$ 6. $0.072 \div 0.09$ 7. $1.96 \div 1.4$

8. $6.24 \div 2.08$ 9. $13.75 \div 1.9$ 10. $2.8 \div 2.3$

11. $0.245 \div 0.7$ 12. $0.114 \div 0.06$ 13. $4.12 \div 1.03$

14. $18.25 \div 3.65$ 15. $3.96 \div 1.7$ 16. $1.024 \div 3.04$

Divide.

17. $6 \div 2.4$ 18. $1.2 \div 0.15$ 19. $54 \div 1.2$

20. $36.5 \div 3.65$ 21. $0.09 \div 0.018$ 22. $5832 \div 9.72$

23. $12 \div 0.4$ 24. $285.6 \div 4.08$ 25. $279.6 \div 0.233$

26. $937.5 \div 6.25$ 27. $14.4 \div 0.24$ 28. $133.7 \div 3.82$

Math Intervention
Book 2 Fractions and Decimals

Name _____ Date _____

Solve the problem. Explain your reasoning.

29. Tim is setting up the course for a **9**-mile walk. He places a sign every **0.15** mile along the path. How many signs will Tim place?

_____
_____
_____

30. You have **$124.50** to divide equally among your employees. You give each employee **$12.45**. How many employees do you have?

_____
_____
_____

31. You spent **$150.94** on **31.25** shares of stock. What was the cost of each share?

_____
_____
_____

DID YOU GET IT?

32. **Fill in the missing words.** When dividing by a decimal, you need to rewrite the division statement so that the _____ is a _____ _____.

33. **Find the error.** Maddox uses the method shown at the right to divide 6 ÷ 0.15. Is he correct? Why or why not?

```
     0.40
15)6.00
   -6 0
      0
```

_____
_____

Math Intervention
Book 2 Fractions and Decimals

LESSON 2-29 Estimate with Decimals

Getting Started In Lessons 2-23, 2-26, and 2-28, you learned how to add, subtract, multiply, and divide with decimals. You can also estimate sums, differences, products, and quotients involving decimals.

Estimating with Decimals You have had practice rounding decimals. To estimate with decimals, the first step is often rounding each decimal to the nearest whole number.

EXAMPLE 1 Estimating a Sum or Difference

Estimate.

a. 3.29 + 1.18   b. 18.34 − 7.87   c. 2.7 + 5.98

Solution

a. 3.29 + 1.18

   3 + 1   Round to the nearest whole number.
   3 + 1 = 4   Add.

ANSWER 4

b. 18.34 − 7.87

   18 − 8   Round to the nearest whole number.
   18 − 8 = 10   Subtract.

ANSWER 10

c. 2.7 + 5.98

   3 + 6   Round to the nearest whole number.
   3 + 6 = 9   Add.

ANSWER 9

TRY THIS Estimate the sum or difference.

1. 4.57 + 1.2   2. 12.15 − 5.48

Name _____ Date _____

Checking for Reasonableness One use of estimation is to check if an answer is reasonable. To check whether the answer is reasonable, first round each decimal to the nearest whole number. Then perform the given operation on the rounded values—add, subtract, multiply, or divide. Finally, compare the rounded answer to the given answer.

EXAMPLE 2 Estimating a Product

Estimate to check the reasonableness of the given product:
$1.89 \times 6.13 = 11.5857$

Solution

$1.89 \times 6.13 = 11.5857$

$2 \times 6 = $ _____   Round to the nearest whole number.

$2 \times 6 = 12$ Multiply the rounded values.

12 is close to **11.5857**.   Compare the rounded answer to the given answer. If they are close, the answer is reasonable. If they are not close, the answer is not reasonable.

ANSWER The given product is reasonable.

EXAMPLE 3 Estimating a Quotient

Estimate to check the reasonableness of the given quotient:
$31.836 \div 3.79 = 10.2$

Solution

$31.83 \div 3.79 = 10.2$

$32 \div 4 = $ _____   Round to the nearest whole number.

$32 \div 4 = 8$ Divide.

8 is much less than **10.2**.   Compare the two quotients. If they are close, the answer is reasonable. If they are not close, the answer is not reasonable.

ANSWER The given quotient is *not* reasonable.

TRY THIS Estimate to check the reasonableness of the given product or quotient.

3. $7.86 \times 3.1 = 24.366$ **4.** $30.06 \div 5.32 = 5.65$

Math Intervention
Book 2 Fractions and Decimals

Name _____ Date _____

> **Summarize**
>
> **Estimating a Sum or Difference**
> Round each decimal to the nearest whole number. Then add or subtract the rounded values.
>
> 1.4 + 6.9 = ____
> 1 + 7 = 8
>
> 5.3 − 2.9 = ____
> 5 − 3 = 2
>
> **Estimating to Check for Reasonableness**
> Round each decimal to the nearest whole number. Then perform the given operation with the rounded values. Compare the rounded answer to the given answer. If the answers are close, the given answer is reasonable. If they are not close, the given answer is *not* reasonable.
>
> 1.8 × 8.2 = 18.76
> 2 × 8 = 16   18.76 is *not* reasonable.
>
> 8.295 ÷ 2.1 = 3.95
> 8 ÷ 2 = 4   3.95 is reasonable.

Practice

Match the given statement with its estimated answer.

1. 4.88 + 4.49 ____   A. 16

2. 19.58 − 3.78 ____   B. 9

3. 4.06 + 1.96 ____   C. 6

Estimate the sum or difference.

4. 3.25 + 8.06   5. 0.69 + 2.9   6. 16.54 − 12.36

7. 8.58 − 3.12   8. 57.95 + 14.95   9. 16.79 − 4.5

Estimate to check the reasonableness of the given sum or difference.

10. 9.45 + 11.87 = 21.32   11. 14.82 + 1.03 = 15.85

12. 5.07 + 7.39 = 14.46   13. 3.67 + 3.21 = 6.88

14. 2.04 + 10.75 = 10.79   15. 8.75 − 6.98 = 1.77

Estimate to check the reasonableness of the given product or quotient.

16. 4.71 × 7.39 = 28.8069   17. 2.38 × 2.65 = 6.307

18. 8.94 × 1.99 = 17.7906   19. 6.25 × 6.67 = 47.9375

20. 3.88 × 7.31 = 21.1988   21. 8.967 ÷ 2.94 = 3.05

22. 15.47 ÷ 4.76 = 3.25   23. 39.69 ÷ 2.02 = 25.65

Math Intervention

Name _____   Date _____

Solve the problem. Use estimation to prove that your answer is reasonable.

24. You have **$15** to spend on drinks and snacks. Do you have enough to buy **3** packs of grape juice and **2** packs of Sweet-and-Salty Mix?

Snacks	
Sweet-and-Salty Mix	$3.95
Pretzels	$1.98
Yogurt Raisins	$4.34
Drinks	
Grape Juice Pack	$2.97
Apple Juice Pack	$1.89
Tropical Pack	$2.51

_____
_____

25. Your mother gives you **40.4** yards of string to distribute evenly among the students in your science lab. You cut equal lengths that measure **5.05** yards each. Your mother assumes that you have **8** students in your science lab. Is she correct?

_____
_____
_____

26. You make **5.75** quarts of iced tea. You fill two **1.5**-quart containers. Do you have enough iced tea left to fill a **0.5**-quart container?

_____
_____
_____

DID YOU GET IT?

27. **Fill in the missing words.** To estimate a sum, first round each _____ to the nearest _____ _____.

28. **Explain your reasoning.** Roberto subtracts **12.78 − 5.94** to get **6.84**. Explain whether his answer is reasonable.

_____
_____

LESSON 2-30
Solve Problems with Decimals

Strategies to Remember

Sometimes a word problem may have too much or too little information:

| Sometimes the facts you are given are *more than you need* to solve a problem. | Other times necessary *facts may be missing*. |

EXAMPLE 1 Solving Problems with Missing Information

If possible, solve the problem. If it is not possible to solve, tell what additional information is needed.

Nathaniel has **$50.25**. He purchases **2 DVDs** for **$24.95** and a CD for **$7.20**.

a. How much money does he have left?

b. How much did each DVD cost?

Solution

Another Way
You can solve the problem a different way. Add the two purchases first. Then subtract that sum from $40.25.

a. **Step 1** **Identify** the operations needed. To find out how much Nathaniel has left, you need to subtract twice.

Step 2 **Calculate.** Subtract the first purchase: $50.25 - 24.95 = 25.30$
Subtract the second purchase: $25.30 - 7.20 = 18.10$

Step 3 **Check** for reasonableness: $50 - 25 = 25; 25 - 7 = 18$. The answer is reasonable.

ANSWER Nathaniel has **$18.10** left.

b. You know that the total cost of the 2 DVDS is **$24.95**, but you are given no information about each DVD individually. So, you don't have enough information to solve this part of the problem.

TRY THIS Fill in the missing information to solve the problem, if possible.

1. Kathy has **$104.29** in the bank. She deposits **$25.60** on Tuesday and **$15.14** on Thursday. How much does she have in the bank on Saturday?

Step 1 You need to _____ twice.

Step 2 Calculate: ▇ + ▇ = ▇   ▇ + ▇ = ▇

Step 3 She has _____ in the bank after she makes the deposit on Thursday. The problem does not give enough information to determine the amount in the account on Saturday.

Math Intervention
Book 2 Fractions and Decimals

Name _____ Date _____

> **EXAMPLE 2** Solving Problems with Extra Information

Solve the problem, if possible. Identify any missing or extra information.

A deli sells turkey for **$7.26** a pound. You buy **10** deli rolls and **3** bags of turkey, each weighing **0.25** pound. How much do you pay for the turkey?

Solution

Step 1 **Identify** the operations needed. Multiply **7.26** by **0.25** to find the cost of **1** bag. Multiply this result by **3** to find the total amount you pay.

Step 2 **Calculate.** Multiply to find the cost of 1 bag: **7.26 × 0.25 = 1.815**
Multiply to find the cost of 3 bags: **1.815 × 3 = 5.445**

Step 3 **Check** for reasonableness. It does not make sense to pay **$5.445**. Round to the nearest hundredths place, or the nearest cent.

ANSWER You pay **$5.45** for the turkey. The information about buying deli rolls was extra. It was not needed to solve the problem.

> **EXAMPLE 3** Solving Problems Using Different Operations

Solve the problem, if possible. Identify any missing or extra information.

A single container of vanilla yogurt costs **$.54**. A grocery store sells a pack of **6** containers for **$3.75**. How much profit does the store make on each six-pack?

Solution

Step 1 **Identify** the operations needed. Multiply **0.54** by **6** to find the cost of a six-pack. Then subtract this amount from **$3.75** to find the profit.

Step 2 **Calculate.** Multiply to find the true cost of 6 containers: **0.54 × 6 = 3.24**
Subtract to find the store's profit: **3.75 − 3.24 = 0.51**

Step 3 **Check** for reasonableness by estimating. At **$.50**, a pack of 6 yogurts costs **$3.00**. If the store charges **$3.75**, they make about **$.75** a pack. The actual answer should be a little lower, so **$.51** is reasonable.

ANSWER The store makes **$.51** on each six-pack of yogurt. All of the information given in the problem was necessary.

TRY THIS Solve the problem, if possible. Explain your reasoning.

2. You work at the library for **$8.12** an hour. Last week you worked **2.5** hours every day for **5** days. How much did you earn? Which days did you work?

_____

_____

Math Intervention
Book 2 Fractions and Decimals

Name _____ Date _____

> **Summarize**
>
> **Solving Word Problems**
> (1) Identify the operation or operations needed.
> (2) Decide whether there is enough information given to solve the problem, or if extra information was provided.
> (3) Perform the calculations to solve the problem, if possible.
> (4) Check your answer for reasonableness.

Practice

Read the problem. Number the steps of the solution to put them in order.

1. A puppy weighs **1.13** pounds. The puppy gains **0.38** pound the first week and **0.44** pound the second week. How much does the puppy weigh after **2** weeks?

   SOLUTION: ____ add: 1.51 + 0.44   ____ add: 1.13 + 0.38

2. A vendor sells raisin mix for **$.29** per ounce. You pay for the raisin mix with a **$10** bill and get **$5.94** in change. How many ounces did you buy?

   SOLUTION: ____ subtract: 10 − 5.94   ____ divide: 4.06 ÷ 0.29

Identify the operation suggested by the phrase.

3. 5 pounds at $1.99 per pound

4. 0.3 liters less than yesterday

5. 1 can at $2.50 for 3 cans

6. Fill in the missing information to solve the problem, if possible. Identify any extra or missing information.

   This morning, Gaby had **$40.50**. She spent **$5.52** on lunch and gave **$2.75** to a friend. Tomorrow, she will be paid **$22.00** for yard clean-up. How much does Gaby have now? What is her hourly pay for yard clean-up?

   a. **Step 1** To find out how much Gaby has now, you need to _____ twice.

      Step 2 Calculate: 40.50 ⬤ 5.52 = ▭   ▭ ⬤ 2.75 = ▭

      Step 3 Gaby has _____ now.

      Step 4 The information about what Gaby will be paid tomorrow _____ (was/was not) needed to decide how much she has now.

   b. The amount Gaby will be paid tomorrow is _____. No information is given about the number of _____ she works. So, the hourly pay _____ (can/cannot) be determined.

Math Intervention
Book 2 Fractions and Decimals

Name _____   Date _____

First identify the operation(s) needed to find the answer. Then solve the problem, if possible. Explain your reasoning.

7. A **2.5**-pound bag of rye flour costs **$1.95**. A **4.5**-pound bag of rye flour costs **$3.25**. A **5**-pound bag of white flour costs **$1.95**. Which size bag of rye flour is the better buy?

   _____
   _____
   _____

8. At a garage sale, you mark two boxes as shown to the right. Someone buys **3** items from Box A and **2** items from Box B. How much do you earn from this sale?

    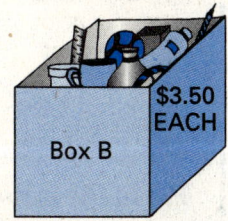

   _____
   _____
   _____

9. Karl makes **$11.15** an hour at a karate school. In April, he worked a total of **8** days for **3.5** hours each day. During the month, he spent part of his earnings. How much did Karl have left at the end of the month?

   _____
   _____

DID YOU GET IT?

10. **Write a word problem.** Write a word problem using the order of the calculations at the right.

    Step 1: $1.50 + $3.40 = $4.90
    Step 2: $4.90 − $.79 = $4.11

    _____
    _____

11. **Explain your reasoning.** Your friend says that the answer to the following problem is **$17.00**. Is your friend's answer reasonable? Explain why or why not.

    A store sells puzzle books for **$.85** each and pencils for **$.19** each. Jerry buys **1** pencil and **3** books. He gives the cashier **$20**. How much change should he get?

    _____
    _____
    _____

Mixed Practice for Lessons 2-23 to 2-30

Vocabulary Review

Match the word with its definition.

Word		Definition
1. dividend	_____	A. a number that is to be divided
2. product	_____	B. an expression that represents a repeated factor
3. power	_____	C. a result of multiplying

Fill in the missing word(s).

4. In the multiplication statement 5.89×0.4, there are a total of three _____ _____ in the factors.

5. To divide by a decimal, multiply the divisor and the dividend by a _____ _____ _____ so that the divisor is a _____ _____.

Shade in the models below to find the product of the decimals.

6. 0.6×0.4 _____

7. 0.5×0.5 _____

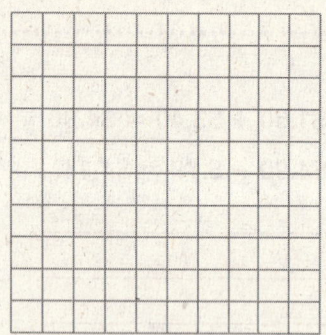
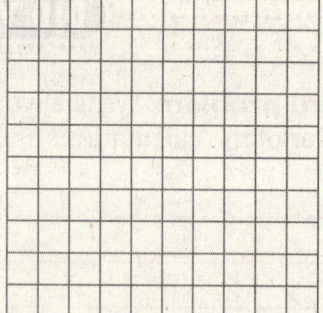

Add, subtract, multiply, or divide.

8. $3.36 \div 4$
9. $0.56 - 0.04$
10. $1.25 + 4.4$

11. 7.542×100
12. $1.487 + 0.3$
13. 0.009×2

14. $4.5 - 2.78$
15. $16.8 \div 16$
16. 6.009×8

17. $0.489 \div 10$
18. $2.9 + 7.972$
19. $21.492 - 6.51$

Math Intervention
Book 2 Fractions and Decimals

Name _____ Date _____

20. Fill in the missing information to solve the problem.

Sam works at an internet catalog company. A batch of orders has a total file size of **575.52** kilobytes. Each order has a file size of **47.96** kilobytes. How many orders are in the batch?

Step 1 You are given the total file size of the batch and the size of each order in the batch. To find the number of orders in the batch, you need to _____ .

Step 2 Calculate: 575.52 ◯ 47.96 = ▭ .

Step 3 There were ▭ orders in the batch.

Step 4 My answer is reasonable because _____ .

Add, subtract, multiply, or divide.

21. 58.43 + 12 **22.** 9.7 − 5 **23.** 0.8 × 0.14 **24.** 0.85 ÷ 1.7

25. 3.48 × 5.7 **26.** 144.78 + 0.7 **27.** 59.22 ÷ 6.3 **28.** 0.98 − 0.0487

Estimate the sum, difference, product, or quotient.

29. 27.3 − 7.4 **30.** 35.7 ÷ 4.2 **31.** 2.43 + 4.58 **32.** 8.4 × 2.86

33. 9.44 ÷ 3.2 **34.** 9.2 × 6.89 **35.** 3.62 + 7.43 **36.** 5.7 − 2.847

Solve the problem, if possible. Identify any extra or missing information. Explain your reasoning.

37. You place several apples on a digital scale. The scale reads **3.48** lb. When you remove a large apple, the reading changes to the amount shown. How much does the large apple weigh? How much does the smallest apple weigh?

_____
_____
_____

38. Last week the manager at a printing company bought **200.65** ounces of ink at **$1.40** an ounce. On average the printing company buys ink every **5** weeks. How much did the manager spend on the ink last week?

_____
_____
_____

McDougal Littell

Math Intervention

Book 3:
Integers and Rational Numbers

McDougal Littell
A DIVISION OF HOUGHTON MIFFLIN COMPANY
Evanston, Illinois • Boston • Dallas

Cover photo © Galina Barskaya/iStock International, Inc.

Illustrations George Barile/McDougal Littell/Houghton Mifflin Company and John Evans/McDougal Littell/Houghton Mifflin Company

Copyright © 2008 by McDougal Littell, a division of Houghton Mifflin Company.
All rights reserved.

Permission is hereby granted to teachers to reprint or photocopy in classroom quantities the pages or sheets in this work that carry a McDougal Littell copyright notice. These pages are designed to be reproduced by teachers for use in their classes with accompanying McDougal Littell material, provided each copy made shows the copyright notice. Such copies may not be sold and further distribution is expressly prohibited. Except as authorized above, prior written permission must be obtained from McDougal Littell, a division of Houghton Mifflin Company, to reproduce or transmit this work or portions thereof in any other form or by any other electronic or mechanical means, including any information storage or retrieval system, unless expressly permitted by federal copyright laws. Address inquiries to, Supervisor, Rights and Permissions, McDougal Littell, P.O. Box 1667, Evanston, IL 60204.

ISBN-13: 978-0-618-90060-2
ISBN-10: 0-618-90060-8

123456789—PBO—11 10 09 08 07

Book 3: Integers and Rational Numbers

Basic Concepts

Lesson 3-1	Integers and the Number Line	2
Lesson 3-2	Opposites and Absolute Value	6
Lesson 3-3	Compare and Order Integers	10
Lesson 3-4	Rational Numbers	14
Lesson 3-5	Compare and Order Rational Numbers	18
	Mixed Practice for Lessons 3-1 to 3-5	22

Operations with Integers and Rational Numbers

Activity 3-6	Adding Integers Using Models	24
Lesson 3-7	Add Integers	26
Lesson 3-8	Subtract Integers	30
Lesson 3-9	Multiply Integers	34
Lesson 3-10	Divide Integers	38
Lesson 3-11	Solve Problems with Integers	42
Lesson 3-12	Rational Number Operations	46
Lesson 3-13	Take Rational Numbers to Whole-Number Powers	50
	Mixed Practice for Lessons 3-7 to 3-13	54

McDougal Littell

Math Intervention

MATH INTERVENTION

- The Math Intervention program includes skill lessons, problem solving lessons, activities, and mixed practice materials covering a wide range of mathematical topics that are needed for success in middle school and high school mathematics.

- There are seven books in the Math Intervention program. Book 3 contains materials on Integer and Rational Number concepts and operations.

- In the Math Intervention books, lessons include worked-out Examples and Try this exercises to help you build understanding of a topic. The Practice section includes a variety of problems to give you the practice you need to develop your math skills. The Did You Get It? section checks your understanding of the lesson.

- Problem solving lessons suggest strategies for approaching real-world problem solving situations and promote the use of estimation to check reasonableness of solutions.

- Activities build your understanding of a topic through the use of models and games.

- Mixed Practice sections include practice of vocabulary, skills, and problem solving methods covering the material in a group of lessons.

- You may complete the work in selected lessons, or cover the book as a whole, as directed by your teacher.

LESSON 3-1: Integers and the Number Line

> **Words to Remember**
>
> *Integer*: Any positive whole number, the opposite of any positive whole number, or zero   −18, −5, 0, 4, 122
>
> *Negative integer*: Any integer that is less than 0   −357, −42, −3
>
> *Positive integer*: Any integer greater than 0   1, 39, 422

Getting Started Previously you learned what whole numbers are and how to graph them on a number line. You can also place integers on a number line. On a number line positive integers are to the right of **0** and negative integers are to the left of **0**.

EXAMPLE 1 Identifying Integers

Identify the integers in the following list.

$3.3, -17, 22, 72\frac{1}{5}$

Solution

3.3 is not an integer since it contains a number after a decimal point.

−17 is an integer since it is the opposite of a positive whole number.

22 is an integer since it is a whole number.

$72\frac{1}{5}$ is not an integer since it contains a fraction, which is not a whole number.

> **Look Ahead**
>
> For more on *opposites*, see Lesson 3-2 on page 6.

TRY THIS

1. Circle the integers in the following list.

   $92, -100.66, \frac{3}{8}, 455, -672$

2. Circle the negative integers in the following list.

   $12, -15, \frac{5}{9}, -2.5, -19, 28.75$

EXAMPLE 2 Graphing Integers on a Number Line

Place the integers −3, 4, 1, and −2 on the number line.

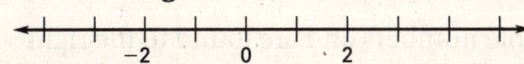

Solution

Step 1 Determine whether each number lies to the right or to the left of **0**.

Negative integers lie to the *left* of **0**: −3 and −2.

Positive integers lie to the *right* of **0**: 4 and 1.

Step 2 Place each integer on the number line.

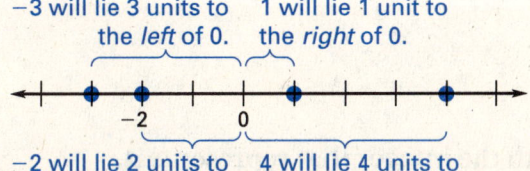

EXAMPLE 3 Modeling a Situation

The high temperature on Monday in San Francisco was 83°F. The high temperature on Tuesday was 72°F. Represent the change in high temperatures from Monday to Tuesday using an integer.

Solution

Step 1 Find the change in temperature from Monday to Tuesday. $83 - 72 = 11°F$

Step 2 Determine whether the temperature change should be positive or negative.

Since the temperature decreased, the sign should be *negative*.

ANSWER The high temperature change was **−11°F**.

TRY THIS

3. Place −1, −4, and 3 on the number line.

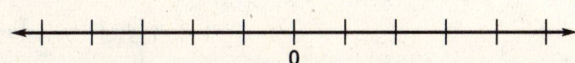

4. Manuel has a piece of ribbon 63 inches long. After removing some of the ribbon for a project, the ribbon is now 44 inches long. Use an integer to represent the change in the length of the ribbon.

Name _____   Date _____

> **Summarize**
>
> An integer is a positive whole number, the opposite of a positive whole number, or zero.
>
> Positive integers are positive whole numbers and are found to the right of zero on a number line.
>
> Negative integers are opposites of positive whole numbers and are found to the left of zero on a number line.
>
> **Modeling Situations with Integers**
>
> Real-world situations can be modeled by integers. When the situation represents a decrease, use a negative integer to describe it. When the situation represents an increase, use a positive integer to describe it.

Practice

Match the description with the integer that represents it.

1. An increase of 11 points _____   A. -30 ft

2. A decrease of 11 points _____   B. 11 points

3. A decrease of 30 feet _____   C. -11 points

4. An increase of 30 feet _____   D. 30 ft

Circle the integers.

5. $-\frac{4}{5}$, 99, 122.55, -37, 14   6. 100.1, 0.5, $45\frac{6}{7}$, -1055, 7

7. 676, -932.9, 12, $\frac{17}{43}$ 8. -15, $-68\frac{33}{51}$, 55.17, $\frac{3}{4}$

9. -722.1, -1434, $222\frac{3}{4}$, 0   10. 10,922, 3.46, -5

Place the integers on a number line.

11. $-1, 0, 2, -5$ 12. $-6, -1, 1, -4$

13. $-2, 3, 5, 6$ 14. $-10, 4, 6, -4$

15. $12, 5, 0, -2$ 16. $-13, 12, 8, -4$

Math Intervention
Book 3 Integers and Rational Numbers

Name _____ Date _____

Tell if the situation represents an *increase* or a *decrease*. Then represent the amount of the increase or decrease by an integer.

17. Karla has **$20** to spend at a jewelry store. After buying a bracelet she has **$6** remaining.

_____

18. Hannah is building a tower of blocks with her younger brother. They currently have **14** blocks stacked in their tower. After her younger brother knocks over the tower there are **4** blocks left standing.

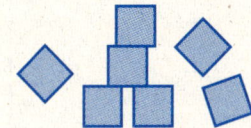

_____

19. Jesse is filling an empty bucket with water. After he fills the bucket there are **3** gallons of water in it.

_____

20. You and a friend order a pizza that has **10** slices in it. After you and your friend finish eating, there are **4** slices remaining.

_____

DID YOU GET IT?

21. Fill in the missing words. To place integers on a number line, graph _____ to the right of zero and graph _____ to the left of zero.

22. Explain your reasoning. What kinds of numbers are integers?

_____
_____
_____

23. Describe. Give an example of a real-life increase and an example of a real-life decrease that can be described by integers. Explain your thinking.

_____
_____
_____

Math Intervention
Book 3 Integers and Rational Numbers

Name _____   Date _____

LESSON 3-2 Opposites and Absolute Value

Words to Remember

Opposites: Two numbers that are the same distance from **0** on a number line, but on opposite sides of **0**

7 and −7 are opposites.
9 and −9 are opposites.

Absolute value of a number: The distance a number is from **0** on a number line.

Remember that distance is always a positive quantity (or zero). Show absolute value with vertical bars on each side of the number, for example |17|.

Getting Started In Lesson 3-1 you learned how to place integers on a number line. Now you will find the distance between a point and zero on the number line to find the *opposite* of a number or the *absolute value* of a number.

EXAMPLE 1   Finding the Opposite of an Integer

Use a number line to find the opposite of 3.

Solution

Step 1 Place **3** on a number line.

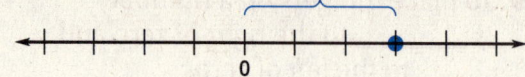

Step 2 Determine how far **3** is from **0**.   3 is 3 units to the right of 0.

Step 3 Find the opposite of **3**. The opposite of a number must be the same distance from **0** as the original number, but in the opposite direction. So, the opposite of **3** must be 3 units to the left of **0**, or at −**3**.

ANSWER The opposite of 3 is −3.

TRY THIS Use a number line to find the opposite of the number.

1. 4   2. −2

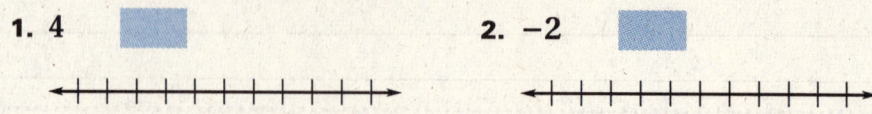

EXAMPLE 2 Finding the Absolute Value of an Integer

Use a number line to find $|-2|$.

Solution

The absolute value of a number is the distance the number is from 0.

Step 1 Graph -2 on a number line.

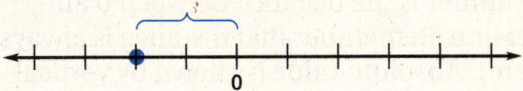

Step 2 Determine how far -2 is from 0. -2 is 2 units to the left of 0.

ANSWER The absolute value of -2 must be 2 because distances are always positive (or 0).

EXAMPLE 3 Finding the Opposite and Absolute Value of an Integer

Use a number line to find the opposite of 4 and to find $|4|$.

Solution

Step 1 Place 4 on a number line.

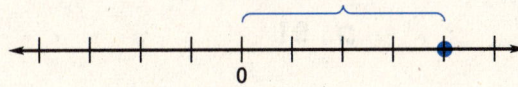

Step 2 Determine how far 4 is from 0.   4 is 4 units to the right of 0.

Step 3 The opposite of 4 must be the same distance from 0 but in the opposite direction. So, the opposite of 4 is -4. The absolute value of 4 must be 4 because distances are always positive (or 0).

ANSWER The opposite of 4 is -4, and $|4| = 4$.

TRY THIS Use a number line to evaluate the expression.

3. $|7| = \boxed{}$

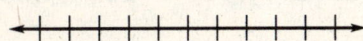

4. The opposite of $-6 = \boxed{}$ and $|-6| = \boxed{}$.

Name _____ Date _____

> **Summarize**
>
> **Opposite**
>
> The *opposite* of a number is a number that is the same distance from zero on a number line as the given number, but on the opposite side of zero.
>
> **Absolute Value**
>
> The *absolute value* of a number is the distance between **0** and the number on a number line. Remember that distance is always a positive quantity (or zero). Absolute value is shown by vertical bars on each side of the number.

Practice

Match the description with the number that represents it. You may use some answer choices more than once or not at all.

1. Opposite of 19 _____   A. -19
2. $|91|$ _____   B. 19
3. $|-19|$ _____   C. -91
4. Opposite of -91 _____   D. 91

Evaluate the expression.

5. Opposite of -7
6. Opposite of 6
7. $|-9|$

8. Opposite of -2
9. $|1|$
10. Opposite of 28

11. Opposite of 44
12. $|-199|$
13. Opposite of -50

14. $|0|$
15. $|-762|$
16. Opposite of 10

17. $|78|$
18. Opposite of 92
19. Opposite of -31

20. Opposite of -74
21. Opposite of 936
22. $|-302|$

23. $|-4002|$
24. Opposite of 76
25. $-|668|$

26. Opposite of 65
27. Opposite of -32
28. $-|-8701|$

Math Intervention
Book 3 Integers and Rational Numbers

Name _____ Date _____

Read and solve the problem. Then explain your answer.

29. Simone told you that she placed a point on a number line that had an absolute value of 15. At what two numbers could she have graphed her point?

_____
_____
_____

30. Julia and Roberto are each holding cards with integers on them. One has a positive integer and the other has a negative integer. The teacher has put a number line on the floor using tape and asks Julia and Roberto to stand on the points that represent their numbers. How can they determine if their numbers are opposites without showing each other their cards?

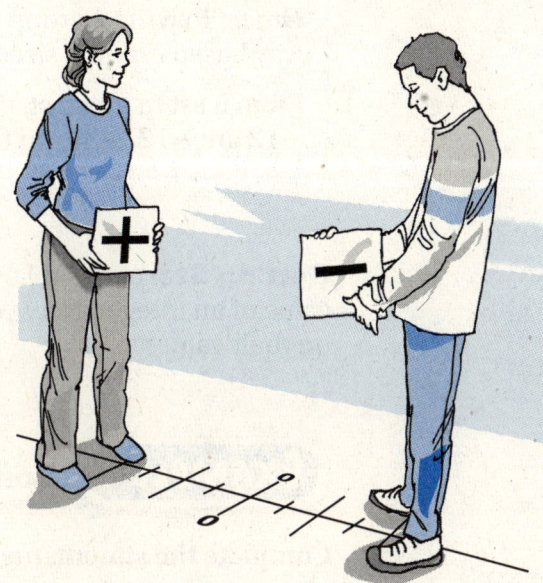

_____
_____
_____

DID YOU GET IT?

31. **Fill in the missing words.** The _____ of a number is the distance between _____ and the number on a number line.

32. **Explain your reasoning.** What is the opposite of the opposite of −3?

_____

33. **Explain your reasoning.** How are the opposite of a number and the absolute value of a number alike? How are they different?

_____
_____
_____
_____

Name _____   Date _____

LESSON 3-3: Compare and Order Integers

> **Words to Remember**
>
> *Compare*: To relate two or more numbers based on their sizes
>
> $-9 < 0;\ -4 > -5$
>
> *Order*: To write a group of numbers in a particular way based on their sizes
>
> From least to greatest, the numbers -3, 6, and -12 are -12, -3, and 6.

Getting Started In Lesson 3-2 you learned how to find the absolute value of an integer. Now you will learn how to order several integers based on their values.

EXAMPLE 1 Comparing Integers

Complete the statements with <, >, or =.

a. -4 2 b. -1 -5

Solution

Step 1 Place the points on a number line.

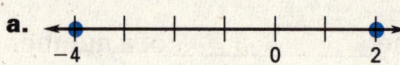 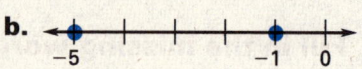

Step 2 Find the integers farthest to the right.

a. 2 is greater than -4 b. -1 is greater than -5

Step 3 Insert the correct inequality sign.

The inequality symbol should open towards the greater integer.

a. $-4\ <\ 2$ b. $-1\ >\ -5$

TRY THIS Complete the statement with <, >, or =.

1. 4 ⬤ -4 2. -7 ⬤ 0

Math Intervention
Book 3 Integers and Rational Numbers

Name _____ Date _____

EXAMPLE 2 Ordering Integers Using a Number Line

Use a number line to order the integers from least to greatest.

4, −5, 3, 0, −2

Solution

Step 1 Place the points on a number line.

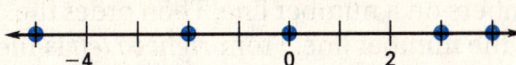

Step 2 Order the integers. Least to greatest is left to right.

−5, −2, 0, 3, 4

EXAMPLE 3 Ordering Integers

Order the integers from greatest to least.

−3, −5, 1, 4, −2

Solution

Step 1 Place the points on a number line.

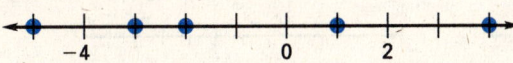

Step 2 Order the integers. Greatest to least is right to left.

4, 1, −2, −3, −5

TRY THIS Order the integers.

3. Least to greatest: 3, −7, 8, −1

4. Greatest to least: −6, 8, 4, −3

Math Intervention
Book 3 Integers and Rational Numbers **11**

Name _____   Date _____

> **Summarize**
>
> **Ordering Integers from Least to Greatest**
>
> Begin by placing the integers on a number line. Then order the points as they appear on the number line. From *left to right* is the order of the integers from *least to greatest*.
>
> **Ordering Integers from Greatest to Least**
>
> Begin by placing the numbers on a number line. Then order the points as they appear on the number line. From *right to left* is the order of the integers from *greatest to least*.

Practice

Use the number line to order the integers from greatest to least.

1. 9, −7, 4, 1, −2
2. 3, 10, −7, 6, −8
3. −12, −6, 4, 0, 1

4. 10, 5, −3, −5, 11
5. −2, −14, −8, −1, −6
6. 0, −13, −25, −11, −22

Use the number line to order the integers from least to greatest.

7. 8, −2, 0, −4, 3
8. −3, 4, 10, −10, 0
9. 8, −8, 0, 7, −7

10. −4, −2, −10, 8, 4
11. 0, −15, −22, 19, −14
12. −18, −20, −2, −30, −13

Name _____ Date _____

Read the problem and answer the questions.

13. Morgan and Mackenzie are comparing their hair length to their friend Jenna's hair length. Morgan states that her hair is +3 inches compared to Jenna's hair and Mackenzie states that her hair is −2 inches compared to Jenna's hair. Who has the shortest hair? Write the girls' names in order of their hair length from shortest to longest.

   _____
   _____
   _____

14. The average temperatures during the winter months in a city are −12°F, 10°F, −2°F, 5°F, and −3°F. What is the order of the temperatures from greatest to least?

   _____
   _____

15. Paige, Amber, and Bailey are running around a track to see how their times compare with the school record. Paige ran −2 seconds as compared to the record, Amber ran +6 seconds as compared to the school record, and Bailey ran +4 seconds as compared to the school record. Who had the fastest time? Write the girls' names in order from fastest to slowest.

   _____
   _____

DID YOU GET IT?

16. **Fill in the missing words.** To order integers from greatest to least using a number line, the greatest integer appears farthest to the _____ and the least integer appears farthest to the _____.

17. **Compare.** How can you compare a positive integer to a negative integer?

   _____
   _____

Name _____ Date _____

LESSON 3-4: Rational Numbers

Words to Remember

Rational number: Any number that can be written as the quotient of two integers when the denominator is not zero. The rational numbers include integers, positive and negative fractions and mixed numbers, and positive and negative terminating or repeating decimals.

Decimals that do not terminate or repeat are not rational numbers.

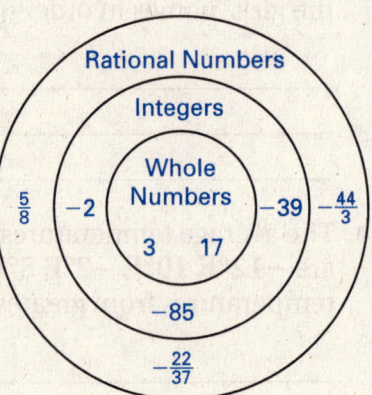

Getting Started In Lesson 3-1 you identified and placed integers on a number line. Now you will identify and graph rational numbers on a number line.

Look Ahead

In a later course you will learn how to write repeating decimals as quotients.
$0.\overline{3} = \frac{1}{3}$, so
$3.\overline{3} = 3\frac{1}{3} = \frac{10}{3}$.
$3.\overline{3}$ is a rational number.

EXAMPLE 1 Writing Integers as Quotients

Show that -3 is a rational number.

Solution

Write -3 as a quotient of integers.

$$-3 = -3 \div 1 = \frac{-3}{1} = -\frac{3}{1} \checkmark$$

EXAMPLE 2 Identifying Rational Numbers

Which numbers listed below are rational numbers?

$-22, \ 0.2, \ 3.4927\ldots, \ 3.\overline{3}$

Solution

-22 is a rational number. It can be written as $-\frac{22}{1}$.

0.2 is a rational number. It can be written as $\frac{2}{10} = \frac{1}{5}$.

$3.4927\ldots$ is not a rational number. The decimal does not terminate or repeat.

$3.\overline{3}$ is a rational number. It is a repeating decimal.

Math Intervention
Book 3 Integers and Rational Numbers

Name _____ Date _____

TRY THIS Circle the rational numbers.

1. $58, 1.77, 3.303003...$
2. $-12.1, 0, 5.\overline{6}$

EXAMPLE 3 Graphing Rational Numbers on a Number Line

Place the rational numbers on a number line.

$$-3.2, 4, \frac{7}{4}, -0.\overline{3}$$

Solution

Step 1 **Identify** any numbers that are not integers. Determine between which two integers they fall.

-3.2 falls between -3 and -4.

4 will be placed on 4.

$\frac{7}{4} = 1.75$ and falls between 1 and 2.

$-0.\overline{3}$ falls between 0 and -1.

Step 2 **Determine** approximately where between the integers you found in Step 1 the rational number should be placed. Then graph the number.

-3.2 lies closer to -3 than to -4.

4 should be placed on 4.

$\frac{7}{4} = 1.75$, which lies closer to 2 than to 1.

$-0.\overline{3}$ lies closer to 0 than to -1.

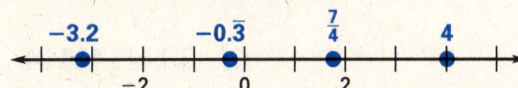

TRY THIS Graph the rational numbers on a number line.

3. $\frac{6}{5}, -2.4, 3\frac{1}{2}$

$\frac{6}{5} = $ ▢, which lies closer to ▢ than to ▢.

-2.4 lies closer to ▢ than to ▢.

$3\frac{1}{2}$ lies between ▢ and ▢.

4. $-3.\overline{6}, -1, \frac{8}{3}$

Math Intervention
Book 3 Integers and Rational Numbers   **15**

Name _____ Date _____

> **Summarize**
>
> A *rational number* is an integer, or the quotient of any two integers when the denominator is not zero. Any decimal that either terminates or repeats is a rational number.
>
> **Placing Rational Numbers on a Number Line**
>
> When the rational number is not an integer, first determine between which two integers the number falls. Next determine where between the two integers it should be placed and then graph it on the number line.

Practice

Match each decimal with its description.

1. -42.455 _____   A. Terminates

2. $6.3471\ldots$ _____   B. Repeats

3. $8.\overline{04}$ _____   C. Neither terminates nor repeats

Tell whether or not the given number is *rational* (R) or *not rational* (N).

4. -52 ____   5. 4.135 ____

6. $2.397\ldots$ ____   7. $\dfrac{14}{5}$ ____

8. $\dfrac{8}{9}$ ____   9. $43.09\overline{74}$ ____

10. 3.21452 ____   11. $6.141141114\ldots$ ____

Place the rational numbers on a number line.

12. $\dfrac{3}{5}, -2.5, 4.9, -1$ 13. $\dfrac{19}{5}, 1.62, -\dfrac{14}{3}, -0.5$

14. $-4\dfrac{1}{5}, -0.22, -1.\overline{4}, 1.4$ 15. $\dfrac{14}{3}, -1.9, -0.\overline{7}, -3$

Determine whether the student's work is correct. Explain your answer. If the student is incorrect, correct the mistake.

16. Shaunda has graphed -0.9 as shown.

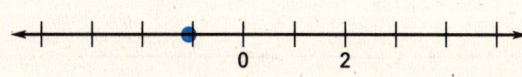

_____
_____
_____

17. Korey states that $7.898898889\ldots$ is a rational number because it is a repeating decimal.

_____
_____
_____

18. Mya states that all whole numbers are rational numbers.

_____
_____
_____

19. Dillan states the numbers $-2, \frac{7}{8}, 0.8, 1\frac{1}{3}, 2.1$ are all examples of rational numbers.

_____
_____
_____

20. **Fill in the missing words.** Any decimal that is either _____ or _____ is a rational number.

21. **Explain your reasoning.** How are whole numbers, integers, and rational numbers related?

_____
_____
_____

LESSON 3-5: Compare and Order Rational Numbers

Words to Remember

Common denominator: When two fractions are written with the same denominator, the denominator is called a *common denominator*

$\frac{2}{7}, \frac{5}{7}$ ← Common denominator

$\frac{3}{15}, \frac{10}{15}$ ←

Getting Started In Lesson 3-3 you compared and ordered integers. Now you are going to compare and order rational numbers.

Comparing Rational Numbers There are several methods for comparing and ordering rational numbers. When the rational numbers have a *common denominator*, compare the numerators. When the rational numbers do not have common denominators, rewrite them so they have common denominators, change them to decimals, or place them on a number line to make the comparison.

EXAMPLE 1 Comparing Two Rational Numbers

Fill in the circle with <, >, or =.

$\frac{18}{5}$ $3\frac{3}{4}$

Solution

$3\frac{3}{4} = \frac{15}{4}$ Write as an improper fraction.

$\frac{18}{5} = 3.6$ and $\frac{15}{4} = 3.75$ Since denominators are not the same, change to decimals for comparison.

$3.6 < 3.75$, so $\frac{18}{5}$ < $3\frac{3}{4}$.   Answer

Another Way

In Example 1, you can write the two fractions with a common denominator of 20 instead. Then compare their numerators.

TRY THIS Fill in the circle with <, >, or =.

1. 12.45 $\frac{249}{20}$

2. -0.22 $-\frac{6}{25}$

Math Intervention
Book 3 Integers and Rational Numbers

Name _____   Date _____

EXAMPLE 2 Ordering Rational Numbers

Use a number line to order the rational numbers from greatest to least.

$2.7, -4\frac{3}{10}, -0.5, \frac{5}{4}, -4.03$

Solution

Step 1 Convert the fractions to decimals so you can place them easily on a number line.

$-4\frac{3}{10} = -4.3, \frac{5}{4} = 1.25$

Step 2 Place and label the points on a number line.

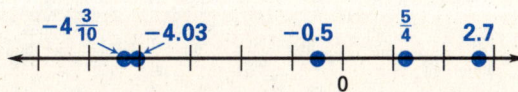

Step 3 Write the numbers as they are placed on the number line from right to left.

ANSWER From greatest to least, the numbers in order are:

$2.7, \frac{5}{4}, -0.5, -4.03, -4\frac{3}{10}$

Remember
The greatest numbers are the farthest to the right on the number line and the least numbers are the farthest to the left on the number line.

TRY THIS
Use a number line to order the numbers from greatest to least.

3. $2.43, -2\frac{7}{10}, -\frac{19}{5}, 1.07, 0.12$

4. $3\frac{7}{20}, -0.8, \frac{17}{3}, -3.82, -\frac{7}{2}$

5. $-\frac{5}{4}, -0.2, 4.31, -3, \frac{5}{2}, -\frac{13}{3}$

Name _____ Date _____

> **Summarize**
>
> **Comparing Rational Numbers**
>
> Write the rational numbers with a common denominator and then compare numerators, or convert them to decimals and compare them.
>
> **Ordering Rational Numbers**
>
> Convert the rational numbers all to the same form, for example decimals. Then compare the decimals, or place the numbers on a number line and then write the order they appear on the number line. The greatest numbers are farthest to the right and the least numbers are farthest to the left.

Practice

Fill in the circle with <, >, or =.

1. -6.5 ◯ $4\frac{1}{8}$

2. $5\frac{9}{25}$ ◯ 5.34

3. $\frac{89}{20}$ ◯ $\frac{9}{2}$

4. $\frac{503}{100}$ ◯ $50\frac{3}{100}$

5. -48.875 ◯ $-\frac{391}{8}$

6. $\frac{3}{5}$ ◯ 0.501

Order the numbers from greatest to least.

7. $-4.2, 3\frac{7}{8}, -4\frac{2}{5}, 2.08$

8. $3.06, 4.1, -\frac{23}{3}, -8.9$

9. $-0.97, -\frac{907}{1000}, -\frac{9}{10}$

10. $104\frac{3}{16}, -10.998, \frac{1049}{10}, -10.99$

Order the numbers from least to greatest.

11. $2.01, \frac{21}{10}, -3.66, -3\frac{2}{3}$

12. $-4\frac{1}{100}, 4.101, -4.101, 4\frac{1}{100}$

13. $\frac{26}{3}, \frac{17}{6}, \frac{33}{12}, \frac{27}{4}$

14. $-13.25, -13\frac{2}{5}, -12.9, -13.09$

Math Intervention
Book 3 Integers and Rational Numbers

Name _____ Date _____

15. Carlos needs a piece of wood for a shelf that is **13.25** feet long. He found one that is $13\frac{3}{20}$ feet long and another one that is $\frac{133}{10}$ feet long. Is either piece of wood long enough for his shelf? If so, which one? If not, how much too short are the pieces he found? Explain.

_____
_____
_____

16. Four members of a model airplane club have brought their model airplanes, of different sizes, to a meeting. The weight of Garrett's airplane is **12.14** pounds, Keisha's airplane weighs $12\frac{11}{25}$ pounds, Tyrei's airplane weighs **10.9** pounds, and the weight of Samuel's airplane is $\frac{59}{5}$ pounds. List the students' names in order of their airplane weights, from least to greatest. Explain your reasoning.

_____
_____
_____

17. You have a rope that is **4** feet long. Your friend has a rope that is $1\frac{2}{3}$ yards long. Who has the longer rope? Explain your reasoning.

_____
_____
_____

DID YOU GET IT?

18. Fill in the missing words. When ordering rational numbers using a number line, the greatest numbers are farthest to the _____ and the least numbers are farthest to the _____.

19. Describe a process. Describe two methods you can use to compare and order rational numbers.

_____
_____

Math Intervention
Book 3 Integers and Rational Numbers

Name _____   Date _____

Mixed Practice for Lessons 3-1 to 3-5

Vocabulary Review

Match the word with its mathematical meaning and its everyday meaning.

Word	Mathematical meaning	Everyday meaning
1. opposite ____, ____	A. any number that can be written in the form $\frac{a}{b}$, where $b \neq 0$	X. an instruction to do something
2. rational ____, ____	B. to compare a set of numbers and sort them by value	Y. facing or across from something
3. order ____, ____	C. a number that is the same distance from zero on a number line as a given number, but in a different direction	Z. clear or sensible thinking

Fill in the word.

4. The _____ of a number is the distance the number is from zero on a number line.

Place the numbers on the number line to order the numbers from least to greatest.

5. $-5, 2, 4, 0, -3$

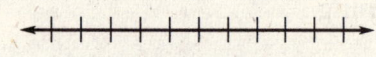

6. $1.4, -\frac{3}{4}, 3\frac{1}{5}, -2.7$

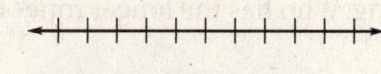

Find the opposite and the absolute value of the number.

7. 16 ▢, ▢

8. -81 ▢, ▢

9. -28 ▢, ▢

10. 72 ▢, ▢

Tell whether the number is *rational* or *not rational* by circling the correct word(s).

11. $0.4239\ldots$ rational, not rational

12. 0.689 rational, not rational

13. -4 rational, not rational

14. $3.7\overline{5}$ rational, not rational

15. $\frac{5}{6}$ rational, not rational

16. $-\frac{1}{12}$ rational, not rational

Math Intervention
Book 3 Integers and Rational Numbers

Name _____ Date _____

Write the number as a rational number in the form $\frac{a}{b}$, where a and b are integers and $b \neq 0$.

17. $5.1 =$ ───

18. $3.3 =$ ───

19. $-0.4 =$ ───

20. $6.88 =$ ───

21. $0.7 =$ ───

22. $5.33 =$ ───

23. $6.4 =$ ───

24. $7.908 =$ ───

25. In golf or miniature golf, *par* is the number of strokes needed by an expert to complete a course. Golf scores can be stated as positive or negative integers to show whether a player's score is above or below par. Eli and four friends play miniature golf. The final scores are Alan: **4**, Marty: **0**, Eli: **−3**, Cade: **−1**, and Ori: **1**. Order the scores from least to greatest. Who won the game?

_____
_____
_____

26. On Macy's monthly bank account statement, a deposit of money is represented by a positive number and a withdrawal of money is represented by a negative number. One month her bank statements showed these transactions:

   −25, 57.75, 23, −42.15, 24.90, 15.55, −80.01

   What was Macy's greatest withdrawal? What was her greatest deposit?

_____
_____
_____

Math Intervention
Book 3 Integers and Rational Numbers

Name _____ Date _____

Adding Integers Using Models

> **Goal:** Use concrete objects to understand how to add integers
> **Materials:** $+1$ and -1 cards.

Getting Started You can use $+1$ and -1 cards to model integer addition. One $+1$ card and one -1 card combine to make zero. This is called a *zero pair*.

$$\boxed{+1}\ \boxed{-1} = 1 + (-1) = 0$$

EXAMPLE

Use the following steps to model $2 + (-5)$ with $+1$ and -1 cards.

Step 1 Model $2 + (-5)$.

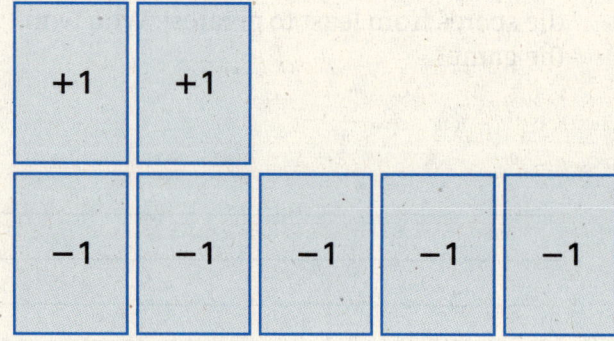

Step 2 Group and remove any zero pairs.

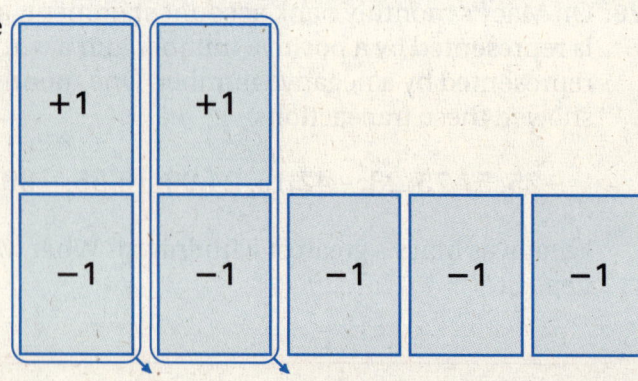

Step 3 Write the result.

ANSWER Since there are $3\ (-1)$ cards remaining, $2 + (-5) = -3$.

Math Intervention
Book 3 Integers and Rational Numbers

Name _____ Date _____

MAKE IT A GAME!

- Form groups of **3** or **4** students, and choose a dealer.
- The dealer gives **5** cards to each person in the group.
- Each person writes the integer addition problem for their hand and finds the sum.
- The person with the greatest sum scores **1** point.
- The players return their cards, and the dealer shuffles and deals again.
- The first person to score **3** points wins the game.

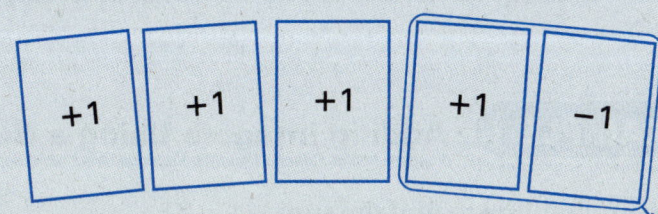

$4 + (-1) = 3$, so the value of this hand is 3.

Practice

Use +1 and −1 cards to find the sum of the positive and negative integers.

1. $5 + (-7)$
2. $3 + (-2)$
3. $3 + (-1)$
4. $1 + (-5)$

5. **Make a Conjecture** Based on your answers to Exercises 1–4, make a conjecture about how to find the sum of a positive and a negative integer without using +1 and −1 cards.

Use your conjecture in Exercise 5 to find the sum.

6. $4 + (-3)$
7. $6 + (-2)$
8. $2 + (-8)$
9. $4 + (-7)$

Use +1 and −1 cards to find the sum of the two negative integers.

10. $-1 + (-2)$
11. $-2 + (-2)$
12. $-3 + (-5)$
13. $-3 + (-1)$

14. **Make a Conjecture** Based on your answers to Exercises 10–13, make a conjecture about how to find the sum of two negative integers without using +1 and −1 cards.

Use your conjecture in Exercise 14 to find the sum.

15. $-5 + (-1)$
16. $-4 + (-2)$
17. $-8 + (-4)$
18. $-20 + (-10)$

DID YOU GET IT? Find the sum of the integers.

19. $-5 + (-3)$
20. $2 + (-8)$
21. $-7 + 5$
22. $-9 + (-11)$

Math Intervention
Book 3 Integers and Rational Numbers

LESSON 3-7 Add Integers

Words to Remember
Inverse property of addition: The sum of a number and its opposite is 0.

$$a + (-a) = 0$$
$$-a + a = 0$$

Getting Started In Activity 3-6 you learned how to add integers using $+1$ and -1 cards. You can also use number lines and absolute values to add integers.

EXAMPLE 1 Adding Integers Using a Number Line

Use a number line to find the sum $-4 + 2$.

Solution

Step 1 Begin at 0 and draw an arrow left to 4 units to represent starting at -4.

Step 2 Begin at -4 and draw an arrow right 2 units to represent adding 2.

Step 3 Write the sum.

$-4 + 2 = -2$ since the end of the arrow after adding 2 to -4 is at -2.

Adding Opposites When you add a number and its opposite on a number line, you draw an arrow away from zero (for example, $+5$ units) and then draw another arrow back in the opposite direction the same number of units (for example, -5 units). The result is 0.

TRY THIS Use a number line to find the sum.

1. $3 + (-2) = \boxed{}$

2. $-5 + 1 = \boxed{}$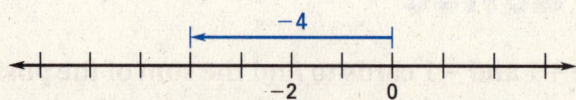

3. $4 + (-4) = \boxed{}$

4. $-1 + (-2) = \boxed{}$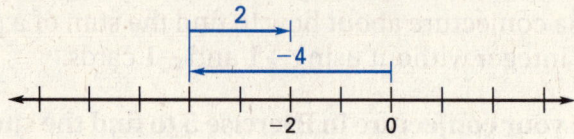

EXAMPLE 2 Adding Integers Using Absolute Values

Use absolute values to find the sum $-6 + (-5)$.

Solution

Step 1 Find the absolute value of each term in the expression.

$$|-6| = 6 \text{ and } |-5| = 5$$

Step 2 Add the absolute values of the integers.

$$6 + 5 = 11$$

Step 3 Write the sum.

Since both of the original terms in the expression are negative, the sum must also be negative.

$$-6 + (-5)$$

ANSWER $-6 + (-5) = -11$

TRY THIS Use absolute values to find the sum.

5. $-7 + (-8) = -(|-7| + |-8|)$

$ = -(\boxed{} + \boxed{})$

$ = -(\boxed{})$

$ = \boxed{}$

Adding Integers with Same Sign Use the sign of the integers in the original expression when using absolute values to add integers with like signs.

Adding Integers with Different Signs It is easiest to add integers with opposite signs using a number line, as shown in Example 1. To use absolute values to add integers that have opposite signs, subtract the least absolute value from the greater absolute value. Use the sign of the integer that has the greatest absolute value.

$3 + (-8) = -(|-8| - |3|)$
$ = -(8 - 3)$
$ = -5$

$|-8| > |3|$, so the final result will have the same sign as -8.

Name _____   Date _____

> **Summarize**
>
> **Using a Number Line to Add Integers**
>
> When an integer is negative, move that many units to the left of **0** or your starting point. When a number is positive, move that many units to the right of zero or your starting point.
>
> **Using Absolute Values to Add Integers**
>
> When the integers have the same sign, begin by finding the absolute values of the integers and then finding their sum. Then use the same sign as the sign of the original integers. When the integers have different signs, subtract the least absolute value from the greater absolute value. Use the sign of the integer with the greater absolute value.

Practice

Match each sum with the number line that represents it.

1. $-4 + 2$ _____   A.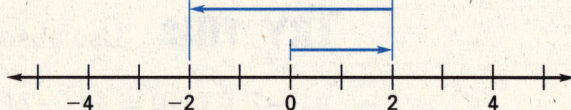

2. $2 + (-4)$ _____   B.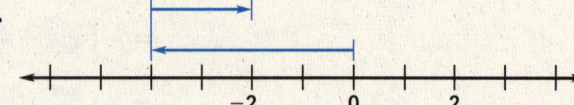

3. $-2 + 4$ _____   C.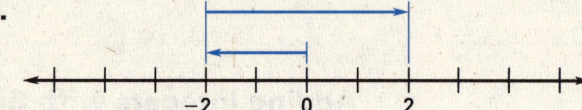

Find the sum using a number line.

4. $3 + (-6) =$ ▢   5. $-7 + 6 =$ ▢   6. $7 + (-2) =$ ▢

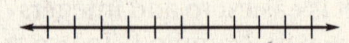

Find the sum using absolute values.

7. $-4 + (-8) =$ ▢   8. $-12 + (-11) =$ ▢

9. $-9 + (-9) =$ ▢   10. $-15 + (-10) =$ ▢

11. $13 + (-6) + (-12) =$ ▢   12. $-70 + (-60) + (-28) =$ ▢

13. $-37 + (-4) + 18 =$ ▢   14. $17 + (-22) + 5 =$ ▢

Math Intervention
Book 3 Integers and Rational Numbers

Name _____ Date _____

Write a sum expression to represent the situation and state whether you would use a *number line* or *absolute values* to find the answer. Then solve the problem. Explain what your answer means.

15. Yoko and Sheila are digging a hole for a fence post. The bottom of their hole is currently 10 inches below the surface of the ground. Yoko digs the hole 5 inches deeper and Sheila digs the hole 8 inches deeper. What is the elevation (in inches) of the bottom of the hole after Sheila is finished?

_____
_____
_____

16. Jasmine and Harley are planting flowers in their flower box. Jasmine fills a watering can with 3 gallons of water. Harley poured 1 gallon of water onto the flowers. How much water is in the watering can after Harley waters the flowers?

_____
_____
_____

DID YOU GET IT?

17. **Fill in the missing words.** To add two integers with opposite signs use a(n) _____. When a number in the sum is negative, then the arrow should move _____. When a number in the sum is positive, then the arrow should move _____.

18. **Explain your reasoning.** When is it usually easiest to use absolute values to add integers?

_____
_____

Name _____ Date _____

LESSON 3-8 Subtract Integers

> **Words to Remember**
>
> *Opposites*: Two numbers that are the same distance from **0** on a number line, but on opposite sides of **0**
>
> 3 and −3 are opposites.
> 8 and −8 are opposites.
>
> *Subtraction Rule*: To subtract an integer, add its opposite.
> $5 - 8 = 5 + (-8) = -3$
> $2 - (-3) = 2 + (3) = 5$

Getting Started In Lesson 3-7 you added integers. Now you will subtract integers using a number line or the subtraction rule.

Using a Number Line When subtracting a *positive integer* using a number line, move to the left of the starting point.

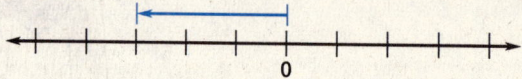

When you are subtracting a *negative integer*, move instead to the right. Because you move to the left when you subtract a positive integer, you move in the opposite direction (to the right) when you subtract a negative integer.

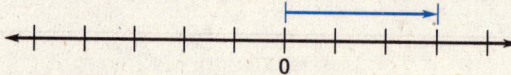

EXAMPLE 1   Subtracting a Positive Integer

Find the difference $4 - 6$ using a number line.

Solution

Step 1 Move 4 units to the right of 0.

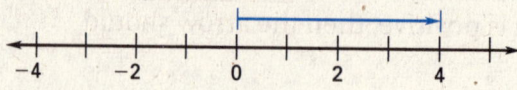

Step 2 Move 6 units to the left of 4.

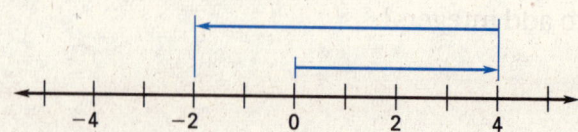

> **Remember**
> When subtracting a positive number, move to the left on the number line.

The final position is −2, so $4 - 6 = -2$.

Step 3 Use the subtraction rule of adding the opposite to check your answer.
$4 - 6 = 4 + (-6) = -2$

Math Intervention
Book 3 Integers and Rational Numbers

EXAMPLE 2 Subtracting a Negative Integer

Use the rule for subtraction to find the difference $2 - (-3)$.

Solution

Step 1 Rewrite as adding the opposite.

$$2 - (-3) = 2 + (+3)$$

Step 2 Add.

$$2 + 3 = 5$$

> **Look Back**
> See Lesson 3-7 for help with adding integers.

EXAMPLE 3 Subtracting a Negative Integer

Use the rule for subtraction to find the difference $-4 - (-2)$.

Solution

Step 1 Rewrite as adding the opposite.

$$-4 - (-2) = -4 + (+2)$$

Step 2 Add.

$$-4 + 2 = -2$$

EXAMPLE 4 Subtracting a Positive Integer

Use the rule for subtraction to find the difference $-6 - 1$.

Solution

Step 1 Rewrite as adding the opposite.

$$-6 - 1 = -6 + (-1)$$

Step 2 Add.

$$-6 + (-1) = -7$$

TRY THIS

Use a number line to find the difference.

1. $3 - 6 =$ ▢

2. $1 - 5 =$ ▢

Use the subtraction rule to find the difference.

3. $3 - (-5) =$ ▢

4. $-5 - 6 =$ ▢

Math Intervention
Book 3 Integers and Rational Numbers

Name _____ Date _____

> **Summarize**
>
> **Subtracting Integers Using a Number Line**
> To subtract a positive integer, move to the left. To subtract a negative integer, move to the right.
>
> **Subtracting Integers Using the Subtraction Rule**
> To subtract an integer, add its opposite.

Practice

Match each difference with the number line that represents it.

1. $-4 - 5$ _____

A.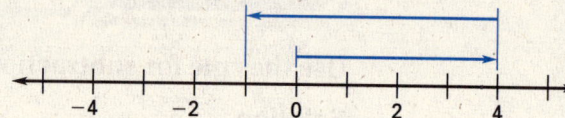

2. $-4 - (-5)$ _____

B.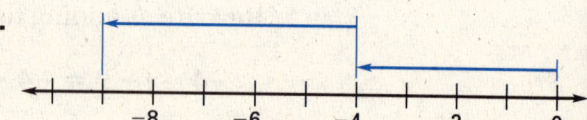

3. $4 - 5$ _____

C.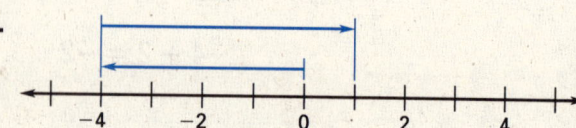

Find the difference using a number line.

4. $3 - 7 =$ ▢

5. $-1 - 2 =$ ▢

6. $-2 - (-2) =$ ▢

Find the difference using the subtraction rule.

7. $-4 - (-8) =$

8. $2 - (-11) =$

9. $-9 - (-9) =$

10. $-15 - 10 =$

11. $3 - 10 =$

12. $12 - (-11) =$

13. $-13 - 13 =$

14. $-85 - (-20) =$

Math Intervention
Book 3 Integers and Rational Numbers

Name _____ Date _____

Write a difference expression to represent the situation. Then solve the problem and explain what your answer means.

15. At noon the temperature was **84°F**. Eight hours later the temperature had dropped **14°F**. What was the temperature at **8:00 P.M.**?

_____
_____
_____

16. Brandon is saving money to buy a bike that costs **$185**. He currently has **$120** in his savings account. How much more does Brandon need to save so he can buy the bike?

_____
_____
_____

17. An elevator is stopped at a floor **20** feet below ground. It descends to another floor **65** feet below ground. What is the change in elevation of the elevator?

_____
_____
_____

DID YOU GET IT?

18. Fill in the missing words. To subtract a positive integer, move to the _____ on a number line. To subtract a negative integer, move to the _____ on a number line.

19. Describe a process. Describe how to use the subtraction rule.

_____
_____

Name _____   Date _____

LESSON 3-9 Multiply Integers

> **Words to Remember**
>
> Multiplication is the same as repeated addition.
>
> $4 \times 2 = 2 + 2 + 2 + 2 = 8$
> $5(-6) = -6 + (-6) + (-6) + (-6) + (-6)$
> $ = -30$

Getting Started In Lesson 3-7 you added integers. Now you will multiply integers by using repeated addition. You will also learn some patterns about the sign of the product of two integers.

EXAMPLE 1 Multiplying Two Integers

Find the product by rewriting it as repeated addition.

a. 3×15

b. $5(-2)$

c. $3 \times (-1)$

Solution

a. $3 \times 15 \quad = 15 + 15 + 15 = 45$

b. $5(-2) \quad = -2 + (-2) + (-2) + (-2) + (-2) = -10$

c. $3 \times (-1) \quad = -1 + (-1) + (-1) = -3$

TRY THIS Use repeated addition to find the product.

1. 5×8

2. $2(-4)$

3. $4(6)$

4. $3 \times (-7)$

Math Intervention
Book 3 Integers and Rational Numbers

Name _____ Date _____

EXAMPLE 2 Finding a Pattern for Multiplication

Look back at Example 1 and at the table below to find a pattern, or rule, for multiplying integers. What do you notice about the product of a positive integer and a negative integer? About the product of two negative integers?

2 × (−3) =	−6
1 × (−3) =	−3
0 × (−3) =	0
−1 × (−3) =	3
−2 × (−3) =	6

Solution

The product of a positive integer and a negative integer is negative.

The product of two negative integers is positive.

TRY THIS Will the product be *positive* or *negative*?

5. 46 × (−8)

   _____

6. (−46) × (−85)

   _____

7. (−46) × (−85) × (−85)

   _____

8. (−46) × (−46) × (−85) × (−85)

   _____

EXAMPLE 3 Multiplying Two Integers

Use the rules for multiplying integers from Example 2 to find the product.

a. 4 × (−4)

b. −5(−7)

Solution

a. 4 × (−4) = −16   The product of a positive integer and a negative integer is negative.

b. −5 × (−7) = 35   The product of two negative integers is positive.

TRY THIS Use the multiplication rules to find the product.

9. 6(−10) = _____

10. −8 × (−4) = _____

Math Intervention
Book 3 Integers and Rational Numbers   **35**

Name _____ Date _____

> **Summarize**
> The product of two negative integers is positive.
> The product of a positive integer and a negative integer is negative.

Practice

Match each product with the repeated addition that represents it.

1. $4 \times (-3)$ _____
2. $3 \times (-4)$ _____
3. 3×4 _____

A. $-3 + (-3) + (-3) + (-3)$
B. $4 + 4 + 4$
C. $-4 + (-4) + (-4)$

Find the product.

4. $10(5) =$
5. $4(-8) =$
6. $-12 \times 11 =$
7. $10 \times (-10) =$
8. $14 \times 3 =$
9. $-42 \times 0 =$
10. $8(-9) =$
11. $-20(-6) =$
12. $-33(1) =$
13. $2(-3)(-1) =$
14. $-3 \times 8 \times 2 =$
15. $12(-3)(5) =$
16. $-6 \times 4 \times 0 =$
17. $-3(2)(-4) =$
18. $-5(-7)(-1) =$
19. $12(2)(-8) =$

Math Intervention
Book 3 Integers and Rational Numbers

Name _____   Date _____

Write a product expression to represent the situation. Decide whether the numbers are positive or negative. Then simplify the expression and explain what the answer means.

20. The temperature drops **2°F** each hour. What is the total change in temperature after **12** hours?

   _____
   _____
   _____

21. Sylvia burns **6** calories per minute when she runs. How many calories does she burn when she runs for **15** minutes?

   _____
   _____
   _____

22. Chandler drives his car **20** miles round trip to work everyday. How many total miles does he drive to and from work in **5** days?

   _____
   _____
   _____

DID YOU GET IT?

23. **Fill in the missing words.** The product of a negative integer and a positive integer is _____. The product of two negative integers is _____.

24. **Explain your reasoning.** Use an example to help you explain how multiplication is like repeated addition.

   _____
   _____

Math Intervention
Book 3 Integers and Rational Numbers

Name _____ Date _____

LESSON 3-10 Divide Integers

Words to Remember

Quotient: The result of dividing two integers

Related problem: You can rewrite a division problem as the related multiplication problem.

$2 \div 4 = 0.5$ ← quotient
$-5 \div 3 = -1.\overline{6}$ ← quotient

$16 \div 8 = 2 \rightarrow 8 \times 2 = 16$

Getting Started   In Lesson 3-9 you multiplied integers. Now you will use multiplication and mental math to divide integers.

EXAMPLE 1   Rewriting Division as Multiplication

Rewrite the division problem as a related multiplication problem.

a. $48 \div (-6) = \underline{?}$

b. $-64 \div 8 = \underline{?}$

Solution

a. $48 \div (-6) = \underline{?}$ is related to the verbal multiplication expression

"Some number times -6 is equal to 48," so $\underline{?} \times (-6) = 48$.

b. $-64 \div 8 = \underline{?}$ is related to the verbal multiplication expression

"Some number times 8 is equal to -64," so $\underline{?} \times 8 = -64$.

Remember
One method for finding the quotient of two integers is to begin by rewriting the division problem as a multiplication problem.

TRY THIS   Rewrite the division problem as a related multiplication problem.

1. $36 \div (-3) = ?$

2. $-15 \div (-5) = ?$

Math Intervention
Book 3 Integers and Rational Numbers

Name _____ Date _____

Rules for the Division of Integers The rules for multiplication of integers also hold true for division. The quotient of two integers with the same sign is positive. The quotient of two integers with different signs is negative.

EXAMPLE 2 Dividing Integers

Determine whether the quotient will be positive or negative.

a. $75 \div (-15) = \underline{\ ?\ }$

b. $-36 \div (-6) = \underline{\ ?\ }$

Solution

a. Since the integers in the expression have *different signs* (one positive and one negative), the quotient will be *negative*.

b. Since the integers in the expression have the *same sign* (both are negative), the quotient will be *positive*.

EXAMPLE 3 Dividing Integers

Rewrite and solve a related multiplication equation for $-40 \div (-8) = \underline{\ ?\ }$.

Solution

Step 1 Think "What number times -8 equals -40?"

   ▨ $\times (-8) = -40$

Step 2 Solve using mental math.

Since the integers -40 and -8 have the same sign, their quotient will be positive.

$\boxed{5} \times (-8) = -40$, so $-40 \div (-8) = 5$

TRY THIS Find the quotient.

3. $88 \div 11 =$ ▨

4. $-32 \div 4 =$ ▨

5. $-125 \div -5 =$ ▨

6. $180 \div (-15) =$ ▨

Math Intervention
Book 3 Integers and Rational Numbers   **39**

Name _____   Date _____

> **Summarize**
>
> **Finding the Quotient of Integers**
>
> The quotient of two integers with the same sign is positive. The quotient of two integers with different signs is negative.
>
> One method for finding the quotient of two integers is to begin by rewriting the division problem as a multiplication problem.

Practice

Tell if the quotient is *positive* (P) or *negative* (N).

1. $15 \div (-3)$ _____
2. $-144 \div (-12)$ _____
3. $-180 \div 18$ _____
4. $155 \div 5$ _____

Rewrite the quotient as a related multiplication problem.

5. $105 \div (-5) = ?$ _____
6. $156 \div (-12) = ?$ _____
7. $-99 \div 11 = ?$ _____
8. $-32 \div (-4) = ?$ _____

Find the quotient.

9. $-5 \div (-1) =$ _____
10. $14 \div (-2) =$ _____
11. $75 \div (-3) =$ _____
12. $-64 \div (-8) =$ _____
13. $21 \div 3 =$ _____
14. $-60 \div (-5) =$ _____
15. $36 \div 4 =$ _____
16. $-36 \div 6 =$ _____

Name _____ Date _____

Write a quotient expression to represent the situation. Then solve the problem. Explain what your answer means.

17. Manuel has some strawberries that he is going to divide equally among himself and **4** friends. Suppose there are **75** strawberries. How many strawberries will each person get?

   _____
   _____
   _____

18. A family of **3** shares the minutes on a cellular telephone equally. Suppose the cellular phone has **675** minutes per month. How many minutes does each person get to use each month?

   _____
   _____
   _____

DID YOU GET IT?

19. **Fill in the missing words.** The quotient of two integers with the same sign will be a _____ number. The quotient of two integers with different signs will be a _____ number.

20. **Compare.** How is dividing integers similar to multiplying integers?

   _____
   _____
   _____

Math Intervention
Book 3 Integers and Rational Numbers

Name _____ Date _____

LESSON 3-11
Solve Problems with Integers

> **Strategies to Remember**
> When you solve a word problem, explain your reasoning:
>
> | **Describe** your thinking. | **Show** your work. |

Getting Started When you explain your reasoning in solving a word problem, you can use steps to give a description of the process used to solve the problem. Often, the final step explains why the solution is a reasonable answer.

EXAMPLE 1   Solving a Division Problem

You are filling balloons with helium for your friend's birthday party. You have 54 feet of ribbon to tie to the balloons. It takes 3 feet for each balloon. How many balloons can you tie with the 54 feet of ribbon? Explain your reasoning.

Solution

Step 1 **Identify** the operation needed.

To find how many equal lengths of 3 feet can be taken from 54 feet, you need to divide.

Step 2 **Divide** 54 feet by 3 feet to find the number of balloons you can tie.

$$54 \div 3 = 18$$

Step 3 **Check** that 18 balloons is a reasonable answer.

Because 20 is slightly more than 18 and 20 balloons × 3 feet = 60 total feet, the total number of feet should be slightly less than 60 feet. Because 54 feet is slightly less than 60 feet, 18 balloons is reasonable.

ANSWER You can use the 54 feet of ribbon to tie ribbons on 18 balloons.

TRY THIS   Solve the problem. Explain your reasoning.

1. A roll of paper towels is 140 feet long. The roll needs to be divided into 4 equal sections for a project. How long will each section be?

_____

_____

Math Intervention
Book 3 Integers and Rational Numbers

Name _____ Date _____

> **Remember**
> See Exercise 25 on page 23 for a discussion of golf scores.

EXAMPLE 2 — Solving a Subtraction Problem

Kiesha has a golf score of -2 after the fourth hole. She decreases her score by 1 more after the sixth hole. What is Kiesha's score after the sixth hole?

Solution

Step 1 **Identify** the operation needed.

The word "decreases" lets you know that you need to use subtraction.

Step 2 **Subtract.** $-2 - 1 = -3$

Step 3 **Check** that a score of -3 is reasonable.

Because she is decreasing her score by 1, her score should be 1 unit to the left of -2 on a number line. -3 is 1 unit to the left of -2 on a number line.

ANSWER Keisha's score after the sixth hole is -3.

EXAMPLE 3 — Solving a Problem Using Multiple Operations

Kaleb has 20 cups of flour. He uses 8 cups to make banana bread. He wants to use the remaining flour to make zucchini bread. Each loaf of zucchini bread uses 3 cups of flour. How many loaves can he make?

Solution

Step 1 **Identify** the operations needed.

Subtract to find the number of cups of flour left after Kaleb makes the banana bread. Then divide by the number of cups needed for each loaf of zucchini bread.

Step 2 **Subtract.** $20 - 8 = 12$ cups

Step 3 **Divide.** $12 \div 3 = 4$ loaves

Step 4 **Check** that 4 loaves is a reasonable answer.

Because $4 \times 3 = 12$, 4 loaves is reasonable.

ANSWER Kaleb can make 4 loaves of zucchini bread.

TRY THIS Solve the problem. Explain your reasoning.

2. The high temperature increases by 3°F each day for 5 days. On Day 1 the high temperature was 67°F. What was the high temperature on Day 6?

_____

_____

Name _____ Date _____

> **Summarize**
> **Solving Word Problems**
> (1) Identify the operation or operations needed.
> (2) Perform the calculations and solve the problem.
> (3) Explain your thinking at each step.
> (4) Check your answer for reasonableness.

Practice

Match the situation with the operation needed to solve the problem.

1. Lyle earned $5 less than Kay. ____
2. 3 curtains each require 4 yards of fabric. ____
3. A 50 yard rope is split into 8 sections. ____
4. Kelli is 4 inches taller than Kim. ____

A. Addition
B. Subtraction
C. Multiplication
D. Division

Identify the operation suggested by the phrase.

5. Twice as many cats
6. 12 more fish
7. 20 fewer flowers
8. One-third as many minutes

Fill in the missing information to solve the problem.

9. The high temperature on a Tuesday in winter is −15°F. The high temperature increases by 8°F on Wednesday. What is the high temperature on Wednesday?

    Step 1 The word "increases" tells you that you need to _____.

    Step 2 Calculate −15 ◯ 8 = _____

    Step 3 The high temperature on Wednesday is _____.

10. Thirteen students each have 4 pets. How many pets do the 13 students have all together?

    Step 1 Since groups are joined together, you need to _____.

    Step 2 Calculate 13 ◯ 4 = _____.

    Step 3 The students have a total of _____ pets.

Math Intervention
Book 3 Integers and Rational Numbers

Name _____ Date _____

Look back at Exercises 2 and 3 on page 44.

11. Explain how to find the number of yards of fabric needed for the curtains.

12. Find the length of rope in each section. Explain your reasoning.

Tell which operation(s) must be used to solve the problem. Then solve the problem. Explain your answer.

13. The eighth grade class is taking a trip to a science museum. There are 75 eighth graders and the school requires that there be 1 chaperone for every 15 students. How many chaperones are needed for the trip?

   _____
   _____
   _____

14. Simon has 3 times as many baseball cards as Trevor. Trevor has 15 baseball cards. Garret has 10 more baseball cards than Simon. How many baseball cards does Garret have?

   _____
   _____

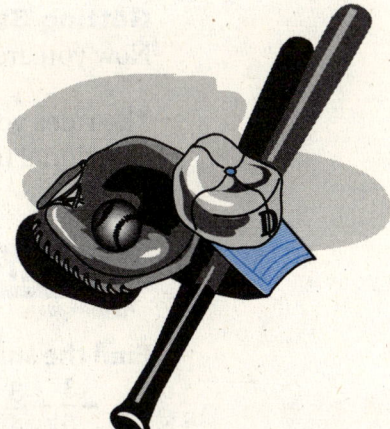

DID YOU GET IT?

15. **Write a word problem.** Write a word problem using the integers below. Then complete the calculations to solve the problem. Explain how you decided what operations to use.

    35 ● 7 = ▇▇▇

16. **Explain your reasoning.** Sometimes a word problem does not contain a key word or phrase that suggests a specific operation. How can you determine what operation should be used?

   _____
   _____
   _____

LESSON 3-12: Rational Number Operations

> **Words to Remember**
>
> *Rational number*: A number that can be written in the form $\frac{a}{b}$, where a and b are integers and $b \neq 0$
>
> So, a rational number is any number that can be represented by a fraction.
>
> $0.75 = \frac{3}{4}$
>
> $2 = \frac{2}{1}$
>
> $-56 = \frac{-56}{1}$
>
> $-0.\overline{6} = -\frac{2}{3}$

Getting Started In Lesson 3-4 you learned what rational numbers were. Now you are going to perform operations with rational numbers.

The rules you use to add, subtract, multiply, and divide integers also apply to rational numbers.

EXAMPLE 1 Adding and Subtracting Rational Numbers

Find the sum or difference.

a. $-\frac{3}{8} + \frac{3}{4}$

b. $2.3 - 5.22$

Solution

a. $-\frac{3}{8} + \frac{3}{4} = -\frac{3}{8} + \frac{6}{8}$ Rewrite using LCD.

$\phantom{-\frac{3}{8} + \frac{3}{4}} = \frac{-3 + 6}{8}$ Add numerators.

$\phantom{-\frac{3}{8} + \frac{3}{4}} = \frac{3}{8}$ Simplify.

b. $2.3 - 5.22 = 2.3 + (-5.22)$ To subtract a number, add its opposite.

$ = -(|5.22| - |2.3|)$ Use rule for adding numbers with different signs.

$ = -2.92$ Simplify.

TRY THIS Find the sum or difference.

1. $-1\frac{1}{10} - \frac{4}{5} = \boxed{}$

2. $-1.125 + 3.721 = \boxed{}$

Math Intervention
Book 3 Integers and Rational Numbers

EXAMPLE 2 Dividing Rational Numbers

Find the quotient $\frac{2}{3} \div -\frac{1}{10}$.

Solution

$\frac{2}{3} \div \left(-\frac{1}{10}\right) = \frac{2}{3} \times \left(-\frac{10}{1}\right)$ Multiply by reciprocal of $-\frac{1}{10}$.

$= -\frac{20}{3}$ Multiply. The numbers have different signs, so their product is negative.

$= -6\frac{2}{3}$ Simplify.

EXAMPLE 3 Multiplying Rational Numbers

Find the product -8.01×4.84.

Solution

$-8.01 \times 4.84 = -38.7684$ Multiply. The numbers have different signs, so their product is negative.

TRY THIS Find the product or quotient.

3. $\frac{3}{4} \div \left(-\frac{1}{16}\right) =$ ▭

4. $-\frac{3}{5} \div 9 =$ ▭

5. $1\frac{5}{9} \div 4\frac{3}{5} =$ ▭

6. $(-7.92) \times (-1.25) =$ ▭

Remember
Just as in Lesson 3-3 when you compared rational numbers, it is easiest to add and subtract rational numbers if they are written in the same form, such as all decimals or all fractions.

EXAMPLE 4 Using Rational Numbers

Find the product and quotient of -2.5 and $\frac{1}{5}$.

Solution

To find the product or quotient, write the numbers in the same form.

Multiply: $-2.5 \times \frac{1}{5} = -2.5 \times 0.2$ Write $\frac{1}{5}$ as 0.2.

$= -0.50$ Multiply.

Divide: $-2.5 \div \frac{1}{5} = -2.5 \div 0.2$ Write $\frac{1}{5}$ as 0.2.

$= -12.5$ Divide.

Math Intervention
Book 3 Integers and Rational Numbers

Name _____ Date _____

> **Summarize**
>
> A *rational number* is a number that can be written in the form $\frac{a}{b}$, where a and b are integers and $b \neq 0$.
>
> **Performing Operations with Rational Numbers**
>
> Rewrite the rational numbers so they are all in the same form, all decimals or all fractions. Then use the rules for performing operations with decimals or fractions.

Practice

Find the sum, difference, product, or quotient.

1. $2.4 - 0.4 = $ ▢

2. $-4\frac{4}{7} + 6\frac{3}{5} = $ ▢

3. $7 \times 6.8 = $ ▢

4. $-10.4 + 2.7 = $ ▢

5. $-\frac{1}{8} \div \frac{3}{4} = $ ▢

6. $-\frac{3}{7} - \frac{3}{7} = $ ▢

7. $98 \times \frac{5}{6} = $ ▢

8. $-\frac{12}{19} - \frac{1}{38} = $ ▢

9. $4.6 + 8.01 = $ ▢

10. $-\frac{7}{8} \div 2 = $ ▢

11. $6\frac{1}{6} + 3\frac{5}{12} = $ ▢

12. $-10.22 - 4.08 = $ ▢

13. $56.701 - (-23.99) = $ ▢

14. $3\frac{13}{15} \times \left(-2\frac{1}{3}\right) = $ ▢

15. $-14\frac{3}{4} \div 3 = $ ▢

16. $-3.24 + 0.625 + (-2.3) = $ ▢

17. $4.42 \times 5.1 \times 0.5 = $ ▢

18. $3.3 + 6.7 - 0.3 = $ ▢

Math Intervention
Book 3 Integers and Rational Numbers

Tell what operation you need to perform to solve the problem. Then write and solve an expression that represents the situation.

19. You and a friend order a pizza. You eat $\frac{3}{10}$ of the pizza and your friend eats $\frac{2}{5}$ of the pizza. What fraction of the pizza did you and your friend eat altogether?

   _____
   _____
   _____

20. Sigourney has a notebook with **150** sheets of colored paper in it. Suppose she uses **0.2** of the sheets. How many sheets does she use?

   _____
   _____
   _____

21. Brady has a box of crackers that weighs **16.8** ounces. Suppose he is going to share the box equally among himself and three friends. How many ounces of crackers will each person have?

   _____
   _____
   _____

DID YOU GET IT?

22. **Fill in the missing words.** A rational number is any number that can be written in the form _____.

23. **Explain your reasoning.** How can you perform operations on rational numbers?

   _____
   _____
   _____

Name _____ Date _____

LESSON 3-13
Take Rational Numbers to Whole-Number Powers

> **Words to Remember**
> In a power the *base* is the repeated factor and the *exponent* is the number of times the factor is repeated.
>
> x^y — exponent on y, base is x
>
> For example, 2^5 means that you are going to multiply 5 factors of 2, or $2 \times 2 \times 2 \times 2 \times 2$.

Getting Started In Lesson 3-12 you learned how to perform operations on rational numbers. Now you are going to learn how to raise a rational number to a power.

EXAMPLE 1 Taking an Integer to a Power

Evaluate the powers.

a. 4^3

b. 3^4

c. 5^2

Solution

Step 1

$4^3 = 4 \times 4 \times 4$ Write in expanded form.
$3^4 = 3 \times 3 \times 3 \times 3$
$5^2 = 5 \times 5$

Step 2

$4^3 = 4 \times 4 \times 4 = 64$ Multiply.
$3^4 = 3 \times 3 \times 3 \times 3 = 81$
$5^2 = 5 \times 5 = 25$

TRY THIS Evaluate the power.

1. $5^3 =$ _____

2. $10^4 =$ _____

Math Intervention
Book 3 Integers and Rational Numbers

EXAMPLE 2 — Raising a Decimal to a Power

Evaluate the powers.

a. $(4.1)^2$

b. $(2.2)^4$

Solution

Step 1 Write in expanded form.

$$(4.1)^2 = 4.1 \times 4.1$$
$$(2.2)^4 = 2.2 \times 2.2 \times 2.2 \times 2.2$$

Step 2 Multiply.

$$(4.1)^2 = 4.1 \times 4.1 = 16.81$$
$$(2.2)^4 = 2.2 \times 2.2 \times 2.2 \times 2.2 = 23.4256$$

TRY THIS Evaluate the power.

3. $(1.8)^2 = $ _____

4. $(2.3)^3 = $ _____

EXAMPLE 3 — Raising a Fraction to a Power

Evaluate the power $\left(\frac{2}{3}\right)^3$.

Solution

$\left(\frac{2}{3}\right)^3 = \frac{2}{3} \cdot \frac{2}{3} \cdot \frac{2}{3}$ Write in expanded form.

$= \frac{2 \cdot 2 \cdot 2}{3 \cdot 3 \cdot 3}$ Multiply numerators and multiply denominators.

$= \frac{8}{27}$ Simplify.

Remember

When a fraction is raised to a power, both the numerator and the denominator are raised to that power.

$\left(\frac{2}{3}\right)^3 = \frac{2^3}{3^3}$

TRY THIS Evaluate the power.

5. $\left(\frac{1}{4}\right)^3 = $ _____

6. $\left(\frac{4}{5}\right)^2 = $ _____

Name _____ Date _____

> **Summarize**
>
> **Raising a Rational Number to a Power**
>
> When you raise a rational number such as an integer, decimal, or fraction to a power, the exponent tells you how many times to use the base as a factor.
>
> When you raise a fraction to a power, remember that both the numerator and the denominator are raised to that power.

Practice

Match the expression and its expanded form.

1. $(5.67)^2$ _____

   A. $5.67 + 5.67$ B. 5.67×2 C. 5.67×5.67 D. $5.67 + 2$

2. $\left(\dfrac{1}{8}\right)^3$ _____

   A. $\dfrac{1}{8} \times \dfrac{1}{8} \times \dfrac{1}{8}$ B. $\dfrac{1}{8} + \dfrac{1}{8} + \dfrac{1}{8}$ C. $\dfrac{1}{8} + 3$ D. $\dfrac{1}{8} \times 3$

Evaluate the power.

3. $2^4 =$ ▢

4. $\left(\dfrac{2}{5}\right)^2 =$ ▢

5. $(5.1)^3 =$ ▢

6. $(7.2)^2 =$ ▢

7. $12^2 =$ ▢

8. $\left(\dfrac{3}{4}\right)^4 =$ ▢

9. $\left(\dfrac{1}{2}\right)^5 =$ ▢

10. $(8.5)^3 =$ ▢

11. $13^3 =$ ▢

12. $(4.8)^2 =$ ▢

13. $5^6 =$ ▢

14. $\left(\dfrac{6}{7}\right)^4 =$ ▢

Math Intervention
Book 3 Integers and Rational Numbers

Name _____ Date _____

Write a power to represent the problem. Then evaluate the power.

5. The area of a square is found by squaring the length of one of the sides. Suppose a side of a square patio has a length of **12.3** feet. What is the area of the top of the patio?

_____
_____

6. A message about softball practice needs to get to members of all of the teams. The coach calls **3** teammates in the morning. Later, each of those **3** people calls **3** more teammates. Finally, each of those teammates calls **3** more people. How many teammates were called in the final, last round of calling?

_____
_____

7. Tori is making a fruit pizza for her mother's birthday. She is halving the recipe, which means that she is making a pizza that requires half of each amount of the ingredients listed. Suppose $\frac{1}{2}$ cup of kiwifruit is needed in the original recipe. How much kiwifruit is needed for Tori's fruit pizza?

_____
_____
_____

DID YOU GET IT?

18. **Fill in the missing words.** To take a rational number to a power, the _____ tells you how many factors of the _____ to _____ together.

19. **Explain your reasoning.** How do you take a fraction to a power?

_____
_____
_____

Name _____   Date _____

Mixed Practice for Lessons 3-7 to 3-13

Vocabulary Review

Match the word with its mathematical meaning and its everyday meaning.

Word	Mathematical meaning	Everyday meaning
1. add ____, ____	A. the operation performed to find a difference	X. somebody that supports a cause
2. subtract ____, ____	B. determines how many times a number is a factor	Y. to withdraw or take away
3. exponent ____, ____	C. the operation performed to find a sum	Z. to say more about something

Fill in the words.

4. When multiplying or dividing two integers, when both integers are negative the result is _____. When one integer is negative and one is positive, then the result is _____.

Add, subtract, multiply, or divide.

5. $-4 + 2 =$ ____

6. $3 \times (-8) =$ ____

7. $-18 \div (-2) =$ ____

8. $5 - (-7) =$ ____

9. $-12 + 19 =$ ____

10. $-5 - (-20) =$ ____

11. $50 \div (-25) =$ ____

12. $-7 \times (-12) =$ ____

13. $-99 \div 11 =$ ____

14. $16 + (-17) =$ ____

15. $-13 \times 4 =$ ____

16. $-18 - 12 =$ ____

Math Intervention
Book 3 Integers and Rational Numbers

Name _____   Date _____

17. Fill in the missing information.

At a softball game $\frac{5}{8}$ of the spectators are fans of the home team. $\frac{1}{5}$ of these fans leave before the end of the game. How many of the fans of the home team, expressed as a fraction of the total spectators, stayed for the entire game?

Step 1 The operations needed are _____ and _____.

Step 2 Calculate $1 \bigcirc \frac{1}{5} = \boxed{}$ of the home team fans stayed.

Step 3 Calculate $\frac{5}{8} \bigcirc \frac{4}{5} = \boxed{}$

Step 4 The fraction of the home team fans that stayed for the entire game is $\boxed{}$ of the spectators.

Simplify the power.

18. $5^3 = \boxed{}$ **19.** $(0.3)^2 = \boxed{}$ **20.** $\left(\frac{3}{4}\right)^4 = \boxed{}$ **21.** $(1.2)^2 = \boxed{}$

Tell what operation(s) you need to find the answer. Then solve the problem. Explain your reasoning.

22. Keith, Justin, and Jamal rent a movie. The total cost is $4.02. If they are going to split the cost equally, how much does each person have to pay?

_____

_____

23. Kara, Emma, and Julia are competing in a high school swim meet. Kara finishes the 100 yard freestyle event in $\frac{19}{20}$ minute, Emma finishes the event in 0.9 minute, and Julia finishes in $\frac{11}{12}$ minute. Who won the event?

_____

_____

McDougal Littell

Math Intervention

Book 4:
Ratios, Rates, Proportions, and Percents

McDougal Littell
A DIVISION OF HOUGHTON MIFFLIN COMPANY
Evanston, Illinois • Boston • Dallas

Cover photo © David Young-Wolff/PhotoEdit and Royalty-Free/Corbis

Illustrations George Barile/McDougal Littell/Houghton Mifflin Company and John Evans/McDougal Littell/Houghton Mifflin Company

Copyright © 2008 by McDougal Littell, a division of Houghton Mifflin Company.
All rights reserved.

Permission is hereby granted to teachers to reprint or photocopy in classroom quantities the pages or sheets in this work that carry a McDougal Littell copyright notice. These pages are designed to be reproduced by teachers for use in their classes with accompanying McDougal Littell material, provided each copy made shows the copyright notice. Such copies may not be sold and further distribution is expressly prohibited. Except as authorized above, prior written permission must be obtained from McDougal Littell, a division of Houghton Mifflin Company, to reproduce or transmit this work or portions thereof in any other form or by any other electronic or mechanical means, including any information storage or retrieval system, unless expressly permitted by federal copyright laws. Address inquiries to, Supervisor, Rights and Permissions, McDougal Littell, P.O. Box 1667, Evanston, IL 60204.

ISBN-13: 978-0-618-90061-9
ISBN-10: 0-618-90061-6

123456789—PBO—11 10 09 08 07

Book 4: Ratios, Rates, Proportions, and Percents

Ratios, Rates, and Proportions

Lesson 4-1	Ratios	2
Lesson 4-2	Rates	6
Lesson 4-3	Convert Units in the Metric System	10
Lesson 4-4	Convert Units in the Customary System	14
Lesson 4-5	Convert Units in Different Measurement Systems	18
Activity 4-6	Making a Scale Drawing	22
Lesson 4-7	Solve Proportions	24
Lesson 4-8	Solve Problems with Proportions	28
	Mixed Practice for Lessons 4-1 to 4-8	32

Percents, Interest, and Probability

Lesson 4-9	Percents	34
Lesson 4-10	Convert Percents, Fractions, and Decimals	38
Lesson 4-11	Find a Percent of a Number	42
Lesson 4-12	Percent of Increase and Decrease	46
Lesson 4-13	Discounts, Tips, Markups, Commissions, and Profit	50
Lesson 4-14	Simple Interest	54
Lesson 4-15	Compound Interest	58
Activity 4-16	Conducting an Experiment	62
Lesson 4-17	Probability	64
	Mixed Practice for Lessons 4-9 to 4-17	68

McDougal Littell

Math Intervention

MATH INTERVENTION

- The Math Intervention program includes skill lessons, problem solving lessons, activities, and mixed practice materials covering a wide range of mathematical topics that are needed for success in middle school and high school mathematics.

- There are seven books in the Math Intervention program. Book 4 contains materials on reading, writing, solving, and using Ratios, Rates, Proportions, and Percents.

- In the Math Intervention books, lessons include worked-out Examples and Try this exercises to help you build understanding of a topic. The Practice section includes a variety of problems to give you the practice you need to develop your math skills. The Did You Get It? section checks your understanding of the lesson.

- Problem solving lessons suggest strategies for approaching real-world problem solving situations and promote the use of estimation to check reasonableness of solutions.

- Activities build your understanding of a topic through the use of models and games.

- Mixed Practice sections include practice of vocabulary, skills, and problem solving methods covering the material in a group of lessons.

- You may complete the work in selected lessons, or cover the book as a whole, as directed by your teacher.

LESSON 4-1 Ratios

> **Words to Remember**
> Ratio: A comparison of two values using division
> Form of a ratio: A ratio can be written in three ways.
>
> $\frac{36 \text{ inches}}{3 \text{ feet}}$ 36 inches to 3 feet   36 inches : 3 feet

Getting Started   In Lesson 2-2 you learned how to work with equivalent fractions. You will use this concept in writing ratios.

EXAMPLE 1 Writing a Ratio in Different Forms

Mason surveys 250 students in a school. Fifty-five of the students' families own a sports utility vehicle. Write a ratio in three different forms to show the number of students whose families own sports utility vehicles compared to the total number of students that Mason surveys.

Solution

$\frac{\text{number of sports utility vehicles}}{\text{total number of students surveyed}}$ Determine the fraction.

$\frac{55}{250}$ Substitute values.

$\frac{55}{250} = \frac{11}{50}$ Simplify.

ANSWER The number of students whose families own sports utility vehicles compared to the total number of students surveyed is $\frac{11}{50}$, or 11 to 50, or 11 : 50.

> **Remember**
> When you work with ratios, they are just like fractions. You must remember to simplify your results.

TRY THIS Write the ratio described in three different forms.

1. In one day, a deli sold 48 sandwiches. Eighteen of these sandwiches were ham and cheese. Write the ratio of ham and cheese sandwiches to total sandwiches.

   _____   _____   _____

2. Terrence attempted to hit 72 baseballs in the batting cage. He actually hit 42. What is his batting average for this practice session? Batting average is $\frac{\text{number of hits}}{\text{number of attempts}}$.

   _____   _____   _____

Math Intervention
Book 4 Ratios, Rates, Proportions, and Percents

EXAMPLE 2 Comparing Ratios

One animal shelter had 45 dogs out of 70 animals. In another shelter the ratio of dogs to all animals was 12:28. Compare the ratios using fractions or decimals and describe the results.

Solution

Write the ratios.

$\frac{45}{70}$ and $\frac{12}{28}$

Compare using the least common denominator of the fractions.

$\frac{45}{70} = \frac{9}{14}$ $\frac{12}{28} = \frac{6}{14}$ The greatest common factor of 70 and 28 is 14.

Notice that $\frac{9}{14} > \frac{6}{14}$, so $\frac{45}{70} > \frac{12}{28}$.

Compare using the decimal form.

$\frac{45}{70} = 0.64$ $\frac{12}{28} = 0.43$ Divide to write as decimals.

Notice that $0.64 > 0.43$, so $\frac{45}{70} > \frac{12}{28}$.

ANSWER The first animal shelter has a greater portion of dogs.

TRY THIS Compare ratios.

3. One fruit basket has 5 oranges out of 25 pieces of fruit. Another basket has a ratio of 3 to 4 for oranges to pieces of fruit. Which basket has the lesser ratio of oranges to total fruit? _____

   Basket 1: $\frac{\text{oranges}}{\text{all fruit}}$ = ☐   Basket 2: $\frac{\text{oranges}}{\text{all fruit}}$ = ☐

4. Kendra has 15 pairs of sports socks out of 35 pairs of socks. Jamilla has a ratio of 4 : 7 of sports socks to total socks. Who has the greater ratio of sports socks to all socks? _____

   Kendra: $\frac{\text{sports socks}}{\text{all socks}}$ = ☐   Jamilla: $\frac{\text{sports socks}}{\text{all socks}}$ = ☐

Name _____ Date _____

> **Summarize**
>
> **Interpreting Ratios**
>
> Write the fraction needed for the answer. Then fill in the appropriate values and simplify the result.
>
> **Comparing Ratios**
>
> Determine the appropriate ratios. Write the ratios as fractions with the same denominator or write them as decimals, then compare.

Practice

1. Write the ratio **21:49** in two other ways. _____ _____

Complete the fraction so that the ratios are equivalent.

2. $\dfrac{3}{5} = \dfrac{12}{\square}$

3. $\dfrac{\square}{36} = \dfrac{7}{18}$

4. $\dfrac{14}{24} = \dfrac{\square}{12}$

In Exercises 5–7, determine the batting average for each of player.

$$\text{Batting average} = \dfrac{\text{number of hits}}{\text{number of attempts}}$$

5. In June, Player **A** came to bat **97** times and hit the ball **36** times. _____

6. In May, Player **B** came to bat **119** times and hit the ball **33** times. _____

7. In March and April, Player **C** went to bat **92** times and hit the ball **29** times. _____

8. Use the results of Exercises 5–7.

   Best batting average: Player _____   Worst batting average: Player _____

Write the ratio in simplest form.

9. Kelly drove **1105** miles on her **3600** mile trip. Write a ratio that shows the number of miles Kelly drove compared to the total length of the trip.

   $\dfrac{\text{distance Kelly drove}}{\text{total length of trip}} = \dfrac{\square}{\square}$

10. A middle school has a total of **950** students. There are **304** students in sixth grade, **290** in seventh grade, and **356** in eighth grade. Write a fraction that shows the ratio of the number of sixth grade students to eighth grade students.

    $\dfrac{\text{number of } \square \text{th grade students}}{\text{number of } \square \text{th grade students}} = \dfrac{\square}{\square}$

Math Intervention
Book 4 Ratios, Rates, Proportions, and Percents

Name _____   Date _____

Compare the ratios. Complete the statement with <, >, or =.

11. $\frac{4}{9}$ ◯ $\frac{2}{3}$ 12. $\frac{8}{20}$ ◯ $\frac{12}{24}$

13. 5 : 6 ◯ 7 : 8   14. 3 to 9 ◯ 4 to 12

Write the ratios. Compare the results. Explain your answer.

15. Willis made **14** of **20** free throw shots in practice. Joe made **8** of **12** free throw shots. Who had the better practice?

_____
_____

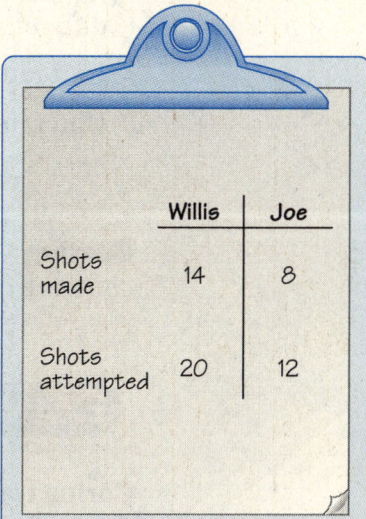

16. Hakim sold a total of **157** cases of fruit for a fundraiser, **82** cases of oranges and **75** cases of grapefruit. Juan also sold **157** cases of fruit, but he sold **103** cases of grapefruit. For the entire fundraiser, the ratio of cases of oranges to total fruit sold was **0.45**. Who came closer to this ratio, Hakim or Juan?

_____
_____
_____

DID YOU GET IT?

17. **Fill in the missing words.** To compare two ratios, write the ratios as _____ or compute the _____ equivalent of the ratios. Then determine the appropriate answer.

18. **Compare ratios.** Jenna read **12** out of the **15** books on her class reading list. Ty read **15** out of the **18** books suggested by the school librarian. Who read the greater portion of books?

_____

19. **Explain your results.** Michael swims **10** laps in **6** minutes. Javier swims **12** laps in **8** minutes. Whose average lap speed (laps to minutes) is greater? Explain your reasoning.

_____
_____
_____

Name _____ Date _____

LESSON 4-2

Rates

> **Words to Remember**
>
> Rate: A ratio of two quantities measured in different units $\frac{45 \text{ miles}}{9 \text{ hours}}$
>
> Unit rate: A rate with a denominator of **1** unit $\frac{5 \text{ miles}}{1 \text{ hour}}$ or 5 mi/h
>
> Unit rates are often read as "per." 5 miles per hour

Getting Started In Lesson 4-1 you learned how to represent and compare quantities as a ratio. A rate is a special type of ratio.

EXAMPLE 1 Simplifying Rates

Corina travels 450 miles from Danville to Big Rock. It takes her 8 hours to make the trip. What is the rate at which Corina traveled?

Solution

Step 1 Write the rate in fraction form. Simplify the fraction if necessary.

$$\frac{450 \text{ miles}}{8 \text{ hours}} = \frac{225 \text{ miles}}{4 \text{ hours}}$$

Step 2 Divide to find the unit rate. Divide the numerator and denominator by 4.

$$\frac{225 \text{ miles} \div 4}{4 \text{ hours} \div 4} = \frac{56.25 \text{ miles}}{1 \text{ hour}}$$

> **Unit Rates**
> Divide the numerator and denominator by the same number to **write the denominator as 1 unit.**

ANSWER Corina traveled at **56.25** miles per hour.

TRY THIS Write a unit rate.

1. Julia was painting notecards for art club. She was able to complete **372** note cards in **12** sessions. What was the average number of notecards she painted in each session?

2. Charlie is building bird houses. He builds **15** bird houses in **5** days. What is his rate for building bird houses?

Math Intervention
Book 4 Ratios, Rates, Proportions, and Percents

Name _____ Date _____

Unit Prices A unit price such as **$1.99** per pound is a special type of unit rate. You can use unit prices to decide which item is the better buy.

EXAMPLE 2 Comparing Unit Prices

A store sells apples packaged in two ways: a bag of 5 pounds for $4.50 or a box of 10 pounds for $8.00. Which is the better buy?

Solution

To find the better buy, compare the unit prices.

5-pound bag: $\dfrac{\$4.50}{5 \text{ pounds}} = \dfrac{\$.90}{1 \text{ pound}}$ Write as a unit rate.

10-pound box: $\dfrac{\$8.00}{10 \text{ pounds}} = \dfrac{\$.80}{1 \text{ pound}}$ Write as a unit rate.

ANSWER Since the **10**-pound box costs less per pound, it is the better buy.

Multi-Step Rates You can use a rate to predict an unknown value or quantity. Multiply or divide by the numerator of the unit rate.

> **Remember**
> When writing rates, the word **per** separates the numerator from the denominator.

EXAMPLE 3 Solving Multi-Step Rate Problems

Alicia read her last book at a rate of 8 pages per day. If she reads a 184-page book at the same rate, how long will it take Alicia to read the book?

Solution

Since the unknown value is "days," which is in the denominator of the unit rate, you *divide* the known values.

$8\overline{)184}^{23}$ Divide the pages in the book by the pages read in 1 day.

ANSWER It will take Alicia **23** days to read the book.

> **Dimensional Analysis**
> In Example 3, you can use the units in the division. **Some units cancel out.**
> 184 pages ÷ $\dfrac{8 \text{ pages}}{1 \text{ day}}$
> = $\overset{23}{\cancel{184 \text{ pages}}} \cdot \dfrac{1 \text{ day}}{\cancel{8 \text{ pages}}}$
> = 23 days

TRY THIS

3. Karen spent **3** hours driving to her grandmother's house. If she drove at an average rate of **60** miles per hour, how many miles did she travel?

   Step 1 The unknown value is "miles," which is in the _____ of the unit rate. So, *multiply* by the numerator of the unit rate, _____.

   Step 2 Multiply 3 × _____ = _____.

   Step 3 Karen drove _____ to her grandmother's house.

Math Intervention
Book 4 Ratios, Rates, Proportions, and Percents

Name _____ Date _____

> **Summarize**
>
> **Simplifying Rates**
>
> Write the fractional form of the rate. Fill in the appropriate values. Simplify if possible.
>
> **Comparing Unit Prices**
>
> You can write the price of items as unit prices to decide which is the better buy.
>
> **Solving Multi-Step Problems with Rates**
>
> Multiply or divide by the numerator of a given unit rate to find a missing value in another rate in the problem.

Practice

1. Which fraction represents a rate? Explain why the others are ratios, but not rates. _____

   A. $\dfrac{12 \text{ inches}}{1 \text{ foot}}$ B. $\dfrac{1200 \text{ words}}{24 \text{ minutes}}$ C. $\dfrac{12 \text{ meters}}{120 \text{ centimeters}}$ D. $\dfrac{3 \text{ hours}}{180 \text{ minutes}}$

2. Which of the following is *not* a unit rate? Explain why not. _____

   A. $\dfrac{5 \text{ miles}}{1 \text{ hour}}$ B. $\dfrac{\$30}{1 \text{ case}}$ C. $\dfrac{32 \text{ pages}}{1 \text{ day}}$ D. $\dfrac{12 \text{ tiles}}{144 \text{ inches}}$

Write the rate in simplest form.

3. Miguel types a **4200** word essay in **105** minutes. What rate describes the number of words per minute that he types?

4. Dora drove from San Mateo to Lemon Heights. The **420** mile trip took her **7** hours. What was Dora's rate in miles per hour for this trip?

5. Michelle spent **3** hours baking **6** batches of muffins. At what rate did Michelle bake a batch of muffins?

6. Joe mowed **8** lawns in **6** hours. What was Joe's rate in lawns per hour?

Find the unit price to the nearest cent.

7. **7** tomatoes for **$3.50**   8. **12** caps for **$52.00**   9. **20** pencils for **$4.25**

Which is the better buy?

10. Used CDs: **8** for **$45** or **12** for **$64**?

11. Pasta: **10** pounds for **$16.38** or **2** pounds for **$3.47**?

Math Intervention
Book 4 Ratios, Rates, Proportions, and Percents

Name _____ Date _____

Determine the rate. Then *multiply* or *divide* to answer the question. Describe how you decided which operation to use.

12. Kyle ran a **5** kilometer race in **40** minutes. If he runs a **10** kilometer race at the same rate, how long will it take Kyle to complete the race?

_____
_____
_____

13. Eunice stuffed envelopes at a rate of **50** per hour. How many envelopes did she stuff in **4** hours?

_____
_____

14. Julio spent a total of **6** hours reading a **216**-page book. How long should it take him to read a **288**-page book if he reads at the same rate?

_____
_____
_____

DID YOU GET IT?

15. Fill in the missing words. When writing a rate in fraction form, the word *per* separates the _____ from the _____ of the fraction.

16. Write a rate. Horatio traveled **146** miles in **40** minutes. At what rate, in miles per hour, did he travel?

_____

17. Explain your results. Cora bought a **24** pack of water bottles for **$3.99**. What would Cora pay for a **36** pack of water bottles at the same rate? Explain why you chose to use *multiplication* or *division* to determine your result.

_____
_____
_____

Math Intervention
Book 4 Ratios, Rates, Proportions, and Percents

Name _____ Date _____

LESSON 4-3 Convert Units in the Metric System

> **Words to Remember**
> Metric system: A system of measurement based on the decimal system
> Some common metric units of measurement are centimeters, meters, kilograms, milliliters, and so on.

Getting Started In Lessons 1-24, 2-24, and 2-27 you learned how to multiply and divide by powers of **10**. In this lesson you will use both of these skills to convert units within the metric system.

Converting Units When you are changing from a larger unit to a smaller unit (say, meters to centimeters, as in Example 1), you *multiply* by a power of **10**. To change from a smaller unit to a larger unit, you *divide* by a power of **10**. The chart below shows meters, but the same method also works for grams and liters.

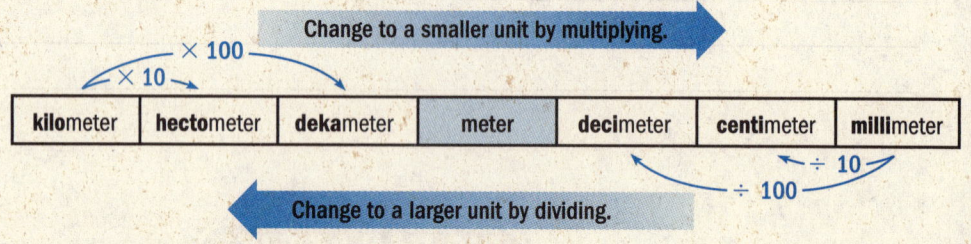

EXAMPLE 1 Converting Metric Units in Symbolic Form

How many centimeters are in 129 meters?

Solution

Step 1 **Identify** the power of **10** you need to use for the conversion from meters to centimeters.

100

Step 2 **Write** an expression for the conversion. Since centimeters are smaller than meters, write an expression showing multiplication by **100**.

129 meters = (129 × 100) centimeters

= 12,900 centimeters

ANSWER There are **12,900** centimeters in **129** meters.

> **Using the Conversion Chart**
> Use the chart above Example 1. You move two steps to the right from meters to centimeters, so multiply by 10^2, or 100.

Name _____   Date _____

TRY THIS Tell whether you would *multiply* or *divide* by a factor to solve the problem. Then identify the factor.

> **Remember**
> When converting to a smaller unit, multiply by the power of 10. When converting to a larger unit, divide by the power of 10.

1. How many meters are in 25 centimeters? _____ by _____
2. How many kilograms are in 320,000 grams? _____ by _____
3. How many deciliters are in 47 liters? _____ by _____

EXAMPLE 2 Computing a Metric Conversion

How many kilograms are in 1500 grams?

Solution

Step 1 Identify the power of 10 you need to use for the conversion from grams to kilograms.

1000

Step 2 Write an expression for the conversion. Since kilograms are larger than grams, write an expression showing division by 1000.

1500 grams = (1500 ÷ 1000) kilograms

= 1.5 kilograms

ANSWER There are 1.5 kilograms in 1500 grams.

> **Review Operations with Powers of 10**
> Recall that when you multiply or divide by a power of 10, you move the decimal point. Add or remove zeros as necessary.

TRY THIS Convert the following metric units.

4. How many grams are in 365 dekagrams?

5. How many millimeters are in 71 centimeters?

6. How many kiloliters are in 49,100 liters?

7. How many hectometers are in 94,000,000 centimeters?

8. How many centigrams are in 137 dekagrams?

Name _____   Date _____

> **Summarize**
>
> **Converting Metric Units**
>
> When you convert from a larger unit to a smaller unit, multiply by the power of 10. When you convert from a smaller unit to a larger unit, divide by the power of 10.
>
> **Writing Metric Conversions in Symbolic Form**
>
> Identify the power of 10 needed for the conversion. Write an expression multiplying or dividing by the power of 10.

Practice

Write the power of 10 needed to make the conversion.

1. kilometer to meter _____
2. meter to millimeter _____
3. decigram to gram _____
4. gram to kilogram _____

Write the expression(s) needed to make the conversion.

5. How many centimeters are in 23 hectometers?
6. How many kilograms are in 1320 dekagrams?
7. How many liters are in 37,500,000 milliliters?
8. How many decimeters are in 2300 centimeters?
9. How many millimeters are in 32 kilometers?
10. How many grams are in 230 dekagrams?
11. How many centiliters are in 1350 milliliters?
12. How many millimeters are in 97 decimeters?
13. How many hectograms are in 34,000,000 centigrams?
14. How many dekaliters are in 7500 liters?
15. How many meters are in 272,000 millimeters?

Complete the statement.

16. 3.9 kL = _____ L
17. 52 m = _____ mm
18. 300 g = _____ kg

Math Intervention
Book 4 Ratios, Rates, Proportions, and Percents

Name _____ Date _____

Tell if you need to *multiply* or *divide* to make the conversion. Then make the conversion. Explain your answer.

19. The drawing shows a set of shelves. What are the dimensions of the set of shelves in decimeters?

_____
_____
_____
_____
_____

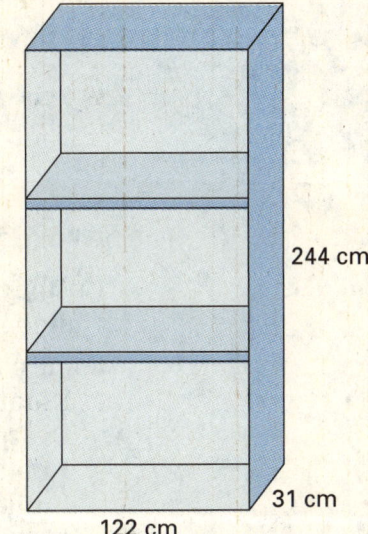

244 cm
31 cm
122 cm

20. A pitcher holds **2000** milliliters of juice. How many liters does the container hold?

_____
_____
_____

21. A piece of wood measures **1.8** meters. How long is the piece of wood in centimeters?

_____
_____
_____

DID YOU GET IT?

22. Fill in the missing words or numbers. To convert from meters to millimeters, _____ by _____.

23. Write an expression. Write the expression to determine how many centigrams are in **230** grams.

_____
_____

24. Explain your results. A batch of muffins requires **237** milliliters of milk. How many liters of milk are needed? Explain your reasoning.

_____
_____
_____

Name _____ Date _____

LESSON 4-4
Convert Units in the Customary System

Words to Remember

Customary system: The system of measurement commonly used in the United States

Some common measurements and conversions:

1 foot (ft) = 12 inches (in.)	1 cup (c) = 8 fluid ounces (fl oz)
1 yard (yd) = 3 feet	1 pint (pt) = 2 cups
1 mile (mi) = 1760 yd	1 quart (qt) = 2 pints
1 mile = 5280 feet	1 gallon (gal) = 4 quarts
1 pound (lb) = 16 ounces (oz)	1 hour (h) = 60 minutes (min)
1 ton = 2000 pounds	1 minute = 60 seconds (sec)

Getting Started In Lesson 4-3 you learned how to convert units in the metric system with multiplication and division. In this lesson, you will learn how to make conversions within the customary system using multiplication and division.

EXAMPLE 1 — Using Expressions to Represent Conversions

How many inches are in 36 feet?

Solution

feet to inches	Identify the conversion needed.
36 × 12 = ?	Multiply by the number of inches in 1 foot.
36 feet = 432 inches	Write the number of inches. 36 × 12 = 432

ANSWER There are 432 inches in 36 feet.

Remember
When converting to a smaller unit, multiply by the conversion amount. When converting to a larger unit, divide by the conversion amount.

TRY THIS Write the expression needed to make the conversion.

1. How many ounces are in 5 pounds?

   5  = _____ , so 5 pounds = _____ ounces.

2. How many miles are in 15,840 feet?

   15,840  = _____ , so 15,840 feet = _____ miles.

Math Intervention
Book 4 Ratios, Rates, Proportions, and Percents

Name _____ Date _____

EXAMPLE 2 Computing a Multi-Step Conversion

The clock shows the number of hours in 1 day. How many minutes are in 1 day?

Solution

Convert days to hours. Then convert hours to minutes.

Step 1 Convert days to hours.

$1 \times 24 = ?$	Multiply by the number of hours in 1 day.
1 day = 24 hours	Write the number of hours. $1 \times 24 = 24$

> **Remember**
> In Example 2, minutes are smaller than days, so multiply by the needed conversions.

Step 2 Convert hours to minutes.

$24 \times 60 = ?$	Multiply by the number of minutes in 1 hour.
24 hours = 1440 minutes	Write the number of minutes. $24 \times 60 = 1440$

ANSWER There are **1440** minutes in one day.

EXAMPLE 3 Computing a Multi-Step Conversion

How many tons are in 40,000 ounces?

Solution

Convert ounces to pounds. Then convert pounds to tons.

$40{,}000 \div 16 = ?$	Divide by the number of ounces in 1 pound.
40,000 ounces = 2500 pounds	Write the number of pounds.
$2500 \div 2000 = ?$	Divide by the number of pounds in 1 ton.
2500 pounds = 1.25 tons	Write the number of tons.

> **Remember**
> In Example 3, tons are larger than ounces, so divide by the needed conversions.

ANSWER There are **1.25** tons in **40,000** ounces.

TRY THIS Convert the following customary units.

3. How many inches are in 6 yards?

4. How many gallons are in 18 pints?

5. How many fluid ounces are in 14 quarts?

Name _____   Date _____

> **Summarize**
>
> **Converting Customary Units**
>
> When you convert from a larger unit to a smaller unit, multiply by the conversion amount. When you convert from a smaller unit to a larger unit, divide by the conversion amount.
>
> **Using Expressions to Represent Conversions**
>
> Identify the conversion(s) needed. Write an expression or expressions multiplying or dividing by the conversion(s) needed.

Practice

Identify the operation and value needed to make the conversion.

1. ounces to pounds

    _____ by _____

2. quart to pint

    _____ by _____

3. hours to minutes

    _____ by _____

4. cups to fluid ounces

    _____ by _____

Write the expression(s) needed to make the conversion.

5. How many hours are in 3 days?

6. How many feet are in 2 miles?

7. How many cups are in 36 fluid ounces?

8. How many gallons are in 10 quarts?

9. How many feet are in 12 yards?

10. How many tons are in 32,000 pounds?

11. How many pints are in 3 gallons?

12. How many seconds are in 12 hours?

13. How many pounds are in 3.5 tons?

14. How many fluid ounces are in 6 cups?

15. How many yards are in 2 miles?

16. How many ounces are in 13 pounds?

Math Intervention
Book 4 Ratios, Rates, Proportions, and Percents

Name _____   Date _____

Tell if you need to *multiply* or *divide* to make the conversion. Then make the conversion. Explain your answer.

17. The distance from school to Tom's house is **23,760** feet. How many miles is it from school to Tom's house?

_____
_____
_____

18. There are **15** days left until vacation. How many minutes do you need to wait?

_____
_____
_____

19. Jade made **8** gallons of punch for the dance. How many cups of liquid did she make?

_____
_____
_____

DID YOU GET IT?

20. Fill in the missing words. To convert from miles to _____, you need to _____ by **5280**.

21. Write the expression. How many feet are in **41** yards?

_____
_____
_____

22. Explain your results. A recipe calls for **5** pounds of flour. How many ounces of flour will the recipe need? Explain your reasoning.

_____
_____
_____

Math Intervention
Book 4 Ratios, Rates, Proportions, and Percents

LESSON 4-5
Convert Units in Different Measurement Systems

Words to Remember
Some common conversions from customary to metric:
1 inch = 2.54 centimeters
1 foot = 0.3048 meters
1 mile ≈ 1.609 kilometers
1 fluid ounce ≈ 29.573 milliliters
1 gallon ≈ 3.785 liters
1 quart ≈ 0.946 liters
1 ounce ≈ 28.35 grams
1 pound ≈ 0.454 kilograms
°Celsius = (°Fahrenheit − 32) ÷ 1.8
1 square foot ≈ 0.093 square meters
1 square mile ≈ 2.59 square kilometers
1 cubic foot ≈ 0.028 cubic meters

Getting Started In Lessons 4-3 and 4-4 you learned how to convert measurements within the same system. In this lesson, you will learn to convert between the metric and the customary systems of measurement.

EXAMPLE 1 Converting from One System to Another

How many inches are in 17.78 centimeters?

Solution

inches to centimeters	Identify the conversion needed.
17.78 ÷ 2.54 = ?	Divide by the number of centimeters in 1 inch.
17.78 cm = 7 in.	Write the number of inches. 17.78 ÷ 2.54 = 7

ANSWER There are 7 inches in 17.78 centimeters.

> **Remember**
> To convert from customary to metric, you multiply by the conversion factor. To convert from metric to customary you divide by the conversion factor.

TRY THIS Multiply or divide by the conversion factor to make the conversion. Round to the nearest hundredth.

1. How many feet are in 16.4 meters?
2. How many gallons are in 2 liters?
3. How many kilograms are in 7.707 pounds?

Math Intervention
Book 4 Ratios, Rates, Proportions, and Percents

Name _____ Date _____

EXAMPLE 2 Comparing Measures Between Systems

Which is warmer, 25°C or 65°F?

Reading
The symbols, °F and °C are read as "degrees Fahrenheit" and "degrees Celsius."

Solution

Step 1 Convert °F to °C.

$°C = (°F - 32) \div 1.8$ Write the temperature conversion formula.

$°C = (65 - 32) \div 1.8$ Substitute 65 for °F.

$= 18.3°C$ Simplify.

Step 2 Compare the two temperatures in °C.

$25°C > 18.3°C$ Compare the values.

ANSWER Since 25°C > 18.3°C and 18.3°C = 65°F, then 25°C > 65°F. So, 25°C is warmer than 65°F.

Remember When comparing measurements in different systems, you only need to convert one measurement. Then compare the results in the same system.

TRY THIS   Compare the measurements with > or <.

4. 5 square miles and 10 square kilometers

   Step 1 5 square miles = _____ square kilometers

   Step 2 So, 5 square miles ◯ 10 square kilometers.

5. 32 gallons and 50 liters

6. 132 cubic feet and 2 cubic meters

7. 12 grams and 2 ounces

Math Intervention
Book 4 Ratios, Rates, Proportions, and Percents

Name _____ Date _____

> **Summarize**
>
> **Converting from One System to Another**
> Determine the conversion needed. Write an expression using multiplication if converting from customary to metric or division if converting from metric to customary. Evaluate the expression.
>
> **Comparing Measures from One System to Another**
> Convert one of the values into its corresponding unit from the other system. Compare the results.

Practice

Which operation is needed to make the conversion, *multiplication* or *division*?

1. feet to meters _____
2. ounces to grams _____
3. milliliters to fluid ounces _____
4. cubic feet to cubic meters _____

Convert units from one system to another.

5. How many cubic feet are in **2.4** cubic meters?
6. How many ounces are in **18** grams?
7. When it is **77°** Fahrenheit, it is _____ degrees Celsius.
8. **15** kilometers is equal to _____ miles.
9. **168** square feet equals _____ square meters.
10. How many liters are in **16** gallons?
11. **318** cubic feet is equivalent to _____ cubic meters.
12. How many square meters are in **168** square feet?

Compare the units.

13. Which is greater, **18** square miles or **45** square kilometers?
14. Which is less, **13** grams or **1** ounce?
15. Which is less, **138** mL or **4** fluid ounces?
16. Which is colder, **48°F** or **7°C**?

Math Intervention
Book 4 Ratios, Rates, Proportions, and Percents

Name _____ Date _____

Determine the operation needed to convert the first unit to the second. Then do the conversion. Explain your answer.

17. Joseph weighs 117 pounds. Kevin's mass is 51 kilograms. Who weighs less?

_____
_____
_____

18. A container can hold 12 cubic meters of liquid. A second container can hold 450 cubic feet of liquid. Which container can hold the most liquid?

_____
_____
_____

19. One path is 40 kilometers long; a second path is 24 miles in length. Which path is longer?

_____
_____
_____

DID YOU GET IT?

20. **Fill in the missing words.** To convert from gallons to _____ you need to _____ by the conversion factor of 3.785.

21. **Write an expression for the conversion.** How many square miles are in 32 square kilometers?

_____
_____
_____

22. **Explain your results.** Which is less, 14 kilograms or 35 pounds? Explain your reasoning.

_____
_____
_____

Math Intervention
Book 4 Ratios, Rates, Proportions, and Percents

Name _____ Date _____

Making a Scale Drawing

> **Goal:** Use scale drawings to explain mathematical reasoning.
>
> **Materials:** A **3** inch by **5** inch notecard or piece of paper, customary ruler, metric ruler, and a **6** inch by **10** inch piece of paper.

Getting Started   In Lesson 4-5 you learned how to convert units between different systems of measures. You can convert measures to create and read a scale drawing. The scale compares the drawing with the actual object.

Reading a Scale   Scales for scale drawings are usually ratios comparing the model size to the actual size. An example is a map with scale **1** inch : **10** miles. This means that for every inch on the map, you would actually travel **10** miles.

EXAMPLE

Use a map to determine actual distances.

What is the actual distance from State Street to Main Street if you travel along College Avenue?

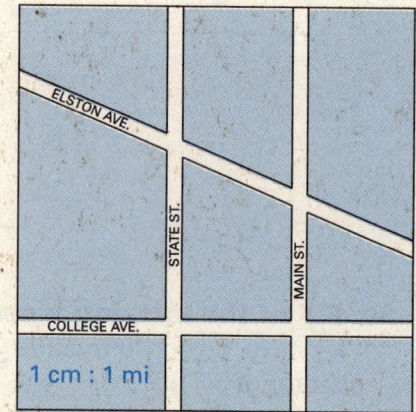

Solution

Step 1 **Measure** the distance on the map.

Using a ruler, the distance from State Street to Main Street along College Avenue is **1.5** centimeters.

Step 2 **Use** equivalent ratios to find the actual distance.

      ×1.5 (1 cm : 1 mi / 1.5 cm : x mi) ×?   Write scale.

      Multiply by 1.5.

Step 3 **Find** the value of x.

1 mi × 1.5 = 1.5 mi, so $x = 1.5$.

ANSWER   The distance from State Street to Main Street along College Avenue is **1.5** miles.

Math Intervention
Book 4 Ratios, Rates, Proportions, and Percents

MAKE IT A GAME!

- Form groups of **2** students.
- Each student creates a **2** inch grid on the **6** inch by **10** inch piece of paper.
- Allow each student **2** minutes to create a simple drawing on a note card or **3** inch by **5** inch piece of paper.
- Trade drawings with a partner and start a timer.
- Each student needs to create a scale of **2** inches : **1** inch for their model. Then recreate the drawing on the larger sheet of paper.
- The student who completes an accurate scale drawing in the shortest amount of time wins.

Practice

The floor plan shows the location of some rooms in a house. Use the floor plan for Exercises 1–4.

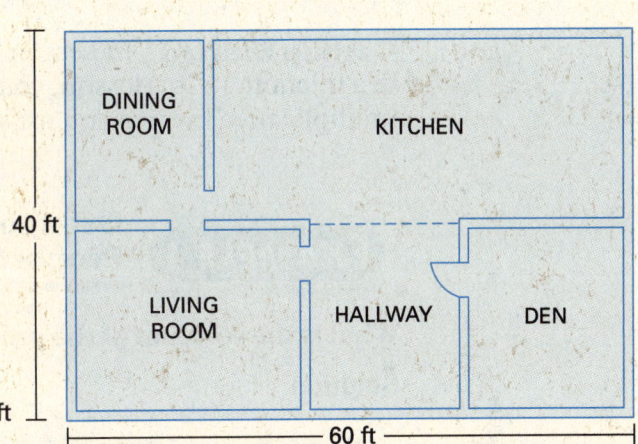

1. What are the dimensions of the den on the model?

2. What are the dimensions of the dining room on the model?

3. What are the actual dimensions of the kitchen?

4. What are the actual dimensions of the living room?

5. Draw a scale model of your classroom. Use the scale of **1** inch : **10** feet.

DID YOU GET IT? Use a map scale.

6. A piece of land is drawn on a map to measure **10** cm by **35** cm. The scale used to create the map is **1** cm : **10** meters. What are the actual dimensions of the piece of land?

Name _____ Date _____

LESSON 4-7 Solve Proportions

Words to Remember

Multiplicative inverse: For the ratio $\frac{a}{b}$ (where $a, b \neq 0$), the multiplicative inverse is its reciprocal, or $\frac{b}{a}$.

Inverse property of multiplication: The product of a number and its multiplicative inverse is **1**.

$\frac{2}{3} \cdot \frac{3}{2} = 1$ $\frac{1}{5} \cdot 5 = 1$

Proportion: An equation stating that two ratios are equivalent $\frac{2}{3} = \frac{x}{7}$

Getting Started In Lesson 2-14 you learned how to find a reciprocal of a fraction. In this lesson, you will use the reciprocal to determine a multiplicative inverse and use this value to solve proportions.

EXAMPLE 1 Using a Multiplicative Inverse to Solve a Proportion

What is the solution of the proportion $\frac{x}{8} = \frac{3}{4}$?

Solution

$\frac{x}{8} = \frac{3}{4}$ Write the proportion.

$\frac{8}{1} \cdot \frac{x}{8} = \frac{3}{4} \cdot \frac{8}{1}$ Multiply each side of the proportion by the multiplicative inverse of the term with the variable.

$x = \frac{24}{4}$ Perform the indicated multiplication.

$x = 6$ Simplify.

ANSWER The solution is 6.

TRY THIS Solve the proportion using multiplicative inverses.

1. $\frac{x}{10} = \frac{6}{5}$ _____   2. $\frac{12}{7} = \frac{x}{14}$ _____

Math Intervention
Book 4 Ratios, Rates, Proportions, and Percents

Solve Proportions using Cross Products A cross product is another operation used to solve a proportion. It is based on the multiplicative inverse. It is especially useful when the variable is in the denominator of one of the fractions.

Cross products property: The cross products of a proportion are equal.

If $\frac{a}{b} = \frac{c}{d}$ where $b \neq 0$ and $d \neq 0$, then $ad = bc$.

EXAMPLE 2 — Using Cross Products to Solve a Proportion

What is the solution of $\frac{3}{x} = \frac{7}{21}$?

Solution

$\frac{3}{x} = \frac{7}{21}$ Write the original proportion.

$3(21) = x(7)$ Use the cross products property.

$63 = 7x$ Multiply.

$\frac{63}{7} = \frac{7x}{7}$ Divide each side by 7.

$9 = x$

ANSWER The solution is 9.

TRY THIS Fill in the missing information to use cross products to solve the proportion.

3. $\frac{5}{7} = \frac{10}{x}$

   ▪ · x = ▪ · ▪

   ▪ · x = ▪

   $\frac{5x}{▪} = \frac{▪}{▪}$

   x = ▪

4. $\frac{x}{9} = \frac{2}{3}$

   x · ▪ = ▪ · ▪

   ▪ · x = ▪

   $\frac{▪}{3} = \frac{18}{▪}$

   x = ▪

Name _____ Date _____

> **Summarize**
>
> **Using Multiplicative Inverses to Solve Proportions**
>
> Determine the multiplicative inverse of the fraction with the variable in it and multiply both sides of the proportion by this fraction. Multiply the fractions and simplify the results.
>
> **Using Cross Products to Solve Proportions**
>
> Write the product created by multiplying the values along both diagonals of the proportion, for example. Perform the multiplication and solve the problem.

Practice

Write the multiplicative inverse of the ratio.

1. $\frac{10}{3}$ _____
2. $\frac{6}{19}$ _____
3. $\frac{7}{5}$ _____
4. $\frac{9}{5}$ _____

Write the multiplicative inverse that you would use to solve the proportion.

5. $\frac{7}{8} = \frac{x}{13}$ _____
6. $\frac{x}{2} = \frac{3}{8}$ _____

Write the cross products for the proportion.

7. $\frac{4}{9} = \frac{x}{7}$

   _____ and _____

8. $\frac{x}{13} = \frac{7}{10}$

   _____ and _____

Match the proportion with its solution.

9. $\frac{x}{12} = \frac{2}{4}$ _____
   - A. 3
   - B. 3.67
   - C. 6
   - D. 13.5

10. $\frac{9}{x} = \frac{5}{3}$ _____
    - A. 15
    - B. 5.4
    - C. 2.4
    - D. 1

Find the solution of the proportion.

11. $\frac{15}{2} = \frac{x}{6}$

12. $\frac{x}{3} = \frac{9}{6}$

13. $\frac{13}{x} = \frac{2}{4}$

14. $\frac{8}{3} = \frac{12}{x}$

Math Intervention
Book 4 Ratios, Rates, Proportions, and Percents

Name _____ Date _____

Solve the problem. Explain your results.

15. Kendra tried to solve the proportion $\frac{5}{7} = \frac{x}{14}$, but did not get the correct answer. Find her mistake and correct it. Kendra's work:

$$\frac{7}{5} \cdot \frac{5}{7} = \frac{x}{14} \cdot \frac{7}{5}$$

$$1 = \frac{7x}{70}$$

$$x = \frac{1}{10}$$

_____
_____
_____

16. A picture measures **8** inches by **9** inches. Sheila wants to enlarge the picture so that the longest side is **18** inches long. She set up the proportion $\frac{8}{9} = \frac{x}{18}$. Solve the proportion to determine the shorter side of the picture. Do you think that Sheila set up the correct proportion?

_____
_____
_____

DID YOU GET IT?

17. Fill in the missing words. To solve proportions using cross products, you _____ the values along each _____ and then solve the resulting equation.

18. Solve a proportion. Find the value of x that makes the proportion $\frac{4}{7} = \frac{x}{14}$ true.

_____
_____

19. Explain your results. Jamal is making a copy of a famous mural that measures **12** feet wide by **18** feet long. He set up the proportion $\frac{12}{18} = \frac{6}{x}$, since his copy is only **6** feet wide. How long is Jamal's copy? Is his proportion correct? Why or why not?

_____
_____

Math Intervention
Book 4 Ratios, Rates, Proportions, and Percents

LESSON 4-8: Solve Problems with Proportions

Strategies to Remember

To use a proportion when you solve a word problem:

(1) **Identify the relationships** in the problem.	(2) **Write a proportion** to represent the relationships.
(3) **Use multiplicative inverses or cross products** to solve the proportion.	(4) **Check** your answer **for reasonableness**.

Getting Started In Lesson 4-6 you learned how to solve a proportion using cross multiplication. In this lesson, you will solve problems involving proportions.

EXAMPLE 1 Solving a Proportion

What is the value of g when $\frac{3}{10} = \frac{g}{12}$?

Solution

$\frac{3}{10} = \frac{g}{12}$ Write the original proportion.

$3(12) = 10g$ Write the cross products.

$36 = 10g$ Multiply.

$g = 3.6$ Divide by 10.

ANSWER The solution is 3.6.

TRY THIS
What is the value of the variable that makes the proportion true?

1. $\frac{8}{c} = \frac{4}{7}$ $8 \cdot \square = c \cdot \square$

    $c = \square$

2. $\frac{13}{15} = \frac{f}{5}$

3. $\frac{16}{21} = \frac{d}{3}$

Math Intervention
Book 4 Ratios, Rates, Proportions, and Percents

Name _____ Date _____

 **Writing a Proportion to Solve a Problem**

The distance from Redding to Sonora is 260 miles. The scale on a map is 1 inch : 150 miles. What is the distance between the cities on the map?

Solution

$\dfrac{1 \text{ inch}}{150 \text{ miles}} = \dfrac{x}{260 \text{ miles}}$ Write a proportion.

$260 = 150x$ Write the cross products.

$x \approx 1.73$ inches   Solve the problem. Make sure to put in the appropriate units.

ANSWER The distance between the cities on the map is approximately **1.73** inches.

Checking Units When you are writing a proportion, make sure that the units used in creating the fractions are consistent. One way to check this is to make sure that the cross products have the same units each time.

In Example 2, for example, the proportion is $\dfrac{1 \text{ inch}}{150 \text{ miles}} = \dfrac{x}{260 \text{ miles}}$, so the cross products are $(1 \cdot 260)$ inch-miles and $(x \cdot 150)$ inch-miles.

TRY THIS Use proportions to find the values.

4. Jennifer is creating a replica of a mural at her school. The actual mural measures **6** feet by **10** feet. The replica that she is creating has a long side of **22** feet. Jennifer used the proportion $\dfrac{6}{10} = \dfrac{x}{22}$. What are the measurements of Jennifer's replica?

   ☐ · ☐ = ☐ · ☐

   ☐ = ☐

5. Korgan was building a replica of the Transamerica Pyramid in San Francisco. The actual building is **260** meters tall. Korgan's model is **32.5** centimeters tall. Set up and solve a proportion to determine how many meters of the real building are equivalent to **10** cm of the model.

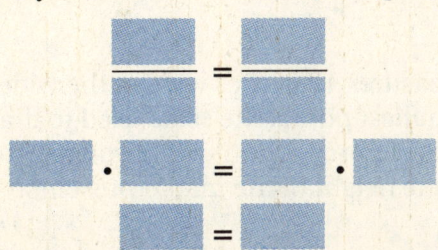

Name _____   Date _____

> **Summarize**
>
> **Solving the Proportion Given in the Problem**
>
> Cross multiply the values in the proportion. Solve the equation using division.
>
> **Writing a Proportion to Solve the Problem**
>
> Set up a proportion to solve the problem. Remember to set each fraction of the proportion up in the same manner. You can check to make sure this is done properly by making sure the products of the units are the same along each diagonal. Use cross products and division to solve the proportion.

Practice

What value makes the proportion correct?

1. $\dfrac{8}{6} = \dfrac{10}{b}$
2. $\dfrac{10}{5} = \dfrac{m}{15}$
3. $\dfrac{h}{7} = \dfrac{9}{21}$
4. $\dfrac{18}{y} = \dfrac{2}{3}$

Solve the proportion.

5. The distance from Jenna's house to the mall is **17.3** miles. She drives at **30** miles per hour. Solve the proportion $\dfrac{30 \text{ miles}}{1 \text{ hour}} = \dfrac{17.3 \text{ miles}}{h \text{ hours}}$ to determine how long it takes Jenna to get to the mall.

6. Henry types at a rate of **45** words per minute. He has a **2000** word essay to type for Language Arts class. Solve the proportion $\dfrac{45 \text{ words}}{1 \text{ minute}} = \dfrac{2000 \text{ words}}{m \text{ minutes}}$ to determine the amount of time it will take Henry to type his essay.

Write a proportion you could use to solve the problem.

7. The ratio of cats to dogs in a neighborhood is **12** dogs : **8** cats. Another neighborhood has an equivalent ratio of cats to dogs. There are **15** dogs in the second neighborhood. What proportion would you use to determine the number of cats in the second neighborhood?

8. A map of Southern California measures **19** inches wide at the widest point and **13.5** inches tall at the tallest point. The scale used to draw the map is **1.5** inches : **40** miles. What proportion would you use to determine the number of miles the height of the map represents?

Math Intervention
Book 4 Ratios, Rates, Proportions, and Percents

Name _____ Date _____

Write a proportion for each problem. Then solve the proportion. Explain how you determined the proportion.

9. Abe is building a model of the Golden Gate Bridge. The total length of the bridge is **8981** feet long and the towers are **746** feet above water. If Abe's scale is **1** inch : **200** feet, how long is Abe's model?

   _____
   _____

10. Isabelle reads a book at a rate of **30** pages in **1** hour. How long will it take her to read a **318** page book?

    _____
    _____

11. On Tuesday, Marco ran **15** miles in **2.5** hours. If he runs at the same rate on Wednesday, how far will he run in **1.5** hours?

    _____
    _____

DID YOU GET IT?

12. **Fill in the missing words.** When setting up a proportion, it is important to write each _____ in the _____ manner.

13. **Describe a process.** Explain the steps in solving the proportion $\frac{3}{k} = \frac{18}{12}$.

    _____
    _____
    _____

14. **Explain your reasoning.** Michael drove **15** miles from school to his grandmother's house at a rate of **35** miles per hour. Does it seem reasonable that it took him **45** minutes to get there? Why or why not?

    _____
    _____
    _____

Name _____ Date _____

Mixed Practice for Lessons 4-1 to 4-8

Vocabulary Review

Match the word with its mathematical meaning and its everyday meaning.

Word	Mathematical meaning	Everyday meaning
1. customary ___, ___	A. a fractional comparison of two values with the same units	X. the amount of something in terms of some other thing
2. rate ___, ___	B. a system of measurement commonly used in the United States	Y. the relation between two quantities
3. ratio ___, ___	C. a fractional comparison of two values with different units	Z. usual, common

Fill in the missing words.

4. _____ is the process of changing from inches to feet or from meters to miles.

5. The fraction $\frac{4}{7}$ is the _____ of $\frac{7}{4}$.

6. When a model is made of a car, the _____ describes the ratio of the model size to the original size.

Write each rate or ratio in simplest form.

7. A pizza parlor made 75 pizzas on a Friday night. 28 of the pizzas were pepperoni. What is the ratio of pepperoni pizzas to total pizzas made?

8. Sofia had 15 hits out of 41 times at bat in her softball season. What is her batting average?

9. It takes Joanna 90 minutes to drive from her house to her sister's college. If the college is 81 miles away, at what rate was Joanna driving in miles per hour?

10. Karl spent 6 hours washing cars this week. If Karl was able to wash 12 cars, how many cars per hour did he wash?

Math Intervention
Book 4 Ratios, Rates, Proportions, and Percents

Name _____ Date _____

Write and solve the expression needed to make each conversion.

11. How many minutes are there in **6** hours?

12. How many meters are there in **7300** centimeters?

13. How many gallons are there in **7.57** liters?

14. How many kilograms are there in **3.5** pounds?

Solve each proportion.

15. $\dfrac{1}{7} = \dfrac{f}{42}$

16. $\dfrac{g}{16} = \dfrac{3}{8}$

17. $\dfrac{5}{9} = \dfrac{10}{r}$

18. $\dfrac{8}{d} = \dfrac{6}{9}$

Write the fraction(s) needed to find the rate(s) or ratio(s). Then use the rate or ratio to solve the problem. Explain your answer.

19. A case of sports drink costs **$13** and contains **24** **20**-ounce bottles. What is the cost per bottle of the sports drink? How much would you expect a case of **36** bottles to cost?

_____
_____
_____

20. Gina spent a total of **$29.60** to put **10** gallons of gasoline in her truck. What is the cost per gallon of gasoline? How much would it cost Gina to put 15 gallons of gasoline in her truck?

_____
_____
_____

21. Warren types a **3400** word essay in **62** minutes. Cristina types a **5000** word essay in **77** minutes. Who types faster?

_____
_____
_____

LESSON 4-9

Percents

Words to Remember

Percent: A ratio whose denominator is 100. Represented by the symbol %

$35\% = \frac{35}{100}$

Getting Started In Lesson 2-21 you learned how to represent decimals as fractions, and in Lesson 2-22 you learned how to represent a fraction as a decimal. In this lesson you will use both of these skills to work with percents.

EXAMPLE 1 Writing Percents as Part of a Hundred in Fraction Form

Write 45% as a fraction.

Solution

$45\% = \frac{45}{100}$ Write the percent as a fraction with a denominator of 100.

$= \frac{9}{20}$ Simplify the fraction.

ANSWER 45% is equivalent to $\frac{9}{20}$.

Don't forget to simplify each fraction. A problem involving fractions is never complete until the fraction is in simplest form.

TRY THIS Write the percent as a fraction.

1. $80\% = \frac{\square}{100} = \frac{\square}{\square}$

2. $65\% = \frac{\square}{100} = \frac{\square}{\square}$

3. $25\% = \frac{\square}{100} = \frac{\square}{\square}$

4. $10\% = \frac{\square}{100} = \frac{\square}{\square}$

Math Intervention
Book 4 Ratios, Rates, Proportions, and Percents

Name _____ Date _____

EXAMPLE 2 — Writing Percents as Part of a Hundred in Decimal Form

Write 30% as a decimal.

Solution

$30\% = \dfrac{30}{100}$ Write the percent as a fraction.

$= 0.30$ Divide.

ANSWER 30% is equivalent to 0.30.

> **Remember**
> Notice that dividing by 100 is the same as moving the decimal point two places to the left.
> $30\% = .30$

TRY THIS Write the percent as a decimal.

5. $20\% = \dfrac{\boxed{}}{100} = 0.\boxed{}$

6. $45\% = \dfrac{\boxed{}}{100} = 0.\boxed{}$

7. $92\% = \dfrac{\boxed{}}{100} = 0.\boxed{}$

8. $13\% = \dfrac{\boxed{}}{100} = 0.\boxed{}$

EXAMPLE 3 — Using a Model to Show a Percent

Draw a model to show 25%.

Solution

Step 1 Write the percent as a fraction. $25\% = \dfrac{1}{4}$

Step 2 Draw a shape and section it into the same number of pieces as the denominator.

Step 3 Shade the same number of pieces as the numerator.

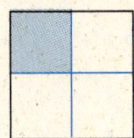

TRY THIS Draw models to show each percent.

9. 30%

10. 75%

11. 60%

12. 10%

Name _____   Date _____

> **Summarize**
>
> **Writing Percents as Fractions**
> Write the percent as a fraction with a denominator of **100**. Simplify the fraction.
>
> **Writing Percents as Decimals**
> Move the decimal point two places to the left.
>
> **Using a Model to Show Percent**
> Write the percent as a decimal. Draw a shape and section it into the same number of pieces as the denominator. Shade the same number of pieces as the numerator.

Practice

Write the percent as a fraction.

1. 15%
2. 35%
3. 50%
4. 85%
5. 5%
6. 40%
7. 60%
8. 95%

Write the percent as a decimal.

9. 25%
10. 10%
11. 42%
12. 87%
13. 32%
14. 9%
15. 77%
16. 53%

17. Which figure represents **20%**?

A.    B. 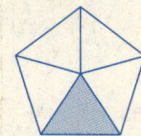   C.    D.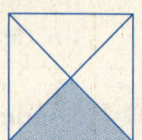

Draw a model to show the percent.

18. 25%
19. 70%
20. 40%
21. 55%

Identify the percent shown.

22.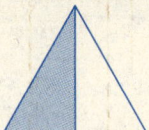

23.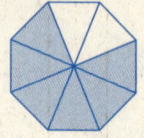

Math Intervention
Book 4 Ratios, Rates, Proportions, and Percents

Name _____   Date _____

Write the percent as a decimal and as a fraction. Then shade the diagram to represent the percent.

24. Carrie wants to plant tomatoes in **40%** of her garden. The diagram models her garden. Shade a part of the garden that Carrie can plant with tomatoes.

_____
_____

25. Marcus wants to use **25%** of a wood board for a project. The diagram models the piece of wood. Shade a part that represents the piece of wood that Marcus needs.

_____
_____

26. Conrad pays more for a bin of scrap metal if the bin is more than **70%** full. The diagram models the bin. Shade the part of the bin that represents **70%** full.

_____
_____

27. Maura is painting a picture in **10%** sections. The diagram models the paint canvas. Shade a piece of the canvas that represents the part she will paint today.

_____
_____

DID YOU GET IT?

28. Shade the figure. What part of the figure represents **90%**?

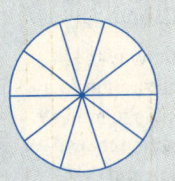

29. Fill in the missing words. To write a percent as a _____ the number before the percent symbol goes in the _____ of the fraction and _____ goes in the _____.

Math Intervention
Book 4 Ratios, Rates, Proportions, and Percents   **37**

Name _____   Date _____

LESSON 4-10
Convert Percents, Fractions, and Decimals

Getting Started In Lesson 4-9 you learned how to turn a percent into a fraction and a decimal. In this lesson you will use these skills to go the other direction and take fractions and decimals and turn them into percents.

Decimals and Percents To write a decimal as a percent, you can multiply by 100. Note that multiplying by 100 is the same as moving the decimal point two places to the right. Add a zero to the right if necessary to move the decimal two places to the right.

EXAMPLE 1 Writing Decimals as Percents

Write the decimal as a percent.

a. 0.27   b. 0.39

Solution

a. Multiply by 100.
$$0.27 = (0.27 \times 100)\%$$ Multiply by 100.
$$= 27\%$$ Simplify.

b. Move the decimal point.
$$0.39 = 39\%$$ Move the decimal point 2 places to the right.

EXAMPLE 2 Writing Fractions as Percents

Write the fraction as a percent.

a. $\frac{13}{20}$ b. $\frac{7}{32}$

Solution

a. $\frac{13}{20} = \frac{13 \times 5}{20 \times 5} = \frac{65}{100}$ Multiply numerator and denominator by 5.

   $= 65\%$ Write as a percent.

   ANSWER $\frac{13}{20} = 65\%$

b. $\frac{7}{32} = 0.21875$ Write fraction as a decimal.
   $= 0.21875$ Move the decimal point 2 places to the right.
   $= 21.875\%$ Write decimal as a percent.

   ANSWER $\frac{7}{32} = 21.875\%$

Another Method

Another way to write a fraction as a percent is to convert the fraction to a decimal, and then convert the decimal to a percent.

Name _____ Date _____

TRY THIS

Write the decimal as a percent.

1. 0.13 = ☐ %
2. 0.91 = ☐ %
3. 0.57 = ☐ %
4. 0.08 = ☐ %

Write the fraction as a percent.

5. $\frac{2}{5}$ = ☐ %
6. $\frac{9}{10}$ = ☐ %
7. $\frac{5}{16}$ = ☐ %
8. $\frac{7}{8}$ = ☐ %

EXAMPLE 3 Determining if Two Values are Equivalent

Is 68% equivalent to $\frac{17}{20}$?

Solution

$\frac{17}{20} \stackrel{?}{=} \frac{68}{100}$ Write a proportion with the given fraction and the percent fraction.

$17 \cdot 100 \stackrel{?}{=} 20 \cdot 68$ Write cross products.

$1700 \neq 1360$ Multiply and compare.

Another Method
You can also convert the percent and the fraction to decimals and compare the two results.

ANSWER The cross products are not equal, so **68%** is not equivalent to $\frac{17}{20}$.

TRY THIS Fill in the missing information to determine if the values are equivalent.

9. $\frac{1}{3}$ and 30%

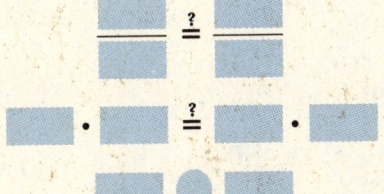

10. 22% and $\frac{11}{50}$

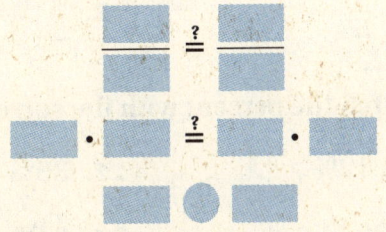

Name _____   Date _____

> **Summarize**
>
> **Writing Decimals as Percents**
> To write a decimal as a percent, move the decimal point **2** places to the right.
>
> **Writing Fractions as Percents**
> Multiply the numerator and denominator by the same factor to rewrite the fraction in the form $\frac{p}{100}$. If the denominator is not a factor of **100**, write the fraction as a decimal, and then write the decimal as a percent.
>
> **Determining if Two Values are Equivalent**
> Write a proportion with the given fraction and the percent fraction. Then compare cross products. An alternative method is to write the percent and the fraction as decimals and compare the results.

Practice

Write the decimal as a percent.

1. 0.67
2. 0.3
3. 0.19
4. 0.26
5. 0.55
6. 0.71
7. 0.33
8. 0.49

Write the fraction as a percent.

9. $\frac{4}{5}$
10. $\frac{1}{4}$
11. $\frac{3}{10}$
12. $\frac{57}{100}$
13. $\frac{5}{6}$
14. $\frac{47}{55}$
15. $\frac{7}{15}$
16. $\frac{12}{33}$

Match the percent with the correct fraction.

17. 60%
18. 25%
19. 80%
20. 75%

A. $\frac{4}{5}$
B. $\frac{3}{5}$
C. $\frac{3}{4}$
D. $\frac{1}{4}$

Match the percent with the correct decimal.

21. 12%
22. 36%
23. 50%
24. 42%

A. 0.5
B. 0.36
C. 0.42
D. 0.12

Math Intervention
Book 4 Ratios, Rates, Proportions, and Percents

Name _____   Date _____

Solve the problem by determining whether the values are equivalent or not. Explain your answer.

25. Ryan scored **87%** on his last quiz. Abby received $\frac{18}{20}$. Who received the better grade on the quiz? How do you know?

    _____
    _____

26. Theo read $\frac{67}{100}$ of a book. Adam read **70%** of his book. Who has read more of his book? How do you know?

    _____
    _____
    _____

27. Beatrice ate $\frac{3}{5}$ of a pizza for lunch. Noah ate **55%** of his pizza for lunch. Who ate more pizza? How do you know?

    _____
    _____
    _____

DID YOU GET IT?

28. **Fill in the missing words.** To determine the percent represented by a fraction, _____ the numerator by the _____. Then move the decimal in the result two places to the _____.

29. **Write the equivalent percent.** _____% is equivalent to $\frac{1}{5}$.

30. **Compare the values.** Jordan ran **96%** of a race at her fastest pace. Kelly ran $\frac{4}{5}$ of the same race at her fastest pace. Who ran her fastest pace the longest? How do you know?

    _____
    _____

LESSON 4-11 Find a Percent of a Number

> **Words to Remember**
> Percent: A ratio whose denominator is 100
> Represented by the symbol %
>
> $35\% = \frac{35}{100} = 0.35$

Getting Started In Lesson 4-9 you learned how to write a percent as a fraction and as a decimal. In Lesson 4-7 you learned how to solve proportions. In this lesson, you will learn several methods you can use to find the percent of a number.

EXAMPLE 1 Finding the Percent of a Number

Find the percent of the number.

a. 20% of 35

b. 25% of 12

Solution

a. Write the percent as a fraction.

$20\% \text{ of } 35 = \frac{20}{100} \cdot 35$ Write 20% as a fraction and multiply.

$= \frac{\overset{1}{20} \cdot 35}{\underset{5}{100}}$ Multiply.

$= \frac{35}{5}$ Simplify.

$= 7$ Simplify.

ANSWER 20% of 35 is 7.

b. Write the percent as a decimal.

$25\% \text{ of } 12 = 0.25(12)$ Write 25% as a decimal and multiply.

$= 3$ Multiply.

ANSWER 25% of 12 is 3.

Math Intervention
Book 4 Ratios, Rates, Proportions, and Percents

Name _____ Date _____

TRY THIS Find the percent of the number.

1. 30% of 18
2. 75% of 6
3. 35% of 20
4. 40% of 8
5. 90% of 10
6. 12% of 30

Proportions You can also find the percent of a number using proportions. Write the percent as a fraction and set it equal to a fraction with the unknown value in the numerator and the given value in the denominator.

EXAMPLE 2 Finding Percents of Quantities

Jerome has 230 baseball cards in his collection. If he plans to sell 20% of his collection, how many cards will Jerome sell?

Solution

To find how many cards Jerome will sell, find **20%** of **230**.

$\dfrac{20}{100} = \dfrac{x}{230}$ Write a proportion.

$20 \cdot 230 = x \cdot 100$ Write the cross products.

$4600 = 100x$ Multiply.

$x = 46$ Solve.

ANSWER Jerome will sell **46** of his baseball cards.

TRY THIS Use a proportion to find the answers.

7. Darnell bought **20%** of the raffle tickets for the school raffle. If **300** tickets were sold, how many did Darnell buy?

8. Elise needs to read a **180** page book. She plans to read **10%** of the book each day. How many pages of the book does Elise read on the first day?

Math Intervention
Book 4 Ratios, Rates, Proportions, and Percents

Name _____ Date _____

> **Summarize**
>
> **Finding the Percent of a Number**
>
> Write the percent as a fraction or decimal and multiply it by the given value.
>
> An alternative method is to write a proportion using the percent as a fraction equal to a fraction with the unknown value over the given value. Solve the proportion.
>
> **Finding Percents of Quantities**
>
> Determine of what value you must take the percent. Write a proportion to solve for this value. Solve.

Practice

Match the question with a correct method for finding the percent of the number.

1. What is 43% of 19? ___
2. What is 17% of 34? ___
3. What is 67% of 123? ___
4. What is 8% of 20? ___

A. $\dfrac{17}{100} = \dfrac{x}{34}$

B. $\dfrac{8}{100} \cdot 20$

C. $\dfrac{43}{100} \cdot 19$

D. $\dfrac{67}{100} = \dfrac{x}{123}$

Find the percent of a number.

5. What is 10% of 35?
6. What is 50% of 18?
7. What is 25% of 8?
8. What is 60% of 10?
9. What is 5% of 20?
10. What is 12% of 100?
11. What is 40% of 15?
12. What is 95% of 30?

Write a proportion for the given situation.

13. Haley owns 132 figurines. She plans to sell 25% of her collection.

14. Jorge mows 10 lawns every week. This week the weather is bad, so he only mows 20% of the lawns.

15. Peter usually walks 8 dogs a day. Today he only walks 25% of the dogs.

Math Intervention
Book 4 Ratios, Rates, Proportions, and Percents

Name _____   Date _____

**Write and solve a proportion for the given situation.
Explain your answer.**

16. Veronica has a collection of **30** famous people's signatures. She wants to sell **10%** of the signatures. How many signatures does Veronica sell?

_____
_____

17. Hyun usually washes **40** cars in a weekend. With bad weather, he only washes **75%** of his normal amount. How many cars does Hyun wash?

_____
_____

18. Cora makes **65%** of the shots she attempts in a basketball game. At today's game, she took **20** shots. How many shots did Cora make in the game?

_____
_____

19. Isaac buys lunch **25%** of the time that he is at work. This month he worked **16** days. How many days did Isaac buy lunch?

_____
_____

DID YOU GET IT?

20. Fill in the missing words. To determine the _____ of a number, you set up a _____ with one fraction being the _____ and the other fraction with the unknown in the _____.

21. Write a proportion. What proportion could you use to find **40%** of **30**?

_____

22. Solve. Hazel has a **200** page book to read. She plans to read **10%** of the book each day. How many pages does Hazel plan to read each day?

_____
_____

Math Intervention
Book 4 Ratios, Rates, Proportions, and Percents

LESSON 4-12
Percent of Increase and Decrease

> **Words to Remember**
>
> **Percent of change:** Shows how much a new amount has increased or decreased from the original amount
>
> **Percent of change** = $\dfrac{\text{amount of change}}{\text{original amount}}$
>
> **Amount of change:** The difference between two quantities
>
> **Percent of increase:** Results when the new amount is greater than the original amount
>
> **Percent of decrease:** Results when the new amount is less than the original amount

Getting Started In Lesson 4-9 you learned how to write a percent as a fraction. In this lesson, you will use a fraction to find a percent of change.

EXAMPLE 1 Finding the Amount of Change

Find the amount of change and determine whether it is an *increase* or a *decrease*.

   a. Original amount: **52**   **b.** Original amount: **120**
      New amount: **70**   New amount: **95**

Solution

Look at the two amounts. The amount of change is the larger number minus the smaller number.

  a. Amount of change = larger number − smaller number
                               = 70 − 52
                               = 18

ANSWER Because the new amount is larger, this is an increase.

  b. Amount of change = larger number − smaller number
                               = 120 − 95
                               = 25

ANSWER Because the new amount is smaller, this is a decrease.

Math Intervention
Book 4 Ratios, Rates, Proportions, and Percents

EXAMPLE 2 Finding the Percent of Increase

At the beginning of the year, Wayne could type 30 words per minute. By the end of the year, Wayne was typing 48 words per minute. What is the percent of increase in the number of words Wayne could type?

Solution

$$\text{Percent of change} = \frac{\text{amount of change}}{\text{original amount}}$$ Use the percent of change equation.

$$= \frac{48 - 30}{30}$$ Substitute values.

$$= \frac{18}{30}$$ Subtract.

$$= 0.6$$ Write the fraction as a decimal.

$$= 60\%$$ Write the decimal as a percent.

Because the new amount is larger, this is a percent of increase.

ANSWER The percent of increase is **60%**.

EXAMPLE 3 Finding the Percent of Decrease

A movie store rented 145 movies in May. The same movie store rented 120 movies in June. What is the percent of decrease in the number of movies rented from May to June?

Solution

$$\text{Percent of change} = \frac{\text{amount of change}}{\text{original amount}}$$ Use the percent of change equation.

$$= \frac{145 - 120}{145}$$ Substitute values.

$$= \frac{25}{145}$$ Subtract.

$$\approx 0.172$$ Write the fraction as a decimal.

$$\approx 17\%$$ Write the decimal as a percent.

Because the new amount is smaller, this is a percent of decrease.

ANSWER The percent of decrease is about **17%**.

Don't Forget
Whether you are looking for a percent of increase or a percent of decrease, the numerator is always the larger number subtracted by the smaller number. The denominator is always the original amount.

TRY THIS Find the percent of increase or decrease.

1. Original amount: 85
   New amount: 102

2. Original amount: 51
   New amount: 45

> **Summarize**
>
> Percent change = $\frac{\text{amount of change}}{\text{original amount}}$
>
> **Finding the Percent of Increase**
>
> Use the percent change equation. The numerator is the new value – the original amount. The denominator is the original amount. Subtract. Write the fraction as a decimal.
>
> **Finding the Percent of Decrease**
>
> Use the percent change equation. The numerator is the original amount – the new value. The denominator is the original amount. Subtract. Write the fraction as a decimal.

Practice

Determine whether the percent of change is an *increase* or a *decrease*.

1. Original amount: 15
   New amount: 36

   _____

2. Original amount: 29
   New amount: 13

   _____

3. Original amount: 42
   New amount: 30

   _____

4. Original amount: 37
   New amount: 51

   _____

Find the percent of increase.

5. Original amount: 85
   New amount: 100

6. Original amount: 23
   New amount: 30

7. Original amount: 8
   New amount: 16

8. Original amount: 15
   New amount: 27

Find the percent of decrease.

9. Original amount: 10
   New amount: 4

10. Original amount: 97
    New amount: 75

11. Original amount: 50
    New amount: 38

12. Original amount: 28
    New amount: 12

Math Intervention
Book 4 Ratios, Rates, Proportions, and Percents

Name _____   Date _____

Decide if the percent of change will be an *increase* or a *decrease*. Then determine the percent of change. Explain your answer.

13. Olivia read 25 books last summer. This summer she read a total of 40 books.

    _____
    _____

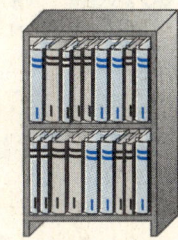

14. This year there are 234 sixth grade students. Last year there were 250 sixth grade students.

    _____
    _____
    _____

15. A garden center sold 132 plants this weekend. Last weekend it sold 115 plants.

    _____
    _____
    _____

16. Ralph hit 32 balls in the batting cage last week. This week he hit 28 balls.

    _____
    _____
    _____

DID YOU GET IT?

17. **Fill in the missing words.** To determine the _____ of change, the _____ of the fraction is the amount of _____ or _____ and the denominator is the _____ amount.

18. **Find the percent of change.** Ursula knew how to play 15 pieces of music. After band camp, she now knows how to play 18 pieces of music. Find the percent of increase or decrease.

    _____
    _____

Name _____ Date _____

LESSON 4-13 Discounts, Tips, Markups, Commissions, and Profit

Words to Remember

Discount: A percent or amount of *decrease* in the price of an item
Sale price = original price − discount

Tip: A percent *earned* by a person for providing a service

Wholesale price: The price a retail store pays the manufacturer
Markup: A percent or amount *increase* a retail store charges to earn a profit
Retail price: The price at which a store sells items to customers
Retail price = wholesale price + markup

Commission: A percent of total sales *earned* by an employee or business
Commission earned = percent commission × total sales

Profit: The difference of the income and the expenses for a business
Profit = income − expenses

Getting Started In Lesson 4-12 you learned how to find percent of change, percent of increase, and percent of decrease. In this lesson, you apply these skills to solve problems.

EXAMPLE 1   Finding a Sale Price

The original price of a shirt is $18. The shirt is on sale for a 20% discount. What is the sale price of the shirt?

Solution

Discount	= 20% of $18	Find the amount of discount.
	= 0.20(18)	
	= 3.60	
Sale price	= original price − discount	Use formula to find sale price.
	= 18 − 3.60	
	= 14.40	

ANSWER The sale price of the shirt is **$14.40**.

 Find the sale price.

1. Original price: $40
   Percent discount: 30%

2. Original price: $75
   Percent discount: 25%

EXAMPLE 2 Finding a Total Cost

Your food bill at a restaurant was $23.50. You leave a 15% tip. What is the total cost of your meal?

Solution

Tip = 15% of $23.50   Find the amount of tip.
   = 0.15(23.50)
   = 3.53

Total cost = 23.50 + 3.53   Add the tip to the food bill.
          = 27.03

ANSWER The total cost of your meal is **$27.03**.

> **Notice**
> **You find total meal costs and retail prices in the same way.** Find the tip or markup amount and add this amount to the food bill or wholesale price.

EXAMPLE 3 Finding a Commission

Anthony receives a 9% commission on magazine subscription sales. Last week, his total sales were $1800. How much commission did he earn?

Solution

Commission = 9% of $1800   Find the amount of commission.
          = 0.09(1800)
          = 162

ANSWER Anthony earned **$162** in commission last week.

EXAMPLE 4 Finding a Profit

You sell fruit drinks at the town field. This past weekend, you collected $107. Your expenses for the fruit drinks were $82. What is your profit?

Solution

Profit = income − expenses   Use formula to find profit.
      = 107 − 82
      = 25

ANSWER Your profit for last weekend is **$25**.

TRY THIS Find the indicated value.

3. Find the retail price.
   Wholesale price: **$50**
   Percent markup: **30%**

4. Find the commission.
   Total sales: **$1600**
   Percent commission: **6%**

Name _____ Date _____

> **Summarize**
>
> **Finding a Sale Price after a Discount**
>
> Find the amount of discount. Subtract the discount amount from the original price.
>
> **Finding a Final Cost after a Tip or Markup**
>
> Find the amount of tip or markup. Add the tip or markup to the original amount.
>
> **Finding a Commission**
>
> Multiply total sales by the percent commission.
>
> **Finding a Profit**
>
> Subtract expenses from income.

Practice

Tell whether you would *add* or *subtract* to find the answer.

1. A store bought **$150** worth of items at wholesale price. The store will markup the items by **120%**. You want to find the retail price. _____

2. The bill at a restaurant is **$45**. You tip **17%**. You want to find the total cost of the meal. _____

3. A movie DVD has an original price of $20. The store is offering a 10% discount on movies. You want to find the sale price. _____

Find the sale price, retail price, or total meal cost.

4. Original price: **$20**
   Discount: **30%**

5. Original price: **$80**
   Discount: **10%**

6. Wholesale price: **$30**
   Percent markup: **120%**

7. Wholesale price: **$85**
   Percent markup: **20%**

8. Food bill: **$55**
   Tip: **18%**

9. Food bill: **$38.40**
   Tip: **15%**

Find the commission.

10. Total sales: **$2000**
    Percent commission: **10%**

11. Total sales: **$1200**
    Percent commission: **5%**

Find the profit.

12. Expenses: **$275**
    Income: **$495**

13. Expenses: **$700**
    Income: **$1050**

Math Intervention
Book 4 Ratios, Rates, Proportions, and Percents

Name _____   Date _____

Solve the problem. Explain your answer.

14. A craft store bought paint for a wholesale price of $100. The store charges a 65% markup. What is the craft store's price for the paint?
    _____
    _____
    _____

15. Sylvano wants to buy a pair of gym shoes that cost $75. The shoes are on sale at a 30% discount. How much will Sylvano spend on the shoes?
    _____
    _____
    _____

16. Howard sold $3500 worth of jewelry this past week. If he earns an 8% commission, how much commission did he earn?
    _____
    _____
    _____

17. A school group collects $194.25 at a fund-raiser. The group spent $53.75 on supplies. How much profit did they earn?
    _____
    _____
    _____

DID YOU GET IT?

18. **Fill in the missing words.** To find the total meal cost, you would _____ the amount of the _____ to the food _____.

19. **Find the sale price.** Original price: $30, Discount: 15%
    _____
    _____

20. **Find the retail price.** A store bought a statue for a $125 wholesale price. The store charges an 85% markup. What is the retail price of the statue?
    _____
    _____

Math Intervention
Book 4 Ratios, Rates, Proportions, and Percents

LESSON 4-14: Simple Interest

> **Words to Remember**
>
> Interest: The amount of money that you pay to borrow money or the amount of money that you earn on a deposit
>
> Annual Interest Rate: The percent of interest that you pay per year for money borrowed, or earn per year for money deposited
>
> Simple interest formula: $I = Prt$ where I is the interest earned, P is the principal or the amount of money that you start out with, r is the annual interest rate as a decimal, and t is the time in years.
>
> Balance: The sum of the principal P and the interest Prt.

Getting Started In Lesson 4-9 you learned how to write percents as decimals. You will use that skill in this lesson to find simple interest.

EXAMPLE 1 — Computing Simple Interest Earned

Dianna deposits $725 into a savings account that pays 2.3% simple annual interest. How much interest will Dianna earn after 18 months?

Solution

In the simple interest formula, time is measured in years. Write 18 months as $\frac{18}{12}$, or 1.5 years. Write the annual interest rate as a decimal.

$I = Prt$ Use the formula for simple interest.

$I = (725)(0.023)(1.5)$ Substitute $725 for P, 0.023 for r, and 1.5 for t.

$I = \$25.01$ Multiply.

ANSWER Dianna will earn $25.01 in interest.

> **Remember**
> There are 12 months in a year. When turning months into years for time, create a fraction $\frac{month}{12}$. The decimal result is the value for t. In Example 1, $\frac{18}{12} = 1.5$ years.

TRY THIS — Find the amount of interest earned.

1. Principal: $550
   Annual rate: 7%
   Time: 4 years
   $I =$ ⬚ · ⬚ · ⬚
     $=$ ⬚

2. Principal: $870
   Annual rate: 3.7%
   Time: 30 months
   $I =$ ⬚ · ⬚ · ⬚
     $=$ ⬚

Math Intervention
Book 4 Ratios, Rates, Proportions, and Percents

EXAMPLE 2 Computing Simple Interest Paid

Josh borrowed $250 from his mother to buy an electric scooter. Josh will pay her back in 1 year with 3% simple annual interest. How much interest will Josh pay?

Solution

$I = Prt$	Use the formula for simple interest.
$I = (250)(0.03)(1)$	Substitute $250 for P, 0.03 for r, and 1 for t.
$I = \$7.50$	Multiply.

ANSWER Josh will pay his mom **$7.50** in interest.

> **Remember**
> Turn all interest rates into decimals when computing simple interest. Also, remember that time must be expressed in years.

Balance When an account earns interest, the interest is added to the money in the account. The *balance A* of an account that earns simple annual interest is the sum of the principal *P* and the interest *Prt*.

$$A = P + Prt$$

EXAMPLE 3 Finding the Balance

You deposit $300 in a savings account that pays 4% simple annual interest. Find your account balance after 9 months.

Solution

Write 9 months as $\frac{9}{12}$ year, or 0.75 year.

$A = P + Prt$	Write the balance formula.
$= 300 + (300)(0.04)(0.75)$	Substitute $300 for P, 0.04 for r, and 0.75 for t.
$= 300 + 9$	Multiply.
$= 309$	Add.

ANSWER Your account balance after 9 months is **$309**.

TRY THIS

Find the amount of interest paid.

3. Principal: $335
   Annual rate: 5.2%
   Time: 2.5 years

4. Principal: $1225
   Annual rate: 8.3%
   Time: 42 months

5. You deposit $800 in a savings account that pays 3.2% simple annual interest. Find your account balance after 15 months.

Name _____   Date _____

> **Summarize**
>
> **Computing Simple Interest**
>
> Use the formula $I = Prt$ where I represents the interest earned or paid, P represents the principal or the amount that you deposit or borrow, r represents the annual interest rate as a decimal, and t represents the time in years.
>
> **Finding the Balance**
>
> Use the formula $A = P + Prt$ where A represents the sum of the principal and the interest earned.

Practice

Write the given time period as a fraction of a year.

1. 4 months _____
2. 6 months _____
3. 21 months _____
4. 32 months _____

Find the simple interest earned.

5. Principal: **$135**
   Annual rate: **4.3%**
   Time: **30 months**

6. Principal: **$575**
   Annual rate: **2.6%**
   Time: **3.3 years**

7. Principal: **$1200**
   Annual rate: **1.9%**
   Time: **5 years**

8. Principal: **$850**
   Annual rate: **5.1%**
   Time: **54 months**

Find the simple interest paid.

9. Principal: **$350**
   Annual rate: **4%**
   Time: **3 years**

10. Principal: **$2575**
    Annual rate: **8.2%**
    Time: **10 years**

11. Principal: **$345**
    Annual rate: **5.5%**
    Time: **42 months**

12. Principal: **$600**
    Annual rate: **6.2%**
    Time: **8 years**

Find the balance of the account.

13. Principal: **$200**
    Annual rate: **3%**
    Time: **2 years**

14. Principal: **$1020**
    Annual rate: **4.1%**
    Time: **18 months**

15. Principal: **$800**
    Annual rate: **2.56%**
    Time: **15 months**

16. Principal: **$1580**
    Annual rate: **3.75%**
    Time: **2.5 years**

Math Intervention
Book 4 Ratios, Rates, Proportions, and Percents

Name _____ Date _____

Write the rate as a decimal. Then find the amount of simple interest. Explain your answer.

17. Anna deposited **$460** into a savings account that pays **3.2%** simple annual interest. In **5** years, how much interest did Anna earn?

_____
_____
_____

18. Michael borrowed **$375** for a new bicycle. He will pay the money back in **18** months with simple annual interest of **5.7%**. How much interest will Michael pay back?

_____
_____
_____

19. Tameka borrowed **$300** to buy a digital music player. She will pay the money back in **1** year at **5%** simple annual interest. How much money will Tameka pay in interest?

_____
_____
_____

20. Victor deposited **$2350** in a savings account that pays **4.5%** simple annual interest. If Victor keeps the money in the account for **30** months, how much interest will he earn?

_____
_____
_____

DID YOU GET IT?

21. Fill in the missing words. To find simple interest you use the formula $I = Prt$ where P stands for _____, r stands for annual interest rate written as a _____, and t stands for _____ in years.

22. Find the balance of the account. Belinda deposits **$550** in an account that pays **3.7%** simple annual interest. If she keeps the money in the account for **2** years, how much will Belinda have in her account after 2 years?

_____
_____

Compound Interest

LESSON 4-15

Words to Remember

Compound interest: Interest that is earned on both the principal and any interest that has been earned previously.

Compound interest formula: $A = P(1 + r)^t$ where A represents the amount of money in the account at the end of the time period, P is the principal, r is the annual interest rate, and t is the time in years.

Balance: The sum of the principal and the interest

Getting Started In Lesson 4-14 you learned how to find simple interest or the total amount of interest earned or paid on the original principal over a period of time. In this lesson you will learn how to find compound interest.

EXAMPLE 1   Computing Compound Interest using Simple Interest

Simon deposits $400 in an account that pays 3% interest compounded annually. What is the balance of Simon's account at the end of 2 years?

Solution

Step 1 Find the balance at the end of the first year.

$I = Prt$ Use the simple interest formula.
$= (400)(0.03)(1)$
$= 12$

Balance $= P + Prt$ Use the balance formula.
$= 400 + 12$
$= 412$

The balance at the end of the first year is **$412**.

Step 2 Find the balance at the end of the second year.

$I = Prt$ Use the simple interest formula.
$= (412)(0.03)(1)$
$= 12.36$

Balance $= P + Prt$ Use the balance formula.
$= 412 + 12.36$
$= 424.36$

ANSWER Simon has **$424.36** in his account after **2** years.

> **Take Note!**
> In Step 2, the principal for the second year is the balance of the first year.

Math Intervention
Book 4 Ratios, Rates, Proportions, and Percents

Name _____ Date _____

> **TRY THIS** Find the balance of the account after *t* years using the simple interest method.

1. Principal: $600, Annual rate: 4%, Time: 3 years

   Balance at the end of the first year is _____.

   Balance at the end of the second year is _____.

   Balance at the end of the third year is _____.

2. Principal: $850, Annual rate: 2.4%, Time: 4 years

   Balance at the end of the first year is _____.

   Balance at the end of the second year is _____.

   Balance at the end of the third year is _____.

   Balance at the end of the fourth year is _____.

EXAMPLE 2 Computing Compound Interest using the Compound Interest Formula

Jackie deposits $325 in an account that pays 4.1% interest compounded annually. How much money will Jackie have in her account after 3 years?

Solution

$A = P(1 + r)^t$ Use the compound interest formula.

$A = 325(1 + 0.041)^3$ Substitute 325 for *P*, 0.041 for *r*, and 3 for *t*.

$A = 325(1.041)^3$ Add.

$A = 366.64$ Simplify.

ANSWER Jackie will have $366.64 in her account after 3 years.

> **TRY THIS** Find the amount in an account after *t* years using the compound interest formula.

3. Principal: $285
   Annual rate: 1.9%
   Time: 6 years

   $A = \underline{} (1 + \underline{})^{\underline{}}$

   $= \underline{}$

4. Principal: $1200
   Annual rate: 8.7%
   Time: 2 years

   $A = \underline{} (1 + \underline{})^{\underline{}}$

   $= \underline{}$

Name _____ Date _____

> **Summarize**
>
> **Computing Compound Interest using Simple Interest**
>
> Compute simple interest for **1** year. Add the interest to the principal. This becomes the principal for year **2**. Repeat these steps for *t* years.
>
> **Computing Compound Interest using the Compound Interest Formula**
>
> Use the formula $A = P(1 + r)^t$ to determine the amount of money in an account after *t* years.

Practice

1. Fill in the missing information to find the balance of the account.
   Principal: **$600**, Annual rate: **4%**, Time: **3** years

   Step 1 The initial principal *P* is _____.

   The interest rate written as a decimal is _____.

   The balance for year **1** is _____.

   Step 2 The principal for year **2** is _____.

   The balance for year **2** is _____.

   Step 3 The principal for year **3** is _____.

   The balance for year **3** is _____.

Find the balance of the account after time *t* using the simple interest method.

2. $375 at 4% interest compounded annually for 3 years

3. $975 at 8.2% interest compounded annually for 2 years

4. $135 at 2.3% interest compounded annually for 7 years

5. $250 at 3.1% interest compounded annually for 4 years

Find the balance of the account after time *t* using the compound interest formula.

6. $1200 at 2.5% interest compounded annually for 8 years

7. $750 at 4.6% interest compounded annually for 4 years

8. $435 at 1.7% interest compounded annually for 10 years

9. $815 at 5% interest compounded annually for 6.5 years

Math Intervention
Book 4 Ratios, Rates, Proportions, and Percents

Name _____ Date _____

In Exercises 12 and 13, how many steps of simple interest need to be performed? Solve the problem.

10. Julio deposits **$345** in an account that earns **3.1%** interest compounded annually. How much money is in the account after **4 years**?

    _____
    _____
    _____

11. Kim deposits **$650** in an account that earns **4%** interest compounded annually. How much money is in the account after **2 years**?

    _____
    _____
    _____

12. Solve the problem using the compound interest formula. Jong deposits **$500** in an account that earns **2.5%** interest compounded annually and keeps the money in the account for **3 years**. Monty deposits **$500** in an account that earns **5.1%** interest compounded annually and keeps the money in the account for **2 years**. Who has more money when he closes his account? Explain your reasoning.

    _____
    _____
    _____

DID YOU GET IT?

13. **Fill in the missing words.** Compound interest is interest that is earned on both the _____ and any _____ that has been earned _____.

14. **Use the compound interest formula.** Nora deposits **$450** in an account that earns **2.4%** interest compounded annually. How much money is in the account after **5 years**?

    _____
    _____

Math Intervention
Book 4 Ratios, Rates, Proportions, and Percents

Name _____ Date _____

Conducting an Experiment

> **Goal:** Use concrete objects to conduct an experiment to determine how likely it is for an event to occur.
>
> **Materials:** a coin, bag of marbles (or other objects in a variety of colors or shapes), or a number cube

Getting Started In Lesson 4-1 you learned how to use ratios to compare related values. You can also use ratios to determine how many times a specific result is likely to occur.

You flip a coin **5** times and get tails **3** times. The ratio of tails to flips is:

$$\frac{\text{number of times tails appeared}}{\text{number of times coin was flipped}} = \frac{3}{5}$$

For this experiment, the *experimental probability* of getting tails is $\frac{3}{5}$.

Use the following steps to perform an experiment for rolling a number cube. Find the probability of rolling a 2.

Step 1 **Create** a table with all possible results listed.

Number	Rolls	Number	Rolls	Number	Rolls
1		2		3	
4		5		6	

Step 2 **Roll** the number cube **50** times and record the results in the table.

Number	Rolls	Number	Rolls	Number	Rolls
1								2									3							
4								5												6									

Step 3 **Calculate** the experimental probability of rolling a 2.

$$\frac{\text{number of times 2 appeared}}{\text{number of times cube was thrown}} = \frac{8}{50} = \frac{4}{25}$$

ANSWER The experimental probability of rolling a 2 is $\frac{4}{25}$, or 4 out of 25 times.

Math Intervention
Book 4 Ratios, Rates, Proportions, and Percents

Name _____   Date _____

MAKE IT A GAME!

- Form groups of three or four students.
- As a group pick an item to use for the experiment. The whole group must choose the same item (coin or number cube, etc.).
- Decide on an experiment and a specific result.

    Coin—how often a heads or tails will appear

    Number cube—how often a specific number will occur

    Bag of marbles—how often a specific color will occur

- Each person should perform the experiment **50** times and record the results in a table.
- Calculate the ratio $\dfrac{\text{number of times specific result occurs}}{50}$ for each person's experiment.
- The player with the greatest ratio wins.

Practice

There are a total of 100 marbles in a bag. Without looking, you pull a marble from the bag 50 times. Each time, you record its color and return it to the bag. Your results are shown in the tables below.

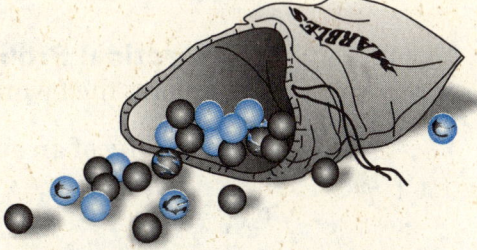

Color	Number of Times Pulled
Blue	8
Yellow	2
White	7

Color	Number of Times Pulled
Green	12
Red	10
Black	11

In Exercises 1–6, use the table to determine the ratio $\dfrac{\text{number of times color chosen}}{50}$ for each color.

1. Blue
2. Green
3. Yellow
4. Red
5. White
6. Black

7. **Make a Conjecture** Based on your answers to Exercises 1–6, make a conjecture about how many green marbles are in the bag.

Name _____ Date _____

LESSON 4-17 Probability

> **Words to Remember**
>
> **Outcomes:** The possible results of an experiment
>
> **Event:** A group of outcomes
>
> **Favorable outcome:** The outcome for a specified event
>
> **Probability of an event:** The likelihood that the event will occur

Getting Started   In Activity 4-16 you learned how to compute *experimental probability*, which is the probability found as the result of an experiment. In this lesson, you will use these same skills to find the *theoretical probability* of an event occurring.

Probability   A probability that an event will occur is a number from **0** to **1**. The closer the probability is to **1**, the more likely it is that the event will occur. You can write probabilities as decimals, fractions, or percents.

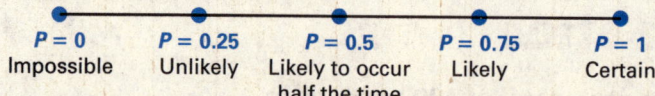

| $P = 0$ | $P = 0.25$ | $P = 0.5$ | $P = 0.75$ | $P = 1$ |
| Impossible | Unlikely | Likely to occur half the time | Likely | Certain |

Theoretical Probability   The theoretical probability of an event compares the favorable outcomes to all the possible outcomes.

Probability of an event = $\dfrac{\text{number of favorable outcomes}}{\text{total possible outcomes}}$

EXAMPLE 1   Finding the Theoretical Probability of an Event

What is the probability of rolling a 5 with a six-sided number cube?

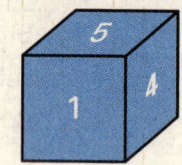

Solution

Step 1   **Use** the probability of an event ratio and make it specific.

Probability of 5 = $\dfrac{\text{number of 5's on a number cube}}{\text{total sides of a cube}}$

Step 2   **Substitute** the values for this problem.

Probability of 5 = $\dfrac{1}{6}$

ANSWER   The theoretical probability of rolling a **5** on a number cube is **1** out of **6**, or $\dfrac{1}{6}$.

Math Intervention
Book 4 Ratios, Rates, Proportions, and Percents

Name _____   Date _____

TRY THIS Use the situation described.

You place 50 slips of paper with pictures on them in a hat. There are 13 suns, 18 frogs, 9 pencils, and 10 bears. Suppose you pull a picture from the bag.

1. The probability of pulling a bear is $\frac{}{50}$, or $\frac{}{}$.

2. What is the probability of pulling a sun? $\frac{}{}$

3. What picture will have the greatest probability of being pulled? the least probability?

Probability of an Event *Not* Occurring The probability that the total possible outcomes of an event will occur is **100%** certain, or **1**. So the probability that a specified outcome will *not* occur is the probability that all other outcomes occur instead. This is the difference of **1** and the probability that the specified outcome *does* occur.

Probability of event *not* occurring = 1 − (the probability of event occurring)

EXAMPLE 2 — Finding the Probability of an Event *Not* Occurring

What is the probability of the spinner *not* landing on a red spot(R)?

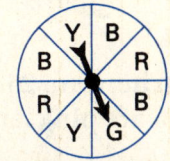

Solution

Step 1 Find the probability of spinning a red.

$$\frac{\text{red sections}}{\text{total sections}} = \frac{2}{8} = \frac{1}{4}$$

Step 2 Find the probability of *not* spinning a red.

The probability of not spinning a red is 1 − (the probability of spinning a red).

$$1 - \frac{1}{4} = \frac{3}{4}$$

ANSWER The probability of *not* spinning a red is $\frac{3}{4}$.

> **Remember**
> A probability can be written in many forms. In Example 2, you can write the probability of spinning a red as $\frac{1}{4}$ or as 0.25. So, you have a 25% chance of spinning a red.

TRY THIS

4. Using the spinner from Example 2, what is the probability of *not* spinning a green(G)?

5. What is the probability of *not* rolling a 2 on a six-sided number cube?

Name _____   Date _____

> **Summarize**
>
> **Determining the Theoretical Probability of an Event**
>
> Use the formula for the probability of an event
> $\frac{\text{number of favorable outcomes}}{\text{total possible outcomes}}$ and substitute the
> information for the problem. Then simplify.
>
> **Finding the Probability of an Event *Not* Occurring**
>
> Find the probability of the event occurring. Then the probability of the event *not* occurring is (1 − the probability of the event occurring).

Practice

Match the situation with its probability written as a decimal, fraction, or percent.

1. Getting heads when coin flipped _____   A. $\frac{1}{8}$

2. Rolling a 6 with an eight-sided number cube _____   B. 0.6

3. Choosing a blue marble from a bag with 3 blue marbles and 2 yellow marbles _____   C. 50%

There are 25 colored cubes placed in a bag. 10 are clear, 6 are blue, 5 are pink, and 4 are marbled. Find the probability of the event.

4. What is the probability that you draw a blue?

5. What is the probability that you draw a clear?

6. What is the probability that you draw a pink?

7. What color cube has the least probability of being drawn?

In Exercises 8–13, use the spinner shown to find the probability of the event described.

8. What is the probability of spinning a red(R)?

9. What is the probability of spinning a yellow(Y)?

10. What is the probability of spinning a blue(B)?

11. What is the probability of *not* spinning a red(R)?

12. What is the probability of *not* spinning a green(G)?

13. What is the probability of *not* spinning a yellow(Y)?

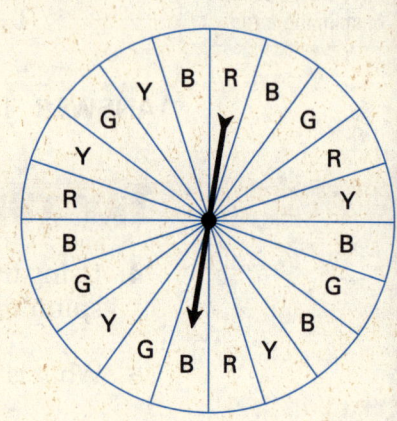

Math Intervention
Book 4 Ratios, Rates, Proportions, and Percents

Name _____ Date _____

Solve the problem using the given information. Explain your answer.

14. What is the probability that you drop a marker onto the board and it lands on a blue square?

_____
_____
_____

15. When you roll a 12-sided number cube with sides numbered 1–12, what is the probability that you do *not* roll a 10?

_____
_____
_____

16. A box contains 75 marbles. There are 15 blue, 13 clear, 20 yellow, 13 pink, 10 speckled, and 4 green marbles. What marble has the greatest probability of being pulled? What marble has the least probability of being pulled? What is the probability of a blue marble being pulled?

_____
_____
_____

DID YOU GET IT?

17. Fill in the missing words. To find the probability of an event occurring, you create a ratio of the _____ over the _____.

18. Find the probability. What is the probability of pulling a pink ribbon from a bag that contains 8 pink ribbons, 2 yellow, and 5 green?

_____
_____

19. Explain your results. What is the probability of *not* pulling a pink ribbon from a bag that contains 8 pink ribbons, 2 yellow, and 5 green? Explain your reasoning.

_____
_____

Mixed Practice for Lessons 4-9 to 4-17

Vocabulary Review

Match the word with its mathematical meaning and its everyday meaning.

Word	Mathematical meaning	Everyday meaning
1. event ____, ____	A. a calculation of a payment to someone for a service, based on a percent of the bill	X. the pointed end of a long slim object
2. interest ____, ____	B. a group of outcomes	Y. curiosity about something
3. tip ____, ____	C. a calculation to determine the amount of money earned or owed, based on a percent of the amount invested or borrowed	Z. an occurrence of some importance

Fill in the missing words.

4. The formula $A = P(1 + r)^t$ is used to compute _____.

5. When finding the _____ of a number, you create a fraction with a denominator of 100.

6. The _____ of an event is the likelihood that the event will occur.

Each value can be written as a percent, fraction, or decimal. Write the other two equivalent forms of the value. Round to the nearest hundredth if necessary.

7. 28%

____, ____

8. $\frac{2}{5}$

____, ____

9. 0.45

____, ____

10. 30%

____, ____

11. 0.35

____, ____

12. $\frac{1}{8}$

____, ____

13. 75%

____, ____

14. $\frac{3}{7}$

____, ____

15. 0.02

____, ____

Math Intervention
Book 4 Ratios, Rates, Proportions, and Percents

Name _____ Date _____

Solve the problem.

16. What is **20%** of **150**?

17. What is **65%** of **50**?

18. Maurice needs to complete **75%** of a model in order to start painting it. The model should take **5** hours to build. How long will it take Maurice before he can begin painting?

19. Ernie had dinner at a restaurant. The bill was **$32.50**. If he leaves the waitress an **18%** tip, how much is the tip?

Find the percent of change. Determine if the change is an *increase* or a *decrease*.

20. Original price: **$35.00**
New price: **$87.50**

21. Original price: **$135.50**
New price: **$95.75**

Find the interest earned.

22. A starting balance of **$575** in an account for **4** years earning **3.7%** simple annual interest.

23. A starting balance of **$1,600** in an account for **6.5** years earning **4.0%** interest compounded annually.

Determine the probability of each event occurring.

24. Rolling a number other than a **5** on a six-sided number cube

25. Spinning a green on a spinner with **6** spaces, where **2** spaces are red, **1** is green, **1** is yellow, and **2** are blue

Tell if you need to add, subtract, or just calculate to find the answer. Find the percent amount. Then solve the problem. Explain your answer.

26. A store purchases **$275** worth of fruit at a wholesale price. The fruit is sold with a **35%** markup. For how much will the store sell the fruit?

_____
_____

27. Cara sold **$3,530** worth of clothes and receives a **6%** commission. What are Cara's total earnings, if she receives **$500** in addition to her commission?

_____
_____

McDougal Littell

Math Intervention

Book 5:
Algebraic Thinking

McDougal Littell
A DIVISION OF HOUGHTON MIFFLIN COMPANY

Evanston, Illinois • Boston • Dallas

Cover photo © A.T. Willett/Alamy

Illustrations George Barile/McDougal Littell/Houghton Mifflin Company and John Evans/McDougal Littell/Houghton Mifflin Company

Copyright © 2008 by McDougal Littell, a division of Houghton Mifflin Company.
All rights reserved.

Permission is hereby granted to teachers to reprint or photocopy in classroom quantities the pages or sheets in this work that carry a McDougal Littell copyright notice. These pages are designed to be reproduced by teachers for use in their classes with accompanying McDougal Littell material, provided each copy made shows the copyright notice. Such copies may not be sold and further distribution is expressly prohibited. Except as authorized above, prior written permission must be obtained from McDougal Littell, a division of Houghton Mifflin Company, to reproduce or transmit this work or portions thereof in any other form or by any other electronic or mechanical means, including any information storage or retrieval system, unless expressly permitted by federal copyright laws. Address inquiries to, Supervisor, Rights and Permissions, McDougal Littell, P.O. Box 1667, Evanston, IL 60204.

ISBN-13: 978-0-618-90076-3
ISBN-10: 0-618-90076-4

123456789—PBO—11 10 09 08 07

CONTENTS
Book 5: Algebraic Thinking

Basic Concepts and Properties

Lesson 5-1	Describe Patterns	2
Lesson 5-2	Recognize a Pattern by its Rule	6
Lesson 5-3	Evaluate Algebraic Expressions	10
Lesson 5-4	Write Algebraic Expressions	14
Lesson 5-5	Properties of Addition and Multiplication	18
Lesson 5-6	The Distributive Property	22
Lesson 5-7	Simplify Algebraic Expressions	26
Lesson 5-8	Solve Addition and Subtraction Equations	30
Lesson 5-9	Solve Multiplication and Division Equations	34
Lesson 5-10	Solve Problems with Equations	38
Lesson 5-11	Solve Inequalities	42
	Mixed Practice for Lessons 5-1 to 5-11	46

Functional Relationships Between Two Quantities

Lesson 5-12	Ordered Pairs	48
Lesson 5-13	Plot Points in the Coordinate Plane	52
Activity 5-14	Plotting Fun Figures	56
Lesson 5-15	Graph Linear Equations	58
Lesson 5-16	Slope	62
Lesson 5-17	Direct Variation	66
Lesson 5-18	Slope-Intercept Form	70
Lesson 5-19	Solve Problems with Linear Equations	74
Lesson 5-20	Nonlinear Relationships	78
	Mixed Practice for Lessons 5-12 to 5-20	82

McDougal Littell

Math Intervention

MATH INTERVENTION

- The Math Intervention program includes skill lessons, problem solving lessons, activities, and mixed practice materials covering a wide range of mathematical topics that are needed for success in middle school and high school mathematics.

- There are seven books in the Math Intervention program. Book 5 contains materials on Algebraic Thinking concepts such as solving simple equations and using a coordinate plane.

- In the Math Intervention books, lessons include worked-out Examples and Try this exercises to help you build understanding of a topic. The Practice section includes a variety of problems to give you the practice you need to develop your math skills. The Did You Get It? section checks your understanding of the lesson.

- Problem solving lessons suggest strategies for approaching real-world problem solving situations and promote the use of estimation to check reasonableness of solutions.

- Activities build your understanding of a topic through the use of models and games.

- Mixed Practice sections include practice of vocabulary, skills, and problem solving methods covering the material in a group of lessons.

- You may complete the work in selected lessons, or cover the book as a whole, as directed by your teacher.

Name _____ Date _____

LESSON 5-1 — Describe Patterns

> **Words to Remember**
> Pattern: A set of rules that can be used to make things such as designs or sequences of numbers
> Congruent: Two figures are congruent if they have the same shape and size.

Getting Started You can continue a pattern of shapes or numbers if you understand how the pattern repeats.

EXAMPLE 1 Extending Patterns Using Shapes

Draw the next two shapes in this pattern.

Solution

Step 1 **Describe** the pattern. The sides in each shape have the same length, so they are congruent. Each shape has one more side than the previous shape.

Step 2 **Draw** the 4th shape. The 4th shape has $5 + 1 = 6$ congruent sides.

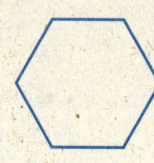

Step 3 **Draw** the 5th shape. The 5th shape has $6 + 1 = 7$ congruent sides.

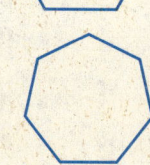

TRY THIS Draw the next two shapes in the pattern.

1.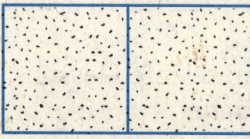

2.

Math Intervention
Book 5 Algebraic Thinking

Name _____ Date _____

EXAMPLE 2 Extending a Numerical Pattern

Find the next three numbers in the pattern 7, 9, 11, 13, ...

Solution

Step 1 **Describe** the pattern. Each number is 2 more than the previous number.

Step 2 **Continue** adding 2.
13 + 2 = 15, 15 + 2 = 17, and 17 + 2 = 19

ANSWER The next three terms are 15, 17, and 19.

TRY THIS
Fill in the missing information to find the next three numbers in the pattern.

3. 4, 7, 10, 13, …

   Step 1 Each number is ____ more than the previous number.

   Step 2 Continuing to add ____, the next three terms are ____, ____, and ____.

4. 3, 6, 12, 24, . . .

   Continuing to _____ each term by 2, the next three terms are ____, ____, and ____.

> **Notice**
> In *Try This* 4, each number is 2 times the previous number.

EXAMPLE 3 Describing a Numerical Pattern

Describe this pattern: 2, 10, 50, 250, ...

Solution

Notice that 2 × 5 = 10. Also, 10 × 5 = 50 and 50 × 5 = 250. Therefore, you start with 2, then multiply each number by 5 to get the next number.

TRY THIS
Fill in the missing information to describe the pattern.

5. 2,   6,   18,   54, …

_____

6. The number of feet on one bird, two birds, three birds, four birds, …

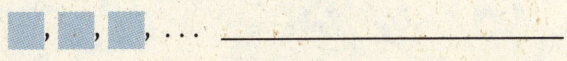

Math Intervention
Book 5 Algebraic Thinking

Name _____   Date _____

> **Summarize**
>
> **Describing and Extending a Visual Pattern**
>
> Identify how the shapes make a pattern. Use this information to draw more figures in the pattern.
>
> **Describing and Extending a Numerical Pattern**
>
> Find what value you use to create the pattern. Do you add, subtract, multiply, or divide by this value? Use the answer to write more numbers in the pattern.

Practice

Which is the next shape or number in the pattern?

1. ☽, ★☽, ★★☽, ★★★☽ _____

    A. ★★★★☽   B. ★★★★   C. ★☽★☽

2. 5, 10, 15, 20, . . . _____

    A. 15   B. 25   C. 30

What are the next two shapes or numbers in the pattern?

3. + × + × × + + + ×

4.

5. 1, 7, 13, 19, . . .

6. 1, 4, 16, 64, . . .

Describe the pattern.

7. Number of ears on one horse, two horses, three horses, four horses, . . .

8.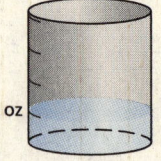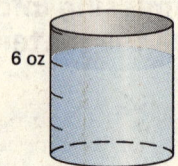

   2 oz   4 oz   6 oz

9. ○△○△△○△△△○

10. 2, 10, 18, 26, . . .

Math Intervention
Book 5 Algebraic Thinking

Name _____ Date _____

Find the fifth number, figure, or letter in the pattern. Explain your reasoning.

11. 9, 13, 17, 21, . . .

_____
_____
_____

12.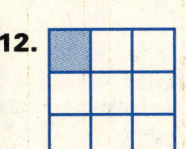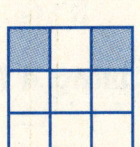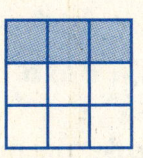

_____
_____
_____

13. A, D, G, J, . . .

_____
_____
_____

DID YOU GET IT?

14. Extend a pattern. Use the given shapes to create a pattern. Then find the next term in your pattern.

   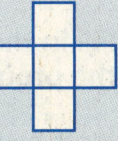

_____
_____
_____

15. Describe a process. Explain how to extend a given pattern of numbers.

_____
_____
_____

Name _____ Date _____

LESSON 5-2: Recognize a Pattern by its Rule

Getting Started In Lesson 5-1 you learned how to describe and extend a pattern of shapes or numbers. You can also describe a pattern by its rule.

EXAMPLE 1 Extending a Pattern Using a Rule

What pattern is described by the rule "the number of legs on a given number of cats"?

Solution

One cat has **4** legs, so two cats would have **8** legs, three cats would have **12** legs, and so on. To generate this pattern you can count by **4**s or multiply the number of cats by **4**.

ANSWER The pattern is **4, 8, 12, 16, ...**

EXAMPLE 2 Describing a Pattern By Its Rule

The pattern 3, 6, 9, 12, ... shows the total number of sides in a given number of triangles. Describe how to create this pattern.

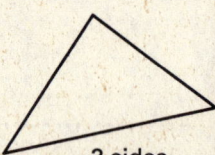
3 sides

Solution

Each triangle has **3** sides. Therefore, the number of triangles can be calculated by counting by **3**s or by multiplying the number of triangles by **3**.

TRY THIS Fill in the missing information to solve the problem.

Remember
A pentagon has 5 points.
Pentagon

1. Describe in words how to create the pattern "the total number of points on a given number of pentagons."

   Step 1 Each pentagon has ▢ points, so you can count by ▢s.

   Step 2 Start with 1 pentagon, then 2 pentagons, and so on. The pattern of points begins ▢, ▢, ...

   Step 3 Continuing to count by ▢s, the pattern is ▢, ▢, ▢, ▢, ...

2. The pattern described by the rule "the number of ears on a given number of pigs" is

   ▢, ▢, ▢, ▢, ...

Name _____ Date _____

Ask a Question
Is a number being *added to* or *subtracted from* a term to get the next term in the pattern? What is this number?

EXAMPLE 3 Describing a Linear Pattern By Its Rule

Write a rule for the pattern 6, 12, 18, 24, 30, ...

Solution

Notice that 6 + 6 = 12. Also 12 + 6 = 18, and 18 + 6 = 24. Therefore, a rule for this pattern is "Start with 6. Then add 6 to a term to get the next term."

TRY THIS Write a rule for the pattern.

3. 100, 75, 50, 25, ...
4. 1, 1.5, 2, 2.5, 3, ...

_____   _____

EXAMPLE 4 Extending a Linear Pattern

Find the 6th term of the pattern 7, 10, 13, 16, ...

Solution

Step 1 **Describe** the pattern by its rule. Starting with 7, add 3 to each term.

Step 2 **Calculate** the 5th term. 16 + 3 = 19

Step 3 **Calculate** the 6th term. 19 + 3 = 22

ANSWER The 6th term of the pattern is 22.

TRY THIS Find terms in a pattern.

5. Fill in the missing information to find the 3rd and 7th terms of the pattern
   50, 46, ▨, 38, ..., ..., ▨, ...

   Step 1 Starting with 50, _____ ▨ from each term.

   Step 2 The 3rd term is 46 ● ▨ = ▨.

   Step 3 The 5th term is ▨. The 6th term is ▨.
   So, the 7th term is ▨.

6. Find the 2nd and 8th terms of the pattern
   6, ▨, 14, 18, ..., ..., ..., ▨, ...

Math Intervention
Book 5 Algebraic Thinking

Name _____ Date _____

> **Summarize**
>
> **Describing a Linear Pattern by Its Rule**
>
> To find a rule, see what number you add or subtract from each term to create the pattern.
>
> **Extending a Pattern Using the Rule**
>
> To extend the pattern using the rule, continue to add or subtract as described in the rule.

Practice

What pattern is described?

1. The number of tires on a given number of racecars

    , ...

2. The number of children in a given number of sets of twins

    , ...

3. The number of dimes in a given number of dollars

    , ...

Describe how to find a term in the pattern.

4. The number of legs on a given number of spiders
   (A spider has **8** legs.)

   Step 1 Each spider has ▣ legs, so you can count by ▣ s.

   Step 2 Start the pattern with **1** spider: ▣ , ...

   Step 3 Continuing to count by ▣ s, the pattern is ▣ , ▣ , ▣ , ▣ , ...

5. The number of minutes in a given number of hours
   (There are **60** minutes in an hour.)

   Step 1 Each hour has ▣ minutes, so you can count by ▣ s.

   Step 2 Start the pattern with **1** hour: ▣ , ...

   Step 3 Continuing the counting by ▣ s, the pattern is ▣ , ▣ , ▣ , ▣ , ...

Math Intervention
Book 5 Algebraic Thinking

Name _____ Date _____

Describe how to find a term in the pattern.

6. The number of days in a given number of weeks

   Step 1 Each week has ▮ days, so you can count by ▮s.

   Step 2 Start the pattern with 1 week: ▮, ...

   Step 3 Continuing the counting by ▮s, the pattern is ▮, ▮, ▮, ▮, ...

Write a rule that describes the pattern. Then use the rule to find the specified term of the pattern.

7. 11, 22, 33, 44, . . . ; 7th term

   _____

8. 19, 21, 23, 25, . . . ; 10th term

   _____

9. 100, 99, 98, 97, . . . ; 8th term

   _____

10. 300, 250, 200, 150, . . . ; 6th term

    _____

11. Explain how you would find the 8th term in the pattern 5, 7, 9, 11, ...

    _____
    _____
    _____

DID YOU GET IT?

12. **Fill in the missing words.** To extend the pattern 6, 15, 24, . . . first find what number must be _____ to 6 to get 15 and to 15 to get 24. Then _____ that number to 24 to get the _____ term.

13. **Explain your reasoning.** Your friend used this rule to describe the pattern 6, 12, 18, 24, . . . : "The number of faces on a given number of number cubes." Was he correct? Explain.

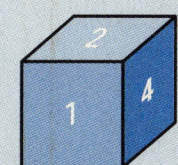

_____
_____
_____

LESSON 5-3

Evaluate Algebraic Expressions

> **Words to Remember**
>
> Variable: A letter or symbol used to represent a number $a, *$
>
> Algebraic expression: An expression involving at least one variable $8x + 3$

Getting Started   In this lesson you will learn how to evaluate algebraic expressions when given values for the variables.

EXAMPLE 1   Evaluating an Algebraic Expression

Evaluate $* + 6$ when $*$ is replaced by 4.

Solution

$* + 6 = 4 + 6$ Substitute 4 for $*$.

$ = 10$ Add.

EXAMPLE 2   Evaluating an Algebraic Expression With More Than One Variable

Evaluate $x - y$ when $x = 6.3$ and $y = 5.71$.

Solution

$x - y = 6.3 - 5.71$ Substitute 6.3 for x and 5.71 for y.

$ = 0.59$ Subtract.

TRY THIS   Evaluate an expression.

1. Evaluate $a + b$ when $a = \frac{3}{4}$ and $b = \frac{1}{8}$.

    $a + b = \boxed{} + \boxed{}$

          $= \boxed{}$

Math Intervention
Book 5 Algebraic Thinking

Name _____ Date _____

Order of Operations In Lesson 1-33 you learned about the order of operations for simplifying numerical expressions. The same order applies when you are evaluating an algebraic expression.

> **Step 1** **Evaluate** expressions inside grouping symbols.
>
> **Step 2** **Evaluate** powers.
>
> **Step 3** **Multiply** and divide from left to right.
>
> **Step 4** **Add** and subtract from left to right.

EXAMPLE 3 — Evaluating an Algebraic Expression Using the Order of Operations

Evaluate $3(5 + 2x)^2$ when $x = 7$.

Solution

$3(5 + 2x)^2 = 3(5 + 2 \cdot 7)^2$ Substitute 7 for x.

$ = 3(5 + 14)^2$ Multiply within parentheses.

$ = 3(19)^2$ Add within parentheses.

$ = 3(361)$ Evaluate power.

$ = 1083$ Multiply.

Using Symbols

The expression "$2x$" means 2 times x.

Use the multiplication symbol $\cdot$ instead of $\times$ in algebraic expressions to avoid confusing $\times$ with the variable x.

TRY THIS Fill in the missing information to evaluate the expression when $x = 3$ and $y = 2$.

2. $8 - 4 + x^2 = 8 - 4 + \square^2$

$ = 8 - 4 + \square$

$ = \square + 9$

$ = \square$

3. $y^2 + 3(x + 2) = \square^2 + 3(\square + 2)$

$ = \square^2 + 3 \cdot \square$

$ = \square + 3 \cdot 5$

$ = 4 + \square$

$ = \square$

Math Intervention
Book 5 Algebraic Thinking

Name _____ Date _____

Summarize

Evaluating an Expression

Replace the variable or symbol with a number. Then simplify.

Evaluate $x + 6 - y$ when $x = 12$ and $y = 8$.
$12 + 6 - 8 = 18 - 8$
$ = 10$

Using the Order of Operations

First you do what is in parentheses, then simplify powers, then multiply and divide from left to right, and finally add and subtract from left to right.

$2^3 - 2 \times 3 = 8 - 2 \times 3$
$ = 8 - 6$
$ = 2$

Practice

Evaluate the expression for the given values of the variables.

1. $8 + * - 5$ when $* = 9$

2. $\triangle + ✿$ when $\triangle = 6$ and $✿ = 10$

3. $♥ - ✿$ when $♥ = 7$ and $✿ = 1$

4. $7(* - ☽)^2$ when $* = 8$ and $☽ = 9$

5. $a + 5$ when $a = 4.68$

6. $3a - b$ when $a = \frac{5}{3}$ and $b = \frac{2}{3}$

7. $4(2x - 3)$ when $x = 2$

8. $6x + 5y$ when $x = 5$ and $y = 18$

Tell which operation you would perform first in evaluating the expression. Then evaluate.

9. $18 \div 9 + 2$

_____
_____
_____

10. $9 + 14 - 7 \times 2$

_____
_____
_____

Evaluate the expression using the order of operations.

11. $2 + 3 \times 6$

12. $16 \div 8 + 4 \times 7$

13. $3^2 - 2 \times 4$

14. $11(10 - 3^2) + 24 \div 4$

Math Intervention
Book 5 Algebraic Thinking

Name _____ Date _____

Substitute and use the order of operations to evaluate the expression.

15. $8a^2 + (b - c)^2$ when $a = 4$, $b = 9$, and $c = 2$

16. $(c + 3d)^2 \div 5 - 3c$ when $c = 12$ and $d = 1$

17. $14y^3 - 6x^2$ when $x = 3$ and $y = 2$

18. $9a + (b - 3c)$ when $a = 10$, $b = 12$, and $c = 4$

19. $(a + 2b) \div c \cdot 6$ when $a = 2$, $b = 5$, and $c = 3$

20. $\dfrac{9m + 2}{5n - 6}$ when $m = 4$ and $n = 5$

21. $\dfrac{1}{2}x + \dfrac{3}{4}y^2 - \dfrac{2}{3}z$ when $x = 8$, $y = 4$, and $z = 9$

22. $2.4c^2 + 5.2(d + 1) - 3.5$ when $c = 1.8$ and $d = 2.5$

23. John evaluated $6a \div 4 \cdot 3$ when $a = 2$, and got 1. What was his mistake? What is the correct answer? Explain your answer.

_____
_____
_____

DID YOU GET IT?

24. **Fill in the missing words.** A variable is a _____ or _____ that represents a _____.

25. **Fill in the missing words.** To evaluate an expression you _____ each variable with the _____ it represents.

26. **Describe a process.** Explain how you would evaluate $(3 + a)^2 - 7b$ when $a = 1$ and $b = 2$, using the order of operations.

_____
_____
_____
_____

Math Intervention
Book 5 Algebraic Thinking

Name _____ Date _____

LESSON 5-4: Write Algebraic Expressions

Words to Remember

You can use key words and phrases to help you decide which operation to use when translating between algebraic expressions and verbal phrases.

KEY WORDS AND PHRASES	OPERATION
Sum, more than, increased by	Add.
Difference, less than, decreased by	Subtract.
Product, times, twice, doubled, of	Multiply.
Quotient, per	Divide.

Getting Started In Lesson 5-3 you evaluated algebraic expressions. In this lesson you will translate between algebraic expressions and verbal phrases.

EXAMPLE 1 Translating a Verbal Phrase

Write an algebraic expression for "four more than a number."

Solution

Let n represent the number.   Always state what variable you are using.

The expression is $n + 4$.   *More than* means addition.

EXAMPLE 2 Translating a Verbal Phrase With Two Operations

Write an algebraic expression for "eight less than twice the number of bananas on a tree."

Solution

Let b represent the number of bananas.

The expression is $2b - 8$.   *Twice* means multiply by 2. *Eight less than* $2b$ means that 8 is subtracted from $2b$.

> **Reading**
>
> $2b$ means 2 times b.
>
> **The order in subtraction makes a difference.** $2b$ is being decreased by 8, not the other way around.

Math Intervention
Book 5 Algebraic Thinking

Name _____ Date _____

TRY THIS Choose a variable and write an algebraic expression for the verbal phrase.

> **Remember**
> The order in division also makes a difference. The quotient of *a* and *b* means $a \div b$ and not $b \div a$.

1. The quotient of a number and 5   ■ ● ■ or ─

2. Six less than 5 times the number of families   ■ • ■ ● ■

Writing a Verbal Phrase   Now you will write a verbal phrase for a given algebraic expression. First, you must know what the variable represents.

EXAMPLE 3   Translating an Algebraic Expression

Write a verbal phrase for $b - 12$, where *b* represents the number of bumblebees in a hive.

Solution

Two possible phrases are "the number of bumblebees decreased by 12" and "12 less than the number of bumblebees."

EXAMPLE 4   Translating an Algebraic Expression With Two Operations

Write a verbal phrase for $3a + 4$, where *a* represents the number of apples you picked.

Solution

Some possible phrases are "four more than 3 times the number of apples," "the sum of 3 times the number of apples and 4," and "3 times the number of apples increased by 4."

TRY THIS   Write a verbal phrase for the algebraic expression.

3. $2t + 16$, where *t* represents the number of T-shirts your class sold

    _____

    _____

4. $\frac{r}{4} - 5$, where *r* represents the number of rabbits in a pen

    _____

    _____

Math Intervention
Book 5 Algebraic Thinking   **15**

Name _____   Date _____

> **Summarize**
>
> **Writing an Algebraic Expression for a Verbal Phrase**
>
> Use a variable to represent an unknown number. Replace words and phrases that represent mathematical operations with the operation symbols.
>
> **Writing a Verbal Phrase for an Algebraic Expression**
>
> Translate the mathematical relationships between variables and other numbers into words.

Practice

Tell whether the word or phrase suggests *addition, subtraction, multiplication*, or *division*.

1. sum
2. quotient
3. product
4. less than
5. more than
6. times
7. divided by
8. decreased by
9. increased by

10. Which algebraic expression represents "the sum of m marigolds and 15"? _____

    A. $15m$ B. $m - 15$ C. $m + 15$

11. Which variable expression represents "the number of jet skis j divided by 6"? _____

    A. $\dfrac{j}{6}$ B. $\dfrac{6}{j}$ C. $6j$

Write an algebraic expression for the verbal phrase. State what the variable represents.

12. Twenty more than the number of fish in an aquarium

    _____

13. The product of a number and 12

    _____

14. The number of helicopters increased by 5

    _____

Math Intervention
Book 5 Algebraic Thinking

Name _____ Date _____

Write an algebraic expression for the verbal phrase. State what the variable represents.

15. The quotient of three times a number and 2

_____

16. Twice the number of zebras in a zoo decreased by 6

_____

17. The difference of 7 times the number of trees in a park and 24

_____

Write a verbal phrase for the algebraic expression.

18. $b + 4$ when b is the number of bicycles at a school

_____

19. $22 - k$ when k is the number of kittens in a pet shop

_____

20. $2p + 8$ when p is the number of potatoes in a bag

_____

21. $\frac{r}{5}$ when r is the number of roses in a garden

_____

22. Write how you would explain to your friend how to write an algebraic expression for "six times the number of cars decreased by 24."

_____
_____

DID YOU GET IT?

23. Fill in the missing words. To translate a verbal phrase into an algebraic expression, replace the unknown quantity with a _____ and replace the operation words with mathematical _____.

24. Fill in the missing information. Let p represent a number of pencils. An algebraic expression for 10 more than the number of pencils is 10 ● ■.

25. Explain your reasoning. Explain why $5n - 2$ represents 2 less than five times a number.

_____
_____

Math Intervention
Book 5 Algebraic Thinking

Name _____   Date _____

LESSON 5-5: Properties of Addition and Multiplication

Words to Remember

Commutative property of addition
$a + b = b + a$
Example: $6 + 7 = 7 + 6$

Associative property of addition
$(a + b) + c = a + (b + c)$
Example: $(6 + 7) + 8 = 6 + (7 + 8)$

Identity property of addition
$a + 0 = a$
Example: $8 + 0 = 8$

Inverse property of addition
$a + (-a) = 0$
Example: $8 + (-8) = 0$

Commutative property of multiplication
$ab = ba$
Example: $6 \cdot 7 = 7 \cdot 6$

Associative property of multiplication
$(ab)c = a(bc)$
Example: $(6 \cdot 7)8 = 6(7 \cdot 8)$

Identity property of multiplication
$a \cdot 1 = a$
Example: $8 \cdot 1 = 8$

Inverse property of multiplication
$a \cdot \frac{1}{a} = 1$
Example: $8 \cdot \frac{1}{8} = 1$

Getting Started In this lesson you will use the properties listed above to simplify expressions.

EXAMPLE 1 Identifying the Property

$3 \times 5 = 5 \times 3$ is an example of what property?

Solution

The commutative property of multiplication

Remember
The commutative properties involve changing the order of two quantities. The associative properties involve regrouping three quantities.

TRY THIS Fill in the missing information to identify a property.

1. $(2 + 8) + \boxed{} = 2 + (\boxed{} + 10)$ is an example of what property?

   _____

2. $5 \cdot \dfrac{1}{\boxed{}} = 1$ is an example of what property?

   _____

Math Intervention
Book 5 Algebraic Thinking

EXAMPLE 2 — Using the Properties

What is the value of $4 + (-4)$? Why?

Solution

$4 + -4 = 0$ by the inverse property of addition.

Simplifying Mental Math These properties can be used to make mental math easier.

EXAMPLE 3 — Using the Properties to Simplify Mental Math

Use the properties to simplify $(25 \times 8) \times 4$. Name the properties or operations you use.

Solution

$(25 \times 8) \times 4 = (8 \times 25) \times 4$ Commutative property of multiplication

$= 8 \times (25 \times 4)$ Associative property of multiplication

$= 8 \times 100$ Multiply.

$= 800$ Multiply.

Using Algebra
Since $25 \times 4 = 100$, group 25×4 to make the multiplication easier.

TRY THIS — Use the properties.

3. Use the properties to simplify $(8 + (-5)) + 5$. Name the properties or operations you use.

$(8 + (-5)) + 5 = 8 + (\square + 5)$ _____

$= 8 + \square$ _____

$= \square$ _____

4. Use the properties to simplify $\frac{2}{3}(10 \times 9)$. Name the properties or operations you use.

$\frac{2}{3}(10 \times 9) = \frac{2}{3}(\square \times 10)$ _____

$= \left(\frac{2}{3} \times \dfrac{\square}{\square}\right) \times 10$ _____

$= \square \times 10$ _____

$= \square$ _____

Name _____   Date _____

> **Summarize**
>
> **Identifying the Properties**
>
> Compare an expression to the properties in this lesson.
>
> **Using the Properties to Simplify Mental Math**
>
> Use the properties to group numbers together that make the arithmetic easier. Look for a number and its additive inverse. Look for a number and its multiplicative inverse.

Practice

Fill in the missing information to identify the property that the statement illustrates.

1. $(2 + 3) \;\square\; 4 = 2 + (3 + 4)$

    _____

2. $2 \times 3 = \square \times 2$

    _____

3. $2 + 0 = \square$

    _____

4. $2 \;\square\; \frac{1}{2} = 1$

    _____

5. $12 + \square = 4 + 12$

    _____

6. $12 \times \square = 12$

    _____

7. $\square + (-12) = 0$

    _____

8. $12 \times (2 \times \square) = (12 \times 2) \times 3$

    _____

9. $3 \;\square\; (4 + 5) = 3 + (\square + 4)$

    _____

10. $\frac{3}{5} \times \frac{5}{3} = \square$

    _____

Find the value of the expression.

11. $-8 + 8$

12. $\frac{1}{8} \times 8$

13. $9 + 0$

14. $\frac{2}{3} \times 1$

Complete the statement.

15. If $3 \times 5 = 15$, then $5 \times 3 =$ _____.

16. If $(8 + 3) + 9 = 20$, then $8 + (3 + 9) =$ _____.

17. If $26 + 19 = 45$, then $19 + 26 =$ _____.

18. If $(9 \times 4) \times 7 = 252$, then $9 \times (4 \times 7) =$ _____.

Math Intervention
Book 5 Algebraic Thinking

Name _____   Date _____

Use the properties and mental math to simplify the expression. Identify the missing numbers and properties in each step.

19. $11 + (56 + (-11)) = 11 + (-11 + \square)$ — Commutative property of addition

$= (\square + \square) + 56$ — Associative property of addition

$= \square + 56$ — Inverse property of addition

$= \square$ — _____

20. $\frac{1}{9} \times (16 \times 9) = \frac{1}{9} \times (9 \times \square)$ — Commutative property of multiplication

$= (\square \times \square) \times \square$ — _____

$= \square \times 16$ — _____

$= \square$ — Identity property of multiplication

21. $(2 \times 17) \times 5 = 2 \times (17 \times 5)$ — _____

$= \square \times (\square \times \square)$ — Commutative property of multiplication

$= (\square \times \square) \times 17$ — _____

$= \square \times 17$ — Multiply.

$= \square$ — _____

DID YOU GET IT?

22. Fill in the missing words. The identity property of addition states that any number plus _____ is _____.

23. Describe a process. Explain how you could use the properties and mental math to simplify $(56 + 74) + (-56)$.

_____
_____

24. Explain your reasoning. Explain how you know that $2 \times 7 = 7 \times 2$ is an example of the commutative property of multiplication.

_____
_____

LESSON 5-6

The Distributive Property

Words to Remember

Distributive property: $a(b + c) = ab + ac$ $6(8 + 7) = 6 \cdot 8 + 6 \cdot 7$
$\phantom{\text{Distributive property: }}a(b - c) = ab - ac$ $6(8 - 7) = 6 \cdot 8 - 6 \cdot 7$

Getting Started   In this lesson you will learn how the distributive property involves two operations.

EXAMPLE 1   Demonstrating the Distributive Property

Use the distributive property to double the number of shapes in ♥♥♦♦♦ two different ways.

Solution

1. Double the hearts and double the diamonds.

   ♥♥   ♦♦♦
   ♥♥   ♦♦♦
   $2(2♥) + 2(3♦) = 4♥ + 6♦$

2. Double the total number of shapes.

   ♥♥♦♦♦
   ♥♥♦♦♦
   $2(2♥ + 3♦) = 4♥ + 6♦$

ANSWER Both methods give $4♥ + 6♦$.

EXAMPLE 2   Recognizing the Distributive Property

Which is an example of the distributive property?

  A. $2(3 + 7) = 2(3) + 7$ **B.** $2(3 + 7) = 2(3) + 2(7)$ **C.** $2(3 + 7) = 2(7 + 3)$

Solution

The correct answer is **B**. The distributive property tells you to multiply both numbers in the parentheses by the number outside, then add.

> **Remember**
> When you use the distributive property you must multiply each term inside the parentheses by the number outside the parentheses.

TRY THIS

1. Which is an example of the distributive property? _____

   A. $7(5 + 4) = 7(5) + 7(4)$

   B. $7(5 + 4) = (7 \times 5) + 4$

   C. $7(5 + 4) = (5 + 4)7$

Math Intervention
Book 5 Algebraic Thinking

EXAMPLE 3 Using the Distributive Property and Mental Math

Use the distributive property and mental math to simplify 4(125).

Solution

$$4(125) = 4(25 + 100) \quad \text{Arithmetic}$$
$$= 4(25) + 4(100) \quad \text{Distributive property}$$
$$= 100 + 400 \quad \text{Multiply.}$$
$$= 500 \quad \text{Add.}$$

EXAMPLE 4 Using the Distributive Property When Adding More Than Two Numbers

Use the distributive property to write the expression $2(-5) + 2(8) + 2(2)$ another way. Then simplify.

Solution

$$2(-5) + 2(8) + 2(2) = 2(-5 + 8 + 2) \quad \text{Distributive property}$$
$$= 2(-5 + (8 + 2)) \quad \text{Associative property of addition}$$
$$= 2(-5 + 10) \quad \text{Add.}$$
$$= 2(5) \quad \text{Add.}$$
$$= 10 \quad \text{Multiply.}$$

TRY THIS Use the distributive property.

2. Use the distributive property to simplify $19(8) + 19(2)$.

$$19(8) + 19(2) = 19(\square + \square)$$
$$= 19(\square)$$
$$= \square$$

3. Use the distributive property to write the expression $8\left(\frac{1}{2} + \frac{3}{4} + 6\right)$ another way. Then simplify the expression.

$$8\left(\frac{1}{2} + \frac{3}{4} + 6\right) = 8 \cdot \square + \square \cdot \frac{3}{4} + \square \cdot \square$$
$$= \square + \square + \square$$
$$= \square$$

Name _____ Date _____

> ## Summarize
> ### Understanding the Distributive Property
> The distributive property is different from the other properties you have learned because it involves both multiplication and addition.
>
> ### Using the Distributive Property
> Suppose you buy a bottle of water and an apple for yourself and a friend. If each bottle of water costs **$1.00** and each apple costs **$.50**, the total cost of the water and apples is:
>
> $2(\$1.00 + \$.50) = 2(\$1.50) = \$3.00$
>
> The distributive property tells you that you can also find the total cost of the water and apples this way:
>
> $2(\$1.00 + \$.50) = 2(\$1.00) + 2(\$.50)$
> $ = \$2.00 + \$1.00$
> $ = \$3.00$

Practice

1. Which is a statement of the distributive property? _____

    A. $a + b = b + a$

    B. $(a + b) + c = a + (b + c)$

    C. $a(b + c) = ab + ac$

Use the distributive property and mental math to simplify the expression.

2. $7(9) + 7(11)$ 　　3. $4(9) + 4(-9)$ 　　4. $5(0.2 + 6)$ 　　5. $-7\left(\dfrac{1}{7} + 3\right)$

6. $8\left(-\dfrac{2}{5}\right) + 8\left(\dfrac{2}{5}\right)$ 　　7. $3(10) - 3(4)$ 　　8. $-6(4) - 6(6)$ 　　9. $20\left(\dfrac{1}{20} + \dfrac{1}{2}\right)$

Use the distributive property to write the expression another way. Then simplify the expression.

10. $15(2) + 15(5) + 15(3)$ 　　　　11. $19(11) + 19(9) + 19(10)$

12. $9\left(\dfrac{1}{2}\right) + 9\left(\dfrac{1}{2}\right) + 9(4)$ 　　　　13. $0.1(4) + 0.1(1) + 0.1(5)$

14. $2(9 + 50 + 100)$ 　　　　15. $4(25 + 3 + 1)$

16. $6(-5 + 10)$ 　　　　17. $12\left(\dfrac{3}{4} + \dfrac{1}{6}\right)$

Math Intervention
Book 5 Algebraic Thinking

Name _____ Date _____

Use the properties of algebra and mental math to simplify the expression. Identify the missing numbers, symbols, or properties in each step.

18. $4(25 + 9) = 4(25)\ \square\ 4(9)$ Distributive property

$= \square + \square$ Multiply.

$= \square$ Add.

19. $\frac{4}{5}(5) + \frac{4}{5}(-12) + \frac{4}{5}(12) = \frac{4}{5}(5 + (-12) + 12)$ _____

$= \frac{4}{5}(5 + (-12 + \square))$ _____

$= \frac{4}{5}(5 + \square)$ _____

$= \frac{4}{5}(\square)$ _____

$= \square$ Multiply.

DID YOU GET IT?

20. Fill in the missing numbers. The distributive property tells you that $11(3 + 7) = 11(\underline{\hspace{1cm}}) + 11(\underline{\hspace{1cm}})$.

21. Write a word problem. Describe a situation that you could represent by the expression $2(3 + 5)$. Then find the value of $2(3 + 5)$ in two different ways. (See the *Summarize* box on page 24.)

_____
_____
_____
_____

22. Explain your reasoning. Which is easier to calculate mentally, $37(95 + 5)$ or $37 \times 95 + 37 \times 5$? Explain.

_____
_____
_____

Name _____   Date _____

LESSON 5-7
Simplify Algebraic Expressions

> **Words to Remember**
>
> Like terms: Terms that have exactly the same variables with exactly the same exponents
>
> **6a** and **9a** are like terms.
>
> Coefficient of a term: The number multiplied by the variable
>
> The coefficient of **3x** is **3**.
>
> Constant term: A term without a variable
>
> In the expression **5x + 2**, **2** is a constant term.
>
> Equivalent expressions: Expressions with equal value
>
> **2x + 5x** and **(2 + 5)x** are equivalent expressions because **2x + 5x = (2 + 5)x**.

Getting Started In this lesson you will use the distributive property to simplify expressions with variables.

EXAMPLE 1 Identifying Coefficients and Terms

Use the expression $5x^2 - 2x + 6$.

a. How many terms are there in the expression?

b. What is the coefficient of x^2?

c. What is the coefficient of x?

d. Which term is a constant term?

Solution

> **Reading Math**
> $5x^2 - 2x + 6 = 5x^2 + (-2x) + 6$, so the coefficient of x is -2.

a. There are three terms: $5x^2$, $-2x$, and 6.

b. Five is multiplied by x^2 so **5** is the coefficient of x^2.

c. Negative 2 is multiplied by x so -2 is the coefficient of x.

d. Six is not multiplied by a variable so **6** is the constant term.

Math Intervention
Book 5 Algebraic Thinking

Name _____ Date _____

TRY THIS Fill in the missing information to solve the problem.

1. Identify the terms and coefficients in the expression $6x^3 + 8x^2 - x + 9$.

    Remember
    $-x$ means $-1x$, so the coefficient of x is -1.

    Step 1 There are ▢ terms in the expression.

    Step 2 ▢ is multiplied by x^3, so ▢ is the coefficient of x^3.

    Step 3 8 is the coefficient of ▢.

    Step 4 The coefficient of x is ▢.

    Step 5 9 is the _____ term.

EXAMPLE 2 Writing Equivalent Expressions

Use the distributive property to write an equivalent expression for $9(a + b)$.

Remember
Since $9a$ and $9b$ are not like terms, $9a + 9b$ cannot be simplified.

Solution

$9(a + b) = 9a + 9b$

TRY THIS Use the distributive property to write an equivalent expression.

2. $15(2m + n) = 15 \cdot$ ▢ ● ▢ $\cdot n$

    $=$ ▢ ● ▢

EXAMPLE 3 Simplifying Expressions By Combining Like Terms

Simplify $8x + 6x + 9$.

Solution

$8x + 6x + 9 = (8x + 6x) + 9$ Group like terms.

$= (8 + 6)x + 9$ Distributive property

$= 14x + 9$ Add.

TRY THIS Simplify the expression.

3. $2y^2 - 4y + 11y$ 4. $12a + 5 + a - 2$

Name _____   Date _____

> **Summarize**
>
> **Identifying Coefficients and Terms in Algebraic Expressions**
>
> Terms are separated by addition and subtraction signs. Terms are like terms if they have exactly the same variables with exactly the same exponents. A constant term has no variable. The coefficient of a term is the number multiplied by the variable.
>
> **Simplifying Expressions**
>
> To simplify an expression, combine all like terms.

Practice

Name the constant term in the expression.

1. $5m + 6$ _____
2. $8y - 13$ _____
3. $15a^2 - 2 + 7a$ _____
4. 19 _____

Name the coefficient of x^2 in the expression.

5. $5x^2 + 6$ _____
6. $9x - 17x^2$ _____
7. $5 + 14x + x^2$ _____
8. $9x^3 - 45x^2 + 2x - 11$ _____

9. Which terms are like terms? _____

    A. $18x$ and $18y$ B. $18b$ and $-5b$ C. $4a^2$ and $9a$

Fill in the missing information to write an equivalent expression for the given expression.

10. $11(c + 2) = \square \cdot c \bigcirc 11 \cdot \square$
11. $3(a - b) = \square \cdot \square \bigcirc \square \cdot \square$
12. $12(x^2 + y) = \square \cdot x^2 \bigcirc \square \cdot \square$
13. $3(m^3 - n^2) = 3 \cdot \square \bigcirc \square \cdot n^2$

Simplify the expression.

14. $8x + 12x$
15. $5a + 9b + 3a + b$
16. $2y^2 - 5y + 7 + 3y^2 + 4y$
17. $4b - 6 + b^2 - 10$
18. $14(2x + y) + 6x$
19. $9(x - 4y) + 5(6x + 2y)$

Math Intervention
Book 5 Algebraic Thinking

Name _____ Date _____

20. Explain how to use the distributive property to add $7x + 15x$.

_____
_____
_____

21. Explain why $2a$ and $2a^2$ are not like terms.

_____
_____
_____

22. An algebraic expression has three terms. The constant term is 11. The coefficient of y is 17 and the coefficient of y^2 is -2. What is the expression?

_____

23. Which of the following expressions is *not* equal to $6(x + 8)$? Explain your reasoning.

    A. $6x + 48$ **B.** $6(x) + 6(8)$ **C.** $6x + 8$ **D.** $48 + 6x$

_____
_____
_____

DID YOU GET IT?

24. Fill in the missing words. In the expression $5a^2 - 2a + 7$, 5 is the _____ of a^2 and 7 is the _____ _____.

25. Find the error. Samantha simplified $4a + 2b - a + 10b$ to $3 + 12b^2$. What were her mistakes?

_____
_____

26. Explain your reasoning. Explain why $6x + 2y$ is equal to $2(3x + y)$.

_____
_____

Math Intervention
Book 5 Algebraic Thinking

Name _____ Date _____

LESSON 5-8: Solve Addition and Subtraction Equations

> **Words to Remember**
>
> Inverse operation: An operation you use to "undo" another operation
>
> Equivalent equations: Equations with the same solution
>
> Solve an equation: To find the value(s) of the variable(s) that make(s) the equation true
>
> Subtraction property of equality: A property that lets you subtract the same number from each side of an equation and produce an equivalent equation
>
> Addition property of equality: A property that lets you add the same number to each side of an equation and produce an equivalent equation

Getting Started In this lesson you will learn how to use the addition and subtraction properties of equality to solve equations. To solve an equation, you want to get the variable alone on one side of the equation.

Using a Property Addition and subtraction are inverse operations. You use the subtraction property of equality to "undo" addition when you solve an equation.

EXAMPLE 1 Solving a Simple Addition Equation

Solve $x + 9 = 15$.

Solution

$x + 9 = 15$	Write the original equation.
$\underline{-9 \quad -9}$	Subtract 9 from each side.
$x + 0 = 6$	Simplify.
$x = 6$	Identity property of addition

Check: $x + 9 = 15$	Write the original equation.
$6 + 9 \stackrel{?}{=} 15$	Substitute 6 for x.
$15 = 15$ ✓	Simplify. The solution checks.

> **Remember**
>
> Subtract 9 from the left side of the equation to "undo" adding 9. This leaves x alone on one side of the equation. The subtraction property of equality says that you must subtract 9 from *each* side of the equation.

Name _____ Date _____

TRY THIS Fill in the missing information to solve the equation.

1. $y + 1 = -10$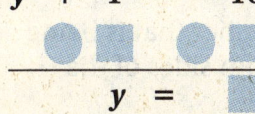

   $y = \square$

2. $25 = m + 15$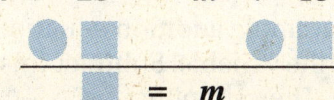

   $\square = m$

Using a Property You use the addition property of equality to "undo" subtraction when you solve an equation.

EXAMPLE 2 Solving a Simple Subtraction Equation

Solve $y - 7 = 8$.

Solution

$y - 7 = 8$	Write the original equation.
$+7 \quad +7$	Add 7 to each side.
$y + 0 = 15$	Simplify.
$y = 15$	Identity property of addition

Check: $y - 7 = 8$	Write the original equation.
$15 - 7 \stackrel{?}{=} 8$	Substitute 15 for y.
$8 = 8$ ✓	Simplify. The solution checks.

Remember
Add 7 to the left side of the equation to "undo" subtracting 7. This leaves x alone on one side of the equation.
The addition property of equality says that you must add 7 to *each* side of the equation.

TRY THIS Fill in the missing information to solve the equation.

3. $x - 11 = -2$

   $x = \square$

4. $6 = a - 3$

   $\square = a$

EXAMPLE 3 Identifying How to Solve an Equation

Tell how to use an inverse operation to solve $5 = z + 9$.

Solution

To undo the addition of 9, subtract 9 from each side of the equation.

TRY THIS Tell how to use an inverse operation to solve the equation. Then solve the equation.

5. $y + 2 = -5$

6. $17 = b - 12$

Name _____   Date _____

> **Summarize**
>
> **Solving a Simple Addition Equation**
>
> To solve a simple addition equation identify the number that is being added to the variable. Subtract this number from both sides of the equation. Then simplify.
>
> **Solving a Simple Subtraction Equation**
>
> To solve a simple subtraction equation identify the number that is being subtracted from the variable. Add this number to both sides of the equation. Then simplify.

Practice

Fill in the missing information to recognize the inverse operation.

Operation	Inverse operation
1. Add 15.	_____ ▢.
2. Subtract ▢.	_____ 2.

Tell how to use an inverse operation to solve the equation.

3. $a + 17 = 19$ 4. $b + 5 = -12$

5. $8 = c + 10$ 6. $d - 11 = 5$

7. $e - 18 = -2$ 8. $4 = f - 9$

Solve the equation. Check your answer.

9. $x + 3 = 9$ 10. $y + 11 = -1$

11. $z + 5 = 2$ 12. $a + 4 = 21$

13. $-18 = b + 17$ 14. $12.13 = c + 2.48$

Math Intervention
Book 5 Algebraic Thinking

Name _____   Date _____

Solve the equation. Check your answer.

15. $\frac{3}{4} = d + \frac{1}{4}$

16. $\frac{2}{3} = e + \frac{1}{3}$

17. $f - 9 = 11$

18. $g - 45 = -6$

19. $h - 31 = 42$

20. $j - 24 = -28$

21. $2.56 = k - 1.94$

22. $5.3 = m - 6.8$

23. $-\frac{3}{5} = n - \frac{2}{5}$

24. $\frac{1}{4} = p - \frac{3}{8}$

25. Marty solved $x + 17 = 9$ by subtracting 9 from each side. Why was his solution incorrect?

_____
_____

DID YOU GET IT?

26. Fill in the missing number. To solve $x + 18 = 5$, subtract _____ from each side.

27. Describe a process. Explain how to solve $y - 2 = -3$.

_____
_____
_____

28. Explain your reasoning. Are $x + 11 = 13$ and $x - 5 = -3$ equivalent equations? Explain.

_____
_____
_____

Math Intervention
Book 5 Algebraic Thinking

Name _____ Date _____

LESSON 5-9 Solve Multiplication and Division Equations

> **Words to Remember**
>
> Multiplication property of equality: A property that lets you multiply each side of an equation by the same number and produce an equivalent equation
>
> Division property of equality: A property that lets you divide each side of an equation by the same number and produce an equivalent equation

Getting Started In this lesson you will learn how to use inverse operations to solve simple multiplication or division equations.

Using a Property Use the division property of equality to "undo" multiplication when you solve an equation.

EXAMPLE 1 Solving a Simple Multiplication Equation

Solve $5x = 30$.

Solution

	$5x = 30$	Write the original equation.
	$\dfrac{5x}{5} = \dfrac{30}{5}$	Divide each side by 5, the coefficient of x.
	$1x = 6$	Simplify.
	$x = 6$	Identity property of multiplication
Check:	$5x = 30$	Write the original equation.
	$5(6) \stackrel{?}{=} 30$	Substitute 6 for x.
	$30 = 30$ ✓	Simplify. The solution checks.

Remember
$\dfrac{5x}{5} = 1x$, and $1x = x$ by the identity property of multiplication.

TRY THIS Solve the equation.

1. $8y = 56$
    $\dfrac{8y}{\blacksquare} = \dfrac{56}{\blacksquare}$
    $\blacksquare y = \blacksquare$
    $y = \blacksquare$

2. $5p = -20$
    $\dfrac{5p}{\blacksquare} = \dfrac{-20}{\blacksquare}$
    $\blacksquare p = \blacksquare$
    $p = \blacksquare$

EXAMPLE 2 Solving a Simple Multiplication Equation with a Negative Coefficient

Solve $-2k = 12$.

Solution

> **Remember**
> Divide each side by the coefficient of the variable.

$-2k = 12$	Write the original equation.
$\dfrac{-2k}{-2} = \dfrac{12}{-2}$	Divide each side by -2.
$1k = -6$	Simplify.
$k = -6$	Identity property of multiplication
Check: $\quad -2k = 12$	Write the original equation.
$(-2)(-6) \stackrel{?}{=} 12$	Substitute -6 for k.
$12 = 12$ ✓	Simplify. The solution checks.

EXAMPLE 3 Solving a Simple Division Equation

Solve $\dfrac{a}{4} = -9$.

Solution

> **Remember**
> The inverse operation of division is multiplication. To "undo" division by 4, multiply each side by 4.

$\dfrac{a}{4} = -9$	Write the original equation.
$4 \cdot \dfrac{a}{4} = 4 \cdot (-9)$	Multiply each side by 4, the divisor of a.
$1a = -36$	Simplify.
$a = -36$	Identity property of multiplication
Check: $\dfrac{a}{4} = -9$	Write the original equation.
$\dfrac{-36}{4} \stackrel{?}{=} -9$	Substitute -36 for a.
$-9 = -9$ ✓	Simplify. The solution checks.

Don't Forget You need to multiply by a negative number when you "undo" division by a negative number.

TRY THIS Solve the equation.

3. $-7x = 63$
$\dfrac{-7x}{\boxed{}} = \dfrac{-63}{\boxed{}}$
$x = \boxed{}$
$x = \boxed{}$

4. $\dfrac{b}{9} = -5$
$\boxed{} \cdot \dfrac{b}{9} = \boxed{} \cdot -5$
$b = \boxed{}$
$b = \boxed{}$

> **Summarize**
>
> **Solving a Simple Multiplication Equation**
> To solve a simple multiplication equation, divide each side by the coefficient of the variable and simplify.
>
> **Solving a Simple Division Equation**
> To solve a simple division equation, multiply each side by the divisor of the variable. Then simplify.

Practice

1. Which value is the solution of $3x = 30$? _____

   A. 90   B. 27   C. 10

2. Which value is the solution of $\dfrac{y}{-4} = 8$? _____

   A. -32 B. -2 C. 12

What number should each side be divided by to solve the equation?

3. $2x = -12$ 4. $8a = 48$

5. $2 = -4y$ 6. $-15 = -5p$

What number should each side be multiplied by to solve the equation?

7. $\dfrac{z}{9} = 1$ 8. $\dfrac{a}{-5} = -2$

9. $17 = \dfrac{b}{6}$ 10. $12 = \dfrac{c}{-3}$

11. Fill in the missing information in the Check that 15 is the solution of $\dfrac{x}{5} = 3$.

    Check: $\dfrac{x}{5} = 3$

    $\dfrac{\blacksquare}{5} \stackrel{?}{=} 3$

    $\blacksquare = \blacksquare$ ✓

Solve the equation. Check your answer.

12. $5a = 45$ 13. $14b = -28$

14. $-11c = 4.4$ 15. $-9d = -90$

Math Intervention
Book 5 Algebraic Thinking

Name _____   Date _____

Solve the equation. Check your answer.

16. $\frac{2}{3}m = 6$

17. $\frac{-3}{4}p = -12$

18. $\frac{r}{16} = 5$

19. $\frac{s}{-3} = 19$

20. $\frac{t}{-4} = -6$

21. $7 = \frac{x}{14}$

22. $6 = \frac{y}{-12}$

23. $0.4 = \frac{z}{-8}$

24. Shawn solved $\frac{2}{3}a = -10$ by multiplying each side by $\frac{2}{3}$. Was he correct? Explain.

_____
_____
_____

DID YOU GET IT?

25. **Fill in the missing words.** To solve $\frac{g}{9} = -2$, you _____ each side by _____.

26. **Fill in the missing words.** To solve $-5y = 25$, you _____ each side by _____.

27. **Explain your reasoning.** Explain why dividing each side of $-6x = 12$ by 6 does not give the solution of the equation.

_____
_____
_____
_____

LESSON 5-10: Solve Problems with Equations

Strategies to Remember

When you solve a word problem use these steps to write an equation:

(1) **Look** at the problem. **Recognize** that some words indicate which operation to use:
  Use *addition* or *multiplication* to combine.
  Use *subtraction* to find how many are left or how many more are needed.
  Use *division* to find numbers in each equal group.
(2) **Write** the words as a verbal equation.
(3) **Choose** a variable and write a mathematical equation.
(4) **Solve** the equation. Show your steps.
(5) **Check** your answer for reasonableness.

EXAMPLE 1 — Solving Word Problems Using a Simple Addition or Subtraction Equation

Lucy has 12 baseball hats after giving 5 to Jim. How many hats did Lucy have before she gave 5 to Jim?

Solution

Step 1 Write the words.

| Number of hats Lucy had | − | Number of hats she gave Jim | = | Number of hats Lucy has left |

Step 2 We do not know how many hats Lucy had. Choose a variable to represent this number.

Let h = the number of hats Lucy had.

Remember: Always state what the variable represents.

Step 3 Write an equation for the words.

$h - 5 = 12$

Step 4 Solve the equation.

$h - 5 = 12$ Write the equation.

$h - 5 + 5 = 12 + 5$ Add 5 to each side.

$h = 17$ Simplify.

ANSWER Lucy had 17 hats.

EXAMPLE 2 Solving Word Problems Using a Simple Multiplication or Division Equation

Sixteen times a number is -144. What is the number? Write and solve an equation to answer the question.

Solution

$16 \times$ a number $= -144$	Write the words.
Let n represent the number.	Tell what the variable represents.
$16n = -144$	Write an equation.
$\dfrac{16n}{16} = -\dfrac{144}{16}$	Solve the equation.
$n = -9$	Simplify.

ANSWER The number is -9.

TRY THIS Write an equation and solve the problem. State what your variable represents.

> **Remember**
> *More than* means addition.

1. Four times the number of horses in a barn is **28**. How many horses are in the barn?

2. One hundred is **14** points more than Bette's quiz grade. What is Bette's quiz grade?

3. Bob has **20** cents less than the amount Jim has. If Jim has **83** cents, how much does Bob have?

EXAMPLE 3 Checking the Reasonableness of a Solution

Fifteen inches less than George's height is **45** inches. Suppose you say that George's height is **30** inches. Is your answer reasonable? Explain.

Solution

No. George's height must be more than **45** inches since you get **45** after you subtract **15**. George's height could not be **30** inches.

TRY THIS Check for reasonableness.

4. Cammy has twelve stuffed bears. The number of bears is **5** more than the number of stuffed dogs she has. How many dogs does Cammy have? Suppose you solved this problem and got **7** for your answer. Is this reasonable?

Math Intervention
Book 5 Algebraic Thinking **39**

Name _____ Date _____

> **Summarize**
>
> **Solving Word Problems Using a Simple Equation**
>
> (1) To solve a word problem using a simple linear equation, you must choose a variable and state what it represents.
>
> (2) Then you write an equation for the problem. Remember the words from Lesson 5-4 that mean addition, subtraction, multiplication, and division. This will help you write an equation for the words.
>
> (3) Solve your equation.
>
> (4) Finally, you need to check to see if your solution is reasonable for the question being asked.

Practice

Write an equation and solve the problem. State what your variable represents.

1. A number increased by **36** is **79**. What is the number?

2. Six times the number of girls in a choir is **90**. How many girls are in choir?

3. The number of apples in a basket divided by **5** is **35**. How many apples are in the basket?

4. When the temperature decreases **7** degrees it will be **−2° F**. What is the temperature now?

5. Martha has a certain number of quarters. The total value of the quarters is **$2.75**. How many quarters does she have?

Math Intervention
Book 5 Algebraic Thinking

Name _____ Date _____

Write an equation and solve the problem. State what your variable represents.

6. A number decreased by $\frac{2}{3}$ is $\frac{1}{2}$. What is the number?

7. Shaunee asked **6** employees to write some letters. If each employee wrote **24** letters, how many letters did they write altogether?

8. Twenty more than the number of kittens in the animal shelter is **33**. How many kittens are in the shelter?

9. Two-thirds of the players at soccer practice are wearing white socks. If **18** players are wearing white socks, how many students are at soccer practice? Suppose you solved this problem and your answer was "**12** students." Is your answer reasonable? Explain.

_____
_____

DID YOU GET IT?

10. **Fill in the missing words.** When solving a word problem, you should state what the _____ represents. Then you should write a(n) _____ for the words that describe the situation.

11. **Write an equation.** Three-fifths of a number is **30**. Write an equation you could use to solve this problem.

_____

12. **Explain your reasoning.** The number of roses in a vase is **8** less than the number of tulips. There are **6** roses. How many tulips are in the vase? To solve this problem, Nanette wrote the equation $6 = 8 - t$. Is her equation correct?

_____
_____

Math Intervention
Book 5 Algebraic Thinking   41

LESSON 5-11: Solve Inequalities

> **Words to Remember**
>
> Inequality: Two expressions separated by an inequality symbol
>
> Inequality symbols: > (greater than), < (less than), ≥ (greater than or equal to), ≤ (less than or equal to)
>
> Solution of an inequality: The numbers that make the inequality true
>
> $x < 6 \quad a \geq 4$

Getting Started You will learn how to solve simple linear inequalities using inverse operations.

EXAMPLE 1 — Solving a Subtraction Inequality and Graphing its Solution

Solve $x - 3 \geq -2$.

Solution

$x - 3 \geq -2$	Write the inequality.
$x - 3 + 3 \geq -2 + 3$	Add 3 to each side to undo *subtract 3*.
$x \geq 1$	Simplify.

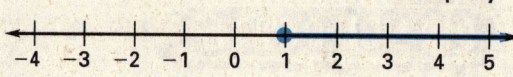

Remember
Use a closed circle when you graph an inequality with ≥ or ≤. In Example 1, the boundary point "1" is included in the solution. The solution shows all numbers greater than or equal to 1.

EXAMPLE 2 — Using an Addition Inequality

Ali wants to eat under 40 grams of sugar today. He has already had 18 grams of sugar. How many more grams of sugar can Ali eat and meet his goal?

Solution

Let s = the number of grams of sugar Ali can eat.

$s + 18 < 40$	Write an inequality.
$s + 18 - 18 < 40 - 18$	Subtract 18 from each side to undo *add 18*.
$s < 22$	Simplify.

ANSWER Ali must eat less than 22 grams of sugar.

Check Since $18 + 22 = 40$, Ali must eat less than 22 grams of sugar to meet his goal.

Multiply or Divide by a Negative Number When you multiply or divide each side of an inequality by a negative number, you must reverse the inequality sign. For example, you know that $-20 < 10$. But if you divide each side by -10, you get $2 > -1$. The inequality sign is reversed.

EXAMPLE 3 — Solving a Multiplication Inequality and Graphing its Solution

Solve $-4x > -12$. Then graph the solution.

Solution

$-4x > -12$ Write the inequality.

$\dfrac{-4x}{-4} < \dfrac{-12}{-4}$ Divide each side by -4 to undo *times* -4. Reverse the inequality sign.

$x < 3$ Simplify.

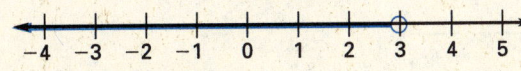

Remember
Use an open circle when you graph an inequality with > or <. In Example 3, the boundary point "3" is not included in the solution. The solution shows all numbers less than 3.

EXAMPLE 4 — Using a Division Inequality

Ali is preparing 4 dinners that will each have no more than 20 grams of protein. If the dinners have the same amount of protein, what is the maximum amount of total protein that can be in the 4 dinners?

Solution

Let $p =$ the total number of grams of protein.

$\dfrac{p}{4} \le 20$ Write an inequality.

$\dfrac{p}{4} \cdot 4 \le 20 \cdot 4$ Multiply each side by 4 to undo *divided by 4*.

$p \le 80$ Simplify.

ANSWER The maximum amount is **80** grams of protein.

Check If there are **80** grams of protein in the **4** meals, then each meal will have $\dfrac{80}{4}$, or **20** grams of protein. Since this is the most protein each meal should have, the **4** meals will have a maximum of **80** grams of protein.

Reading
"No more than 20" means the quantity must be 20 or less, so $\dfrac{p}{4} \le 20$.

TRY THIS

Solve the inequality and graph its solution.

1. $x + 3 > 5$
2. $\dfrac{m}{-2} < 3$

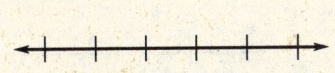
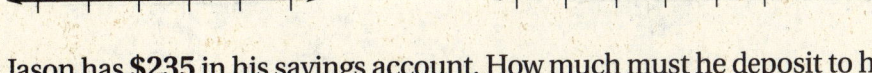

3. Jason has **$235** in his savings account. How much must he deposit to have at least **$275** in his account? Check that your solution makes sense.

Reading
"At least $275" means the quantity must be 275 or more.

Name _____ Date _____

> **Summarize**
>
> **Solving a Simple Linear Inequality**
>
> To solve a simple linear inequality you use inverse properties just as you do when solving linear equations. You want to get the variable by itself on one side of the inequality.
>
> **Multiplying or Dividing by a Negative Number**
>
> When you solve an inequality, if you multiply or divide each side of the inequality by a negative number the inequality sign switches direction.

Practice

1. Which is a solution of $x < 7$? _____

   A. 5   B. 7   C. 9

2. Which is the graph of $x \geq 2$? _____

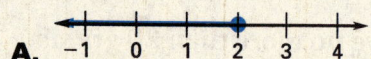
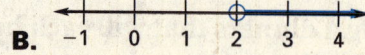

Solve the inequality. Graph the solution.

3. $x + 9 < 2$

4. $a + 5 \geq -7$

5. $d - 6 > 3$

6. $e - 12 \leq 23$

7. $8h > 32$

8. $9j < -27$

9. $\dfrac{n}{6} < 9$

10. $\dfrac{p}{-2} \geq 1.5$

11. $g - 1.5 \leq -3.75$

12. $-w < 5$

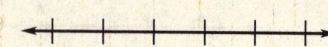

Math Intervention
Book 5 Algebraic Thinking

Name _____ Date _____

Use an inequality to solve the problem. Check that your answer makes sense.

13. Ramon wants to run at least 18 miles this week. If he runs the same distance for 5 days, how far should he run each day?

14. Jen needs less than 80 cubic feet of topsoil for her garden. She already has 15 cubic feet of topsoil. How much more does she need?

15. Kinsley has some baseball cards. She wants to give 25 away. After she gives the cards away, she will have more than 180 cards left. What is the minimum number of cards Kinsley could have now?

16. To get a grade of A, Tyler's quiz total must be at least 450. So far his quiz total is 358. How many more points does he need to receive a grade of A?

17. Explain how you would solve the inequality $\frac{2}{3}x \leq -6$.

_____
_____

DID YOU GET IT?

18. **Fill in the missing words.** To solve $-5x < -15$, you _____ each side by -5. The inequality sign will _____.

19. **Describe a process.** Explain how you would graph the solution of $y + 2 > -3$.

_____
_____
_____

20. **Explain your reasoning.** Is this the correct graph of the solution of $2x > 6$? Explain.

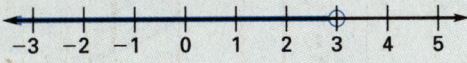

_____
_____
_____

Name _____   Date _____

Mixed Practice for Lessons 5-1 to 5-11

Vocabulary Review

Match the word with an example that illustrates the word.

Word		Example
1. linear equation	____	A. 2 in $2a + 6$
2. linear inequality	____	B. 6 in $2a + 6$
3. coefficient	____	C. $2x + 6$
4. constant term	____	D. $2x + 6 < 12$
5. algebraic expression	____	E. $2x + 6 = 12$

Fill in the missing word(s).

6. $2(3 + 7) = 2(3) + 2(7)$ is an example of the _____ property.

7. $2(3 + 7) = 2(7 + 3)$ is an example of the _____ property of _____.

8. $3 \cdot \frac{1}{3} = 1$ is an example of the _____ property of _____.

9. Find the next three numbers in the pattern 9, 15, 21, ...

10. Describe the pattern of the number of feet in 1 yard, 2 yards, 3 yards, ...

11. Find the next shape in the pattern.

12. Find a rule for the pattern 36, 18, 9, ...

13. Describe how to create the pattern "the number of leaves on a given number of four-leaved clovers."

14. Evaluate $3 \cdot ☺ + 10$ when ☺ is replaced by 4.

15. Evaluate $\frac{x + 2y}{3z}$ when $x = -8$, $y = 12$, and $z = 4$.

16. Write an algebraic expression for "six more than twice the number of shirts s."

Math Intervention
Book 5 Algebraic Thinking

Name _____ Date _____

17. Write a verbal phrase for $m - 7$ where m represents the number of monkeys in the zoo.

18. Simplify $8(-4) + 8(4)$ using the distributive property and mental math.

19. Write an equivalent expression for $8(2a - b)$ using the distributive property.

Solve the equation or inequality.

20. $x - 11 = 26$ **21.** $\dfrac{k}{3} = -9$ **22.** $-\dfrac{3}{4}y = -12$

23. $17 = a + 19$ **24.** $m + 2 = -50$ **25.** $y - \dfrac{3}{4} = \dfrac{1}{2}$

26. $2 = \dfrac{b}{7}$ **27.** $-6x = 15$ **28.** $p - 3 < -4$

29. $12 + y \geq 5$ **30.** $-7g \geq 21$ **31.** $\dfrac{x}{6} > 1$

Solve the problem using an equation. State what the variable represents.

32. Miranda had 104 baseball cards. After she bought another package she had 129 baseball cards. How many cards were in the package she bought?

_____
_____
_____

33. Seven times the amount a tree grew the first year is 84 inches. How many inches did the tree grow the first year?

_____
_____
_____

Math Intervention
Book 5 Algebraic Thinking

Name _____ Date _____

LESSON 5-12
Ordered Pairs

Words to Remember

Ordered pair: A pair of numbers represented by *x* and *y* and written in the form (*x*, *y*)

Input: The values of *x* or of the first numbers in the ordered pairs

Output: The values of *y* or of the second numbers in the ordered pairs

Equation in two variables: A rule relating input and output values

Getting Started You can use a rule to describe how the output values are related to the input values. The ordered pairs from the rule can be displayed in an input-output table.

EXAMPLE 1 Making an Input-Output Table

Complete the input-output table for the rule $y = x - 1$.

Solution

Substitute each input value for *x* in the rule. Then simplify to find the output values *y*.

Input, *x*	−3	−1	0	5
Output, *y*	$-3 - 1 = -4$	$-1 - 1 = -2$	$0 - 1 = -1$	$5 - 1 = 4$

TRY THIS Make a table.

1. Complete the input-output table for the rule $y = 2x$.

Input, *x*	−2	0	1	4
Output, *y*				

2. Complete the input-output table for the rule $y = x + 5$.

Input, *x*	−3	−1	2	4
Output, *y*				

Math Intervention
Book 5 Algebraic Thinking

EXAMPLE 2 Writing Ordered Pairs from a Table

Write the values in the table as ordered pairs.

x	−3	−1	0	2	5
y	1	3	4	6	9

Remember
In an ordered pair, you write the x-values first and the y-values second.

Solution

$(-3, 1), (-1, 3), (0, 4), (2, 6), (5, 9)$

TRY THIS Write ordered pairs.

3. Write the values in the table as ordered pairs.

x	−15	−5	0	10
y	−3	−1	0	2

EXAMPLE 3 Writing a Rule from an Input-Output Table

Look for a Pattern
How can the y-values be obtained from the corresponding x-values?

Write a rule that shows how y relates to x.

x	−6	−3	0	5
y	−2	1	4	9

Solution

The y-values are 4 more than the corresponding x-values. Therefore, the rule is $y = x + 4$.

TRY THIS Write a rule.

4. Write a rule that shows how y relates to x.

x	−2	−1	0	1	2
y	−6	−3	0	3	6

5. Write a rule that shows how y relates to x.

x	−4	−2	0	2	4
y	−7	−5	−3	−1	1

Summarize

Making an Input-Output Table
Using a rule describing a relationship between two values x and y, substitute input values for x to find the corresponding output values for y.

Writing Ordered Pairs from a Table
The x-values or input values are the first number in each ordered pair. The y-values or output values are the second.

Writing a Rule from an Input-Output Table
Look for a relationship between the x-values and the y-values. Find the pattern that determines how each value of y can be obtained from the corresponding value of x.

Practice

Complete the input-output table using the given rule.

1. $y = 4x$

Input, x	1	2	5	7
Output, y				

2. The number of sailboats x is 20 less than the number of speed boats y.

Sailboats, x	0	2	3	5
Speed boats, y				

Write the values in the table as ordered pairs.

3.

x	−6	−2	1	4
y	−8	−4	−1	2

_____

4.

x	−3	−2	−1	0
y	4	5	6	7

_____

Math Intervention
Book 5 Algebraic Thinking

Name _____   Date _____

Write a rule that shows how y relates to x.

5.
x	−1	0	1	2
y	4	0	−4	−8

_____

6.
x	−1	0	1	2
y	−2	−1	0	1

_____

7.
x	−3	0	6	12
y	−1	0	2	4

_____

8. Explain how to identify the input values in the ordered pairs $(-2, -1)$, $(7, 6)$, and $(10, 9)$.

_____
_____

9. The distance d that Maria travels in h hours can be described by the rule $d = 50h$. Write three ordered pairs that make the rule true.

_____

DID YOU GET IT?

10. **Fill in the missing words.** In the ordered pair (x, y), the value of _____ is the input and the value of _____ is the output.

11. **Describe a process.** How would you write a rule that shows how y relates to x?

x	−2	−1	0	1
y	−8	−4	0	4

    _____
    _____

12. **Explain your reasoning.** Can the relationship between the number of weeks that have passed and the number of years that have passed be described by a rule relating two variables w and y? Explain.

    _____
    _____

Math Intervention
Book 5 Algebraic Thinking

Name _____ Date _____

LESSON 5-13
Plot Points in the Coordinate Plane

Words to Remember

x-axis: The horizontal axis

y-axis: The vertical axis

Origin: The point (0, 0), where the horizontal and vertical axes intersect

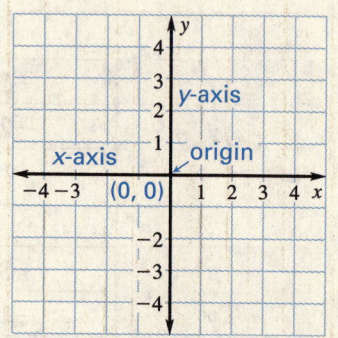

Getting Started In Lesson 5-12 you learned how to write ordered pairs from an input-output table. In this lesson you will graph ordered pairs in a coordinate plane.

EXAMPLE 1 Identifying Points in a Coordinate Plane

Name the two points on the graph with the coordinates (−4, 0) and (1, −3).

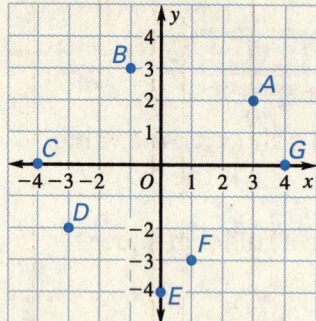

Remember

A point with *y*-coordinate 0 lies on the *x*-axis. A point with *x*-coordinate 0 lies on the *y*-axis.

Solution

Starting at the origin, if you move left 4 units, then up 0 units, you get to *C*. Point *C* has coordinates (−4, 0).

Starting at the origin, if you move right 1 unit, then down 3 units, you get to *F*. Point *F* has coordinates (1, −3).

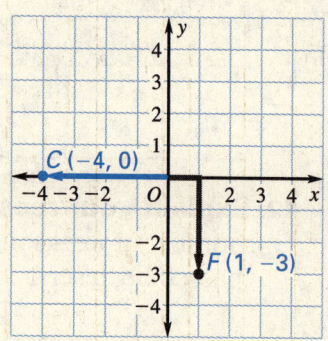

Math Intervention
Book 5 Algebraic Thinking

TRY THIS Use the graph in Example 1 to name the point with the given coordinates.

1. (4, 0)

   If you move _____ 4 units, then up ☐ units you get to point _____. Point _____ has coordinates (**4, 0**).

2. (−3, −2)

   If you move left ☐ units, then _____ 2 units you get to point _____. Point _____ has coordinates (**−3, −2**).

EXAMPLE 2 Graphing Points in a Coordinate Plane

Graph the points $A(-5, 2)$, $B(4, 1)$, and $C(0, -3)$.

Solution

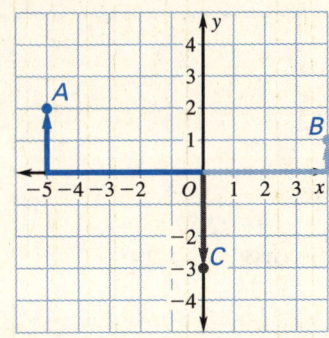

To graph A move left 5 units.
Then move up 2 units.

To graph B move right 4 units.
Then move up 1 unit.

To graph C do not move right or left.
Just move down 3 units.

> **Remember**
> When you graph a point, always start at the origin. Move right or up for positive coordinates. Move left or down for negative coordinates. First move along the horizontal axis. Then move up or down.

TRY THIS

3. Graph the points $X(-2, -4)$, $Y(-1, 3)$, and $Z(2, 0)$.

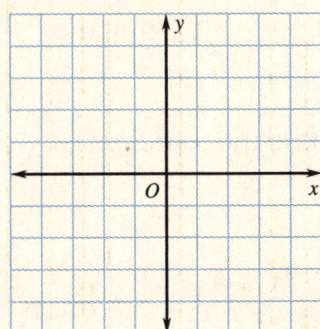

To graph X move left ☐ units.
Then move _____ 4 units.

To graph Y move _____ 1 unit.
Then move up ☐ units.

To graph Z just move _____ ☐ units. Do not move _____ or _____.

Summarize

Identifying Points in a Coordinate Plane

(1) To name the coordinates of a point on a coordinate graph, first find the *x*-coordinate by counting how many units the point is to the left or right of the origin.

(2) Then find the *y*-coordinate by counting how many units the point is above or below the origin.

(3) Write the coordinates as an ordered pair with the *x*-coordinate first and the *y*-coordinate second.

Plotting a Point in a Coordinate Plane

(1) To plot a point, start at the origin and move right or left the number of units corresponding to the *x*-coordinate. Move right if the *x*-coordinate is positive, move left if it is negative.

(2) Then move up or down the number of units corresponding to the *y*-coordinate. Move up if the *y*-coordinate is positive, move down if it is negative.

(3) Make a dot at this location.

Practice

In Exercises 1–7, write the coordinates of the points.

1. Point *A* is **1** unit right and **6** units down from the origin, so the coordinates of *A* are _____.

2. Point *B* is **4** units right and **1** unit up from the origin, so the coordinates of *B* are _____.

3. Point *C* is ▢ units right and **3** units _____ from the origin, so the coordinates of *C* are _____.

4. Point *D* is ▢ units _____ and ▢ units _____ from the origin, so the coordinates of *D* are _____.

5. Point *E* is ▢ units _____ from the origin, so the coordinates of *E* are _____.

6. The coordinates of *F* are _____.

7. The coordinates of *G* are _____.

Name _____ Date _____

Plot the point.

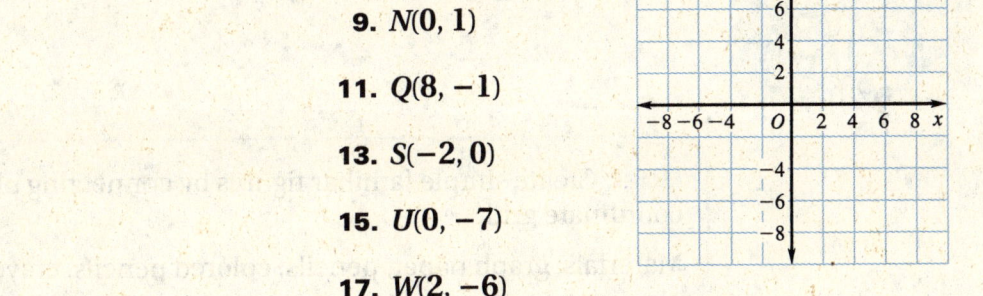

8. $M(-6, 2)$
9. $N(0, 1)$
10. $P(-3, -4)$
11. $Q(8, -1)$
12. $R(5, 6)$
13. $S(-2, 0)$
14. $O(0, 0)$
15. $U(0, -7)$
16. $V(-1, 8)$
17. $W(2, -6)$
18. $X(0, -2)$
19. $Y(3, 1)$

20. Describe the coordinates of a point that lies on either the x-axis or the y-axis.

_____
_____
_____
_____

21. **Fill in the missing words.** The horizontal axis in a coordinate plane is called the _____ and the vertical axis is called the _____.

22. **Describe a process.** How would you explain to your friend how to graph the point $(6, -1)$?

_____
_____

23. **Explain your reasoning.** Fred says the coordinates of point M are $(4, -2)$. Vicki says the coordinates are $(-2, 4)$. Who is correct? Explain.

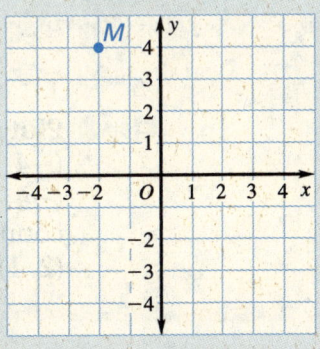

_____
_____

Math Intervention
Book 5 Algebraic Thinking **55**

Name _____   Date _____

Plotting Fun Figures

> **Goal:** Create simple familiar figures by connecting plotted points on a coordinate grid.
>
> Materials: graph paper, pencils, colored pencils, crayons

Getting Started In Lesson 5-13 you learned how to plot points. In this activity you will plot points to draw fun figures.

EXAMPLE

Use the following steps to draw a familiar figure.

Step 1 Plot the points (−6, 4), (−8, 4), (0, 9), (8, 4), (6, 4), (6, −5), (−6, −5), (−6, 4) and connect them in order.

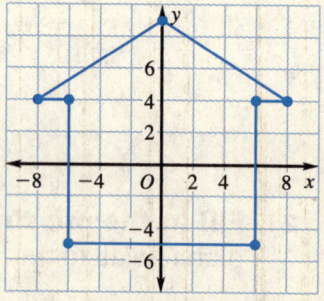

Step 2 Plot and connect (−1, −5), (−1, −1), (1, −1), (1, −5), and (−1, −5) in order.

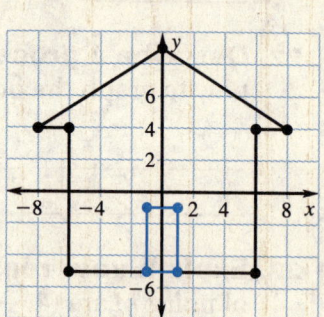

Step 3 Plot and connect (−4, 1), (−4, 3), (−2, 3), (−2, 1), and (−4, 1) in order. Then plot and connect (4, 1), (4, 3), (2, 3), (2, 1), and (4, 1) in order.

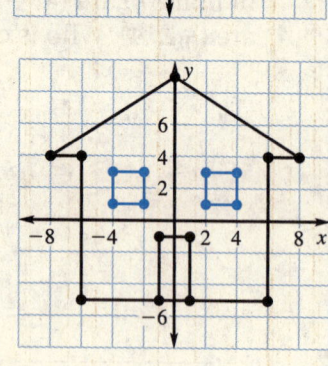

Step 4 Identify the figure.

The figure is a house.

Math Intervention
Book 5 Algebraic Thinking

Name _____ Date _____

MAKE IT A GAME!

- Form pairs of students.
- Each student creates a set of points with drawing instructions to create a fun figure.
- Students switch papers with their partner and draw the figure they are given.
- Students color their creations and exhibit them in the classroom.
- Students vote on the best design.

Practice

Plot the points in each group and connect them in order to draw a familiar figure. Name the figure created.

1. Group 1: $(-7, 0)$, $(-9, 1)$, $(-6, 4)$, $(4, 4)$, $(4, 3)$, $(6, 3)$, $(7, 2)$, $(7, 1)$, $(6, 2)$, $(4, 2)$, $(4, 1)$, $(-5, 1)$, $(-5, 2)$, $(-7, 0)$

   Group 2: $(-4, 1)$, $(-5, -3)$, $(-4, -3)$, $(-3, 1)$, $(-3, -3)$, $(-2, -3)$, $(-2, 1)$

   Group 3: $(2, 1)$, $(1, -3)$, $(2, -3)$, $(3, 1)$, $(3, -3)$, $(4, -3)$, $(4, 1)$

   Group 4: $(-7, 3)$, $(-6, 5)$, $(-6, 4)$

   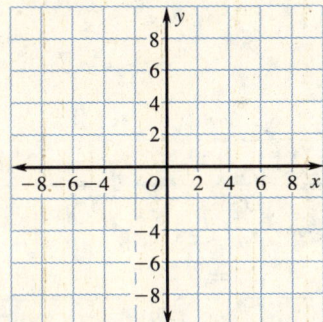

2. Group 1: $(-4, -1)$, $(-4, 5)$, $(5, 5)$, $(5, -1)$, $(-4, -1)$

   Group 2: $(-4, 5)$, $(0.5, 7)$, $(5, 5)$

   Group 3: $(5, 4)$, $(7, 4)$, $(7, 1)$, $(5, 1)$, $(5, 2)$, $(6, 2)$, $(6, 3)$, $(5, 3)$

   Group 4: $(-4, 0)$, $(-7, 3)$, $(-6, 4)$, $(-4, 1)$

   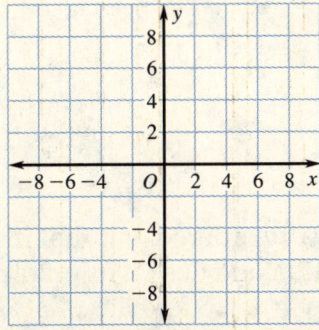

LESSON 5-15 Graph Linear Equations

Words to Remember

Graph of a linear equation: All the points in the coordinate plane that are solutions of the equation

The graph is a horizontal, vertical, or diagonal line.

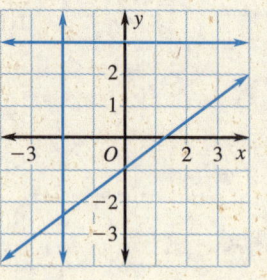

Getting Started In Lesson 5-13 you learned how to plot points in a coordinate plane. In this lesson you will learn how you can plot points to graph a line.

 **Graphing Linear Equations Using a Table of Values**

Use the table of values to graph $y = x + 3$. Interpret the graph by explaining how you know that the point (10, 13) also lies on the graph of the line.

Solution

Step 1 Complete the table.

> **Remember**
> Find y by substituting each value of x in the equation $y = x + 3$.

x	−2	−1	0	1
y	$y = x + 3$ $y = -2 + 3$ $= 1$	$y = x + 3$ $y = -1 + 3$ $= 2$	$y = x + 3$ $y = 0 + 3$ $= 3$	$y = x + 3$ $y = 1 + 3$ $= 4$
(x, y)	(−2, 1)	(−1, 2)	(0, 3)	(1, 4)

Step 2 Plot the points.

Step 3 Draw a line through the points.

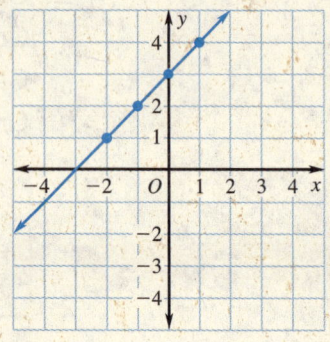

Step 4 Interpret the graph. Every ordered pair that makes $y = x + 3$ true is a solution of the equation and lies on its graph. Since $13 = 10 + 3$, (10, 3) is a solution of $y = x + 3$ and lies on its graph.

Math Intervention
Book 5 Algebraic Thinking

Name _____   Date _____

TRY THIS   Use the equation $y = 2x + 1$.

1. Fill in the missing information to graph $y = 2x + 1$.

   Step 1 Complete the table.

x	−2	0	1
y	$y = 2x + 1$ $y = 2 \cdot \square + 1$ $= \square$	$y = 2x + 1$ $y = 2 \cdot \square + \square$ $= \square$	$y = \square$ $y = \square \cdot \square + \square$ $= \square$
(x, y)	(□, □)	(□, □)	(□, □)

   Step 2 Plot the points (□, □), (□, □), and (□, □). Then draw a line through the points.

2. The point (−8, −15) also lies on the graph of $y = 2x + 1$ because □ = 2 · □ + □.

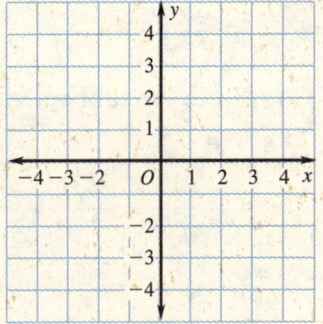

EXAMPLE 2   Graphing Horizontal and Vertical Lines

Use three ordered pairs to determine whether the graphs of $y = -4$ and $x = 3$ are horizontal or vertical.

Solution

Choose 3 values for x. Notice that y is always −4.

y = −4		
(−2, −4)	(0, −4)	(1, −4)

Choose 3 values for y. Notice that x is always 3.

x = 3		
(3, −4)	(3, 0)	(3, 3)

ANSWER The graph of $y = -4$ is a horizontal line.

The graph of $x = 3$ is a vertical line.

TRY THIS   Use three ordered pairs to determine whether the graph is horizontal or vertical.

3. $x = -2$ _____   4. $y = 1$ _____

Math Intervention
Book 5 Algebraic Thinking   **59**

Name _____ Date _____

> **Summarize**
>
> **Graphing a Linear Equation**
>
> To graph a linear equation, make a table of values and plot the points. Graph at least three points to determine the line.
>
> **Graphing a Vertical or Horizontal Line**
>
> For a vertical line, *x* will have the same value for all values of *y*. For a horizontal line, *y* will have the same value for all values of *x*.
>
> | Vertical line | Horizontal line | Diagonal line |
> |---|---|---|
> | $x = 2$ $x = -0.5$ | $y = -10$ $y = 12$ | $y = x - 5$ $y = -4x + 1$ |

Practice

Complete the table of values to draw the graph.

1. $y = x - 1$

x	−2	−1	0
y	$y = x - 1$ $y = \boxed{} - 1$ $= \boxed{}$	$y = x - 1$ $y = \boxed{} - \boxed{}$ $= \boxed{}$	$y = $ $y = \boxed{} - \boxed{}$ $= \boxed{}$
(x, y)	(□ , □)	(□ , □)	(□ , □)

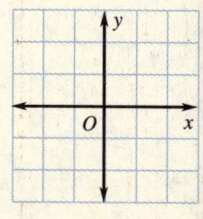

2. $y = x + 7$

x	−2	0	2
y			

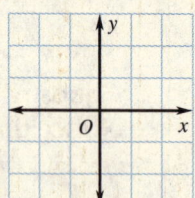

3. $y = 2x - 5$

x	2	3	4
y			

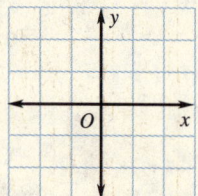

4. $y = 4x + 2$

x	−1	0	1
y			

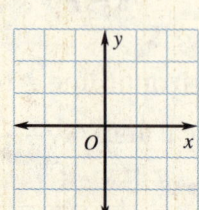

5. $y = -\dfrac{3}{5}x - 1$

x	−5	0	5
y			

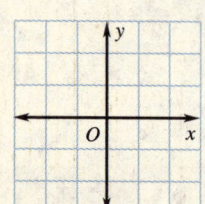

Math Intervention
Book 5 Algebraic Thinking

Name _____   Date _____

Complete the table of values to draw the graph.

6. $x + y = 4$

x	−1	0	1
y			

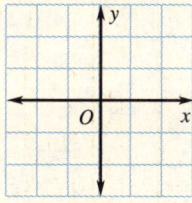

7. $3x + y = 6$

x	1	2	3
y			

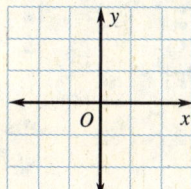

8. $y = 1.5$

x			
y	1.5	1.5	1.5

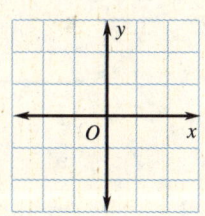

9. $x = −2$

x	−2	−2	−2
y			

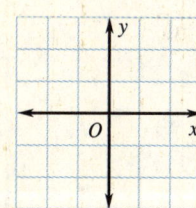

Tell whether the graph of the equation is a *vertical, horizontal,* or *diagonal* line. Explain your reasoning.

10. $y = 3$ _____

_____

11. $x = 4$ _____

_____

12. $y = 2x − 6$ _____

_____

DID YOU GET IT?

13. **Fill in the missing words.** The graph of a linear equation is a _____ , _____ , or _____ line.

14. **Describe a process.** How would you graph $y = \frac{1}{2}x + 3$?

_____

_____

15. **Explain your reasoning.** Your friend said that the graph of $x = 2$ is a horizontal line. Is she correct?

_____

_____

_____

LESSON 5-16 Slope

Words to Remember

Slope: $\dfrac{\text{vertical change}}{\text{horizontal change}} = \dfrac{\text{rise}}{\text{run}} = \dfrac{y_2 - y_1}{x_2 - x_1}$

Slope can be positive, negative, zero, or undefined.

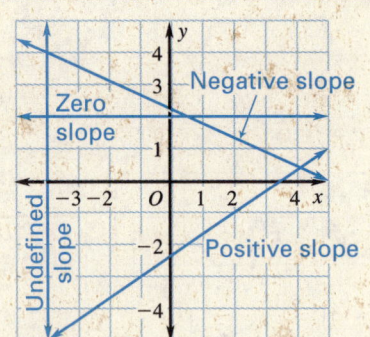

Getting Started In this lesson you will use graphs of linear equations to find the slopes of the lines.

EXAMPLE 1 — Finding the Slope of a Line Using the Ratio $\dfrac{\text{Rise}}{\text{Run}}$

Find the slope of the line through (3, 3) and (6, 5).

Solution

Step 1 Find the ratio of rise to run between (3, 3) and (6, 5).
$\dfrac{\text{rise}}{\text{run}} = \dfrac{2}{3}$

Step 2 Check the slope using (3, 3) and (0, 1).
$\dfrac{\text{rise}}{\text{run}} = \dfrac{-2}{-3} = \dfrac{2}{3}$

ANSWER The slope is $\dfrac{2}{3}$.

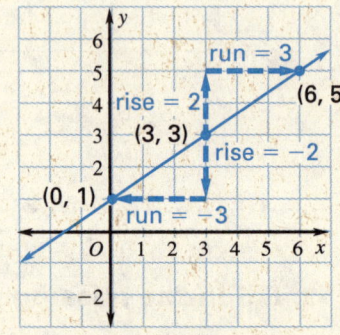

Remember
The slope of a line is the same between any two points on the line.

Notice
A rise and a run can be either positive or negative.

EXAMPLE 2 — Understanding the Slope of Horizontal and Vertical Lines

Find the slope of $y = 3$ and $x = -2$.

Solution

There is no vertical change between the points on the line $y = 3$. Therefore $\dfrac{\text{rise}}{\text{run}} = \dfrac{0}{\text{run}} = 0$. The slope of $y = 3$ is 0.

There is no horizontal change between the points on the line $x = -2$. Therefore $\dfrac{\text{rise}}{\text{run}} = \dfrac{\text{rise}}{0}$. Since division by zero is not allowed, the slope of the line $x = -2$ is undefined.

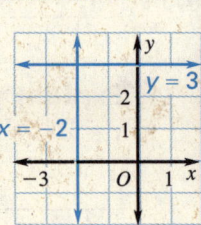

Math Intervention
Book 5 Algebraic Thinking

Name _____   Date _____

TRY THIS Fill in the missing information to find the slope of the line.

> **Notice**
> **The slope** of any horizontal line is 0.

1.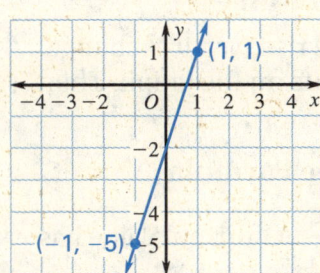

   slope = $\dfrac{\text{rise}}{\underline{}}$

   = $\dfrac{\square}{2}$ = $\square$

   The slope is $\square$.

2.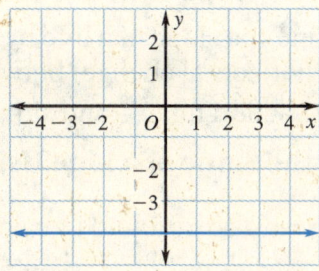

   The line has no $\square$ change. Therefore

   $\dfrac{\text{rise}}{\text{run}} = \dfrac{\square}{\text{run}} = \square$.

   The slope is $\square$.

Slope Formula The slope of a line containing the points (x_1, y_1) and (x_2, y_2) can be found by using this formula: **slope** = $\dfrac{y_2 - y_1}{x_2 - x_1}$.

EXAMPLE 3 Using the Slope Formula

What is the slope of the line containing the points $(5, 7)$ and $(-2, 4)$?

Solution

slope = $\dfrac{y_2 - y_1}{x_2 - x_1}$ Slope formula

= $\dfrac{4 - 7}{-2 - 5}$ Substitute values for y_2, y_1, x_2, and x_1.

= $\dfrac{-3}{-7}$ Simplify.

= $\dfrac{3}{7}$ Simplify.

> **Remember**
> When calculating the slope from the coordinates of two points, subtract the x-values in the same order that you subtract the y-values.

TRY THIS Find the slope of the line containing the given points.

3. $(28, 2)$ and $(6, 9)$

   slope = $\dfrac{y_2 - y_1}{x_2 - x_1}$

   = $\dfrac{9 - \square}{\square - 28}$

   = $\dfrac{\square}{\square} = \square$

   The slope is $\square$.

4. $(8, 2)$ and $(8, 23)$

   slope = $\dfrac{y_2 - y_1}{x_2 - x_1}$

   = $\dfrac{\square - 2}{8 - \square}$

   = $\dfrac{\square}{\square}$

   The slope is $\square$.

> **Notice**
> **The slope** of any vertical line is undefined.

Name _____   Date _____

Summarize

Finding the Slope of a Line using Rise over Run

You can find the slope of a line by counting the rise (vertical change) and run (horizontal change) between two points on the graph. Then write the fraction for $\frac{\text{rise}}{\text{run}}$ and simplify.

Finding the Slope of a Line Using the Slope Formula

The slope can also be found by calculating $\frac{y_2 - y_1}{x_2 - x_1}$. A horizontal line has **0** slope. A vertical line has undefined slope. A line sloping up to the right has a positive slope. A line sloping down to the right has a negative slope.

Practice

Tell whether the slope of the line is *positive*, *negative*, *zero*, or *undefined*.

1. 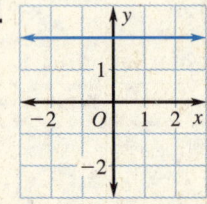   2. 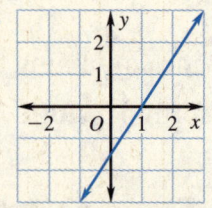   3. 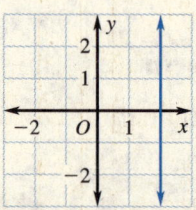   4.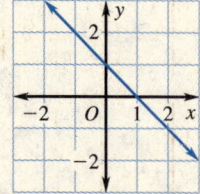

Fill in the missing information to find the slope of the line.

5.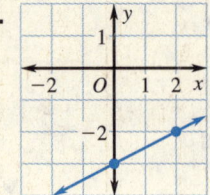

slope = $\frac{}{\text{run}}$

= $\frac{1}{\boxed{}}$

The slope is $\frac{\boxed{}}{\boxed{}}$.

6.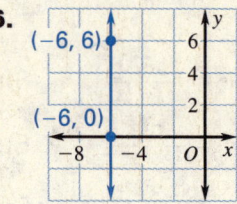

The line has no

_____ change.

So $\frac{\text{rise}}{\text{run}} = \frac{\text{rise}}{\boxed{}}$

Division by $\boxed{}$ is undefined. Therefore, the slope is _____.

Find the slope of the line.

7. 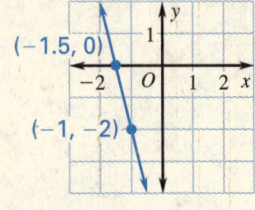   8.   9.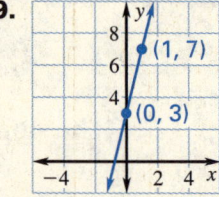

Name _____   Date _____

Find the slope of the line containing the given points.

10. $(0, 5)$ and $(-1, 4)$

slope $= \dfrac{y_2 - y_1}{x_2 - x_1}$

$= \dfrac{4 - \square}{\square - 0}$

$= \dfrac{\square}{\square}$

$= \square$

The slope is $\square$.

11. $(3, 6)$ and $(8, 6)$

slope $= \dfrac{y_2 - y_1}{x_2 - x_1}$

$= \dfrac{\square - 6}{3 - \square}$

$= \dfrac{\square}{\square}$

$= \square$

The slope is $\square$.

12. $(2, 5)$ and $(2, -1)$

13. $(-11, -9)$ and $(-8, -3)$

14. $(-12, -2)$ and $(-9, 13)$

15. $(-2, -6)$ and $(8, -12)$

16. $\left(-\dfrac{1}{3}, \dfrac{1}{2}\right)$ and $\left(-\dfrac{1}{2}, \dfrac{2}{3}\right)$

17. $\left(-\dfrac{2}{5}, -\dfrac{3}{4}\right)$ and $\left(\dfrac{3}{5}, \dfrac{1}{4}\right)$

DID YOU GET IT?

18. Fill in the missing words. The slope of a line can be found by writing the word fraction "_____ over _____."

19. Find the error. Lihue found the slope of the line containing $(5, 6)$ and $(3, 9)$ to be $-\dfrac{2}{3}$. What was his mistake?

_____
_____
_____

20. Explain your reasoning. A line contains $(2, 4)$ and $(-3, 5)$. You found the slope using $\dfrac{5 - 4}{-3 - 2}$. Your friend found the slope using $\dfrac{4 - 5}{2 - (-3)}$. Who is correct? Explain.

_____
_____
_____

LESSON 5-17

Direct Variation

> **Words to Remember**
>
> **Direct variation:** An equation of the form $y = kx$, where k represents a constant and $k \neq 0$
>
> **Varies directly as:** In a direct variation relationship, such as $y = 3x$, we say that "y varies directly as x."

Getting Started In Lesson 5-15 you learned how to graph linear equations. In this lesson you will graph lines that pass through the origin. The equations of these lines are direct variations.

EXAMPLE 1 Graphing Quantities with the Same Ratio

There are three feet in a yard. Graph the relationship between the number of feet and the number of yards.

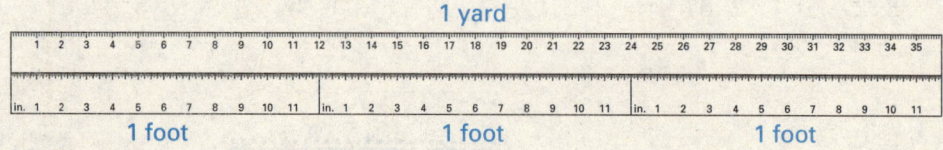

Solution

Step 1
Make a table of values.

Number of yards, x	Number of feet, y
1	3
2	6
3	9

Step 2
Draw the graph.

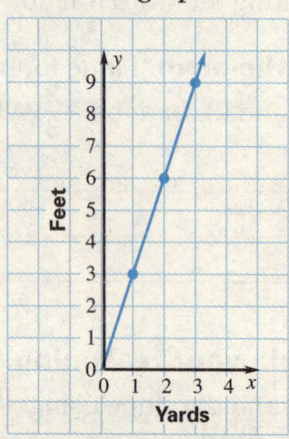

> **Remember**
> The pattern will continue, so draw a line through the points on the graph.

Direct Variation Notice that in Example 1 $\frac{\text{feet}}{\text{yards}} = \frac{3}{1} = \frac{6}{2} = \frac{9}{3}$. The slope of the line you graphed is also $\frac{3}{1}$ or 3. The graph of a linear direct variation relationship is a line that contains the origin. The slope of the line is the ratio between the two variables. This ratio is called the *constant of variation*.

Math Intervention
Book 5 Algebraic Thinking

Name _____ Date _____

> **EXAMPLE 2** Graphing a Direct Variation

Suppose one gallon of gasoline costs $4.00. Graph the relationship between the number of gallons of gasoline and the cost.

Solution

Use a table of values to draw the graph.

Number of gallons, g	Cost in dollars, c
0	0
1	4
4	16
10	40

> **Notice**
> The cost is directly related to the number of gallons.

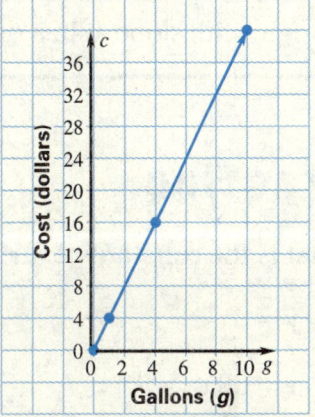

> **EXAMPLE 3** Writing a Direct Variation Equation

Write a direct variation equation for Example 2.

Solution

In each ordered pair, $c = 4g$, so a direct variation equation is $c = 4g$.

TRY THIS

1. Fill in the missing information to graph the direct variation between inches and feet.

    Step 1 1 foot = ☐ inches

    ☐ feet = 36 inches

    7 feet = ☐ inches

    Step 2 Plot the points (1, ☐),

    (☐, 36), and (☐, ☐).

    Then draw a line through the points.

2. In Try This Problem 1, $\dfrac{\text{inches}}{\text{feet}} = \dfrac{☐}{1} = \dfrac{36}{☐} = \dfrac{☐}{7}$.

    The slope of the line in Try This Problem 1 is also $\dfrac{☐}{1}$ or ☐.

3. In Try This Problem 1, in each ordered pair, $y =$ ☐ x. A direct variation equation is ☐ = ☐ x.

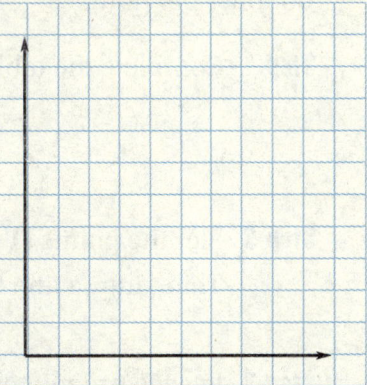

Math Intervention
Book 5 Algebraic Thinking

Name _____ Date _____

> ## Summarize
> ### Writing a Direct Variation Equation
> A direct variation equation is an equation of the form $y = kx$, where $k \neq 0$; k is the constant of variation.
>
> ### Graphing a Direct Variation Equation
> The graph of a direct variation equation is a line passing through the origin with slope k. In a direct variation $y = kx$, so $\frac{y}{x} = k$.

Practice

What is the constant of variation for the direct variation?

1. $y = 2x$
2. $y = -3x$
3. $y = 60x$
4. $y = 4x$

Give the slope of the line.

5. $y = 5x$
6. $c = 16b$
7. $m = \frac{1}{5280}f$
8. $y = \frac{4}{9}x$

Graph the relationship between the quantities. Then write a direct variation equation for the relationship.

9. Graph the relationship between miles and hours, if Josh travels at 60 miles per hour.

   Step 1 Complete the table of values.

Number of hours, h	1	☐	6
Number of miles, m	☐	180	☐

   Step 2 Plot the points (1, ☐), (☐, 180), and (☐, ☐). Then draw a line through the points.

   Step 3 In each ordered pair, $m =$ ☐ h. A direct variation equation is ☐ $=$ ☐ h.

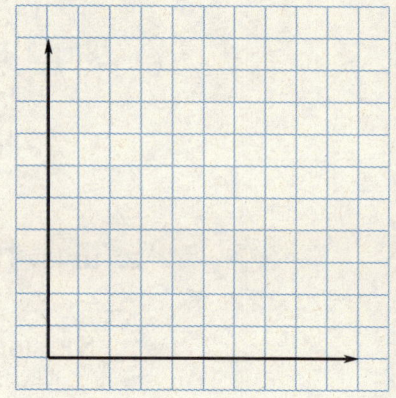

Math Intervention
Book 5 Algebraic Thinking

Name _____ Date _____

Graph the relationship between the quantities. Then write a direct variation equation for the relationship.

10. Graph the relationship between words and minutes, if May can type **50** words per minute on her computer. _____

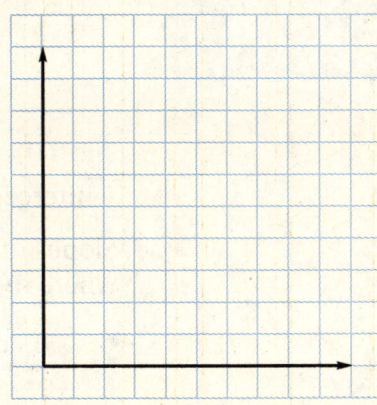

11. Graph the relationship between cost and minutes, if the telephone company charges **$3.00** for each **10** minutes of a long distance call. _____

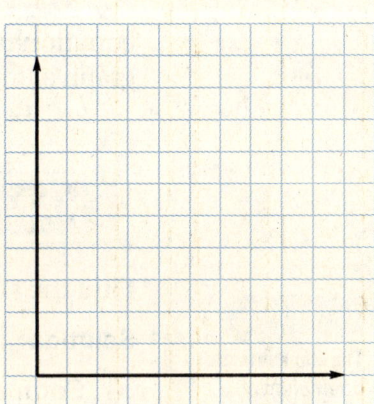

DID YOU GET IT?

12. **Fill in the missing words.** A direct variation equation relates two quantities whose ratio is always the _____. This ratio is the _____ of the line.

13. **Give an example.** Give an example of a direct variation equation.

    _____
    _____
    _____

14. **Explain your reasoning.** Does this graph show a direct variation? Explain.

    _____
    _____
    _____

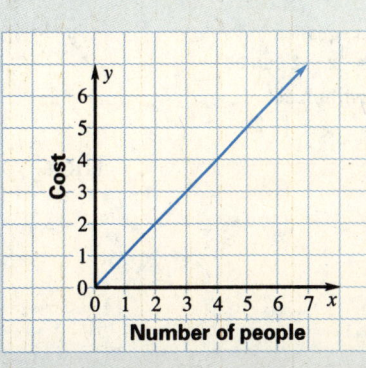

Math Intervention
Book 5 Algebraic Thinking

Slope-Intercept Form

LESSON 5-18

Words to Remember

y-intercept: The *y*-value of the point where a line crosses the *y*-axis

Slope-intercept form: The equation of a line in the form $y = mx + b$, where **m** is the slope of the line and **b** is the *y*-intercept

Getting Started In Lesson 5-15 you learned how to graph a linear equation using a table of values. In this lesson you will learn another way to graph a linear equation.

EXAMPLE 1 — Finding the Slope and *y*-Intercept

Find the slope and *y*-intercept of the line $y = 3x + 5$.

Solution

Compare the equation to $y = mx + b$.

$y = mx + b$ *m* is the slope; *b* is the *y*-intercept.

$y = 3x + 5$ In this equation, $m = 3$ and $b = 5$.

ANSWER The slope *m* is 3. The *y*-intercept *b* is 5.

> **Remember**
> The slope *m* is the coefficient of *x*.

TRY THIS — Fill in the missing information to solve the problem.

1. Find the slope and *y*-intercept of the line $y = \frac{3}{4}x - 2$.

   Compare $y = \frac{3}{4}x - 2$ to $y = mx + \boxed{}$.

   $y = mx + \boxed{}$ *m* is the slope; $\boxed{}$ is the *y*-intercept.

   $y = \boxed{} x \bigcirc (-2)$ In the equation $y = \frac{3}{4}x - 2$, $m = \boxed{}$, and $b = \boxed{}$.

   The slope *m* is $\boxed{}$. The *y*-intercept *b* is $\boxed{}$.

> **Remember**
> The equation $y = \frac{3}{4}x - 2$ can be rewritten as $y = \frac{3}{4}x + (-2)$.

EXAMPLE 2 Graphing a Line in Slope-Intercept Form

Graph the line $y = 4x + 3$.

Solution

Step 1 **Identify** the slope and y-intercept.
Compare $y = 4x + 3$ to $y = mx + b$.
This shows you that the slope m
is 4 and the y-intercept b is 3.

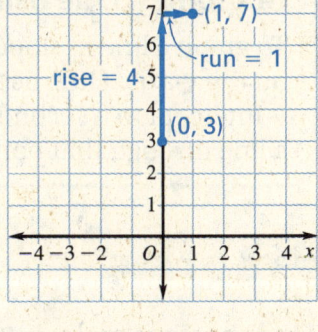

Step 2 **Plot** the y-intercept at $(0, 3)$.

Step 3 **Use** the slope to graph a second point.
slope = $\frac{\text{rise}}{\text{run}} = \frac{4}{1}$
From $(0, 3)$ move 4 units up and
1 unit right to $(1, 7)$.
Graph this point.

> **Remember**
> Write the slope as the fraction $\frac{4}{1}$ to identify the rise and the run.

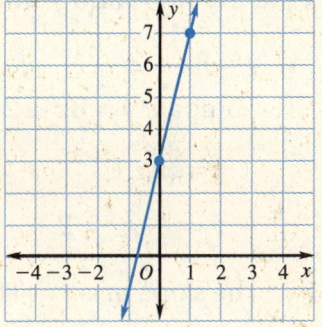

Step 4 **Draw** the graph of the
line between the two points.

Don't Forget You will need to move *down* from
the y-intercept if the slope is negative.

TRY THIS Fill in the missing information.

2. Follow these steps to graph $y = -\frac{1}{2}x - 1$.

   Step 1 Identify the slope and _____.

   Rewrite $y = -\frac{1}{2}x - 1$ as $y = -\frac{1}{2}x \boxed{} - 1$.

   Compare $y = -\frac{1}{2}x \boxed{} \boxed{}$ to $y = mx + b$.

   This shows you that the slope m is $\boxed{}$

   and the y-intercept is $\boxed{}$.

   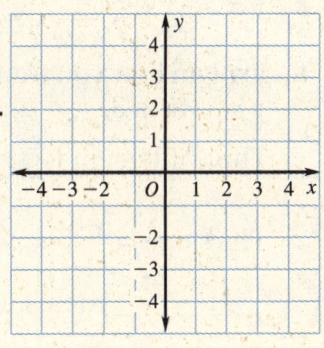

   Step 2 Plot the y-intercept at ($\boxed{}$, $\boxed{}$).

   Step 3 Use the slope to graph a second point.

   slope = $\frac{\phantom{\text{rise}}}{\text{run}} = \frac{\boxed{}}{2}$.

   From b move $\boxed{}$ unit down and $\boxed{}$ units right.

   This takes you to the point ($\boxed{}$, $\boxed{}$). Graph this point.

   Step 4 Draw the graph of $y = -\frac{1}{2}x - 1$ between ($\boxed{}$, $\boxed{}$) and the
   y-intercept.

Name _____   Date _____

Summarize

Finding the Slope and y-Intercept

When an equation is in the form $y = mx + b$, the value of m is the slope and the value of b is the y-intercept.

Graphing a Line Using the Slope and y-Intercept

To graph a line in slope-intercept form, first plot the y-intercept on the y-axis. Then use the rise and the run to move from the y-intercept to a second point on the line. Graph this point and draw a line through that point and the y-intercept.

Practice

Find the slope and y-intercept of the line.

1. $y = 8x + 2$

    Compare $y = 8x + 2$ to $y = mx +$ ▢.

    $y = mx +$ ▢ m is the slope; ▢ is the y-intercept.

    $y =$ ▢ x ◯ $2.$ In the equation $y = 8x + 2$, $m =$ ▢ and $b =$ ▢.

    The slope m is ▢. The y-intercept b is ▢.

2. $y = \frac{1}{5}x - 3$ _____   3. $y = -7x - 4$ _____

4. $y = -\frac{2}{3}x + \frac{1}{2}$ _____   5. $y = x - 10$ _____

6. Explain how you would use the slope and y-intercept to graph $y = -4x + 3$.

    The y-intercept is ▢, so graph (▢, ▢).

    The slope $= \frac{\text{rise}}{\underline{}} = \frac{▢}{1}$, so from the y-intercept, move ▢ units _____ then 3 units _____.

    Draw a line through this point and (▢, ▢).

Graph the line using the slope and y-intercept.

7. $y = 3x + 1$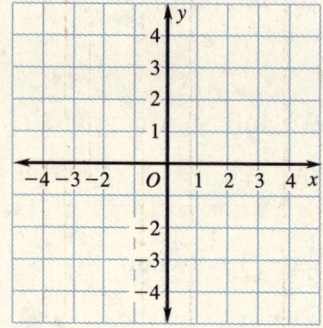

8. $y = \frac{1}{2}x - 2$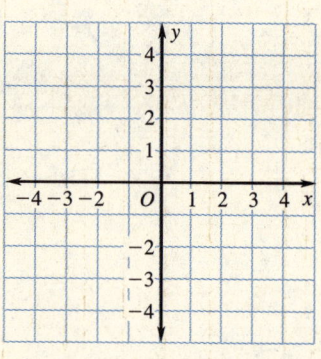

Math Intervention
Book 5 Algebraic Thinking

Name _____ Date _____

Graph the line using the slope and *y*-intercept.

9. $y = -x - 6$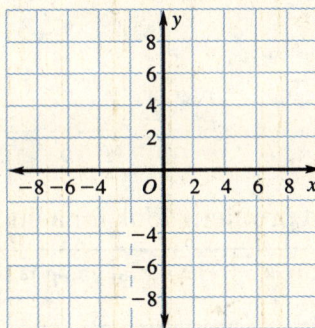

10. $y = 4x - 6$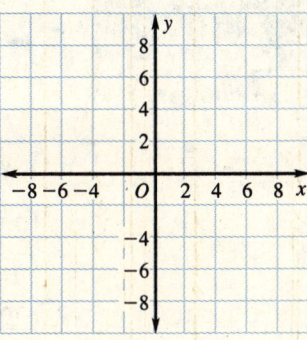

11. $y = x$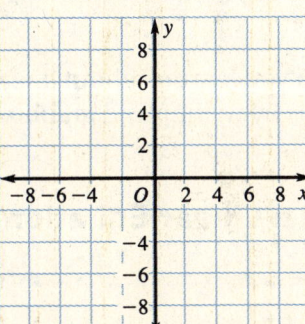

12. $y = x + 3$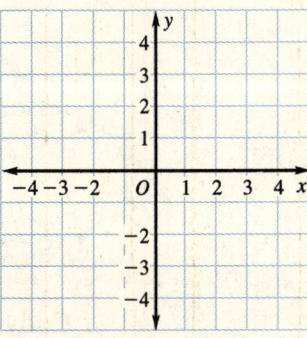

13. $y = \frac{3}{5}x + 2$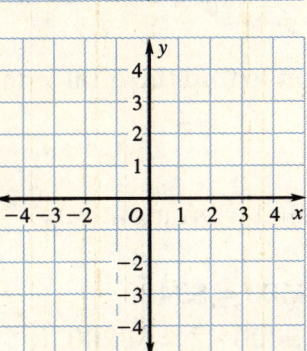

14. $y = -\frac{2}{3}x + 4$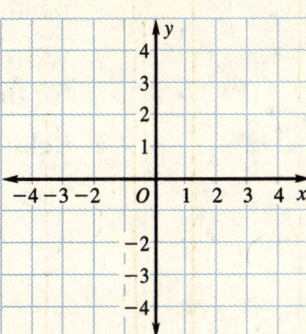

DID YOU GET IT?

15. **Fill in the missing words.** In the equation $y = 2x + 6$, **2** is the _____ and **6** is the _____. This equation is in _____ form.

16. **Explain your reasoning.** Do you think it would be easier to graph the line $y = \frac{2}{3}x + 1.4$ using a table of values or the slope and *y*-intercept? Explain.

_____
_____
_____

LESSON 5-19: Solve Problems with Linear Equations

> **Strategies to Remember**
> To make a graph to solve a word problem, look for a linear relationship:
>
> | The **constant change** in the problem is the slope of the line. | The **initial value** is the *y*-intercept. |

Getting Started In Lesson 5-15 you learned about linear equations. In this lesson you will solve word problems by writing and graphing linear equations.

 Graphing a Linear Equation to Solve a Problem

Cody paid $3000 cash for his car. In addition he also makes monthly payments of $400 on a car loan.

Write and graph a linear equation to find the total amount Cody has paid for the car at the end of a year.

Solution

Step 1 **Calculate** total amounts after a few months.
After 0 months: $3000
After 1 month: $3000 + $400 = $3400
After 2 months: $3000 + $400 · 2 = $3800
After 3 months: $3000 + $400 · 3 = $4200

Step 2 **Graph** the points and continue the pattern on the graph.

The total amount increases $400 each month.

Step 3 **Interpret** the graph. The ordered pair (12, 7800) tells you that Cody has paid $7800 at the end of 12 months or a year.

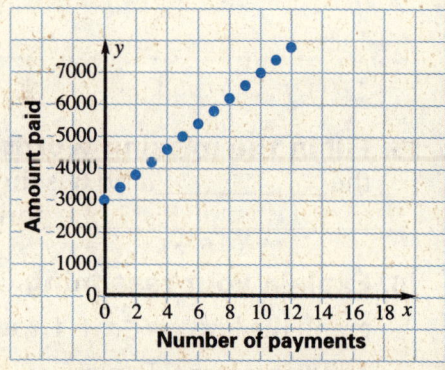

Step 4 **Write** a linear equation to check your answer. Use the pattern from Step 1.

$$y = 3000 + 400x$$
$$\stackrel{?}{=} 3000 + 400(12)$$
$$= 7800 \checkmark$$

Math Intervention
Book 5 Algebraic Thinking

Name _____ Date _____

TRY THIS Max orders CDs by mail for $9 each plus a $5 shipping charge. Use this information to find the missing information and solve the problems.

1. Graph a linear equation to find the total cost of buying **8** CDs.
   Graph the point (**1**, ▢) to show the cost of **1** CD.
   Graph the point (**2**, ▢) to show the cost of **2** CDs.
   Graph the point (▢, ▢) to show the cost of **3** CDs.

   Continuing the pattern, graph the next **5** points: (**4**, ▢), (**5**, ▢), (▢, **59**), (▢, ▢), and (▢, ▢).
   The total cost of **8** CDs is ▢.

2. Write a linear equation to check your answer to Try This Problem 1.

   $y = \square x + \square$
   $ = \square \cdot \square + \square$
   $ = \square$ ✓

EXAMPLE 2   Estimating Unknown Quantities Graphically

The graph shows the relationship between the width of a rectangle and the perimeter of the rectangle. Estimate the perimeter of the rectangle when the width is **5** inches.

Notice
The width of a rectangle cannot be 0, so there is an open circle on the graph.

Solution
The graph appears to contain the point (**5, 30**). This means the perimeter is **30** inches when the width is **5** inches.

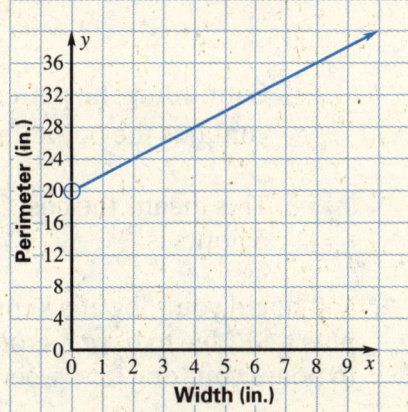

TRY THIS Use the graph in Example 2 to fill in the missing information.

3. Estimate the perimeter of the rectangle when its width is **3.5** inches.

   The graph appears to contain the point (**3.5**, ▢). This means the perimeter is ▢ inches when the width is ▢ inches.

Math Intervention
Book 5 Algebraic Thinking **75**

Name _____ Date _____

Summarize

Graphing a Linear Equation to Solve a Problem

(1) From the given situation determine a few points on the graph.

(2) Continue the pattern on the graph.

(3) Interpret the graph to find the point that answers the question in the problem.

(4) Write an equation to check your answer.

Estimating Unknown Quantities Graphically

For any given value of x estimate the corresponding value of y by locating the point on the graph.

Practice

Graph a linear equation to solve the problem.

1. Mark rents a boat at the lake. He must pay a security deposit of **$50** plus rental fee of **$10** per hour. How much does it cost him to rent the boat for **5** hours?

    Step 1 The cost for **1** hour is **50 +** ☐ **=** ☐.

    Step 2 The cost for **2** hours is ☐ **+ 2 ·** ☐ **=** ☐. The cost for 3 hours is ☐ **+ 3 ·** ☐ **=** ☐.

    Step 3 Represent these costs by graphing the points (**1,** ☐), (**2,** ☐), and (☐ , ☐).

    Step 4 Continuing the pattern on the graph, the graph contains the point (**5,** ☐).

    Step 5 This means the cost for renting the boat for **5** hours is ☐.

    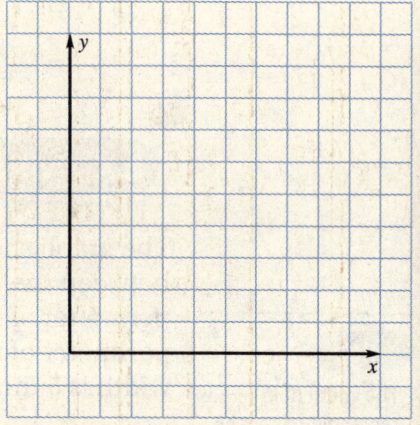

2. You board your dog at a kennel for **$8** per day plus a **$12** fee to have it groomed. What is the cost to board your dog for a week?

    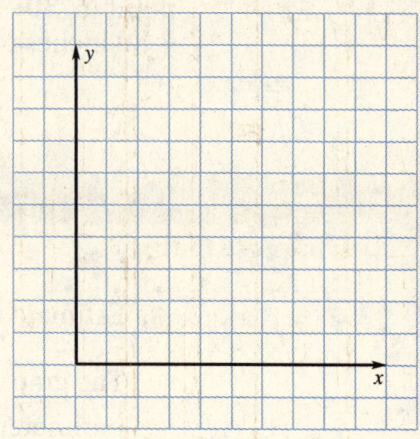

Math Intervention
Book 5 Algebraic Thinking

Name _____ Date _____

The graph shows the amount Steve still owes on his digital camera. He pays $20 each week.

3. How much does Steve owe after **9** weeks?

4. What does the ordered pair (**15, 100**) represent?

5. After how many weeks does Steve owe **$320**?

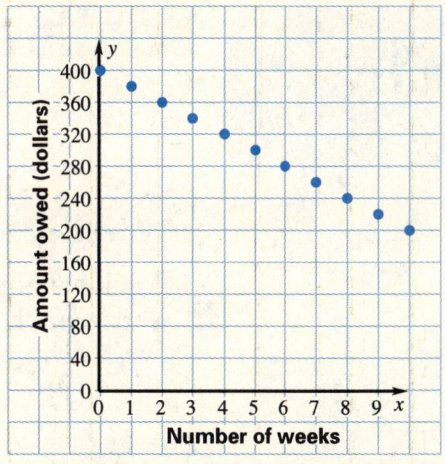

An air pump pumps 1 cubic foot of air into a rubber raft every 2 minutes. The raft holds 10 cubic feet of air.

6. Use the graph to estimate the amount of air in the raft after pumping for **5** minutes.

7. The amount of air in the raft y is given by the equation $y = \frac{1}{2}x$ where x is the number of minutes the air has been pumped in. Use the equation to check your answer to Exercise 6.

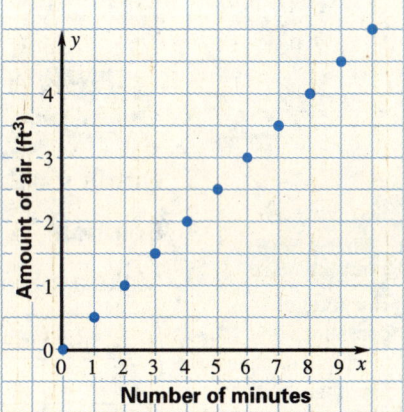

DID YOU GET IT?

8. **Fill in the missing words.** The equation $y = 10x - 50$ represents the profit y that Nan makes at an art show when she sells x pictures. The amount she sells each picture for is _____ and her fixed cost to enter the show is _____.

9. **Describe a relationship.** A cell phone company charges **$20** per month plus **$.10** per minute for calls. How would you write a linear equation to represent this situation?

   _____
   _____

10. **Explain your reasoning.** Explain how you would use the graph to estimate the cost of printing **500** calendars.

    _____
    _____

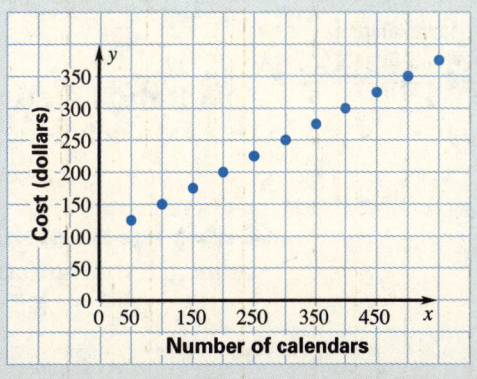

Math Intervention
Book 5 Algebraic Thinking

LESSON 5-20

Nonlinear Relationships

> **Words to Remember**
> Nonlinear equation: An equation whose graph is not a line $y = x^2,\ y = 2x^3$

Getting Started   In Lesson 5-15 you learned how to graph linear equations. In this lesson you will graph some equations that are not linear.

EXAMPLE 1 — Graphing Nonlinear Equations of the Form $y = nx^2$ and $y = nx^3$

Graph $y = 2x^2$ and $y = 2x^3$.

Solution

Make a table of values for each equation.

> **Remember**
> The order of operations tells you to square or cube x first, then multiply by 2.

$y = 2x^2$					
x	−2	−1	0	1	2
y	8	2	0	2	8

$y = 2x^3$					
x	−2	−1	0	1	2
y	−16	−2	0	2	16

Plot the points for each graph and draw a smooth curve through all the points.

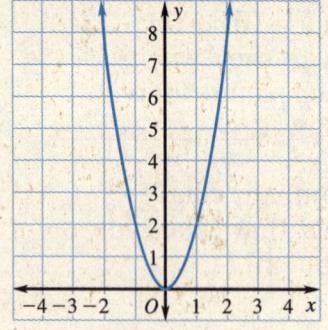
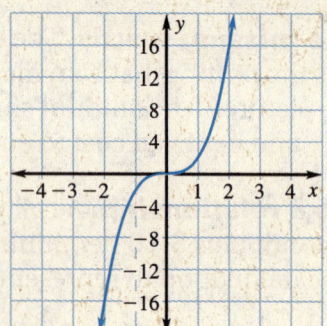

> **Check Your Work**
> A negative number raised to an even power is positive. A negative number raised to an odd power is negative.

Quadratic Relationships   An equation of the form $y = nx^2$, where $n \neq 0$, is called a quadratic equation. Its graph is a special curve called a *parabola*.

Cubic Relationships   An equation of the form $y = nx^3$, where $n \neq 0$ is called a cubic equation. Its graph is a curve.

Math Intervention
Book 5 Algebraic Thinking

TRY THIS Graph the equation.

1. $y = -x^2$

Step 1 Fill in the missing numbers in the table of values.

x	−2	−1	0	1	2
y					

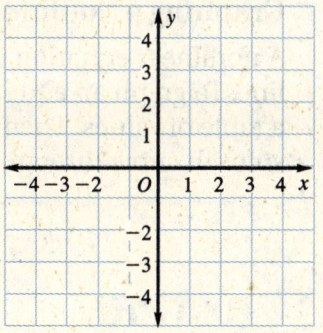

Step 2 Plot the points. Then draw a smooth curve through the points.

2. $y = x^3$

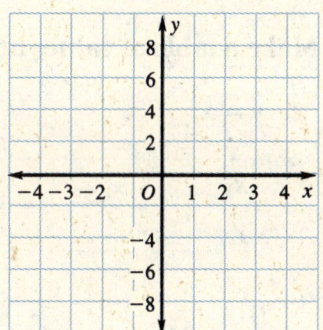

EXAMPLE 2 Using the Graph of a Nonlinear Equation to Solve a Problem

Half of the graph of $y = 3x^2$ shows the area y of a rectangle x units wide (and $3x$ units long). Use the graph to estimate the area of the rectangle if it is 15 feet wide.

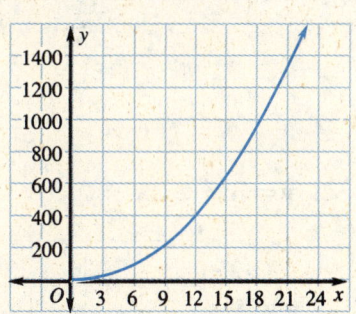

Solution

When $x = 15$, y appears to be about **700**. This means the area is about **700** square feet when the width is **15** feet.

TRY THIS Use the graph shown in Example 2.

3. Fill in the missing information so you can estimate the area of a rectangle whose width is 10 meters.

When $x =$ ▢ , y appears to be about ▢ . This means the area is about ▢ square meters when the width is ▢ meters.

Math Intervention
Book 5 Algebraic Thinking

Name _____   Date _____

> **Summarize**
>
> **Graphing a Nonlinear Equation**
>
> A nonlinear equation is an equation whose graph is not a straight line. To graph an equation of the form $y = nx^2$ or $y = nx^3$, first make a table of values. Then plot the points in your table. Finally, draw a smooth curve through the points.

Practice

1. Which equation is nonlinear? _____

   A. $y = 5x^2$ B. $y = 5x$ C. $y = x + 5$

Make a table of values and graph the equation.

2. $y = x^2$

3. $y = -\dfrac{1}{3}x^2$

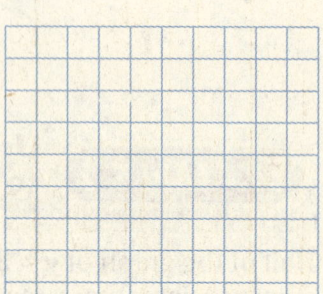

4. $y = 3x^2$

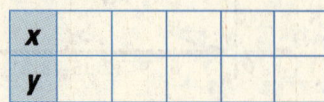

5. $y = -2x^3$

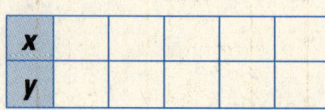

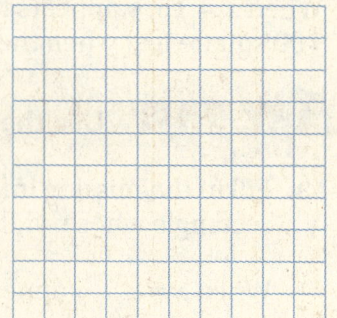

Name _____   Date _____

Make a table of values and graph the equation.

6. $y = -x^3$

x				
y				

7. $y = \frac{1}{2}x^3$

x				
y				

8. Half the graph of $y = 4x^2$ shows the area y of a rectangle x units wide and $4x$ units long. Use the graph to estimate the area of the rectangle if it is 10 meters wide.

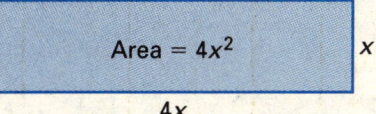

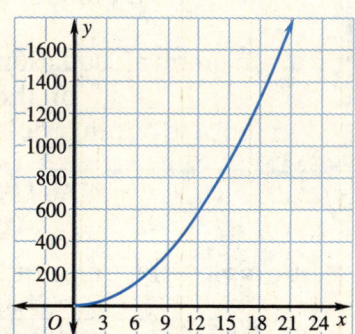

DID YOU GET IT?

9. **Fill in the missing words.** The equation $y = 6x^2$ is a _____ equation because its graph is not a _____.

10. **Describe a process.** How do you graph $y = x^3$?
_____
_____

11. **Explain your reasoning.** Angus graphed the equation $y = -4x^2$ and got a diagonal line sloping down to the right. Was he correct? Explain.
_____
_____

Math Intervention
Book 5 Algebraic Thinking

Name _____ Date _____

Mixed Practice for Lessons 5-12 to 5-20

Vocabulary Review

Match the word with its mathematical meaning.

Word   **Mathematical meaning**

1. linear equation ____ **A.** The ratio rise over run
2. slope ____ **B.** An equation of the form $y = kx$
3. y-intercept ____ **C.** An equation whose graph is a straight line
4. direct variation ____ **D.** The point where a line crosses the y-axis

Fill in the missing word(s).

5. The first number in an ordered pair is the _____ -value and the second number is the _____ -value.

6. To graph an equation in slope-intercept form you first plot the _____ on the y-axis and then use the _____ ratio to move to another point on the line.

7. Complete the input-output table for the rule $y = 3x - 1$.

Input	-3	-1	0	2	5
Output					

8. Write a rule for the ordered pairs in the table.

x	-2	-1	0	1	2
y	-10	-5	0	5	10

9. Plot the points $A(-4, 0)$, $B(3, 4)$, $C(1, -3)$, and $D(-2, -1)$.

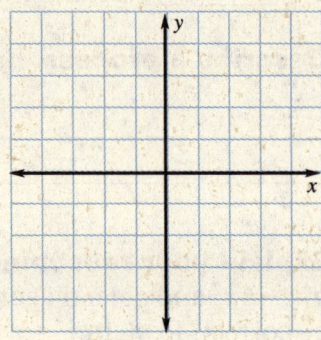

Math Intervention
Book 5 Algebraic Thinking

Name _____   Date _____

Graph the line or curve.

10. $y = 2x - 4$

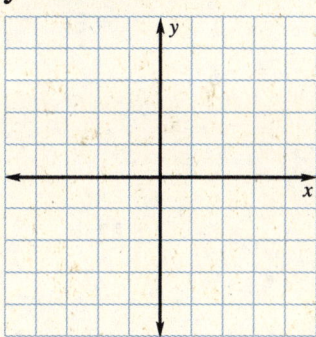

11. $x = 4$

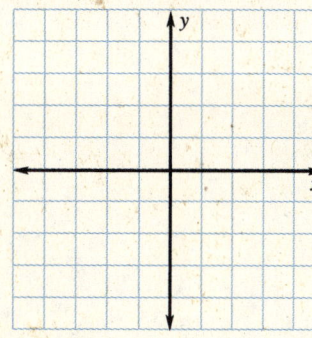

12. $y = -2$

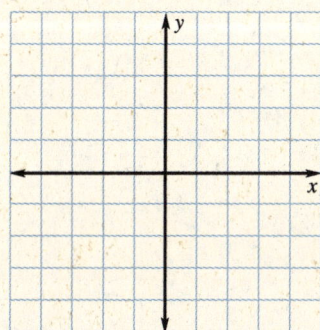

13. $y = x^2$

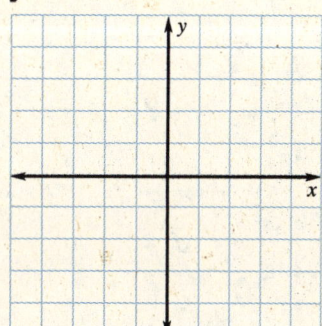

Find the slope and y-intercept of the line.

14. $y = \frac{1}{2}x + 3$

15. $y = -x + 8$

16. Jack paid **$1000** cash toward a new car. In addition, each month he pays **$500** on a loan for the car. Write a linear equation to express the total amount **y** he has paid after **x** months.

17. Luigi can pick **1** pint of blueberries in **30** minutes. Write a direct variation equation to express the number of pints of blueberries **y** Luigi can pick in **x** minutes.

18. Explain how you would find the slope of the line containing the points (**2**, **8**) and (**7**, **−2**).

_____
_____
_____

19. Which equation will have a graph that is a line sloping down to the right? Explain your reasoning.

   A. $y = \frac{3}{4}x - 6$ B. $y = -7x + 1$

   C. $y = x^2 - 3$ D. $y = -4$

_____
_____

Math Intervention
Book 5 Algebraic Thinking

McDougal Littell

Math Intervention

Book 6:
Data Analysis and Geometry

McDougal Littell
A DIVISION OF HOUGHTON MIFFLIN COMPANY
Evanston, Illinois • Boston • Dallas

Cover photo © Photodisc Green/Getty Images

Illustrations George Barile/McDougal Littell/Houghton Mifflin Company and John Evans/McDougal Littell/Houghton Mifflin Company

Copyright © 2008 by McDougal Littell, a division of Houghton Mifflin Company.
All rights reserved.

Permission is hereby granted to teachers to reprint or photocopy in classroom quantities the pages or sheets in this work that carry a McDougal Littell copyright notice. These pages are designed to be reproduced by teachers for use in their classes with accompanying McDougal Littell material, provided each copy made shows the copyright notice. Such copies may not be sold and further distribution is expressly prohibited. Except as authorized above, prior written permission must be obtained from McDougal Littell, a division of Houghton Mifflin Company, to reproduce or transmit this work or portions thereof in any other form or by any other electronic or mechanical means, including any information storage or retrieval system, unless expressly permitted by federal copyright laws. Address inquiries to, Supervisor, Rights and Permissions, McDougal Littell, P.O. Box 1667, Evanston, IL 60204.

ISBN-13: 978-0-618-90077-0
ISBN-10: 0-618-90077-2

123456789—PBO—11 10 09 08 07

 **Book 6: Data Analysis and Geometry**

Data Analysis

Lesson 6-1	Sort Objects and Data	**2**
Lesson 6-2	Record Data	**6**
Lesson 6-3	Represent Data	**10**
Lesson 6-4	Compare Data Sets	**14**
Lesson 6-5	Probability Experiments	**18**
	Mixed Practice for Lessons 6-1 to 6-5	**22**

Length and Area

Lesson 6-6	Measure Length	**24**
Lesson 6-7	Find Perimeter	**28**
Lesson 6-8	Area of a Rectangle	**32**
Lesson 6-9	Area of a Parallelogram	**36**
Lesson 6-10	Area of a Triangle	**40**
Activity 6-11	Working with Circles and Diameters	**44**
Lesson 6-12	Circumference of a Circle	**46**
Lesson 6-13	Area of a Circle	**50**
	Mixed Practice for Lessons 6-6 to 6-13	**54**

Surface Area and Volume

Activity 6-14	Finding Surface Area Using Models	**56**
Lesson 6-15	Surface Area of a Rectangular Prism	**58**
Lesson 6-16	Volume of a Rectangular Prism	**62**
Lesson 6-17	Volume of a Triangular Prism	**66**
Lesson 6-18	Volume of a Cylinder	**70**
	Mixed Practice for Lessons 6-15 to 6-18	**74**

CONTENTS cont.

Other Geometry Concepts

Lesson 6-19	Angles	76
Lesson 6-20	Classify Angles	80
Lesson 6-21	Complementary and Supplementary Angles	84
Lesson 6-22	Classify Triangles	88
Activity 6-23	Finding the Sum of the Angles in a Triangle	92
Lesson 6-24	Angles in a Triangle and Quadrilateral	94
Lesson 6-25	Square Roots	98
Lesson 6-26	Pythagorean Theorem	102
Lesson 6-27	Converse of the Pythagorean Theorem	106
Lesson 6-28	Parallel and Perpendicular Lines	110
Lesson 6-29	Congruent Figures	114
Lesson 6-30	Similar Figures	118
	Mixed Practice for Lessons 6-19 to 6-30	122

McDougal Littell

Math Intervention

MATH INTERVENTION

- The Math Intervention program includes skill lessons, problem solving lessons, activities, and mixed practice materials covering a wide range of mathematical topics that are needed for success in middle school and high school mathematics.

- There are seven books in the Math Intervention program. Book 6 contains materials on Data Analysis and Geometry concepts such as representing data and classifying and measuring geometric figures.

- In the Math Intervention books, lessons include worked-out Examples and Try this exercises to help you build understanding of a topic. The Practice section includes a variety of problems to give you the practice you need to develop your math skills. The Did You Get It? section checks your understanding of the lesson.

- Problem solving lessons suggest strategies for approaching real-world problem solving situations and promote the use of estimation to check reasonableness of solutions.

- Activities build your understanding of a topic through the use of models and games.

- Mixed Practice sections include practice of vocabulary, skills, and problem solving methods covering the material in a group of lessons.

- You may complete the work in selected lessons, or cover the book as a whole, as directed by your teacher.

Name _____   Date _____

LESSON 6-1
Sort Objects and Data

> **Words to Remember**
> Object: A thing that you can touch and feel
> Groups: Collections of objects or numbers
> Assemble: To place objects or numbers in a group
> Attribute: Something about the object or number that allows it to fit into a group
> Data: A collection of numbers

Getting Started You can assemble objects by their attributes. An object's *shape* is an attribute.

EXAMPLE 1 Assembling Objects Into Groups

Assemble the following objects into groups based on *shape*.

football   soccer ball
basketball   tennis racket
baseball bat   tennis ball

Solution

Step 1 **Define** the groups.

  Round, Not round   Use shape to name groups for these objects.

Step 2 **Assemble** the objects into the defined groups.

Round group	Not round group
basketball	football
soccer ball	baseball bat
tennis ball	tennis racket

Remember
An object can have many attributes.

TRY THIS Use the data in Example 1.

1. Group the objects above based on *size*:

   Large group _____   Small group _____

Math Intervention
Book 6 Data Analysis and Geometry

Name _____ Date _____

Attributes Don't forget that you can assemble objects or numbers into many different groups based on their attributes. You also must be able to define the groups. You could say that a basketball is large. Because the basketball is larger than a baseball, you could then say that a baseball is small.

Data The numbers listed in Example 2 are *data*. You can assemble the data into different groups by defining the *type* of number, the *order* of the number, and so on.

EXAMPLE 2 Recognizing Attributes of Numbers

Assemble the following numbers into groups.

2, 4, 5, 7, 9, 12, 20, 31, 32, 36, 45, 50

Solution

Step 1 **Define** the group.

Odd, Even	Determine attributes.
Less than 10, Greater than 10	Sub-divide groups, if you choose.
Odd < 10, Even < 10, Odd > 10, Even > 10	Determine group names.

> **Remember**
> *Less than* uses a < symbol and *greater than* uses a > symbol.

Step 2 **Assemble** the numbers into the groups.

Odd < 10	Even < 10
5, 7, 9	2, 4

Odd > 10	Even > 10
31, 45	12, 20, 32, 36, 50

TRY THIS Use the data in Example 2.

2. Suppose the data in Example 2 lists people's ages. Assemble the data into groups with the following attributes:

   Younger than my age   My age   Older than my age

Math Intervention
Book 6 Data Analysis and Geometry   **3**

Name _____ Date _____

> **Summarize**
>
> Objects are things that you can touch and feel.
> Groups are collections of objects or numbers.
> You can assemble objects or numbers into groups.
> Groups of data are often made up of numbers.
> An attribute about an object is something that allows it to be grouped with other objects. For example, *round* is an attribute about an object.
> An attribute about a number is something that allows it to be grouped with other numbers. For example, *even* is an attribute about a number.

Practice

1. Assemble a group of all of the odd numbers from the list:

    8, 10, 5, 7, 16, 36, 39, 44, 23, 19, 28, 98, 99

    _____
    _____

2. Assemble a group of all of the even numbers from the list:

    4, 8, 10, 5, 7, 16, 36, 39, 44, 23, 19, 28, 56, 66

    _____
    _____

3. Select the round objects from the list:

    football, dinner plate, baseball, shoe box, soup can, car, dartboard, bridge

    _____
    _____

4. Select the numbers from the list that are multiples of 5:

    45, 26, 32, 56, 75, 25, 10, 19, 42, 30, 100, 63

    _____
    _____

5. Select the numbers from the list that are divisible by 10:

    35, 20, 50, 87, 19, 110, 25, 230, 49, 70, 185, 90

    _____
    _____

Math Intervention
Book 6 Data Analysis and Geometry

Name _____ Date _____

Objects and numbers may often be listed together.

6. Select the objects from the list:

   3, 42, tennis ball, 8, balloon, banana, 52, 82, golf ball, 98, 33, 21, pen, pencil, 47, 52, watch

   _____
   _____

7. Select the numbers from the list:

   3, 42, football, 8, pen, ring, 48, 82, phone, 97, 33, 21, radio, spoon, 47, 52, 65

   _____
   _____

8. Select the objects from the list that are not round:

   cereal box, cell phone, fork, basketball, tennis ball, bicycle tire, Ferris wheel, picture frame

   _____
   _____

DID YOU GET IT?

9. **Write a sorting problem.**

   Give a list of objects or numbers. _____

   Identify attributes of your list. _____

   Assemble your list into groups. _____

   _____

Fill in the missing words.

10. An attribute about an object is something that allows it to be grouped with other _____.

11. An attribute about a number is something that allows it to be grouped with other _____.

12. Groups are collections of _____.

13. Objects are _____.

14. Groups of data are often made up of _____.

Math Intervention
Book 6 Data Analysis and Geometry

Name _____ Date _____

LESSON 6-2

Record Data

Words to Remember

Record: To write down
Frequency: How often something occurs
Order: To assemble in a defined way
Collect: To assemble into a group

Getting Started You can count how often certain numbers occur in a group and record their *frequency*.

EXAMPLE 1 Determining Frequency

Determine the frequency of each of the numbers in the list and record the result.

10, 4, 5, 10, 2, 4, 10, 4, 5, 4, 2, 2, 10, 4, 10

Solution

Step 1 **Determine** the frequency of each number.

2	4	5	10	List each different number.
3	5	2	5	Count the number of times each number occurs.

Step 2 **Collect and record** the results.

The number 2 occurs 3 times.

The number 4 occurs 5 times.

The number 5 occurs 2 times.

The number 10 occurs 5 times.

Remember
Less than uses a < symbol and *greater than* uses a > symbol.

TRY THIS Use the data in Example 1.

1. Collect the different numbers.

   Less than 4 _____ Greater than 4 _____

2. What is the number with the greatest frequency that is > 4? _____

Math Intervention
Book 6 Data Analysis and Geometry

Name _____   Date _____

Collect Don't forget that you can use many ways to show your results when you are determining the frequencies of numbers, including making a list.

EXAMPLE 2 Keeping Track of What is Counted

Count, order, and record the frequencies of the numbers that are less than or greater than 50.

51, 48, 50, 57, 99, 48, 20, 99, 49, 36, 49, 50,
86, 74, 44, 99, 86, 57, 36, 86, 57, 74, 86, 57

Solution

Step 1 **Determine** the numbers less than or greater than **50**.

Less than 50:
48, 20, 49, 36, 44

Greater than 50:
51, 57, 99, 86, 74

Step 2 **Place** the numbers in numerical order.

Less than 50:
20, 36, 44, 48, 49

Greater than 50:
51, 57, 74, 86, 99

Step 3 **Record** the frequencies of the numbers. Show the frequency in parentheses ( ).

Less than 50:
20 (1), 36 (2), 44 (1), 48 (2), 49 (2)

Greater than 50:
51 (1), 57 (4), 74 (2), 86 (4), 99 (3)

TRY THIS Use the data in Example 2.

3. Suppose the data in Example 2 represents the scores of a basketball team. How many times has this team scored:

< 50 points	50 points	> 50 points

Math Intervention
Book 6 Data Analysis and Geometry   7

Name _____ Date _____

> **Summarize**
> **Collecting Data**
> Record your result by writing it.
> Count how often something occurs. This is the frequency.
> Order numbers by assembling them in a defined way.
> Collect numbers by assembling them into a group.

Practice

The following is a list of numbers that are not in order. Use the list for Exercises 1–3.

25, 88, 53, 67, 11, 36, 39, 64, 73, 19, 28, 98, 99

1. Record the list of numbers in numerical order.

   _____

2. Identify the odd numbers that are less than **62** from the list in Exercise 1.

   _____

3. Identify the even numbers that are greater than **62** from the list in Exercise 1.

   _____

4. Determine the frequency of each of the numbers in the list below and record the result.

   25, 18, 30, 32, 30, 18, 24, 25, 18, 30, 30, 24, 25

Number					
Frequency					

5. Collect and record the results of Exercise 4.

   _____
   _____
   _____

Math Intervention
Book 6 Data Analysis and Geometry

Name _____ Date _____

Sometimes knowing the frequency of a certain number is important. Use the following list for Exercises 6–8.

3, 42, 256, 8, 120, 256, 52, 82, 21, 98, 33, 21, 82,
120, 98, 21, 52, 3, 21, 42, 3, 120, 42, 3, 8, 42, 8

6. Record the three most frequent numbers in the list. Give their frequencies.

   _____

7. Record the odd numbers with a frequency > **1** from the list.

   _____

8. Record the even numbers with a frequency > **2** from the list.

   _____

DID YOU GET IT?

Use the following list for Exercises 9–11.

13, 48, 256, 16, 120, 256, 58, 82, 24, 98, 35, 24, 82,
120, 98, 24, 28, 13, 24, 48, 13, 120, 48, 13, 16, 48, 16

9. **Determine frequency.** How often does an odd number occur in the list? Repeats are allowed.

   _____

10. **Record data.** Record the frequencies of the numbers greater than **80**.

    _____

11. **Order data.** Make a list in numerical order from the data in Exercise 10.

    _____

Fill in the missing words.

12. Frequency is how often something _____.

13. If you write something, you _____ it.

14. To assemble numbers in a defined way is to _____ them.

15. You _____ numbers by assembling them into a group.

LESSON 6-3

Represent Data

Words to Remember
Represent: Use a method to show data
Display: To list, show
Methods: Lists, graphs, tally charts, tables, bar graphs, pictographs, and so on
Frequency: A count of an object or number

Getting Started   You can use different methods to show data.

EXAMPLE 1   Representing Data Using Different Methods

Suppose a car dealer has red (R), silver (S), black (B), and white (W) cars in stock on the lot in the following order:

R R S B W S R R R W W W B B B W W W B S S S S S B B B R B W B
B R R W W W W S R W W W W R S B S R R B B R S R S R W W W W W

Solution

Method 1   Count the individual items and record the results as a simple list.

   red (15), silver (12), black (14), white (22)

Method 2   Represent the data in another way. Use a tally chart.

red													
silver											
black													
white																			

Tally Marks
Record a tally mark (|) for each data value. Indicate each 5th value by a cross-mark (—).

TRY THIS   Use the data in Example 1.

1. Display the data as a bar graph. Draw bars and give the heights of each bar. (*Red* is done for you.)

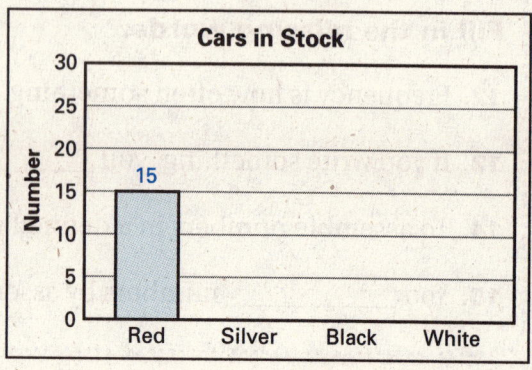

Math Intervention
Book 6 Data Analysis and Geometry

Methods Don't forget that you can use many different methods to display data. Some common examples of these methods are tally charts, graphs, diagrams, bar graphs, lists, and tables.

EXAMPLE 2 — Using a Table

> **Remember**
> A table is one method for displaying data.

Find the frequency of each number and use a table with headings to display the result.

50, 4, 7, 7, 4, 20, 20, 7, 36, 32, 36, 7, 50
7, 7, 20, 32, 7, 2, 32, 2, 7, 50, 2, 20, 20

Solution

Step 1 **Determine** how many different numbers are in the list. Add **1** to get the number of rows.

7 numbers + 1 = 8 rows

Step 2 **Determine** the number of columns in the table and decide on the headings.

Columns: **2**
Headings: Number, Frequency

Step 3 **Count** how many of each number there are and display the frequencies in a table.

Number	Frequency
2	3
4	2
7	8
20	5
32	3
36	2
50	3

TRY THIS   Use the data in Example 2.

2. Suppose the data is a code for different color cars in a parking lot. If the code for a green car is **20**, how many green cars are there in the lot?

3. Which numbers have a frequency of 3?

Math Intervention
Book 6 Data Analysis and Geometry

Name _____   Date _____

> **Summarize**
> **Representing Data**
> Showing or displaying data is representing data.
> Methods for representing data include lists, graphs, tally charts, tables, and so on.

Practice

1. Parking Lot **1** contains **9** blue cars, **16** red cars, **6** green cars, and **5** silver cars. Represent the data as a tally chart.

2. Parking Lot **2** contains **10** blue cars, **6** red cars, **6** green cars, and **7** silver cars. Represent the data as a table.

3. Parking Lot **3** contains **17** blue cars, **15** red cars, **18** green cars, and **12** silver cars. Show the data using a method different than Exercise 1 or Exercise 2.

4. Fill in the bar graph below showing the total number of blue, red, green, and silver cars in Parking Lots 1–3.

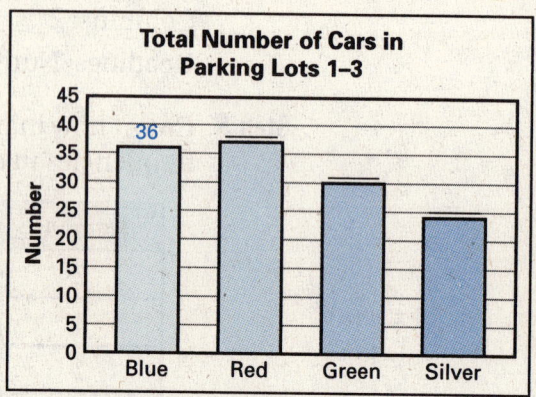

5. The pictograph shows the number of songs on many of the CDs in Caroline's collection. Make a tally chart for the data. How many songs are there altogether?

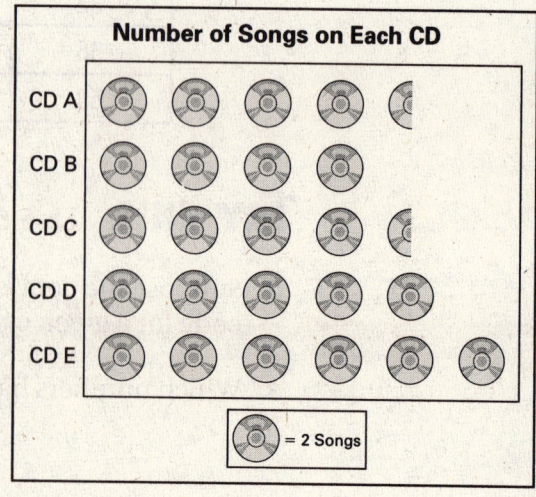

Math Intervention
Book 6 Data Analysis and Geometry

Name _____ Date _____

Use the following list of numbers for Exercises 6–8.

5, 4, 7, 8, 4, 2, 7, 6, 9, 6, 7, 5,
8, 7, 2, 3, 7, 2, 2, 2, 7, 5, 2, 2, 8

6. How many different numbers are in the list? List them in order.

7. Find the frequency of each number in the list and represent it as a table with a heading.

8. Suppose the data are different shoe sizes of students in the class. How many students wear size 7? size 2?

DID YOU GET IT?

9. **Describe a process.** Explain how to make a frequency table of data.

   _____
   _____

10. **Make a graph.** Use a bar graph to display the answer for CDs A, B, C, D, and E of Exercise 5.

    Number of Songs on Each CD

    Number

    CD

Fill in the missing words.

11. Data can be represented by using _____.

12. How often an object or number appears in a list is its _____.

Name _____ Date _____

LESSON 6-4: Compare Data Sets

> **Words to Remember**
>
> **Data set:** A group of data
> **Fraction:** Part of a whole (Examples: $\frac{1}{4}, \frac{1}{2}$, or **0.25, 0.5**)
> **Percent:** Part of **100** (Examples: $\frac{57}{100}$, **57%**)

Getting Started You can represent and compare data in different ways by using pictures, bar graphs, tally charts, or picture graphs.

EXAMPLE 1 — Representing and Comparing Data

Suppose a shoe store has flip-flops (F), athletic shoes (A), and sandals (S) on the shelves as shown below. Determine which type of shoes has the most stock.

F A A A F F S S S F F A A A A A F F F A A S S S S A
A A A F F F F F F F F F S S S S S S F A A A A F F A

Solution

Step 1 Tally the individual items and record the results in a tally chart.

Type	Amount
Flip-flops	‖‖‖ ‖‖‖ ‖‖‖ ‖‖‖
Athletic shoes	‖‖‖ ‖‖‖ ‖‖‖ ‖‖‖ ‖‖
Sandals	‖‖‖ ‖‖‖ ‖‖‖

Step 2 Compare the results of the tally. There are **20** pairs of flip-flops, **22** pairs of athletic shoes, and **14** pairs of sandals.

ANSWER 14 < 20 < 22, so the store has more athletic shoes than the other types.

TRY THIS — Use the data in Example 1.

1. The store orders more stock if inventory falls below **20** pairs of one item. What should they order?

Math Intervention
Book 6 Data Analysis and Geometry

Name _____   Date _____

EXAMPLE 2 Comparing Data with Fractions

Remember
A fraction is part of a whole.

The picture graph shows the distribution of a Little League baseball team by grade. What fraction of the team is composed of 6th graders?

6th grade	7th grade	8th grade
⚾⚾⚾ ⚾⚾⚾⚾	⚾⚾⚾⚾ ⚾⚾⚾⚾	⚾⚾⚾ ⚾⚾⚾⚾

Solution

Step 1 **Count** how many team members are in each grade. Add.

6th grade: 7   7th grade: 8   8th grade: 7

There are 22 members on the team.

Step 2 **Show** the comparison as a fraction.

7 is the number of 6th graders and 22 is the team size.

ANSWER $\frac{7}{22}$

EXAMPLE 3 Comparing Data in a Bar Graph

Display the data below in bar graphs. What number appears most often?

Data set 1: 50, 50, 7, 7, 20, 50

Data set 2: 50, 7, 20, 20, 7, 7, 20, 7, 50, 7

Solution

Graph the data in each set.

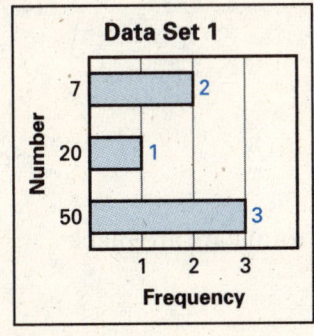
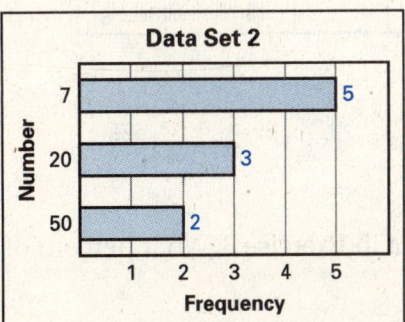

ANSWER 7 appears most often.

TRY THIS Use the data in Example 3.

2. What percent of the data in Data set 2 is the number 7?

$\frac{\square}{\square} = 0.\square\square = \underline{}\%$

Math Intervention
Book 6 Data Analysis and Geometry

Name _____ Date _____

> **Summarize**
> **Comparing Data**
> A data set is a group of data.
> A fraction is part of a whole (such as $\frac{1}{4}$, $\frac{1}{2}$, or **0.25, 0.5**).
> A percent is part of **100**.

Practice

1. A shoe store has **200** pairs of flip-flops, **200** pairs of athletic shoes, and **600** pairs of sandals. What percent of the total number of shoes is the number of flip-flops?

2. Using the data in Exercise 1, what fraction shows how the number of athletic shoes compares to the number of sandals?

   $\dfrac{\text{athletic shoes}}{\text{sandals}} = \dfrac{\square}{\square} = \dfrac{\square}{\square}$

3. Cars in a parking lot have the colors shown in the tally chart. What percent of red cars is the number of blue cars?

Car Color	Tally
blue	ﬀﬀ ﬀﬀ ﬀﬀ ﬀﬀ ﬀﬀ
green	ﬀﬀ ﬀﬀ ﬀﬀ ﬀﬀ ﬀﬀ II
silver	ﬀﬀ ﬀﬀ ﬀﬀ ﬀﬀ II
black	ﬀﬀ ﬀﬀ ﬀﬀ ﬀﬀ
red	ﬀﬀ ﬀﬀ ﬀﬀ ﬀﬀ ﬀﬀ ﬀﬀ

   $\dfrac{\square}{\square} = 0.\square\square\square = \underline{\hspace{1cm}}\%$

4. Use the data in Exercise 3. What percent of the total cars are black or green?

   $\dfrac{\square}{\square} = 0.\square\square\square = \underline{\hspace{1cm}}\%$

Name _____   Date _____

5. Use the data in Exercise 3. What fraction of cars in the lot are red? What fraction are silver?

6. Bob has **100** CDs in his collection. **25** of his CDs have over **10** songs. What percent of his CD collection has **10** songs or less?

7. Jane likes the color red. She has **12** red dresses and **8** dresses of other colors. What fraction of her dresses are red?

8. Jim collects marbles. He has three different boxes that contain red, blue, green, and yellow marbles. The number of each color (in order) is shown in the lists. What percent of the marbles is yellow?

         R   B   G   Y

Box 1: **40, 38, 18, 25**

Box 2: **30, 33, 29, 34**

Box 3: **50, 17, 15, 31**

9. Use the data in Exercise 8. Which of the three collections of marbles is the largest?

DID YOU GET IT?

10. **Explain your reasoning.** Using the data in Exercise 8, explain how to find the fraction of total marbles that are in Box 2.

_____
_____

11. **Display data.** Use a bar graph to display the number of marbles by color for all the data in Exercise 8 combined.

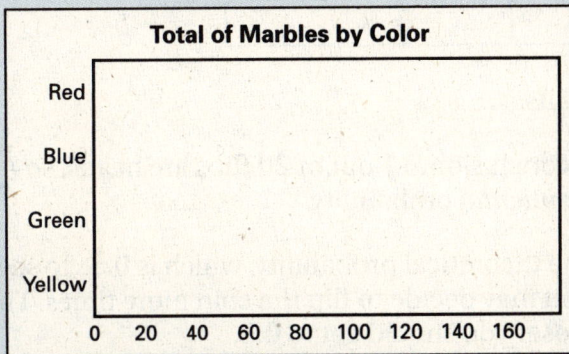

Name _____ Date _____

LESSON 6-5 Probability Experiments

> **Words to Remember**
>
> Event: Something that happens or something that may happen
> Probability: How likely it is that an event will happen
> Outcome: The result of an event such as tossing a coin
> Theoretical probability: The probability of an event based on the number of possible and the total number of outcomes

Getting Started In Activity 4-16 you found experimental probabilities of events. In this lesson, you will conduct experiments to find the probability that an event will happen.

EXAMPLE 1 Conducting a Simple Probability Experiment

Determine the probability that when you flip a coin, the result will be heads. Express the result as a number between 0 and 1.

Heads

Tails

Solution

Step 1 Flip a coin 20 times and record the results in a tally chart.

Coin side	Frequency
Heads	|||| ||||	
Tails	|||| |||

Step 2 Analyze the results.

Step 3 Determine the conclusion. 11 out of 20 flips are heads, so $\frac{11}{20}$ or 0.55 is the *experimental* probability.

This result is close to the theoretical probability, which is **0.5**. To see if you can get closer to **0.5**, you may decide to flip the coin more times. The more you flip the coin, the closer you should get to **0.5**.

> **Remember**
>
> The theoretical probability of getting heads when you flip a coin is
>
> $\dfrac{1 \text{ possible outcome (Heads)}}{2 \text{ total outcomes (Heads or tails)}} = \dfrac{1}{2} = 0.5.$

Math Intervention
Book 6 Data Analysis and Geometry

Name _____ Date _____

TRY THIS Use the approach in Example 1.

Remember
The probability of an event is a number between 0 and 1.

1. Flip the coin 100 times, keep track with a tally chart, and determine the probability of getting heads. Analyze the results.

EXAMPLE 2 Displaying the Results

Determine how often you will roll a 4 on a number cube. Event: roll a 4.

Solution

Step 1 Select a number cube with numbers 1, 2, 3, 4, 5, 6.

Step 2 Roll the cube 50 times and record the results in a tally chart.

Number	Frequency	Number	Frequency
1										4											
2												5								
3										6							

Step 3 Display the results using a bar graph.

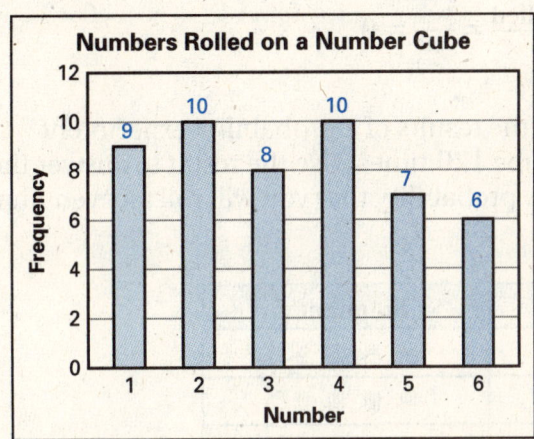

Step 4 Analyze the results. For this experiment, the probability of rolling a 4 is $\frac{10}{50} = \frac{1}{5}$, or 0.2.

TRY THIS Use the data in Example 2.

Remember
You can review the material in Activity 4-16.

2. What is the experimental probability that you will roll a 6? Compare this to the theoretical probability.

3. What is the experimental probability that you will roll an even number? Compare this to the theoretical probability.

Math Intervention
Book 6 Data Analysis and Geometry

Name _____   Date _____

> **Summarize**
>
> **Doing a Probability Experiment**
>
> An outcome is the result of an event such as tossing a coin.
>
> Probability is how likely or unlikely something will occur.
>
> A probability experiment involves determining the conclusion from events involving probability.

Practice

1. Use a number cube.

    a. Odd numbers on the cube: ☐, ☐, and ☐.

    b. Roll a number cube **20** times.

    c. Record how many rolls are odd numbers. _____

    d. Find the probability of rolling an odd number.

    $$\frac{\text{odd numbers rolled}}{\text{all rolls}} = \frac{\boxed{}}{\boxed{}} = 0.\boxed{}$$

2. The tally chart shows the results of a probability experiment that rolls a number cube **120** times. Use the result to answer the question, "What is the probability that you will roll an even number on the next roll?"

Number	Frequency
1	‖‖‖‖ ‖‖‖‖ ‖‖‖‖ ‖‖‖‖ ‖
2	‖‖‖‖ ‖‖‖‖ ‖‖‖‖ ‖‖‖
3	‖‖‖‖ ‖‖‖‖ ‖‖‖‖ ‖‖‖‖
4	‖‖‖‖ ‖‖‖‖ ‖‖‖‖ ‖‖‖‖ ‖‖
5	‖‖‖‖ ‖‖‖‖ ‖‖‖‖ ‖‖‖
6	‖‖‖‖ ‖‖‖‖ ‖‖‖‖ ‖‖‖‖

3. Use the data in Exercise 2. What is the probability of rolling an odd number?

    $$\frac{\text{odd numbers rolled}}{\text{all rolls}} = \frac{\boxed{}}{\boxed{}} = 0.\boxed{}$$

4. Compare your answer to Exercise 3 with the theoretical probability of rolling an odd number.

5. Use the data in Exercise 2. What is the probability of rolling a **4** or a **6**? Explain your reasoning.

6. **Probability experiment:** Flip **2** coins at least **50** times and record the results in the tally chart below.

Outcome	Frequency
Heads, Heads	
Heads, Tails	
Tails, Tails	
Tails, Heads	

Using your results, find the following experimental probabilities.

Event A: getting **2** heads
Event B: getting one head and one tail
Event C: getting **2** tails

7. Use the data from Exercise 6. Make a conjecture about the theoretical probability of getting **2** heads. Explain your reasoning.

8. Suppose you have a marble collection that contains **40** red, **38** blue, **18** green, and **25** yellow marbles. Suppose you put all of the marbles in a box and shake the box to distribute the marbles. What is the probability that you will draw a red marble?

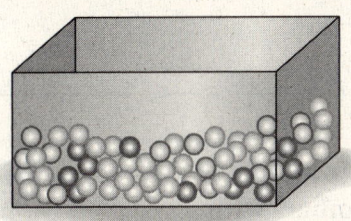

DID YOU GET IT?

9. **Do an experiment.** Roll a number cube **24** times. What is the experimental probability that you roll a **6**? What is the theoretical probability?

10. **Fill in the missing words.** How likely something is to happen is its _____. An _____ is the result of an event. A **50** per cent chance represents a _____.

Name _____ Date _____

Mixed Practice for Lessons 6-1 to 6-5

Vocabulary Review

Match the word with its mathematical and everyday meanings.

Word	Mathematical meaning	Everyday meaning
1. frequency ____, ____	A. how likely an event is to happen	X. how many of something
2. probability ____, ____	B. count of an object or number	Y. chance of something happening

Fill in the missing word(s).

3. An _____ is a thing that you can touch and feel.

4. An _____ is something about an object that would allow it to fit into a group.

5. Data is a collection of _____.

6. Assemble a group of all of the odd numbers from the list:

   18, 20, 5, 17, 16, 35, 39, 44, 26, 27, 28, 98, 99

   _____

   _____

Use the data in Exercise 6 to determine the frequency of numbers with the attribute described.

7. Odd < 40   8. Even > 30   9. Multiple of 3

10. Even   11. Numbers < 20   12. Numbers > 50

13. Determine the frequency of each of the numbers in the list and record the result in a frequency chart with headings.

   25, 28, 33, 30, 28, 17, 25, 25, 28, 32, 30, 30, 25

Number						
Frequency						

Math Intervention
Book 6 Data Analysis and Geometry

Name _____ Date _____

Suppose you have a group of objects that has a football, a tennis ball, a baseball bat, a soccer ball, a basketball, and a tennis racquet. Determine which objects would be in the group described.

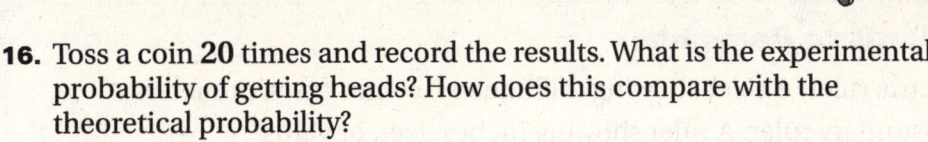

14. Not round objects

15. Round objects

16. Toss a coin **20** times and record the results. What is the experimental probability of getting heads? How does this compare with the theoretical probability?

_____
_____
_____

Suppose that you have 25 red marbles, 20 blue marbles, 35 green marbles, and 20 yellow marbles in a jar and they are well mixed together. You reach in and choose a random marble. What is the probability that you draw the marble described?

17. A red or blue marble

$$\frac{\text{Red or blue}}{\text{Total marbles}} = \frac{}{}$$

18. A green marble

$$\frac{\text{Green}}{\text{Total marbles}} = \frac{}{}$$

Solve the problem. Then explain your answer.

19. A shoe store has **200** pairs of boots, **500** pairs of shoes, and **300** pairs of sandals. What is the percent of shoes out of the total footwear items?

_____
_____
_____

20. Jane has a collection of **280** CDs. She has **120** CDs with more than **14** songs and **160** CDs with fewer than **14** songs. What percent of her CDs have fewer than **14** songs?

_____
_____
_____

Math Intervention
Book 6 Data Analysis and Geometry

LESSON 6-6

Measure Length

> **Words to Remember**
> Metric ruler: A ruler showing millimeters, centimeters, or meters
> Customary ruler: A ruler showing inches, feet, or yards
> Line segment: A part of a line with a definite length. The endpoints may be labeled.

Getting Started You can measure length using the customary system in the U.S. or you can measure length using the metric system.

EXAMPLE 1 Using a Customary Ruler

Use a customary ruler to measure the length of the rectangle to the nearest inch.

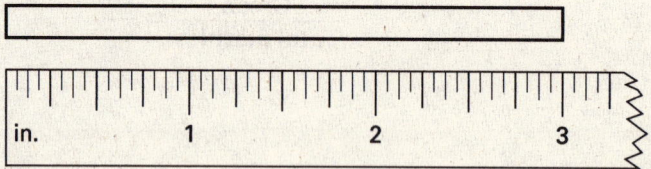

Solution

Step 1 **Select** a customary ruler that is **12** inches long.

Step 2 **Place** the **0** point of the ruler even with the left edge of the rectangle.

Step 3 **Read** the number on the ruler that is closest to the right edge of the rectangle.

Step 4 **Note** that the number on the ruler that is closest to the right edge of the rectangle is **3**.

The rectangle may not be exactly **3** inches in length. You are rounding to the nearest whole inch.

Remember
A customary ruler and a metric ruler use different systems for measurement.

TRY THIS Use the approach in Example 1.

1. Use a metric ruler to measure the length of the rectangle in Example 1 to the nearest whole centimeter.

Math Intervention
Book 6 Data Analysis and Geometry

Remember
Coordinates are an ordered pair of numbers that identify a point on a coordinate plane. Points (x, y) are found along horizontal and vertical lines.

 **Finding the Length of a Horizontal Line Segment**

Each unit in the coordinate grid represents 1 inch. Calculate the length of the line segment from point A to point B.

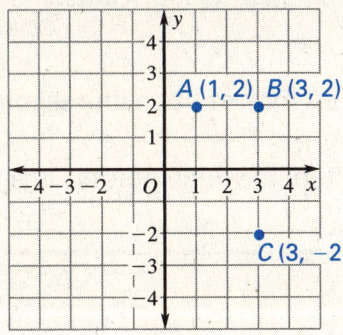

Solution

Step 1 Give the *x*-coordinates for each point.

    1 and 3   The *x*-coordinate is the first coordinate in the ordered pair (*x*, *y*).

Step 2 Find the distance between points.

    3 − 1 = 2   Subtract 1 from 3.

ANSWER The length of the line segment from *A* to *B* is 2 inches.

Remember
You can use *y*-coordinates to find a vertical distance.

EXAMPLE 3 **Finding the Length of a Vertical Line Segment**

Refer to the graph in Example 2. Calculate the length of the vertical line segment from point *B* to point *C*.

Step 1 Give the *y*-coordinates for each point.

    2 and −2   The *y*-coordinate is the second coordinate in an ordered pair (*x*, *y*).

Step 2 Find the distance between points.

    2 − (−2) = 4   Subtract −2 from 2 or count the distance.

ANSWER The line segment from *B* to *C* is 4 inches long.

Look Back
See Lesson 4-5 for help with conversion.

TRY THIS Refer to Step 2 of Example 3.

2. Convert the distance between points *B* and *C* to centimeters. Use 1 inch = 2.54 centimeters.

Math Intervention
Book 6 Data Analysis and Geometry

Name _____ Date _____

> **Summarize**
>
> **Using a Ruler**
>
> A metric ruler is used to measure length in millimeters, centimeters, or meters.
>
> A customary ruler is used to measure length in inches, feet, or yards.
>
> **Finding the Length of a Segment**
>
> A line segment is a part of a line. A line continues forever but a line segment has a definite length.
>
> A coordinate plane or a coordinate grid is a system in which points (x, y) are found along horizontal and vertical lines.

Practice

1. Use a customary ruler to measure the length of the rectangle in inches.

2. Measure the length of the rectangle with a metric ruler in centimeters.

3. Use a customary ruler to measure the length of the base of the triangle in inches.

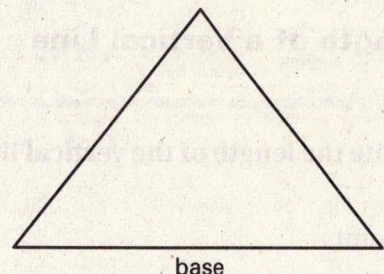

4. Measure the length of the base of the triangle in Exercise 3 in centimeters with a metric ruler.

5. Each unit in the coordinate grid represents one inch. Calculate the length of the line segment from point A to point B in inches.

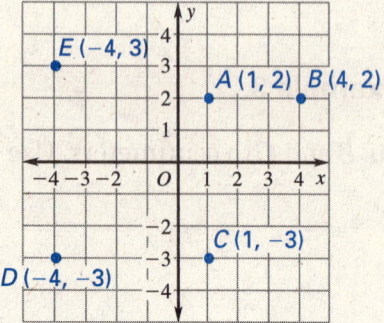

Math Intervention
Book 6 Data Analysis and Geometry

6. Using the coordinate grid in Exercise 5, convert the distance between points *A* and *B* to centimeters. Use 1 inch = 2.54 centimeters.

7. Using the coordinate grid in Exercise 5, calculate the length of the line segment between point *D* and point *C* in inches.

8. Using the coordinate grid in Exercise 5, calculate the length of the line segment between point *D* and point *E* in inches.

9. Using a customary ruler, measure the length of a desk or table to the nearest inch. Then remeasure the desk to the nearest centimeter using a metric ruler. Which measurement do you think is the most accurate? Why?

DID YOU GET IT?

Fill in the missing words.

10. A metric ruler can be used to measure a line segment in _____, _____, or _____.

11. A customary ruler can be used to measure a line segment in _____, _____, or _____.

Compare.

12. How does an inch compare to a centimeter?

_____

_____

_____

13. If you measure a line segment with a customary ruler and then with a metric ruler, which measurement will be more accurate?

_____

_____

_____

LESSON 6-7

Find Perimeter

> **Words to Remember**
>
> Polygon: A closed figure formed from line segments that meet only at their endpoints
>
> Perimeter: The sum of the lengths of the sides of a figure

Getting Started In this lesson, you will find the perimeter of a polygon and you will use a coordinate grid to represent a simple figure.

EXAMPLE 1 Finding the Perimeter of a Polygon

Find the perimeter of the rectangle.

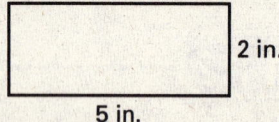

2 in.
5 in.

Solution

Step 1 **Find** the lengths of all sides. Since a rectangle has opposite sides equal, the lengths are 2 inches, 2 inches, 5 inches, and 5 inches.

Step 2 **Add** the lengths. $2 + 2 + 5 + 5 = 14$

ANSWER The perimeter is 14 inches.

TRY THIS

1. Find the perimeter of a rectangle with side lengths 6 inches and 4 inches.

    Perimeter = ☐ + ☐ + ☐ + ☐

    = ☐ inches

2. Find the perimeter of a triangle with side lengths 3 inches, 4 inches, and 4 inches.

    Perimeter = ☐ + ☐ + ☐

    = ☐ inches

Math Intervention
Book 6 Data Analysis and Geometry

Name _____   Date _____

Remember
Coordinates are ordered pairs of numbers that identify a point on a coordinate grid.

EXAMPLE 2   **Graphing a Polygon On a Coordinate Grid**

Graph the rectangle whose endpoints are $(-3, 2)$, $(4, 2)$, $(4, -1)$, and $(-3, -1)$.

Solution   Plot each of the points on the coordinate grid and connect them.

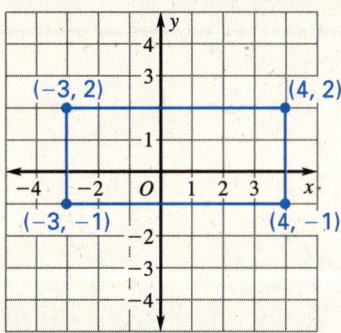

EXAMPLE 3   **Finding Perimeter on a Coordinate Grid**

Remember
You can use x-coordinates to find horizontal distance and y-coordinates to find vertical distance.

Refer to the coordinate grid in Example 2. Find the perimeter.

Solution

Step 1   **Find** the length of the vertical segments. Since one pair of vertical segments has coordinates $(-3, 2)$ and $(-3, -1)$, the length is the difference of the y-coordinates, $2 - (-1)$, or 3.

Step 2   **Find** the length of the horizontal segments. Since one pair of horizontal segments has coordinates $(-3, 2)$ and $(4, 2)$, the length is the difference of the x-coordinates, $4 - (-3)$, or 7.

ANSWER   The perimeter of the rectangle is $3 + 3 + 7 + 7 = 20$ units.

TRY THIS

3. In Example 3, suppose the coordinates of the rectangle are $(-1, 3)$, $(2, 3)$, $(2, -1)$, and $(-1, -1)$. Graph the rectangle.

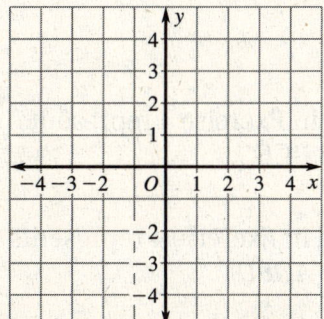

4. Find the perimeter of the rectangle in Try this Exercise 3.

Math Intervention
Book 6 Data Analysis and Geometry   **29**

Name _____ Date _____

> **Summarize**
>
> **Finding the Perimeter of a Polygon**
>
> A polygon is a closed figure formed from line segments that meet only at their endpoints.
>
> The perimeter of a polygon is the sum of the lengths of the sides.

Practice

1. Find the perimeter of the rectangle.

   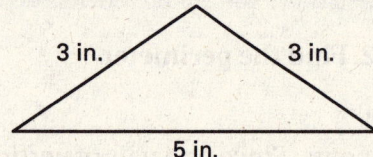

2. Find the perimeter of the triangle.

   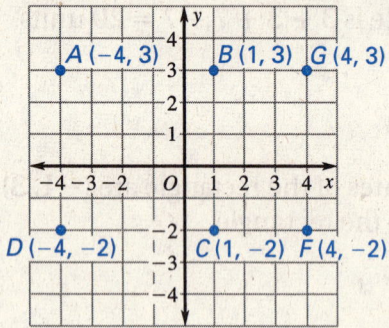

3. Find the perimeter of the polygon in Exercise 2 in centimeters.
   1 inch = 2.54 centimeters

4. Suppose each unit in the coordinate grid represents one inch. Find the perimeter of the rectangle ABCD.

5. Suppose each unit in the coordinate grid in Exercise 4 represents one inch. Find the perimeter of rectangle BCFG.

6. Suppose each unit on the coordinate grid in Exercise 4 represents one inch. Find the perimeter of rectangle AGFD.

7. In Exercise 4, suppose the coordinates of A and D are A(−2, 3) and D(−2, −2). Find the perimeter of AGFD.

Math Intervention
Book 6 Data Analysis and Geometry

Name _____ Date _____

8. A polygon has endpoints $R(-1, 2)$, $S(3, 2)$, $T(3, -3)$, and $U(-1, -3)$. Graph the polygon on a coordinate grid.

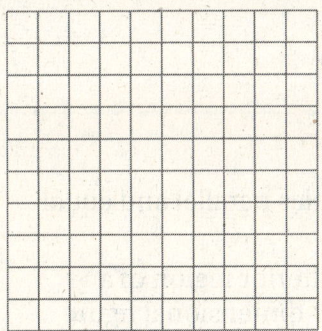

9. Suppose each unit in the coordinate grid for Exercise 8 represents one centimeter. What is the perimeter of the polygon?

10. A five sided polygon is called a pentagon. Explain how to find the perimeter of a pentagon.

_____
_____
_____

DID YOU GET IT?

Describe a process.

11. How do you find the perimeter of a polygon?

_____
_____
_____

12. In a coordinate grid, how do you find the perimeter of a polygon whose sides are vertical or horizontal segments?

_____
_____
_____

Fill in the missing words.

13. Triangles and rectangles are examples of _____.

14. A point on a coordinate grid has ___ and ___ coordinates.

Name _____ Date _____

LESSON 6-8
Area of a Rectangle

> **Words to Remember**
>
> Rectangle: A 4-sided figure with opposite sides parallel and equal and with four right angles
>
> Area: The measure, in square units, of the interior region of a 2-dimensional figure or of the surface of a 3-dimensional figure
>
> Square inch: The area of a square one inch long and one inch wide

Getting Started In Lesson 2-6 you used a metric ruler and a customary ruler. In this lesson, you will measure the sides of a rectangle and find the area using square units such as square inches, square centimeters, square yards, and square meters.

EXAMPLE 1 — Measuring the Area of a Rectangle

Use a customary ruler to measure the sides of the rectangle and calculate the area in square inches.

Solution

Step 1 **Measure** the sides of the rectangle.

    4 inches   Find the length.
    1.25 inches   Find the width.

Step 2 **Calculate** the results.

    4 inches × 1.25 inches = 5 square inches

> **Area Formula**
> For a rectangle:
> Area = length × width

TRY THIS Use the rectangle in Example 1.

1. Measure the sides using a metric ruler. What is the area in square centimeters?

Math Intervention
Book 6 Data Analysis and Geometry

Name _____   Date _____

 **Drawing a Rectangle and Calculating the Area**

Remember
One inch converts to 2.54 centimeters.

Draw a rectangle that is 3 inches long and 2.5 inches wide. Calculate the area in square inches and in square centimeters.

Solution

Step 1 **Draw** the rectangle using a customary ruler.

Step 2 **Calculate** the area in square inches.

   Area = 3 inches × 2.5 inches
        = 7.5 square inches

Step 3 **Calculate** the area in square centimeters.

   3 inches × 2.54 = 7.62 centimeters
   2.5 inches × 2.54 = 6.35 centimeters

   Area = 7.62 centimeters × 6.35 centimeters
        = 48.387 square centimeters

TRY THIS

2. Draw a rectangle that is 5 inches long and 4 inches wide. Calculate the area in square inches and in square centimeters.

   Area = ▢ inches × ▢ inches
        = ▢ square inches

   Area = ▢ centimeters × ▢ centimeters
        = ▢ square centimeters

Math Intervention
Book 6 Data Analysis and Geometry

Name _____ Date _____

> **Summarize**
>
> **Finding the Area of a Rectangle**
>
> A rectangle is a 4-sided figure with opposite sides parallel and equal and with four right angles.
>
> Area is the measure, in square units, of the interior region of a 2-dimensional figure or of the surface of a 3-dimensional figure.
>
> A square inch is the area of a square that is one inch long and one inch wide.

Practice

1. Using a customary ruler, measure the sides of the rectangle to the nearest inch and determine the area of the rectangle in square inches.

2. Determine the area of the rectangle in Exercise 1 in square centimeters. Use 1 inch = 2.54 centimeters.

3. Using a metric ruler, measure the sides of the rectangle to the nearest centimeter and determine the area of the rectangle in square centimeters.

4. Using a customary ruler, draw a rectangle that is **3.5** inches long and **2** inches wide. Then find its area in square inches.

5. Using a metric ruler, draw a rectangle that is **8.9** centimeters long and **4.5** centimeters wide. Then find its area in square centimeters.

Math Intervention
Book 6 Data Analysis and Geometry

Name _____ Date _____

6. What is the area of the rectangle in Exercise 4 in square centimeters?

7. Find the area of the rectangle in square inches. Round to the nearest square inch.

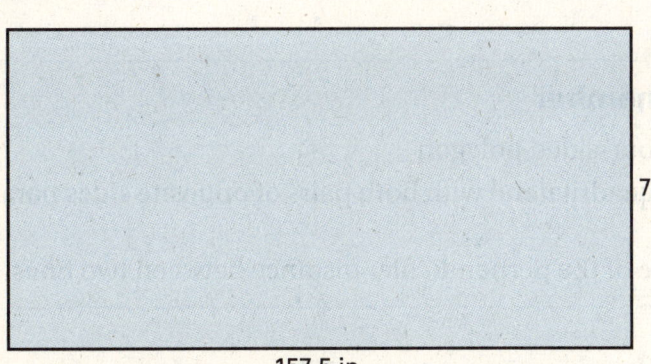

78.7 in.
157.5 in.

8. Using the rectangle in Exercise 7, calculate the area in square feet. Round to the nearest square foot. (1 inch = $\frac{1}{12}$ foot)

9. Find the area of the rectangular garden.

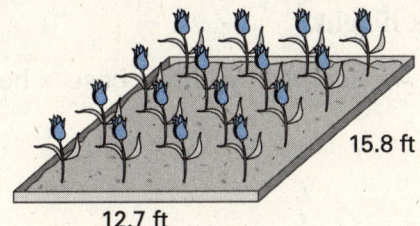

15.8 ft
12.7 ft

DID YOU GET IT?

10. **Describe a process.** How do you convert the area of a rectangle from square inches to square centimeters?

   _____
   _____

Fill in the missing words.

11. A square yard is equal to _____ square feet.

12. The area of a rectangle is _____ × _____ square units.

13. The area is a measure, in _____ units, of the interior region of a _____ figure, or the surface of a 3-dimensional figure.

Math Intervention
Book 6 Data Analysis and Geometry

LESSON 6-9
Area of a Parallelogram

> **Words to Remember**
>
> Quadrilateral: A four-sided polygon
>
> Parallelogram: A quadrilateral with both pairs of opposite sides parallel and equal
>
> Height: A measure of the perpendicular distance between two lines

Getting Started In Lesson 6-8 you found the area of a rectangle. In this lesson, you will compare the area of a rectangle to the area of a parallelogram.

Key Concept: If you label the sides of a rectangle "**base**" and "**height**", then the area of the rectangle is **base × height**.

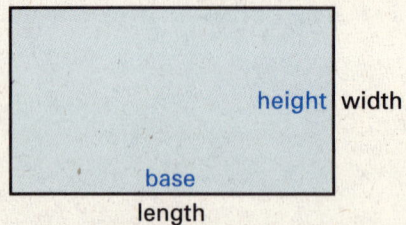

A = length × width = base × height

EXAMPLE 1  Deriving the Formula for the Area of a Parallelogram

Find the area of a parallelogram that has a base of 4 centimeters and a height of 1.8 centimeters.

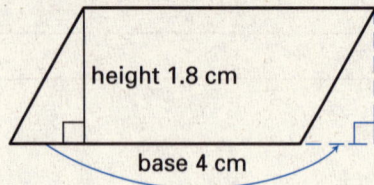

Solution

Step 1 **Cut** the right triangle from the parallelogram and move it to the other side to make a rectangle with the same base and the same height. The area of the parallelogram is the same as the area of the rectangle.

Step 2 **Find** the area. Since the area of the rectangle is **base × height,** the area of the parallelogram is **base × height**.

ANSWER The area is **4 × 1.8 = 7.2** square centimeters.

Math Intervention
Book 6 Data Analysis and Geometry

Area of a Parallelogram The formula for the area of a parallelogram is $A = \textbf{base} \times \textbf{height}$, or $A = bh$.

TRY THIS

1. The area of a rectangle is **18** square centimeters. What is the area of a parallelogram with the same length base and height?

   Area of rectangle = ☐ × ☐

   Area of parallelogram = ☐ × h

   = ☐ square centimeters

EXAMPLE 2 Finding the Area of a Parallelogram

Find the area of the parallelogram.

Solution

Step 1 Find the dimensions of the parallelogram.

   4 inches   base b

   1.5 inches   height h

Step 2 Substitute into the formula.

   $A = bh$ Area formula for a parallelogram

   $A = 4 \times 1.5 = 6$ Substitute for b and h.

ANSWER The area is **6** square inches.

TRY THIS

2. Find the area of a parallelogram with base **0.5** meter and height **0.3** meter.

   Area of parallelogram = ☐ × h

   = ☐ × ☐

   = ☐ square meter

Name _____   Date _____

> **Summarize**
>
> **Identifying a Parallelogram**
>
> A quadrilateral is a four-sided polygon.
>
> A parallelogram is a quadrilateral with two pairs of opposite sides parallel and equal.
>
> **Finding the Area of a Parallelogram**
>
> The area of a parallelogram is base times height, or $A = bh$.

Practice

1. Find the area of the parallelogram.

   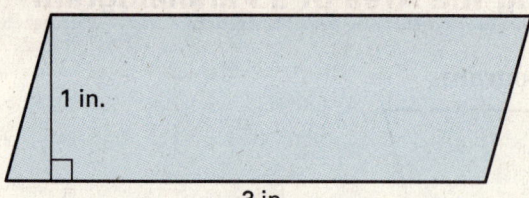

2. Using the parallelogram in Exercise 1, draw and label a rectangle with the same area. Find the area of the rectangle.

3. Find the area of the parallelogram.

   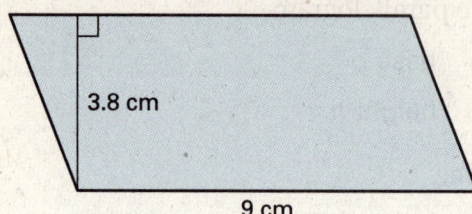

4. Using the parallelogram in Exercise 3, draw and label a rectangle with the same area. Find the area of the rectangle.

5. Draw and label a parallelogram that has a height of **2** inches and a base of **5** inches. Find the area of the parallelogram.

6. Draw and label a parallelogram that has a height of **4.5** centimeters and a base of **2.5** centimeters. Find the area of the parallelogram.

Find the area of the parallelogram described.

7. base = 3.4 cm, height = 8 cm

8. base = 9 ft, height = 3.5 ft

9. base = 4 m, height = 9 m

10. base = 6.25 in., height = 8.5 in.

Math Intervention
Book 6 Data Analysis and Geometry

Name _____ Date _____

11. Describe and correct the error in finding the area of the parallelogram.

| $A = bh$
 $= 8 \times 5$
 $= 40$ | 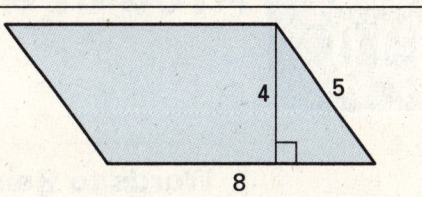 |

_____
_____

12. Show two different ways to find the area and compare your results.

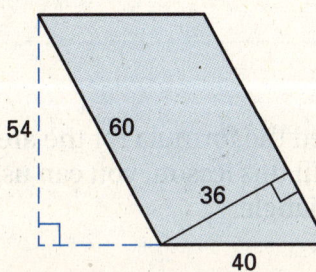

Method 1	Method 2
_____	_____
_____	_____

DID YOU GET IT?

Fill in the missing words.

13. A parallelogram is a quadrilateral with _____ pairs of opposite sides _____ and _____.

14. The area of a parallelogram is _____ × _____.

15. Describe a process. How would you find the height of a parallelogram with area 24 square centimeters if the base is 6 centimeters?

_____
_____
_____

16. Explain your reasoning. Ronny says that a rectangle is also a parallelogram. Explain how he knew this.

_____
_____
_____

LESSON 6-10 Area of a Triangle

> **Words to Remember**
>
> Area of a parallelogram: **base × height**, or $A = bh$
> Triangle: A polygon with three sides
> Area of a triangle: $\frac{1}{2}$ × **base** × **height**,
> or $A = \frac{1}{2}bh$

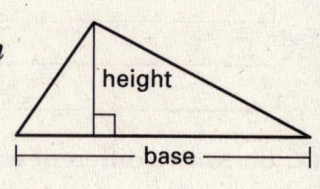

Getting Started In Lesson 6-9, you derived the formula for the area of a parallelogram from the area of a rectangle. In this lesson, you can use the area of a parallelogram to find the area of a triangle.

EXAMPLE 1 Comparing a Triangle to a Parallelogram

Find the area of a triangle with base 4 inches and height 1.5 inches.

Solution

Step 1 **Draw** the triangle described. Then add a second triangle by copying the first, flipping it over and placing it against the first triangle, as shown.

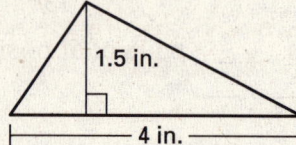 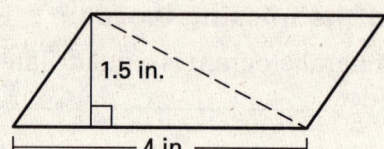

Step 2 **Notice** that the two triangles together form a parallelogram with the same base and height. So, the area of either triangle is one half of the area of the parallelogram.

Step 3 **Find** the area of the triangle.

$A = bh$ Area formula for a parallelogram

$A = \frac{1}{2}bh$ Area formula for a triangle

$= \frac{1}{2} \times 4 \times 1.5$ base = 4, height = 1.5

$= 3$ square inches

ANSWER The area of the triangle is **3** square inches.

Name _____ Date _____

TRY THIS

1. The area of a parallelogram is **32** square centimeters. What is the area of a triangle with the same length base and height?

   Area $= \frac{1}{2}bh = \frac{1}{2} \cdot \boxed{} = \boxed{}$

EXAMPLE 2 Calculating the Area of a Triangle

Find the area of the triangle.

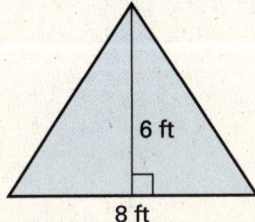

Solution

$A = \frac{1}{2}bh$ Area formula for a triangle

$= \frac{1}{2} \times 8 \times 6$ base = 8, height = 6

$= 24$

ANSWER The area is **24** square feet.

EXAMPLE 3 Calculating the Area of a Triangle

Find the area of a triangle with base 12 centimeters and height twice the base.

Solution

The height is twice **12**, or $12 \times 2 = 24$.

$A = \frac{1}{2}bh$ Area formula for a triangle

$A = \frac{1}{2} \cdot 12 \cdot 24$ base = 12, height = 24

$A = 144$

ANSWER The area is **144** square inches.

TRY THIS   Find the area of the triangle described.

2. $b = 12$ cm, $h = 10$ cm   3. $b = 2.3$ m, $h = 1.8$ m

Name _____ Date _____

> **Summarize**
>
> **Finding the Area of a Triangle**
> A triangle is a polygon with three sides.
> The area of a triangle is $A = \frac{1}{2} \times$ base $\times$ height, or $A = \frac{1}{2}bh$.

Practice

1. Find the area of the triangle.

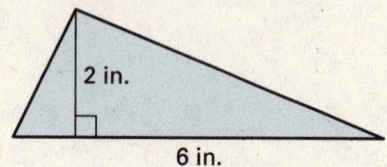

2. Using the triangle in Exercise 1, draw and label a parallelogram with the same base and height. Find the area of the parallelogram.

3. Find the area of the triangle.

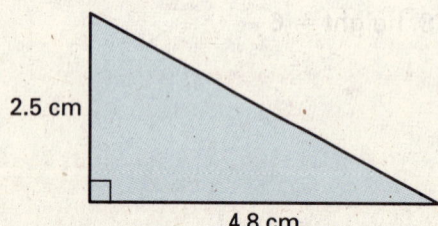

4. Using the triangle in Exercise 3, draw and label a parallelogram with the same base and height. Find the area of the parallelogram.

5. Draw and label a triangle that has a height of 2 inches and a base of 5 inches. Find the area of the triangle.

6. Draw and label a triangle that has a height of 3.5 centimeters and a base of 7 centimeters. Find the area of the triangle.

Find the area of the triangle described.

7. base = 2.4 cm, height = 6 cm

8. base = 8 ft, height = 3.2 ft

9. base = 3 m, height = 7 m

10. base = 5.25 in., height = 7.5 in.

Math Intervention
Book 6 Data Analysis and Geometry

Name _____ Date _____

11. Describe and correct the error in finding the area of the triangle.

$A = \frac{1}{2}bh$

$= \frac{1}{2} \times 5 \times 6$

$= 15$

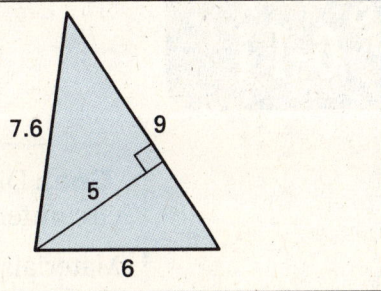

_____
_____

12. How would you find the height of a triangle with area **32** square centimeters if the base is **16** centimeters?

$A = \frac{1}{2}bh$

$\square = \frac{1}{2} \cdot \square \cdot h$

$\square = \square \cdot h$

$\square = h$

DID YOU GET IT?

Fill in the missing words.

13. A triangle is a polygon with _____ sides.

14. The area of a triangle is ____ × _____ × _____.

15. Compare methods. Show two different ways to find the area and compare your results.

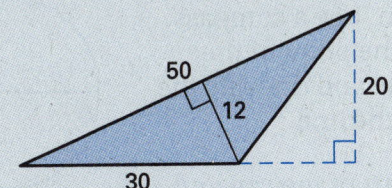

Method 1	Method 2

16. Explain your reasoning. Georgeann says that the area of a triangle is a one half the area of a rectangle. Explain how she knew this.

_____
_____

Math Intervention
Book 6 Data Analysis and Geometry **43**

Name _____ Date _____

Working with Circles and Diameters

> **Goal:** Discover the relationship between the diameter and circumference of a circle.
>
> Materials: scissors, string, paper, ruler, compass, four cans of different sizes (such as soup cans)

Getting Started Plan to use a ruler and strings to measure cans. These measures will be diameters and circumferences of circles.

Definitions

The **circumference** is the distance around a circle, and the **diameter** is the distance across a circle through the center point.

Example

Find the ratio of the diameter to the circumference of a circle.

Step 1 **Select** a can and find the diameter by using a ruler to measure across the middle of the top of the can. Diameter: ▮ inches.

Step 2 **Use** the ruler to draw a line on paper the same length as the diameter of the can. Use a compass to construct a circle by putting the point of the compass at the middle of the line and drawing the circle through the endpoints of the line.

Check Your Work

The can should fit perfectly into the circle you drew on paper.

Step 3 **Tie** a string around the round part of the can and cut it so that it is equal to the distance around the can. Then measure the length of the string. Circumference: ▮ inches.

Step 4 **Divide** the diameter into the length of the string (the circumference of the circle). The ratio should be about $\frac{22}{7}$, or **3.14**, and is called pi (π).

$$\frac{\text{length of string}}{\text{diameter}} = \frac{}{} \approx \underline{}$$

Math Intervention
Book 6 Data Analysis and Geometry

Name _____ Date _____

MAKE IT A GAME!

- Form teams of two students.
- Your team will use a ruler and string to measure each of the four cans.
- Find the ratio of diameter to circumference for each can. Write your answers to four decimal places.
- The team that has a number closest to the exact value of π (using four decimal places) wins.

Practice

Use the formula $C = \pi d$ in these exercises where C is the circumference, $\pi \approx 3.14$, and d is the diameter.

1. Find the circumference of a circle that has a diameter of **6** inches.

2. Find the circumference of a circle that has a diameter of **10** centimeters.

3. Use a customary ruler to measure the diameter of the circle below to the nearest inch. Then find the circumference.

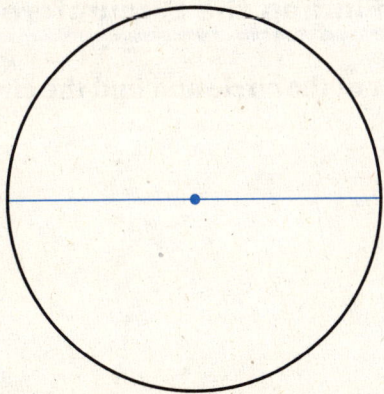

4. Find the diameter of a circle that has a circumference of **25.12** centimeters.

5. Find the diameter of a circle that has a circumference of **12.56** inches.

6. **Make a Conjecture** Based on your answers to Exercises 1–5, make a conjecture about how to find the formula for the circumference of a circle given the radius.

Definition

The **radius of a circle** is the distance from the center to the edge of the circle, or $\frac{1}{2}$ the diameter.

LESSON 6-12: Circumference of a Circle

Words to Remember

Center: A point that is the same distance from all points on a circle

Circle: A closed curve in a plane whose points are the same distance from a fixed point called the center

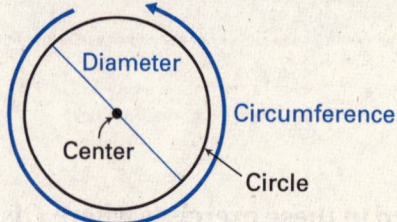

Circumference: The perimeter of a circle, or the distance around a circle

Diameter: The length of the segment through the center of the circle connecting two points of the circle

Getting Started In Activity 6-11 you learned that circumference of a circle is pi (π), the ratio of the circumference to the diameter, times the diameter. You used $\pi \approx \frac{22}{7}$ or **3.14**. In this lesson, you will find the actual value and an estimated value of the circumference of a circle.

EXAMPLE 1 Finding the Circumference of a Circle

Measure the diameter of the circle and find the circumference.

Solution

The diameter is **3** centimeters. Use the circumference formula.

$C = \pi d$
$\approx (3.14) \cdot 3$ Use $\pi \approx 3.14$.
$= 9.42$ centimeters

Approximating π
The actual circumference is 3π.
9.42 is an estimate.

TRY THIS

1. What is the circumference of a circle with diameter **8** centimeters?

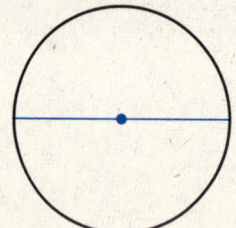

Name _____ Date _____

Definition

The radius of a circle is always $\frac{1}{2}$ the diameter. You can use either the radius or the diameter to find the circumference.

EXAMPLE 2 — Finding Circumference Using the Radius

Draw a circle that has a radius of 1.5 inches and find the circumference. Use $\pi \approx \frac{22}{7}$.

Solution

Step 1 Draw a line 1.5 inches long. Draw a circle using a compass by placing the points at each end of the line and then drawing the curve.

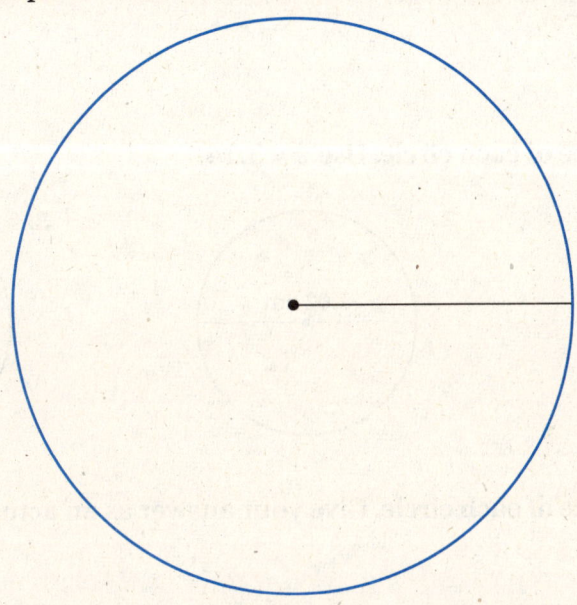

Step 2 Calculate the circumference using the radius.

$$C = 2\pi r$$
$$\approx 2 \times \frac{22}{7} \times 1.5 \text{ inches}$$
$$= 9.43 \text{ inches}$$

Formula

$C = 2\pi r$ can be used to find the circumference C with radius r. The actual circumference is 3π. 9.43 is an estimate.

TRY THIS

Find the circumference. Give the actual value and an estimate.
Use $\pi \approx 3.14$ for the estimate.

2. diameter = 5.8 cm

   $C = \pi d \approx$ ☐ · ☐ = ☐ ____

3. radius = 8.2 ft

   $C = 2\pi r \approx$ ☐ · ☐ · ☐ = ☐ ____

Find the diameter.

4. Circumference = 21.98 in.   5. radius = 4.5 cm

Math Intervention
Book 6 Data Analysis and Geometry   **47**

Name _____   Date _____

> **Summarize**
>
> Circle: A closed curve in plane whose points are the same distance from a fixed point called the center
>
> **Finding the Circumference of a Circle**
>
> $C = \pi d$ or $C = 2\pi r$
>
> You can estimate the circumference if you use $\pi \approx 3.14$ or $\pi \approx \frac{22}{7}$.

Practice

Find the circumference of each circle. Use $\pi \approx 3.14$.

1.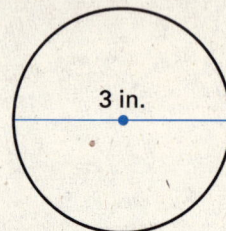
3 in.

2.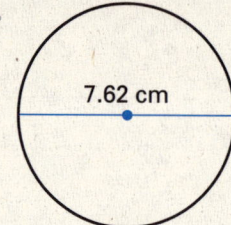
7.62 cm

3.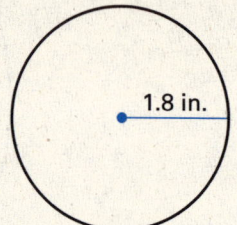
1.8 in.

Find the circumference of each circle. Give your answer as an actual value in terms of π.

4.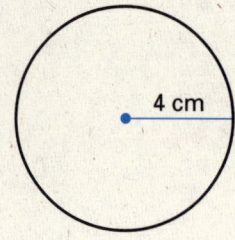
4 cm

5.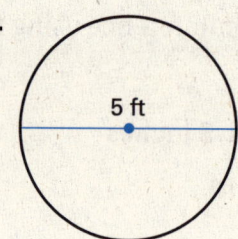
5 ft

6.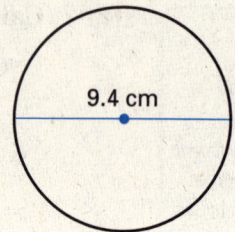
9.4 cm

Find the circumference of each circle. Use $\pi \approx \frac{22}{7}$.

7. radius = 7 in.
8. diameter = 21 cm
9. radius = 14 ft

10. diameter = 28 m
11. radius = 42 cm
12. diameter = 35 in.

Find the diameter of each circle. Use $\pi \approx 3.14$.

13. Circumference = 15.7 in.
14. radius = 6 cm

15. Circumference = 18.84 ft
16. radius = 8.2 in.

Math Intervention
Book 6 Data Analysis and Geometry

Name _____ Date _____

17. Suppose the diameter of the circle in Exercise 1 is twice as big. Will the circumference of that circle be twice as big? Explain.

_____
_____
_____

18. Suppose the radius of a circle is **4** times the radius of a smaller circle. How will their circumferences compare?

_____
_____
_____

DID YOU GET IT?

19. Write the formula. When using the diameter of a circle the formula for calculating the circumference is _____.

20. Write the formula. When using the radius of a circle the formula for calculating the circumference is _____.

21. Fill in the missing words. The center of a circle is the _____ distance from each point of the circle. The radius of a circle is _____ the diameter.

22. Describe a process. Explain how to find the diameter of a circle if you know the circumference.

_____
_____
_____

23. Explain your reasoning. Gerry says that if the diameter of one circle is three times the diameter of another circle, the circumference will be three times as much. Is she right? Explain your reasoning.

_____
_____
_____

Math Intervention
Book 6 Data Analysis and Geometry

Name _____ Date _____

LESSON 6-13 Area of a Circle

Words to Remember

Area: The measure, in square units, of the interior region of a 2-dimensional figure or of the surface of a 3-dimensional figure

Getting Started In Lesson 6-12 you found the actual and estimated circumference of a circle given its diameter or radius. You used $\pi \approx \frac{22}{7}$ or 3.14. In this lesson, you will also find the actual value and an estimated value of the area of a circle.

EXAMPLE 1 Finding the Area of a Circle

Measure the radius of the circle and find the area.

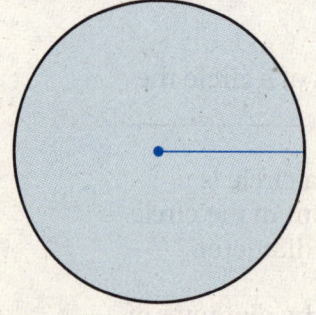

Area Formula

$A = \pi r^2$ can be used to find the area A with radius r. The actual area is 4π.

12.56 is an estimate.

Solution

The radius is 2 centimeters. Use the formula for calculating the area.

$A = \pi r^2$
$\approx (3.14)(2)^2$ Use $\pi \approx 3.14$.
$= (3.14)(4)$
$= 12.56$ square centimeters

TRY THIS

1. What is the area of a circle with radius 8 centimeters? Use $\pi \approx 3.14$.

   $A = \pi r^2$
   $\approx \boxed{} \cdot \boxed{}^2$
   $= \boxed{}$ square centimeters

2. What is the actual area of a circle with radius 5 feet?

Math Intervention
Book 6 Data Analysis and Geometry

Name _____ Date _____

EXAMPLE 2 **Finding the Area of a Circle Using the Diameter**

Draw a circle that has a diameter of 3 inches and find the area. Use $\pi \approx 3.14$.

Solution

Step 1 Draw a line 3 inches long. Use a compass to draw a circle through its endpoints.

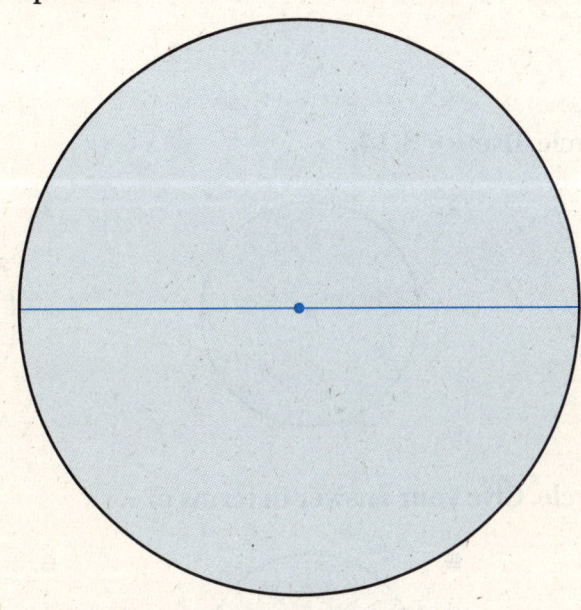

Step 2 Divide by 2 to get the radius.

$3 \div 2 = 1.5$

Notice
The actual area is 2.25π.

Step 3 Calculate the area using the standard formula.

$A = \pi r^2$

$\approx (3.14)(1.5)^2$ Use $\pi \approx 3.14$.

$= (3.14)(2.25)$

$= 7.065$ square inches

TRY THIS

Find the area. Give the actual value and an estimate. Use $\pi \approx \frac{22}{7}$ for the estimate.

3. diameter = 14 cm

4. radius = 2.1 ft

Find the radius.

5. Area = 9π in.²

6. Area = 3.14 cm²

Math Intervention
Book 6 Data Analysis and Geometry

Name _____ Date _____

> **Summarize**
>
> **Finding the Area of a Circle**
>
> The area of a circle is the measure, in square units, of the interior region of the 2-dimensional figure.
>
> **Area:** $A = \pi r^2$ You can estimate the area if you use $\pi \approx 3.14$ or $\pi \approx \frac{22}{7}$.

Practice

Find the area of the circle. Use $\pi \approx 3.14$.

1.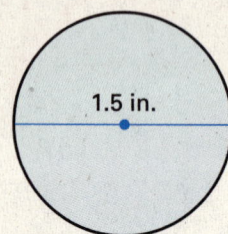
   1.5 in.

2.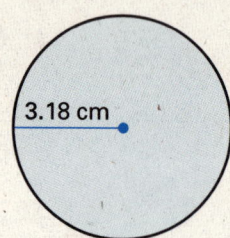
   3.18 cm

3.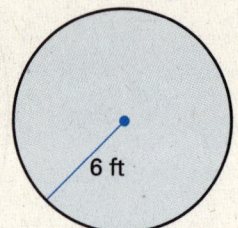
   6 ft

Find the area of the circle. Give your answer in terms of π.

4.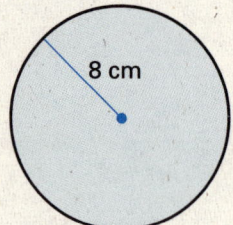
   8 cm

5.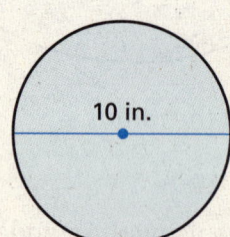
   10 in.

6.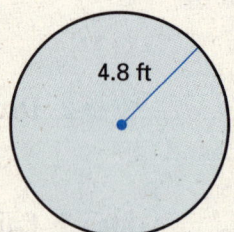
   4.8 ft

Find the area of the circle described. Use $\pi \approx \frac{22}{7}$.

7. radius = 7 in.

8. diameter = 28 cm

9. radius = 1 ft

10. diameter = 5 cm

11. radius = 4.1 in.

12. diameter = 7 cm

Find the radius. (In Exercises 17 and 18, use $\pi \approx 3.14$.)

13. Area = 16π in.²

14. Area = 121π cm²

15. Area = 49π ft²

16. Area = 25π in.²

17. Area = 28.26 cm²

18. Area = 200.96 cm²

Math Intervention
Book 6 Data Analysis and Geometry

Name _____   Date _____

19. Suppose the radius of the circle in Exercise 1 is twice as large. Will the area of that circle be twice as large? Explain.

_____
_____
_____

20. Suppose the radius of a circle is **4** times the radius of a smaller circle. How will their areas compare?

_____
_____
_____

21. Suppose the area of a circle is **4** times the area of a smaller circle. How do their radii compare?

_____
_____
_____

22. Explain how to find the area of a CD with a diameter of **12** centimeters.

_____
_____
_____

DID YOU GET IT?

23. Write the formula. When using the radius of a circle the formula for finding the area is _____.

24. Fill in the missing words. The area of a circle is the _____ of the radius times π. The area of a circle with diameter **8** is _____ times π.

25. Explain your reasoning. Kyle says that if the radius of one circle is three times the radius of another circle, the area will be three times as much. Is he right? Explain your reasoning.

_____
_____

Math Intervention
Book 6 Data Analysis and Geometry

Name _____   Date _____

Mixed Practice for Lessons 6-6 to 6-13

Vocabulary Review

Match the word with its meanings.

Word	Mathematical meaning	Everyday meaning
1. polygon ___, ___	A. closed figure whose sides meet at the endpoints	X. the distance around a circle
2. circumference ___, ___	B. diameter times π	Y. a figure with 3 or more sides

Fill in the missing word(s).

3. A _____ ruler is for linear measure based on the metric system.

4. A _____ ruler is for linear measure based on the customary system.

5. A _____ is four-sided polygon.

Measure the length of each side of the triangle in centimeters.

6.    7.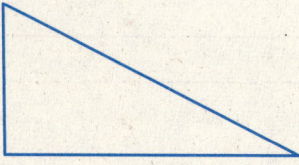

8. Find the perimeter of the triangle in Exercise 6.

Calculate the perimeter and area of the rectangle with the given length and width.

9. 5 in., 3 in.

10. 2 cm, 8 cm

11. 6 m, 3.8 m

12. 1.5 cm, 2.5 cm

For Exercises 13–15, a polygon has endpoints $A(-3, 2)$, $B(4, 2)$, $C(4, -3)$, and $D(-3, -3)$.

13. Graph the polygon on a coordinate grid.

14. Find the length of each side.

15. Find the area of the polygon if each unit in the coordinate grid represents one inch.

Math Intervention
Book 6 Data Analysis and Geometry

Name _____ Date _____

Find the area of the given parallelogram with base b and height h.

16. $b = 7$ in., $h = 4$ in.
17. $b = 9$ cm, $h = 8$ cm
18. $b = 18$ m, $h = 12$ m
19. $b = 3$ cm, $h = 6$ cm
20. $b = 11$ in., $h = 4$ in.
21. $b = 2$ m, $h = 5$ m

22. Draw and label a parallelogram that has a base of **10** centimeters and a height of **5** centimeters. Find the area of the parallelogram.

Find the area of each triangle with base b and height h.

23. $b = 4$ in., $h = 8$ in.
24. $b = 2$ cm, $h = 6$ cm
25. $b = 7$ m, $h = 8$ m
26. $b = 10$ m, $h = 2$ m
27. $b = 12$ in., $h = 3$ in.
28. $b = 9$ cm, $h = 6$ cm

Find the circumference of the given circle with diameter d or radius r. Use $\pi \approx 3.14$.

29. $d = 9$ in.
30. $r = 6$ m
31. $d = 12$ ft
32. $r = 3$ ft
33. $d = 4$ in.
34. $r = 4$ m

Find the area of the given circle with diameter d or radius r. Use $\pi \approx 3.14$.

35. $d = 8$ in.
36. $r = 10$ m
37. $r = 8$ ft
38. $d = 10$ cm
39. $r = 7$ in.
40. $d = 2$ m

Solve the problem. Then explain your answer.

41. Suppose a public park is in the shape of a circle and you want to walk all the way around the park. If the diameter of the park is two miles, how many miles will you have to walk? What is the area of the park in square miles?

_____
_____

42. Suppose that another park in your city is bordered by streets that form a rectangle. The lengths of the streets are **100** yards and **150** yards. What is the area of the park in square yards?

_____
_____

Math Intervention
Book 6 Data Analysis and Geometry

Name _____ Date _____

Finding Surface Area Using Models

> **Goal:** Find the surface area of a cube and a rectangular box using a model.
>
> **Materials:** construction paper, scissors, tape, Patterns for Cube and Box

Getting Started   In Lesson 6-8 you learned how to find the area of a rectangle. In this activity you will use this knowledge to find the surface area of a cube and of a rectangular box.

Find the surface area of a cube.

Step 1 **Draw** this pattern to scale on a piece of construction paper.

Using a Pattern
The pattern drawn here is not shown at the actual size. See your teacher for a pattern you can trace onto construction paper. On that pattern, each square is actually 2 inches by 2 inches.

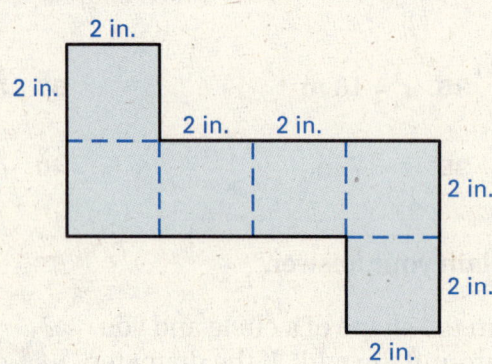

Step 2 **Cut** out your pattern and fold it on the dotted lines. Tape the edges together to make a cube.

Step 3 **Find** the area of each square face.

$A = b \times h$
$= \square \times \square$
$= \square$ square inches

Step 4 **Add** these areas together. This is the surface area of the cube.

Surface area = ___ + ___ + ___ + ___ + ___ + ___
= ___ square inches

Math Intervention
Book 6 Data Analysis and Geometry

MAKE IT A GAME!

- Form groups of four students.
- One or two groups will make a pattern for a cube that has surface area **6** square centimeters, one or two groups will make a pattern for a cube that has surface area **54** square centimeters, and one or two groups will make a pattern for a cube with surface area **96** square centimeters.
- Exchange patterns with another group, cut out the pattern you receive, make the cube, and verify its surface area.

Practice

1. What is the surface area of the cube that will be created by this pattern?

2. The cube in Exercise 1 has ▢ faces. Each face has area ▢^{2}. So, the surface area is ▢ · ▢^{2} = ▢.

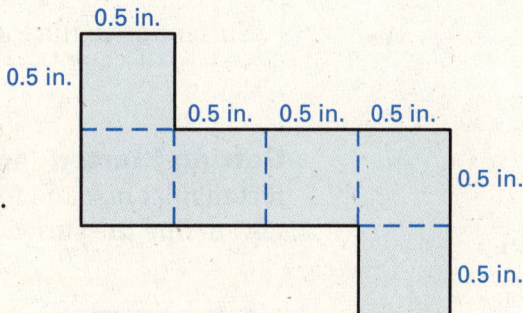

3. **Make a Conjecture** Based on your answers to Exercises 1 and 2, make a conjecture about a method to find the surface area of a cube.

Using a Pattern
See your teacher for a pattern you can use for Exercise 4.

4. Draw this pattern to scale on construction paper, cut it out, and fold it on the dotted lines. Tape the edges together to make a rectangular box. Find the surface area of the box.

5. Find the surface area of the rectangular box formed by this pattern.

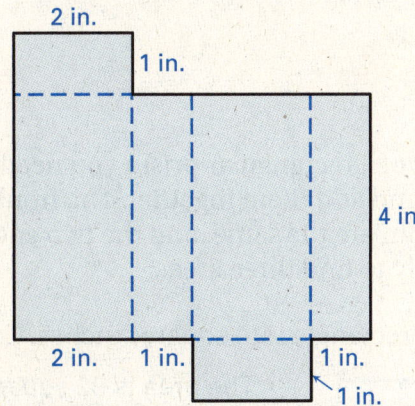

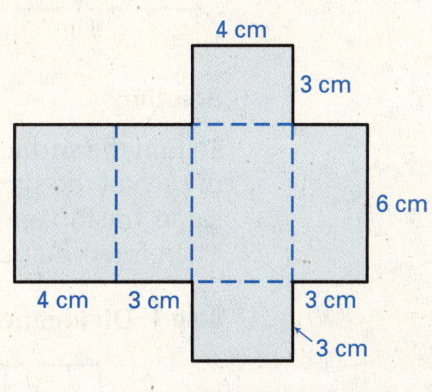

6. **Make a Conjecture** Based on your answer to Exercise 5, make a conjecture about how to find the surface area of a rectangular box.

Name _____ Date _____

LESSON 6-15 Surface Area of a Rectangular Prism

> **Words to Remember**
>
> Prism: a three-dimensional figure with two parallel bases that are the same polygons
>
> Lateral face: a face of a prism that is not a base
>
> Rectangular prism: a prism with six rectangular faces
>
> Faces: the polygons that are surfaces of a prism; *ABCD, EFGH, AEFB, DHGC, AEHD, BFGC*
>
> Surface area: the total area of all the faces

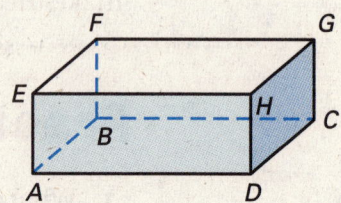

Getting Started In Activity 6-14 you constructed a cube and a rectangular box and found their surface areas. In this lesson you will learn how to find the surface area of a rectangular prism.

EXAMPLE 1 Finding Surface Area by Counting Squares

Find the surface area of the prism shown.

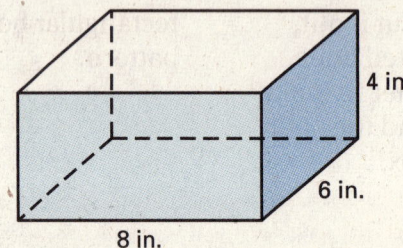

Solution

To find the surface area of a rectangular prism you need to find the area of each of the six faces and add them together. The front and back are the same, the top and bottom are the same, and the two ends are the same. Therefore, you need only to find three areas.

Step 1 **Divide** the front rectangle into squares inches. Count the squares.

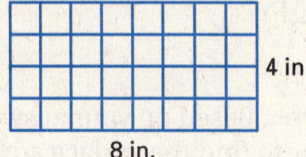

The area is 32 square inches.

(continued)

Math Intervention
58 Book 6 Data Analysis and Geometry

Step 2 Divide the bottom rectangle into square inches. Count the squares.

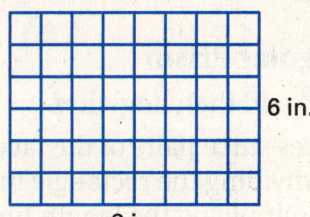

The area is 48 square inches.

Step 3 Divide the end rectangle into square inches. Count the squares.

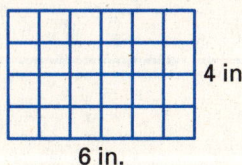

The area is 24 square inches.

> **Remember**
> Units for area are square inches or square centimeters, and so on. Units for surface area are also square inches, square centimeters, and so on.

Step 4 Add the areas.

ANSWER The surface area is 2(32) + 2(48) + 2(24) = 64 + 96 + 48 = 208 square inches.

EXAMPLE 2 Finding Surface Area Using a Formula

Find the surface area of the rectangular prism.

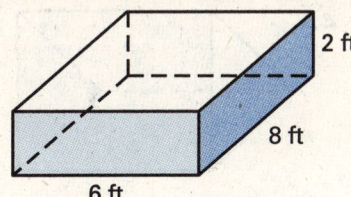

The area of each rectangle is length l times width w, or $A = lw$.

Front: 6 × 2 = 12 ft²
Bottom: 6 × 8 = 48 ft²
End: 8 × 2 = 16 ft²

ANSWER The surface area is 2(12) + 2(48) + 2(16) = 24 + 96 + 32 = 152 square feet.

TRY THIS Find the surface area of the rectangular prism.

1.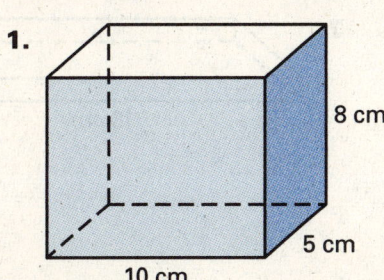

2.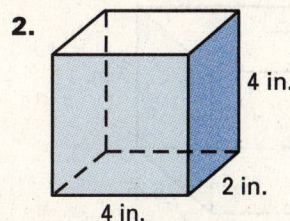

Math Intervention
Book 6 Data Analysis and Geometry

Name _____   Date _____

> **Summarize**
>
> **Finding the Surface Area of a Rectangular Prism**
>
> Find the area of each rectangular face and add them together.
>
> You only need to find the area of three faces since pairs of the faces are congruent. You can find each area by dividing the rectangle into squares and counting the squares or by multiplying the length times the width.
>
> Units for surface area are square inches, square feet, square centimeters, and so on.

Practice

Tell whether the figure is a rectangular prism.

1.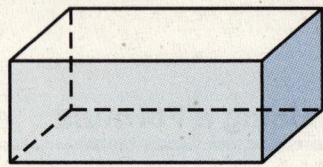

2.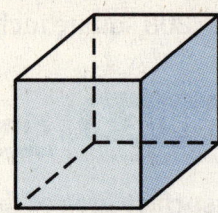

3.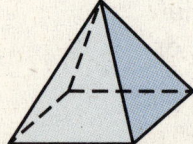

4.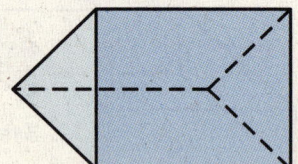

5. Name the faces of the prism.

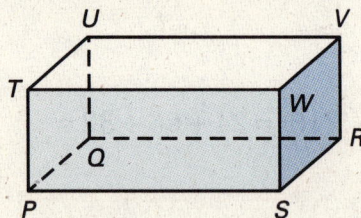

Find the surface area of the rectangular prism.

6.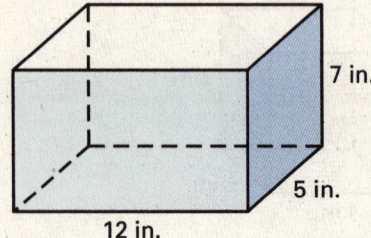

7.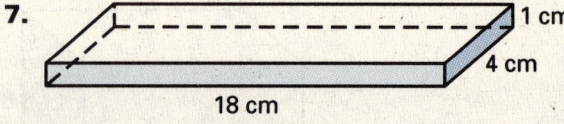

Math Intervention
Book 6 Data Analysis and Geometry

Name _____ Date _____

Find the surface area of the rectangular prism.

8.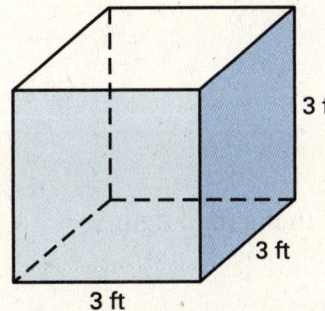

9.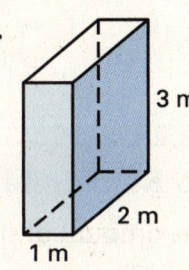

10. Nora was wrapping the birthday present shown for her friend. What is the least amount of wrapping paper she needs? Explain how you got your answer.

_____
_____
_____

DID YOU GET IT?

11. **Fill in the missing words.** A rectangular prism is a three-dimensional figure that has _____ bases which are _____. Its surface area is the sum of the area of the six _____.

12. **Describe a process.** Explain how you would find the surface area of the rectangular prism.

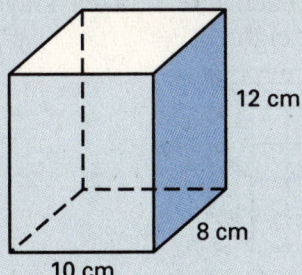

_____
_____
_____

Name _____ Date _____

LESSON 6-16 Volume of a Rectangular Prism

> **Words to Remember**
> Volume: The amount of space inside a three-dimensional figure
> Base of prism: The top or bottom face
> Height of prism: The distance between the bases
>
>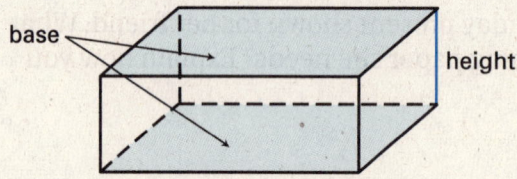

Getting Started   In Lesson 6-15 you learned how to find the surface area of a rectangular prism. In this lesson you will learn how to find the volume.

EXAMPLE 1   Finding Volume by Counting Cubes

Find the volume of the rectangular prism.

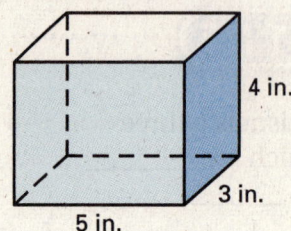

Solution

Step 1 **Divide** the prism into cubes 1 inch on each side. It takes 4 layers of 15 cubes to make the prism the right height.

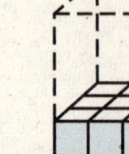 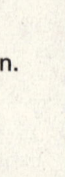 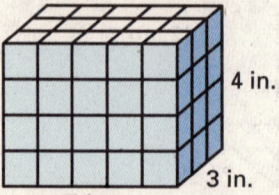

Step 2 **Count** the cubes.

4 layers of 15 cubes = 4 · 15 = 60 cubes

ANSWER The volume of each cube is 1 cubic inch. The volume of the rectangular prism is 60 cubic inches.

Units for Volume

For volume you use cubic units. This could be cubic inches, written in.³, or cubic feet, written ft³, or cubic centimeters, written cm³, and so on.

Name _____   Date _____

TRY THIS

1. Find the volume of the prism.

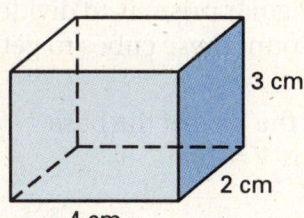

Volume Formula for a Rectangular Prism To find the volume of a rectangular prism you can find the number of cubes that will fit on the bottom and multiply that number by the height, since you are stacking rows of these cubes on top of each other until you reach the top. Therefore, the formula for the volume of a prism is $V = Bh$ where B is the area of the base and h is the height.

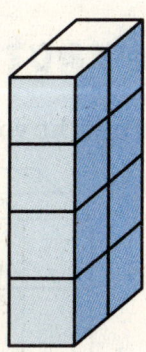

EXAMPLE 2 Finding Volume by Using a Formula

Volume Formula

Since the area of the base of a rectangular prism is $l \times w$, the volume of the prism can also be found using the formula $V = l \times w \times h$.

Find the volume of the prism.

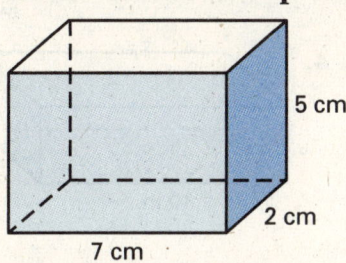

Solution

$B = l \times w$; $B = 7 \times 2 = 14$ cm²   Area of base formula

$V = Bh$; $V = 14 \times 5 = 70$ cm³   Volume formula

TRY THIS

2. Find the volume of the prism.

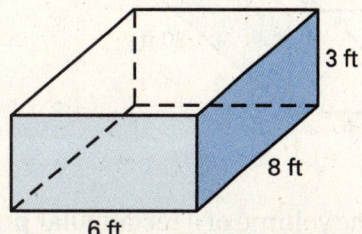

Math Intervention
Book 6 Data Analysis and Geometry

Name _____   Date _____

> **Summarize**
>
> **Finding the Volume of a Rectangular Prism**
>
> One method of finding the volume of a rectangular prism is to divide the prism into cubes one unit on each side. Count these cubes to get the volume.
>
> Another method to find the volume is to find the area of the base and multiply that by the height. The formula is **V = Bh**.
>
> Volume is expressed in cubic units.

Practice

Find the volume of the prism.

1.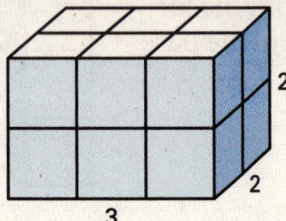

2.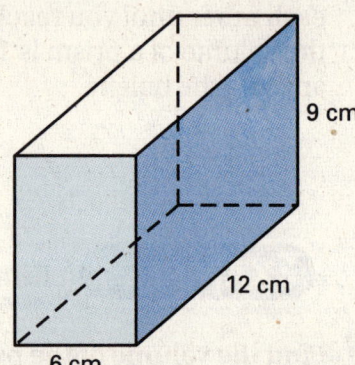

3.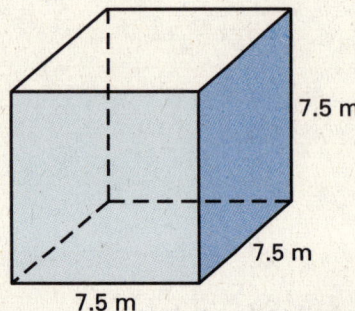

4.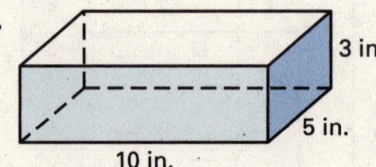

5.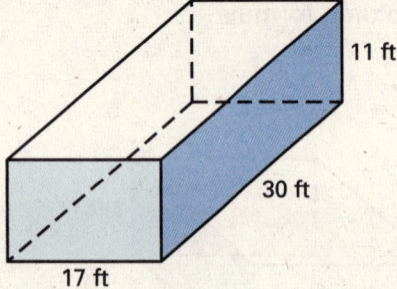

6.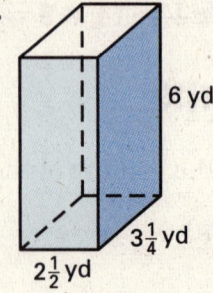

7. Find the volume of a rectangular prism with a length of 4 centimeters, a width of 5 centimeters, and a height of 2 centimeters.

Name _____   Date _____

Find the volume of the given rectangular prism with length *l*, width *w*, and height *h*.

8. $l = 7$ in., $w = 6$ in., $h = 4$ in.

9. $l = 12$ cm, $w = 8$ cm, $h = 3$ cm

10. $l = 6.5$ m, $w = 2$ m, $h = 5$ m

11. $l = 9$ ft, $w = 11$ ft, $h = 7.25$ ft

12. How many bags of $\frac{1}{2}$ cubic foot of sand are needed to fill Jerome's sandbox shown? Explain how you found your answer.

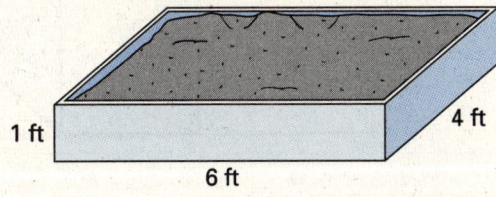

_____
_____
_____

DID YOU GET IT?

13. **Fill in the missing words.** The volume of a three-dimensional figure is the amount of _____ that it will _____.

14. **Fill in the missing words.** A method of finding the volume of a rectangular prism is to _____ the prism into cubes _____ unit on each side, and then _____ the total number of cubes.

15. **Fill in the missing words.** The volume of a rectangular prism can be found by multiplying the _____ of the _____ by the _____.

16. **Explain your reasoning.** Which swimming pool can hold more water? How much more? Explain your reasoning.

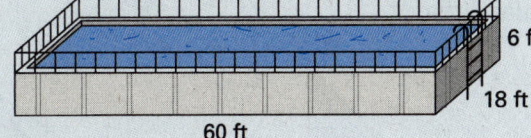 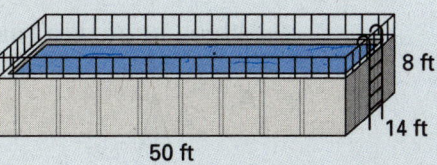

_____
_____
_____

Math Intervention
Book 6 Data Analysis and Geometry

Name _____ Date _____

LESSON 6-17
Volume of a Triangular Prism

Words to Remember
Triangular prism: a prism with two bases that are triangles

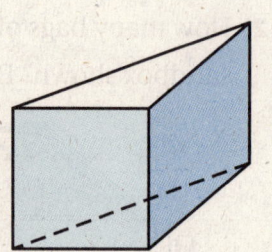

Getting Started In Lesson 6-16 you learned how to find the volume of a rectangular prism. In this lesson you will learn how to find the volume of a triangular prism.

EXAMPLE 1 Identifying a Triangular Prism

Which figure is a triangular prism?

A. 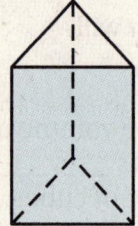   B. 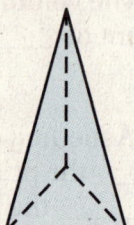   C.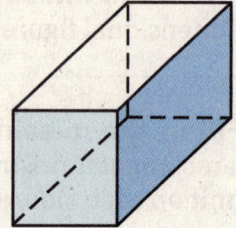

Solution

The answer is figure **A**. It is a prism with bases that are triangles. Figure **B** is not a prism. Figure **C** is a prism with bases that are rectangles.

TRY THIS

1. Which figure is a triangular prism?

A. 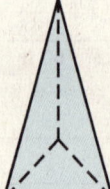   B. 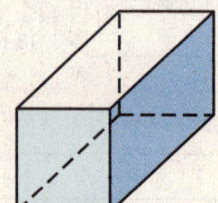   C.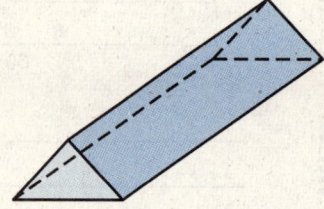

Math Intervention
Book 6 Data Analysis and Geometry

Volume of a Triangular Prism The volume of a triangular prism is found by multiplying the area of the base by the height: $V = Bh$.

EXAMPLE 2 — Finding the Volume of a Right Triangular Prism

Find the volume of the prism.

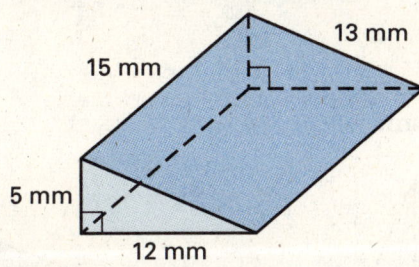

Solution

Each base of the prism is a right triangle. The area of each base is found by taking one half the product of the lengths of the two sides that form the right angle.

> **Remember**
> The area of a triangle is one half the product of its base and its height. The base of a triangle is different from the base of a prism.

$B = \frac{1}{2}bh$ Write the area of triangle formula.

$ = \frac{1}{2} \cdot 5 \cdot 12$ Substitute in values.

$ = 30 \text{ mm}^2$ Simplify.

$V = Bh$ Write the volume formula.

$ = 30 \cdot 15$ Substitute in values.

$ = 450 \text{ mm}^3$ Simplify.

TRY THIS

Find the volume of the triangular prism.

2.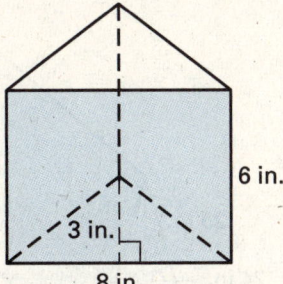

3.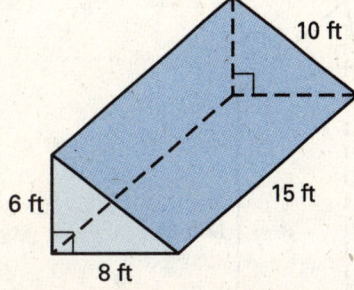

Math Intervention
Book 6 Data Analysis and Geometry

Name _____ Date _____

> **Summarize**
>
> **Finding the Volume of a Triangular Prism**
>
> The volume of a triangular prism is found by multiplying the area of the base times the height. Since the base is a triangle, its area is found by one-half the product of its base times its height.

Practice

Tell whether the figure is a triangular prism.

1.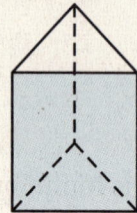
2.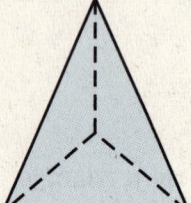
3.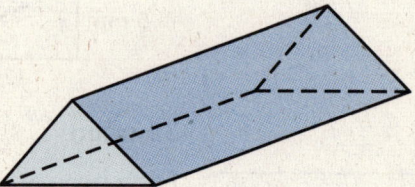

4.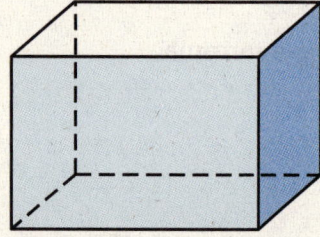
5.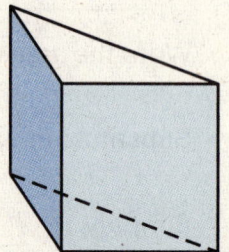
6.

Find the volume of the prism.

7.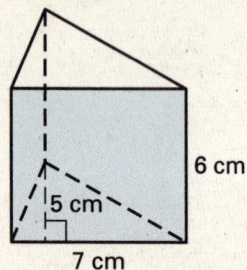
   6 cm, 5 cm, 7 cm

8.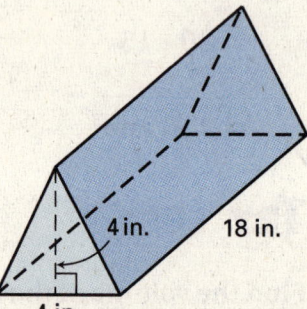
   4 in., 18 in., 4 in.

9.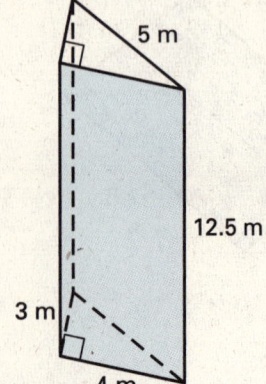
   5 m, 12.5 m, 3 m, 4 m

10.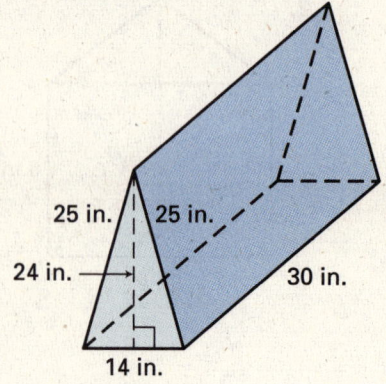
    25 in., 25 in., 24 in., 30 in., 14 in.

Math Intervention
Book 6 Data Analysis and Geometry

Name _____ Date _____

11. How is the volume of a triangular prism similar to the volume of a rectangular prism? How are they different? Explain.

_____
_____
_____

12. Compare the volumes of the prisms shown.

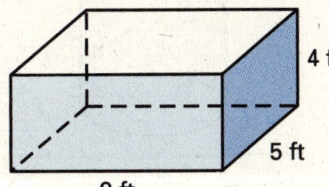 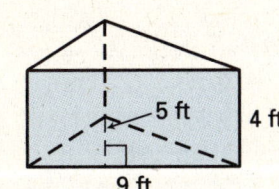

_____
_____
_____

DID YOU GET IT?

13. Fill in the missing words. A triangular prism is a three-dimensional figure that has _____ bases which are _____.

14. Fill in the missing words. The volume of a triangular prism is found by multiplying the _____ of the _____ times the _____.

15. Describe a process. Explain how you would find the volume of the prism.

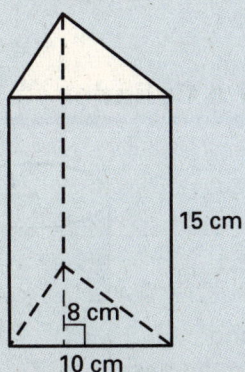

_____
_____

Name _____ Date _____

LESSON 6-18: Volume of a Cylinder

Words to Remember

Cylinder: a three-dimensional figure with two parallel bases that are circles

Getting Started In Lesson 6-16 you learned how to find the volume of a rectangular prism. In this lesson you will find the volume of a cylinder. The formula for the volume of a cylinder is the same as the formula for a prism except the base is a circle, not a rectangle. Therefore, the formula for finding the area of the base is different.

EXAMPLE 1 Identifying a Cylinder

Which figure is a cylinder?

A. 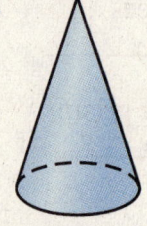   B.    C.

Solution

The answer is **B**. The top and bottom bases are circles.

EXAMPLE 2 Finding the Volume of a Cylinder

Find the volume of the cylinder.

Solution

$V = Bh$ Write the volume formula.

$B = \pi r^2 = \pi(4)^2 = 16\pi$ Substitute in values and simplify to find area of the base.

$V = 16\pi(8)$ Substitute into volume formula.

$= 128\pi$ in.³   Simplify.

$\approx 128(3.14) = 401.92$ in.³   Substitute 3.14 for π and multiply.

Remember

The base is a circle so you can find its area by multiplying π by the square of the radius. Another formula for the volume of a cylinder is $V = \pi r^2 h$.

Math Intervention
Book 6 Data Analysis and Geometry

Try This

1. Which figure is a cylinder? _____

   A. 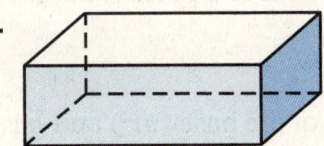 B.  C.

Check Given Information

The diameter of 10 cm is given, not the radius. It needs to be divided by two to find the radius before you can find the area of the base.

2. Find the volume of the cylinder.

   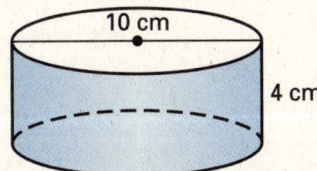

Example 3 Using Volume

Juan is filling an aquarium with water from a cylindrical container. About how many containers of water will it take to fill the aquarium? Round your answer up to a whole number.

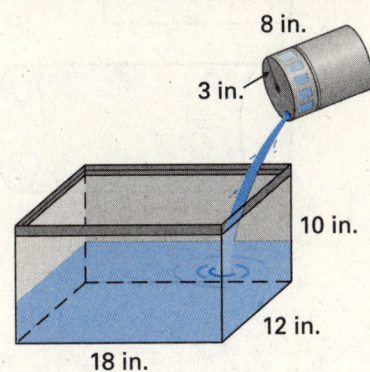

Solution

$V = Bh$	Write the volume formula.
$= (18)(12)(10)$	Substitute in values for aquarium.
$= 2160 \text{ in.}^3$	Simplify.
$= \pi(3)^2(8)$	Substitute in values for cylinder.
$= 72\pi \approx 226.08 \text{ in.}^3$	Simplify.
$2160 \div 226.08 \approx 9.55$	Divide volumes.

Remember

Divide the volume of the aquarium by the volume of the container to find how many containers of water are needed.

ANSWER Juan will need about **10** containers to fill the aquarium.

Name _____ Date _____

> **Summarize**
>
> **Identifying a Cylinder**
>
> A cylinder is a three-dimensional figure that has two parallel bases that are circles.
>
> **Finding the Volume of a Cylinder**
>
> Use the formula $V = Bh$ where B is the area of the base (πr^2) and h is the height.

Practice

Tell whether the figure is a cylinder.

1.

2.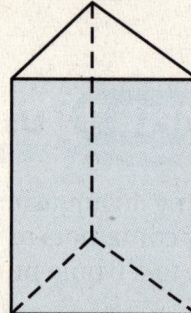

3.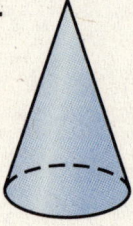

4.

Find the volume of the cylinder.

5.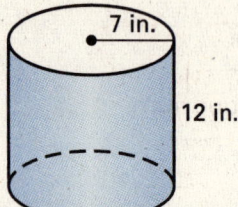

6.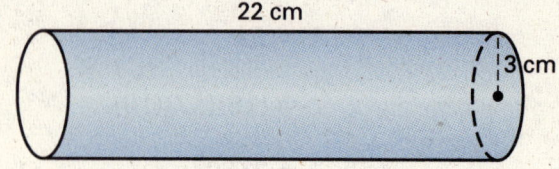

7.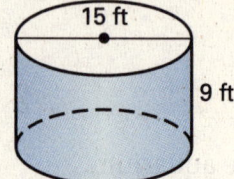

8.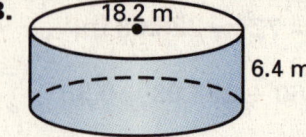

Math Intervention
Book 6 Data Analysis and Geometry

Name _____ Date _____

Find the volume of the cylinder described.

9. A cylinder with radius 6 in., height 12 in.

10. A cylinder with diameter 20 cm, height 4 cm

11. A cylinder with radius 15 cm, height 5 cm

12. A cylinder with diameter 8 in., height 7 in.

13. Marie has a box of rice that is 4.8 inches by 6 inches by 1.8 inches. How many cylindrical containers with diameter 4 inches and height 2.5 inches can she fill? Round your answer down to a whole number. Explain how you found your answer.

    _____

    _____

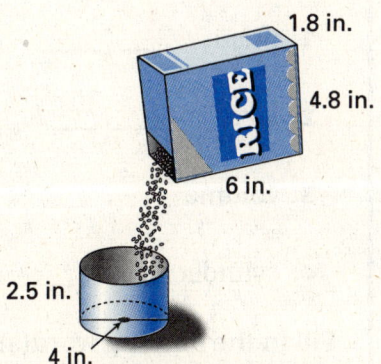

DID YOU GET IT?

14. **Fill in the missing words.** A cylinder is a three-dimensional figure with _____ bases that are _____.

15. **Describe a process.** Describe how you would find the volume of a cylindrical garbage can with height 3 feet and radius 1 foot.

    _____

    _____

16. **Explain your reasoning.** Jeff has a cylinder 35 centimeters tall with a diameter of 18 centimeters and a rectangular prism with height 35 centimeters, width 15 centimeters, and length 18 centimeters. Which has the greater volume? Explain.

    _____

    _____

    _____

Name _____   Date _____

Mixed Practice for Lessons 6-15 to 6-18

Vocabulary Review

Match the word with its mathematical meaning and its everyday meaning.

Word	Mathematical meaning	Everyday meaning
1. prism ___, ___	A. surface of a prism	W. chamber in an engine
2. face ___, ___	B. solid with two parallel circular bases	X. loudness or softness
3. volume ___, ___	C. solid with two parallel polygonal bases	Y. transparent body to decompose light
4. cylinder ___, ___	D. space contained in a solid	Z. front part of head

Fill in the missing word(s).

5. The volume of a prism is found by multiplying the _____ of the _____ by the height.

Identify the figure.

6.

7.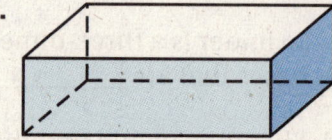

8.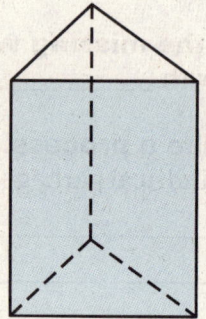

Find the surface area of the figure.

9.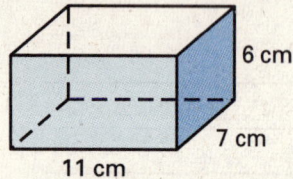
6 cm, 7 cm, 11 cm

10.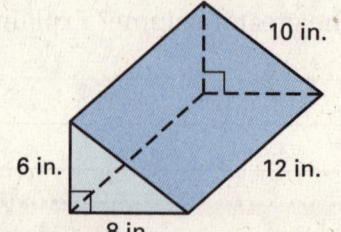
10 in., 6 in., 12 in., 8 in.

11.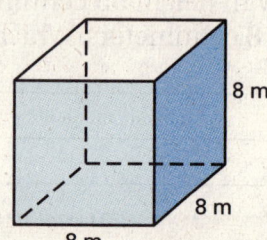
8 m, 8 m, 8 m

12. Find the surface area of a rectangular prism with length **8** inches, width **3** inches, and height **2** inches.

13. Find the surface area of a triangular prism **5** feet high if the base has side lengths **6** feet, **6** feet, and **6** feet and area **15.6** square feet.

Math Intervention
Book 6 Data Analysis and Geometry

Name _____ Date _____

Find the volume of the figure. Use 3.14 for π. Round to the nearest tenth if needed.

14.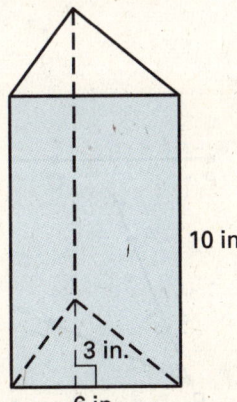

15.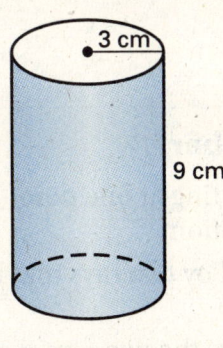

16.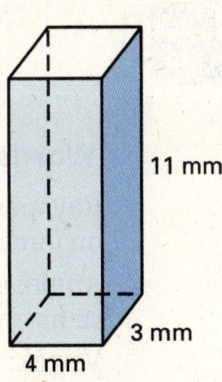

17. Zach has two containers for his turtle. One is a rectangular prism with length 30 inches, width 12 inches, and height 15 inches. The other is a cylindrical container with radius 9 inches and height 22 inches. Find the volume of each. Which has the greater volume? How much greater?

_____
_____

18. Petra is painting stands to display her plants. Which stand will require more paint? Explain your answer.

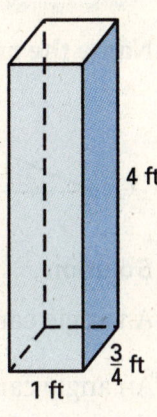 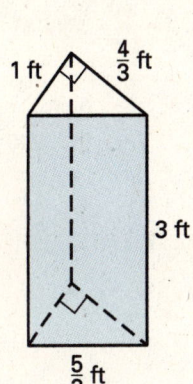

_____
_____

19. What is the volume of Donnie's toy box shown? Explain how you found your answer.

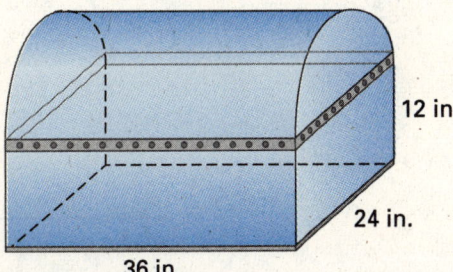

_____
_____

Math Intervention
Book 6 Data Analysis and Geometry

LESSON 6-19 Angles

> **Words to Remember**
>
> **Ray:** part of a line, starting at one point and going on forever in one direction
>
> **Angle:** a figure formed by two rays that have the same endpoint; ∠ABC
>
> **Vertex:** the point where the two rays meet; B

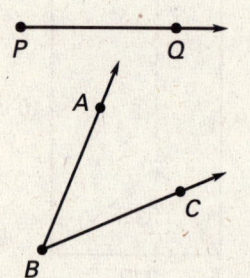

Getting Started In this lesson you will learn about angles. The symbol ∠*ABC* is read "angle *ABC*." The symbol $\overrightarrow{AB}$ is read "ray *PQ*" or "the ray from *P* through *Q*."

EXAMPLE 1 Naming an Angle

Name the angle shown.

Solution

An angle can be named by the letter at its vertex. ∠*X*

An angle can also be named by a point on each ray and the vertex. The letter at the vertex must be in the middle. ∠*WXY* or ∠*YXW*

TRY THIS Name the angle three ways.

1.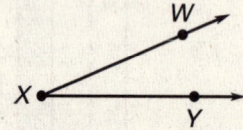

2.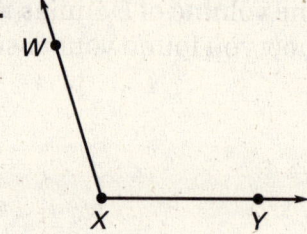

1.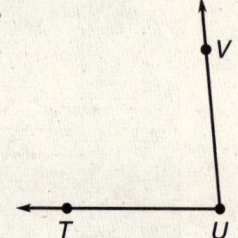

2.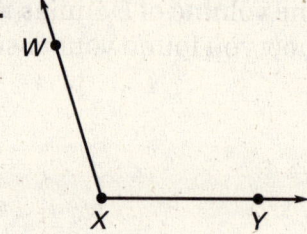

Measuring Angles An angle is measured in degrees using a *protractor*. The measure of angle *A* is written *m*∠*A*. If the measure of angle *A* is 60 degrees, you write *m*∠*A* = 60°.

Math Intervention
Book 6 Data Analysis and Geometry

Name _____ Date _____

EXAMPLE 2 Measuring an Angle Using a Protractor

Measure the angle shown.

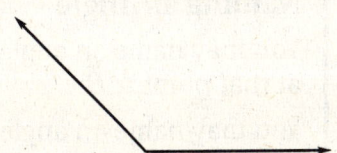

Solution

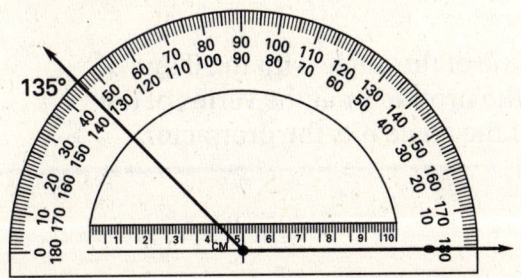

Line up one side of the angle on the 0 line of the protractor.

Place the vertex of the angle at the center of the protractor.

Read where the other side of the angle intersects the protractor.

The measure is 135°.

EXAMPLE 3 Drawing an Angle Using a Protractor

Draw an angle with measure 20°.

Solution

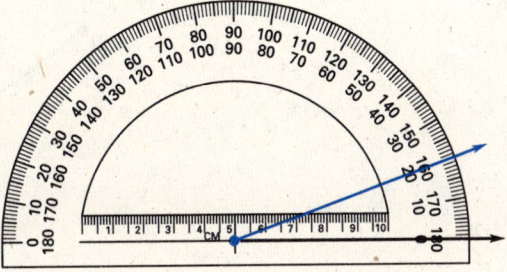

Draw a ray.

Place the center of the protractor at the vertex.

Line up the ray on the 0 line of the protractor.

Mark where 20° is on the protractor.

Draw a ray from the vertex to that point.

Remember
Mark 20° using the same scale that includes the 0 which you used to line up the given ray.

TRY THIS

Be Careful
Be sure to read the scale of the protractor that corresponds to the one where you lined up the side of the angle with 0.

Measure the angle with your protractor.

3.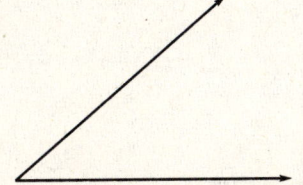

4.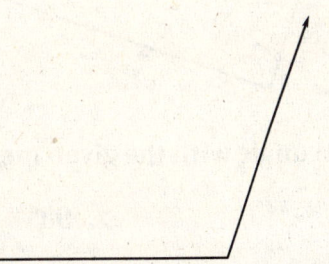

5. Draw an angle with measure 55°.

Math Intervention
Book 6 Data Analysis and Geometry   77

Name _____   Date _____

> **Summarize**
>
> **Naming an Angle**
>
> You may name an angle using the vertex letter if there is only one angle at that point. ∠B
>
> You may name an angle using three points, one at the vertex and one on each side of the angle. ∠ABC, ∠CBA
>
> **Measuring an Angle**
>
> To measure an angle, line up one side of the angle with the **0** line of the protractor. Place the center of the protractor at the vertex of the angle. Read where the other side of the angle hits the protractor.

Practice

Name the angle three ways.

1.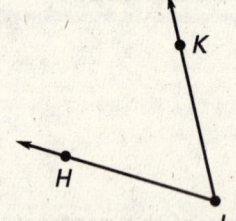
2.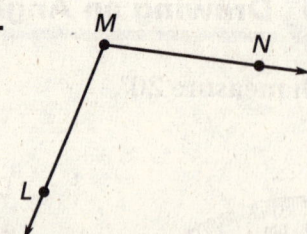
3.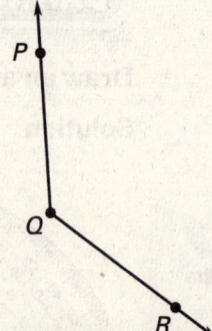

Measure the angle with your protractor.

4.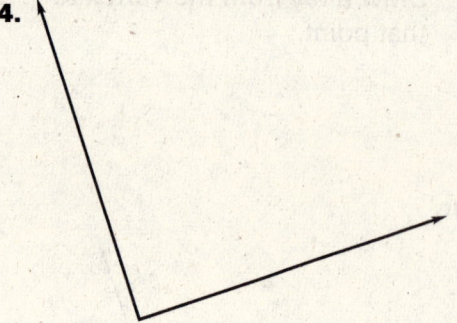
5.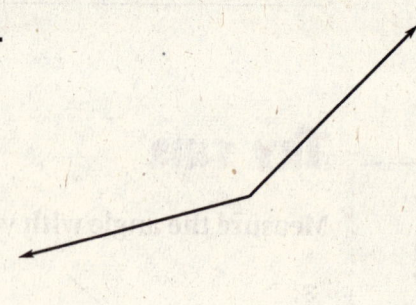

Draw an angle with the given measure.

6. 5°
7. 98°
8. 162°
9. 76°
10. 89°
11. 120°
12. 64°
13. 137°

Math Intervention
Book 6 Data Analysis and Geometry

Name _____   Date _____

There are three angles in this figure. Use this figure for Exercises 14–16.

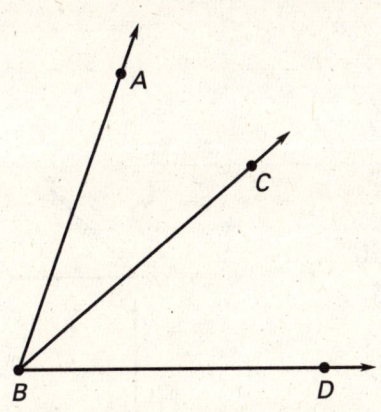

14. Tammy named one of the angles ∠B. Explain why that is not a good name for her to use.
_____
_____
_____

15. Name the three angles in the figure.
_____

16. Measure the three angles.
_____
_____

DID YOU GET IT?

17. **Fill in the missing words.** An angle is formed by _____ that have the _____ _____.

18. **Find the error.** Martin measured the angle shown and got 140°. Explain his mistake. What is the measure of this angle?

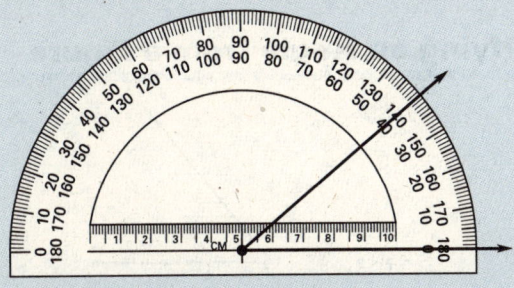

_____
_____

Math Intervention
Book 6 Data Analysis and Geometry   **79**

LESSON 6-20

Classify Angles

Words to Remember

Acute angle: angle with measure less than **90°**

Right angle: angle with measure **90°**

Obtuse angle: angle with measure greater than **90°** and less than **180°**

Straight angle: angle with measure **180°**

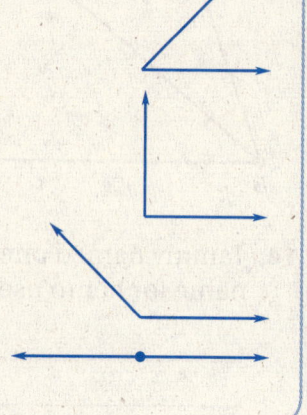

Getting Started In Lesson 6-19 you learned how to measure an angle. In this lesson you will learn names for different types of angles.

EXAMPLE 1 Classifying an Angle

The measure of an angle is 100°. What type of angle is it?

Solution

Since **100°** is between **90°** and **180°**, the angle is obtuse.

TRY THIS Classify an angle with the given measure.

1. 90°   2. 74°   3. 180°   4. 126°

EXAMPLE 2 Classifying an Angle from a Figure

What type of angle is ∠X?

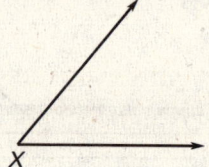

Solution

Measure ∠X with your protractor.

Since the measure is **50°**, the angle is acute.

Math Intervention
Book 6 Data Analysis and Geometry

Name _____   Date _____

TRY THIS   Find the measure of the given angle. Then classify the angle as acute, right, obtuse, or straight.

5.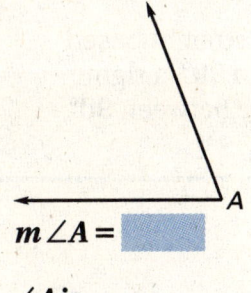

$m\angle A =$ ▭

$\angle A$ is _____.

6.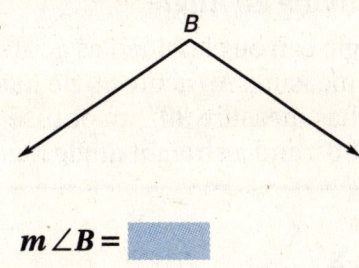

$m\angle B =$ ▭

$\angle B$ is _____.

Recognizing Angles   To tell if an angle is a right angle, you can place the corner of a sheet of paper in the angle. The sides of the angle should line up with the sides of the paper. To tell if an angle is a straight angle, you can place a straightedge along it. It should be a straight line.

Symbol

To indicate that an angle is a right angle, draw a small box at its vertex.

EXAMPLE 3   Identifying a Right Angle

Which angle is a right angle?

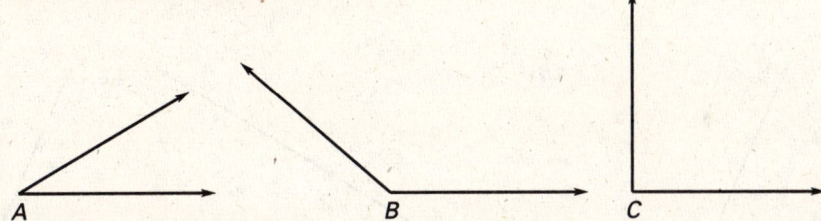

Solution

$\angle C$ is a right angle since it lines up with the sides of a piece of paper.

TRY THIS   Classify the angle as acute, right, obtuse, or straight.

7.

8.

9.

10.

Math Intervention
Book 6 Data Analysis and Geometry   **81**

Name _____ Date _____

> **Summarize**
> **Classifying an Angle**
> An angle can be classified as acute, right, obtuse, or straight based on its measure. An acute angle has measure less than **90°**, a right angle has measure **90°**, an obtuse angle has measure between **90°** and **180°**, and a straight angle has measure **180°**.

Practice

Classify the angle as acute, right, obtuse, or straight.

1. 82°
2. 97°
3. 150°
4. 90°
5. 180°
6. 84°

7.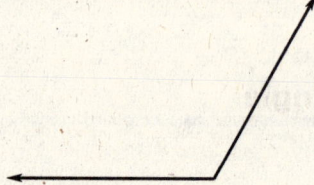
8.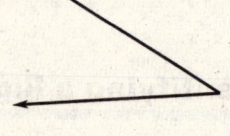
9.

10.
11.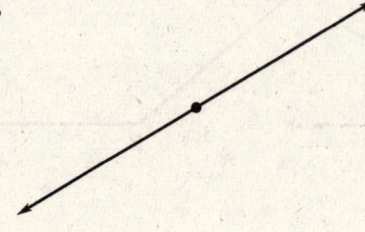
12.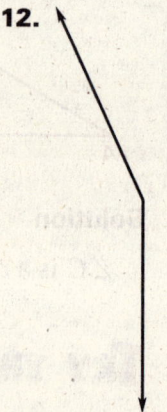

13.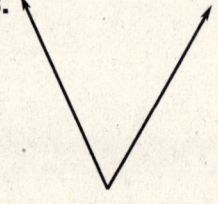
14.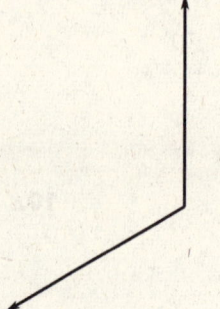
15.

Math Intervention
Book 6 Data Analysis and Geometry

Name _____   Date _____

16. Explain how you could use the corner of a piece of paper to identify an obtuse angle.

_____
_____
_____

17. Explain what a straight angle looks like.

_____
_____
_____

18. Name a common object in addition to the corner of a piece of paper that you could use to classify angles.

_____
_____
_____

DID YOU GET IT?

19. Fill in the missing words. An angle with measure less than 90° is called an _____ angle, while an angle with measure more than 90° and less than 180° is called an _____ angle.

20. Draw a diagram. Given that $m\angle ABC = 45°$ and $m\angle CBD = 45°$, where D is not on $\overrightarrow{BA}$, draw a figure to illustrate these angles.

21. Explain your reasoning. Classify $\angle ABD$ in the figure you drew for Exercise 20. Explain how you obtained your answer.

_____
_____
_____

Name _____ Date _____

LESSON 6-21
Complementary and Supplementary Angles

Words to Remember

Complementary angles: two angles whose sum is **90°**; example: **30°** and **60°**

Supplementary angles: two angles whose sum is **180°**; example: **30°** and **150°**

Getting Started In Lesson 6-20 you learned how to classify an angle. In this lesson you will learn how to classify pairs of angles.

EXAMPLE 1 Identifying Pairs of Angles

Is the pair of angles complementary, supplementary, or neither?

a. $m\angle C = 68°$, $m\angle D = 112°$ b. $m\angle P = 32°$, $m\angle Q = 58°$

Solution

a. $m\angle C + m\angle D = 68° + 112°$ Substitute measures.
   $= 180°$ Add.

   ANSWER Angles C and D are supplementary because their sum is **180°**.

b. $m\angle P + m\angle Q = 32° + 58°$ Substitute measures.
   $= 90°$ Add.

   ANSWER Angles P and Q are complementary because their sum is **90°**.

TRY THIS Are the angles complementary, supplementary, or neither?

1. 10°, 80°   2. 60°, 130°
3. 98°, 82°   4. 6°, 174°

Complementary and Supplementary Angles When two angles are complementary, one is the *complement* of the other. When two angles are supplementary, one is the *supplement* of the other.

Math Intervention
Book 6 Data Analysis and Geometry

EXAMPLE 2 Finding the Complement of an Angle

Find the measure of the complement of the angle.

a. $m\angle A = 64°$ b. $m\angle B = 27°$

Solution

a.
$64 + ? = 90$ Complementary angles add up to 90°.
$64 + ? - 64 = 90 - 64$ Subtract 64 from each side.
$? = 26$ Simplify.

ANSWER The complement of $\angle A$ has measure **26°**.

b.
$27 + ? = 90$ Complementary angles add up to 90°.
$27 + ? - 27 = 90 - 27$ Subtract 27 from each side.
$? = 63$ Simplify.

ANSWER The complement of $\angle B$ has measure **63°**.

> **Alternate Method**
> To find the complement of an angle you can subtract the given angle measure from 90°.
> $90° - 64° = 26°$

EXAMPLE 3 Finding the Supplement of an Angle

Find the measure of the supplement of the angle.

a. $m\angle C = 104°$ b. $m\angle D = 121°$

Solution

a.
$104 + ? = 180$ Supplementary angles add up to 180°.
$104 + ? - 104 = 180 - 104$ Subtract 104 from each side.
$? = 76$ Simplify.

ANSWER The supplement of $\angle C$ has measure **76°**.

b.
$121 + ? = 180$ Supplementary angles add up to 180°.
$121 + ? - 121 = 180 - 121$ Subtract 121 from each side.
$? = 59$ Simplify.

ANSWER The supplement of $\angle D$ has measure **59°**.

> **Alternate Method**
> To find the supplement of an angle you can subtract the given angle measure from 180°.
> $180° - 104° = 76°$

Not All Angles have Complements When the measure of an angle is greater than 90° it will not have a complement.

> **Notice**
> The measure of the supplement of an angle is 90° more than the measure of the complement of the same angle.

TRY THIS Find the measures of the complement and the supplement of the angle, if possible.

5. 15°   6. 71°

7. 120°   8. 42°

Math Intervention
Book 6 Data Analysis and Geometry

Name _____   Date _____

> **Summarize**
>
> **Identifying Pairs of Angles as Complementary or Supplementary**
>
> To identify complementary or supplementary angle pairs, add their measures. If the sum is **90°**, they are complementary. If the sum is **180°**, they are supplementary.
>
> **Solving Problems with Complementary and Supplementary Angles**
>
> To find the complement of a given angle, find what angle must be added to it to get **90°**. To find the supplement of a given angle, find what angle must be added to it to get **180°**.

Practice

Is the pair of angles complementary, supplementary, or neither? Use a protractor if necessary.

1. 17°, 63°

2. 9°, 81°

3.
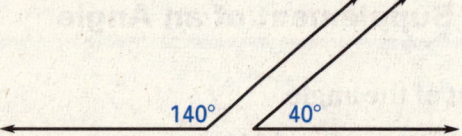

4.
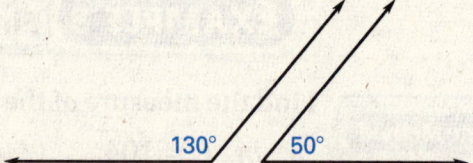

5.
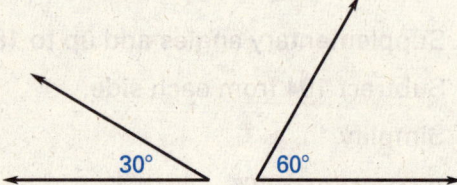

6.
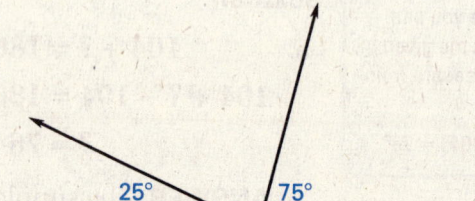

7.
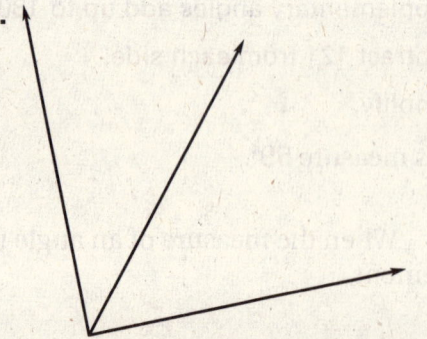

8.
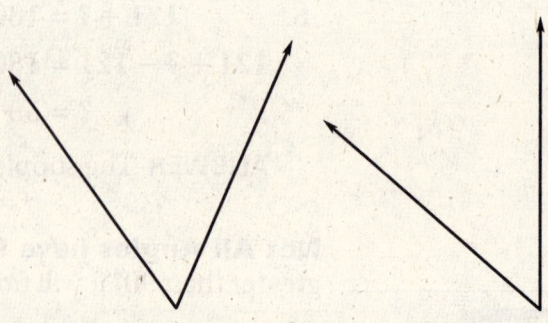

Find the measures of the complement and supplement of the angle, if possible.

9. 26°   10. 1°   11. 84°   12. 110°

Math Intervention
Book 6 Data Analysis and Geometry

Name _____   Date _____

13. Can two angles be complementary and equal in measure? Explain.
_____
_____
_____

14. Can two angles be supplementary and both acute? Explain.
_____
_____
_____

15. Can a complementary angle be obtuse? Explain.
_____
_____
_____

DID YOU GET IT?

16. Fill in the missing words. Two angles are _____ if the sum of their measures is **90°**.

17. Fill in the missing words. Two angles are _____ if the sum of their measures is **180°**.

18. Find the error. Angela says the complement of a **54°** angle is **126°**. Is she correct? Explain.
_____
_____
_____

19. Explain your reasoning. Can two right angles be complementary or supplementary? Explain your reasoning.
_____
_____
_____

Math Intervention
Book 6 Data Analysis and Geometry

Lesson 6-22: Classify Triangles

Getting Started In Lesson 6-20 you learned how to classify angles. In this lesson you will learn how to classify triangles. Triangles can be classified by their angles or by their sides.

Key Concept

Acute triangle: a triangle with all three angles acute

Obtuse triangle: a triangle with one obtuse angle

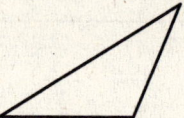

Right triangle: a triangle with one right angle

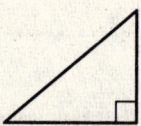

EXAMPLE 1 — Classifying a Triangle by its Angles

Remember
For a triangle to be obtuse, it only needs to have one obtuse angle. But for it to be acute, all three angles must be acute.

Tell whether the triangle is acute, obtuse, or right.

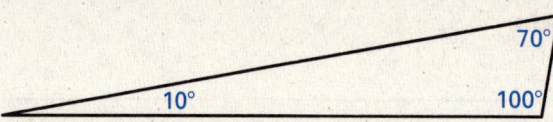

Solution

Since one angle is more than **90°**, the triangle is obtuse.

TRY THIS — Classify the triangle by its angles.

1.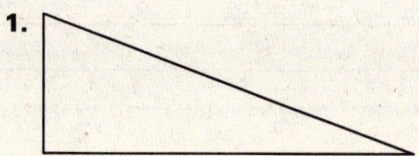

2.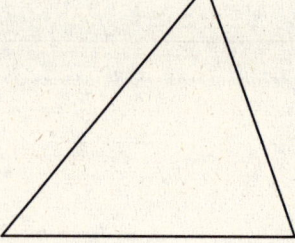

Key Concept

Scalene triangle: a triangle with no equal sides

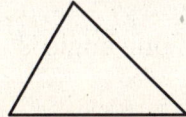

Isosceles triangle: a triangle with at least two equal sides

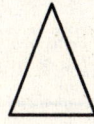

Equilateral triangle: a triangle with three equal sides

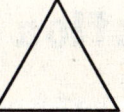

EXAMPLE 2 Classifying a Triangle by its Sides

Tell whether the triangle is equilateral, isosceles, or scalene.

Solution

Since two sides are equal, the triangle is isosceles.

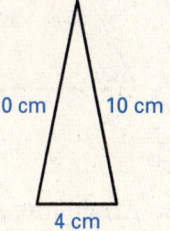

TRY THIS Classify the triangle by its sides.

3.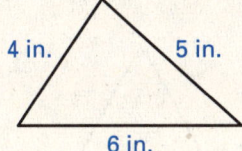

4.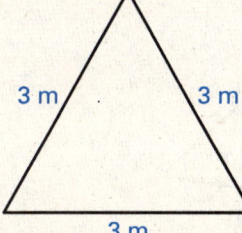

EXAMPLE 3 Drawing a Triangle

Draw an equilateral triangle.

Solution

Draw a segment. Make intersecting arcs from each endpoint with your compass using that segment length for the radius. Connect the points to draw the triangle.

> **Notice**
> You know the triangle is equilateral because you constructed it with all three sides the same length.

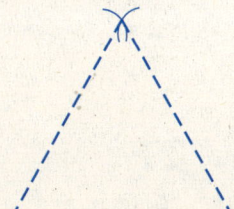

Name _____ Date _____

> **Summarize**
>
> **Classifying a Triangle by its Angles**
>
> A triangle is acute if all three angles are acute. It is obtuse if one angle is obtuse. It is right if one angle is right.
>
> **Classifying a Triangle by its Sides**
>
> A triangle is equilateral if all three sides are equal. It is isosceles if at least two sides are equal. It is scalene if no sides are equal.

Practice

Classify the triangle as acute, right, or obtuse.

1.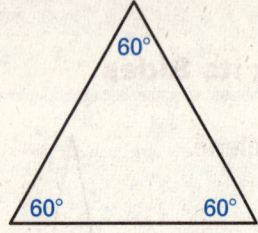

2.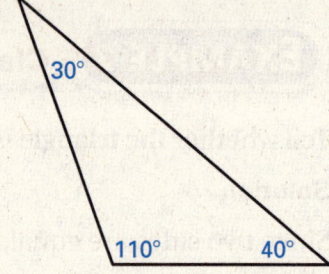

3. Angle measures 5°, 15°, 160°

4. Angle measures 17°, 90°, 73°

Classify the triangle as equilateral, isosceles, or scalene.

5.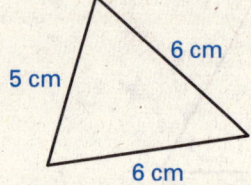

6.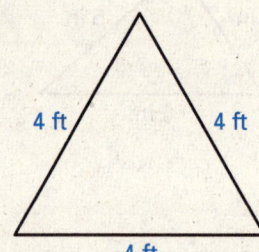

7. Side lengths 5 in., 12 in., 13 in.

8. Side lengths 7.2 cm, 8 cm, 7.2 cm

Draw the described triangle.

9. Triangle with angles 50°, 50°, and 80°

10. Triangle with sides 2 in., 2 in., 2 in.

11. Isosceles right triangle

Math Intervention
Book 6 Data Analysis and Geometry

Name _____ Date _____

12. Can a triangle be isosceles and obtuse? Explain.
_____
_____
_____

13. Look at the triangle you drew in Exercise 10. Use a protractor to measure its angles. Explain why the triangle might be called *equiangular*.
_____
_____

14. What can you say about the measures of the angles of an isosceles right triangle? What do you think they measure?
_____
_____
_____

DID YOU GET IT?

15. Fill in the missing words. An equilateral triangle has _____ sides. An isosceles triangle has _____ sides. An obtuse triangle has _____ angle _____ than _____.

16. Describe a process. A triangle has angles with measure 62°, 58°, and 60°. How can you determine whether it is acute, right, or obtuse?
_____
_____
_____

17. Explain your reasoning. Can a triangle have two right angles? Explain your reasoning.
_____
_____
_____

Name _____ Date _____

Finding the Sum of the Angles in a Triangle

> **Goal:** Find the sum of the measures of the angles of a triangle and a quadrilateral.
> **Materials:** protractor, straightedge, scissors, Triangle Patterns

Getting Started In Lesson 6-22 you learned how to classify a triangle by its angles. Now you will investigate the sum of the angles of a triangle. You will use this information in Lesson 6-24.

Use a model of a triangle to find the sum of its angles.

Step 1

Draw a triangle on a sheet of paper and cut it out. Label the angles.

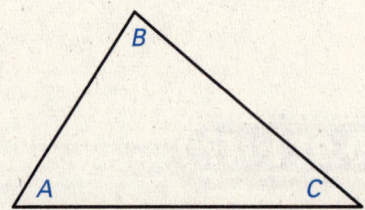

Step 2

Tear off the corners and rearrange them so all the vertices are next to each other.

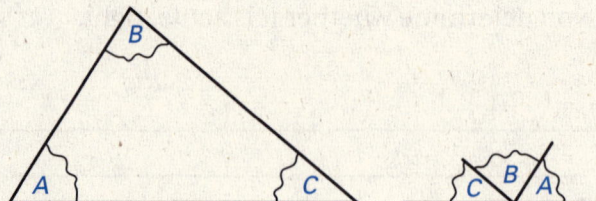

Step 3

Line up a straightedge by your triangle pieces. What angle do they form? What is its measure?

ANSWER A _____ angle with measure _____.

Math Intervention
Book 6 Data Analysis and Geometry

MAKE IT A GAME!

- Form groups of four students.
- One student in each group creates an obtuse triangle, one an acute triangle, one a right isosceles triangle, and one a right scalene triangle.
- The group completes the example in the activity.
- Compare the sums of the measures of the angles of the triangles. What do you notice?

Practice

Use a protractor to measure the angles in the triangle. Find the sum of the measures.

1.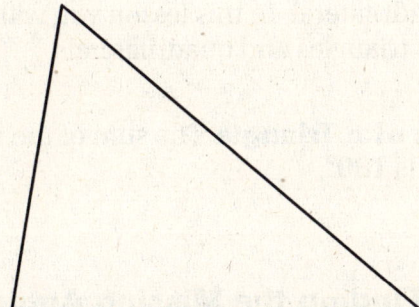

2.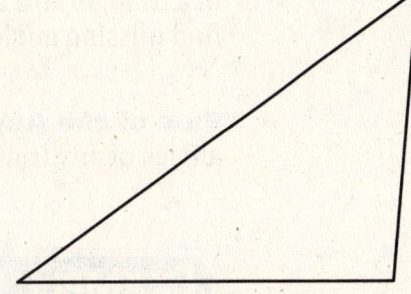

3. **Make a Conjecture** Based on your answers to Exercises 1 and 2, make a conjecture about the sum of the measures of the angles in any triangle.

4. A quadrilateral is a polygon with four sides. Cut a quadrilateral out of a sheet of paper. Tear off all four corners and arrange them with the vertices together as in the example in this activity. What appears to be the sum of the angles of this quadrilateral?

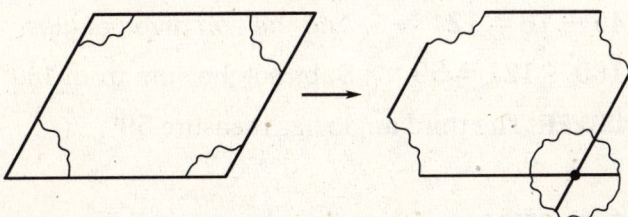

5. **Make a Conjecture** Based on your answer to Exercise 4, make a conjecture about the sum of the measures of the angles in any quadrilateral.

Math Intervention
Book 6 Data Analysis and Geometry

LESSON 6-24: Angles in a Triangle and Quadrilateral

Words to Remember

Quadrilateral: a polygon with 4 sides

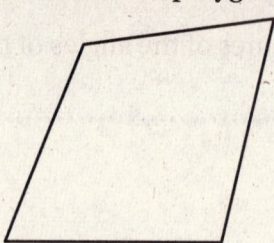

Getting Started In Activity 6-23 you investigated the sum of the angles of a triangle and a quadrilateral. In this lesson you will use the angle sums to find missing angles of triangles and quadrilaterals.

Sum of the Angles of a Triangle The sum of the measures of the angles of any triangle is **180°**.

EXAMPLE 1 — Finding the Missing Angle of a Triangle

A triangle has angles with measure 45° and 76°. What is the measure of the third angle?

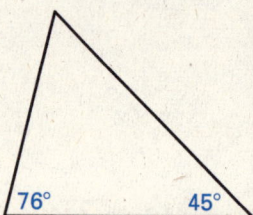

Solution

$45 + 76 = 121$ Add the two given angles.

$180 - 121 = 59$ Subtract the sum from 180°.

ANSWER The third angle has measure 59°.

Notice
It does not matter what kind of triangle it is. The sum of the three angles is still 180°.

TRY THIS Find the measure of the third angle of a triangle having the two given angles.

1. 16°, 100°
2. 42°, 42°

Math Intervention
Book 6 Data Analysis and Geometry

Name _____ Date _____

EXAMPLE 2 Determining if Three Given Angles Form a Triangle

Can a triangle have angles of measure 19°, 19°, and 152°?

Solution

19 + 19 + 152 = 190   Add the angles.
190 ≠ 180   Compare the sum to 180.

ANSWER No, a triangle cannot have these angle measures.

TRY THIS Can a triangle have the given angle measures?

3. 70°, 60°, 50°
4. 50°, 50°, 78°

Sum of the Angles of a Quadrilateral A quadrilateral can be divided into two triangles as shown. Since the sum of the measures of the angles in each triangle is 180°, the sum of the measures of the angles of the quadrilateral is 2(180°) = 360°.

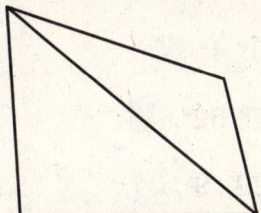

EXAMPLE 3 Finding the Missing Angle of a Quadrilateral

A quadrilateral has angles with measure 36°, 111°, and 74°. What is the measure of the fourth angle?

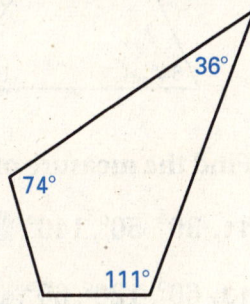

Solution

36 + 111 + 74 = 221   Add the angles.
360 − 221 = 139   Subtract from 360.

ANSWER The fourth angle has measure 139°.

Remember
The angles of a quadrilateral add up to 360°, not 180°.

TRY THIS Find the measure of the missing angle of the quadrilateral.

5. 76°, 98°, 154°
6. 22°, 22°, 170°

Math Intervention
Book 6 Data Analysis and Geometry

Name _____   Date _____

> **Summarize**
>
> **Finding a Missing Angle in a Triangle**
>
> The sum of the measures of the angles of any triangle is **180°**. To find the measure of a missing angle, first add the two given angle measures. Then subtract that total from **180°** to find the measure of the third angle of the triangle.
>
> **Finding a Missing Angle in a Quadrilateral**
>
> The sum of the measures of the angles of any quadrilateral is **360°**. To find the measure of a missing angle, first add the three given angle measures. Then subtract that total from **360°** to find the measure of the fourth angle of the quadrilateral.

Practice

Find the measure of the third angle of the triangle.

1. 30°, 50°, ▪
2. 17°, 34°, ▪
3. 96°, 70°, ▪
4. 20°, 4°, ▪
5. 82°, 12°, ▪
6. 47°, 52°, ▪
7. 39°, 101°, ▪
8. 128°, 9°, ▪

9.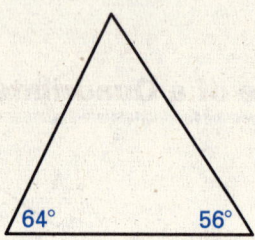

10.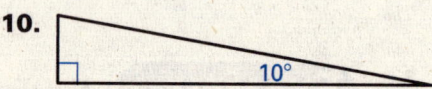

Find the measure of the fourth angle of the quadrilateral.

11. 30°, 50°, 140°, ▪
12. 84°, 86°, 88°, ▪
13. 60°, 120°, 60°, ▪
14. 24°, 110°, 150°, ▪
15. 98°, 72°, 56°, ▪
16. 42°, 81°, 112°, ▪
17. 107°, 66°, 29°, ▪
18. 163°, 79°, 87°, ▪

19.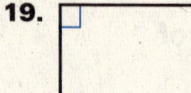

20.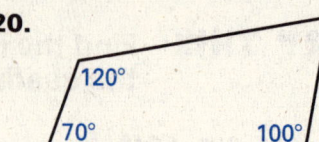

Math Intervention
Book 6 Data Analysis and Geometry

Name _____ Date _____

Can the given measures be angles of a triangle?

21. 36°, 36°, 72°

22. 56°, 87°, 37°

23. 62°, 39°, 79°

24. 43°, 71°, 93°

Can the given measures be angles of a quadrilateral?

25. 108°, 84°, 84°, 84°

26. 100°, 100°, 100°, 100°

27. 130°, 142°, 31°, 77°

28. 152°, 28°, 76°, 104°

29. All three angles of an equilateral triangle have the same measure. What is the measure? Explain how you found your answer.

_____
_____
_____

DID YOU GET IT?

30. **Fill in the missing words.** The sum of the measures of the angles of a triangle is _____, while the sum of the measures of the angles of a quadrilateral is _____.

31. **Describe a process.** Explain how to find the measure of the third angle of a triangle if two of the angles have measure 90° and 48°.

_____
_____

32. **Explain your reasoning.** Howard divided a quadrilateral into four triangles as shown. He argued that the sum of the angles of the quadrilateral must be 4 times 180° or 720° since the sum of the angles of each triangle is 180°. Explain his mistake.

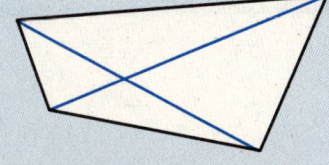

_____
_____

Name _____ Date _____

LESSON 6-25: Square Roots

> **Words to Remember**
>
> **Perfect square:** a number that is the square of a positive integer; **1, 4, 9, 16,** and so on.
>
> **Square root:** The square root of a number p is a number q such that $q^2 = p$. The square roots of 9 are 3 and −3 because $3^2 = 9$ and $(-3)^2 = 9$.
>
> **Square root symbol:** You can write the square root of 9 as $\sqrt{9}$: $\sqrt{9} = 3$ and $-\sqrt{9} = -3$.

Getting Started In Lesson 1-32 and Lesson 3-13 you learned how to square numbers. In this lesson you will learn how to take the square root of a number. These are opposite operations.

EXAMPLE 1 Evaluating the Square Roots of a Perfect Square

Find the square roots of 25.

Solution

Since $5^2 = 25$, 5 is a square root of 25.

Since $(-5)^2 = 25$, −5 is a square root of 25.

ANSWER The square roots of 25 are 5 and −5.

TRY THIS Find the square roots of the number.

1. 81: ____ and ____
2. 49: ____ and ____

EXAMPLE 2 Evaluating a Square Root

Find $\sqrt{36}$.

Solution

Since $6^2 = 36$, $\sqrt{36} = 6$.

> **Note**
> The symbol $\sqrt{36}$ indicates the positive, or principal, square root of 36 only. The symbol $-\sqrt{36}$ indicates the negative square root of 36 only.

TRY THIS Find the square root.

3. $\sqrt{16} =$ ____
4. $-\sqrt{100} =$ ____

Math Intervention
Book 6 Data Analysis and Geometry

Name _____ Date _____

> **EXAMPLE 3** **Evaluating Square Roots of Non-Perfect Squares**

Find $\sqrt{56}$ to the nearest whole number and to the nearest tenth.

Solution

Use your calculator.

Enter 56. Then press the square root key.

$\sqrt{56} \approx 7.483314774$

$\sqrt{56} = 7$ Round to the nearest whole number.

$\sqrt{56} = 7.5$ Round to the nearest tenth.

Remember
When rounding 7.4833 to the nearest tenth, look at the number to the right of the number in the tenths' place. This number is 8. Since it is 5 or larger, the number 4 in the tenths' place rounds up to 5.

TRY THIS

Find the square root. Round your answers to the nearest whole number and to the nearest tenth.

5. $\sqrt{150}$ 6. $\sqrt{2}$ 7. $-\sqrt{19}$

8. What is the nearest perfect square less than $\sqrt{85}$? greater than $\sqrt{85}$?

9. How could you use your answer to Exercise 8 to estimate $\sqrt{85}$ without a calculator?

Memorize You may want to memorize all the perfect squares from 1 through 225 (there are 15 of them). This will make finding square roots easier.

Number	Square	Number	Square
1	1	11	121
2	4	12	144
3	9	13	169
4	16	14	196
5	25	15	225
6	36	16	256
7	49	17	289
8	64	18	324
9	81	19	361
10	100	20	400

Math Intervention
Book 6 Data Analysis and Geometry

Name _____ Date _____

> **Summarize**
>
> **Finding the Square Root of a Perfect Square**
> Find the number that when squared gives you the perfect square.
> The square roots of 36 are 6 and −6. $\sqrt{36} = 6$; $-\sqrt{36} = -6$
>
> **Finding the Square Root of a Non-Perfect Square**
> Use your calculator. Round your answer as specified.
> $\sqrt{40} \approx 6.32455532$ or 6.3 $\sqrt{48} \approx 6.92820323$ or 7

Practice

Find the square roots of the number.

1. 121
2. 4
3. 400
4. 1
5. 196
6. 10,000

Find the square root.

7. $\sqrt{0}$
8. $\sqrt{64}$
9. $-\sqrt{25}$
10. $\sqrt{625}$
11. $-\sqrt{144}$
12. $\sqrt{16}$
13. $\sqrt{81}$
14. $-\sqrt{169}$
15. $\sqrt{361}$

Use your calculator to find the square root. Round to the nearest whole number and to the nearest tenth.

16. $\sqrt{5}$
17. $\sqrt{182}$
18. $\sqrt{74}$
19. $\sqrt{13}$
20. $\sqrt{95}$
21. $\sqrt{41}$
22. $\sqrt{1000}$
23. $\sqrt{6.32}$

Use your calculator to find the square root. Do not round.

24. $-\sqrt{96.04}$
25. $-\sqrt{635.04}$
26. $-\sqrt{2313.61}$
27. $-\sqrt{342.25}$

28. Nancy knows that $\sqrt{121} = 11$. How can she use this information to help her find $\sqrt{1.21}$? Explain.

_____
_____
_____

Math Intervention
Book 6 Data Analysis and Geometry

Name _____   Date _____

29. Explain how you would find $\sqrt{\frac{4}{9}}$.

_____
_____
_____

30. Use your knowledge of square roots to find $\sqrt{3} \cdot \sqrt{3}$. Explain your reasoning.

_____
_____
_____

31. Explain why you cannot take the square root of -4.

_____
_____
_____

DID YOU GET IT?

32. Fill in the missing words. $\sqrt{225}$ equals _____ because _____ equals _____.

33. Describe a process. How could you find an approximate value for $\sqrt{93}$ without a calculator?

_____
_____
_____

34. Explain your reasoning. Randy says $\sqrt{15}$ is between 3 and 4. Explain how he knew this.

_____
_____
_____

35. Explain a concept. Why are there two square roots of 4 but $\sqrt{4}$ has only one value?

_____
_____
_____

Name _____ Date _____

LESSON 6-26: Pythagorean Theorem

Words to Remember

Hypotenuse: the side of a right triangle opposite the right angle

Legs: the sides of a right triangle that form the right angle

Pythagorean theorem: In a right triangle, the sum of the squares of the lengths of the legs is equal to the square of the length of the hypotenuse. $a^2 + b^2 = c^2$

Getting Started In Lesson 6-25 you learned how to evaluate square roots. In this lesson you will learn about the Pythagorean theorem and use it to find missing sides of a right triangle. You will use square roots in this process.

EXAMPLE 1 — Finding the Hypotenuse of a Right Triangle

Find c.

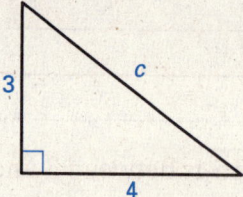

Order of Operations
You must square the numbers before you add them together. And you must add them together before you take the square root.

Solution

$a^2 + b^2 = c^2$	Write the Pythagorean theorem.
$3^2 + 4^2 = c^2$	Substitute in values.
$9 + 16 = c^2$	Evaluate powers.
$25 = c^2$	Add.
$5 = c$	Take the square root.

TRY THIS

1. Find c.

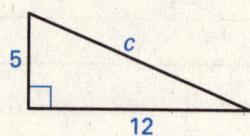

Math Intervention
102 Book 6 Data Analysis and Geometry

EXAMPLE 2 — Finding a Leg of a Right Triangle

Find x.

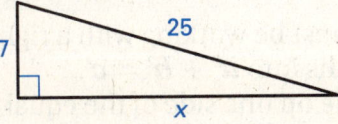

Solution

$a^2 + b^2 = c^2$	Write Pythagorean theorem.
$7^2 + x^2 = 25^2$	Substitute in values.
$49 + x^2 = 625$	Evaluate powers.
$49 + x^2 - 49 = 625 - 49$	Subtract 49 from each side.
$x^2 = 576$	Subtract.
$x = 24$	Take the square root.

Notice
The square of the hypotenuse must always be alone on one side of the equal sign.

TRY THIS

2. Find x.

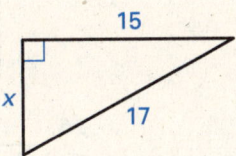

EXAMPLE 3 — Finding A Missing Length

Find the diagonal of a rectangle with length 20 inches and width 6 inches. Round to the nearest tenth of an inch.

Solution

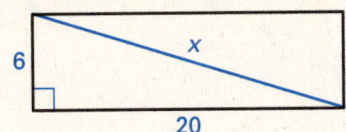

Draw and label a figure.

$a^2 + b^2 = c^2$	Write the Pythagorean theorem.
$6^2 + 20^2 = x^2$	Substitute in values.
$36 + 400 = x^2$	Evaluate powers.
$436 = x^2$	Add.
$\sqrt{436} = x$	Take the square root.
$20.9 \approx x$	Evaluate the square root to the nearest tenth.

Notice
The diagonal of the rectangle forms two right triangles so you can use the Pythagorean theorem on one of the triangles.

ANSWER The diagonal is approximately **20.9** inches.

TRY THIS

3. Draw a square and label the sides 7 meters. Then find the length of the diagonal. Round to the nearest tenth.

Name _____   Date _____

> **Summarize**
>
> **Using the Pythagorean Theorem**
>
> To use the Pythagorean theorem you must be working with a right triangle. Substitute the given side lengths into $a^2 + b^2 = c^2$. Evaluate the powers. Isolate the variable on one side of the equal sign. Take the square root. Round your answer if necessary.

Practice

Find the missing side of the triangle. Round your answer to the nearest tenth if necessary.

1.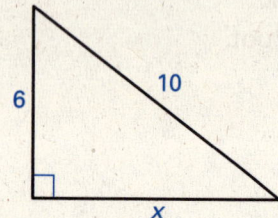

2.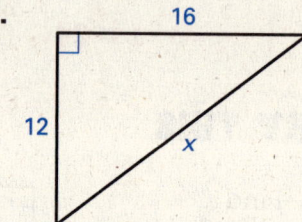

3.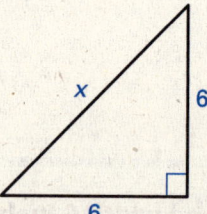

4.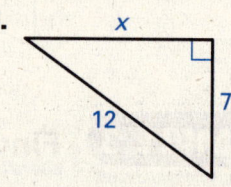

5. Find the length of the diagonal of a rectangle if the length is 15 centimeters and the width is 9 centimeters. Round to the nearest tenth of a centimeter.

Find the value of x. Round to the nearest tenth.

6.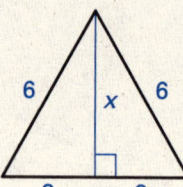

7.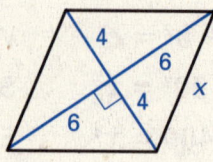

8.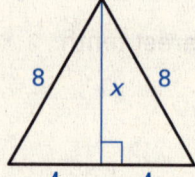

9.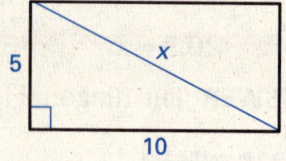

Math Intervention
Book 6 Data Analysis and Geometry

Name _____ Date _____

Find the missing value for right triangle *ABC*. Round to the nearest tenth if necessary.

10. $a =$ ▢, $b = 48$, $c = 50$

11. $a = 16$, $b = 30$, $c =$ ▢

12. $a = 2.5$, $b =$ ▢, $c = 6.5$

13. $a =$ ▢, $b = 7$, $c = 9$

14. $a = 4$, $b = 8$, $c =$ ▢

15. Explain why you cannot use the Pythagorean theorem to find the missing side in this triangle.

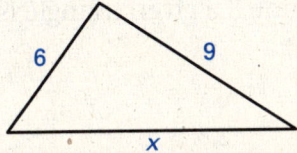

_____
_____
_____

DID YOU GET IT?

16. **Fill in the missing words.** If $a = 3$ and $b = 6$ in _____ triangle *ABC*, then $3^2 +$ _____ = _____ by the _____ theorem.

17. **Find the error.** Mark wrote the equation $6^2 + 10^2 = x^2$. Then he simplified and got $6 + 10 = x$. What was his mistake?

_____
_____
_____

18. **Explain your reasoning.** One leg of a right triangle has length 8 inches and the hypotenuse has length 12 inches. Would you use the equation $8^2 + 12^2 = x^2$ or the equation $8^2 + x^2 = 12^2$ to find the length of the other leg? Explain your reasoning.

_____
_____
_____

LESSON 6-27 Converse of the Pythagorean Theorem

Words to Remember

Converse: The converse of an if-then sentence is obtained by reversing the two parts of the sentence.

Statement: If a, then b.
Converse: If b, then a.

Getting Started In Lesson 6-26 you learned how to use the Pythagorean theorem. In this lesson you will use the Converse of the Pythagorean theorem. The converse can be used to determine if a given triangle is a right triangle.

Converse of the Pythagorean Theorem

Pythagorean Theorem: If △ABC is a right triangle with sides *a*, *b*, and *c*, then $a^2 + b^2 = c^2$.

Converse of Pythagorean Theorem: If $a^2 + b^2 = c^2$, then △ABC is a right triangle.

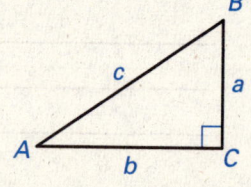

EXAMPLE 1 Writing the Converse of an If-Then Statement

Notice
In Example 1, the original statement is true but the converse is false. However, both the Pythagorean theorem and its converse are true.

Write the converse of the sentence: If $x = 2$, then $x < 3$.

Solution

If $x < 3$, then $x = 2$.   Reverse the if and then parts.

TRY THIS Write the converse of the sentence.

1. If today is Monday, then John has orchestra practice.

   If _____,

   then _____.

2. If a number is a multiple of 2, then the number is even.

   If _____,

   then _____.

Math Intervention
Book 6 Data Analysis and Geometry

EXAMPLE 2 — Using the Converse of the Pythagorean Theorem

A triangle has sides of length 24 centimeters, 32 centimeters, and 40 centimeters. Tell whether the triangle is a right triangle.

Solution

$a^2 + b^2 \stackrel{?}{=} c^2$ Write the Pythagorean theorem.

$24^2 + 32^2 \stackrel{?}{=} 40^2$ Substitute in values.

$576 + 1024 = 1600$ Evaluate powers.

$1600 = 1600$ ✓   Add and compare.

Remember
The largest number must be the **hypotenuse** and must be substituted in the equation for *c*.

ANSWER Yes, the triangle is a right triangle.

TRY THIS

3. A triangle has sides of length 15 inches, 18 inches, and 20 inches. Is the triangle a right triangle? Explain.

EXAMPLE 3 — Using the Converse of the Pythagorean Theorem to Form a Right Angle

Randy needs to make a rectangular border around his garden. To be sure he has a right angle he measures 3 feet on one side, 4 feet on the other side, and then arranges the edging until the distance between these two points is 5 feet. Why does this make a right angle?

Solution

$a^2 + b^2 \stackrel{?}{=} c^2$ Write Pythagorean theorem.

$3^2 + 4^2 \stackrel{?}{=} 5^2$ Substitute in values.

$9 + 16 = 25$ Evaluate powers.

$25 = 25$ ✓   Add and compare.

ANSWER Because these numbers are the lengths of the sides of a right triangle, the angle formed is a right angle.

TRY THIS

4. A triangular table has sides of length 10 inches, 24 inches, and 26 inches. Is the table a right triangle? Explain.

> **Summarize**
>
> **Writing the Converse of an If-Then Statement**
>
> To write the converse of an if-then statement, reverse the two parts of the statement. The converse of a true statement may or may not also be true.
>
> **Using the Converse of the Pythagorean Theorem**
>
> You can use the converse of the Pythagorean theorem to determine whether three given lengths could be the sides of a right triangle. Substitute the values into the Pythagorean theorem. If the equation is true, then the lengths form a right triangle.

Practice

Write the converse of the statement.

1. If today is Saturday, then Lois does not have school.

2. If a triangle has three equal sides, then it is equilateral.

3. If a quadrilateral has four right angles, then it is a rectangle.

4. If $x + 6 = 15$, then $x = 9$.

Are the given lengths the sides of a right triangle? Write *yes* or *no*.

5. 9, 12, 15
6. 12, 16, 18
7. 25, 60, 65
8. 2.5, 6, 6.5
9. 3, 6, 7
10. 9, 10, 12
11. 7, 24, 25
12. 8, 8, 8
13. 21, 35, 28

14. A triangle has side lengths of 9 centimeters, 11 centimeters, and 14 centimeters. Is the triangle a right triangle? Explain.

_____

_____

_____

15. Explain how you could use measurements of **6** inches, **8** inches, and **10** inches to build a picture frame with a right angle.

_____
_____
_____

16. A parallelogram has sides of **8** inches and **12** inches, and a diagonal of **15** inches. Is the parallelogram a rectangle? Explain your answer.

_____
_____
_____

17. A triangular area between three streets has dimensions **90** feet by **400** feet by **410** feet. Is the area a right triangle? Justify your reasoning.

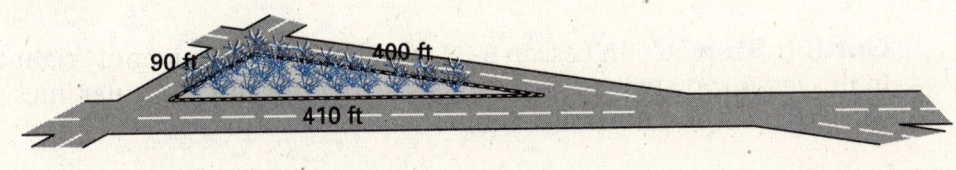

_____
_____
_____

DID YOU GET IT?

18. Fill in the missing words. The _____ of the Pythagorean theorem says: If $a^2 + b^2 = c^2$, then triangle *ABC* is a _____ triangle.

19. Give an example. Write an if-then statement that is true, but that has a false converse. Write the converse.

_____
_____
_____
_____

20. Explain your reasoning. Explain how you know that a triangle with sides **8** centimeters, **15** centimeters, and **17** centimeters is a right triangle.

_____
_____

Name _____ Date _____

LESSON 6-28
Parallel and Perpendicular Lines

> **Words to Remember**
>
> Parallel lines: Lines in the same plane that do not intersect
>
>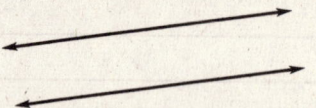
>
> Perpendicular lines: Lines that intersect to form four right angles
>
>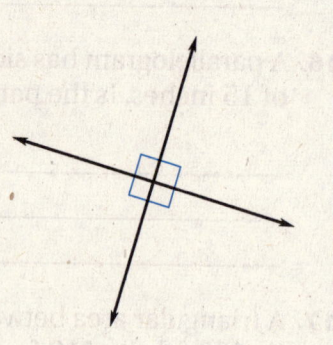

Getting Started In Lesson 6-20 you learned how to identify right angles. In this lesson you will use right angles to identify perpendicular lines. You will also learn about parallel lines.

EXAMPLE 1 Recognizing Parallel and Perpendicular Lines

Tell whether the lines are parallel, perpendicular, or neither.

a.
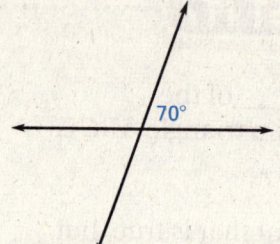

ANSWER Neither; they intersect but the angle is not 90°.

b.
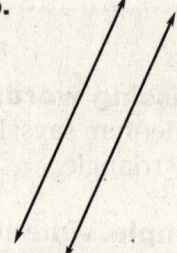

ANSWER Parallel; they do not intersect.

TRY THIS
Tell whether the lines are parallel, perpendicular, or neither.

1.
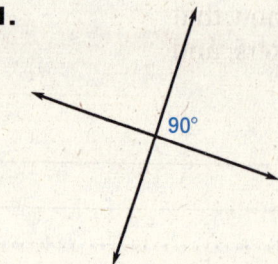

2. lines a and b
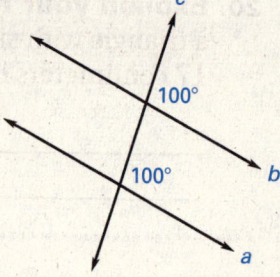

Math Intervention
Book 6 Data Analysis and Geometry

Notation

You can write the line passing through B and C as $\overleftrightarrow{BC}$, read "line BC."

EXAMPLE 2 Constructing a Perpendicular Line

Construct a line perpendicular to $\overleftrightarrow{BC}$. A construction uses only a compass and straightedge.

Solution

Step 1 Open compass more than half the distance from B to C.

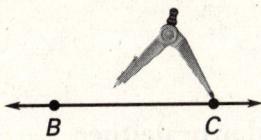

Step 2 Make arcs from B and C that intersect on each side of the line.

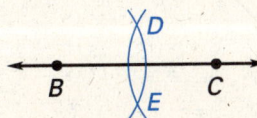

Step 3 Draw a line through the two intersection points. This line is perpendicular to $\overleftrightarrow{BC}$.

$\overleftrightarrow{DE} \perp \overleftrightarrow{BC}$

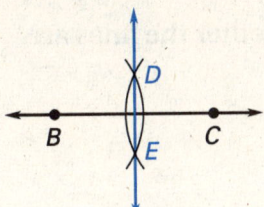

Symbols

The symbol for perpendicular lines is $\perp$. If lines a and b are perpendicular, you write $a \perp b$.

EXAMPLE 3 Drawing a Parallel Line

Draw a line parallel to $\overleftrightarrow{JK}$ through X.

Solution

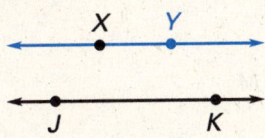

The line must be at the same angle as $\overleftrightarrow{JK}$.
$\overleftrightarrow{XY} \parallel \overleftrightarrow{JK}$

Symbols

The symbol for parallel lines is $\parallel$. If lines a and b are parallel, you write $a \parallel b$.

TRY THIS Use the diagram shown.

3. Construct a line perpendicular to $\overleftrightarrow{MN}$.

4. Draw a line parallel to $\overleftrightarrow{MN}$ through P.

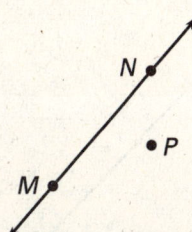

Name _____ Date _____

> **Summarize**
>
> **Identifying Parallel and Perpendicular Lines**
> Parallel lines are lines in the same plane that do not intersect.
> Perpendicular lines are lines that intersect to form four right angles.

Practice

Tell whether the lines are parallel, perpendicular, or neither.

1. 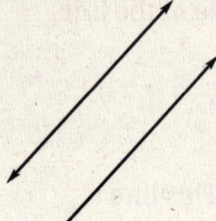   2. 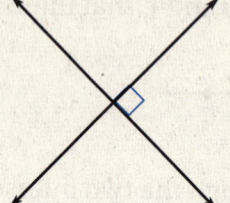   3.

Use the diagram for Exercises 4 and 5. Tell whether the lines are parallel, perpendicular, or neither.

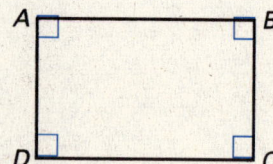

4. $\overleftrightarrow{AB}$ and $\overleftrightarrow{BC}$ 5. $\overleftrightarrow{AD}$ and $\overleftrightarrow{BC}$

Construct a line perpendicular to the line shown.

6. 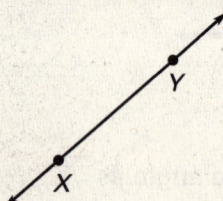   7.

Draw a line parallel to the line shown.

8. 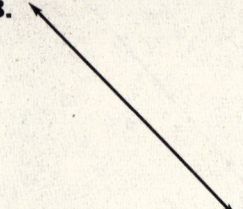   9. ←───────

Math Intervention
Book 6 Data Analysis and Geometry

Name _____ Date _____

10. Explain how you could construct a line through B perpendicular to $\overleftrightarrow{BC}$.

_____
_____
_____

11. In Exercise 10, how many distinct lines could you have drawn through B perpendicular to $\overleftrightarrow{BC}$? Explain.

_____
_____
_____

12. If you constructed a line through B perpendicular to $\overleftrightarrow{BC}$ in Exercise 10 and a line through C perpendicular to $\overleftrightarrow{BC}$, how could you then construct a line parallel to $\overleftrightarrow{BC}$?

_____
_____
_____

DID YOU GET IT?

13. Fill in the missing words. Two lines in the same plane are parallel if they do not _____. They are perpendicular if they intersect to form four _____ _____.

14. Describe a process. Explain how to construct a line perpendicular to a given line.

_____
_____
_____

15. Explain your reasoning. Trudy says that two lines that are not perpendicular must be parallel. Is she correct? Explain.

_____
_____
_____

Math Intervention
Book 6 Data Analysis and Geometry

Name _____ Date _____

LESSON 6-29
Congruent Figures

> **Words to Remember**
>
> Congruent figures: Figures that have the same size and shape
>
>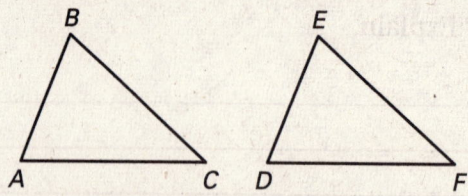
>
> Corresponding parts: The sides or angles that are in corresponding positions in congruent figures

Getting Started If two figures are congruent, then their corresponding sides have the same length and their corresponding angles have the same measure. The symbol for congruent is ≅. If triangle *ABC* is congruent to triangle *DEF* you write △*ABC* ≅ △*DEF*.

EXAMPLE 1 Identifying Congruent Figures

Which triangle is congruent to △XYZ?

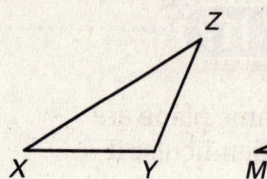 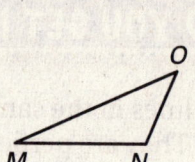 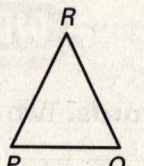 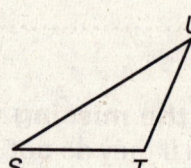

Solution

△*STU* ≅ △*XYZ* because they are the same size and shape.

Remember
The figure could be rotated or flipped over and still be congruent to the other one.

TRY THIS

1. Which figure is congruent to the one shown?

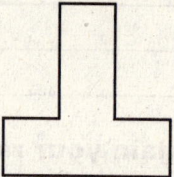

A. 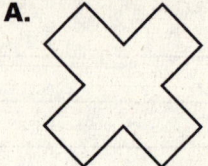   B. 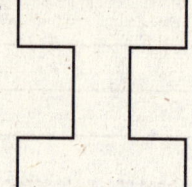   C.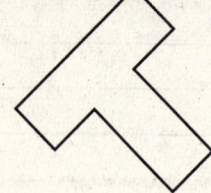

Math Intervention
Book 6 Data Analysis and Geometry

Name _____ Date _____

EXAMPLE 2 — Naming Corresponding Angles and Sides in Congruent Figures

Given △MNO ≅ △XYZ, name the corresponding parts.

Solution

$\overline{MN} \cong \overline{XY}$, $\overline{MO} \cong \overline{XZ}$, $\overline{NO} \cong \overline{YZ}$ — Pairs of corresponding sides

∠M ≅ ∠X, ∠N ≅ ∠Y, ∠O ≅ ∠Z — Pairs of corresponding angles

> **Corresponding Parts**
> The order of the letters tells you which points correspond in the congruent figures.

TRY THIS

2. Name the corresponding parts if △GHK ≅ △QRP.

> **Notation**
> You write $\overline{MN}$ to name segment MN. The length of $\overline{GF}$ is written GF.

EXAMPLE 3 — Finding Sides and Angles in Congruent Figures

Given ABCD ≅ FGHJ, find GF and m∠J.

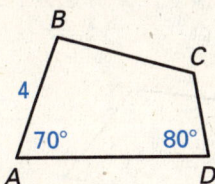
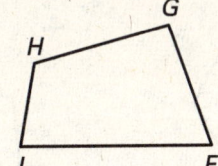

Solution

$\overline{GF} \cong \overline{BA}$, so GF = 4   Corresponding sides are congruent.

∠J ≅ ∠D, so m∠J = 80°   Corresponding angles are congruent.

TRY THIS

3. Given △XYZ ≅ △PQR, find m∠Q and PQ.

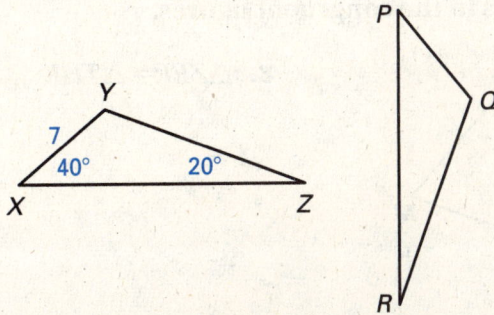

(Hint: Use the fact that the sum of the angles of a triangle is 180°.)

Math Intervention
Book 6 Data Analysis and Geometry

Name _____   Date _____

> **Summarize**
>
> **Identifying Congruent Figures**
>
> Figures are congruent if they have the same shape and are the same size.
>
> **Finding Corresponding Parts in Congruent Figures**
>
> Corresponding sides and angles are those in the same relative positions in congruent figures. The corresponding sides have the same length and the corresponding angles have the same measure.

Practice

Tell whether the figures are congruent or not. Explain your reasoning.

1.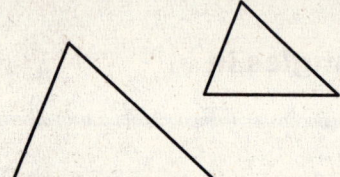

2.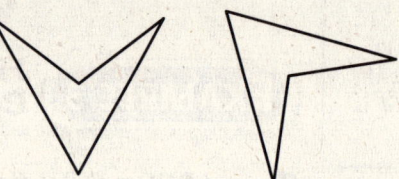

3.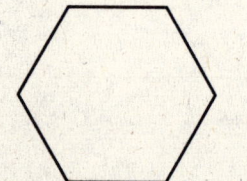

4.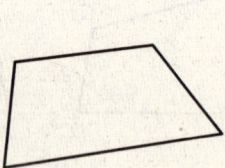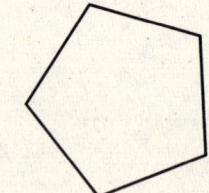

3.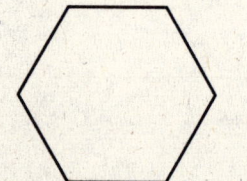

4.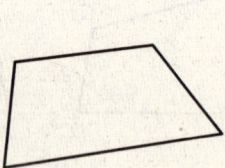

(Additional figures: 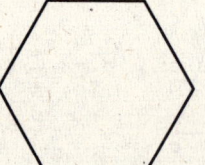)

Name the corresponding sides in the congruent figures.

5.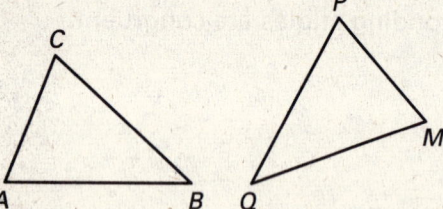

6. $\triangle ZER \cong \triangle THK$

Name the corresponding angles in the congruent figures.

7.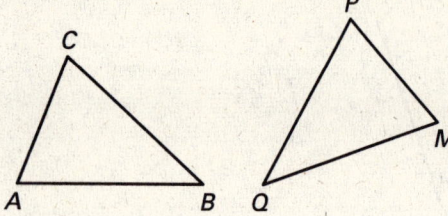

8. $\triangle ZER \cong \triangle THK$

Math Intervention
116 Book 6 Data Analysis and Geometry

Name _____   Date _____

Find the indicated measures.

9. △ABC ≅ △DEF

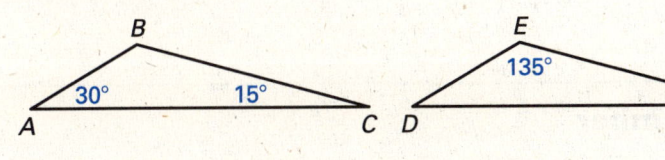

Find m∠F and m∠B.

10. △GHI ≅ △JKL

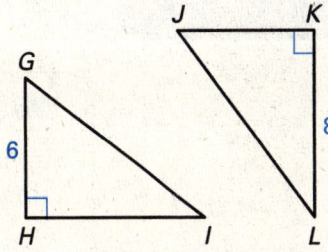

Find HI, GI, JK, and JL.

11. Must two equilateral triangles be congruent? Explain.

_____
_____
_____

12. Must two right triangles with legs **6** inches and **8** inches be congruent? Explain.

_____
_____
_____

DID YOU GET IT?

13. Fill in the missing words. Two figures are congruent if they are the same _____ and the same _____.

14. Fill in the missing words. Corresponding sides in congruent figures have the same _____. Corresponding angles in congruent figures have the same _____.

15. Explain your reasoning. If triangle *KLM* is congruent to triangle *PRQ*, which angle is congruent to ∠*L*? Explain.

_____
_____
_____

Name _____   Date _____

LESSON 6-30: Similar Figures

Words to Remember

Similar figures: Figures that have the same shape but not necessarily the same size

Getting Started In Lesson 4-6 you learned how to solve proportions. Now you will use proportions to solve for missing side lengths in similar figures.

EXAMPLE 1 Using a Proportion to Solve a Problem

Julie uses a recipe that makes 36 rolls with 1.5 teaspoons of yeast. How much yeast will she need to use to make 54 rolls?

Solution

$\dfrac{36}{1.5} = \dfrac{54}{x}$ Write a proportion.

$36x = 1.5(54)$ Write the cross products.

$36x = 81$ Multiply.

$\dfrac{36x}{36} = \dfrac{81}{36}$ Divide each side by 36.

$x = \dfrac{9}{4}$ Simplify.

ANSWER Julie will need $\dfrac{9}{4}$, or **2.25** teaspoons of yeast.

Remember
When you set up the proportion, corresponding quantities must go in the same place on both sides of the equal sign.

TRY THIS

1. Eric can run 3 miles in 16 minutes. At this rate, how long would it take him to run 5 miles?

Math Intervention
Book 6 Data Analysis and Geometry

Name _____   Date _____

Symbols
You can use the symbol ~ ("is similar to") to show that two figures are similar.

Similar Figures When two figures are similar their corresponding angles are congruent and their corresponding sides are proportional. The ratio between their corresponding sides is called the *ratio of similarity*.

EXAMPLE 2 Finding a Side in Similar Figures

If △ABC ~ △DEF, find DF and the ratio of similarity.

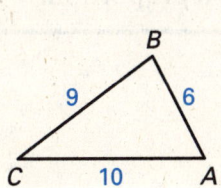
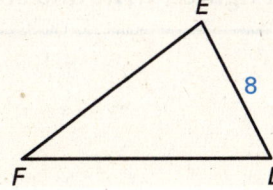

Note
Since 6 is a side of △ABC and it is in the numerator, then 10, which is also a side of △ABC, must be in the numerator of the other fraction.

Solution

$\frac{6}{8} = \frac{10}{x}$ Write a proportion.

$6x = 80$ Write the cross products.

$\frac{6x}{6} = \frac{80}{6}$ Divide each side by 6.

$x = 13\frac{1}{3}$ Simplify.

ANSWER DF is $13\frac{1}{3}$. The ratio of similarity is $\frac{6}{8} = \frac{3}{4}$.

TRY THIS

2. Find EF in Example 2.

EXAMPLE 3 Identifying Similar Figures

Which figure is similar to this one?

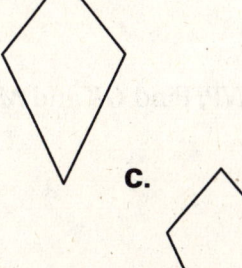

A.   B.   C.

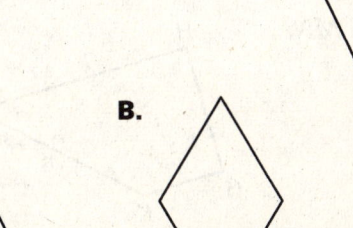

Solution

The answer is **C**.   The shapes are the same; one is just smaller than the other. They are not congruent but they are similar.

Name _____ Date _____

> **Summarize**
>
> **Identifying Similar Figures**
>
> Similar figures have the same shape but may be different sizes. Corresponding angles in similar figures are congruent and corresponding sides are proportional.
>
> **Finding Sides in Similar Figures**
>
> To find a missing side in similar figures, write and solve a proportion.

Practice

Solve the proportion.

1. $\dfrac{2}{x} = \dfrac{10}{15}$
2. $\dfrac{a}{20} = \dfrac{9}{10}$
3. $\dfrac{6}{10} = \dfrac{y}{15}$

Tell whether the figures are similar.

4.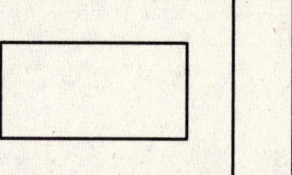

5.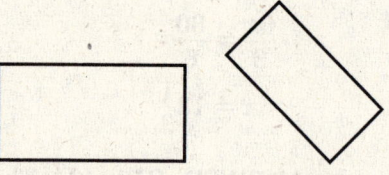

Find the missing sides of the similar figures shown or described. Give the ratio of similarity.

6. △ABC ~ △DEF; Find DE and AC.

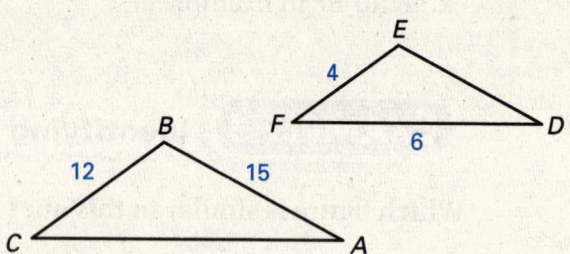

7. GHJK ~ LMNP; Find GK and MN.

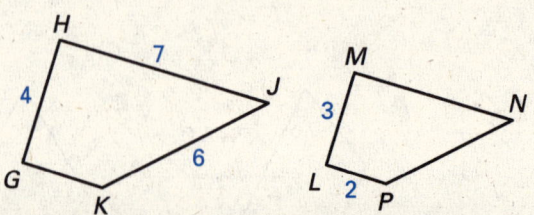

8. △XYZ ~ △MNP, XY = 8, YZ = 10, XZ = 15, and MN = 4; Find MP and NP.

9. △RST ~ △WXY, m∠R = 50°, m∠S = 60°; Find m∠T, m∠W, m∠X, and m∠Y.

Math Intervention

Book 6 Data Analysis and Geometry

Name _____   Date _____

10. Draw two figures that are similar but not congruent.

11. Can two figures be congruent but not similar? Explain.

_____
_____
_____

DID YOU GET IT?

12. Fill in the missing word. Two figures are similar if they are the same _____.

13. Fill in the missing words. Corresponding sides of similar figures are _____ and corresponding angles are _____.

14. Write a reason. Explain why the ratio of similarity between two congruent figures is 1 to 1.

_____
_____

15. Explain your reasoning. Given △XYZ ~ △STW. Will WT be less than or greater than ZY? Explain.

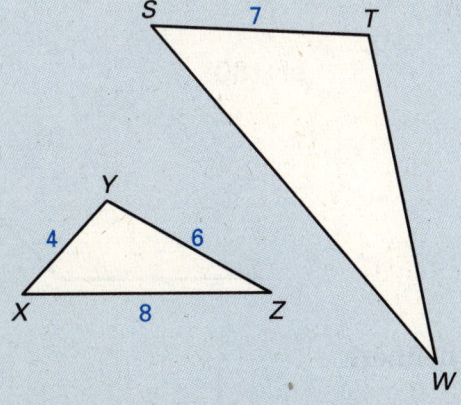

_____
_____

Math Intervention
Book 6 Data Analysis and Geometry   **121**

Name _____ Date _____

Mixed Practice for Lessons 6-19 to 6-30

Vocabulary Review

Match the word with its mathematical meaning and its everyday meaning.

Word	Mathematical meaning	Everyday meaning
1. angle ____, ____	A. point where rays intersect	X. point of view
2. vertex ____, ____	B. sides of a right triangle	Y. supporting limbs
3. legs ____, ____	C. figure formed by 2 rays with a common endpoint	Z. highest point

Fill in the missing word(s).

4. Two angles that have a sum of **90** degrees are _____ .
   Two angles that have a sum of **180** degrees are _____ .

Use ∠MNP for Exercises 5 and 6.

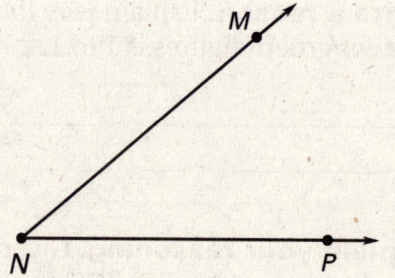

5. Name the angle three ways.

6. Find the measure of the angle in Exercise 5.

Classify the angle as acute, obtuse, right, or straight.

7. 50° 8. 172° 9. 180°

10. 90° 11. 12.

Are the angles complementary, supplementary, or neither?

13. 154°, 26° 14. 70°, 100°

15. 36°, 54° 16. ∠ABC, ∠CBD

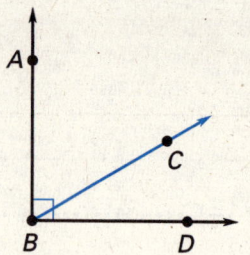

Math Intervention
122 Book 6 Data Analysis and Geometry

Name _____   Date _____

17. Find the measure of the complement and the supplement of an angle with measure 17°.

Tell whether the triangle is acute, obtuse, or right.

18. 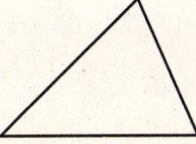   **19.** 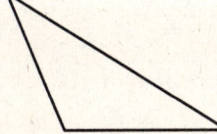   **20.**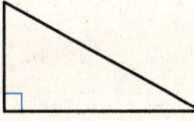

Tell whether the triangle is equilateral, isosceles, or scalene.

21. 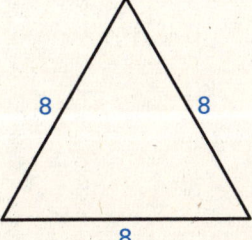   **22.** 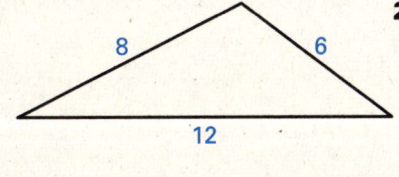   **23.**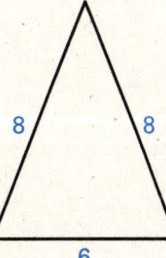

Find the square root. Round to the nearest tenth if necessary.

24. $\sqrt{16}$ **25.** $-\sqrt{144}$ **26.** $\sqrt{92}$

27. Give the square roots of 4.

Find the missing side of the triangle.

28. 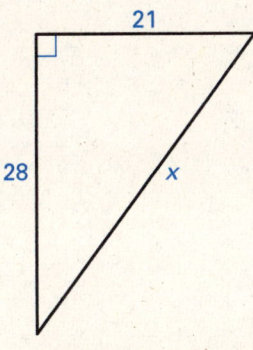   **29.**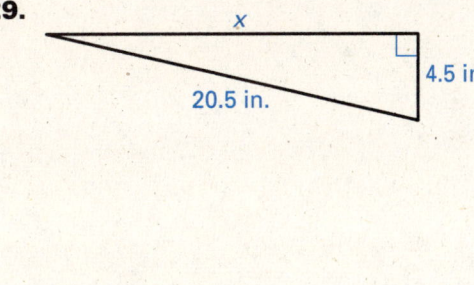

30. A triangle has sides of length 16 inches, 30 inches, and 34 inches. Is it a right triangle? Explain.

_____
_____

31. Which figures are congruent? Which figures are similar? Explain.

A. 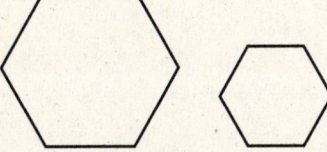   **B.**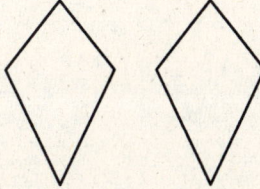

_____
_____

Math Intervention
Book 6 Data Analysis and Geometry

McDougal Littell

Math Intervention

Book 7:
Getting Ready for Algebra

McDougal Littell
A DIVISION OF HOUGHTON MIFFLIN COMPANY
Evanston, Illinois • Boston • Dallas

Cover photo © Purestock/Getty Images

Illustrations George Barile/McDougal Littell/Houghton Mifflin Company and John Evans/McDougal Littell/Houghton Mifflin Company

Copyright © 2008 by McDougal Littell, a division of Houghton Mifflin Company.
All rights reserved.

Permission is hereby granted to teachers to reprint or photocopy in classroom quantities the pages or sheets in this work that carry a McDougal Littell copyright notice. These pages are designed to be reproduced by teachers for use in their classes with accompanying McDougal Littell material, provided each copy made shows the copyright notice. Such copies may not be sold and further distribution is expressly prohibited. Except as authorized above, prior written permission must be obtained from McDougal Littell, a division of Houghton Mifflin Company, to reproduce or transmit this work or portions thereof in any other form or by any other electronic or mechanical means, including any information storage or retrieval system, unless expressly permitted by federal copyright laws. Address inquiries to, Supervisor, Rights and Permissions, McDougal Littell, P.O. Box 1667, Evanston, IL 60204.

ISBN-13: 978-0-618-90078-7
ISBN-10: 0-618-90078-0

123456789—PBO—11 10 09 08 07

Book 7: Getting Ready for Algebra

Solving Multi-Step Equations and Inequalities

Lesson 7-1	Write Equations	**2**
Lesson 7-2	Solve Multi-Step Equations	**6**
Lesson 7-3	Solve Problems with Multi-Step Equations	**10**
Lesson 7-4	Solve Multi-Step Inequalities	**14**
Lesson 7-5	Solve Problems with Multi-Step Inequalities	**18**
	Mixed Practice for Lessons 7-1 to 7-5	**22**

Properties of Exponents

Activity 7-6	Looking for Exponent Patterns	**24**
Lesson 7-7	Zero and Negative Exponents	**26**
Lesson 7-8	Product of Powers	**30**
Lesson 7-9	Power of a Power	**34**
Lesson 7-10	Power of a Product	**38**
Lesson 7-11	Quotient of Powers	**42**
Lesson 7-12	Power of a Quotient	**46**
Lesson 7-13	Fractional Exponents with a Denominator of 2	**50**
Lesson 7-14	Fractional Exponents with any Denominator	**54**
	Mixed Practice for Lessons 7-7 to 7-14	**58**

McDougal Littell

Math Intervention

MATH INTERVENTION

- The Math Intervention program includes skill lessons, problem solving lessons, activities, and mixed practice materials covering a wide range of mathematical topics that are needed for success in middle school and high school mathematics.

- There are seven books in the Math Intervention program. Book 7 contains materials on Getting Ready for Algebra concepts such as writing and solving multi-step equations and inequalities and using properties of exponents.

- In the Math Intervention books, lessons include worked-out Examples and Try this exercises to help you build understanding of a topic. The Practice section includes a variety of problems to give you the practice you need to develop your math skills. The Did You Get It? section checks your understanding of the lesson.

- Problem solving lessons suggest strategies for approaching real-world problem solving situations and promote the use of estimation to check reasonableness of solutions.

- Activities build your understanding of a topic through the use of models and games.

- Mixed Practice sections include practice of vocabulary, skills, and problem solving methods covering the material in a group of lessons.

- You may complete the work in selected lessons, or cover the book as a whole, as directed by your teacher.

Name _____   Date _____

LESSON 7-1 Write Equations

> **Words to Remember**
> Word sentence (or verbal sentence): A relationship or situation described in words
> Equation: A mathematical sentence showing that two quantities are equal
>
> Five more than a number n equals 60.
>
> $5 + n = 60$

Getting Started In Lesson 5-4 you learned how to write algebraic expressions. You can use the same methods to write equations.

 **Writing an Equation From a Word Sentence**

Write an equation to represent this sentence: Two less than a number is 12.

Solution

Let x represent the number.

Two less than the number would be $x - 2$.

The statement ends in "is 12," so the expression must be set equal to 12.

ANSWER The equation is $x - 2 = 12$.

 **Writing an Equation From a Word Sentence**

Write an equation to represent this sentence: A number two thirds more than four times another number is 30.

Solution

Let x represent the number.

Four times the number would be $4x$.

Two thirds more means to add $\frac{2}{3}$.

The statement ends in "is 30," so the expression must be set equal to 30.

ANSWER The equation is $4x + \frac{2}{3} = 30$.

Math Intervention
Book 7 Getting Ready for Algebra

Name _____ Date _____

Vocabulary
Consecutive means next. The next odd integer is two more than the previous odd number.
$15 = 13 + 2$
$17 = 15 + 2$
… and so on
…13, 15, 17,…

EXAMPLE 3 Writing an Equation for a Relationship

Write an equation to describe this relationship: The sum of two consecutive odd integers is 108.

Solution

Let x represent an odd integer.

Then $x + 2$ is the next odd integer.

$x + (x + 2)$ is the sum of the two odd integers.

The statement ends in "is 108," so the expression must be set equal to 108.

ANSWER The equation is $x + (x + 2) = 108$.

EXAMPLE 4 Writing an Equation Using Only One Variable

Write an equation to describe this relationship: Tara is 3 years older than her sister. Their ages together add up to 27.

Solution

Let s represent the age of Tara's sister.

Then $s + 3$ represents Tara's age.

$s + (s + 3)$ is the sum of the two girls' ages.

Since the girls' ages add up to 27, the expression must be set equal to 27.

ANSWER The equation is $s + (s + 3) = 27$.

TRY THIS Replace the word sentence with an equation.

1. A number six times as great as r equals 90. _____

2. Three less than eight times a number is 21. _____

3. A number decreased by one half equals 7. _____

4. Four more than twice a number b equals 16. _____

5. The sum of two consecutive integers is 25. _____

6. A number decreased by one third of the number is 18. _____

Math Intervention
Book 7 Getting Ready for Algebra   3

Name _____ Date _____

> **Summarize**
>
> **Writing a Verbal Sentence as an Equation**
> (1) Start with a word sentence describing a mathematical relationship.
> (2) Use numbers and algebraic symbols to represent the words.
> (3) Replace each word with the corresponding number or algebraic symbol.

Practice

Match the word sentence with the correct equation.

1. A number increased by **6** equals **10**. _____

2. A number decreased by **6** equals **10**. _____

3. Six is **10** more than a number. _____

A. $x + 10 = 6$ **B.** $x + 6 = 10$ **C.** $x - 6 = 10$

Replace the word sentence with an equation.

4. Four more than a number equals 7. _____

5. Five less than a number equals **16**. _____

6. Three eighths of a number is **24**. _____

7. A number divided by **3** equals **10**. _____

8. The sum of two consecutive even integers is **66**. _____

9. A number decreased by two thirds of the number equals **50**. _____

10. Three less than four times a number is **12**. _____

11. Eight more than a number is three less than two times the number. _____

12. Four times the sum of a number and two is five times the number. _____

13. Two boxes together weigh **36** pounds, and one box weighs five times what the other box weighs. _____

Math Intervention
Book 7 Getting Ready for Algebra

Name _____ Date _____

Write an equation for the relationship. Explain your reasoning.

14. John has **2** sacks of apples that together contain **42** apples. The second sack has **8** fewer apples than the first sack.

_____
_____
_____

15. Mary opened a box of light bulbs and found that **48** light bulbs were damaged. This number was one fifth of the light bulbs in the box.

_____
_____
_____

16. Chris is **2** years younger than Jim. The sum of their ages is **30**.

_____
_____
_____

DID YOU GET IT?

17. **Fill in the missing words.** When writing an equation you must replace each of the words in the _____ with algebraic _____.

18. **Describe a process.** Explain how to change the equation $2x = 5x - 4$ into a word sentence.

_____
_____
_____

19. **Explain your reasoning.** Your friend says that $2x + 8 = 10$ is the same as $2x + 10 = 8$. Is your friend correct? Explain why or why not.

_____
_____
_____

Name _____ Date _____

LESSON 7-2 Solve Multi-step Equations

Words to Remember

Terms: In an expression, the items separated by addition or subtraction symbols

Like terms: Two variable terms that have the same variable parts or two *constant terms*

Like terms	Not like terms
$x, 4x$	$3x, 3$
$-2, 8$	xy, x

Coefficient: In a term, the number multiplied by the variable

Combining like terms: Using the distributive property to combine coefficients of like terms

$5x + 2x = (5 + 2)x = 7x$

Getting Started In Lesson 5-8 you learned how to solve addition and subtraction equations. In Lesson 5-9 you learned how to solve multiplication and division equations. In Lesson 5-10 you learned how to solve problems using equations. You can combine these methods to solve multi-step equations.

EXAMPLE 1 Solving a Two-Step Equation

Properties
You can use the properties of equality you have learned to get the variable alone on one side of the equation.

Solve the equation $2x + 6 = 10$. Graph the solution.

Solution

$2x + 6 = 10$	Original equation
$2x + 6 - 6 = 10 - 6$	Subtract 6 from each side.
$2x = 4$	Simplify.
$\dfrac{2x}{2} = \dfrac{4}{2}$	Divide each side by 2.
$x = 2$	Simplify.

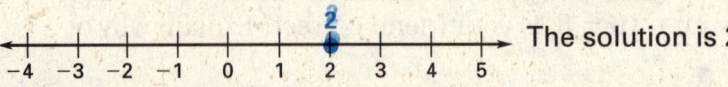

The solution is 2.

TRY THIS Solve the equation. Graph the solution.

1. $4x - 7 = 13$ 2. $6x + 15 = 3$ 3. $14 = 5x + 5$

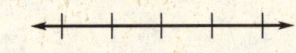 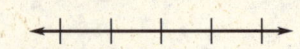 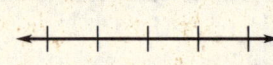

Name _____   Date _____

Coefficients

Notice that the term *k* has a coefficient of 1. So $k - 3k = (1-3)k = -2k$.

EXAMPLE 2 — Combining Like Terms

Solve the equation $k + 2 - 3k = -4k + 11$. Graph the solution.

Solution

$k + 2 - 3k = -4k + 11$	Original equation
$-2k + 2 = -4k + 11$	Combine like terms.
$-2k + 2 + 4k = -4k + 11 + 4k$	Add $4k$ to each side.
$2k + 2 = 11$	Simplify.
$2k + 2 - 2 = 11 - 2$	Subtract 2 from each side.
$2k = 9$	Simplify.
$\dfrac{2k}{2} = \dfrac{9}{2}$	Divide each side by 2.
$k = 4.5$	Simplify.

The solution is 4.5.

EXAMPLE 3 — Using the Distributive Property

Solve the equation $4(x + 3) - 2(3x - 1) = 8$. Graph the solution.

Solution

$4(x + 3) - 2(3x - 1) = 8$	Original equation
$4x + 12 - 6x + 2 = 8$	Distributive property
$-2x + 14 = 8$	Combine like terms.
$-2x + 14 - 14 = 8 - 14$	Subtract 14 from each side.
$-2x = -6$	Simplify.
$\dfrac{-2x}{-2} = \dfrac{-6}{-2}$	Divide each side by -2.
$x = 3$	Simplify.

The solution is 3.

TRY THIS — Solve the equation. Graph the solution.

4. $5x - 2 + 3x = 2x + 6$

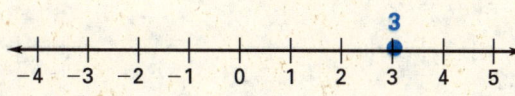

5. $5(p - 10) = 8(p + 2)$

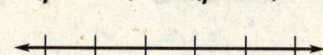

Math Intervention
Book 7 Getting Ready for Algebra

Name _____   Date _____

> **Summarize**
>
> **Solving a Multi-step Equation**
> (1) Simplify expressions and combine like terms on each side of the equation if possible.
> (2) Use the properties of equality to isolate the variable.

Practice

Match the equation with the graph of its solution.

1. $5x - 3x = 10$ _____   A. (number line with point at 5, marks 3-7)

2. $3x - 5x = 10$ _____   B. (number line with point at $2\frac{3}{5}$, marks 0-4)

3. $5x - 3 = 10$ _____   C. (number line with point at -5, marks -7 to -3)

Solve the equation. Graph the solution.

4. $7x - 3 = 18$

5. $3 + 8x = 15$

6. $8x + 2x = 16 + 4$

7. $2x + 16 = 36 - 3x$

8. $n - 2n + 4 = 3n - 1$

9. $8n + 5 = -4n - 19$

10. $3n + 7n = -47 + 17$

11. $4(k + 2) = 3(k - 1)$

12. $6(r - 3) = 8(r - 4)$

13. $7b - 3(b + 1) = 2(3b + 1)$

14. $8(2x - 2) = -3(4x + 10)$

15. $7(k - 3) - 2(2k + 4) = 10$

Math Intervention
Book 7 Getting Ready for Algebra

Name _____ Date _____

Write an equation to model the situation. Then solve the equation. Explain your reasoning.

16. Jared has a **530**-page book to read. He has read **50** pages of this book. If he reads **32** pages a day, how many days will it take him to finish the book?

   _____
   _____
   _____

17. Kyle and Sara are training for a marathon. Kyle has already run **11** miles and Sara has run **6** miles in the first week. If Kyle wants to increase how many miles he runs by **3** miles each week and Sara wants to increase how many miles she runs by **4** miles each week, how many weeks will it take them to be running the same number of miles each week?

   _____
   _____

DID YOU GET IT?

18. **Fill in the missing words.** When solving an equation you must always get the _____ by _____ on one side of the equation.

19. **Describe a process.** Explain the steps you would use to solve the equation $3(x + 5) - (x - 7) = 14$.

   _____
   _____

20. **Explain your reasoning.** Your friend says that the equations $5x + 8 = -17$ and $-5x - 8 = 17$ have the same solution. Is your friend correct? Explain why or why not.

   _____
   _____
   _____

Math Intervention
Book 7 Getting Ready for Algebra

LESSON 7-3: Solve Problems with Multi-step Equations

Strategies to Remember

To get a variable by itself when you solve a multi-step linear equation, undo whatever was done to the variable.

To undo addition: • subtract	To undo subtraction: • add
To undo multiplication: • divide	To undo division: • multiply

Getting Started In Lesson 7-1 you learned how to write equations and in Lesson 7-2 you learned how to solve multi-step equations. You will combine these methods to solve problems using multi-step equations.

EXAMPLE 1 Solving a Multi-step Equation

Janelle has $160 in the bank. She deposits $8 each week. In how many weeks will Janelle have $248 in the bank?

Solution

Let w represent the number of weeks.

$8w + 160 = 248$ Write an equation to fit the problem.

$8w = 88$ Subtract 160 from each side.

$w = 11$ Divide each side by 8.

CHECK for reasonableness 11 weeks of saving $8 is $88. Add the $160 she had in the bank to get $248. So, 11 weeks is a reasonable solution.

TRY THIS Fill in the missing information to solve the problem.

1. Brad has $329 saved up. Of that money he spends $16 a week. In how many weeks will Brad have $89 left?

   Step 1 Let ___ represent the number of weeks.

   Step 2 Spending $16 a week for ___ weeks means you subtract ___.

   Step 3 Brad starts with $ _____ .

   Step 4 Solving the equation $329 - $ ___ $=$ _____ , Brad will have $89 left after _____ weeks.

Math Intervention
Book 7 Getting Ready for Algebra

EXAMPLE 2 — Writing and Solving a Multi-step Equation

Jerry has a board 15 feet long. He cuts off 2 boards that are the same length. His original board is now 7 feet long. What are the lengths of the boards Jerry cut off?

Solution

Let b represent the length of each board that is cut off.

$15 - 2b = 7$ Write an equation to fit the problem.
$-2b = -8$ Subtract 15 from each side.
$b = 4$ Divide each side by -2.

Remember
The integer 15 is positive so it needs to be subtracted from each side of the equation.

CHECK for reasonableness 2 boards that are each 4 feet long make 8 feet. 8 feet cut off a board 15 feet long will leave 7 feet. So, 4 feet is a reasonable solution.

EXAMPLE 3 — Writing and Solving a Multi-step Equation

Ginny earns d dollars per week babysitting. Of that she spends $2 per week at school. If she has $84 at the end of 6 weeks, how much does she earn per week?

Solution

Because Ginny earns d dollars per week and spends **$2.00**, she saves $(d - 2)$ dollars per week.

$6(d - 2) = 84$ Write an equation to fit the problem.
$6d - 12 = 84$ Distributive property
$6d = 96$ Add 12 to each side.
$d = 16$ Divide each side by 6.

ANSWER Ginny earns $16 per week.

TRY THIS Solve the problem. Explain your reasoning.

2. A portable DVD player that Jessica wants costs $179. She has already saved $35. Each week, Jessica earns d dollars and spends $6 of her paycheck. She saves the rest of her paycheck. If it takes 8 weeks for Jessica to save enough for the DVD player, how much does she earn per week?

$\square(d - \square) + 35 = 179$

$d = \$\square$

Name _____ Date _____

> **Summarize**
>
> **Solving Word Problems**
> (1) Read the problem carefully.
> (2) Decide what operations are needed.
> (3) Write an equation.
> (4) Solve the equation.
> (5) Check your answer for reasonableness.

Practice

Fill in the missing symbols +, −, ×, ÷ for the situation described.

1. Beth spent $\frac{1}{2}$ of her **$250** paycheck. $\frac{1}{2}$ ◯ 250

2. Bill gave away **55** of his baseball cards to his **11** friends. They each got the same amount.   55 ◯ 11

3. Gaige has some CDs. He gave **2** to his friend then bought **3** more. He now has **12** CDs. x ◯ 2 ◯ 3 = 12

4. Kaitlyn has **5000** miles on her car. She drives the same number of miles for each of **3** days and then has **5600** miles on her car. 5000 ◯ $3x$ = 5600

Identify the first step used to solve each of these equations.

5. $2x + 7 = 10$ 6. $3x - 8 = 13$ 7. $\frac{x}{2} - 4 = 6$

   _____   _____   _____

8. Fill in the missing information to solve the problem. Mark has **$6420** in his savings account. He deposited **$350** then made a withdrawal. He now has **$6210** in his account. How much money did Mark withdraw?

   Let x represent the amount withdrawn.

   Step 1 Since **$350** was deposited you need to _____ 350; since an amount was withdrawn you need to _____ x.

   Step 2 Write an equation. 6420 ◯ 350 ◯ x = 6210

   Step 3 Solve for x by first _____ 6420 and 350.

   Step 4 Next add x to each side and _____ 6210 from each side.

   Step 5 Mark withdrew $ _____ .

Math Intervention
Book 7 Getting Ready for Algebra

Name _____ Date _____

Write an equation. Solve the equation. Explain your reasoning.

9. A family is on a vacation in which they are traveling **3000** miles. They have already traveled **900** miles. If they travel **700** miles a day, how many more days will it take them to reach their destination?

   _____
   _____
   _____

10. Brent works for a company that pays him **$10** an hour plus **$7** for transportation and **$9** for meals if he works on Saturdays. Last Saturday he made **$68.50**. How many hours did he work on Saturday?

    _____
    _____
    _____

11. A local outlet store had a contract with Mr. Johnson to have him provide the store with **10,000** reclaimed golf balls. He has already provided them with **4000** golf balls. If he finds **500** golf balls per week, how many more weeks will he need to complete the contract?

    _____
    _____
    _____

DID YOU GET IT?

12. **Write a word problem.** Write a word problem for the equation $458 = 178 + 70d$. Solve the equation. Explain how you came up with the situation.

    _____
    _____
    _____

13. **Explain your reasoning.** Your friend says that the answer to the following problem is **30** days. Is your friend correct? Why or why not? Larry was planting evergreen trees on the edge of his acreage for a windbreak. He has **190** trees planted already and plants **28** trees a day. In how many days will Larry have **638** trees planted?

    _____
    _____
    _____

Name _____   Date _____

LESSON 7-4 Solve Multi-step Inequalities

Words to Remember

Inequality: A relationship involving the symbols >, <, ≥, or ≤

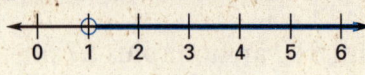
$x > 1$
greater than 1

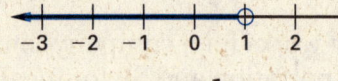
$x < 1$
less than 1

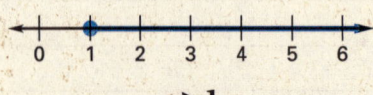
$x \geq 1$
greater than or equal to 1

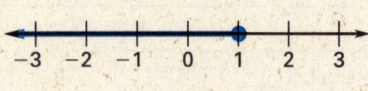
$x \leq 1$
less than or equal to 1

Getting Started In Lesson 5-11 you learned how to solve one-step linear inequalities. In Lesson 7-2 you learned how to solve multi-step equations. Combine these methods to solve multi-step inequalities.

EXAMPLE 1 Solving a Two-Step Inequality

Solve the equation $4x \leq 7x + 18$. Graph the solution.

Solution

$4x \leq 7x + 18$ — Original inequality

$4x - 7x \leq 7x + 18 - 7x$ — Subtract 7x from each side.

$-3x \leq 18$ — Simplify.

$\dfrac{-3x}{-3} \geq \dfrac{18}{-3}$ — Divide each side by −3 and reverse symbol.

$x \geq -6$ — Simplify.

Remember
Reverse the inequality symbol when you multiply or divide by a negative.

ANSWER The solution is all real numbers greater than or equal to −6.

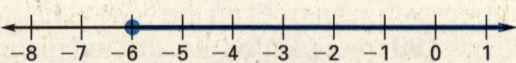

TRY THIS Solve the inequality. Graph the solution.

1. $6x - 7 < -4$ 2. $15x > 3x + 20$ 3. $2x \leq 10 - 3x$

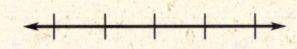   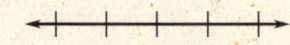   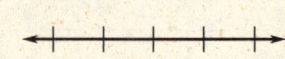

Math Intervention
Book 7 Getting Ready for Algebra

Name _____ Date _____

EXAMPLE 2 — Combining Like Terms

Solve the inequality $20 + 7n \geq 2n - 8 - 9n$. Graph the solution.

Solution

$20 + 7n \geq 2n - 8 - 9n$	Original inequality
$20 + 7n \geq -7n - 8$	Combine like terms.
$20 + 7n + 7n \geq -7n - 8 + 7n$	Add $7n$ to each side.
$20 + 14n \geq -8$	Simplify.
$20 + 14n - 20 \geq -8 - 20$	Subtract 20 from each side.
$14n \geq -28$	Simplify.
$\dfrac{14n}{14} \geq \dfrac{-28}{14}$	Divide each side by 14.
$n \geq -2$	Simplify.

ANSWER The solution is all real numbers greater than or equal to -2.

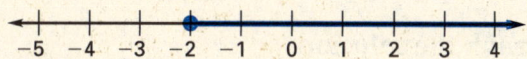

EXAMPLE 3 — Using the Distributive Property

Solve the inequality $4(2z + 3) + 2(z - 7) < 13$. Graph the solution.

Solution

$4(2z + 3) + 2(z - 7) < 13$	Original inequality
$8z + 12 + 2z - 14 < 13$	Distributive property
$10z - 2 < 13$	Combine like terms.
$10z - 2 + 2 < 13 + 2$	Add 2 to each side.
$10z < 15$	Simplify.
$\dfrac{10z}{10} < \dfrac{15}{10}$	Divide each side by 10.
$z < 1.5$	Simplify.

ANSWER The solution is all real numbers less than 1.5.

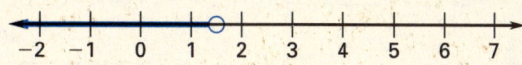

TRY THIS — Solve the inequality. Graph the solution.

4. $4x - 6 + 3x < 4 - 3x$

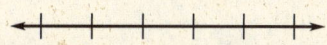

5. $2(3x - 10) \leq 5(x - 5)$

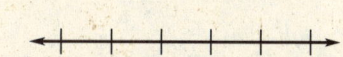

Name _____   Date _____

> **Summarize**
>
> **Solving a Multi-step Inequality**
>
> (1) Simplify expressions and combine like terms on each side of the inequality if possible.
> (2) Use the properties of equality to isolate the variable.
> (3) Reverse the inequality symbol when multiplying or dividing by a negative number.

Practice

Match the inequality with the graph of its solution.

1. $3x + 5 < 11$ _____
2. $x + 8 < 5x$ _____
3. $4x + 3 > -5$ _____

A. number line from −3 to 1, open circle at 2 (shaded left)
B. number line from −1 to 3, open circle at 2 (shaded right)
C. number line from 1 to 5, open circle at 2 (shaded right)

Solve the inequality. Graph the solution.

4. $3x - 4 < 8$ _____

5. $2x + 5 \geq 17$ _____

6. $-4x + 13 < -3$ _____

7. $-3q + 6 < -10q$ _____

8. $5p + 8 < 7p$ _____

9. $-6t + 10 \leq -5t$ _____

10. $-12 + 3x \leq 6 - 3x$ _____

11. $-3p - 9 \geq 5p + 3$ _____

12. $-6r - 14 > 3 + 4r - 5$ _____

13. $5(2 - n) > -15$ _____

14. $4x + 3 \geq 3(x + 6)$ _____

15. $7(x - 3) \leq -3(8 - 2x)$ _____

Math Intervention
Book 7 Getting Ready for Algebra

Name _____   Date _____

Write an inequality to model the situation. Then solve the inequality. Explain your reasoning.

16. Beth needed her washing machine fixed. She called a repairman who charges **$25** an hour in addition to a service fee of **$35**. How many hours could the repairman have worked if Beth's bill was less than **$85**?

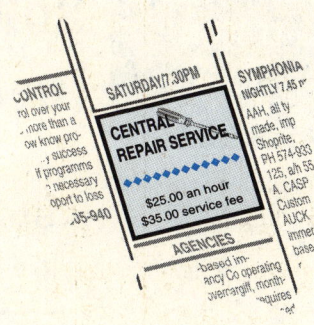

_____
_____
_____

17. James called a repairman to fix his dryer. The repairman's hourly rate was **$30** and his service fee was **$25**. How many hours could the repairman have worked if James' bill was less than **$115**?

_____
_____
_____

DID YOU GET IT?

18. **Fill in the missing words.** When solving a linear inequality, if you _____ or _____ by a _____ number, you must _____ the inequality symbol.

19. **Compare.** Explain the similarities and differences in solving the two inequalities $3x - 5 < 7$ and $-3x - 5 < 7$.

_____
_____

20. **Compare.** Explain the difference between the two solutions graphed here.

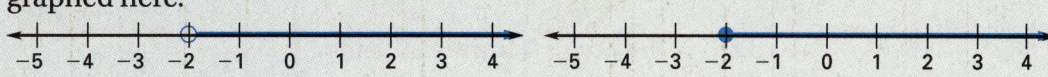

_____
_____

21. **Explain your reasoning.** Do the inequalities $-3x + 1 > -9x + 5$ and $-x + 6 > 2(x + 4)$ have the same solution? Explain why or why not.

_____
_____

Name _____ Date _____

LESSON 7-5
Solve Problems with Multi-step Inequalities

> **Strategies to Remember**
> To write inequalities with the correct inequality symbol:
>
> | Use < when the problem says:
• less than (or fewer than)
• under | Use > when the problem says:
• more than (or greater than)
• over |
> |---|---|
> | Use ≤ when the problem says:
• less than or equal to
• no more than
• at most | Use ≥ when the problem says:
• greater than or equal to
• no less than
• at least |
>
> When solving an inequality, reverse the inequality symbol when you multiply or divide by a negative number.

Getting Started In Lesson 7-1 you learned how to write equations and in Lesson 7-4 you learned how to solve multi-step inequalities. You will combine these two methods to solve problems using multi-step inequalities.

EXAMPLE 1 Solving a Multistep Inequality

A crate weighs 8 pounds. An apple weighs about $\frac{1}{4}$ pound. How many apples can be put in the crate if the total weight must be under 40 pounds?

Solution

Let a represent the number of apples.

$8 + \frac{1}{4}a < 40$ Write the inequality.

$\frac{1}{4}a < 32$ Subtract 8 from each side.

$a < 128$ Multiply each side by 4.

CHECK for reasonableness $\frac{1}{4}$ of $128 = \frac{1}{4} \cdot 128 = 32$. After adding the 8 pounds, the crate weighs 40 pounds. For the weight to be under 40 pounds, there must be fewer than 128 apples.

TRY THIS Solve the problem. Explain your reasoning.

1. Jackie has $20. She spends $12 on one item. She also wants some bracelets that cost $2 each. What is the greatest number of bracelets she can buy?

Math Intervention
Book 7 Getting Ready for Algebra

Name _____ Date _____

EXAMPLE 2 Solving a Multi-step Inequality

Becky is ordering shirts to sell for a school fundraiser. She needs at least 450 shirts. She has already ordered 200 shirts. To get a discounted price, she must order 50 shirts at a time. How many more groups of 50 shirts must she order?

Solution

Let s represent the number of groups of 50 shirts.

$200 + 50s \geq 450$	Write the inequality.
$50s \geq 250$	Subtract 200 from each side.
$s \geq 5$	Divide each side by 50.

CHECK for reasonableness 5 more orders of 50 shirts is 250 shirts, plus the 200 shirts Becky already ordered adds to 450 shirts. So, Becky must order at least 5 more groups of 50 shirts.

EXAMPLE 3 Solving a Multi-step Inequality

Dave must have at least $500 in his checking account to avoid paying a service charge. He now has $1025 in his account. He wrote one check for $375 and then he wrote 2 more checks that were for the same amount. What is the largest amount he could use to write the next 2 checks?

Solution

Let x be the amount of each of the 2 checks.

$1025 - 375 - 2x \geq 500$	Write the inequality.
$650 - 2x \geq 500$	Combine like terms.
$-2x \geq -150$	Subtract 650 from each side.
$x \leq 75$	Divide each side by -2.

> **Remember**
> When dividing by a negative number you must reverse the inequality symbol.

CHECK for reasonableness 75 times 2 is 150; subtracting both 150 and 375 from 1025 gives 500. So, Dave's next 2 checks must be no more than $75 each.

TRY THIS Use Example 3.

2. Suppose Dave deposits an additional $1000 into his account before writing any checks. How many checks for $375 can he write and still keep a minimum balance of $500? Explain your reasoning.

Name _____ Date _____

> **Summarize**
> **Solving Word Problems**
> (1) Read the problem carefully.
> (2) Decide what operations and inequality symbols are needed.
> (3) Write an inequality.
> (4) Solve the inequality.
> (5) Check your answer for reasonableness.

Practice

Fill in the correct inequality symbol for the situation described.

1. The baby's height, h, is no more than 21 inches. $h \bigcirc 21$

2. In Sarah's junior year of high school basketball, her average points per game, a, was over 32 points. $a \bigcirc 32$

3. The sum of 2 consecutive even integers is less than 62. $n + (n + 2) \bigcirc 62$

4. Brittney wants to drink at least 10 glasses of water today. She has already had 4 glasses. Each time she drinks water, she drinks 2 glasses. $2g + 4 \bigcirc 10$

Identify the first step to solve each of these inequalities.

5. $3x - 6 \leq 4$ 6. $6x - 2 \geq 10$ 7. $5x + 4 < 9$

_____   _____   _____

8. Fill in the missing information to solve the problem.
Laura is saving money to buy an MP3 player. After comparison shopping, she determined she needs at least $225 to get the one she wants. She has already saved $100. She plans to save money for another 5 weeks. How much money must she save each week?

Let w represent the amount to save each week.

Step 1 The words "at least" tells you the inequality symbol you need is $\bigcirc$.

Step 2 Write an inequality. $100 + 5w \bigcirc 225$

Step 3 Solve for w by first _____ 100 from each side.

Step 4 Next _____ each side by 5.

Step 5 Simplifying gives $w \geq$ ▢.

Step 6 Laura must save $▢ each week to buy the player she wants.

Math Intervention
Book 7 Getting Ready for Algebra

Name _____ Date _____

Write an inequality. Solve the inequality. Explain your reasoning.

9. Bob knew the route of a 4-day trip he took was at most **2650** miles. The first day he traveled **700** miles. Then he traveled the same number of miles on each of the remaining three days. What was the greatest amount of miles he traveled in each of the remaining days?

   _____
   _____
   _____

10. The sum of **2** consecutive integers is at least **47**. What are the two smallest integers possible?

    _____
    _____
    _____

11. Gary can play at most **54** holes with his golf cart when it is fully charged. He has already played **29** holes of golf. If he plays **5** holes an hour, how many hours will it take until his golf cart needs to be recharged?

    _____
    _____

DID YOU GET IT?

12. **Write a word problem.** Write a word problem for the inequality $50 + 25m \geq 200$. Solve the inequality. Explain how you came up with your situation.

    _____
    _____

13. **Explain your reasoning.** Your friend says that the answer to the following problem is at least **18** miles per day. Is your friend correct? Why or why not? Jessica is training to run a marathon. She wants to run at least **85** miles in **5** days. If she ran **31** miles the first **2** days, how much must she run each of the remaining days?

    _____
    _____

Math Intervention
Book 7 Getting Ready for Algebra

Mixed Practice for Lessons 7-1 to 7-5

Vocabulary Review

Match the word with its mathematical meaning and its everyday meaning.

Word	Mathematical meaning	Everyday meaning
1. variable ___, ___	A. the answer to a multiplication problem	X. something that changes or fluctuates
2. difference ___, ___	B. a letter used to represent an amount	Y. output of an industry
3. product ___, ___	C. the answer to a subtraction problem	Z. characteristic distinguishing one from another

Fill in the missing word(s).

4. In solving a multistep equation, whatever is done to one side of the equation must be done to the _____ side of the equation.

5. To solve $5x + 8 = 18$, the first step is to _____ 8 from each side.

6. When you are solving an inequality, if you multiply or divide by a negative number you must _____ the inequality symbol.

Write an equation or inequality to model the situation. Then solve the equation.

7. Seven less than a number is less than 20.

8. Five more than two times a number is 8.

9. Meredith has $200 in her savings account. If she saves $30 per week, how many weeks will it take for her to save at least $500 in her account?

Solve the equation. Graph the solution.

10. $3x = 9$ _____

11. $\dfrac{x}{5} = 8$ _____

12. $x - 6 = 7$ _____

13. $x + 5 = 10$ _____

Math Intervention
Book 7 Getting Ready for Algebra

Name _____ Date _____

Solve the equation or inequality. Graph the solution.

14. $2x + 7 = 13$ _____

15. $7x - 1 = 6$ _____

16. $2x + 4 < 8$ _____

17. $-3x + 5 \geq 17$ _____

18. Fill in the missing information to solve the problem. Jeremy's cell phone allows him to talk for at most **90** minutes before it needs to be recharged. He has used **45** minutes so far. If he talks for the same length of time to **3** more people, how long can he talk to each person?

Step 1 The phrase "at most" tells you the inequality symbol you should use is .

Step 2 Write an inequality: ▢ $+ 3m$ ● 90

Step 3 Solve for m by first _____ 45 from each side.

Step 4 Next _____ each side by 3.

Step 5 $m \leq$ ▢

Step 6 Jeremy can talk for **15** or _____ minutes to each of the **3** people.

Solve the equation or inequality.

19. $\dfrac{x}{3} = 8$ **20.** $3x + 6 = 5x$ **21.** $7x + 2 < 9$

22. $2x - 1 = -11$ **23.** $15x + 4 > 14x + 9$ **24.** $x + 3 + 2x = 21$

Write an equation or inequality. Then solve the problem. Explain your reasoning.

25. A farmer wants to have **52** rows of sweet corn in his field. He has already planted **12** rows. If his tractor plants **8** rows per round, how many more rounds does he need to get **52** rows?

_____
_____
_____

26. Trevor is **4** years older than his sister. The sum of their ages is at most **42**. What is the oldest Trevor and his sister can be?

_____
_____
_____

Name _____   Date _____

Looking for Exponent Patterns

> **Goal:** Understand the meaning of zero and negative exponents by seeing a pattern
>
> Materials: Powers of 4 cards

Getting Started In Lesson 1-25 you learned how to multiply and divide by 10 and powers of 10. In Lesson 5-1 you learned to describe and extend a numerical pattern. You can also use patterns to understand the meaning of zero and negative exponents.

EXAMPLE

Find the pattern in the table, then complete the table.

n	10^n	Value of 10^n
4	10^4	10,000
3	10^3	1000
2	10^2	100
1	10^1	10
0	10^0	1
−1	10^{-1}	$\frac{1}{10}$
−2	10^{-2}	$\frac{1}{100}$
−3	10^{-3}	
−4	10^{-4}	

Pattern: _____

Notice that the zero power of 10 is 1.

Notice that negative powers of 10 are fractions with positive integer powers.

Powers of 4 The pattern involving powers of 10 that you saw in the Example above can be extended to powers of other numbers. You can use a pattern involving powers of 4 in the Game described on page 25.

Name _____   Date _____

MAKE IT A GAME!

- Form groups of **2** to **3** students and choose a dealer.
- The dealer shuffles the cards and lays them face down on the table.
- The first player turns over **2** cards and decides if they are equal. If they are equal, that player gets those **2** cards and then gets another turn. If they are not equal, the player turns them face down where they were.
- The next player takes a turn and does the same thing. Play continues until all the cards have been matched up and are gone.
- All players should watch what cards are turned over by the other players and try to remember where the cards are so they can find the most matches.
- Players get one point for each pair they have.
- The player with the greatest number of points wins.

$$4^{-2} = \frac{1}{16}$$

$$4^0 = 1$$

Practice

In Exercises 1–6, use the cards to find the value of the power.

1. 4^2
2. 4^{-2}
3. 4^{-1}
4. 4^1
5. 4^0
6. 4^{-3}

7. **Make a Conjecture** Let x be a positive integer. Based on your answers to Exercises 1–6, make a conjecture about the value of the expression x^0.

8. **Make a Conjecture** Let x and n be positive integers. Based on your answers to Exercises 1–6, make a conjecture about x^{-n} compared to the value of x^n.

DID YOU GET IT? Find the value of the power.

9. 5^0
10. 3^{-2}
11. 2^{-3}

Math Intervention
Book 7 Getting Ready for Algebra

Name _____ Date _____

LESSON 7-1
Zero and Negative Exponents

> **Words to Remember**
>
> A power has a base and an exponent.
>
> base → 3^{-2} ← exponent
> power
>
> For any nonzero number b, $b^0 = 1$.
>
> For any nonzero number b, b^{-n} is the reciprocal of b^n, so $b^{-n} = \dfrac{1}{b^n}$.

Getting Started In Lesson 1-32 you learned to work with positive exponents. All of the same rules of exponents apply for zero and negative exponents. Zero exponents make the power equal to 1. With negative exponents, you take the reciprocal of the power.

EXAMPLE 1 Using Negative Exponents

Write 6^{-2} as a simple fraction without a negative exponent.

Solution

$6^{-2} = \dfrac{1}{6^2}$ Negative exponent property

$= \dfrac{1}{36}$ Simplify.

EXAMPLE 2 Using Negative Exponents

Write $\dfrac{1}{81}$ as an integer with a negative exponent. Use the smallest integer possible.

Solution

$\dfrac{1}{81} = \dfrac{1}{3^4}$

$= 3^{-4}$ Negative exponent property

Another Way

Notice that $\dfrac{1}{81}$ can also be written as 9^{-2}.

TRY THIS Write the expression without a negative exponent.

1. 3^{-1}
2. 4^{-3}
3. 2^{-4}

Math Intervention
Book 7 Getting Ready for Algebra

EXAMPLE 3 Using Zero Exponents

Simplify 4^0.

Solution

$4^0 = 1$ Zero exponent property

EXAMPLE 4 Rewriting Without Negative Exponents

Rewrite the expression without negative exponents.

a. $r^5 \cdot t^{-3}$ b. $3n^{-4} \cdot a^3$

Solution

a. $r^5 \cdot t^{-3} = r^5 \cdot \dfrac{1}{t^3}$ Negative exponent property

$= \dfrac{r^5}{t^3}$ Simplify.

b. $3n^{-4} \cdot a^3 = 3 \cdot \dfrac{1}{n^4} \cdot a^3$ Negative exponent property

$= \dfrac{3a^3}{n^4}$ Simplify.

TRY THIS

Write with a negative exponent.

4. $\dfrac{1}{49} =$ ____   5. $\dfrac{1}{32} =$ ____   6. $\dfrac{1}{27} =$ ____

Simplify and rewrite without negative exponents.

7. 8^0 8. $b^5 \cdot c^{-2}$ 9. $4c^{-3} \cdot b^{-1}$

10. 3^0 11. $h^{-5} \cdot k^3$ 12. $2a^3 \cdot c^{-2}$

Complete using >, <, or =.

13. $7^0 \bigcirc 7^1$ 14. $4^3 \bigcirc 4^{-3}$ 15. $\dfrac{1}{27} \bigcirc 3^{-3}$

16. $12^{-1} \bigcirc 12^0$ 17. $6^{-4} \bigcirc 6^{-3}$ 18. $\dfrac{1}{3} \bigcirc 12 \cdot 6^{-2}$

Name _____ Date _____

> **Summarize**
>
> Zero exponents: Any number or variable to the zero power equals **1**.
> Examples: $4^0 = 1$ $n^0 = 1$
>
> Negative exponents: Any number or variable to the negative power equals one over that number to the positive power.
> Examples: $8^{-3} = \frac{1}{8^3}$ $x^{-2} = \frac{1}{x^2}$

Practice

Match the expression with the correct integer or fraction.

1. 3^{-2} _____
2. 4^0 _____
3. 2^{-3} _____

A. $\frac{1}{8}$
B. $\frac{1}{9}$
C. 1

Write each fraction as an integer with a negative exponent.

4. $\frac{1}{25} =$ ____
5. $\frac{1}{216} =$ ____
6. $\frac{1}{125} =$ ____

Simplify.

7. $x^{-2} \cdot z^3$
8. $a^{-3} \cdot b^2$
9. $3^{-3} \cdot 4^2$
10. $2^2 \cdot 3^{-2}$
11. $3^0 \cdot x^0$
12. $3n^3 \cdot m^{-4}$

Write as a simple fraction without a negative exponent.

13. $3^{-2} =$ ____
14. $7^0 =$ ____
15. $x^{-3} =$ ____

16. $5^{-3} =$ ____
17. $y^{-1} =$ ____
18. $2^0 =$ ____

Tell whether the equation is true or false.

19. $6^{-2} = \frac{1}{6} \cdot \frac{1}{6}$ _____
20. $2^{-5} = \frac{1}{5} \cdot \frac{1}{5}$ _____
21. $4^{-3} = 1 \div (4 \cdot 4 \cdot 4)$ _____

Match the expression with the graph of its value.

22. 2^{-2}
23. 8^0
24. 3^{-1}

A.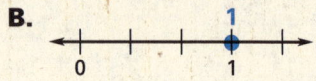

B.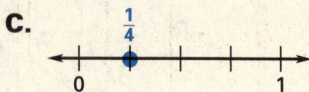

C.

Write each number as a power using a positive or negative exponent.

25. One of Robert's ancestors was from Ireland. So Robert is $\frac{1}{32}$ Irish.

    $\frac{1}{32} =$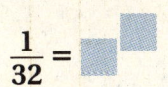

26. A millisecond, or $\frac{1}{1000}$ of a second, is used to measure the time needed to write information to a CD-ROM.

    $\frac{1}{1000} =$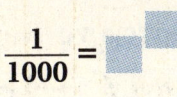

27. A one-pound box of a certain type of nail contains **49** nails.

    $49 =$

28. Yarn for sweaters and other items is described by a number that is $\frac{1}{1600}$ times the length of one pound of the yarn.

    $\frac{1}{1600} =$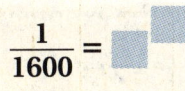

29. There are **144** eggs in a crate, and $\frac{1}{144}$ of the eggs are broken.

    $\frac{1}{144} =$

DID YOU GET IT?

30. **Fill in the missing words.** Any number raised to the _____ power equals **1**. The _____ of b^{-n} is b^n.

31. **Describe a process.** Explain how $4^{-2} = \frac{1}{16}$ by using a pattern of repeated division. Show what happens at each step.

    _____
    _____
    _____

32. **Explain your reasoning.** Your friend says $3^{-1} + 3^{-6} + 4^{-2} = \frac{1}{3} + \frac{1}{729} + \frac{1}{8}$. Is your friend correct? Explain why or why not.

    _____
    _____
    _____

Name _____ Date _____

LESSON 7-8 — Product of Powers

> **Words to Remember**
>
> Power: 4^5 → 4 is the base, 5 is the exponent
> $4^5 = 4 \cdot 4 \cdot 4 \cdot 4 \cdot 4$
>
> Notice that $x^3 \cdot x^4 = (x \cdot x \cdot x) \cdot (x \cdot x \cdot x \cdot x) = x \cdot x \cdot x \cdot x \cdot x \cdot x \cdot x$.
>   3 factors   4 factors   7 factors
>
> So, $x^3 \cdot x^4 = x^{3+4} = x^7$.
>
> Product of powers property: To multiply powers having the same base, add the exponents.
>
> $x^a \cdot x^b = x^{a+b}$

Getting Started In Lesson 1-32 you learned to work with positive exponents. You will now multiply variable expressions that each have exponents.

EXAMPLE 1 Multiplying Powers with the Same Base

Simplify $x^6 \cdot x^4$. Show two different methods.

Solution 1 Use multiplication.

$x^6 \cdot x^4 = (x \cdot x \cdot x \cdot x \cdot x \cdot x) \cdot (x \cdot x \cdot x \cdot x)$ Write without exponents.

$= x \cdot x \cdot x \cdot x \cdot x \cdot x \cdot x \cdot x \cdot x \cdot x$ Combine product.

$= x^{10}$ Simplify.

Solution 2 Use the property.

$x^6 \cdot x^4 = x^{6+4}$ Product of powers property

$= x^{10}$ Simplify.

TRY THIS Simplify. Use either multiplication or the product of powers property.

1. $x^7 \cdot x^2 = x^{\square}$
2. $y^3 \cdot y^7 = y^{\square}$
3. $n^5 \cdot n^5 = n^{\square}$
4. $p^{12} \cdot p^3 = p^{\square}$
4. $r^{10} \cdot r^{-4} = r^{\square}$
6. $t^7 \cdot t^6 = t^{\square}$

Name _____ Date _____

EXAMPLE 2 — Simplifying Powers When the Bases Are Not the Same

Simplify $b^4 \cdot n^2 \cdot b^3 \cdot n$.

Solution 1 Use multiplication.

$b^4 \cdot n^2 \cdot b^3 \cdot n = (b \cdot b \cdot b \cdot b) \cdot (n \cdot n) \cdot (b \cdot b \cdot b) \cdot n$ Write without exponents.

$= (b \cdot b \cdot b \cdot b) \cdot (b \cdot b \cdot b) \cdot (n \cdot n) \cdot n$ Commutative property of multiplication

$= b^7 \cdot n^3$ Simplify.

Solution 2 Use the property.

$b^4 \cdot n^2 \cdot b^3 \cdot n = b^4 \cdot b^3 \cdot n^2 \cdot n$ Commutative property of multiplication

$= b^{4+3} \cdot n^{2+1}$ Product of powers property

$= b^7 \cdot n^3$ Simplify.

EXAMPLE 3 — Simplifying Powers

Simplify $4^2 \cdot 4^{-1} \cdot 4^5$.

Solution

$4^2 \cdot 4^{-1} \cdot 4^5 = 4^{2+(-1)+5}$ Product of powers property

$= 4^6$ Add.

$= 4096$ Simplify.

TRY THIS Simplify.

7. $a^3 \cdot b^2 \cdot a^5 \cdot b^3 = a^{\square} \, b^{\square}$

8. $c^4 \cdot n^3 \cdot c^5 = c^{\square} \, n^{\square}$

9. $b^6 \cdot b^5 \cdot d^{-3} \cdot d^4 = b^{\square} \, d^{\square}$

10. $5^1 \cdot 5^2 \cdot 5^3$

11. $2^9 \cdot 2^{-3} \cdot 2^{-2}$

12. $c^8 \cdot d^5 \cdot c^2 \cdot d^3$

13. $3^1 \cdot 3^{-2} \cdot 3^4$

Name _____ Date _____

> **Summarize**
>
> **Finding the Product of Powers**
>
> (1) To find the product of two powers with the same base, add the exponents. Keep the base the same.
>
>   Example: $b^3 \cdot b^4 = b^7$
>
> (2) A product of powers with different bases cannot be simplified.
>
>   Example: $a^4 \cdot b^5$ cannot be simplified.

Practice

Match the expression with the correct product.

1. $a^3 \cdot b^5 \cdot a^4$ _____
2. $a^7 \cdot b^5 \cdot a^5$ _____
3. $a^5 \cdot b^3 \cdot a^4$ _____

A. $a^{12} \cdot b^5$
B. $a^9 \cdot b^3$
C. $a^7 \cdot b^5$

Tell whether the equation is true or false.

4. $a^5 \cdot b^5 \cdot a^5 = a^{25} \cdot b^5$
5. $c^{-5} \cdot d^8 \cdot c^8 = c^{-5} \cdot d^{16}$
6. $n^2 \cdot t^9 \cdot t^5 = n^2 \cdot t^{14}$

_____ _____ _____

Simplify.

7. $x^3 \cdot x^5$
8. $x^0 \cdot x^4$
9. $x^0 \cdot y^0 \cdot z^3$

10. $a^2 \cdot b^3 \cdot a^3$
11. $n^2 \cdot m^3$
12. $c^4 \cdot b^7 \cdot b^3$

13. $a^3 \cdot a^{-2}$
14. $b^5 \cdot c^3 \cdot b^{-2}$
15. $x^3 \cdot y^2 \cdot x^4$

16. $n^2 \cdot n^8$
17. $d^{-4} \cdot f^2 \cdot d^5 \cdot f^3$
18. $a^2 \cdot b^{-1} \cdot b^3 \cdot a^4$

19. $2^3 \cdot 2^2$
20. $x^5 \cdot x^{-2}$
21. $c^2 \cdot c^5$

22. $3^7 \cdot 3^{-1} \cdot 3^2$
23. $4^{-2} \cdot 4^4$
24. $b^{15} \cdot b^{-3} \cdot b^{-2}$

Evaluate the expression when $x = 2$. Match the result with the correct graph.

25. $x^{-3} \cdot x^6$ _____
26. $x^{-4} \cdot x^8$ _____
27. $x^0 \cdot x^2$ _____

A.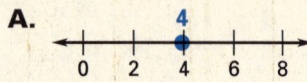

B.
```
  ←—+—+—+—●—+—+—+→
    2   4   6   8   10
              8
```

C.
```
  ←—+—+—●—+—+→
    8  12  16  20  24
           16
```

Name _____ Date _____

Model the situation by substituting values for the variables in the given equation. Then solve the equation. Explain your reasoning.

28. Suppose some bacteria triple in number every hour. There are 300 bacteria in the beginning. After h hours there will be B bacteria. Use the formula $B = 300 \cdot 3^h$. How many bacteria will there be after 2 hours?

_____
_____
_____

29. The expression 2^x represents the approximate number of limestone and granite blocks that make up the Great Pyramid in Egypt. The average mass in kilograms of one of these blocks is represented by the expression 2^y. Use the equation $M = 2^x \cdot 2^y$ to approximate the total mass in kilograms M of the Great Pyramid if $x = 21$ and $y = 11$.

_____
_____
_____

DID YOU GET IT?

30. Fill in the missing words. When multiplying powers with the same base, _____ the exponents; the _____ stays the same.

31. Describe a process. Explain how to simplify the expression $6^3 \cdot 6^{-3} \cdot 6^2$.

_____
_____
_____

32. Explain your reasoning. Your friend says that the product of x^4 and x^3 equals x^{12}. Is your friend correct? Explain why or why not.

_____
_____
_____

Name _____   Date _____

LESSON 7-9
Power of a Power

> **Words to Remember**
>
> Power of a power: A number with an exponent is raised to a power $(3^2)^3$
> Notice that $(3^2)^3 = 3^2 \cdot 3^2 \cdot 3^2 = (3 \cdot 3) \cdot (3 \cdot 3) \cdot (3 \cdot 3) = 3^6$
> So, $(3^2)^3 = 3^{2 \cdot 3} = 3^6$.
> Power of a power property: To find a power of a power, multiply the exponents.

Getting Started In Lesson 1-32 you learned how to work with positive exponents. In Lesson 7-8 you found the product of powers. You can combine these methods to find the power of a power.

EXAMPLE 1   Finding the Power of a Power

Simplify $(x^3)^2$. Show two different methods.

Solution 1 Use multiplication.

$(x^3)^2$ means (x^3) is multiplied by itself 2 times.

$(x^3)^2 = (x \cdot x \cdot x) \cdot (x \cdot x \cdot x)$ Write without exponents.

$ = x \cdot x \cdot x \cdot x \cdot x \cdot x$ Write without parentheses.

$ = x^6$ Simplify.

Solution 2 Use the property.

$(x^3)^2 = x^{3 \cdot 2}$ Power of a power property

$(x^3)^2 = x^6$ Simplify.

TRY THIS   Simplify. Use either multiplication or the power of a power property.

1. $(x^5)^2$ 2. $(k^9)^3$ 3. $(x^3)^{11}$

4. $(t^4)^8$ 5. $(p^7)^4$ 6. $(m^{10})^2$

7. $(b^2)^1$ 8. $(c^0)^5$ 9. $(g^{12})^3$

Math Intervention
Book 7 Getting Ready for Algebra

EXAMPLE 2 Multiplying Powers

Simplify $2b^5 \cdot (b^2)^3$.

Solution 1 Use multiplication.

$2b^5 \cdot (b^2)^3 = 2 \cdot (b \cdot b \cdot b \cdot b \cdot b) \cdot (b \cdot b) \cdot (b \cdot b) \cdot (b \cdot b)$ Write without exponents.

$ = 2 \cdot (b \cdot b \cdot b \cdot b \cdot b \cdot b \cdot b \cdot b \cdot b \cdot b \cdot b)$ Combine product.

$ = 2 \cdot b^{11} = 2b^{11}$ Simplify.

Solution 2 Use the property.

$2b^5 \cdot (b^2)^3 = 2 \cdot b^5 \cdot b^{2 \cdot 3}$ Power of a power property

$ = 2 \cdot b^5 \cdot b^6$ Simplify.

$ = 2b^{11}$ Product of a power property

EXAMPLE 3 Simplify Expressions With Powers Raised to Powers

Simplify $3^{-10} \cdot (3^4)^5$.

Solution

$3^{-10} \cdot (3^4)^5 = 3^{-10} \cdot 3^{4 \cdot 5}$ Power of a power property

$\phantom{3^{-10} \cdot (3^4)^5} = 3^{-10} \cdot 3^{20}$ Simplify.

$\phantom{3^{-10} \cdot (3^4)^5} = 3^{-10+20}$ Product of powers property

$\phantom{3^{-10} \cdot (3^4)^5} = 3^{10}$ Add.

TRY THIS Simplify.

10. $4a^3 \cdot (a^2)^2 = \square \cdot a^{\square}$

11. $3n^3 \cdot (n^4)^5 = \square \cdot n^{\square}$

12. $6p^7 \cdot (p^3)^7 = \square \cdot p^{\square}$

13. $(2^8)^2$

14. $7 \cdot (p^3)^4 \cdot 3$

15. $(x^3)^2$

16. $5 \cdot (t^3)^8 \cdot 2^2$

17. $(6^2)^8$

18. $2^3 \cdot (x^2)^4 \cdot (x^1)^5 \cdot 3^2$

Name _____ Date _____

> **Summarize**
>
> **Finding the Power of a Power**
>
> To find the power of a power, multiply the exponents and keep the base the same.
>
> Example: $(x^m)^n = x^{mn}$, where x is a real number and m and n are positive integers.
>
> Example: $(b^2)^4 = b^8$

Practice

Match the expression with the correct form of a power of a power.

1. $a^3 \cdot a^3$ _____   **A.** $(a^2)^2$

2. $a^2 \cdot a^2 \cdot a^2$ _____   **B.** $(a^2)^3$

3. $a^2 \cdot a^2$ _____   **C.** $(a^3)^2$

Match the expression with the correct answer after simplifying.

4. $(x^4)^{10}$ _____   5. $(x^2)^7$ _____   6. $(x^3)^3$ _____

A. x^{40} **B.** x^9 **C.** x^{14}

Tell whether the equation is true or false.

7. $2 \cdot (c^2)^3 = 2c^5$ 8. $3 \cdot (d^5)^2 = 3d^{10}$ 9. $(r^3)^2 \cdot (r^2)^3 = r^{12}$

Simplify.

10. $(m^7)^4$ 11. $(p^3)^6$ 12. $(z^4)^5$

13. $(t^3)^3$ 14. $(x^7)^0$ 15. $(s^4)^2$

16. $3v \cdot (v^2)^3$ 17. $2^3 \cdot t \cdot (t^4)^6$ 18. $6 \cdot (n^8)^5$

Evaluate when $x = 4$.

19. $(x^3)^2$ 20. $2 \cdot (x^2)^1$ 21. $3x \cdot (x^2)^2$

Simplify.

22. $(3^3)^4$ 23. $(x^2)^7$ 24. $3^3 \cdot (b^2)^4$

25. $(a^{10})^4$ 26. $5x \cdot (x^3)^5$ 27. $4^2 \cdot (p^3)^2$

Math Intervention
Book 7 Getting Ready for Algebra

Name _____ Date _____

Write an expression or equation to model the situation. Then simplify the expression or equation. Explain your reasoning.

28. A cube has side lengths as shown.

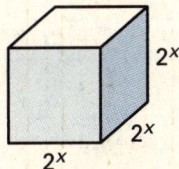

The volume of a cube can be found by multiplying the length times the width times the height. Write an expression for the volume of the cube. Then find the volume when $x = 3$.

_____
_____

29. A cube has side lengths as shown.

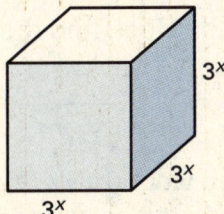

The volume of a cube can be found by raising a side length to the third power. Write an expression for the volume of the cube. Then find the volume when $x = 2$.

_____
_____

DID YOU GET IT?

30. **Fill in the missing words.** When raising a power to a _____, you must _____ the exponents.

31. **Describe a process.** Explain how to simplify $[(x^3)^2]^4$.

_____
_____

32. **Explain your reasoning.** Your friend says that the product of 7 and $(x^5)^2$ equals $7 \cdot x^7$. Is your friend correct? Explain why or why not.

_____
_____
_____

Math Intervention
Book 7 Getting Ready for Algebra

LESSON 7-10: Power of a Product

Words to Remember

Power of a product: When a product is raised to a power $(bn)^5$

Notice that $(bn)^5 = (b \cdot n) \cdot (b \cdot n) \cdot (b \cdot n) \cdot (b \cdot n) \cdot (b \cdot n)$

$$= \underbrace{(b \cdot b \cdot b \cdot b \cdot b)}_{\text{5 factors}} \cdot \underbrace{(n \cdot n \cdot n \cdot n \cdot n)}_{\text{5 factors}}$$

$$= b^5 \cdot n^5$$

So, $(bn)^5 = b^5 n^5$.

Power of a product property: To find the power of a product, find the power of each factor and multiply.

Getting Started In Lesson 1-32 you learned how to work with positive exponents. In Lesson 7-8 you found the product of powers. You can combine these methods to find the power of a product.

EXAMPLE 1 Simplifying Expressions Involving Powers of Products

Simplify $(xy)^4$. Show two different methods.

Solution 1 Use multiplication.

$(xy)^4 = (x \cdot y) \cdot (x \cdot y) \cdot (x \cdot y) \cdot (x \cdot y)$	Write without exponents.
$(xy)^4 = x \cdot y \cdot x \cdot y \cdot x \cdot y \cdot x \cdot y$	Combine product.
$= x \cdot x \cdot x \cdot x \cdot y \cdot y \cdot y \cdot y$	Commutative property of multiplication
$= x^4 \cdot y^4$	Simplify.

Solution 2 Use the property.

$(xy)^4 = x^4 \cdot y^4$	Power of a product property

TRY THIS
Simplify. Use either multiplication or the power of a product property.

1. $(ab)^5 = a^{\square} \cdot b^{\square}$
2. $(2c)^2 = {\square} \cdot c^{\square}$
3. $(3r)^4 = {\square} \cdot r^{\square}$
4. $(cd)^{10} = c^{\square} \cdot d^{\square}$
5. $(xz)^8 = x^{\square} \cdot z^{\square}$
6. $(2y)^3 = {\square} \cdot y^{\square}$

Math Intervention
Book 7 Getting Ready for Algebra

Name _____ Date _____

EXAMPLE 2 Rewriting Without Parentheses and Simplifying

Rewrite $\frac{1}{2}(4n)^3$ **without parentheses and simplify.**

Solution 1 Use multiplication.

$\frac{1}{2}(4n)^3 = \frac{1}{2}(4 \cdot n) \cdot (4 \cdot n) \cdot (4 \cdot n)$ Write without exponents.

$= \frac{1}{2}(4 \cdot n \cdot 4 \cdot n \cdot 4 \cdot n)$ Combine product.

$= \frac{1}{2}(4 \cdot 4 \cdot 4 \cdot n \cdot n \cdot n)$ Commutative property of multiplication

$= 32 \cdot n^3$ Simplify.

Solution 2 Use the property.

$\frac{1}{2}(4n)^3 = \frac{1}{2}(4^3) \cdot (n^3)$ Power of a product property

$= \frac{1}{2}(64) \cdot (n^3)$ Simplify.

$= 32 \cdot n^3$ Simplify.

EXAMPLE 3 Evaluating Products With Powers

Evaluate $(3x)^3$ **when** $x = 2$.

Solution

$(3x)^3 = (3 \cdot 2)^3$ Substitute 2 for x.

$= (6)^3$ Simplify within parentheses.

$= 216$ Simplify.

TRY THIS

Rewrite without parentheses and simplify.

7. $(abc)^2$
8. $3(2y)^3$
9. $15(6mnt)^0$

Evaluate the expression when $r = 3$.

10. $0.5(2r)^4$
11. $7(5r)^0$
12. $4(3r)^2$

> **Remember**
> Any number or expression raised to the zero power is 1.

Name _____ Date _____

> **Summarize**
>
> **Finding the Power of a Product**
> To find the power of a product, raise each factor to the power. Then multiply.
> Example: $(cdf)^3 = c^3 \cdot d^3 \cdot f^3$

Practice

Match the expression with the correct answer after simplifying.

1. $2(xyz)^3$ _____   A. $8x^3 \cdot y^3 \cdot z^3$

2. $(2xyz)^3$ _____   B. $4x^2 \cdot y^2 \cdot z^2$

3. $(2xyz)^2$ _____   C. $2x^3 \cdot y^3 \cdot z^3$

Tell whether the equation is true or false.

4. $4m(mp)^5 = 4m^6p^5$ _____   5. $2(cft)^7 = 2cft^7$ _____   6. $(nr^3)^2 \cdot (nr)^3 = n^5r^9$ _____

Simplify.

7. $(2m)^4$ 8. $(gt^2)^3$ 9. $(ad)^3$

10. $(abc^2)^5$ 11. $(4x^3)^2$ 12. $(c^2x^3)^8$

13. $2n \cdot (b^3n)^6$ 14. $5 \cdot (ms^4)^2$ 15. $3^2 \cdot r \cdot (vr^2)^0$

Evaluate when $x = 3$.

16. $(2x^3)^2$ 17. $4 \cdot (2x)^2$ 18. $5x \cdot (3x^2)^0$

Rewrite without parentheses and simplify.

19. $(3x^3)^4$ 20. $(bx^2)^3$ 21. $2^3 \cdot (ab^2)^5$

22. $(6af)^3$ 23. $3x \cdot (cx^2)^3$ 24. $5t \cdot (pt^3)^2$

Which graph is the solution of the expression when $n = 2$?

25. $(2n)^2$ _____   26. $\frac{1}{2}(4n)^0$ _____   27. $\frac{1}{3}(3n)^2$ _____

A.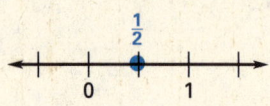

B.
```
       16
<--+---+---+---+---+-->
   8  12  16  20  24
```

C.
```
          12
<--+---+---+---+---+-->
   8  10  12  14  16
```

Name _____ Date _____

Write an expression to model the situation. Then simplify the expression. Explain your reasoning.

28. A square has side lengths as shown.

    The area of a square is the square of its side length. What is the area of the square?

    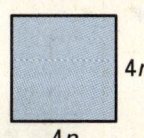

    _____
    _____
    _____

29. Two cubes have side lengths as shown. The length of a side of the second cube is twice the length of a side of the first cube.

    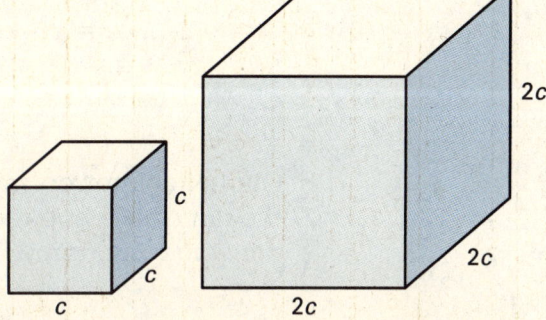

    The volume of a cube can be found by raising a side length to the third power. The volume of the larger cube is how many times larger than the volume of the smaller cube?

    _____
    _____
    _____

DID YOU GET IT?

30. **Fill in the missing words.** When finding the power of a _____, every term in _____ must be raised to the power.

31. **Compare.** Explain the difference between the two expressions $2(x)^2$ and $(2x)^2$.

    _____
    _____

32. **Explain your reasoning.** Is the product $(x^3y)^2$ equal to $(x^2y)^3$? Explain why or why not.

    _____
    _____

Name _____ Date _____

LESSON 7-11
Quotient of Powers

Words to Remember

Quotient of powers: Dividing two numbers with the same base and exponents that are the same or different

Notice that $\dfrac{x^5}{x^2} = \dfrac{x \cdot x \cdot x \cdot x \cdot x}{x \cdot x}$

$\phantom{Notice that \dfrac{x^5}{x^2}} = x^3$

So, $\dfrac{x^5}{x^2} = x^{5-2} = x^3$.

Quotient of powers property: To find the quotient of two powers with the same base, subtract the exponents. The common base must be a nonzero real number.

Getting Started In Lesson 7-8 you worked with the product of powers and added the exponents when the bases were the same. You will now study the quotient of powers and subtract the exponents when the bases are the same.

EXAMPLE 1 Dividing Expressions Involving Exponents with a Common Base

Divide $\dfrac{p^7}{p^3}$. Show two different methods.

Solution 1 Use division.

$\dfrac{p^7}{p^3} = \dfrac{p \cdot p \cdot p \cdot p \cdot p \cdot p \cdot p}{p \cdot p \cdot p}$  Write without exponents.

$\phantom{\dfrac{p^7}{p^3}} = p \cdot p \cdot p \cdot p$ Divide out common factors.

$\phantom{\dfrac{p^7}{p^3}} = p^4$ Simplify.

Solution 2 Use the property.

$\dfrac{p^7}{p^3} = p^{7-3}$ Quotient of powers property

$\phantom{\dfrac{p^7}{p^3}} = p^4$ Simplify.

Applying the Quotient of Powers Property In Example 1, the greater exponent was in the numerator of the fraction. You can also apply the quotient of powers property when the greater exponent is in the denominator.

Math Intervention
Book 7 Getting Ready for Algebra

Name _____   Date _____

EXAMPLE 2   **Dividing When the Greater Exponent Is in the Denominator**

Simplify $\dfrac{x^4}{x^6}$.

Solution 1 Use division.

$\dfrac{x^4}{x^6} = \dfrac{x \cdot x \cdot x \cdot x}{x \cdot x \cdot x \cdot x \cdot x \cdot x}$ Write without exponents.

$\phantom{\dfrac{x^4}{x^6}} = \dfrac{1}{x \cdot x}$ Divide out common factors.

$\phantom{\dfrac{x^4}{x^6}} = \dfrac{1}{x^2}$ Simplify.

Solution 2 Use the property.

$\dfrac{x^4}{x^6} = x^{4-6}$ Quotient of powers property

$\phantom{\dfrac{x^4}{x^6}} = x^{-2}$ Simplify.

$\phantom{\dfrac{x^4}{x^6}} = \dfrac{1}{x^2}$ Write using a positive exponent.

EXAMPLE 3   **Dividing Powers When the Bases Are Not the Same**

Simplify $\dfrac{3a^3b^4c^2}{9ab^2c^6}$.

Remember
$a = a^1$

Solution

$\dfrac{3a^3b^4c^2}{9ab^2c^6} = \dfrac{3}{9} \cdot \dfrac{a^3}{a} \cdot \dfrac{b^4}{b^2} \cdot \dfrac{c^2}{c^6}$ Rewrite as a product of fractions.

$\phantom{\dfrac{3a^3b^4c^2}{9ab^2c^6}} = \dfrac{1}{3} \cdot a^{3-1} \cdot b^{4-2} \cdot c^{2-6}$ Quotient of powers property.

$\phantom{\dfrac{3a^3b^4c^2}{9ab^2c^6}} = \dfrac{1}{3} \cdot a^2 \cdot b^2 \cdot c^{-4}$ Simplify.

$\phantom{\dfrac{3a^3b^4c^2}{9ab^2c^6}} = \dfrac{a^2b^2}{3c^4}$ Write using positive exponents.

TRY THIS

Suppose you write each quotient as an integer raised to a power. Predict whether the integer will be raised to a positive or a negative power.

1. $\dfrac{6^3}{6^2}$ 2. $\dfrac{10^7}{10^9}$ 3. $\dfrac{2^{11}}{2^3}$

Divide.

4. $\dfrac{r^8}{r^3} = r^{\boxed{}}$ 5. $\dfrac{m^{10}}{m^2} = m^{\boxed{}}$ 6. $\dfrac{t^2}{t^6} = t^{\boxed{}}$

Simplify.

7. $\dfrac{4x^3}{6x^2}$ 8. $\dfrac{d^3f^5}{d^2f^{10}}$ 9. $\dfrac{2c^2d}{4c}$

Name _____ Date _____

> **Summarize**
>
> **Finding the Quotient of Powers**
>
> (1) To find the quotient of two powers with the same base, subtract the exponents and keep the base the same.
>
> Example: $\dfrac{b^8}{b^2} = b^{8-2} = b^6$
>
> (2) A quotient of powers with different bases cannot be simplified.
>
> Example: $\dfrac{c^5}{a^3}$ cannot be simplified.

Practice

Match the expression with the correct quotient.

1. $\dfrac{a^7}{a^4}$ _____
2. $\dfrac{a^4}{a^7}$ _____
3. $\dfrac{a^{15}}{a^4}$ _____

A. a^{11}
B. a^3
C. $\dfrac{1}{a^3}$

Suppose you write each quotient as an integer raised to a power. Predict whether the integer will be raised to a positive or a negative power.

4. $\dfrac{5^8}{5^7}$
5. $\dfrac{3^2}{3^9}$
6. $\dfrac{11^2}{11^5}$

Tell whether the equation is true or false.

7. $\dfrac{2b^3}{2b^2} = 2b$ _____
8. $\dfrac{m^8}{m^{10}} = m^2$ _____
9. $\dfrac{3n^6}{3n^3} = n^3$ _____

Divide and simplify. Write with positive exponents.

10. $\dfrac{a^3 c}{2a^2 c}$
11. $\dfrac{6d^3}{9d^5}$
12. $\dfrac{b^8}{b^3}$

13. $\dfrac{c^3 f^5}{cf^2}$
14. $\dfrac{8n^8}{4n^4}$
15. $\dfrac{r^6}{r^{10}}$

16. $\dfrac{7b^4 c}{b^3}$
17. $\dfrac{5r^3}{5r^2 s^5}$
18. $\dfrac{18a^3 b^3 d^4}{6a^2 b^6 d}$

Evaluate.

19. $\dfrac{5^3}{5^2}$
20. $\dfrac{4^6}{4^3}$
21. $\dfrac{3^3}{3^5}$

22. $\dfrac{3^5}{3^3}$
23. $\dfrac{8^4}{8^2}$
24. $\dfrac{2^9}{2^6}$

Math Intervention
Book 7 Getting Ready for Algebra

Name _____ Date _____

25. Sam and **7** of his friends together purchase a card table with **4** chairs as a wedding gift for **$256**. How much does each person have to pay? Set this up using the quotient of powers with **2** as your base number.

Step 1 How many people are purchasing the wedding gift? _____

Step 2 Write this number as a power of **2**: _____ = $2^{\square}$

Step 3 Write the cost $256 as a power of **2**: 256 = $2^{\square}$

Step 4 Divide the cost by the number of people:

$$\frac{2^{\square}}{2^{\square}} = 2^{\square - \square} = 2^{\square}$$

Step 5 How much does each person pay? _____

26. In Jane's math class, she has to divide **243** by **27**. She has to solve it using powers of **3**. How will she solve this?

_____
_____

DID YOU GET IT?

27. **Fill in the missing words.** When simplifying $\frac{x^a}{x^b}$, if the larger power is in the numerator the result is a _____ power of x. If the larger power is in the _____ the result is a negative power of x.

28. **Explain your reasoning.** Division by **0** is not possible. Is it possible to divide a number by n^0, where n is a positive integer? Explain your reasoning.

_____
_____
_____

29. **Find the error.** Your friend says that the quotient $\frac{c^5}{c^8}$ equals c^3. Is your friend correct? Explain why or why not.

_____
_____
_____

LESSON 7-12: Power of a Quotient

Words to Remember

Power of a quotient: Raising a quotient (fraction) to a power

$$\left(\frac{x}{3}\right)^2 = \left(\frac{x}{3}\right) \cdot \left(\frac{x}{3}\right) = \frac{x^2}{3^2} = \frac{x^2}{9}$$

Power of a quotient property: To find the power of a quotient, find the power of the numerator and the power of the denominator and divide. Simplify if possible.

$$\left(\frac{x}{y}\right)^a = \frac{x^a}{y^a}$$

Getting Started In Lesson 7-10 you worked with the power of a product property. The power of a quotient property is similar. It lets you find powers of fractions.

EXAMPLE 1 Writing Fractions Raised to Powers as Simple Fractions

Write $\left(\frac{3}{4}\right)^3$ as a simple fraction. Show two different methods.

Solution 1 Use multiplication.

$\left(\frac{3}{4}\right)^3 = \left(\frac{3}{4}\right) \cdot \left(\frac{3}{4}\right) \cdot \left(\frac{3}{4}\right)$ Write without exponents.

$= \frac{3 \cdot 3 \cdot 3}{4 \cdot 4 \cdot 4}$ Multiply the fractions.

$= \frac{27}{64}$ Simplify.

Solution 2 Use the property.

$\left(\frac{3}{4}\right)^3 = \frac{3^3}{4^3}$ Power of a quotient property

$= \frac{27}{64}$ Simplify.

TRY THIS Write as a simple fraction.

1. $\left(\frac{5}{8}\right)^2 =$  $=$ ____

2. $\left(\frac{1}{3}\right)^4$

Math Intervention
Book 7 Getting Ready for Algebra

Name _____   Date _____

EXAMPLE 2 — Rewriting as a Single Fraction

Rewrite $4 \cdot \left(\dfrac{2a}{b}\right)^3$ as a single fraction.

Solution

$$4 \cdot \left(\dfrac{2a}{b}\right)^3 = 4 \cdot \dfrac{(2a)^3}{b^3} \quad \text{Power of a quotient property}$$

$$= 4 \cdot \dfrac{2^3 a^3}{b^3} \quad \text{Power of a product property}$$

$$= 4 \cdot \dfrac{8a^3}{b^3} \quad \text{Simplify.}$$

$$= \dfrac{32a^3}{b^3} \quad \text{Simplify.}$$

Remember
You can think of 4 as $\dfrac{4}{1}$. Then just multiply the fractions.

EXAMPLE 3 — Evaluating a Fraction

Evaluate $\left(\dfrac{2x}{7}\right)^2$ when $x = 3$.

Solution

$$\left(\dfrac{2x}{7}\right)^2 = \left(\dfrac{2 \cdot 3}{7}\right)^2 \quad \text{Substitute.}$$

$$= \left(\dfrac{6}{7}\right)^2 \quad \text{Simplify.}$$

$$= \dfrac{6^2}{7^2} \quad \text{Power of a quotient property}$$

$$= \dfrac{36}{49} \quad \text{Simplify.}$$

TRY THIS

Rewrite as a single fraction.

3. $\left(\dfrac{3x}{4}\right)^3$

4. $\dfrac{1}{8} \cdot \left(\dfrac{2c}{de}\right)^2$

5. $81b^4 \cdot \left(\dfrac{a}{3b}\right)^4$

Evaluate the expression when $x = 2$.

6. $\left(\dfrac{x}{3}\right)^3$

7. $\left(\dfrac{5x}{7}\right)^2$

8. $\left(\dfrac{3x}{4}\right)^3$

Name _____   Date _____

> **Summarize**
> **Finding the Power of a Quotient**
> (1) To find the power of a quotient, find the power of the numerator and the power of the denominator and divide.
>
> (2) Simplify if possible.
> Example: $\left(\dfrac{a}{4}\right)^3 = \dfrac{a^3}{4^3} = \dfrac{a^3}{64}$
>
> Example: $\left(\dfrac{d}{f}\right)^8 = \dfrac{d^8}{f^8}$
>
> (3) To evaluate a variable expression in which a fraction is raised to a power, first substitute the given value for the variable. Perform operations inside parentheses, apply the power of a quotient property, and simplify the resulting expression as needed.

Practice

Match the expression with the correct quotient.

1. $\left(\dfrac{b}{2}\right)^4$ _____
2. $\left(\dfrac{2}{b}\right)^4$ _____
3. $2^4 \cdot \left(\dfrac{b}{2}\right)^4$ _____

A. $\dfrac{16}{b^4}$
B. b^4
C. $\dfrac{b^4}{16}$

Tell whether the equation is true or false.

4. $\left(\dfrac{a}{3}\right)^6 = \dfrac{a^6}{3^6}$ _____
5. $\left(\dfrac{a}{3}\right)^6 = \dfrac{a^6}{729}$ _____
6. $\left(\dfrac{a}{3}\right)^6 = \dfrac{a^6}{3}$ _____

Rewrite as a single fraction.

7. $\left(\dfrac{ab}{2}\right)^7$
8. $2^3 \cdot \left(\dfrac{m}{8}\right)^3$
9. $\left(\dfrac{3}{n}\right)^4$

10. $\left(\dfrac{2c}{2}\right)^8$
11. $3^2 \cdot \left(\dfrac{a}{9}\right)^1$
12. $4^5 \cdot \left(\dfrac{t}{4}\right)^4$

Evaluate when $b = 2$.

13. $\left(\dfrac{b}{3}\right)^3$
14. $\left(\dfrac{6}{b}\right)^5$
15. $\left(\dfrac{12}{b}\right)^2$

Evaluate when $c = 3$.

16. $\left(\dfrac{3c}{10}\right)^3$
17. $\left(\dfrac{5c}{8}\right)^2$
18. $\left(\dfrac{2c}{5}\right)^4$

Math Intervention
Book 7 Getting Ready for Algebra

Name _____ Date _____

Write an expression to model the situation. Then simplify the expression. Explain your reasoning.

19. Kaliah reduces a page she is copying to $\frac{2}{3}$ of its original size, then decides she wants to reduce it to $\frac{2}{3}$ of the resulting size. What is the total reduction? Write your answer as a power of a quotient.
   _____
   _____

20. Jared has a cube-shaped decoration on his desk with the measurements shown.

   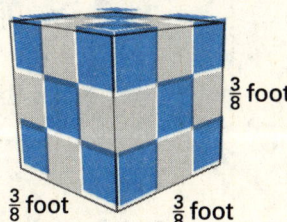

   Use the fact that the volume of a cube can be found by raising a side length to the third power to express the volume of the cube as the power of a quotient.
   _____
   _____
   _____

DID YOU GET IT?

21. **Fill in the missing words.** When a fraction is raised to a power, both the _____ and _____ are raised to the power.

22. **Describe a process.** Explain how you can find the value of $\left(\frac{c}{d}\right)^0$ without knowing the value of c or d. Assume c and d are positive integers.
   _____
   _____
   _____

23. **Explain your reasoning.** Kaitlyn thinks that $\left(\frac{b}{6}\right)^2$ is equal to $\frac{b^2}{6}$. Is Kaitlyn correct? Explain why or why not.
   _____
   _____
   _____

Name _____ Date _____

LESSON 7-13
Fractional Exponents with a Denominator of 2

Words to Remember

Fractional exponent: An exponent that is a fraction

A number raised to the $\frac{1}{2}$ power means you take the square root of the number:

Example: $100^{\frac{1}{2}} = \sqrt{100^1} = \sqrt{100} = 10$

Getting Started In Lesson 7-8 you simplified and evaluated expressions that included exponents. Fractional exponents with a denominator of 2 will be similar. After taking a number to the power in the numerator, you then take the square root.

EXAMPLE 1 Simplifying Expressions with Fractional Exponents with a Denominator of 2

Simplify $16^{\frac{1}{2}}$.

Solution

$16^{\frac{1}{2}} = 16^{1 \cdot \left(\frac{1}{2}\right)}$ Write the fractional exponent as a product of an integer and $\frac{1}{2}$.

$= \sqrt{16^1}$ Simplify.

$= \sqrt{16}$ Simplify.

$= 4$ Simplify.

TRY THIS Simplify.

1. $64^{\frac{1}{2}}$
2. $144^{\frac{1}{2}}$
3. $\left(\frac{25}{49}\right)^{\frac{1}{2}}$

Perfect Squares In Example 1, you were able to simplify $\sqrt{16}$ because 16 is a perfect square. Sometimes an expression cannot be simplified, as in Example 2.

Math Intervention
Book 7 Getting Ready for Algebra

Name _____ Date _____

EXAMPLE 2 — Rewriting Without a Fractional Exponent

Rewrite $13^{\frac{1}{2}}$ without a fractional exponent.

Solution

$13^{\frac{1}{2}} = \sqrt{13^1}$ Definition of fractional power

$\phantom{13^{\frac{1}{2}}} = \sqrt{13}$ Simplify.

$\sqrt{13}$ cannot be simplified further because 13 is not a perfect square.

EXAMPLE 3 — Multiplying Terms with Fractional Exponents

Multiply $36^{\frac{1}{2}} \cdot 4^{\frac{1}{2}}$.

Solution

$36^{\frac{1}{2}} \cdot 4^{\frac{1}{2}} = \sqrt{36^1} \cdot \sqrt{4^1}$ Definition of fractional power

$\phantom{36^{\frac{1}{2}} \cdot 4^{\frac{1}{2}}} = \sqrt{36} \cdot \sqrt{4}$ Simplify.

$\phantom{36^{\frac{1}{2}} \cdot 4^{\frac{1}{2}}} = 6 \cdot 2$ Simplify.

$\phantom{36^{\frac{1}{2}} \cdot 4^{\frac{1}{2}}} = 12$ Simplify.

Remember

Since the numerator is 1 and that is the power, 36 and 4 must both be raised to the first power. Since the denominator is 2 and that is the root, you must then take the square root of both 36 and 4.

EXAMPLE 4 — Rewriting Without a Fractional Exponent

Rewrite $4^{\frac{3}{2}}$ without a fractional exponent.

Solution

$4^{\frac{3}{2}} = 4^{3 \cdot \frac{1}{2}}$ Write the fractional exponent as a product of an integer and $\frac{1}{2}$.

$\phantom{4^{\frac{3}{2}}} = \sqrt{4^3}$ Definition of fractional power

$\phantom{4^{\frac{3}{2}}} = \sqrt{64}$ Simplify.

$\phantom{4^{\frac{3}{2}}} = 8$ Simplify.

TRY THIS Rewrite without a fractional exponent.

4. $51^{\frac{1}{2}}$ 5. $144^{\frac{1}{2}} \cdot 25^{\frac{1}{2}}$ 6. $9^{\frac{3}{2}}$

Math Intervention
Book 7 Getting Ready for Algebra

Name _____   Date _____

Summarize

Simplifying Fractional Exponents

(1) Raising an expression to the fractional power $\frac{1}{2}$ is the same as taking the square root of the expression.

Example: $25^{\frac{1}{2}} = \sqrt{25} = 5$

Example: $17^{\frac{1}{2}} = \sqrt{17}$, which cannot be simplified.

(2) The numerator of the fractional power is the power and the denominator is the root.

(3) You can think of the fractional exponent in a power such as $x^{\frac{3}{2}}$ as a product of an integer and $\frac{1}{2}$.

Example: $36^{\frac{3}{2}} = 36^{3 \cdot \frac{1}{2}}$

$= \sqrt{36^3}$

$= \sqrt{46{,}656} = 216$

Practice

Match the expression involving fractional exponents with its correct value.

1. $121^{\frac{1}{2}}$ _____
2. $11^{\frac{1}{2}}$ _____
3. $121^{\frac{1}{2}} \cdot 4^{\frac{1}{2}}$ _____

A. 22   B. 11   C. $\sqrt{11}$

Tell whether the equation is true or false.

4. $16^{\frac{1}{2}} \cdot 1^{\frac{1}{2}} = 16$ _____
5. $36^{\frac{1}{2}} \cdot 0^{\frac{1}{2}} = 1$ _____
6. $0^{\frac{1}{2}} \cdot 49^{\frac{1}{2}} = 0$ _____

Simplify.

7. $4^{\frac{1}{2}}$
8. $3^2 \cdot 36^{\frac{1}{2}}$
9. $\left(\frac{16}{25}\right)^{\frac{1}{2}}$
10. $\left(\frac{36}{121}\right)^{\frac{1}{2}}$
11. $49^{\frac{1}{2}} \cdot 16^{\frac{1}{2}}$
12. $144^{\frac{1}{2}} \cdot 9^{\frac{1}{2}}$

Rewrite without a fractional exponent.

13. $15^{\frac{1}{2}}$
14. $\frac{1}{4} \cdot 49^{\frac{1}{2}}$
15. $47^{\frac{1}{2}}$
16. $\frac{1}{5} \cdot 25^{\frac{1}{2}}$
17. $23^{\frac{1}{2}}$
18. $196^{\frac{1}{2}}$
19. $25^{\frac{3}{2}}$
20. $16^{\frac{3}{2}}$
21. $4^{\frac{5}{2}}$

Name _____ Date _____

Write an equation to model the situation. Then solve the equation. Explain your reasoning.

22. Cassie has a square shaped mirror sitting on her bureau with the area shown.

    Find the length of the side of the mirror, *x*, using fractional exponents.
    _____
    _____

23. Aaron has a dog kennel with a square door that has an area of **49** square feet.

    Find the length of each side of the dog kennel door, *y*, using fractional exponents.
    _____
    _____

24. A square wall in James's office cubicle has area **2500** square inches. Find the length of each side of the cubicle opening, *z*, using fractional exponents.
    _____
    _____

DID YOU GET IT?

25. **Fill in the missing words.** When a fractional power has a denominator of **2**, you must take the _____ root of the expression. Only perfect squares will give answers that are _____ numbers.

26. **Describe a process.** Explain why $81^{\frac{1}{2}}$ means you take the square root of **81**.
    _____
    _____
    _____

27. **Explain your reasoning.** Jaylynn thinks that $4^{\frac{1}{2}}$ is equal to **2**. Is Jaylynn correct? Explain why or why not.
    _____
    _____
    _____

Math Intervention
Book 7 Getting Ready for Algebra

Name _____ Date _____

LESSON 7-14
Fractional Exponents with Any Denominator

> **Words to Remember**
>
> Fractional exponent: An exponent that is a fraction.
>
> Cube root: b is a cube root of a if $b^3 = a$ $\sqrt[3]{27} = 3$ because $3^3 = 27$
>
> The cube root of a can be written as $\sqrt[3]{a}$ or as $a^{\frac{1}{3}}$.

Getting Started In Lesson 7-13 you simplified expressions that included fractional exponents with a denominator of **2**. In this lesson you will simplify expressions that involve other fractional exponents.

EXAMPLE 1   Finding Roots

Simplify if possible.

a. $\sqrt[3]{1000}$ b. $\sqrt[4]{16}$ c. $\sqrt[3]{4}$

Solution

a. Look for an integer b such that $b^3 = 1000$.

   $\sqrt[3]{1000} = 10$ because $10^3 = 1000$.

b. Look for an integer b such that $b^4 = 16$.

   $\sqrt[4]{16} = 2$ because $2^4 = 16$.

c. $\sqrt[3]{4}$ cannot be simplified further because there is no integer value of b such that $b^3 = 4$.

TRY THIS   Simplify if possible.

1. $\sqrt[3]{125}$ 2. $\sqrt[5]{32}$ 3. $\sqrt[4]{27}$

Other Fractional Exponents In lesson 7-13, you learned that $x^{\frac{1}{2}}$ means $\sqrt{x}$. The expression $x^{\frac{1}{3}}$ means $\sqrt[3]{x}$ and the expression $x^{\frac{1}{4}}$ means $\sqrt[4]{x}$, or the fourth root of x. The expression $x^{\frac{3}{4}}$ means $\sqrt[4]{x^3}$.

Name _____ Date _____

EXAMPLE 2 — Simplifying Expressions with Fractional Exponents with Any Denominator

Simplify $8^{\frac{2}{3}}$. Show two methods.

Solution 1 Take the power first and then the root.

$8^{\frac{2}{3}} = 8^{2 \cdot \frac{1}{3}}$ Write the fractional exponent as the product of 2 and $\frac{1}{3}$.

$8^{\frac{2}{3}} = \sqrt[3]{8^2}$ Definition of fractional power

$\phantom{8^{\frac{2}{3}}} = \sqrt[3]{64}$ Square 8.

$\phantom{8^{\frac{2}{3}}} = 4$ Take the cube root of 64.

Solution 2 Take the root first and then the power.

$8^{\frac{2}{3}} = 8^{2 \cdot \frac{1}{3}}$ Write the fractional exponent as the product of 2 and $\frac{1}{3}$.

$8^{\frac{2}{3}} = \left(\sqrt[3]{8}\right)^2$ Definition of fractional power

$\phantom{8^{\frac{2}{3}}} = (2)^2$ Take the cube root of 8.

$\phantom{8^{\frac{2}{3}}} = 4$ Square 2.

EXAMPLE 3 — Multiplying Terms with Fractional Exponents

Multiply $16^{\frac{1}{2}} \cdot 81^{\frac{3}{4}}$. Simplify each term first then multiply.

Solution

$16^{\frac{1}{2}} \cdot 81^{\frac{3}{4}} = \sqrt{16^1} \cdot \left(\sqrt[4]{81}\right)^3$ Definition of fractional power

$\phantom{16^{\frac{1}{2}} \cdot 81^{\frac{3}{4}}} = \sqrt{16} \cdot 3^3$ Simplify.

$\phantom{16^{\frac{1}{2}} \cdot 81^{\frac{3}{4}}} = 4 \cdot 27$ Simplify.

$\phantom{16^{\frac{1}{2}} \cdot 81^{\frac{3}{4}}} = 108$ Simplify.

TRY THIS Simplify.

4. $16^{\frac{3}{4}}$

5. $32^{\frac{2}{5}}$

6. $27^{\frac{2}{3}}$

7. $243^{\frac{1}{5}} \cdot 25^{\frac{1}{2}}$

8. $256^{\frac{1}{4}} \cdot 27^{\frac{1}{3}}$

9. $49^{\frac{1}{2}} \cdot 1^{\frac{1}{2}}$

Name _____   Date _____

> **Summarize**
> **Simplifying Fractional Exponents**
> (1) The cube root of a number x is written as $\sqrt[3]{x}$. Other roots can be found as well, such as the fourth root of x, written as $\sqrt[4]{x}$.
>
> Example: $\sqrt[3]{8} = 2$ because $2 \cdot 2 \cdot 2 = 8$
>
> Example: $\sqrt[4]{10,000} = 10$ because $10 \cdot 10 \cdot 10 \cdot 10 = 10,000$
>
> (2) The expression $x^{\frac{1}{3}}$ means $\sqrt[3]{x}$. The expression $x^{\frac{1}{4}}$ means $\sqrt[4]{x}$.
>
> Example: $8^{\frac{1}{3}} = \sqrt[3]{8} = 2$
>
> Example: $(10,000)^{\frac{1}{4}} = \sqrt[4]{10,000} = 10$
>
> (3) You can think of the fractional exponent in a power such as $x^{\frac{2}{3}}$ as a product of an integer and a fraction with a denominator of 1. Rewriting the exponent can help you evaluate the power.
>
> Example: $8^{\frac{2}{3}} = 8^{2 \cdot \frac{1}{3}}$
>
> (4) The expression $8^{\frac{2}{3}}$ can be written as $\sqrt[3]{8^2}$ or as $\left(\sqrt[3]{8}\right)^2$. To evaluate $8^{\frac{2}{3}}$, you can find the cube root of 8^2 or find the square of the cube root of 8.

Practice

Match the expression involving fractional exponents with its correct value.

1. $81^{\frac{1}{2}}$ _____

2. $125^{\frac{1}{3}} \cdot 16^{\frac{1}{4}}$ _____

3. $125^{\frac{1}{2}} \cdot 1^{\frac{1}{7}}$ _____

A. 10

B. $\sqrt{125}$

C. 9

Tell whether the equation is true or false.

4. $8^{\frac{1}{3}} \cdot 8^{\frac{2}{3}} = 8$ _____

5. $27^{\frac{2}{3}} \cdot 36^{\frac{1}{2}} = 18$ _____

6. $64^{\frac{1}{3}} \cdot 64^{\frac{1}{2}} = 64$ _____

Simplify.

7. $\sqrt[3]{27}$

8. $\sqrt[3]{0}$

9. $\sqrt[4]{10,000}$

10. $9^{\frac{1}{2}}$

11. $2^4 \cdot 125^{\frac{2}{3}}$

12. $\left(\dfrac{27}{64}\right)^{\frac{1}{3}}$

13. $25^{\frac{1}{2}} \cdot 216^{\frac{1}{3}}$

14. $81^{\frac{1}{2}} \cdot 32^{\frac{2}{5}}$

15. $81^{\frac{1}{4}} \cdot 8^{\frac{1}{3}}$

Math Intervention
Book 7 Getting Ready for Algebra

Name _____   Date _____

Rewrite without a fractional exponent.

16. $28^{\frac{1}{3}}$

17. $\frac{5}{6} \cdot 36^{\frac{1}{2}}$

18. $\frac{1}{2} \cdot 33^{\frac{1}{4}}$

Write an equation to model the situation. Then solve the equation. Explain your reasoning.

19. Kyle has a cube-shaped container in which he stores food for his parrot. The volume and the length of a side, *t*, are shown.

    The volume formula is length times width times height. Find the length of the side of the container, *t*, using fractional exponents.

    _____

    _____

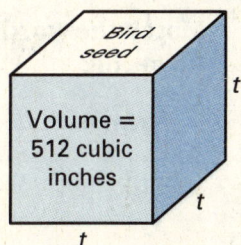

20. Jenna has a cube-shaped container which she uses for storage. The cube has the volume shown.

    The volume formula is length times width times height. Find the length of each side of the container, *m*, using fractional exponents.

    _____

    _____

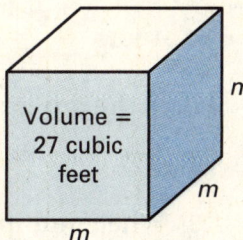

DID YOU GET IT?

21. **Fill in the missing words.** When working with a fractional power, the numerator is the _____ and the denominator is the _____.

22. **Describe a process.** Explain how to simplify $64^{\frac{2}{3}}$ using mental math.

    _____

    _____

    _____

23. **Explain your reasoning.** John says it is easier to simplify $16^{\frac{3}{4}}$ by taking the root first and then the power. Jeff says it is easier to simplify it if you take the power first then the root. Which one is correct? Explain why.

    _____

    _____

    _____

Name _____ Date _____

Mixed Practice for Lessons 7-7 to 7-14

Vocabulary Review

Match the word with its mathematical meaning and its everyday meaning.

Word	Mathematical meaning	Everyday meaning
1. power ___, ___	A. a number less than zero	X. the underground part of a plant
2. negative ___, ___	B. a quantity taken an indicated number of times as an equal factor	Y. marked by denial or refusal
3. root ___, ___	C. exponent, number of times a factor occurs	Z. possession or control, authority

Fill in the missing words.

4. Any positive integer to the _____ power is one.

5. When multiplying powers with the same base, _____ the exponents and leave the base the same.

6. Raising a number to the $\frac{1}{2}$ power is the same as taking the _____ root of the number.

Write the equation that is shown using exponents.

7. $(7 \cdot 7 \cdot 7) \cdot (7 \cdot 7 \cdot 7 \cdot 7) = 7 \cdot 7 \cdot 7 \cdot 7 \cdot 7 \cdot 7 \cdot 7$

   $7^{\square} \cdot 7^{\square} = 7^{\square}$

8. $(x \cdot x) \cdot (x \cdot x \cdot x) \cdot (x \cdot x \cdot x) = x \cdot x \cdot x \cdot x \cdot x \cdot x \cdot x \cdot x$

   $x^{\square} \cdot x^{\square} \cdot x^{\square} = x^{\square}$

9. $\frac{n \cdot n \cdot m}{n \cdot m \cdot m} = \frac{n}{m}$

   $\frac{n^{\square} \cdot m^{\square}}{n^{\square} \cdot m^{\square}} = \frac{n^{\square}}{m^{\square}}$

10. $\left(\frac{2}{3}\right)^4 = \frac{2 \cdot 2 \cdot 2 \cdot 2}{3 \cdot 3 \cdot 3 \cdot 3}$

    $\left(\frac{2}{3}\right)^{\square} = \frac{2^{\square}}{3^{\square}}$

Math Intervention
Book 7 Getting Ready for Algebra

Name _____   Date _____

Multiply or divide and simplify.

11. $x^3 \cdot x^5$
12. $\dfrac{x^6}{x^4}$
13. $\dfrac{a^2b}{ab^2}$
14. a^0b^0

15. $(x^2)^3$
16. $(x^4)^2$
17. $(2r)^3$
18. $(x^2y)^2$

19. $b^5 \cdot b^{-3}$
20. $(r^4)^3$
21. $a \cdot a^5$
22. $(b^3)^9$

23. Fill in the missing information to solve the problem.

   Suppose certain bacteria double in number every hour. There are 400 bacteria in the beginning. After h hours there will be B bacteria. Use the formula $B = 400 \cdot 2^h$. How many bacteria will there be in 3 hours?

   Step 1 In the formula $B = 400 \cdot 2^h$, ____ stands for the number of hours.

   Step 2 Substitute ____ for h.

   Step 3 Simplify to get $B =$ _____.

   Step 4 In 3 hours there will be _____ bacteria.

Rewrite as a single fraction.

24. 5^{-2}
25. 4^0
26. $\left(\dfrac{c}{p}\right)^2$
27. $\left(\dfrac{b^2}{d}\right)^3$

Simplify.

28. $9^{\frac{1}{2}}$
29. $8^{\frac{2}{3}}$
30. $16^{\frac{1}{4}}$
31. $125^{\frac{1}{3}} \cdot 16^{\frac{1}{2}}$

Write an equation. Then solve the equation. Explain your reasoning.

32. The area of the square shown is **100** square feet. Find x, the length of a side of the square.

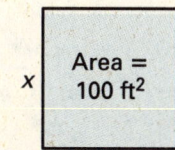

_____
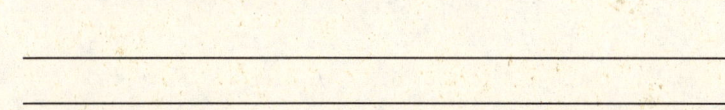

33. The volume of the cube shown is **216** cubic centimeters. Find y, the length of a side of the cube.

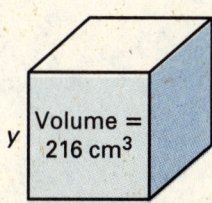

_____
_____
_____